Music and Poetry
in a Colombian Village

Music and Poetry in a Colombian Village

A Tri-Cultural Heritage

GEORGE LIST

Indiana University Press

Bloomington

Publication of this book was assisted by a grant from the Publications Program of the National Endowment for the Humanities, an independent federal agency.

Manufactured in the United States of America

Library of Congress Cataloging in Publication Data

List, George, 1911-
    Music and poetry in a Colombian village.

    Bibliography: p.
    1. Folk music--Colombia--Evitar--History and criticism.
2. Folk-songs, Spanish--Colombia--Evitar--History and criticism. 3. Music and literature. I. Title.
ML3575.C7L55 1983   781.7861'1   82-48534
ISBN 0-253-33951-0
1 2 3 4 5 87 86 85 84 83

TO MY WIFE

EVE EHRLICHMAN LIST

WITH AFFECTION AND GRATITUDE

CONTENTS

PART III. THE MUSIC AND POETRY

PART IV. SYNTHESIS

FIGURES

Unless otherwise indicated, all photographs were made in Evitar by George List. The year in which the photograph was made, of the drawing if it was made *in situ*, is indicated in parentheses, as is the location if it was not Evitar.

When a photograph or drawing has been published previously, this information is offered in most cases in the form of a citation. The reader who wishes further information should refer to the audiography or bibliography. The term *reproduced from* indicates that what is reproduced here is a photographic copy of what is found in the source cited. The term *also published in* indicates that although the photograph or drawing was published previously, what is reproduced here is not a photographic copy from that source but represents a different print from the same negative or a copy of the original drawing.

TRANSCRIPTIONS

TABLES

PROLOGUE

We discovered Evitar on November 1, 1964. I use the term *discovery* advisedly. Evitar was *tierra incognita* to everyone in the region with whom I had any acquaintance before that date. Even the name, Evitar, was unknown to Manuel Zapata Olivella and his sister, Delia Zapata Olivella, who introduced me to the region. These two Colombian folklorists are natives of the Costa Atlántica and had themselves collected widely in the countryside. Nor were the *choferes*, the taxi drivers whose services we constantly employed in our field work, much better informed in this direction. They are noted for their knowledge of the countryside, but during my four expeditions to the region I found only one who had heard of Evitar, and he was unsure of its location, not having been there himself. This is not strange, since the location of the village is indicated in only the most detailed of maps.

We "discovered" Evitar in the following manner: I had begun my field work in the region the previous week, utilizing Cartagena as a base. Delia Zapata had joined me there to act as my field assistant. I had decided to focus my initial investigations on the *cumbia* complex, and the previous weekend we had visited Soplaviento, where we had worked for two days with the *conjunto de cumbia* of that community. Delia had had contact in the past with a similar group in Mahates led by a man named Roque Arrieta. Thus we planned a visit to Mahates the following Sunday, a day when we could be confident that the members of the *conjunto* would be at home rather than working in the fields. We arose early and were met by the *chofer* for whose services we had contracted for the day. We were in the midst of the rainy season. The day was fortunately clear, but it was very hot and humid, and pools of water lay on all sides. Driving south on the paved highway, we crossed the Dique Canal and after passing Malagana turned onto the dirt road leading to Mahates. Here our progress was considerably slower, but after an extended period during which we either jolted over ruts or skidded through mud, we finally arrived at our destination.

In Mahates we soon located two members of Roque Arrieta's *conjunto*, the *tambolero* and the *bombero*, but not Roque, the *pitero* and leader. From the first two we learned that some months previously Roque had moved to Cartagena, whence we came. The *con-*

junto, lacking a leader, was now inactive. The sun was now high
in the sky. What should we do? Should we return to Cartagena or
should we search the countryside further in hope of locating a
conjunto de cumbia? At this juncture the *bombero* informed us that
Roque had learned to play the *pito* from a man who lived in Evitar,
and that he believed there was a *conjunto de cumbia* in that village. Since neither Delia nor our *chofer* had ever heard of Evitar,
they were inclined to doubt the existence of a community with such
a peculiar name. However, the *bombero* assured us that Evitar did
indeed exist and that it in fact was located only a short distance
from Mahates. Thus reassured, we decided that we would visit
Evitar, and the *bombero* instructed the *chofer* concerning the route
he should follow.

We set out again, driving south from Mahates on the road to
Calamar. After a short distance we turned onto an unmarked dirt
road which in this season seemed a mere muddy double track. Our
chofer, skilled in such matters, negotiated some four kilometers
with only minor mishaps, and Evitar, half-drowned in water, then
appeared before us. Upon inquiring at the first *bahareque,* we
were informed that there was indeed a *cumbia* in Evitar and that
its leader, Santiago Ospino, lived across the street. We immediately repaired to the house to which we had been directed. We
were hospitably received by Santiago's wife, who informed us that
although it was Sunday, Santiago was nevertheless working in the
fields. While a child went to fetch him we were invited to seat
ourselves in a fiber hammock, there being no chairs in the room.
After a considerable lapse of time Santiago appeared and greeted
us amiably. Yes, he did have a *cumbia* which frequently played in
Evitar and the surrounding area, but unfortunately he was *en luto*
for a brother who had recently died. Under these circumstances
he was unable to perform for us. If we would contact him when the
period of mourning was over, he would be glad to arrange for the
conjunto to play for us.

It was now considerably past noon, and lunch was indicated. We
made our way to the *almacén,* Evitar's only store, where the woman
who operated it graciously permitted us to use her facilities to
prepare and consume the food and drink that we had brought with
us. As we ate I suggested to Delia that we look no further that
day for *cumbia.* It was nearly two o'clock in the afternoon, and
the search would probably be fruitless. Surely there must be
individuals in this village in addition to the members of the *conjunto de cumbia* who made music. Let us find them and record whatever they had to offer. Delia agreed. Word was quickly spread
through the village of our desire to record those who wished to
sing or play for us. Through the good offices of the proprietress
of the *almacén* we secured the key to the school for girls, which,
since it was Sunday, was not in use. This served as our "studio,"
offering some barrier to wandering, grunting pigs and whispering
and giggling swarms of children.

There was no lack of response from the *evitaleros,* and we were
soon recording *décimas, zafras, vaquería, arrullos,* and *cantos del
velorio de angelito.* As night fell we stopped briefly to eat prepared sandwiches and to purchase candles at the *almacén.* Lighting
these, we set them upright in their own drippings on the wooden

table of the schoolhouse and in this flickering illumination continued our recording session. It was late at night when I packed
my equipment for the long ride back to Cartagena. Knowing that
there was still much we had not recorded, we made arrangements to
return the next Sunday, and on that day recorded children's game
songs, *gavilán*, *bullerengue*, *fandango*, and further songs utilized
during the *velorio de angelito*. Such were the circumstances from
which there developed, *en fin*, an investigation in depth of the
music and poetry of the village of Evitar.

ACKNOWLEDGMENTS

During the many years spent in the preparation of this volume,
was fortunate in having the assistance of a large number of individuals, institutions, and agencies. My appreciation must first
be extended to the people of Evitar for their friendliness and
their tolerance of this prying *gringo* in their midst. Second only
to the *evitaleros* themselves I must express my gratitude to another
costeño, Manuel Zapata Olivella, physician, novelist, folklorist,
vagabond, and opener of all gates, for his unfailing help in all
matters large and small. It was he who brought me together with
his sister Delia and "Willy" Caballero, my other two field assis-
tants, to whom I am also deeply indebted. Delia Zapata was my
first tutor in *costeño* life and custom, and Caballero worked with
me on this research project not only in Colombia but later while
studying folklore at Indiana University. There is one other person with whom my family and I have had close association, Rosa
Zapata, *colombiana* and *catalana*, whom I wish to thank for her
interest and help, most importantly in keeping a watchful eye on
my son, Michael, while his parents were out of Bogotá.

Among other Colombians I owe the largest debt of gratitude to
Joaquín Piñeros Corpas, then *director* of the Comisión para Inter-
cambio Educativo, who offered me many courtesies during my year's
tenure as Fulbright scholar. Other Colombians to whom I am
grateful for advice or other assistance are Guillermo Espinosa,
then chief, Music Division, Pan-American Union; Fabio González
Zuleta, then *director*, Conservatorio Nacional de Música; Francisco
Márquez Yáñez, *subdirector*, Instituto Colombiano de Antropología;
and Octavio Marulanda, *director*, Instituto de Cultura Popular of
Cali. Victor Manuel Patiño, Secretaría de Desarollo y Fomento,
Cali, and Alvaro Fernández Pérez, *director*, Instituto Nacional de
Ciencias Naturales, kindly furnished the scientific names of
various plants and animals native to the Costa Atlántica.

While in Spain in 1970 I received valuable assistance from Pilar
García de Diego, *directora*, and José Pérez Vidal of the Instituto
de Dialectología y Tradiciones Populares, Consejo Superior de In-
vestigaciones Científicas, and from Nieves de Hoyo, *directora*,
Museo del Pueblo Español. I am particularly grateful for the
opportunity to make use of the excellent libraries of these two
institutions. Later I was privileged to receive by letter from D.

Gaizka Barandiaran of San Sebastián references to published works and other data concerning the *décima española* and from the afore-mentioned Pilar García de Diego similar materials referring to both the *décima* and the *vaquerada*. Concerning the *décima*, the following Spanish scholars, D. Jesús Bal y Gay, José Pérez Vidal, and Arcadio de Larrea Palacín, kindly offered information based on their field work which Pilar García de Diego transmitted to me.

A number of other scholars also furnished materials developed in their field work and research. Of these I am most indebted to Gerhard Kubik, Institut für Völkerkunde, Vienna, for sharing with me both verbally and in writing his rich field experience in Africa and for sending me many beautifully documented photographs of musical instruments. I owe many thanks to Klaus Wachsmann, formerly of Northwestern University, who provided references and field data concerning African musical instruments and to Kenneth A. Gourlay, School of African and Oriental Studies, University of London, who made available to me considerable data he had collected concerning the musical bow in Africa. I much appreciate the generosity of Geneviève Dournon, Département d'Ethnomusicologie, Musée de l'Homme, Paris, who sent me data concerning drums in the museum's collection and photographs of them, and that of David Ames, San Francisco State College, who provided me with informa-tion concerning Igbo drums and a photograph thereof. My grati-tude must also be extended to Jacoba van Oven, formerly at Women's Teachers College, Port Loko, Sierra Leone, and James Rosellini, formerly of the Archives Sonores, Centre Voltaïque de Recherche Scientifique, Ouagadougou, Upper Volta, for sending me photographs and other data concerning musical instruments of these two coun-tries. I am equally indebted to Donald B. Tayler, Pitt Rivers Museum and Department of Ethnology and Prehistory, University of Oxford, who sent me a photograph of the Kogi Indians of Colombia made in cooperation with Brian Moser.

I am doubly indebted to Gerard Béhague, Department of Music, University of Texas. He sent me references concerning the *aboio* in Brazil and Portugal and a tape recording of this genre which he had made in Brazil. He also read and offered criticism of the initial version of this work. Many of his useful suggestions have been incorporated into the later revisions. I am also grateful to Merle Simmons, Department of Spanish and Portuguese, Indiana University, for his critical reading of the sections on Spanish versification in chapters 5-6. Lois Anderson, Music Department of the University of Wisconsin, was kind enough to check my recordings of *zafras* and *vaquería* for North African influences.

I acknowledge with thanks the assistance of a number of friends and colleagues at Indiana University. I received references and other data concerning Spain and Latin America from Merle and Connie Simmons, Luis and Ann Beltrán, John Lombardi, Anya Royce, Emma Simonson (now deceased), and Joseph Ricapito (now at Tulane University). Similar assistance concerning sub-Saharan Africa was received from Charles Bird, Robert Port, Ivan Karp, and Alan P. Merriam (now deceased). I am also grateful for assistance rendered by Peter Gold, Curator, University Museum. I wish especially to acknowledge the most generous assistance received from Thomas Glastras, Reference Librarian, Graduate Library.

My largest debt of gratitude is owed to the staff of the Indiana University Archives of Traditional Music, an institution of which I was director for many years. Frank Gillis, who succeeded me as director and is now retired, extended me many courtesies. Louise Spear, the assistant director, edited the initial version of the audiography and bibliography and aided me in innumerable ways, as did Marilyn Graf, who provided invaluable assistance in editing, typing, and proofreading the initial version of the work. Amy Novick, the Archives' librarian, materially assisted in finding and documenting the Archives' holdings listed herein.

I am also grateful for assistance received from a number of graduate students. While engaged in field work in Africa, Carol Robertson (now a member of the faculty of the University of Maryland, College Park) sent me drawings and data concerning musical instruments in Ghana; Ruth Stone (now a member of the faculty of Indiana University, Bloomington) sent me photographs and descriptions of musical instruments in Liberia. Valerie Christian (now Valerie Merriam) shared with me knowledge concerning performance techniques of the *bounkam*, gained while working at the Archives Sonores in Upper Volta. Verlon Stone helped in the selection of photographs to be utilized as illustrations and in the frame-by-frame analysis of drumming in the *cumbia*. He collaborated with Ruth Stone in the preparation of the graphic realization of this analysis. Mellonee Burnim made available to me a copy of her master's thesis, *Songs in Mende Folktales*. Joyce Hendrixson shared with me her field experience in Nigeria. Thomas Avery translated for me portions of scholarly works in Portuguese. Barbara Seitz copied music illustrations, proofread, and assisted in other ways in the preparation of the initial version of this work, as did Abraham Cáceres, and Nancy Fogal. Deborah Schwartz, Robert Fogal, and Roberta Singer assisted in its first and full revision and the latter in the partial second revision. Other students who assisted in one manner or another were Elena Fraboschi and John Hasse.

I acknowledge with much appreciation financial support received from the following institutions and agencies: The field work of 1964 and 1965 was carried on while I held a Fulbright Research Fellowship. In 1964 the Instituto de Cultura Popular of Cali provided released time for Delia Zapata to accompany me in the field. In 1965 the Universidad Nacional de Colombia offered me a small grant to assist in the field work. My field work of 1968 was financed by the Indiana University Latin American Studies Program with research funds provided by the Ford Foundation. The field work in 1970 and the research in Spain during the same year were carried on while I was on sabbatical leave from Indiana University and with additional assistance from the Latin American Studies Program. The first version of part I was written and the transcriptions offered in part III prepared in 1974, while I was holding a Senior Fellowship from the National Endowment for the Humanities. Additional assistance was received from the Indiana University Office of Research and Graduate Development in 1974 and from the College of Arts and Sciences in 1974-75. Further funds were received from the Office of Research and Graduate Development during the years 1978-81.

Some data, photographs, drawings, musical illustrations, and transcriptions included in this work were previously published in the same or different form in articles by this author in the *Journal of the International Folk Music Council*, the *Yearbook of the International Folk Music Council*, the *Journal of the Society for Ethnomusicology*, *Revista Musical Chilena*, the *Latin American Music Review*, *Grove's New Dictionary of Music and Musicians*, *Folklore Today: a Festschrift for Richard M. Dorson*, and in the album *Cantos Costeños* (see audiography). Photographs and drawings from the works of other authors published by the Österreichische Akademie der Wissenschaften of Vienna and the Fundação Calouste Gulbenkian and the Sociedade de Geografia of Lisbon are also included. Permission for use from the publisher is gratefully acknowledged in each case. Specific visual credits are given in the list of figures and the list of transcriptions.

CAMERA-READY PREPARATION

The camera-ready copy from which this book was produced was prepared under the supervision of the author with funds provided by the National Endowment for the Humanities, the Indiana University Foundation, and the following agencies of Indiana University: the Office of Research and Graduate Development, the Office of International Programs, and the Department of Learning Resources. I wish to express my gratitude to these agencies for their support of this work, and my appreciation of the efforts of Dean Walter Meserve of the Office of Research and Graduate Development and Natalie Wrubel, Managing Editor of the Indiana University Press, in assisting me to secure these funds. The latter and Harriet Curry, Production Manager of the Indiana University Press, offered most patient and useful guidance in the preparation of the camera-ready copy. To this David Zablodowsky and Judith McCulloh added words of counsel concerning typefaces and indexing.

My principal assistant in this project was Roberta Singer. She made invaluable contributions to its success through her careful attention to all relevant detail and her assistance in coordinating the efforts of the other individuals involved. Others who assisted in proofreading and other aspects of the work were Marc Satterwhite, Abraham Cáceres, Diana Barber, and Vincent Sorisio. Jane Shelly was a painstaking copy editor and the most cooperative of collaborators in the arduous task of preparing the index. Beverly Clinkingbeard negotiated all the complex problems presented by this work with the aplomb of a skilled and veteran typist.

The music copying is the work of two excellent calligraphers, William Buckmaster and Timothy McAlpine. The photographs and drawings were prepared by divisions of Instructional Systems Technology of Indiana University. The majority of the photographs reproduced were processed by Photographic Services. George Bostick of Graphics prepared the maps and fingering charts and Mary Blizzard, also of Graphics, was responsible for the layout of the figures. I am also indebted to Mary Blizzard for instructing Roberta Singer in the delicate art of stripping in visuals and for permitting the use of the facilities at Graphics for this purpose.

INTRODUCTION

ORGANIZATION AND GOALS

Due to its geographic isolation at the time of my field work, Evitar seems to have preserved a greater proportion of its traditional music practice than had neighboring communities. However, Evitar is not viewed here as an isolated phenomenon but as a microcosm representative of the folk culture of the northern portion of the Departamento de Bolívar and, to a lesser extent, of the Costa Altántica as a whole. The view then expands to other cultures or culture regions--the Spanish-European, the sub-Saharan African, and the Amerindian--which historically may have influenced the development of *costeño* song and instrumental music.

This study focuses upon two aspects of *costeño* culture, its music and its sung poetry. Both take the form of structured sound. When heard simultaneously in the form of a song, neither can be fully understood without the consideration of the other. All other phenomena--the people, their environment, their musical instruments, and the occasions when music is performed--are discussed in part I, "The Context." They are of interest in their own right, but they are considered here primarily as the means of developing an understanding of the two interrelated sound structures which form the principal subject of investigation. I have discussed this approach in some detail in a previous publication (List 1979:1-4).

This is the first work of any length in the English language concerning any aspect of the folk culture of the *costeño*. It is also, to my knowledge, the first attempt to assess the contributions of three diverse cultures to the musical life of a particular community. This study, of necessity, is interdisciplinary in nature. It primarily combines the approaches of the ethnomusicologist and folklorist, but it also makes some use of concepts and methods derived from other fields of study within both the humanities and the social sciences. This work may therefore be expected to be of interest to readers with a wide variety of backgrounds, only a few of whom will possess all the skills and knowledge requisite for its fullest understanding.

With this in mind I have endeavored to make the material offered as accessible as possible by avoiding the use of technical terms,

xxix

especially those of the social sciences, when this is feasible.
Those readers who do not possess Spanish are provided with translations of the song texts and of any Spanish terms appearing elsewhere. Should the reader be concerned with aspects of music as a
sound structure, he or she must, of course, be familiar with the
notation system employed in Western music and the basic terminology
used to describe such music. Some knowledge of the terminology
utilized in describing poetry would also be useful, but it is not a
requisite. Assuming this minimum of skill and knowledge on the
part of the reader, I have endeavored to supply reasonably detailed
explanations of the technical terms and methods employed in dealing
with both the music and the sung poetry and the concepts and theories upon which they are based. Obviously, it would be best if
part III, "The Music and Poetry," were unencumbered with such explanation so that the reader already equipped to follow a certain
line of inquiry would not need to precede it with the reading of
what he or she already knows. I have, therefore, gathered together the greater part of the explanatory material in chapters
5-6, which form part II, "Methodology." However, the introductions
to both of these chapters should be read before proceeding to part
III, since they provide basic information necessary to the understanding of the remainder of the work. Chapters 5-6 are organized
in outline form and are preceded by an outline of their contents
in which the page upon which the discussion of each topic begins is
also indicated. Throughout the remainder of the work reference is
made to the relevant explanatory section or sections of part II by
means of the symbols assigned to them in this outline. For ready
reference these symbols are also given at the head of each page of
these two chapters.

The six chapters of part III are concerned with the various
genres comprising the song and instrumental repertory of the
evitaleros. The first part of each chapter is descriptive in
nature, offering transcriptions, translations, and other data concerning performance of specific genres. The second part of each
chapter, "Commentary," begins with a discussion of those characteristics which differentiate one genre from another or the performance of one informant from that of a second. It then proceeds to
the assessment of possible cultural sources of the various stylistic elements displayed in the performances transcribed. A summa-
tion of the latter discussion will be found at the close of each
of these six chapters.

Part IV, "Synthesis," views what has been offered previously
from a broader perspective. Chapter 13 is concerned with the
costeño repertory as a whole, with the similar and contrasting
traits displayed by the various genres. Chapter 14 offers a sum-
mation of the specific contributions of the three parent cultures
to *costeño* music and sung poetry. Judgments are then made concerning the degree of influence exerted by each parent culture,
and possible reasons are presented for the ranking thus produced.

My experience over many years as director of the Indiana University Archives of Traditional Music has made me acutely conscious
of the need for detailed and accurate documentation of field recordings. My field recordings which are transcribed or mentioned
are each identified by LF plus a number. These are correlated in

an appendix with the identifying numbers of copies on deposit in the Archives of Traditional Music. Some of the items offered in chapters 7-9 are found in a commercial disc recording issued through the Archives of Traditional Music and are also correlated by side and band numbers. A similar issue offering items found in chapters 10-12 is planned.

All of the recordings transcribed or discussed, whether field recordings or commercial issues, are identified in the running text, and a fuller reference, when necessary, is supplied in the audiography. Only publications cited are listed in the latter and in the bibliography. Finally, a detailed index of the entire work is provided.

The Spanish word *negro* is the equivalent of the English *black*. Negro is an honorific title in the Costa Atlántica and the *evitaleros* thus refer to themselves as *negros* (see TR 46, p. 413). With ample justification, North Americans of African descent who are speakers of English prefer to be called Blacks. Since this work is concerned with the music and poetry made by individuals who speak Spanish, I have used the term *negro* when referring to them (it is not capitalized in Spanish) and the word Black in my occasional reference to the music of English-speaking North Americans of African descent.

Opinion differs as to whether the actual names of informants should be given in a work of this nature or pseudonyms employed to preserve anonymity. I have chosen the former course. If the discussion of musical families, of the effect of kinship upon the transmission of musical practices, was to be included, this approach was to a great extent required. In addition, I am of the opinion that the use of actual names rather than pseudonyms adds a useful sense of reality to the exposition. It impresses the reader with the fact that those discussed are living, breathing human beings rather than fictitious characters forming an anonymous aggregate. I do not believe that members of such an open society will object to the use of their names.

All discussion of musical practices, customs, and physical and economic conditions in Evitar and the surrounding region refers to a period ending in 1971. As indicated in the epilogue (p. 573), there has been considerable alteration in these circumstances since that time.

THE INVESTIGATION

This study is based upon both primary and secondary sources. Data for the first type were secured in four field trips to the Costa Atlántica. These occurred during October and November of 1964, February and March of 1965, June through August of 1968, and February through April of 1970. Other materials were drawn from published sources, in part during a three-month period in Spain in 1970. Further data were secured from field recordings and documentation on deposit in the Archives of Traditional Music and from commercially issued disc albums held by that institution. A number of scholars also most courteously made available to me unpublished materials which they had collected in the field.

During the four field expeditions I visited every locality
marked on the map given in fig. 1 (p. 4) and collected materials
in all but four: Barranquilla, Santa Marta, Valledupar, and La
Paz. I made no attempts to collect in the first three, all capi-
tals of *departamentos*. In La Paz I was unable to work with a
vallenato ensemble as planned. I later recorded such an ensemble
in Bogotá.

I initially focused on the collection of material concerning
the *cumbia* complex. This was soon expanded to the wider purpose
of securing as representative and as well documented a collection
as possible of *costeño* folksong and instrumental music. In addition, I recorded 75 tales and a large number of interviews concerning the *velorio* custom. The full collection comprises 125
rolls of recorded magnetic tape, ten reels of 8 mm. sound film,
250 slides and photographs, and 20 musical instruments. The recordings are on deposit in the Archives of Traditional Music and
the instruments in the Indiana University Museum.

I had worked in Evitar in both 1964 and 1965, but it was only
when I studied the materials collected during these two expeditions that I conceived the idea of using the village of Evitar as
the focal point of a wider study of *costeño* music and sung poetry.
Thus when I returned to Colombia in 1968 I placed more emphasis
on field work in Evitar, although I also collected materials in
other parts of the region. In 1970 I devoted all my time to working in Evitar or in studying the materials collected there.

In my field work I was in most cases accompanied by a native
of the region who acted as an intermediary or field assistant. In
1964 I was accompanied by Delia Zapata Olivella, in 1965 by Manuel
Zapata Olivella, and in 1968 and 1970 by Winston Caballero Salguedo. The Zapatas were and continue to be active as folklorists.
Caballero has an undergraduate degree in sociology and later came
to Indiana University for formal training in folklore. Manuel
Zapata had some command of English, the other two none. These
individuals were of assistance in many ways, but most importantly
they acted as intermediaries in interviews. I began my field
work with a fund of academically learned Spanish, which improved
steadily as my work progressed. However, the rural *costeño,* and
those of the lower economic class in the cities, speak a dialect
of Spanish which Colombians native to other regions of the country
find difficult to understand. It was in this direction that I
required the greatest assistance.

In my early field work I used a numbered questionnaire as a
guide for the two of us. It was constantly necessary to add questions, and this method became too cumbersome. I soon discarded it
for a less structured form of interview. Beginning in 1965 I myself carried on interviews with more and more frequency. On occasion I was assisted by my wife, Eve, when she accompanied me into
the field.

In almost all cases it was I who tape-recorded, photographed,
and filmed. In all field expeditions, except in 1968, I employed
a Nagra III tape recorder with a full-track recording head. In
1968 I also used an Uher 4000 Reporter with a dual-track head. All
music was recorded at 7 1/2 i.p.s., the greater part of the interview at 3 3/4 i.p.s. The camera used during the first three expe-

ditions was a Honeywell Pentax H3, in the field work of 1970 an
Olympic -10EE-2. A Fairchild Cinephonic sound camera was utilized
in filming in 1964 and 1965.

Although recordings of music made in context offer certain
types of information not easily secured by other means, they are
rarely useful for transcription or detailed study. This is particularly true in the case of performances by ensembles where a balanced recording is an absolute requisite. On occasion we therefore
brought the larger ensembles from the country to Cartagena, where
I recorded their performances in large rooms in hotels or in the
studios of Radio Miramar. In 1970 we recorded *evitaleros* in Mahates
performing *danza de negro, bullerengue,* and *fandango* in the semi-
seclusion of an outdoor motion picture theater. Through the courtesy of the *alcalde* (mayor) a *policía* (policeman) was stationed at
the entrance to ward off unwanted visitors. A photograph of this
recording session appears on the cover of *Ethnomusicology Newsletter,* vol. IV, no. 3.

The informants were paid for their services in cash; but some
volunteered their services or refused the proffered payment. The
amount paid was established on the basis of prevailing wages or
through negotiation. Drinks and cigarettes also were usually provided. When informants were brought from the countryside to Cartagena, the cost of their food and lodging was defrayed.

Cartagena was my base in all four expeditions to the Costa
Atlántica. When I worked in other *departamentos* I used their
capital as a temporary base. In most cases I visited the nearby
rural communities during weekends, when the men were less likely
to be dispersed in the fields. Field work is the art of achieving
the possible. An extended residence in Evitar would have proved
very useful. I could have observed most of the occasions during
which music was performed, learned to play the musical instruments,
and possibly participated in musical performance. Unfortunately,
this was not feasible. I had family and academic responsibilities,
I was in my fifties, and, most importantly, I had not developed the
adult *costeño's* ability to ward off tropical organisms. In 1964
and 1965 I attempted short stays in other rural communities, but my
limited capacity to adapt to these circumstances was rather forci-
bly impressed upon me.

For purposes of this investigation, Winston Caballero made three
trips to Evitar while I was not in Colombia. Two of these followed
my expedition of 1968 and one that of 1970. In all three Caballero
was accompanied by his brother-in-law Hector Díaz Herazo. Those
of 1968 were made at Caballero's suggestion. He thought that he,
as a *costeño*, alone rather than accompanied by a *gringo,* would more
expeditiously be able to secure certain data. He was also of the
opinion that by working alone he could develop rapport which would
be found useful in further field work in which he might accompany
me. He was proved to be correct in both assumptions. His third
visit to Evitar was made at my request. Unrest following national
elections in 1970 produced martial law and a curfew and made it
impossible for me to carry out a planned visit to Evitar. For all
field work on Caballero's part I provided funding and instructions
as to the data and material I wished him to collect. Some of the
data he collected are incorporated in the following pages, and

three of the transcriptions are of recordings made by Caballero
and Díaz.

While working in Evitar I did have opportunity to observe some
dances and song games. I recorded one of these occasions with
8 mm sound film and photographed others. Of necessity, then, data
not secured by observation had to be secured by interview. Special
efforts were exerted to assure the reliability of the information
drawn from the latter. Two aspects of the investigation facilitated these efforts. The first was that almost all interviews were
recorded. I thus could hear what actually occurred as frequently
as I desired. The second was that my visits to Evitar spanned a
period of six years. I was therefore able to follow the same line
of inquiry not only with a number of informants but with the same
informant after a considerable lapse of time. All interviews were
transcribed. The typed transcripts provided a convenient means of
comparing responses made to the same line of inquiry by the same
or different informants. The recordings offered subtler insights
into meaning and intention as gauged by inflection and timing. I
checked for misunderstandings, for misconceptions concerning the
meaning of questions, and for "leading questions" on our part
which themselves suggested what answers should be made. I attempted
to determine whether the statements made represented actual observation or merely opinion. Nevertheless, there remain instances
where the reliability of the data is moot. In such cases, what I
have included and how it is stated can represent no more than my
best judgment.

The best results are achieved when further field work follows
transcription and study of the material previously collected.
With the knowledge thus gained the investigator is in a much better
position to determine what further paths of inquiry should be followed. Unfortunately, between my visits to the Costa Atlántica
I could find time only to work on interviews and song texts. The
music transcriptions offered in this volume were not made until
1974, and their analysis was not completed until some time later.
I had planned a further field trip to Evitar once this process was
completed, but this did not prove possible. Although I did not
know this at the time, such a return visit would not have been very
fruitful. By that date most of my informants had either left the
village or died (see "Epilogue," p. 573).

My informants, of course, could offer me little assistance in
the determination of the degree to which each parent culture had
contributed to the musical life of Evitar and the vicinity. Such
information was necessarily secured from a wide variety of other
sources. A number of years were spent in accumulating data concerning possible sources of stylistic and structural traits, but
there is obviously no end to such a task. To arrive at conclusions
it was necessary to assume that the evidence I had accumulated was
sufficient for my purpose and that contrary evidence did not exist.
Such an assumption is basic to all empirical study and requires
no apology. As in other cases, new data will undoubtedly come to
light which will require modification of some of my conclusions.

One further assumption had to be made. The processes of diffusion and acculturation which produced the *costeño* folk culture
began several centuries in the past. Historical data bearing upon

these processes come primarily from European sources, but even
these offer few specifically analogous items. Relations between
the *costeño* and the three parent cultures therefore must be based
almost entirely upon data accumulated in this century. The assumption here is that since the time of cultural contact, the stylistic
characteristics of sub-Saharan West African music and Amerindian
music of this region of the New World have remained reasonably constant. Lacking appropriate historical records, there is no means
of proving this to have been the case. However, in societies which
have been primarily non-literate, a certain continuity of practice
can be assumed.

Indiana University, Bloomington   GEORGE LIST

March 1983

PART I.
The Context

I. The Setting

THE REGION

The village of Evitar is located in the Corregimiento de Mahates, Departamento de Bolívar, Colombia. The village forms part of a cultural-geographic region whose inhabitants are referred to as *costeños*. This region, known in Colombia as the Costa Atlántica, lies between the Caribbean Sea and the inland ranges of the Andes. The bulk of the population resides in the departamentos of Atlántico, Bolívar, Cesar, Córdoba, Magdalena, and Sucre. The marshy coast lands of the departamentos of Antióquia and Chocó are sparsely populated, and the Guajira Peninsula is a desert populated primarily by partially acculturated Indians.

The greater part of the region is a low-lying plain. However, a lone mountain mass with snow-capped peak, the Sierra Nevada de Santa Marta, rises abruptly from the sea in northern Magdalena, reaching a height of 19,000 feet. On the plain the climate is tropical, averaging 27 to 28 degrees centigrade (approximately 82 to 84 degrees Fahrenheit). It is very humid, since precipitation in general exceeds evaporation. Thus there are many shallow lakes (*ciénagas*), some of which are formed by overflow from the Magdalena, Colombia's principal river, which empties into the Caribbean Sea. There are no seasons as known in temperate climes. Instead the year is divided into four alternating periods of greater or lesser rainfall.

The Spaniards discovered this coast very early in their exploration of the New World. Columbus was the first European to land on these shores, during his voyages between 1499 and 1503. Amerigo Vespucci apparently followed soon thereafter. The first permanent European settlement was established in 1525 at Santa Marta, present capital of the Departamento de Magdalena, where there exists a small but excellent harbor. Cartagena de Indias, present capital of the Departamento de Bolívar, was founded in 1533 and became one of Spain's principal military bases in the New World.

During the first quarter century of colonization, the only period during which an exact record was kept, some five thousand Spaniards came to the New World. The largest number of these came from southern Spain, from Andalucía, Badajoz (Extremadura), and the Canary Islands. It can be assumed that this trend continued,

3

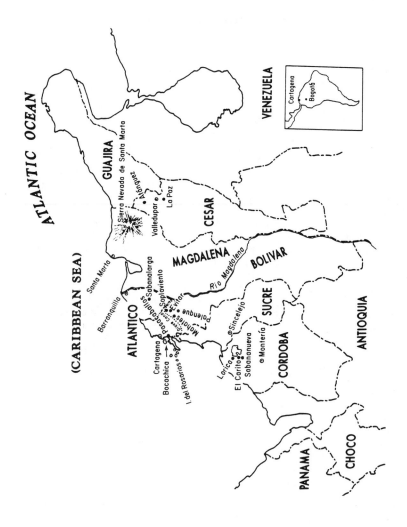

Fig. 1. The Atlantic coastal region of Colombia

since the pronunciation of Spanish as it developed in the New
World is closer to that of southern Spain than that of central or
northern Spain. The slaves brought to Colombia came from western
Africa, from the northern countries of Senegal, Gambia, and
Guinea-Bissau and from other countries along the west coast as
far south as Gabon, Congo, Angola, and Zaire.

In the first decade of the seventeenth century Cartagena was
the scene of an insurrection of Negro slaves. Led by an enslaved
African prince, Benko, many escaped from the city and fled into
the interior, where they formed a *palenque* (fortified settlement),
now known as Palenque de San Basilio. The *palenqueros* remained
independent throughout the entire period of Spanish rule. Living
in isolation, they developed a mixed Spanish and pan-African culture. Among the costeños Palenque is believed to be the principal
source of African traditions persisting in the region.

When the Spaniards arrived the lowlands of the Costa Atlántica
were occupied by a large number of Indian tribes. During the
early period of colonization many Indians were enslaved. However,
Indians were not accustomed to the institution of slavery and its
concomitant heavy labor in mines and fields. Many died in cap-
tivity, others in battle with the Spaniards for possession of their
lands. As great a decimation was caused by the diseases brought
by the Spaniards. Those Indians who remained soon lost their identity through intermarriage or acculturation, and the tribes as such
became extinct. However, the tribal names remain as those of communities or of geographical points: Calamar, Turbaco, Tolú,
Mompás, and Sinú.

Only those tribes who lived on land unsuited for agriculture
still maintain their identity. Thus tribes speaking their own
language are found almost entirely in mountain, desert, and marshy
areas, the Motilón in the Sierra de Perijá on the Venezuelan border, the Kogi and Ika in the Sierra Nevada de Santa Marta, the
Guajiro on the Guajira Peninsula, and the Cuna along the Darien
Gulf near Panamá.

After centuries of intermarriage the contemporary costeño displays a mingling in varying degrees of the racial heritages of
the African Negro, the Amerindian, and the Spanish Caucasian. The
degree of prominence of particular racial traits differs from area
to area as well as within the same community. In the towns and
villages that I have visited in rural northern Bolívar, Negro
physical characteristics seem more pronounced than those of the
other two races. However, the faces of some inhabitants seem to
display predominantly Amerindian or Caucasian features.

The city of Cartagena was the first in Colombia to declare its
independence from Spain, in 1809. Similar declarations soon followed in other areas of the colony. A lengthy struggle with Spain
then ensued under the leadership of Simón Bolívar, known in
Colombia as *el libertador* (the Liberator). Independence was
achieved in 1819.

Although Cartagena and Santa Marta have natural harbors, the
principal port of Colombia is the city of Barranquilla, capital of
the Departamento de Atlántico. Until recent times the Magdalena
River formed the main artery of commerce in Colombia. Barranquilla
is located a short distance inland from the mouth of the Magdalena

and possesses a large man-made harbor. The Magdalena also dis-
charges its water into the sea through several channels across
the lowlands south of Cartagena. Over millennia the river has
changed its course several times. One of these ancient channels
empties into the Bahía de Cartagena. This channel was dredged
to make it navigable by river boats and has since been known as
the Canal del Dique (Reymond 1942:417). At present neither the
Magdalena nor the Canal del Dique is much used for transport.
Some cargo brought to the ports is delivered inland by rail, but
most transport is by truck.

Large-scale mechanized commercial farming has developed along
the Sinú River valley in the Departamento de Córdoba and in the
valley surrounding the capital city of Valledupar in the Departamento de Cesar. This type of agriculture is also practiced in
the Sábana de Bolívar, the southern part of that departamento,
but the northern part of the departamento is devoted primarily to
cattle raising and small-scale farming. The *campesinos* (country
people) of this area have therefore experienced somewhat less
change in their mode of life and, as a corollary, in folk music
practice. However, in the last two decades generator-operated
phonographs have been slowly replacing the traditional folk instrumental ensembles in providing music for rural *fiestas*. In
1970 the transistor radio had only recently made its appearance
and was beginning to affect musical taste.

THE MUNICIPIO

In Colombia the political division similar to the state or
province of other countries is the *departamento*. Each departamento in turn is divided into smaller political divisions known
as *municipios*. The administrative center of the municipio, usually its largest town, carries the same name as the municipio as
a whole. The smaller towns or villages within the municipio are
known as *corregimientos*. Thus Evitar is a corregimiento of the
Municipio de Mahates, of which the town of Mahates is the *cabeza
de corregimiento* (administrative center).

Political administration is highly centralized in Colombia, a
legacy of Spanish rule. The executive officer of the municipio
is the *alcalde* (mayor). The alcalde of the municipio is appointed
by the *gobernador* (governor) of the departamento, who in turn is
appointed by the *presidente* (president) of the Republic of
Colombia. In turn the alcalde appoints the administrative offi-
cers of the other communities found within the municipio, alcaldes
for towns of some size and *inspectores* for the villages. Thus all
administrators are normally members of the political party in
power. The municipio also has a *juez* (judge), who is appointed
by the judicial authorities in the capital, and a *concejo* (council),
which is elected by the citizens of the municipio.

As its largest community, the town of Mahates was the municipio's market center. It was principally to Mahates that the residents of Evitar brought their produce for sale, and it was here
that they made most of their purchases. It was also here that the
hacendados (large landowners) had their residences and carried on
their business. Colombia is a Catholic country. The church of

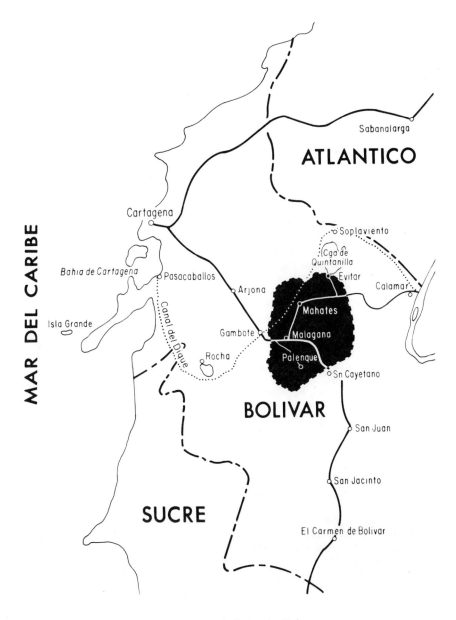

Fig. 2. The municipio de Mahates

the municipio is located in the town of Mahates, and until recently
only the priests connected with this church were available to perform the Catholic sacraments for the residents of the neighboring
villages.

THE VILLAGE

In Spanish, Evitar is the infinitive form of the verb "to avoid."
Several legends have arisen to explain the origin of this curious
name, each linking Evitar with Mahates. Since the consonant h is
silent in Spanish and the final s of a word is rarely pronounced in
the costeño dialect, Mahates is heard as "mate." In fact, the name
of the town is spelled thus in an early map originally published in
France in 1827 (Instituto...Codazzi 1967:137). *Mate* is the third
person singular present subjunctive of the verb *matar* (to kill), a
form also used as an imperative. The following legend utilizes
this murderous interpretation of the meaning of the name Mahates:
   Shortly after the founding of Cartagena, two soldiers left that
city and made their way south, seeking a site for a new settlement.
One of the soldiers was an exceedingly quarrelsome fellow and the
other, considering his trade, was a rather peaceable individual.
The first soldier disagreed in a most disputatious manner with
every suggestion made by the second. Thus their quest was interrupted by bickering and heated argument, and they finally nearly
came to blows. Tired of the constant strife, the second soldier
parted from his companion and after traveling a short distance
found a site to his liking and named it Evitar, thus indicating
his desire to avoid further conflict. The first soldier set off
in the opposite direction and, selecting his own site, vented his
fury by naming it Mahates (¡mate!).
   Evitar has been, and still is, a remarkably isolated community.
Until 1962 there was no road into Evitar, only a track or path
connecting the village with Mahates which one followed on foot or
on a burro or a mule if one had such an animal at one's disposal.
In that year a road was constructed which connects Evitar and some
haciendas to the east with the Mahates-Calamar road. The road to
Evitar is not marked. Since it leads to no other community, it is
little traveled. It had not been repaired since it was first
graded, and by 1970 it had become a mere double dirt track, almost
impassable during the rainy seasons. Since the ciénaga is immediately north of Evitar, the road skirts the village and turns
east and passes the village's cemetery. This small body of water
leads through various channels to a number of ciénagas and the
Canal del Dique, providing the *evitaleros* with sites for fishing
and transport by water to the town of Soplaviento. This watery
area presents a considerably different appearance during the dry
seasons than during the rainy seasons, and the inhabitants of
Evitar know the portions of this watery maze by quite different
names from those found on published maps.
   The population of Evitar is not listed in any publication.
Such information is published concerning the population of entire
municipios, not of the corregimiento that forms part of a municipio unless the former is of considerable size. Estimates of the
population of Evitar varied from 1,000 to 1,200, of the number of

Fig. 3. The road to Evitar

Este pueblo evitalero	This village, Evitar,
es un pueblo embotellado	Is an embottled village
como nadie no se imagina.	As no one can imagine.
. . .	
Ya carretera tenemos.	Now we have a road.

Pedro Cueto Pimientel

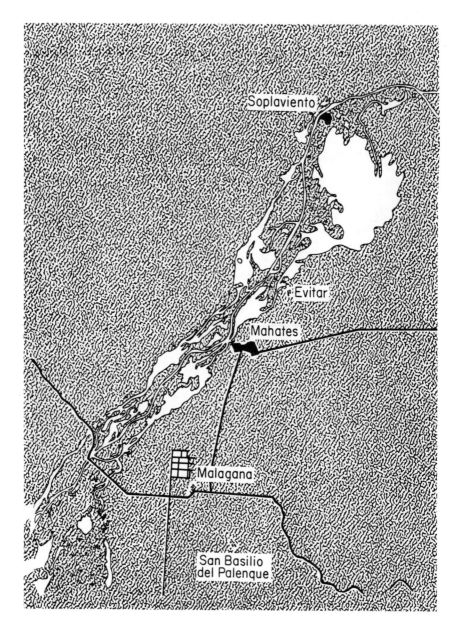

Fig. 4. The waterways

households in the village from 140 to 160. Some 200 evitaleros
were eligible to vote in the last election. Evitar is a Liberal
village; that is, the majority of its citizens vote for the
Liberal rather than the Conservative Party. It is the duty of
the inspector of the village to supervise the elections and to
see that each individual voting has the proper *cédula* (identification card). There seems little need for the maintenance of law
and order in a village like Evitar, and the inspector in 1970,
Herculano Pimientel, had no office and spent most of his time
working as an agriculturist.

The streets of Evitar are not marked, but they are known by
various names by its inhabitants. The three public buildings,
the school for boys, the recently constructed school for girls,
and the unfinished chapel, are located on a slight eminence and
overlook the village. The houses are built close to the street,
each having a yard demarcated by a *cerca* (fence) made of stakes
of *caña brava* (*Arundo donax 1.*), a heavy bamboo. The yard serves
as home base for the family's fowl, goats, and pigs. There is
usually an opening in the cerca through which the animals exit
to search through the streets for food.

The houses in Evitar are of the *bahareque* type common to this
tropical region. However, the inhabitants refer to them as *chozas*
or *ranchos*, not as bahareques. The chozas or ranchos of Evitar
have pitched roofs thatched with palm leaves, plastered walls, and
dirt floors. The windows are open apertures which are closed at
night by heavy wooden shutters. Most chozas are rectangular and
contain two rooms, one used as a living room and the other as a
bedroom. A cooking hut is found in back of the house within the
cerca. It is similar in construction to the choza but has no
walls.

At night the house is illuminated by either *velas* (candles)
or *mecheros* (kerosene lamps). The latter are preferred, since
they provide light at less expense and can also be used out of
doors. During fiestas or *velorios* light is provided in back or in
front of the house by hanging mecheros in doorways or on the
cerca.

The principal economic activity in Evitar is agriculture.
However, there are few men in Evitar who own land in addition
to that upon which their houses are built. The greater part of
the land near the village is the property of hacendados, who use
it primarily for cattle grazing. Most of the men in the village
cultivate small tracts of land which have been lent to them by
the hacendados for a period of one to three years. In return for
the use of the land the man cultivating it must clear it of all
growth but large trees and must sow grass when his period of use
is about to terminate.

The primary crops raised by the evitaleros are *maíz* (corn),
arroz (rice), *yuca* (cassava), and *ajonholí* (sesame). Among other
crops raised are *millo* (millet) and *piña* (pineapple). Most of the
crops raised are consumed within the village. The men sell a
portion of them, principally yuca and maíz, to buyers who live
outside the village. Because of difficulties in transport they
cannot expect a large or regular income from this source.

Those men who own boats fish in the water of the ciénagas.

Fig. 5. The bahareque of Santiago Ospino Caraballo

Fig. 6. Street scene looking east on Calle
del Cementerio. The almacén is to the right.

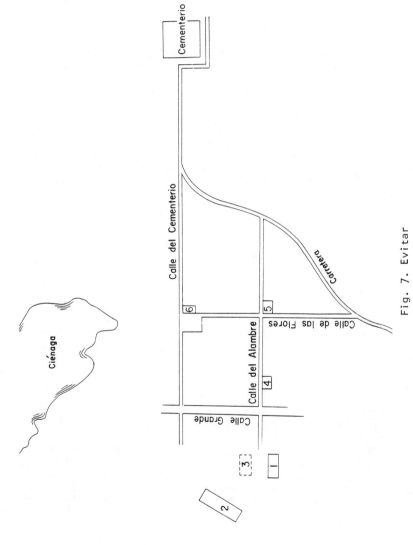

Fig. 7. Evitar

(1) schoolhouse for boys (2) schoolhouse for girls (3) unfinished chapel
(4) bahareque of the inspector (5) almacén (6) bahareque of Abraham Herrera.

This is done early on Saturday mornings. When the men return with their catch they are usually met by woman vendors who have come to buy fish to sell elsewhere. A few men own shotguns and hunt both for food and for pelts to sell elsewhere. That part of his catch which the fisherman cannot sell to the woman vendors and which cannot be consumed by his family, he will attempt to sell to other villagers. Hunters who bag larger game also attempt to sell within the village that part of the meat which their family cannot consume. Occasionally a domestic animal such as a pig or a goat is slaughtered and the surplus flesh sold on a table placed in front of the door of the house.

Most of the work required by the neighboring hacendados is done by *peones*, men who work regularly for them. However, the evitaleros do work with some frequency for one or another of these large landholders. Occasionally they will be employed by the hacendado as *vaqueros* (cattle herders). However, this is infrequent, since cattle are now more likely to be moved by truck than on foot.

There is only one *almacén* (store) in Evitar, and it is managed by a woman. The almacén has a limited stock, and the evitaleros must shop in other communities for most of their clothes, cooking utensils, and other necessities. A number of other men and women ply their various trades. There are two men who build chozas, three dressmakers and a tailor, three *rezanderas* (women who recite prayers at the velorio, or wake), and four midwives, of which three are women and one a man. All the above are part-time occupations. The only individuals in the village who receive full-time compensation are the two teachers, the *maestro* of the school for boys and the *maestra* of the school for girls.

Formal, legal marraige is the exception rather than the rule in Evitar. In the majority of cases the couples enter into a de facto union without sanction of either religious or civil authorities. Following a formal marriage there is always a fiesta given by the father of the bride. In de facto marriage there is no ceremony and no fiesta. Both sexes prefer a de facto rather than a legal marriage. In a de facto marriage neither partner is permanently attached to the other. If the man feels he is not treated well by the woman, he is free to leave her. The woman is equally free to leave the man if he does not treat her in the manner which she believes appropriate. If they are legally married neither partner will feel free to leave the other. Marriage is a holy sacrament, and they will fear punishment in the hereafter if they do not abide by it.

In sexual relations, as in other matters, the man is dominant, at least overtly. This fact is illustrated by the custom of the *baile de cuota*, a dance sponsored by a household in order to earn money. Only unattached women attend, and they pay no admission fee. The man of the household will invite as many unattached women as possible, since it is their presence which attracts the men who do pay admission. The men who attend may be unattached or may have a formal union with a woman or a de facto union with one or more women. In the latter cases the woman or women will not attend the dance but will remain at home. On the basis of contacts made at the baile de cuota a man may form new sexual unions or break old ones.

Custom decrees that a man support any woman with whom he has a

union and any children that he has fathered. In Evitar, if a man
leaves his woman as soon as she becomes pregnant, a fairly common
occurrence, or does not support his woman or women and his children, social pressure will be brought to bear to see that he meets
his responsibilities. It will be difficult for him not to comply
unless he leaves the village.

Not only do plants thrive in this tropical climate, but organisms of all types flourish as well. There is much standing water
and thus a profusion of mosquitos, which fortunately in this area
do not carry malaria. Rain water is used for drinking whenever
possible, but during the dry seasons water must be taken from the
ciénaga. Sanitary facilities, even privies, are unknown. Infant
dysentery is common, and infant mortality is high. Individuals
who reach the age of eight or nine develop sufficient immunity to
disease to carry them through many more years.

Evitar has two schools, one for boys and one for girls. The
schoolhouse for boys was built in 1960 and consists of one room
only. It is a solid brick building with a corrugated asbestos roof
and barred windows. The new schoolhouse for girls was built in
1969 and is, without a doubt, the most impressive structure in
Evitar. It is constructed of cement block and has a corrugated
asbestos roof supported by light metal girders. There are three
rooms, with a blackboard mounted on the wall of each.

Domingo Polo Venecia, the maestro of the boys' school when I
was there, had received his *bachillerata*, which represents five
years of elementary and six years of secondary education. Carmen
Escamilla Barragán, the maestra of the girls' school, had received
education through the third year of the bachillerata. Two years
of schooling were offered until 1963, after which three years were
available. In 1968 there were 52 students enrolled in the boys'
school and 80 in the school for girls. The curriculum includes
the reading and writing of Spanish, arithmetic, and some history
of Colombia. In addition, all students receive the required five
hours a week of instruction in the Catholic religion.

Some children do not attend school. The majority are boys,
who begin to work in the fields at an early age. More boys than
girls also drop out before completing the three years of schooling
offered.

Evitar has neither priest nor chapel. If they desire the services of a priest, the villagers must travel to a location where
one is available or pay a priest to come to Evitar from Mahates.
The latter course is more expensive than most families in Evitar
can afford. To come to Evitar from Mahates a priest charges a
fee larger than the amount a man can earn in a week's hard labor.
His fee has to be paid in advance and is the same whether the
priest comes for a short period or for the day. Thus for a baptism, a mass, or a wedding the evitaleros usually go to Mahates
and employ the services of a priest attached to the church in
that town. A child who has not been baptized is referred to as a
moro (Moor) or affectionately as a *morín*. In January many of the
villagers contribute to the cost of bringing a priest to officiate
in the celebration of the fiesta of San Sebastián, the patron
saint of Evitar. Since the priest is already in the village, he
will offer additional services at a small fee. Many parents wait

Fig. 8. Schoolhouse for boys, maestro Polo in the doorway.

Fig. 9. Schoolhouse for girls, rear view.

Fig. 10. The unfinished chapel

for this occasion to have their children baptized.

Since there is no chapel the village's wooden images of the
Virgin Mary and San Sebastián are kept in the boys' schoolhouse.
It is to San Sebastián that the evitaleros appeal when in difficulty. A man may pray that his badly wounded arm be healed, a
woman that her lost *vaquita* (cow) be found. In return for his
services they promise the saint a velorio (wake) or a *milagro*
(miracle). The latter is a small replica in semiprecious metal
of what has been saved or returned. A string of such milagros is
suspended from the right arm of the image of the saint.

Most of the men have a poor opinion of priests, but many women
are more devout. Those evitaleros who are strongly religious have
always desired that there be a chapel in Evitar. Several attempts
have been made to construct one. The last attempt began in 1963
and terminated in 1969. It resulted in an unfinished chapel consisting of a cement floor and partially constructed concrete block
walls.

Although there has rarely been a religious celebration of Sunday in the village, Sunday has always been a day of rest for the
men. On this day they don their best clothes, white shirt and
white trousers, and visit with their friends. Such conviviality
often ends with drunkenness, since the men drink on all festive
occasions, of which Sunday is the most frequent. The women also
wear their best clothes on Sunday, but, unlike the men, they do
not drink.

Fig. 11. View within the cemetery

When an evitalero dies his or her passing is observed by a velorio. A velorio is a night or a series of nights spent without sleep in the company of the body or spirit of an individual who no longer lives on earth. The velorio for an adult lasts nine nights, and its principal purpose is to assist the soul of the deceased in moving from purgatory into heaven. Thus, *rosarios* (prayers) are recited twice or three times each night by a rezandera. In order to stay awake, those who attend the velorio play games and tell *cuentos* (tales). The family, wishing them to remain, provides what food and drink it can afford. Traditionally, rum is distributed both to the guests and to the neighbors. Velorios thus at times become somewhat boisterous.

While the men of the family go to the cemetery to dig the grave, the women prepare an altar in the *sala* (living room) of the choza. A sheet is hung against the wall and a table covered by a sheet placed against it. A wooden cross and pictures of the Virgin Mary are leaned against the wall. Its condition permitting, the corpse of the deceased is washed and dressed in white. If contagion is feared, the body is buried immediately. Otherwise it is displayed in its coffin for one night. The open coffin is placed at a right angle to the table with the head of the corpse adjacent to it. Velas are inserted in the tops of bottles; one bottle is placed at each corner of the coffin, and the candles are lit. When the coffin is later removed, the bottles with their candles remain in the same position and continue to form part of the altar.

Only men go to the cemetery to be present at the burial of the deceased. The women remain at home. Once erected, the altar remains intact throughout the velorio. If the body is not displayed, the bottles and candles are placed in such a manner as to outline the position of the coffin that would have been present. It is believed that the spirit of the deceased remains in the house until the altar is dismantled, which occurs on the final night of the velorio shortly before daybreak. This process is called *levantar el cuerpo* (raising the body) and signals the departure of the spirit of the deceased from the house to the cemetery.

2. Musical Instruments and Ensembles

Although costeño culture is itself a product of the past mingling of three diverse cultural strains and has undoubtedly been subjected to additional influences over the years, a visitor to Evitar during the early part of this century would have found fairly stable traditions of music and dance. Escalante in his study of Palenque offers brief descriptions of most of the instruments which I found in Evitar or which I was informed had existed there in the past. Escalante also describes the dances *cumbia*, *bullerengue*, and *danza de negro* and the ensembles which accompany each. He includes descriptions of both the *conjunto de cumbia* and the *conjunto de gaitas*, since both accompanied the dance cumbia in Palenque (Escalante 1954:293-97). All of these dances and ensembles could have been seen and heard in Evitar or in almost any village or town in the immediate area during the early part of this century.

With the increasing development of means of transport and communication, new influences were more frequently felt. These had their earliest and greatest impact on the urban areas and only later and to a lesser degree on the countryside. The Cuban *sexteto* with its *rumba* and *bolero* had its period of popularity and then disappeared. The *banda de vientos* (wind band) also had its day, but it retained its popularity only in the Departamento de Córdoba. Neither ensemble had a lasting effect upon musical practice in rural northern Bolívar, particularly in such a poor and isolated community as Evitar. It was rather the phonograph which has exerted the most permanent influence. This mechanical music maker invaded the countryside in the 1950's and has slowly caused the disappearance of certain folk musical practices. The gasoline-powered phonograph produces more volume and a greater variety of music for dancing than any of the traditional musical ensembles.

Because of its isolation and homogeneity, the disintegration of traditional musical culture has proceeded at a somewhat slower pace in Evitar than in most communities in the immediate area. However, the movement toward dependence upon commercially provided rather than self-produced musical fare, like the dependence upon manufacturered goods in general rather than on local artisanry, began many years before I first visited the village.

In order to document this process of change, a description follows of not only those musical instruments, ensembles, and dances

that were observed and recorded during the period of the investigation, but also those which we were told existed in Evitar in the
past. In one case, that of the *vallenato*, I am describing an ensemble which was just making its influence felt and which possibly
came into existence after my departure. In thus providing what
amounts to a recent history of musical practice in Evitar, I have
added to the data obtained in the village itself corroborative
information secured in my field work elsewhere in the region and
the little available in published form.

MUSICAL INSTRUMENTS

With the exception of the *marímbula*, an import from Cuba, all
the instruments described are traditional in the area. Unless
otherwise noted, the instruments were constructed by those who
played them.

IDIOPHONES

Palmetas (figs. 12-13).

As the name suggests, this instrument is utilized as a substitute for handclapping (*palmadas*). Two *palmetas* are used simultaneously and are clapped together like hands. Fig. 13 shows
Enríquez Sánchez Palacio playing them. The palmeta is made of a
thin board of *ceiba* (*Bombacopsis quinata*) about 1 centimeter thick
and is shaped like the paddle used in ping-pong. The paddle is
approximately 9 centimeters in length and 7.5 centimeters at its
widest point.

I have found no information concerning the use elsewhere of
the clapping together of two paddles instead of the clapping of
the hands. The instrument was possibly devised in this region.

Guacharaca (figs. 14-15).

The *guacharaca* is a rasp. The sound of the instrument is believed to be similar to the call of a bird of the same name
(*Ortalis guttata*), and it was therefore given the same name as
this bird. The instrument used in the performances of the danza
de negro in 1970 was made of a section 49 centimeters long and 2
centimeters wide of the stem of the *lata* (*Bactris minor* Jacq.),
a small palm tree. The stem of the lata is a thin, hard-walled,
dark brown tube filled with pith. To make the rasp, the central
and larger portion of the section of the lata stem is cut in half
lengthwise and the pith removed. This central section is 33.5
centimeters in length, the uncut portions at either end 8.5 and 9
centimeters in length, respectively. On the outside of the half-
tube forming the central section of the instrument, incisions are
made to form the rasp.

The guacharaca is played by drawing a *trinche* (fork) back and
forth across the incisions of the half-tube. The trinche consists of seven pieces of wire of differing lengths inserted into a
wooden handle. The full length of the trinche is 26 centimeters,
of which the handle occupies 15 centimeters and the longest wire of

Figs. 12-13. Palmeta; playing the palmetas.

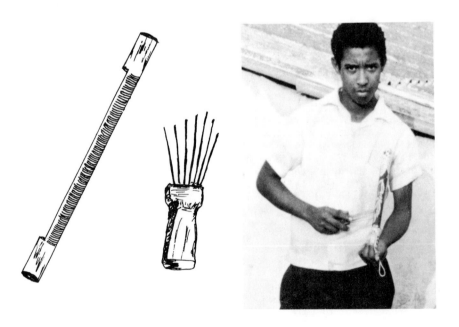

Figs. 14-15. Guacharaca and trinche; playing the guacharaca.

the fork 11 centimeters. In performance the left hand holds the
rasp part of the instrument at its lower extremity at about waist
level, the tube rising vertically with incisions forward, the
upper extremity leaning against the chest below the left shoulder.
The trinche is drawn up and down over the rasp with the right hand.
Fig. 15 is a photograph of Carlos Castellón Patino of Cartagena
playing the instrument.

The rasp or rubbed notched stick is known both in Africa and in
the New World. It was known among the Aztecs and is widely dispersed in Mexico and the western United States. However, there is
no archeological or documentary evidence that it existed among the
Indians of South America in pre-Colombian times. In South America
it is found among Indian tribes, such as the Cayapá of Coastal
Ecuador, who have had close contact with *negro* populations
(Izikowitz 1935:160-61). On the basis of the evidence it would
seem that the costeño guacharaca had its source in Africa. However, diffusion from Amerindian sources to the north cannot be
completely ruled out.

Guacho (figs. 16-17, and 66).

The *guacho* is a tubular rattle filled with seeds. In Evitar
the term refers specifically to such a rattle constructed of
metal. However, the term is also employed rather loosely in the
region to refer to any large rattle utilized in musical performance. Thus, when I asked a player in Evitar if he had ever seen
a guacho made of wood rather than metal, as I had in another community not far from Evitar, he replied that he had seen a guacho
made of *totumo* (*Crescentia cujete*). As will be seen below, he
was referring to the *maraca*, which is quite different in shape
from the guacho proper. In Evitar, as far as is known by those
questioned, the guachos have always been made of metal and have
always been played in pairs.

The guacho evitalero is a closed cylinder constructed of lata.
Lata is a term having many meanings in the region. It refers to
a tin plate, to a tin bucket, to a tin can whether filled with
food or empty, to the lata palm, which produces edible fruit, and
to food in general. In this case it refers to the tin plate from
which the guacho is fashioned. The discs which form the ends are
soldered to the cylinder. The guacho measured is 31 centimeters
in length and 5.5 centimeters in diameter. Four lines, each consisting of ten small holes, are punched along the side of the
cylinder. The lines are 8 centimeters apart, and the holes making
up the lines are approximately 2.5 centimeters apart. That part
of the guacho which is grasped by the hand is left intact. The
two end plates of the guacho are pierced with five holes each in
a geometric pattern. The guacho is filled with the dried seeds of
the *gapacho*, or *capacho* (*Canna coccinea*) plant. When these seeds
are not available small pebbles are employed as a substitute.

One guacho is held in each hand, and they are usually played
while standing rather than sitting. In a *ritmo* (music for a
particular dance) with a relatively slow tempo the two guachos are
shaken up and down simultaneously just above waist level (fig.
66). In a faster tempo they are shaken up and down alternately

Fig. 16. Guachos played by
Juan Ospino Jiménez of Evitar

Fig. 17. Guachos made by Juan
Ospino Jiménez of Evitar

in the same position (fig. 16). When a sustained shake is desired
the two instruments are held aloft and shaken simultaneously.
Repeated, accented shakes of shorter duration are occasionally
produced by twirling the guachos in opposite directions.

Tubular rattles made of bamboo or reeds, closed at both ends
and filled with hard seeds or pebbles, are found both in Africa
and in the Americas. The tubular rattle found in Togo and among
the Pangue (of Gabon) is made of sections of bamboo or reed cut
in half lengthwise and then fastened together with nails (Izikowitz 1935:146). The seeds or pebbles strike the nails when the
rattle is shaken, and an additional sound element is thus produced.
Those Indian tribes whose tubular rattles display African influence
insert palm needles through the wall of the rattle for the same
purpose. This is done among the Cuna and the Chocó, for example
(Izikowitz 1935:144). The tubular wooden rattle known as the *guasá*
used by the negro people of the Pacific coastal region of Colombia
is constructed in the same manner.

The only tubular bamboo rattle that I observed and recorded in
the Atlantic coastal region was played in the conjunto de cumbia
in Soplaviento. This guacho was played in the same manner as the
guasá; that is, it was held horizontally by hands placed at each
end of the tube. Unlike the guasá, it had no needles thrust
through its wall. It apparently represented the Indian tradition
influenced by the African. The guacho evitalero is made of tin
plate and is held in a different manner, and no nails or needles
are used. This seems to be a contemporary development of the
Indian tubular rattle. On the other hand, there has been metal-
working of this type among both the Europeans and the Africans
but not among the Amerindians. This may indicate that all three
cultures contributed to this particular development.

Maraca   (figs. 18-19, 53, 56-57, and 68).

The *maraca* was no longer in use in Evitar at the time of the
investigation. However, it had been employed in the recent past
in company with the *gaita*. The maraca as seen in other towns and
villages of the region is made from the dried rind of the gourd-
shaped fruit of the totumo tree. One maraca collected at San
Jacinto measures approximately 27 centimeters in length and 14
centimeters at its greatest diameter. Like the guacho described
above, it is filled with dried gapacho seeds. The wooden handle
is larger in diameter than its extension which passes through the
totumo rind, thus securing the latter at that end. The gourd-
shaped rind is secured at the upper end by a short, thin metal
rod which pierces the protruding extension of the handle and by
wire wound around this end of the handle. When played with gaitas
the maraca is held erect in the right hand of the player of the
gaita macho (fig. 68, p. 89). It is shaken back and forth, or sustained shakes are produced by twirling the instrument.

The maraca used in the conjunto de gaitas of San Jacinto (fig.
37) is randomly pierced with small holes throughout its circumference. A similar, smaller instrument is in use among the Spanish-
speaking descendants of the Atánquez Indians in the village of that
name. This instrument displays the same random pattern of holes as

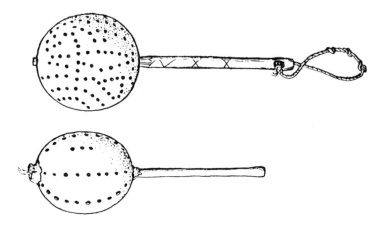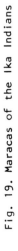

Fig. 19. Maracas of the Ika Indians

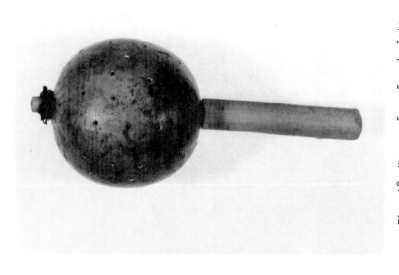

Fig. 18. Maraca from San Jacinto

the maraca of San Jacinto and, like that instrument, is employed
in company with two duct flutes to accompany dance (fig. 57, p. 70).

Gourd rattles are found among various Amerindian groups, who use
them singly primarily in ritual dance and shamanistic practices.
Gourd rattles are also in use in Africa. I believe the maraca
costeña to be indigenous for two reasons: 1) it occurs in common
association with paired duct flutes, which also seem to be indigenous (see gaita, pp. 65-71), and 2) the calabashes of the maracas
which accompany these duct flutes are randomly pierced with holes
throughout. Among Indian tribes of South America gourd rattles
are pierced with designs, squares, figure eights, or lines. However, as far as I can determine, rattles with small holes pierced
throughout the calabash are characteristic of only the region
under discussion.

Fig. 19 is a drawing of Ika maracas. Note that the Ikas possess
maracas of both types, with the holes pierced in a design and with
the holes randomly pierced throughout the whole calabash. Tayler
describes a maraca utilized by the kindred Kogi in association
with two flutes known as *kuizi*. This instrument is about 8 inches
long and consists of a round calabash of totumo which is punctured
with multiple holes. The wooden handle pierces through the gourd
and is kept from slipping out at the narrow end by a wad of beeswax (Tayler 1968:vi).

Marimba (marímbula) (fig. 20).

Of all the instruments in use in sub-Saharan Africa, the lamellaphone or thumb piano is the only one believed to have had its origin
in that continent. The instrument diffused to the Americas with the
importation of slaves from Africa and is known in Brazil, Haiti, the
Dominican Republic, Cuba, Puerto Rico, and Curaçao (Thompson 1971:
105-14). The lamellaphone diffused from Cuba to Colombia in the
late 1920's by audio-visual means (see p. 90). In the former
country it is most commonly known as the marímbula, in the latter
as *marimba*. It was no longer in use in Evitar when I first visited
that community in 1964, nor, as far as I could determine, had it
been in use in other parts of the region for many years. In 1965
a marimba was constructed and played for me by individuals who had
made and played the instrument in the past. This marimba will be
described later in this section.

The African lamellaphone consists of a number of forged iron
strips of different lengths mounted on a board. In most instruments one end of each of these metal keys is fixed by insertion
within metal bridges. The keys are plucked by the thumb and
forefinger, hence the name thumb piano. Small instruments are
played while held in the palms of the two hands; larger ones are
held on the lap. The board may be placed in an open calabash
which acts as the resonator, or the metal keys may be mounted on a
wooden box rather than on a board. The Cuban-Colombian instrument
is of the latter type.

In the Americas the term *marimba* is more frequently applied to
the xylophone than to the lamellaphone. In the Pacific coastal
region of Colombia, for example, *marimba* refers to a xylophone
rather than a lamellaphone. In Africa, however, related names are

Fig. 20. Marimba (marímbula) played by
José Isabel Castillo Martínez of Cartagena

applied to both instruments. In Bantu languages the stem or root
rimba or *limba* signifies a tone, a sounding key, a slat, or a
lamella. In Mozambique and Malawi, for example, one-tone gourd-
resonated xylophones are played in groups. Each such instrument
is referred to as a limba. A cumulative prefix, such as *ma-*, is
added when referring to an instrument possessing more than one
key. Thus *marimba* or *malimba* refers to tones, sounding keys,
slats, or lamellae and thus to the keyboard or the instrument as
a whole. Bantu musicians conceive the lamellaphone to be a small
relative of the xylophone, a kind of portable form of the latter.
Thus in Zanzibar the box-resonated xylophone is known as marimba
and the similarly resonated lamellaphone as *marimba madogo,* the
latter equaling "small marimba" (Kubik 1979:36-37). Other cumulative prefixes such as *si-*, *va-*, and *u-* are added to the stem or
root *rimba* or *limba* by other Bantu groups. The term *mbila* is
also applied to either the lamellaphone or the xylophone (Kubik
1980:682). In some areas distinctly different terms are applied
to the two instruments. The marimba-malimba complex is not in
use in most of the Bantu-speaking areas. Nevertheless, it has
achieved almost complete currency in the Americas. The most
common names applied to the lamellaphone in the Caribbean area
are, for example, marimba, malimba, *manimba, marimb'la, marimbola,*
marímbola, and marímbula (Thompson 1971:104).

The resonator box of the marimba made for me in Cartagena in 1965 consists of boards 1.5 centimeters thick nailed to a wooden frame. In dimension the box is 52.5 centimeters long, 33 centimeters wide, and 29 centimeters high. A sound hole is cut in one of the long sides of the box. Below this hole are three bridges consisting of thin metal rods fastened to the box by loops of wire which penetrate the side of the box and are fastened within it. The instrument constructed for me has seven keys of different lengths cut from the winding spring of an old phonograph. The keys are inserted between the upper and central bridges and pass over the lower bridge, the pressure of the opposing bridges holding in place the piece of spring forming the key. The player sits on the instrument in such a manner that his hands can reach the keys (fig. 20). The thumb and fingers push down the extremities of the keys and then glide off, thus causing them to vibrate. The keys, which vary in length from 13 to 16.5 centimeters, are tuned by adjusting their position within the bridges. According to José Isabel Castillo Martínez, the man who played the instrument for me in Cartagena in 1965, the less skilled players used marimbas with four, five, and six keys, the more skilled players instruments with seven, eight, ten, twelve, or even fourteen keys (for further information see List 1968b).

MEMBRANOPHONES

Tambor mayor (figs. 21-23, 28, 66, and 68).

Tambor is the generic term for drum in Spanish. This particular drum is given the added denomination *mayor* to distinguish it from its smaller counterpart, the *llamador*, but it is often referred to merely as the tambor. The tambor mayor is a slightly conical drum with a single head, which covers the upper opening of the shell. The lower end of the shell is left open. A tambor utilized in an ensemble of Evitar recorded in 1970 was 63 centimeters high, 28 centimeters in diameter at the head, and 26 centimeters in diameter at the foot. The *caja* (shell) was made from the trunk of the *banco* (*Gyrocarpus americanus* Jacq., Hernandiáceas) tree. In order of preference, the *parche* (head) is cut from the skin of a calf not yet born, the stomach of a large alligator, deerskin, or goatskin. The availability of the materials listed was in reverse order to the preference. There are few cows in the village, and the large variety of alligator had almost completely disappeared from the region. On the other hand, hunters still found deer, and domestic goats were in good supply. After the shell has been prepared the skin to be used is shaved and cut to the approximate size needed. The skin is fastened in place by two *aros* (hoops). The informants refer to these hoops merely as the lower and the upper, but I shall employ the technical terms, flesh hoop and counter hoop. Both hoops are usually fashioned from a strong *bejuco* (vine or creeper). Thread is wrapped around it where the two ends overlap as a means of keeping it in place. In the drums in use in San Jacinto the counter hoops are formed from heavy copper wire rather than bejucos (fig. 21).

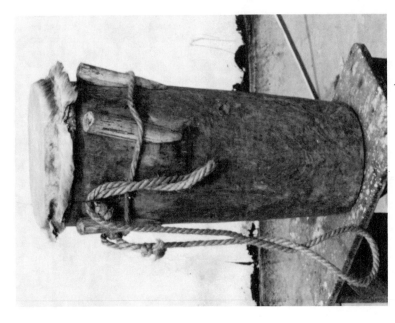

Fig. 22. Tambor mayor made by José del
Carmen Pimientel Martínez of Evitar

Fig. 21. Tambor mayor made
by José Lara of San Jacinto

The skin is wetted and placed over the opening in the top of the shell. The counter hoop is placed over the head and slid a short distance down the shell. The outer portion of the skin forming the head is then folded up and over the flesh hoop, and the counter hoop is placed above it. The counter hoop now holds the flesh hoop and skin in place, with the remainder of the skin emerging upward behind the counter hoop. The skin is then trimmed about 6 centimeters above the top aro.

The circumference of the drum is encircled by a girdle 18 to 20 centimeters below the flesh hoop, or approximately one-third the distance down the side of the shell. The girdle is usually fashioned of two or three windings of *cabuya*, a strong rope or cord made of *pita*, the fiber of the *agave*. Cabuya is purchased, not made locally. In Palenque the girdle is fashioned of two or more bejucos around which a very thin bejuco has been twisted.

Two methods are commonly employed in connecting the girdle and the counter hoop, both making use of cabuya. In the first method a single long section of rope connects the counter hoop and the girdle in a zigzag fashion, first looping over one and then the other (fig. 21). In the second method individual pieces of cabuya are cut, and after being passed over the hoop and girdle the ends are knotted together to form vertically stretched loops. The *tambolero* of the conjunto de cumbia of Evitar had introduced a modification of this second method. He replaced the loops of cabuya with sections of strong wire with hooks at each end by which the lengths of wire were attached to the hoop and girdle (fig. 22). In either case, the vertical connections are evenly spaced around the drum.

Wood *cuñas* (wedges) are now thrust down into the girdle mid-way between the points of the v's formed by the zigzag lacing or midway between the vertical connections made by rope or wire. The wedges are pounded down between the girdle and the shell with a stone or a hammer, and the head is thus tightened.

In my field work in the region I recorded 11 ensembles in which the tambor mayor was played. All of the drums I saw employed this wedge-girdle tension method.

When seated the player holds the drum between his legs and rests it upon the floor or ground (fig. 23). When it is played while standing or walking it is held in place by a rope sling passing over the shoulder. The ends of the carrying sling are attached to the girdle and the counter hoop. The tambor mayor is played with the hands. Usually the head is struck with the open palm, less frequently with the hand in slightly cupped position, and occasionally with the flat of the fingers only. There are two areas in which the head is commonly struck, near the edge in front of the player and just off center. The term *canto* (edge) is used in referring to the first area. Should these two areas be struck with blows of equal strength, greater resonance will be produced by those struck on the canto. However, a sharply accented blow struck in the center of the head produces a rather metallic, cracking sound which has considerable carrying power. Another type of tone can be produced, a soft, stopped, harmonic-like sound, by striking the very edge of the head with a glancing blow of the fingers only.

Fig. 23. Tambor mayor played by José
del Carmen Pimientel Martínez of Evitar

Fig. 24. Chocó drum

When the player is seated, the bottom opening of the drum is
closed by the floor or ground upon which it rests. It thus
produces somewhat less resonance than when played while standing
or walking. The seated player takes advantage of this situation
and varies his tone production by occasionally raising the drum
from the floor or ground and thus producing greater resonance.
This is accomplished by grasping the shell with the legs and
lifting the feet onto their toes. The two positions, and the two
different tone qualities thus produced, are referred to as *tapado*
(closed) and *destapado* (not closed, open).

The characteristic feature of this single-headed drum is the
method used to produce tension upon the head, wooden wedges
thrust down into a girdle which is connected by one means or
another to the counter hoop. Such drums are found in the Pacific
coastal region of Colombia (List 1980:574), Venezuela (Aretz 1967:
Tabla II), Brazil and Panamá (Howard 1967:123, 120, respectively),
Cuba (Ortiz 1954:21), and other areas of Latin America where
there are large negro populations. These include not only other
islands of the Caribbean but also the northern coastal region of
Ecuador.

Drums employing the wedge-girdle type of tension are also
found among a few Indian groups in northern South America. Fig. 24
is an example of such a drum used by the Chocó of the Pacific
coastal region of Colombia. Drums of this nature are also found
among the Kogi of the Atlantic coastal region of Colombia and the
Cayapá of the northern coastal region of Ecuador (Izikowitz 1935:
179). Izikowitz is inclined to believe that the Indians had
single-headed, tubular drums in pre-Colombian times and adopted

the wedge-girdle tension system from negro drums (1935:180). This
is very likely. Large negro populations have lived for centuries
in the areas adjacent to those occupied by the Kogi, Chocó, and
Cayapá. The latter also possess the negro marimba (xylophone).

African analogues of the type of drum being discussed were
described by Ankermann at the turn of the century. He terms this
tension mechanism *keilringspannung* and offers four drawings of
drums on which it was employed. One drum was collected from the
Ekoi people of northwest Cameroon, the second from the Bakundu,
and the third from the Ogowe (Ogooué) region of Gabon. The
fourth is merely identified as being collected in Cameroon (Ankermann 1901:57).

Von Hornbostel describes this method of securing tension in a
single-headed drum as "wedge-bracing." He indicates that it is
found in West Africa and the Congo (1933:287). Wieschhoff also
offers drawings of drums of the keilringspannung type (1933:15,
47). He details their distribution in Africa as the west coast
from the mouth of the Ogowe River north to the Niger and in the
interior as far north as the Benuë (1933:25-26). Von Hornbostel
indicates that this type of drum is also found in Indonesia, and
Wieschhoff documents a wide distribution in that area. Sachs,
who refers to the wedge-girdle tension as *spannkeile*, implies
that it diffused from Indonesia to Cameroons (1928:134). This
drum must have diffused to the New World from Africa rather than
Indonesia, since it was Africans rather than Indonesians who
were brought to the Americas in great numbers.

Kubik, whose field work has taken him across Africa from east
to west, also believes the drum with keilringspannung to have a
limited distribution in Africa. He has found such drums in the
Upper Sangha River region in the southwest portion of the Central
African Republic and in Congo-Brazzaville (People's Republic of
the Congo) near the border of the former country. In this large
area it is found among both the pygmies and Bantu-speaking groups.
Kubik believes this type of drum will also be found in Gabon and
Spanish Guinea among related cultural groups (information based
on data collected in joint field work by Gerhard Kubik and Maurice
Djenda). Kubik is certain that this type of drum is not found in
East Africa. Although von Hornbostel gives the Congo as an area
of distribution of the "wedge-bracing" type of drum, it is apparently unknown in Zaire. In some 500 photographs of drums from
the Belgian Congo and Rwanda-Buruti in the Teruen collection published by Olgibun, none display wedges thrust into a girdle (1951).
On the other hand, several single-headed drums employing this
tension system which were collected in Congo-Brazzaville are
found in the collection of instruments at the Musée de l'Homme in
Paris (information from Geneviève Dournon, Department de Ethnomusicologie).

Fig. 25 is a photograph of two different-sized drums of the
type known as *ndumu* of the Bangombe group of the Pygmies of the
Upper Sangha area of the Central African Republic. (The Pygmies
are referred to as Bamphenga and Babinga by the Bantu-speaking
people of the area and the French, respectively.) Both drums are
slightly conical in shape, and the girdles and wedges are approximately the same distance from the head as those of the tambor.

Fig. 25. Ndumus of
the Bangombe Pygmies

Fig. 26. Playing the ndumus

Specimens of the taller drum measure from 50 centimeters to a meter compared with 63 centimeters for the tambor mayor measured. The lacing which connects the girdle and the head is somewhat different in the two drums; the bottom of the larger drum is open and that of the smaller is closed. Fig. 26 shows one method of playing the drums. The heads of the drums are raised from the ground by a log placed under the upper part of the instruments. The men straddle the drums in seated position and strike the heads with their hands (Djenda 1968b:35).

This drum is considered characteristic of the Pygmies by the taller Bantu-speaking people who also inhabit this large area, which forms the so-called northern Bantu borderland. Kubik and Djenda found both the Mpyemo and the Pomo of this Bantu group to possess a similar instrument. The Mpyemo are found in the Upper Sangha area of the Central African Republic and in the southeast portion of Cameroon. They are believed to have moved to this area from Congo-Brazzaville some 150 years in the past to escape slave raids. They say that they adopted the wedge-girdle type of drum which they call *bokinda* from the Pygmies.

The bokinda is the same shape as the pygmy ndumu, and specimens range from 60 to 70 centimeters in height. The girdle, which is made of a *liana,* is in approximately the same relationship to the head as that of the tambor mayor. The bokinda is thus analogous to the tambor mayor in a number of respects. In addition, it is laced in zigzag fashion. However, in the bokinda the two sides of the inverted v's of the zigzag lacing are separated to some extent when they reach the head rather than coming to a point as in the tambor mayor. This drum also differs from the Colombian instrument in being furnished with a stand with short legs and in not being played with the hands. While the drum is in an upright position it is struck with a stick made of rafia held in the right hand and dampened with the left (Kubik n.d.:33-35).

The Pomo live on both sides of the border separating Congo-Brazzaville and the Central African Republic. They make use of a wedge-girdle type of drum which they call *kohn*. The shell of this drum is of a more pronounced conical shape, and a stand permits it to be played in an upright position. It is played by two men. One strikes the shell of the drum with a stick, and the other strikes the head with a stick and dampens it with the other hand (information based on data obtained in the field by Gerhard Kubik and Maurice Djenda).

Fig. 27 is a photograph of two Igbo men from the town of Obino in the Nsuka distict of southern Nigeria. Of the two drums being played, the larger or female drum is called *nwunye* and the shorter or male drum *oke*. Both are open at the bottom. Like the tambor mayor, both are carried by means of a rope sling passed over the shoulder and are played with both hands. When played in a seated position the drums are also played with the hands. The nwunye is laid upon the lap with the head to the right and is held in position by pressure of the left forearm near the elbow. The oke is held on the left thigh with the head facing to the right and is held in position in the same manner (information based on data collected in the field by David W. Ames).

Although the route of the Niger River within Nigeria is quite

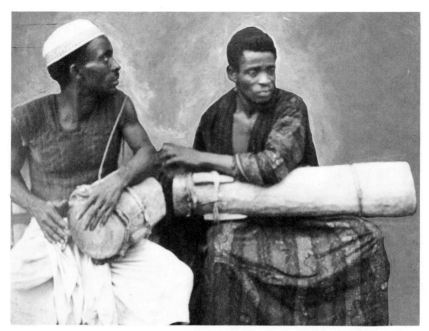

Fig. 27. Nwunye (right) and oke (left) played by Igbo

irregular, the Nsuka region can be said to lie to its south. The
African drums so far discussed therefore fall within the restricted
distribution area from the Ogowe River in Gabon to the Niger, as indicated by Wieschhoff. The Upper Sangha River area was in the
past part of German Cameroons. The distribution in the Congo mentioned by von Hornbostel is represented by drums of this type found
in Congo-Brazzaville and in immediately adjacent areas of the
Central African Republic.

Nevertheless, a drum using the wedge-girdle tension mechanism
and played in very much the same manner as the tambor mayor is
found considerably north of this supposedly restricted area of distribution. Fig. 28 offers in juxtaposition photographs of Colombian and African drummers. The photograph on the left is of a man
in the Atlantic coastal region of Colombia playing the tambor
mayor; the photograph on the right is of a man of the Susu people
of the Kafu Bullom Chiefdom, Port Loko district, Sierra Leone playing the *sangbei*. Both drums are open at the bottom. The sangbei
differs from the tambor mayor in that the former has wood cut away
from its lower portion to form a foot. The lacing of the sangbei
is in the zigzag pattern employed in some specimens of the tambor
mayor, but as in the bokinda of the Mpyemo the two sides of the
inverted v's do not converge at the flesh hoop.

The sangbei is often played in sets of three, each of a different size. However, none of the three plays a steady pulse as does
the llamador. This is usually the function of an additional drum.
The wedge-girdle type of drum is in use among a number of groups in

Fig. 28. Left, tambor mayor played by evitalero; right, sangbei played by Susu.

Sierra Leone. The Susu and Mende call it the sangbei, the Taeno and the Temne the *sangba*. The Susu also refer to this drum as the *yimbei* (information based on data collected in the field by Jacoba van Oven).

Both the sangbei and the tambor mayor are played with the hands only, and in each case the drummer produces various timbres both by hitting the drum head in a particular location and by the manner in which the stroke is produced. The latter techniques seem very common in West Africa. I have no exact information concerning the timbres produced with the hands in the playing of the sangbei by the Susu, of the nwunye or the oke by the Igbo, or of the ndumu by the Pygmies. However, the complex hand playing of the *sogo* by the Ewe of southeastern Ghana has been well documented.

The sogo is a single-headed drum, but tension is not produced by wedges thrust into a girdle. According to A. M. Jones, the head of the sogo is divided into three zones, and different timbres are produced by strokes directed to each zone (1959:63). Further timbres can be produced by complex movements of the hands (Jones 1959:plates 13-17). Serwadda and Pantaleoni also describe in detail hand playing of the sogo and offer notations of the hand patterns employed (1968:48-51). There therefore seems little doubt that the source of the tambor mayor is West Africa. There are no European analogues. The only hand-struck drum in common use in Europe during the colonial period was the tambourine. The few Amerindian analogues are found among groups which have had long and continued contact with negros.

However, the tambor mayor displays one trait, the counter hoop, which seems to have been derived entirely from Europe. As far as I can determine, the counter hoop is employed in producing tension in all European drums. Fig. 29 shows how tension is applied to the head of the kohn of the Pomo. The outer extremity of the skin forming the head is curled around a hoop. A cord running above the hoop next to the shell descends behind the hoop through a hole in the skin, loops under the girdle, and returns whence it came, and then continues further around the shell. At equal intervals it descends and returns in the same manner and then continues its progress around the shell above the hoop. Thus when equally spaced wedges are thrust down into the girdle, even pressure is exerted upon the head by the cord running above the flesh hoop.

Such detail cannot be seen in the drawing of the bokinda of the Mpyemo in the unpublished manuscript cited, in the drawings published by Ankermann and Wieschhoff, nor in any of the photographs of African drums reproduced in this volume (figs. 25-29, and 38). My assumption that none of these drums is furnished with a counter hoop is based upon my close examination of 12 African drums found in the collections of the Indiana University Museum. Five of these are from Nigeria, three from Liberia, two from Ghana, one from Southwest Africa, and one is merely marked Hausa. Some are single-headed and some double-headed; they may be conical, cylindrical, or hourglass-shaped. They are of various sizes, and there is a great variety of lacing and of methods of producing tension, but in none is a counter hoop employed. In all cases pressure is applied upon the hoop to which the head is attached by cords or leather thongs which ascend behind this hoop, run above

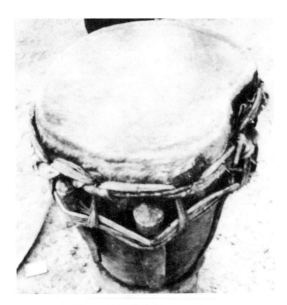

Fig. 29. Tension system
of the kohn of the Pomo

it along the shell, and then run down again in approximately the
manner seen in the photograph of the kohn of the Pomo (fig. 29).
    In four photographs of drums of the wedge-girdle type collected
in Congo-Brazzaville sent to me by the Musée de l'Homme, this
means of applying pressure upon the head is clearly discernible.
However, it seems to be applied in a slightly different manner in
the bokinda and in the sangbei. Both drums have a zigzag lacing
like that found in some specimens of the tambor mayor. In the
latter the two sides of the inverted v's come to a point where
the lacing is looped over the counter hoop. In the two African
drums the two sides of the v do not meet at the head but are
somewhat separated. It seems likely, therefore, that in the
African instruments the cord forming one side of the inverted
v runs upward through a hole in the skin behind the hoop, runs
for a short distance above it along the shell, and then descends
to form the other side of the inverted v. In this manner equal
pressure can also be exerted upon the head by the wedges thrust
down into the girdle.
    Like the tambor mayor, the ndumu of the Pygmies and nwunye
and oke of the Igbo are carried by means of rope slings passing
over the shoulder. In the tambor mayor one end of the sling is
attached to the girdle and the other to the counter hoop. In
the ndumu one end of the sling is attached to the girdle and the
other to one of the ropes connecting the girdle and the head.
This would indicate that there is no counter hoop to which it

could be attached. If it were attached at any point to the cord
running above the flesh hoop it would tend to produce an imbalance
in the pressure being applied upon the head. No detail is available concerning the points at which the sling is attached to the
Igbo drums.

In summary, all traits but one of the tambor mayor seem to have
their source in Africa. The instrument is analogous to African
drums in its use of the wedge-girdle tension mechanism, in the
means by which it is carried, and in the varied timbres produced
when playing with both hands. In some cases the lacing and the
material used in making the hoops are also similar. Its one
European trait is the use of a counter hoop.

Llamador (figs. 30-32, 66, and 68).

The llamador (caller) is so named because its function is to
play a steady beat and to thus hold an ensemble together. In
almost all cases the instruments played for me in the region were
small replicas of the tambor mayor and displayed a similar variation in the form of the lacing and in the material employed in
the girdles and hoops. However, the instruments in use in Evitar
were not of this type. The wedge-girdle tension mechanism has
been discarded in favor of other means of tightening the head.

The llamador played in the conjunto de cumbia in 1965 was a
replica of one the player had seen at a performance of *vallenato*
at San Jacinto (fig. 31). To retain the tightness of the head in
a drum with the wedge-girdle tension system it is necessary to
frequently remove the head, wet it, and replace it on the drum.
This also requires removing the wedges, lacing, and hoops and
their later replacement. The llamador seen in San Jacinto was
so constructed as to obviate this necessity. The player thought
this a very good feature and had one made for him. In constructing the tension mechanism the maker used the claws and
screws designed for producing tension in a commercially manufactured bass drum. The claws are hooked over the counter hoop and
the screws passed through wire loops protruding from small holes
in the shell. A nut is placed on each screw below the wire loop.
Tension is exerted upon the head by tightening the nuts against
the wire loops.

The apparatus used for producing tension in the llamador
employed in the performance of bullerengue and *fandango* in 1970
was an adaptation of the same principle utilized in the drum
previously described, but some of the parts were probably made by
a blacksmith rather than in a factory (fig. 32). Plates with
vertically placed sleeves or half-tubes in their middle are
screwed to the shell. Threaded bolts are passed through the
sleeves of the plates, their heads resting against the top end
of the sleeve. Loops of wire extend downward from the counter
hoop to the plates, where they are wound around the heads of the
bolts. Nuts are placed on the threaded lower ends of the bolts
and tightened against the lower ends of the sleeves of the plates,
thus exerting tension upon the drum head. This was the only
llamador played by an evitalero that was measured. It is 21
centimeters in diameter at the head, 20 centimeters in diameter

Fig. 30

Fig. 31

Fig. 32

Fig. 30. Llamador made in San Jacinto played by Angel Ospino Santana of Evitar; fig. 31. the llamador alone; fig. 32. llamador from Evitar.

at the foot, and 25.5 centimeters in height.

The llamador is struck with the open palm of the hand. When
played in a seated position the instrument is usually supported
by the thigh of the left leg, held in place by the left arm, and
struck with the right hand (fig. 30). When played while standing
or walking the instrument is held under the arm or by means of a
short rope sling. The player may, on occasion, alternately tap
the head with the hand that is holding the drum. This is done
to assist the player in keeping the beat. These taps are so light
that they cannot be heard when the ensemble is playing.

Drums with the wedge-girdle tension system are commonly employed
in sets of different sizes in both Africa and Latin America. The
Bangombe Pygmies of the Upper Sangha and the Igbo of southern
Nigeria make simultaneous use of two such drums and the Susu of
Sierra Leone three. Thus the llamador is the smallest member of
a battery of this type. African influence is also probably manifest in the occasional reference to the llamador as *macho* (male)
and to the tambor mayor as *hembra* (female), as is customary among
the Igbo. On the other hand, in construction the llamador shows a
much greater influence of urban technology than does the tambor
mayor.

Bombo (figs. 33-34, 36-37, and 66).

The *bombo* is a large drum with a cylindrical shell and two
heads which is struck with sticks rather than the hands. Like
the bass drum, it is held so that the heads are in vertical relationship with the ground or floor. The shell of the bombo, like
that of both the tambor mayor and the llamador, is made from a
hollowed-out section of the banco tree. The heads utilized on
the bombo are cut from deerskin, goatskin, or sheepskin. Although
larger, the heads and hoops are made and applied in very much the
same manner as in the other two drums described. Again, there is
variety in the material used in making the counter hoops. In the
bombos played for me in Soplaviento and Cartegena the counter
hoops were formed from bejucos; in Evitar they were made of heavy
copper wire. The bombo played for me in Sabanalarga was exceptional in having counter hoops shaped from a single thin piece of
wood, as in European drums.

The two heads are connected by a zigzag lacing fashioned of
cabuya. In the bombo of Sabanalarga the lacing passes through
equidistant holes bored into the counter hoop. In the other bombos
the lacing itself does not pass over the counter hoops. Rather,
short strips of rawhide or cabuya in the form of loops are passed
over the counter hoops, and the lacing is pulled through them. In
the bombo of Evitar these small loops are fashioned from rawhide,
in Soplaviento from cabuya, and in Cartagena double loops of
cabuya were employed. In the process of lacing the rope is also
passed through other loops of rawhide or cabuya in such a manner
that near one side of the shell such a loop encircles the lower
part of each v. The rope lacing is then pulled tight, and an
extension of the rope is passed around the shell parallel to the
heads. On its way it is looped around the sides of the v's formed
on the other side of the shell. The rope is then pulled tight and

Fig. 33. Bombo made by Manuel Pimientel Pacheco of Evitar

Fig. 34. Bombo played by Manuel Pimientel Pacheco of Evitar

fastened, thus pulling apart the v's around which it is looped at their wider part. The small loops surrounding the lower and narrow parts of the other v's are now pushed toward the center of the drum, pulling together the lower sides of the v's. Thus in tightening the drum head two contrasting but complementary methods of producing tension are applied to alternate v's formed by the lacing, the first widening the upper parts of the v's, the second pulling the lower sides together. The shell of the bombo collected in Evitar is quite asymmetrical in shape, and the lacing required to tighten the head is necessarily arranged in an equally asymmetrical fashion (figs. 33-34).

A lozenge-shaped sound hole is pierced in the shell of each bombo, usually equidistant from the two heads. Its purpose is to maintain the equilibrium of air pressure within the drum.

When played in a seated position the bombo is supported by the left thigh and held in place by the left arm resting on the top of the drum (fig. 66, p. 85). If a small stool or bench is available the drum may be rested upon this instead of the player's thigh. When the player is standing or walking, the bombo is held by a rope sling attached to the center ropes of the instrument (fig. 34). When the sling is placed over the shoulder, the drum is held in a position in front of but slightly to the left of the player. This permits free movement of the right arm. Whether carried or played while seated, the drum is always positioned so that the sound hole appears on the top of the instrument.

The bombo is struck with two *bolillos* (drum sticks) without heads. The bolillos are cut from the branches of the *guayabo* or *guayacán*. The latter has the hardest wood of any tree found in the region. The bombo is struck either on the right head or on the shell near that head. The right hand is held free, while the left hand rides on top of the bombo in such a position that an adjustment of the wrist permits a blow to be struck on either the head or the wood of the shell. Both head and shell are struck with either hand. If one hand is striking the head and the other the wood, the right hand strikes the former and the left hand the latter. Strongly accented blows on the head can only be struck by the right hand.

The heads of the bombo played in the conjunto de cumbia of Evitar in 1964 are approximately 45 centimeters in diameter. The width of the shell is 43 centimeters. The bombos utilized in the conjuntos de cumbia of Cartagena and Sabanalarga were considerably larger. The sound hole pierced in the shell of the Evitar bombo is 4 by 8 centimeters. The bolillos used in Evitar are 1.8 centimeters in diameter and 46 and 47 centimeters, respectively, in length.

Reproductions on vases and references in the literature indicate that two-headed drums were in use in Perú in pre-Colombian times (Izikowitz 1935:184). Two-headed drums covered almost entirely with skin have also been found in excavations in northern Chile (Grebe 1974:25). There is no evidence that two-headed drums existed in the rest of South America before the coming of the Europeans. During the post-Colombian period, and most notably in this century, double-headed drums played with sticks have been

observed throughout the Andean region, the northwest Pacific coast
of South America, and the Atlantic coastal region of Colombia. All
of these instruments seem to be derived from European or African
models with one possible exception, a small drum found among the
Chocó Indians of Colombia which is played by women and apparently
with the hands or fingers only (Izikowitz 1935:192 and Bermúdez
and Abadía 1966:23). In northern South America double-headed
drums are almost without exception played with sticks rather than
with the hands. In addition, in this area and in the Iberian
peninsula and West Africa, the playing of drums is almost entirely
a prerogative of the male.

Izikowitz believes that the drums played by the Aymara or
Quechua-speaking Andean Indians are imitations of European models.
This is possible. I have observed among the Quechua-speaking
Salasacas Indians of Ecuador a performance in which one man simul-
taneously played both a drum and a vertical flute. The instrument,
resembling a bass drum, was suspended in front of him by a sling.
He struck the head with a ball-tipped stick held in his right
hand and played the flute with his left. This "pipe and tabor"
combination is reminiscent of European folk practice, in which,
however, a smaller drum was usually used. On the other hand, the
Guambiano Indians of the Andean region of Tierradentro in southern
Colombia perform on similar drums in a manner which seems more
African than European. The Guambiano, who are not Quechua
speakers, make simultaneous use of several such drums, employing
two sticks without balls and striking both head and shell (information based on data collected in the field by Elsie Fardig
Córdoba). This is the manner in which the bombo is played in both
the Atlantic and Pacific coastal regions of Colombia.

The term *bombo* is applied to the bass drum in both Spain and
Portugal. The instrument was in common use in the countryside in
Portugal in this century, but no information seems to be available concerning its use in Spain. Since the two countries occupy
the same peninsula and historically have had close cultural and
political ties, it can be assumed that similar drums were found in
Spain in the past. The following information concerning the
Portuguese instruments is taken from Veiga de Oliveira (1966:
188-90).

Portuguese bombos vary considerably in size, depending upon
the region in which they are found, ranging in diameter from
approximately 80 to 30 centimeters. However, they are generally
quite similar in construction. Although occasionally made of
sheet metal, the shell is usually formed from a wide, thin piece
of wood which is wetted or heated while being fashioned into a
drum, and the two ends are held together by staples or nails.
The flesh hoops are formed from thin, flexible branches and the
counter hoops from thin, narrow, flat strips of wood rounded into
shape in the same manner as the shell and attached at the two
ends. Heads made of goatskin or kidskin are preferred, but skins
of other animals, such as the burro, are also used. The extremities of the heads are curled around the flesh hoops and occasionally sewn into place.

In the most common form of the Portuguese bombo, equidistant
holes are pierced in the two counter hoops. They are then placed

Fig. 36. Portuguese bombo

Fig. 35. Portuguese tamboril

above the flesh hoops in such a manner that the holes in one
counter hoop align with the spaces between the holes in the
other counter hoop. A cord or rope is tied to a hole in one of
the counter hoops and then passed back and forth in zigzag fashion
through the holes in the two hoops until it is finally secured
where it began. It can thus be seen that the counter hoops and
the methods of connecting them in the bombo of Sabanalarga are
similar to those of the Portuguese bombos.

Tension is exerted upon the rope lacing, and thus upon the two
heads, by two methods which are different in some respects from
and similar in others to those employed in the costeño bombos. In
the first such method the lacing at the points of the v's is encircled by small loops of leather, skin, or rope which are pushed
toward the center of the shell to pull the two lower sides of the
v together (fig. 36). These small loops are usually located on
only one side of the instrument, as in the costeño bombos, but
occasionally are located on the second side as well. The second
and alternative method of producing tension is to run a second
piece of rope laterally around the shell about one-third of the
distance from one of the heads. This rope loops around the lower
sides of the v's and pulls them together, producing approximately
the same result as the little leather loops. This lateral, running rope can be seen in fig. 35, which is a photograph of a
Portuguese *tamboril*, a smaller drum with gut snares on both heads.
In costeño bombos the lateral rope usually pulls the upper sides
of the v's apart rather than the lower sides together. In the
Portuguese bombos only one method of tension is employed--either
the small loops or the lateral rope, not both. In costeño bombos
both methods of securing tension are applied simultaneously.

The *massetas* (drum sticks) utilized by the Portuguese *bomberos*
are usually furnished with balls containing cotton, cork, kapok,
or a similar soft substance. At times the ball may consist only
of an enlargement of the wood at the striking end of the masseta.
One or two drum sticks may be used. If only one is employed it
is held in the right hand and strikes the *batedeira* (the principal
drum head). When the bombero makes use of two massetas, the one
held in the left hand is usually smaller than that held in the
right. The *berboeira* (the lesser drum head) is struck with this
smaller drum stick. Alternatively, both drum sticks can be used
to strike the batedeira. In contrast, the drum sticks used by
costeño bomberos are not tipped with balls and strike either the
right head or the wood of the shell.

The instruments of both regions are analogous in one aspect of
their construction: a sound hole is located in the shell equidistant between the two heads.

A wide variety of two-headed drums have been in use in West
Africa. Their bodies or shells usually consist of hollowed-out
and carved tree trunks of appropriate size. A few of these two-
headed drums are of a size and shape similar to the costeño bombo.
Such a drum, for example, is in use among a number of groups in
Sierra Leone. The Temne call this instrument the *tempe*. The
Limba term is *huban*. The intertribal designation is *ban*.

The ban is usually struck with two headless sticks. The two
sticks may be used in striking one head, or the drummer may beat

on both heads. Frequently one stick is used to strike a head and
the other the wood of the adjacent shell. Finally, one head may
be struck with a stick and the other with the hand. However, the
drummer always uses at least one drumstick; the ban is never struck
with the hands only. The function of the ban is to play a steady
beat or a repeated rhythm as an accompaniment to a group of different drums which perform more complex rhythms. The shell of the
instrument consists of a portion of hollowed-out tree trunk; more
recently, the musicians have made use of oil drums (information
based on data collected in the field by Jacoba van Oven).

A similar, but smaller, double-headed, cylindrical drum is found
among various groups in Liberia. The Kpelle refer to this instrument as the *gbùn-gbùn*. The Bai call it the *gbei-gbei*. The Gola
use the same term as the Bai, while the Loma refer to it as the
gbei-gbei-gi. The Kpelle say that the name used represents the
sound produced when the instrument is played. The head of a gbùn-
gbùn collected among the Kpelle, and now in the Indiana University
Museum, measures 33.7 centimeters and the shell 31.1 centimeters
in width. This instrument is therefore much smaller than the
bombo and, judging from photographs, than the ban of Sierra Leone.
The shell of the gbùn-gbùn is made of light cork wood, the head
of deerskin, and the lacing from cord woven of oil palm fiber.
The hoops are fashioned from rattan.

When the player is seated, the gbùn-gbùn is held between the
knees with the heads in horizontal relationship with the ground.
It is played with two sticks without heads. The stick held in
the right hand is struck against either the head or the shell,
that held in the left hand against the head only. In standing
or walking position the drum is suspended beneath the armpit by
means of a cord passing over the shoulder, and thus the head is
vertical to the ground. The Kpelle say that the gbùn-gbùn serves
in the same relationship to the master drum as the chorus to the
soloist. It never varies its basic rhythmic pattern except to
occasionally cue the end of a section (information based on data
collected in the field by Ruth Stone).

Examination of a photograph of the ban indicates that the zigzag lacing is attached to two free-standing hoops, which in turn
are attached to the heads by means of double vertical cords. This
tension system is similar to the system employed in the gbùn-gbùn,
which can be described in detail since the drum itself is available for examination. In the gbùn-gbùn there are two hoops for
each head, as in both the costeño and Portuguese bombos. One of
these hoops is used to fasten the skin in place, the other to
produce tension. However, the relationship of the hoops to each
other is quite different from that found in the bombos. Instead
of being placed above the hoop around which the skin is folded
or curled, the second hoop of the gbùn-gbùn is located a short
distance below the first hoop, where it stands free from the
shell. It is to these free-standing rattan hoops that the lacing
is attached (fig. 38). The skin curled around the first hoop is
held in place by a cord running immediately above the hoop. At
regular intervals this cord descends behind the hoop through holes
in the skin, runs under the free-standing hoop, loops over it, and
returns whence it came. After running further above the skin and

Fig. 38. Gbũn-gbũn of the Kpelle

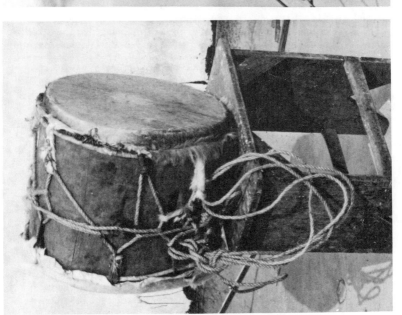

Fig. 37. Bombo from Evitar

first hoop for a short distance, it repeats the process, reaching downward and connecting with the second hoop and returning. This is the same method used in the kohn of the Pomo in connecting the head with the girdle (see p. 39).

The lacing which connects the two free-standing hoops, as in the bombos, produces a series of v's and inverted v's. The lacing passes under the rattan hoop, between the two cords which form the loop which connects this hoop with the head, then over this hoop and on to the opposite hoop near the other end of the drum. After the zigzag lacing is completed, the remainder of the single, long cord is run around the middle of the shell of the drum, looping around the diagonal cords and providing tension after the end of the cord has been tied firmly in place. In the costeño bombos individual little loops of rope or rawhide are used to narrow the v's made by the lacing, whereas the lateral extension of the lacing is looped around the v's and pulled to make them wider. No rawhide or rope loops of this type are used in the gbùn-gbùn. Instead, the extension of the lacing runs around the drum twice, looping around the diagonal cords in a different manner each trip. In the first trip it pulls on the v's in such a manner as to widen them; the second time around it pulls them together. Thus the cord looped laterally around the shell in the gbùn-gbùn produces the same double and complementary tension as the lateral rope and small loops in the costeño bombos (compare figs. 37 and 38).

It can now be seen that similar principles of construction are operative in the costeño, Iberian, and West African drums discussed. This is not surprising, since double-headed drums have a long and complex history in the Middle East and Mediterranean areas. Large drums of the type were known in Egypt in the Middle Kingdom. The double-headed drum was also known by the Romans and widely diffused by them. The type now known as the side or snare drum was brought to Europe during the Crusades. A larger drum, with heads in vertical relationship to the ground, apparently developed in Turkey, and there is evidence of its having been in use in that country as early as 1500. This drum was known in Europe as the Turkish drum until the nineteenth century, after which the term bass drum was applied to it (Marcuse 1975b:123-29). However, the existence of drums of similar construction in the Iberian peninsula and sub-Saharan West Africa can more specifically be attributed to the spread of Islam from North Africa to both areas. The later differentiated types were then diffused to Colombia, and the costeño bombo represents a merging of their various traits plus, as usually occurs, some independent development. What influence Amerindian drums may have had upon this syncretism cannot be established because of insufficient evidence. The following summary is therefore concerned only with the apparent relationships of the costeño bombos to the Portuguese and African drums discussed.

1. Certain features of the costeño bombo could have been derived from either Europe or Africa. The drums in all three areas are laced in zigzag fashion, and in all three areas a laterally running rope is employed to apply tension by modifying the shape of the v's produced by the lacing (compare figs. 35-38).

2. Traits specifically derived from the Iberian bombos are
the employment of counter hoops and the provision of sound holes.
The free-standing hoops of the African drums cannot be considered
counter hoops because they are not located above the flesh hoops
and do not apply pressure downward upon them. Holes pierced in
the body or shell of the instrument--found primarily in single-
headed drums--are seen in African instruments in museums, but in
actual use these holes were covered with a vibrating membrane
and therefore do not serve the same function as the sound holes
in the Iberian and costeño bombos (information from Klaus Wachsmann).

3. Traits specifically derived from West Africa are the use
of a tree trunk as the material for the shell and the use of
sticks, lacking balls, which are struck upon the wood as well as
upon the head of the drum. To my knowledge, European drums of
the bass drum type are struck only upon the head, not upon the
shell, with drum sticks tipped with balls.

4. The methods employed in the costeño bombo to modify the
lacing in order to produce tension are both a combination of and
a variation upon those used in the Iberian and African instruments. The placement around the lower parts of the v's of small
loops which produce tension when pushed toward the center of the
shell seems to be a European trait, whereas the use of a lateral
rope looping around the sides of the v's for a similar purpose
is found in both African and European drums. However, in the
African drums one method--the use of the lateral rope--produces
the same results as the application of both methods--the lateral
rope plus the small loops--in the costeño drums (compare figs. 35-
38). As in the African drums the flesh hoops of the costeño
drums are made of vine. Although the employment of a counter hoop
is a European trait, in two of the costeño bombos the counter
hoops are also made of vine. In a third the counter hoop is
formed of copper wire. I know of no Iberian or African drums in
which hoops were made of this material. Nevertheless, this is
not necessarily a European influence. The mining of copper and
its fabrication in various forms were known in Africa before the
period of the Atlantic slave trade.

5. Although the connections of the lacing in the bombo from
Sabanalarga are the same as in the Portuguese bombos, what would
seem to be an independent development is employed in the other
three costeño bombos. Small loops of rope or rawhide are passed
over the counter hoops, and it is through these that the lacing
runs rather than through holes in a counter hoop.

AEROPHONES

Caña de millo (figs. 39-42, and 66).

The *caña de millo* (cane of millet) is also known as the *pito*,
a term applied to several aerophones but most frequently to the
caña de millo. In Evitar the instrument is always called the
pito, although my reference was understood when I referred to the
instrument as caña de millo. The instrument is a transverse,
ideoglottic clarinet. It consists of a short tube open at both

ends with the reed cut from the tube near one extremity and four
fingerholes pierced near the other (fig. 39). The drawing in
fig. 39 is of an instrument made by Roque Arrieta, a *pitero* whom
I recorded in Cartagena but who was a native of Mahates. According
to Arrieta, different types of cane were used in making pitos in
various areas. In northern Bolívar they were made of lata, in the
Departamento de Atlántico of millo, and in the Sabana de Bolívar
(which later became the Departamento de Sucre) of *carrizo*. The
latter is a form of cane commonly used in many areas of Colombia
in making flutes. The term *caña de millo* is used elsewhere in
northern Bolívar in referring to the instrument. In fact, Roque
Arrieta himself used this appellation on occasion. Possibly all
of these instruments in the region were originally made of millo.
However, my own experience corroborated Arrieta's statement as
far as northern Bolívar and Atlántico were concerned. The four
piteros I recorded in northern Bolívar did indeed play pitos made
of lata. Fig. 40 shows such pitos made by Santiago Ospino Caraballo of Evitar. The one player I recorded in Atlántico, Gabriel
de los Reyes Mendoza, did indeed utilize an instrument he made
of millo. I did not observe or record pitos in the Sabana de
Bolívar, and I therefore have no personal knowledge of the material
used in this area in making the instrument.

I was informed by both Roque Arrieta and Santiago Ospino
Caraballo that the advantage of using lata rather than millo is
that an instrument made of the former material has much greater
carrying power. As Ospino stated the matter: "With the lata
everyone in the plaza can hear you." I was also informed by both
Arrieta and Ospino that the instrument made of lata is much more
difficult to play than one made of millo, that much more exertion
of the lungs is required to play one made of lata. An instrument
fashioned from lata also requires additional care. If not played
with some frequency, the reed may become hard and not respond.
The instrument is then soaked in water for a short period of time
to soften the reed.

In making a pito of lata a section of the proper length is first
cut from the stem of the palm with a machete. The soft pith is
then removed and the tube allowed to dry. The reed is then cut at
a distance of two finger widths from one extremity of the tube with
a penknife. The fourth fingerhole (fig. 43) is first pierced at a
distance of three finger widths from the other extremity of the
tube. The four fingerholes are spaced one finger width apart.
The fingerholes are produced by applying to the tube the heated
head of a nail. They are thus of the same size. An instrument
which was made and played by Santiago Ospino (the longer instrument
in fig. 40) is 33 centimeters in length and 1.5 centimeters in
diameter. The wall of the tube is approximately .15 centimeters
thick. The reed is 3.5 centimeters in length and .5 centimeters
in width. The distance from the point where the reed merges with
the tube to the nearest extremity of the tube is 4.2 centimeters.
The fingerholes are approximately .8 centimeters in diameter and
from center to center are approximately 3 centimeters apart. The
center of the fingerhole most distant from the reed is located 6
centimeters from the adjacent extremity of the tube.

The fingerholes are usually covered with the fingers of the

Fig. 39. Pito made by Roque Arrieta of Cartagena

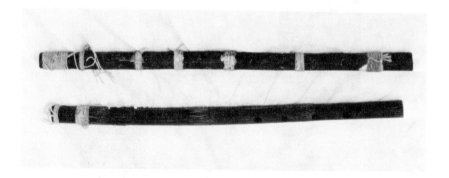

Fig. 40. Pitos of lata from Evitar

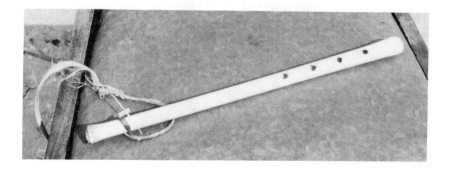

Fig. 41. Pito of millo from Sabanalarga

Fig. 42. Pito played by Santiago
Ospino Caraballo of Evitar

right hand and the instrument held to the mouth with the left hand
(fig. 42). The holes are covered with the flat of the finger, not
with the tip. The mouth covers the reed in such a manner that the
latter is entirely within the oral cavity. Thin string or heavy
thread is tightly wound around the tube in a band, the inner edge
of which meets the reed at the point where it merges with the tube.
This band serves two functions: it prevents the lengthening
through vibration of the incisions which form the reed, and it
causes the reed to vibrate with greater ease. In some instruments
collected or observed, several of the strings or threads forming
this band have long ends which hang down along the side of the
instrument. When present, these hanging ends serve no function
but adornment. Other bands of string may be wound around the
tube in various places when there is danger of its cracking (fig.
40).

A single and separate piece of string or thread is placed
beneath the reed, its ends extending 6 or 7 centimeters from each
side of the reed (fig. 39). When the player wishes to "tune"
his instrument, he grasps the two ends of this thread and adjusts
the position of the thread under the reed. The reed of a particular instrument vibrates most readily when the thread is placed
in a particular position under the reed. This is usually not
far from the point where the reed and tube merge. Reeds are
difficult to control. The player occasionally finds it necessary
to adjust the thread so that the reed continues to vibrate easily.
This is usually done between performances. However, while I was
recording Santiago, the pitero of Evitar, he once found it
necessary to stop playing during a performance (see TR 62, p. 498)
in order to make such an adjustment.

Santiago Ospino was not very articulate when questioned concerning the technique of playing the pito. However, I had gathered
considerable information in this regard in separate interviews
the previous year, 1964, with Roque Arrieta and his cousin Erasmo
Arrieta, also a pitero. I recorded interviews with Roque Arrieta
in Cartagena and with Erasmo Arrieta in Bogotá. However, they
are both natives of Mahates, and both had played the pito in
ensembles in that community before moving to the city. Roque
had learned to play the pito in Mahates from an older relative,
Manuel Arrieta. According to Roque, Manuel had learned to play
the instrument in Evitar. That Manuel Arrieta had indeed lived
in Evitar is attested by the fact that Felipe Jaramillo gave
his name as the player of the claves in the sexteto which is
described later in this chapter (p. 90). I therefore believe
that we can assume the technique of performance employed by
Santiago Ospino and the two Arrietas to be similar in most respects. This assumption is further strengthened by the fact that
an instrument made for me by Roque Arrieta is almost identical to
the one made by Santiago Ospino which was previously described.
In addition, in studying recordings of performances by the three
piteros, I found their playing style to be substantially alike.

In my interview with Roque Arrieta in 1964 I had asked him to
play for me the various pitches that could be produced with all
possible fingerings. I had not made the same request of Erasmo
Arrieta, whom I interviewed during the same year. I then wrote

to Manuel Zapata in Bogotá in 1974 and asked that he make a recording of Erasmo Arrieta doing the same. He did so, and it is upon
these three recordings made of the Arrietas, those I made of the
two in 1964 and the one made of Erasmo Arrieta by Manuel Zapata in
1974, that the following discussion is based.

The caña de millo has three registers, which Roque Arrieta
referred to as *grave* (bass), *agudo* (tenor), and *sobreagudo* (treble).
These terms are not usually applied to the registers of instruments but refer to the clefs in which the parts for the male
church choir are written. Grave represents the bass clef, agudo
the treble clef with an 8 attached below it to indicate that it
sounds an octave lower, and sobreagudo the treble clef in which
the parts for boys' voices are written. Neither Santiago nor
Erasmo was familiar with the terms that Roque applied to the
registers; however, I find it convenient to utilize Roque's terms.
In performance in the grave register the tube is closed at the
extremity nearest the reed. This is done with the thumb or palm
of the left hand. The tones of the agudo register are produced
with both extremities of the tube open. In both cases the reed
is set in vibration by the exhalation of air. In producing the
sobreagudo register the tube remains open, but the air is inhaled
through the reed rather than exhaled through it.

The fingering chart in fig. 43 offers the pitches produced in
the three registers while utilizing the most common fingering
combinations. A circle indicates an open hole, a blacked-in
circle a hole covered by a finger. The capital letter R identifies
those pitches produced by Roque Arrieta and the E those produced
by Erasmo Arrieta. In the recording sessions each pitero was
asked to play pitches in the same register with the same fingering
several times but not successively. There was some variation from
performance to performance in the pitch produced by the same
player using the same fingering and the same register. The pitches
offered for each fingering combination in fig. 43 are the ones most
commonly heard in the recordings.

For purposes of comparison the sets of pitches played by each
pitero have been transposed. Those recorded by Roque Arrieta are
slightly flat in comparison to those offered in the chart. Those
performed by Easmo Arrieta are a semitone lower than given. The
latter's instrument was apparently slightly longer than that utilized by Roque. (For the meaning of the arrows above the notes
see chapter 5, I.E.1.5.) In the chart the numbers above the four
fingerholes represent the fingers of the right hand used to cover
them. Number 1 represents the index finger. The various combinations of open and closed fingerholes are identified by the
letters from A through E.

Santiago began each performance with a sustained b^1 (center
line, treble clef), fingering E in the chart in the agudo register.
This is a signal for the remaining members of the ensemble to be
ready to join the pitero in performance (see chapter 12, p. 479).
A sonograph made of a recording of his performance of this signal
indicated that he was producing a first overtone. Thus the closed
tube produces the fundamental and the open tube the first overtone. It can therefore be assumed that the pitches produced in
the sobreagudo register represent the second overtone. (For a

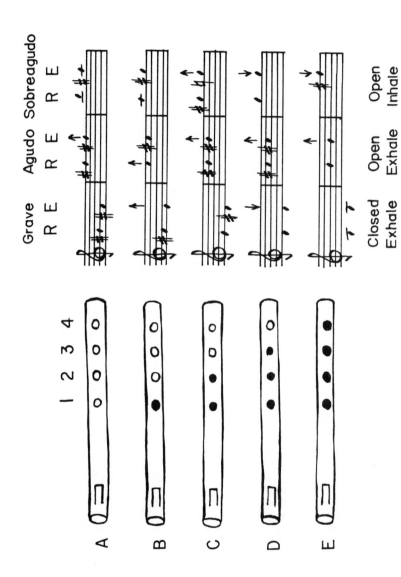

Fig. 43. Fingering chart, caña de millo

discussion of the overtone series see chapter 6, IV.A.1.1.) It
will be noted that the pitches produced by the same fingering
combination in the grave and agudo registers are at times somewhat less than a perfect 8ve apart. The first overtone is therefore often produced flat in comparison to the fundamental. Since
the sobreagudo register is the most difficult to produce, the
second overtone is still flatter in comparison with acoustic
expectation. Only in fingering E does the interval between the
first and second overtones approach the expected perfect 5th.
In other cases the interval may be as small as a major 3rd.

Experiments in playing the pitos which I brought with me when
I returned to the United States indicated that a chromatic scale
with the range of a major 3rd could be produced with fingering A
in the agudo register by increasing breath pressure and tightening the embouchure by drawing back the corners of the lips.
Thus, should the player so desire, other pitches than those
offered in Fig. 43 can be produced with the same fingering.

In performance the pitches of the agudo register are those
primarily utilized. The sobreagudo register is employed sparingly,
since it is difficult to produce. The tones of the grave register are of low intensity and do not carry well over the sounds
of the *repercusión*, the percussion section of the ensemble. In
the recordings of the performances by Santiago Ospino, he utilized
only one pitch in the grave register, $f\#^1$ (transposed to d^1 in the
transcriptions), and this is seen in one transcription only (see
TR 65, m. 13, p. 503).

In performing the melodic major triad, the piteros frequently
employ the cross fingerings given in fig. 44. As can be seen in
fig. 44, the open fingerhole nearest the reed is the basic deter-
minant of the pitch produced. Cross fingering, the closing of an
adjacent fingerhole, does not seem to affect pitch in playing the
caña de millo as it would, for example, in playing a flute. Since
b^1 in the agudo register, fingering E in fig. 43, is difficult to
produce, piteros prefer to keep the fourth finger down. An examination of the transcriptions of Santiago's opening signal, a sustained b^1 (given as a transposed g^1 in the transcriptions), will
indicate how this tone fluctuates when it is sustained (see
chapter 12).

I found that the primary pitch of Santiago's opening signal
varied somewhat as the recording session progressed. In his
first few performances the pitch was very close to b^1, approximately 500 cps. He then adjusted the string below the reed of
his instrument, and the initial pitch produced was slightly flat
in comparison with those previously produced. A further adjustment again slightly flattened the initial pitch. However, these
changes do not seem to have materially affected the intonation of
his scale in the performances following the sounding of the initial signal pitch.

There is no evidence that the clarinet existed in South America
in pre-Colombian times. There are no archeological findings of
clarinets, no reproductions of clarinets on artifacts, and no
references to such an instrument in the early historical literature. The earliest data concerning the use of the clarinet in
South America are found in seventeenth-century sources (Izikowitz

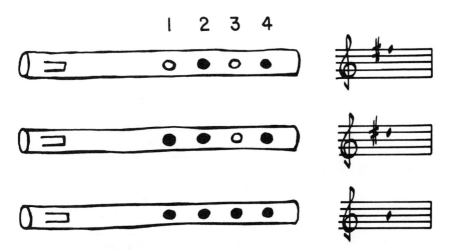

Fig. 44. Cross fingerings, caña de millo

1935:262). To my knowledge, a transverse, ideoglottic clarinet,
that is, a clarinet held horizontally with the reed cut from and
remaining attached to the tube of cane, is found in the Western
Hemisphere only in the Atlantic coastal region of Colombia. It
is apparently played only by the Spanish-speaking people of the
lowlands, not by the Indians. Vertical clarinets are played
among a number of tribal groups in South America, including the
Guajiro, but none possess a horizontal clarinet (Aretz 1967:267-
68 and Izikowitz 1935:262-65). Nor have I found a reference to
the use of such an instrument in Europe.

The instrument seems fairly common in the Western Sudan, in
the grasslands south of the Sahara. This is the area in which
millet is grown. As its name implies, the caña de millo was originally made of millet, not of lata. In the transverse clarinets
made of millet found in Africa, the reed is cut from the wall of
the instrument at one end of the tube, as it is in the caña de
millo. In both cases the reed is completely covered by the oral
cavity in performance. In other aspects the African and Colombian
instruments differ. Fig. 45 is a photograph of a Fulbe (Fulani)
man of Upper Volta playing the *bobiyel*. This instrument is made
of a long, thin stalk of millet cane and has no fingerholes. The
reed, cut from the side of the cane near one end of the stalk, is
covered by the mouth of the player. The bobiyel is on occasion
accompanied by a small drum.

Fig. 46 is a photograph of the *bounkam* of the Bissa people of
Upper Volta. The instrument is 70 centimeters in length. It is
made of a millet stalk much greater in diameter than that used
in making the bobiyel, and it is furnished with two gourd resonators. One piece of cord is tied around the tube at the point
where the reed joins it and serves the same function as in the
caña de millo. The other string is used to tie the reed in place
so that it will not be broken when the instrument is being carried.

Fig. 45. Bobiyel played by a Fulbe (Fulani) of Upper Volta

Fig. 46. Bounkam of the Bissa of Upper Volta

Either cord can be wrapped around a finger to support the instrument while playing.

The instrument was photographed in Ouagadougou, the capital of Upper Volta. The player (fig. 50) was the only extant performer of the instrument. He was a professional who played without accompaniment at dances and ceremonies during the Ramadan season. There is one finger hole on the back of the instrument. Change in pitch can also be produced by covering the hole in the gourd resonator which is the most distant from the reed and by inhalation as well as exhalation of breath. It is probable, as in the caña de millo, that pitch can also be changed by tightening or loosening the embouchure. In a recording made of the playing of the man shown in the photograph, a rather unusual pentatonic scale is heard. The intervals, beginning with the lowest, are a minor 3rd followed by three major 2nds or whole tones (information based on data collected in the field by James Rossellini and Valerie Christian).

Fig. 47 offers drawings of two types of the *kamkō* of the Kasera-Nakari people, who live in northern Ghana quite close to the Upper Volta border. This instrument is played by children, young farmers, and shepherds during the millet harvest season, from November to August. A freshly cut cane must be used, since in this dry climate the cane is likely to split within a two-week period. In both instruments shown in the drawing the left end of the tube is closed with wax. Pitch can be changed by opening and closing the openings in the gourd resonators or by moving the string back and forth under the reed (see the enlargement of this portion of the instrument in fig. 48).

The form of the kamkō shown in the upper drawing of fig. 47 is usually played by opening and closing the holes in the gourd with both hands. At times the left hand continues to cover the opening on the top of the gourd while the right hand is brought to the right of the mouth. Here it grasps the string by wrapping it around the index finger. With a slight movement of the finger the string is pulled back and forth, thus controlling the length of the reed that is vibrating. In the lower drawing in fig. 47 the right hand continually manipulates the string under the reed and the left hand the gourd, which has only one opening. There is also a type of this instrument known as *mankō*, which, like the bounkam, has two gourds, one at each end of the tube. This instrument is played in the same manner as the kamkō in the upper drawing of fig. 47 (information based on field data collected by Carol Robertson).

The Dendi of Dahomey have an instrument, the *papo*, which seems identical to the bounkam of the Bissa people of Upper Volta (Bebey 1975:79).

The distribution of the ideoglottic clarinet is apparently not restricted to the grasslands of the Sudan (that area of Africa lying to the south of the Sahara Desert). Fig. 49 is a drawing of an instrument very much like the bounkam of the Bissa which is found among the Warua people of Togo. The transverse pipe of the instrument is made of cane and the resonators found at both ends from fruit rinds or gourds. As in the bounkam there is a fingerhole near one end of the cane and a tongue cut from the

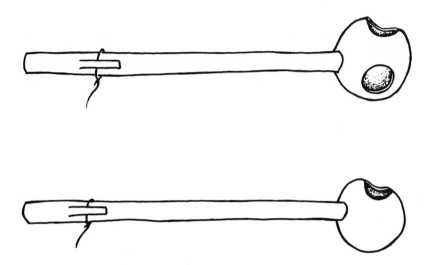

Fig. 47. Kamkō of the Kasera-Nakari of northern Ghana

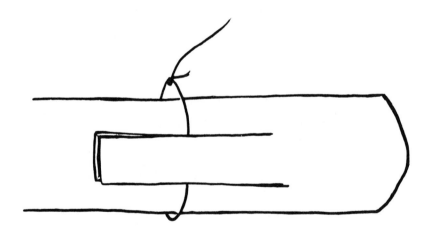

Fig. 48. Detail of the reed of the kamkō

Fig. 49. Ideoglottic clarinet of the Warua of Togo

cane near the other end. However, each gourd is perforated with three holes. The tongue is 3 centimeters long and 3 millimeters wide and vibrates when blown through (Ankermann 1901:47-48).

Fig. 50 contrasts the playing of the bounkam of Upper Volta with that of the caña de millo of the Atlantic coastal region of Colombia. The caña de millo is played by Erasmo Arrieta. It can be seen in these two juxtaposed photographs that the position of the mouth and the general method of holding the instrument are the same in both cases. This evidence leaves little doubt that the source of the caña de millo is Africa and that clarinets like the bobiyel, the bounkam, and the kamkõ are its progenitors. However, one question remains--whence the four fingerholes? This would seem to be an indigenous influence. The great majority of both transverse and vertical flutes in use among the Amerindians in Colombia have four fingerholes, as does the gaita, to be discussed next. Since the caña de millo served the same function in the past as the *gaita hembra*, that is, to provide the melodic part in the instrumental accompaniment for the dance cumbia, this association may have provided the impetus for the adoption of fingerholes as a means of producing changes of pitch.

Gaita (figs. 51-53, and 68).

In Spanish-English dictionaries bagpipe is given as the equivalent of the Spanish term *gaita*. In folk usage in Spain, however, *gaita* is a generic term for pipes. It is applied not only to the bagpipe but to the shawm (a type of oboe) and to the hornpipe (a type of clarinet) (Marcuse 1975a:197). In Colombia this name is applied to a vertical duct flute. The tube of the gaita consists of a dried section of *cardón* (*Selencereus grandiflorus*), a cactus, from which the pith has been removed. To the upper extremity of the tube is attached a head made of beeswax mixed with vegetal carbon. A cut duck or turkey quill is inserted in the head of the gaita in such a manner that the stream of air blown through the quill breaks on the upper edge of the tube of cardón, with part of the stream entering the tube and part escaping though an orifice in the head provided for this purpose (fig. 52).

Felipe Jaramillo of Evitar was a *gaitero*, but he had not played the gaita at any specific event in the village for many years. When Jaramillo was interviewed in 1971 he had no instrument. However, I previously had recorded performances of gaitas in San Jacinto, Cartagena, and on Isla Grande of the Islas de Rosario. In almost all cases the instrument is played in pairs, the gaita hembra (female flute) and *gaita macho* (male flute). The hembra

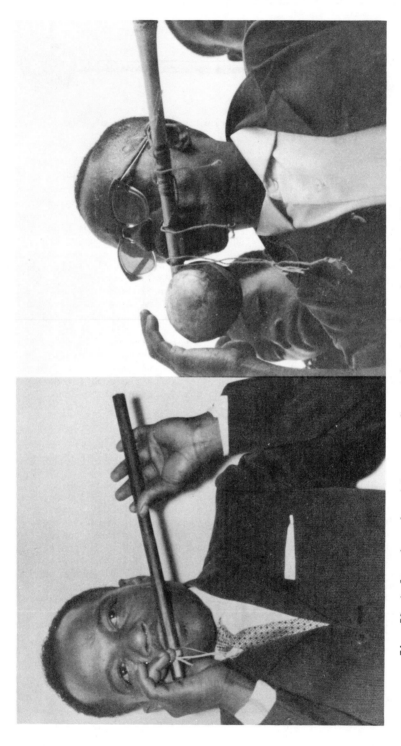

Fig. 50. Left, pito played by a costeño; right, bounkam played by a Bissa of Upper Volta.

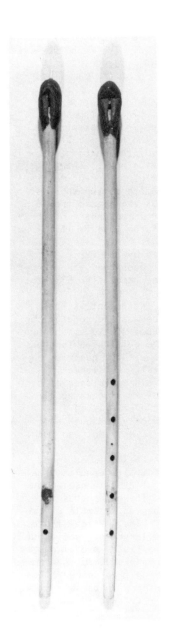

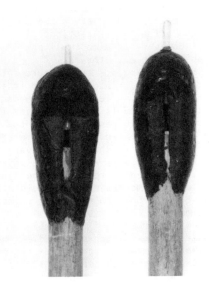

Fig. 52. Heads of the gaitas shown in fig. 51.

Fig. 51. Gaitas
from San Jacinto

Fig. 53. Gaitas and maraca played by Juan
Lara and Antonio Fernández of San Jacinto.

and macho are identical except in the number of fingerholes. The
hembra has five fingerholes, but only four are in use at any one
time. Either the highest or lowest fingerhole is closed with
wax. Most machos observed had one fingerhole. The macho utilized
in San Jacinto was exceptional in having two fingerholes (fig.
51). However, in almost all performances one of the two fingerholes was closed with wax.

The following are the measurements of a pair of gaitas collected in San Jacinto and shown in fig. 51. The instruments are
90 centimeters in length and 2.9 centimeters in diameter. The
wall of the tube is .4 centimeters thick. The head occupies
approximately 10 centimeters of the length of the instrument,
and the quill extends 1.5 centimeters from the head. The fingerholes are oval in shape. They vary from .91 to .96 centimeters
at the longest axis and measure .85 centimeters at the shortest
axis. From center to center the fingerholes are spaced from 6.5
to 6.65 centimeters apart. The distance from the center of the
lowest fingerhole to the lower extremity of the tube is 11.6
centimeters.

The fingerholes of the hembra are covered by the first two
fingers (index finger and middle finger) of each hand, the fingerhole of the macho by the index finger of one hand (fig. 53) (for
further information see List 1973b).

The peculiarity of construction of this instrument is its
head. This unique feature is modeled of beeswax and vegetal carbon and is mounted on the upper end of a tube. The duct through
which the air is blown is fashioned from the quill of a feather
and is inserted in the head. This flute is without question
indigenous. I can find no firm evidence of its existence in
Europe or Africa. García Matos, the late folk music specialist
at the Conservatorio Nacional in Madrid, informed me categorically
in 1970 that no instrument of this type had ever existed in Spain.
According to Izikowitz, this flute is found only in South and
Central America among the Ika, Cágaba (Kogi), Motilón, and Cuna
Indians (1935:372-73).

Fig. 54 is a photograph of paired flutes called *tolos* found
among the Cuna in Panama. The hembra has four fingerholes, the
macho one. Fig. 55 is a drawing of similar flutes in use among
the Ika, with a cross section of the head. The hembra has five
fingerholes, the macho one. Tayler describes an ensemble of two
Kogis playing kuizis and maraca (fig. 56): "The vertical flutes
called *kuizi* by the Kogi, are from a single length of cane about
one inch in diameter and two feet long. The flutes are always
played in pairs and are referred to by the Spanish terms *hembra*
or female and *macho* or male, the former having five spaced holes,
the latter one. The heads of both are covered with beeswax with
a turkey quill reed inserted so that the air current in the quill
touches the end of the cane tube. These cane flutes are played
by two men, the elder playing the five-holed flute with the fingers of both hands, the younger playing the single-holed flute
with the index finger of his right hand and shaking the *maraca*
in the left hand" (1968:vi).

In 1965 I recorded two Spanish-speaking men of Indian descent
playing two carrizos and a maraca in the village of Atánquez on

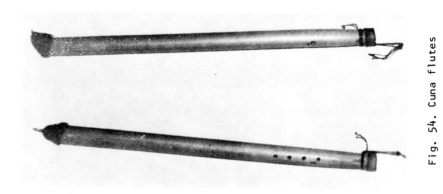

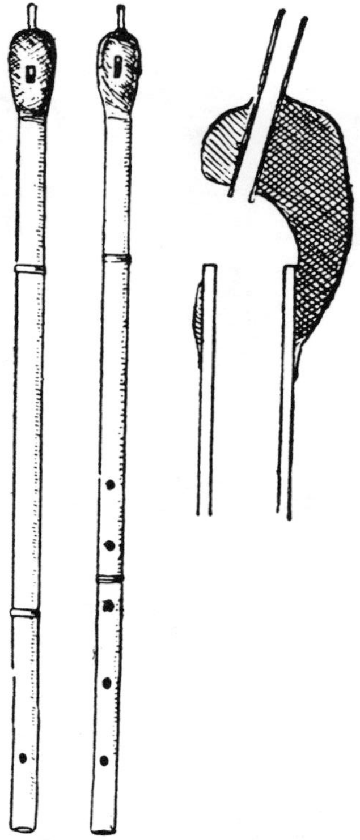

Fig. 55. Ika flutes

Fig. 54. Cuna flutes

Fig. 57. Conjunto de carrizos of Atánquez.

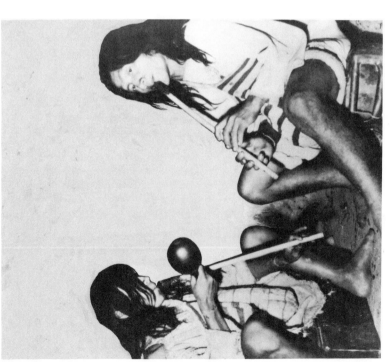

Fig. 56. Kuizis and maraca played by Kogis

the eastern slope of the Sierra Nevada de Santa Marta (fig. 57).
This ensemble is called *conjunto de carrizos* and accompanies a
round dance known as *chicote*. The instruments are known as
carrizos because they are made from the cane of that name. These
flutes are similar in size to the kuizis played by the Kogi.

I should add that similar paired flutes are found among the
Noanamá Chocoan group in the region of Guapi on the Pacific Coast
of Colombia near the Ecuadorian border (Bermudez and Abadía 1966:
22-23). A similar flute made of cane, wax, and quill is found at
present in Mexico. This Huaxteca flute has five fingerholes,
the upper of which is stopped with wax. The wax is pierced with
a small hole and covered with the membrane of a spider's egg
(information secured in the field by Charles L. Boilès).

CHORDOPHONES

   Marimba (figs. 58 and 60).

In this case the term *marimba* refers to the musical bow,
which, in this area, is known by no other name. When I first
visited Evitar in 1964 I was informed that there was an old man,
Juan Martínez by name, who had formerly played the musical bow
but who no longer played the instrument. Martínez was absent
from the village during my first period of field work, and I was
unable to interview him. He was no longer alive when I again
returned to Evitar.

According to my informants in Evitar, the bow played by Juan
Martínez was large, the size of a hunting bow with which one
shoots arrows. The cord tied to the extremities of the bow was
held between the lips, the oral cavity thus forming a resonance
chamber. The cord was struck with one piece of wood and stopped
with a second. The bow was made from a branch of the *chupa-chupa*
(sorrel) tree, the branches of which are particularly flexible.
There was some difference of opinion concerning the material
utilized as the cord. An older informant, Abraham Herrera, said
that the cord was shaped from *napa* of the *iraca* (*Carludovica
palmata*) palm. Napa is the stem of the palm leaf and in its
extension becomes the center vein of the leaf. To make the cord
and the musical bow the napa was first separated from the leaf,
and then a long strip was peeled from it. This strip was washed
in water and then scraped with a knife until it was of the right
thickness. A younger informant, Simon Herrera, said that the
cord was made from *matamba* (Desmoneus), a non-erect vinelike palm.
Both informants agreed that the *varilla,* the little rod with
which the cord was struck, was fashioned from the stem of the lata
palm.

I recorded two players of the musical bow in the Costa Atlántica, Rafael Terán in Palenque in 1964 and Antonio Palomino Robles
on Isla Grande of the Islas del Rosario in 1968. The instrument
described as having been played by Juan Martínez in Evitar was
very similar to those recorded in Palenque and on Isla Grande.
The *marimberos* recorded played the instrument in the same manner.
The bow is rested on the left thigh and is held with the left
hand. It is positioned so that the portion of the string near the

Fig. 58. Marimba (musical bow)
played by Rafael Terán of Palenque.

right extremity of the bow--right from the player's point of view--
is held between the lips. The mouth is partially open and the lips
slightly parted. Thus the bowstring is not in acutal contact with
the mouth and is free to vibrate. Tone is initiated by beating the
cord immediately to the right of the mouth with a thin, long *varita*.
(Varita and *varilla* are different forms of the diminuitive of *vara*,
a rod or stick.) The *palito*, a short, dowel-like piece of wood
held in the left hand, is used to stop the string in one place,
producing a fundamental a semitone higher than that produced by
the open string. By expanding and contracting his oral cavity,
the player strengthens a particular overtone of the fundamental
being produced by the string as a whole (see chapter 6, IV.A.1.6).
These are usually the third, fourth, or fifth overtones, but occasionally the sixth is also amplified.

Fig. 59. Fundamentals and overtones produced by the marimba.

Thus two musical lines are heard simultaneously, the first consisting of the two fundamentals, the second utilizing overtones
derived from these fundamentals. The overtones are of course of
less amplitude than the fundamentals. The two melodic lines are
rhythmically the same, since rhythm is produced by one means
only, the beating of the cord by the varita.

In Palenque the marimbero made his bow from a peeled branch
of *negrillo* (elm) or *palma iraca*, his cord from the napa of an
unspecified palm tree. He informed me that the napa breaks if
allowed to dry out and that he always carries a spare. For the
varita he used a section of the napa of the *palma amarga* (*Sabal
mauritiiformis*), which is less flexible than the type of napa he
utilized for the cord. The palito or piece of wood used to stop
the string was a short section of a peeled branch of the guayabo
(for further information see List 1966).

The marimbero recorded on Isla Grande utilized for his bow a
branch of chupa-chupa, or *negrito* or *canilla de venado*. (Again,
negrito and *negrillo* are alternate forms of a diminutive, in
this case of *negro*.) He fashioned his cord from the napa of the
palma de coco or palma amarga or from a vine he called *pituguia*.
He used palma amarga or palma lata in making his varilla and
fashioned his palito or bolillo from any kind of wood. The bow
which he played for me was made of canilla de venado, which he
preferred above the other woods mentioned because of its strength.

Fig. 60. Marimba: detail of
attachment of string to bow

The cord used was of pitugüia. He would have preferred a cord made
from the napa of the palma amarga, which he said had a better tone.
However, as he was lame he found it difficult to climb the palm to
secure the napa.

Both marimberos attached the cord to the bow by the same means:
the cord was wetted, the bow bent, and the cord wound around the
extremities of the bow in such a manner as to be held in place by
its own tension when the bow was released (fig. 60).

The following are the measurements of the musical bow used by
Antonio Palomino Robles when I recorded him on Isla Grande in
1968. The curved length of the bow is 119 centimeters. A direct
line from one extremity of the bow to the other measures 111
centimeters. The bow is 2.5 centimeters in diameter. The
varilla is more or less round and .5 centimeters in diameter. In
length it is 39.5 centimeters. The palito is also round, 2 centimeters in diameter and 16 centimeters in length. The cord is
very thin and flat and is .3 centimeters in width.

The marimba does not produce a large volume of sound. Performances are usually for the self-gratification of the individual
player. Rafael Terán of Palenque informed me that at times some
of the boys of the village would gather around and listen to him
play. The ears of such listeners would need to be within two to
three feet of the player's mouth in order to distinguish the
sounds produced. Nevertheless, Terán insisted that he had in the
past played the marimba to accompany dancing in an ensemble which
included drums. In his study of Palenque, Escalante indicated

that he was informed that such a practice had existed there in
the past (1954:297). The other instruments of the ensemble were
two drums and a guacho. On Isla Grande, Antonio Palomino also
informed me that he was accustomed to playing the marimba in an
ensemble with drums. There were drummers present, and I indicated that I would like to record such an ensemble. Palomino
asked a tambolero and a player of the llamador to join him. I
attempted to record the ensemble, but because of the softness
of the tones produced by the musical bow I could not make a
recording in which all three instruments could be heard.

My experience in recording the musical bow has led me to
doubt its utility as the melodic instrument in an ensemble containing drums. Perhaps it is a matter of pride for marimberos
to insist that their instrument is capable of fulfilling this
function. No mention was made in Evitar of the marimba's forming
part of an ensemble. If indeed the musical bow was in the past
used in an ensemble with drums, I would think that its participation was more ceremonially than musically significant.

The musical bow is very widely distributed. It is found in
Oceania, in Australia, and in southern Asia, Africa, and North
and South America. Although it is basically a very simple
instrument, there is great variation in the methods employed in
constructing and playing it. These complexities add to the
difficulty of establishing whether its existence in the New World
is due to polygenesis or diffusion, that is, whether the instrument developed independently in the Americas or whether it was
diffused to the New World from a region where it was already
established, such as Africa. There is much evidence concerning
the existence of the musical bow in South America, Central
America, and Mexico in this and the past centuries. We have no
firm evidence, either archeological or documentary, to indicate
that the musical bow existed in the Americas in pre-Columbian
times. Lack of such evidence of course does not represent complete proof that the instrument did not exist during that period.
To quote Izikowitz, "If the musical bow is pre-Columbian it
would be the only string instrument known in America before
Columbus. The simplicity of the instrument and the fact that the
Indians were acquainted with the bow and arrow renders fairly
great the probablility of its pre-Columbian occurrence in
America" (1935:301).

In the Atlantic coastal region of Colombia there are two
Indian tribes which possess the musical bow, the Guajiro and the
Motilón. These groups live in both Colombia and Venezuela. The
Motilón inhabit the Sierra de Perijá, which forms the border
between the two countries. The Guajiro live on the Guajira
Peninsula, a narrow northeastern strip of which forms part of
Venezuela. The following data concerning the Motilón come pri-
marily from Colombian sources, those concerning the Guajiro from
Venezuelan sources.

Among the Motilón the musical bow is played by both men and
women. The curved bow is made from a flat piece of bamboo and
the cord from a fiber called *fique*. The oral cavity, the mouth,
is used as the resonating chamber. The player supports the bow
with the left hand, and the thumb of this hand is used to stop the

string. The other end of the wood of the bow is held against the
player's teeth, the cord remaining free of contact with the face.
With his right hand the player rubs a stick back and forth across
the cord as one would a violin bow, but near his mouth. This
stick is occasionally moistened with saliva in order to produce
better friction (Reichel-Dolmatoff 1945:43).

The Guajiro have a similar bow, which is apparently played only
by men. The arch of the bow is made of a short section of vine
cut in two lengthwise and sharpened at each end. A cord made
from the hairs of a horse's mane is stretched from one end to the
other (Aretz 1967:110). The Guajiro play the bow in the same
manner as the Motilón except that the Guajiro moisten the string
itself with saliva rather than the stick rubbed upon it (Izikowitz
1935:204). In photographs viewed, the Motilón bow is held immediately projecting in front of the body, whereas the bow as played
by the Guajiro is held at an angle to the left. In both cases the
bow is held at a somewhat higher level than the bowstring. Thus
the stick that rubs the string passes under the bow (see Moser and
Tayler 1972:plates 13-14 and Perez Piñango n.d.:back cover).

The bow played by the Motilón and the Guajiro is much smaller
than that played by the Spanish-speaking inhabitants of the lowlands. The curved length of the bow which I collected at Isla
Grande is 119 centimeters. The length of a Motilón bow on exhibi-
tion in the Instituto Nacional de Antropología in Bogotá is 68
centimeters (measurement courtesy of Carlos Garibello Adano).
The curved length of two Guajiro musical bows measured by Aretz
is 28 and 35 centimeters respectively (Aretz 1967:110). The
oral cavity is used as the resonator in all cases. However, in
Palenque and Isla Grande the cord of the bow is placed between
the parted lips and itself imparts vibrations to the oral cavity.
Conversely, in the Indian instruments the oral cavity receives
the vibration through the end of the wooden bow placed against
the teeth. In the lowlands the cord is vibrated by being beaten
with a thin rod. The cord of the Indian bow is vibrated by
rubbing it with a stick placed across it.

A distinction can also be made between the bows of the Indians
and those of the Spanish-speaking lowlanders on the basis of
what is played on the instrument. The lowlander plays *toques*
(two-voiced pieces), which he learns by listening to others perform them. Animal names for toques are common, for example
"Mono prieta" (brown monkey), "Maguá," and "Toche" (the latter
two are named for local birds). However, the toques are primarily
melodic in character and are not specifically descriptive of
sounds made by the animals for which they are named. In one case
only, that of the toque "Toche," was I informed that the piece
was inspired by the singing of this particular bird. On the other
hand, the Motilón and the Guajiro do not amplify certain overtones in such a manner as to produce melodies. Rather, what they
perform seems to represent actual imitations of the sounds produced by various animals found in their environment: birds, frogs,
and cattle.

Reichel-Dolmatoff is of the opinion that the Motilón musical
bow is indigenous rather than African, and Aretz holds the same
opinion concerning the musical bow of the Guajiro. Their belief

is that bows whose cords are rubbed with a stick are indigenous
and that those whose cords are beaten are African in origin
(Reichel-Dolmatoff 1945:43 and Aretz 1967:111).

This view seems amply justified, although neither author
offers much evidence to back their opinion. I can find no
reference to the use of a bow in West Africa in the playing of
which friction is applied to the bowstring by rubbing it with a
stick. On the other hand, this method of producing tone is quite
common among Indian groups in South America. It is found among
the Jívaro of the Ecuadorian Amazon, among the Araucanians
(Mapuche) of western Argentina and Chile, and among the Indian
groups found in the Chaco and Patagonia (Izikowitz 1935:204).
Beating the cord with a rod seems to be the common method of
producing tone in the African mouth bow (this term is applied
to a musical bow in which resonance is produced by the oral
cavity). The playing of bows in which tone is produced in this
manner has been observed in Senegal among the Diola (Thomas
1959:381) and the Fulani/Tukulor (Beárt 1955:679), in Liberia
among the Kpelle (Stone and Stone 1972:B3), the Bassa (Okie 1955:
A4), and the Gbunde (Schwab 1947:153), in Nigeria among the
Bakwiri (Boulton 1957:87-B) and the Igbira (Meek 1975:156-57),
and in French Equatorial Africa among the Mboko (Rouget 1946:
Side II Band 3). Such a bow was observed in Nigeria as early
as 1819 (Bowdich 1966:362-63).

In all of these instruments the cord is held between the lips
and beaten with a thin rod. The stopping of the bowstring with
the other hand is usually done with some type of stick or other
implement but occasionally with the thumb or other fingers. A
rather full description is given of the bow of the Bakwiri of
Nigeria. The lower end of the bow is held by the second, third,
and fourth fingers of the left hand, while the first finger and
thumb hold the stick used to stop the string. The bowstring is
struck with a stick or reed held in the right hand. The cord
is held between the open lips but does not touch them. By
leaving the string open or by stopping it with the stick held
in the left hand, two fundamentals are produced. These are constantly accompanied by amplified overtones which "may be said to
produce the effect of two consecutively progressive chords....
The fundamental tones are at an interval of a major 2nd" (Boulton
1957:87-B).

An examination of the published photograph of the Mboko bow
indicates that it is held and played in exactly the same manner
as the Bakwiri bow described by Boulton. By listening to the
recording, I also determined that the two fundamentals employed
are approximately a major 2nd part. The player of the Mboko bow
produces a rather broken upper melodic line, amplifying the third,
fourth, and fifth overtones of the open string and the second,
third, fourth, fifth, and sixth overtones of the stopped string
(Rouget 1946:Side II Band 3).

In African mouth bows a section of the bowstring rather close
to the tip of the bow or one toward the middle is placed across
the mouth (Nketia 1974:98-99). The former is the case, for
example, in the Mkobo bow from French Equatorial Africa and the
latter in the *gbong-kpala*, the bow of the Kpelle of Liberia

(information from Ruth Stone). A player of the mouth bow of the
Baule of the Ivory Coast, as viewed in a sound film, places between his lips that section of the string nearest to the tip of
the bow. In its kinetic aspects this performance is analogous in
all respects to that of the marimbero of Palenque, which I also
documented on sound film. The interval between the fundamentals
produced by the open and stopped string of the Baule bow is very
close to a semitone. However, there are no clearly amplified
overtones, since the player produces various sound effects by
manipulating the string with his lips (Himmelhaber 1970).

From the standpoint of the overtones produced, more exact
analogues of the costeño bows can be found further south. Fig. 62
is a photograph of a man of the Fang people of Gabon playing the
beng, fig. 63 a man of the Mpyemo of the Upper Sangha playing the
agwong. When these two photographs are compared with that of the
marimbero of Palenque (fig. 61) it will be seen that the manner
of holding the instrument and the method of beating and stopping
the cord are identical. Note that the cord is attached to the
bow in very much the same manner as it is in a costeño bow
(fig. 60).

In both African instruments the interval separating the two
fundamentals employed as a semitone. In the *beng* of the Fang all
amplification is of the third, fourth, and fifth overtones: $\underline{c}$ $\underline{e}$ $\underline{g}$
and $\underline{d}^{\flat}$ $\underline{f}$ $\underline{a}^{\flat}$ (Kubik 1968:51). In the transcription of the pitches
produced on the *agwong* of the Mpyemo, the fundamentals are given
as $\underline{c}$ and $\underline{c}^{\sharp}$. In playing this instrument, the first and second
overtones are apparently utilized as well as the third, fourth,
and fifth of each fundamental (Kubik n.d.:35). The Mpyemo live
in the southwestern part of the Central African Republic and in
the southeastern part of Cameroon. They migrated to that area
from Congo-Brazzaville (People's Republic of the Congo). The
Fang live not only in Gabon but in Guinea Equatorial (formerly
Spanish Guinea). This type of mouth bow and its particular
playing technique therefore probably have a wider distribution
in this region of Africa than the two cited examples necessarily
indicate.

There are also similarities in the fashioning of the costeño
bows and those of West Africa in general. Like that of the bow
of Isla Grande, the cord of the Fang and Mpyemo bows is made from
a vine or a creeper. This is also the case with the bows of the
Bassa of Liberia (Okie 1955:A4) and of the Mboko of French Equatorial Africa (Rouget 1946: Side II Band 3). The marimbero of
Palenque fashions both the cord of his bow and the varita with
which he strikes it from the napa or rib of a palm leaf. The
Igbira of Nigeria fashion the cord of their bow from a palm leaf;
the Diola of Senegal strike the cord of their bow with a beater
fashioned from a leaf rib (Meek 1971:156-57; Thomas 1959:81).

There is thus no question that the musical bow in use by the
costeño of northern Bolívar had its source in Africa. Although
mouth bows of this type are found in many areas of West Africa,
the closest analogues to the costeño instrument seem to be in
use in central West Africa.

Fig. 61. Marimba played by a costeño

Fig. 62. Beng played
by a Fang of Gabon

Fig. 63. Agwong played by a
Mpyemo of the Upper Sangha

Carángano (earth bow) (figs. 64-65)

The *carángano* was no longer played in Evitar when I first
visited the village in 1964. However, Marcelina Sánchez
Pimientel informed me that her mother had played the instrument,
and Abraham Herrera Pacheco indicated that his aunt had also
done so. According to Herrera, a carángano consisted of a cord,
a pole, and a resonator. One end of the cord was tied to a bent
sapling or a flexible pole inserted into the ground; the other
end was attached to a resonator in the form of an old kettle or
gasoline tin. The player sat upon the resonator and plucked
the string with the hand.

The carángano seems to be the only musical instrument customarily played by women in this region. In Mahates a carángano
was made and played for us by an elderly woman, Emilia Beltrán.
The instrument was assembled in the yard of a bahareque next to
the cerca. Beltrán utilized as a resonator a wooden box in
which candles had been shipped. The top of the box was removed,
the box was turned over, and a small hole was made near one end
of what was originally the bottom of the box. One end of a
length of cotton string was tied around the middle of a short
stick. The free end of the string was then passed through the
hole in the box from the inside and the string pulled through
until the stick pressed against the wood. The box was then
placed open side down on the ground next to the cerca, where a
branch of the totumo tree had previously been tied to one of
the bamboo stakes. The free end of the string was then tied to
the extremity of this branch. The branch was bent down while this
was done, and when released it pulled the string taut (fig. 64).
Beltrán sat on the box with the string extending vertically
between her legs. She caused the string to vibrate by plucking
its lower portion with a wooden plectrum held in her right hand.
She produced different pitches by pinching the upper portion of
the string in various places between thumb and fingers, thus
changing the length of the lower vibrating portion of the string
(fig. 65).

The box used as a resonator was made of *cativo* (*Prioria
copaifera*) boards approximately 1 centimeter thick and was 30.4
centimeters high by 23 centimeters wide and 41 centimeters long.
The piece of cotton string used was approximately 1.4 meters in
length. The branch of totumo was 133 centimeters in length and
ranged from 3.3 to 2 centimeters in diameter from butt to tip.
The plectrum was made of hard wood and was 5.5 centimeters in
length and .08 centimeters thick.

A carángano was also made for me in El Carmen by Olegario
Camargo. This instrument differed in two respects from the instrument made by Emilia Beltrán in Mahates. The resonating chamber in
this case consisted of a small pit dug in the ground near a cerca
and covered with a piece of tin. The piece of tin was considerably
larger than the pit and was held in place by stones placed upon it
where it rested on the ground around the circumference of the pit.
The string emerging from the tin was tied to a bent stake of the
bamboo cerca rather than to a branch tied to such a stake. Camarga
had seen the instrument made and played many years in the past.

Fig. 64. Carángano made by Emilia Beltrán.

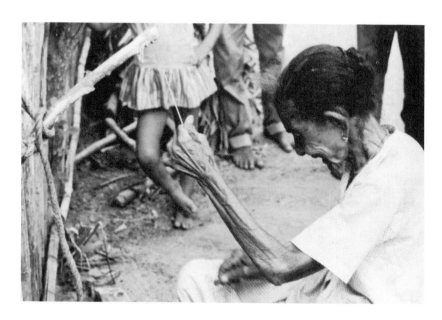

Fig. 65. Carángano played by Emilia Beltrán

However, he had never made one before, nor had he ever played the instrument.

According to Emilia Beltrán, and to informants I questioned concerning the carángano in El Carmen de Bolívar, the instrument was primarily used to accompany singing. Beltrán was recorded accompanying her two daughters in the singing of *merengues* and fandangos. At times she joined the singing. No information is available as to the type of ensemble in which the carángano was utilized in Evitar.

The earth bow is found with some frequency in Africa. According to Bebey, a hole is dug in the ground and covered with a board or a piece of bark. A flexible pole is inserted in the ground nearby. A string is stretched between the end of the bent pole and the board or bark, with the cavity in the ground acting as a resonator when the string is struck or plucked (1975:64). The instrument is usually made and played by children or youths. It is struck with a stick or the index finger or plucked with the thumb and index finger (information based on data collected in the field by Gerhard Kubik). Versions of the instrument in which there is no real resonator are found in northern Ghana and among the Mpyemo of the Central African Republic. In the first case the string is merely buried in the ground and at times is secured with a stone (Nketia 1974:98). In the *angedeng* of the Mpyemo the string is attached to a piece of wood driven into the ground. A bow employing a resonator consisting of a pit in the ground covered with bark is found in the northern Congo area and among the Azande of Zaire. The rectangular piece of bark is held in place by crosspieces staked at the end with forked sticks. A strip of rattan is used as the string (Djenda 1968a:44).

The Gbaya-Bogoto of the Central African Republic and Eastern Cameroon possess an earth bow with the suggestive name *korongoe*. The Gbaya-Bogoto speak a Sudanese language and are believed to originally have inhabited a region south of Lake Chad, possibly in northern Cameroon. Djenda describes a korongoe made and played by a fourteen-year-old boy of this ethnic group:

A round hole some 20 centimeters deep and 25 to 30 centimeters wide is dug in the ground, and a branch a meter or more in length is planted in the ground a meter distant from the hole. One end of a string about 80 centimeters in length is attached to the end of the branch and the other to a tin can through a hole in its top. The bottom of the can is open, and the string is attached to the top of the can either by means of a knot or by tying it to a wooden stick. The branch is bent by pulling on the string, and the can is lowered into the cavity until its open end touches bottom. The player sits with the bow to his left and holds the can in place with the soles of his feet. He strikes the string with the index finger of his right hand, using either single strokes or a back-and-forth motion. Pitch is changed by stopping the string in various places with the thumb and index finger of the left hand. The player also produces lower sounds and glissandi by bending down the branch with his left hand while beating the string with his right (1968a:44).

It is interesting to note that in its diffusion from Africa to Colombia the social function of the earth bow changed. It is no

longer an instrument played by children or young men for their
own amusement but one played by women to accompany singing.

Marcuse states that although the earth bow is now found only
in Africa, there is evidence that in Neolithic times it was found
on several continents (1975a:350-51). Since, to my knowledge,
the first work in which the existence of the earth bow in Colombia
is discussed was published in 1980 (List:570), Marcuse could not
have been aware of its existence in that country.

ENSEMBLES

Cumbia is a concept central to costeño music, dance, and festivity. The term has many connotations. It refers to the ensemble that plays for the dance, to the ritmo or music that is performed, and to the dance itself. A *gran cumbia* or *cumbia completa*
refers to a festivity in which much music is performed, in which
much dancing takes place, and in which the entire community parti-
cipates. A man may refer to himself as a *cumbiambero*, implying
that he is by inheritance a musician; that is, his father and
possibly his grandfather before him performed the cumbia.

The dance known as cumbia takes place at night. The dancing
couples revolve counterclockwise in a circle around the musicians
seated in the center. The women occupy the perimeter of the
circle, illuminating the proceedings with a packet of lit candles
wrapped in a colorful handkerchief and carried in each uplifted
right hand. Their dance is a rapid shuffle of short steps. Their
movement is usually to one side or the other but occasionally
forward as well. The man dances around his partner in a zigzag
pattern, leaning on his left foot and propelling himself with his
right. The partners rarely touch but often pass each other back
to back. On occasion, the man reaches up his right arm to support
that of the woman holding the candles. After this brief physical
contact the couple executes a full turn, and the man immediately
retires to his position within the ring (Escalante 1954:297).

The dance is believed to have been derived from the Spanish
fandango, in which a man dances around a woman who remains in more
or less the same location as she dances (Zapata Olivella 1962:189-
90; Ballanoff 1971:45-47). This is probable, since couple dancing
is characteristic of European rather than of African or Amerindian
dances (Kurath 1949:283-84 and 1956:293-94).

The music for the dancing may be provided by either of two ensembles. In one the caña de millo or pito is the melodic instrument, in the other the gaita hembra serves this function. In
northern Bolívar the first ensemble is known as cumbia or conjunto
de cumbia. In the Departmento de Atlántico it is referred to as
cumbiamba. The ensemble utilizing the gaita is referred to as
conjunto de gaitas or merely as gaita. Since it serves the same
function as the conjunto de cumbia, the conjunto de gaitas may on
occasion also be referred to as cumbia or cumbiamba. The man who
refers to himself as a cumbiambero may perform on any instrument
found in either ensemble, although the appellation is most commonly applied to players of the pito or gaita.

In the past the ritmo played by the conjunto de gaitas to
accompany the dance was known as gaita and that used for this

purpose by the conjunto de cumbia was known as cumbia. At that
time the cumbia was apparently a purely instrumental piece, as
the gaita still is. Escalante in his discussion of the performance
of these ritmos in Palenque does not mention singing as part of the
performance (1954:295-96). However, during the period of investigation *cuartetos* (quatrains) with or without choral response formed
part of the performance of some cumbias in Evitar and in other
localities where I recorded this ritmo. An additional development
had taken place: the conjunto de cumbia now performed ritmos which
were differentiated as cumbia and gaita. A similar but not as
clearly defined development had taken place in the repertory of
the conjunto de gaitas. Of the three ensembles of this type that
I recorded, one played two ritmos which were distinguished as
gaita corrida and cumbia, a second played only gaita corrida, and
the third played only cumbia.

EXISTING ENSEMBLES (1964-71)

   Conjunto de cumbia (fig. 66).

   There are five players in this ensemble. The leader plays the
only melodic instrument, the caña de millo or pito. The other
instruments are the tambor mayor, the bombo, the guachos, and the
llamador. Among the four conjuntos that I recorded in the region,
the only variable in the instrumentation of the ensemble was the
type of rattles employed. In Evitar two cylindrical metal guachos
were employed, in Soplaviento one cylindrical guacho made of bamboo, in Cartagena two maracas, and in Sabanalarga one maraca.
According to Escalante, the guacho in use in this conjunto in
Palenque was cylindrical in shape and pierced with holes, but he
does not indicate of what material it was made (Escalante 1954:
296).
   The traditional ritmos played by this conjunto are the cumbia,
gaita, *porro,* and *puya.* When called upon to do so the ensemble
of Evitar will also play danza de negro and bullerengue.

   Danza de Negro.

   The danza de negro is one of the *comparsas* of musicians and
dancers that participated in the *carnaval* in Evitar. Such a group
was also active during the carnaval in other communities of the
area. Escalante describes a performance of the group in Palenque
(1954:293-94), and we were accosted by such a comparsa in Mahates
on Ash Wednesday in 1970. Although the danza de negro is occasionally performed during other fiestas, it is primarily an
aspect of the celebration of the carnaval. I shall therefore
defer describing the dance as such until the discussion of the
carnaval in the succeeding chapter. Here I shall be concerned
only with the group of musicians which provides the music.
   The ensemble from Evitar which I recorded in Mahates in 1970
consisted of five men, a vocal soloist and four instrumentalists,
who also sang the choral refrain. The instruments utilized were
tambor mayor, guacharaca, and palmetas. A fourth man reinforced
the part of the palmetas by striking together two bombo sticks.

Fig. 66. Conjunto de cumbia of Evitar. Pito, Santiago Ospino Caraballo; tambor mayor, José del Carmen Pimientel Martínez; bombo, Manuel Pimientel Pacheco; guachos, Juan Ospino Jiménez; llamador, Angel Ospino Santana.

Fig. 67. Abraham Herrera Pacheco and Juana
García Blanquiset dancing the bullerengue

The recording session occurred in April. In February of the same
year I observed a performance of the danza de negro in Evitar
during the period in which the carnaval normally takes place. I
photographed the dancers and musicians but made no attempt to
record the music. A larger number of men participated in the
music making. There was the same vocal soloist as recorded on
the later occasion, Agostín Pallares Hernández, but a different
tambolero, Andrés Herrera. I did not obtain the names of the
other participants. One man played what was apparently an improvised substitute for the guacharaca. He rubbed a stick over a
flat, circular sieve woven of fiber which is used to separate
the hulls from grain. A number of men clapped, and three held
pairs of sticks in their hands which they struck together. No
one played palmetas.

Bullerengue.

The ensemble that performs the music of the bullerengue consists of a *cantante*, a chorus which sings the refrain and simultaneously claps, and players of the tambor mayor and llamador.
The drummers are seated. The soloist and chorus stand behind
them. The dancing takes place in front of the drummers. Musicians and dancers are encircled by onlookers. I was told that
the cantante could be a man or a woman. Both Juana García
Blanquiset and Marcelina Sánchez Pimientel indicated that they
at times sang the solo or cantante part. However, while I was
in Evitar, and in recording sessions, the cantante was always
Abraham Herrera Pacheco. Some men did occasionally participate
in singing the choral refrain, but in recording sessions it was
sung entirely by women. The latter were referred to as either
cantadoras or *contestadoras*.

The following description of the dancing of the bullerengue
is based primarily upon motion film made of a performance in
Evitar on November 8, 1964. There is only a single couple
dancing at any one time. At frequent intervals one of the
partners of the dancing couple is alternately replaced by one of
the onlookers. As the man or woman enters the ring he or she
immediately begins dancing, and the partner being replaced
immediately stops dancing and leaves the ring. On occasion, the
partners may be replaced simultaneously by a couple entering the
ring. At times all or part of the onlookers join the contestadoras in clapping, bending and straightening their legs with the
knees in time to the music.

Except for occasional turns, the partners dance facing each
other. At no time do they touch. Both dance in short, shuffling
steps, usually to one side or the other and less frequently in a
forward direction. Either may revolve in place. The man may
dance around the woman and revolve once or twice as he goes,
while she revolves in place. The man often holds his arms high
above the shoulders, especially when entering the ring (fig. 67).
The woman may dance with one or both hands raised, but never
higher than the shoulder. The torsos are held erect, and there
is little leaning over even during turns. However, in the
dancing of both sexes there is a continuous rotary motion of hips

and loins. At times the woman will raise her skirt with one hand
and dance in this manner facing the man.

Fandango.

The term *fandango*, like the term *cumbia*, has many connotations.
It is generally applied to dances done through the streets. The
place where people meet to begin such a dance is also known as a
fandango, as is the festivity as a whole of which the dance is a
part. In Evitar the term carries these general connotations, but
it apparently is also applied to a specific song genre accompanied
by drums. I was unable to establish any specific relationship
between this musical genre and a particular dance pattern.

The ensemble from Evitar recorded in 1970 performing fandango
was similar to that which performed bullerengue except that the
drums utilized were tambor mayor and bombo rather than tambor
mayor and llamador. However, the instrumentation seems variable.
When asked to list the instruments used in the various ensembles,
one experienced cumbiambero in Evitar, Felipe Jaramillo, included
all three of these drums in the ensemble utilized in performing
fandango.

ENSEMBLES EXISTING IN THE PAST (Pre-1964)

Conjunto de gaitas (fig. 68).

As indicated previously, this ensemble is part of the cumbia
complex, and its original function, like that of the conjunto de
cumbia, was to accompany the dance cumbia. This ensemble is
composed of four musicians. One plays the principal melodic
part on the gaita hembra. A second plays two instuments simultaneously: a secondary melodic part on the gaita macho held in
his left hand and a rhythmic part with a maraca held in his
right. The other two instrumentalists play the tambor mayor and
the llamador.

There existed in Evitar in the 1930's a conjunto de gaitas in
which Manuel Jaramillo Tijera played the gaita hembra. In 1939
Manuel's son Felipe Jaramillo returned from a sojourn in Barranquilla. Felipe, then a young man, joined the conjunto, playing
the gaita macho and the maraca. Upon his father's death he
assumed direction of the group and replaced his father as player
of the gaita hembra. This conjunto was active until the 1950's.
Andrés Herrera played the gaita macho and maraca or, on occasion,
the tambor mayor. However, the usual tambolero was one of
Felipe's cousins, Dionisio Jaramillo. I assume a fourth man was
found to play the llamador as needed. This was the procedure
followed by the three permanent members of the conjunto de gaitas
of San Jacinto. This is a feasible procedure, since the only
ability required of the player of the llamador is to keep steady
time.

In addition to the two previously discussed ritmos played by
the conjunto de gaitas, the gaita corrida and the cumbia, the
ensembles recorded also played the traditional ritmos, porro
and puya.

Fig. 68. Conjunto de gaitas of San Jacinto. Gaita hembra,
Juan Lara; gaita macho and maraca, Antonio Fernández; tambor
mayor, José Lara; llamador, Enrique González of Cartagena.

Danza de indio.

This ensemble forms part of the *comparsa de indios*, a band of
dancers and musicians representing Indians who participate in
the carnaval. Since the dance is rarely performed at any other
festivity, it will be described in the succeeding chapter.
According to Felipe Jaramillo, who had been active as the gaitero
in such a comparsa in Evitar, the instruments utilized were the
gaita hembra and the guacho. He was using the latter term in
its generic rather than in its specific sense. The rattle in
question was the type described previously as a maraca.

Sexteto.

The sexteto was an ensemble modeled on the Cuban groups, in
particular that known as the Sexteto Habanera, which performed in
commercial sound films shown in the principal cities of the region
beginning in 1927 or 1928. Conjuntos organized in imitation of
the Cuban sextetos sprang up in the cities (see List 1968b:55-56.),
and their influence was eventually felt in the villages. Felipe
Jaramillo had become familiar with such ensembles when he lived
in Barranquilla for a short period as a young man. A few years
after he returned from Barranquilla to Evitar a sexteto from
Soplaviento played in the village. Thus inspired, Jaramillo
founded his own sexteto. This ensemble was in existence from
1943 through 1946 and performed in neighboring towns and villages
as well as in Evitar. Jaramillo played the marimba (marímbula).
Other instruments used in the sexteto were *guitarra* (guitar),
corneta (cornet), maracas, on timbales, and claves. The timbales
are a group of two or three cylindrical or slightly conical
drums of contrasting sizes. They are tuned by adjusting the
pegs to which the heads are attached. They are struck with
sticks or with the hands and at times are mounted on a bar of
wood. The claves are two short lengths of round hardwood. One
is held in each hand, and they are beaten together.
The ritmos performed by the sexteto were those which had
been made popular by the Cuban ensembles. Among others, they
included the rumba, the bolero, and the *guaracha*.

Banda de vientos.

In the 1930's and 1940's there was a movement to establish
bandas de vientos (wind bands) in many areas of the Costa
Atlántica. In most cases these attempts were not successful,
and, in general, such bands persist only in the Departamento de
Córdoba, where I heard and observed such an ensemble during a
political rally in Lorica in 1970. These bands are not usually
very large. The instruments are primarily of the brass and percussion families--cornets, trombones, some member of the tuba
family, and drums. Performance is by rote or by ear.
During the latter part of the period mentioned--one informant
placed the date as 1948--an attempt was made to establish a
banda de vientos in Evitar. The venture met with very little
success and was soon abandoned. The leader of the group was

Manuel Pimientel Sánchez, who was no longer alive at the time
the above information was obtained in 1968.

PROJECTED ENSEMBLE

   Vallenato.

   This ensemble developed in the late 1940's in the valley of the
Cesar River in and near the city of Valledupar, which is now the
capital of the recently established Departamento de Cesar.   There
were three musicians in the early vallenato.   The first, the
leader, played the accordion and sang the *coplas*.   The other two
played the *caja* and the guacharaca, respectively.   *Caja* (box or
chest) is a term loosely applied to drums in general.   When
reference is made to a particular part of a drum, *caja* denotes
shell.   In the early vallenato the term specifically referred to
a drum with two heads, somewhat smaller in size than the llamador.
The instrument was usually held on the left thigh and played with
two short sticks without balls.
   The ensemble and its music gained great popularity through the
issue of commercial recordings of a number of such groups.
Vallenatos were soon in existence in other areas of the country.
The caja was then replaced with a commercially fabricated drum
with a single head, similar in form and size to the llamador and
also played with the hands.   Later other instruments were added
to the ensemble.
   When I visited Valledupar and the surrounding region in 1965
the vallenato ensemble was almost nonexistent in the area of its
origin.   However, I was able to record such a group a few months
later in Bogotá.   The leader of the group, Victor Soto Daza, was
a costeño who was a native of the region in which the vallenato
had developed.   He informed me that the precursor of the vallenato
was an ensemble known as the *conjunto de carrizos*, which included
one or two gaitas, caja, and guacharaca.   As previously indicated,
while in Atánquez in 1965 I recorded an ensemble called a conjunto
de carrizos made up of two men who played gaita-like flutes and
maraca.   During the same period I also recorded a group called
conjunto de gaita.   This ensemble consisted of a gaita hembra (an
exact duplicate of the hembra used in the conjunto de carrizos),
the caja with two heads, and a cantante.   The flutes used in both
ensembles were made of the cane known as carrizo.   The instruments are shorter and smaller in diameter than the gaitas made
of cardón played in the coastal lowlands.
   The characteristic ritmos of the vallenato were the merengue
and the *pasillo*.   The first was the most popular, and the terms
vallenato and *merengue* became almost synonymous.   The pieces
played were composed, and the composers known by the performers,
but the music does not always exist in published form.   Pieces
were often learned by listening to recordings.
   Simón Herrera of Evitar had lived for a short period in
Valledupar.   During our visits in 1968 and 1970 he spoke of his
plans to establish a vallenato in Evitar.   In 1971 he sang several
popular merengues while accompanying himself on a llamador-like
drum.   Whether he later found an accordionist to join him in such

an ensemble is not known. There were members of the Pimientel family in the village who were said to play both accordion and caja.

ELECTRONIC REPRODUCTION

Picó.

Picó is the local pronunciation of the English work "pickup." The term refers to a portable gasoline-powered phonograph. The apparatus consists of three parts: the motor and the generator of electricity which it operates, the turntable, and the speaker. The division of the equipment into three physically separated components makes it more portable in transport and flexible in arrangement. A picó I observed in Evitar in 1970 was set up with the speaker on the ground in front of a bahareque and the turntable and motor-generator within. In this case, an additional speaker in the shape of a horn was hung from the eaves of the house. In 1970 two evitaleros owned picós, and both sets with accompanying records were for rent by the hour or for a lump sum for use during a night of dancing from 7:00 PM to 4:00 AM. The ritmos heard on the records provided were vallenatos, *rancheras, charangas,* and a few *tangos.* According to the informants, these are popular dance forms originating in different countries and areas. The vallenato is Colombian, the ranchera is Mexican, the charanga comes from the Antilles, and the tango is Argentinian. I was also informed that the latter ritmo is not much liked in Evitar.

When I asked the villagers why the picó was preferred to a conjunto composed of live musicians for accompanying dancing, they offered three reasons. The first was that the picó produced a greater volume of tone. The second was that a greater variety of music can be heard. The third and last reason offered for this preference was that the picó, unlike live musicians, did not need to rest.

Transistor radio.

During my visits to Evitar from 1964 through 1970 I saw only two portable battery-operated transistor radios and no radios that were not portable. The small transistor radios seen in the village during that period were not capable of producing as much volume of tone as the picó and, as far as could be determined, were not used to accompany dancing. During the period of investigation the transistor radio was apparently having little impact on thought and musical taste in the village. I assume that with the later development of less costly portable battery-operated radios of greater power, its effect was increased.

SOURCES OF THE ENSEMBLES

The sources of the ensembles are, in general, determined by those of the instruments of which they are composed. Almost

without exception, the traditional instruments in use in Evitar
are of the types found in Africa or among the Amerindians rather
than those found in Europe. Some European traits have been
incorporated into these instruments, such as the counter hoop in
the case of the tambor mayor and the llamador. Further European
methods of producing tension have lately been applied to the
latter. However, of all the instruments traditionally in use,
only the bombo can be said to have a European progenitor. I am,
of course, omitting consideration of the accordion. Although I
was given the names of individuals in the village who were said
to play the accordion, at no time was there any evidence of the
existence of an ensemble such as the vallenato in which this
instrument would play a part.

During the principal ceremony of the carnaval, *la conquista*,
the danza de indios is accompanied by gaita hembra and a maraca,
while the danza de negros is accompanied by the tambor mayor,
guacharaca, singing, and clapping. In this the popular view
coincides with the conclusions which I have drawn from the ethnographic data. The guacharaca is the sole instrument in the latter
ensemble which could have been derived from either African or
Amerindian sources. With the exception of that which accompanies
the danza de indios, all of the ensembles contain some instruments
of mixed heritage. Thus in the conjunto de gaitas the two gaitas
and maraca are purely Indian, while the tambor mayor and llamador,
although primarily African, display at least one European trait:
the counterhoop. Nevertheless, this ensemble remains almost
entirely a mixture of Indian and African traits. Posada Gutiérrez,
writing in 1865, offers an account of how this mixed cultural
derivation may have occurred:

In the early part of the nineteenth century, there were great
festivities in Cartagena which began on the day of Nuestra
Señora de Candelaria, the second of February. The inhabitants of
some wealth and social position danced within a pavilion especially constructed for the occasion to music provided by regimental
bands. Those of the lower classes danced *al fresco*, in the open
air. Two dances of the latter strata of society occurred simultaneously. The dancers in one case were negros or *pardos* (individuals of mixed racial inheritance) and in the other case were
Indians. The dance of negros and pardos, then known as the
currulao, was a circle dance of couples very much like the present
day cumbia. In it, as in the cumbia, the women often held aloft
lit candles wrapped in a handkerchief. The dance of the Indians,
on the other hand, was a closed circle in which women and men
alternated and joined hands. In both cases the musicians performed
in the center of the ring. The dance of the negros was accompanied
by two or three hand-beaten drums and a chorus of women, who also
clapped. That of the Indians was accompanied by gaitas. By 1865,
the two castes had lost much of their mutual antagonism and combined in dancing what was then known as the *mapalé*. Thus the
tamboleros and the gaiteros joined forces in accompanying the
dance (Escalante 1964:149-51 quoting Posada Gutiérrez 1929:11-
195).

It can be seen from the preceding discussion that the bullerengue as an ensemble is derived entirely from African sources. It

duplicates the composition of the ensemble which Posada describes
as accompanying the currulao, two or more hand-beaten drums, singing, and clapping. The bullerengue is believed by the inhabitants
of the region to have had its origin in Palenque.

The ensemble which performed fandango for me was similar to
that of the bullerengue except for the substitution of the bombo
for the llamador. It therefore remains primarily African in
derivation. Of the five instruments of which the conjunto de
cumbia is composed, there is little question that three, the caña
de millo, the tambor mayor, and the llamador, are primarily
derived from Africa. As has been seen, the guacho has progenitors both in Africa and among the Amerindians, and the bombo in
both Europe and Africa. Thus, Africa has exerted the greatest
influence in the composition of the conjunto de cumbia. Further,
ensembles containing a large number of percussion instruments are
not characteristic of musical practice of the Amerindians of the
region being discussed, while such ensembles are widely distributed in West Africa.

3. Music Occasions

This chapter is concerned with the more structured occasions during which music was performed in Evitar both during and previous to the period of investigation. Although other musical genres not discussed in this chapter (such as lullabies, children's game songs, and work songs) serve specific social functions, they occur with some spontaneity, and little or no preparation is required prior to their performance. The contexts in which such genres are performed will be discussed in later chapters.

Beginning in the 1950's, at the latest, the rising tide of inflation in Colombia has imposed an ever greater strain on the economy of the rural costeño. As he has become more and more dependent upon manufactured goods such as metal pots, cloth, and kerosene, he has simultaneously found it more and more difficult to obtain the necessary cash with which to purchase them. The inhabitants of an isolated village like Evitar are at a particular disadvantage. Because of the lack of transport they have no ready market for their produce. Thus it is not only the growth of technology and of urban influence which has affected costeño folk culture but increasing poverty as well. Communal customs which require a generous outlay of cash are now rarely celebrated or have fallen completely into disuse. In Evitar during the period of investigation the gran cumbia or cumbia completa, requiring many candles and much rum, seems to have been celebrated only during the fiesta of the patron saint of the village. La conquista, the culminating event of the carnaval, had not been seen for some years. It required a number of fairly elaborate costumes and the construction of a temporary palace for the *reina* (queen).

RITES OF PASSAGE

The rites of passage are those ceremonies pertaining to the principal events of the life cycle: birth, puberty, marriage, and death. The Catholic Church provides a rite for each of these occasions--baptism, confirmation, the marriage sacrament, and the requiem mass. The inhabitants of Evitar in the past have had limited access to these services. Nor do they expect the Church to furnish music for these occasions. Traditionally, the evitaleros themselves have provided the music at the celebration of two particular rites of passage, marriage and the *velorio de angelito*.

MARRIAGE

Following a formal wedding, but not following the establishment of a de facto union, there is always a fiesta sponsored by the parents of the bride. Such a fiesta normally takes place at the home of the parents of the bride, and all expenses are defrayed by her father. Rum and food are served to the invited guests and music is provided for dancing. In former times music for dancing was furnished by a conjunto de cumbia or a conjunto de gaitas. Some years prior to my first visit to the village, the conjuntos were replaced by the picó as the customary means of providing music for dancing at a wedding.

VELORIO DE ANGELITO

The velorio for a child differs in many respects from that for an adult. These differences arise from the belief, based primarily upon the teachings of Catholicism, that the child does not suffer after death. A child, although baptized and thus a Christian, is still incapable of committing sins of sufficient magnitude that his soul after death need pass through purgatory before reaching heaven. Instead, the soul of a child moves directly to heaven. It is for this reason that the wake for a child is called velorio de angelito (wake for a little angel) and no rosarios are recited. If a child dies before baptism, it is believed that he does not go to heaven but becomes a *duende* (fairy), a free spirit without care. The velorio for a child is therefore considered a joyous occasion by most of those who attend. The parents, and perhaps very close relatives, do not necessarily share this approach to the occasion, especially the mother, who remains weeping by the body of the child during the greater part of the period during which it is displayed before burial.

The altar for the deceased child is similar in most aspects to that for the adult. However, the child is displayed upon the table, rather than in a coffin. The child is wrapped in a piece of white cloth or dressed in that color. Other colors may be used, but never black. The hands are folded on the chest and tied together with a ribbon of any color but black. Wild flowers are gathered and placed around the child. One is placed in the mouth and one or more between the middle fingers of the clasped hands. It is believed unlucky to bury a child with his eyes closed. If the child's eyes are not open in death, they are propped open by toothpicks broken to the size needed. To avoid contagion the body may be placed upon a board which is in turn placed upon the top of the table. Two lit candles in bottles are placed on the table, one on each side of the corpse. No glass of water is provided for the spirit of the child.

The child's little coffin is placed under the table. It is painted white and decorated with cutouts of tin foil pasted over the paint. These consist of lines running lengthwise and stars

and half-moons placed between the lines. As in the case of an
adult, the corpse of a child is displayed for only one night.
At dawn it is placed in the coffin, the cover is nailed on, and
the coffin is taken by men to the cemetery and buried.

The velorio for an infant lasts for only one night. If the
infant dies at night, the velorio will be celebrated for the
remainder of that night and the infant will be buried in the
morning. For older children the velorio may be of greater
duration. According to Rosina Aguirre, one of the three rezanderas
in the village, the general custom is to celebrate one night of
velorio for children not more than five years of age at death and
six nights of velorio for children who die at ages six through
nine. She could remember only a few cases where velorios were
celebrated for children who were past the age of nine at death.
One was held in 1969 for an eleven-year-old girl. The velorio
was celebrated for nine nights like that for an adult, but
Aguirre did not recite rosarios. Instead, she sang *versos de
santo*. These were sung in the early morning only. At the time of
the interview Aguirre was *en luto* (in mourning) for a son who had
recently died, and therefore she could not sing the versos for us.
She did recite the text of one, which follows:

¡Campo alegre!	Fields of joy!
Cadáver de que cruza	Cadaver that crosses
las inmensas llanuras del	The immense plains of the
mar	seas
y felices que cruz no la	And what happiness that one
usa,	does not bear the cross,
que en los cielos	That one is able
se puede entrar!	To enter heaven!

Campo alegre is a term applied in a laudatory sense to a particular neighborhood or region. The general argument of the verse is
that while the adult must earn the right to enter heaven through
suffering, the child, without undergoing the same experience, is
able to traverse the vast distance between earth and heaven and to
enter therein.

The refreshments served at the velorio de angelito are similar
to those served at a velorio for an adult. Since the former is
considered by the guests to be a joyous occasion, rather than a
time for lamenting, many games are played. These games are similar in many respects to those played by children. However, at
the velorio for a child the games are played by the men and women
present, not by the children. The latter do not attend velorios,
and in Evitar it is not thought appropriate that children play
these particular games. The adults play these games in the street
in front of the house, not in the rancho itself. Light is provided by mecheros hung in the doorway and on the nearby cerca. In
some of the games played the words are sung, in others they are
spoken or recited. The song games will be discussed in chapter 7.
Here I will describe only one of the recited games, *jétepie,* since
it seems related to the purpose of the velorio.

This game is played by the men who gather at the cemetery while
the grave is being dug. As soon as this work is completed two

files are formed, each man placing his hands upon the shoulders of
the one in front of him. As the men proceed toward the village a
lone man, the *caballo* (horse), walks between the two files, carrying a pole between his legs. All march in rhythm to the cry
"jétepie," uttered by the caballo and repeated after him by the
other men in chorus. As he marches along the caballo occasionally
lashes out with his pole and attempts to hit men in one or the
other file in the shins. The latter are on the alert and either
jump or draw aside to avoid being struck by the pole.

This antic procession makes its way from the cemetery to the
house where the corpse of the deceased child is on display. Upon
arriving, the men enter the house and form a half-circle around
the corpse and altar. The caballo then addresses the corpse, and
the others respond in chorus:

Caballo:	¿Se va, ño mango?	You're leaving, Mango?
Chorus:	¡Se va!	He's leaving!
Caballo:	¿Se va, ño Mango?	You're leaving, Mango?
Chorus:	¡Se va!	He's leaving!
Caballo:	La gurupera.	The pillion.
Chorus:	¡la gurupá!	The croup!

The last two lines are repeated several times. The men then leave
the house and continue to play jétepie or begin a new game.

Mango is a term often applied to children, since they are very
fond of this sweet fruit. *Ño* is a term employed by country people
instead of *señor* (mister). In an equivalent situation no term of
address would be used in English. *Gurupera* is a dialect form of
grupera, a pillion or extra seat behind the rider of a horse.
Gurupá is a dialect form of *grupa,* the croup or rump of a horse.
When we asked the informants what the meaning was of *jétepie,* we
were told that it meant *este pie* (this foot). When they were
asked why the caballo suggested that the dead child mount and
leave with him, the only reply was "That is the way the game is
played." It is probable that this game originally had some ritu-
alistic significance. It seems to reflect an ancient belief that
the soul of the deceased is transported to the other world on a
horse or by a horseman. I have found no reference to this belief
in works on Spanish folklore, but it seems to have been widespread
in southern Europe. The early Romans considered the horse to be a
funerary animal. The proto-Slavic tribes believed it to possess
chthonic characteristics, those of the underworld. On many
Etruscan monuments a man is depicted being carried by a horse.
In the opinion of some scholars, the horsemen carved on Bosnian
gravestones represent the carriers of the souls of the dead
(Zečević 1974:133-34). Christianity has also employed the horse
as a symbol of death. In Revelation 6:8, death is described as
riding on a pale horse.

The wake is a widespread phenomenon, and there are a number of
similarities between the funerary practices of the European, the
African, the Amerindian, and the costeño: the vigil through the
night, the display of the corpse, the belief that the spirit of
the deceased is present, and the provision of entertainment and
food and drink. In Spain the wake was known as the *velatorio.*

There are data concerning its existence in that country in the past,
but little data more recent than the first quarter of this century
(Casas Gaspar 1947:337-43). In Africa the type and degree of
funerary activity engaged in depend upon the age and status of
the deceased. Among the Jívaro of Ecuador the type of burial
given the corpse differs when the deceased is a child, a woman,
or a father (Karsten 1935:156). No evidence could be found, however, that the wake itself differed in the case of a child. Only
in Spain does there seem to be a considerable difference between
the celebration of a wake for a child and one for an adult
(Capmany 1931:320-22).

In Spain the child is also referred to as an *angelito*. The
velatorio for an angelito has been found primarily in southern
Spain, in the provinces along the Mediterranean, Extremedura, and
the Canary Islands. In Valencia, Alicante, and Murcia the observance was known as an *auroro*. In the auroro the corpse of the child
was wrapped in a shroud of gauze or chiffon ornamented with silver
thread, and the mother applied color to the cheeks and lips to
simulate life. The corpse was displayed in a coffin filled with
white flowers spangled with gold and placed on the dining room
table, which was covered with a sheet and a bedspread. At night-
fall friends and neighbors arrived, some carrying guitars and
castanets. The front of the cottage was illuminated. The younger
members of the crowd formed a wide circle and danced and sang to
the accompaniment of the instruments. This merriment continued
until dawn (Casas Gaspar 1947:340-42).

In the 1860's Charles Davillier and Gustavo Doré witnessed a
similar observance in Alicante, and the latter published a drawing
he made of the scene (fig. 69). In this case a lit candle was
placed in each corner of the table. In the *baile de angelito*
the young people were dancing a *jota* to the accompaniment of
guitar, *bandurria,* singing, and clapping (Davillier 1881:324).

CALENDRIC OBSERVANCES

There are various occasions during the year when music is traditionally performed. All are religious in character with the
exception of the carnaval, and the dates upon which they occur
are determined by the calendar of the Catholic Church. Christmas
and the days of saints are fixed. They occur each year on the
same date. Others, like the carnaval and the Sábado de Gloria,
are dependent upon the date when Easter occurs during a particular
year and thus are variable. As in Spain, the celebration of any
particular festival begins on its eve, that is, after sundown.
Because of the intense heat of the day in this area, very little
of any festivity takes place during the day. The celebration of
a particular fiesta therefore customarily begins at sundown of the
previous day and lasts until the dawn of the day listed in the
calendar as the day of the event. The same pattern is customarily
followed in each day of an observance of greater length than a
single day.

In character the calendric observances are a mixture of Christian and pre-Christian traditions. In its spread through Europe,
Christianity adapted for its own purposes many preexistent prac-

Fig. 69. Baile de angelito in Alicante. Drawing by Gustavo Doré.

tices. The celebration of the nativity of Jesus replaced winter
solstice rites, incorporating in the process the twelve-day celebration of this period in Scandinavia. Substituted for the summer
solstice rites of purification by fire and water was the celebration of the day of St. John the Baptist, who purified through a
water rite. The celebration of the death and resurrection of the
Savior replaced the fertility rites of the vernal equinox.

All Spanish fiestas had both their religious and popular
aspects. Like Spain during the period of investigation, Colombia
was legally a Catholic country. However, religious services were
not as widespread as they were in Spain. Neither Evitar nor
Palenque had a chapel nor a priest in residence. Both would have
been found in any community of equivalent size in Spain. Thus
the observances in Evitar are necessarily more popular than religious in character. In addition, the activities carried on during
a fiesta often differ considerably from those customary on the
particular occasion in Spain. Many of the customs followed are
those seen in Europe on one occasion or another but not necessarily
this occasion. However, as has been seen, the traditional ensembles which performed on these occasions in Evitar were derived from
African and Amerindian rather than European sources.

DIA DE SAN SEBASTIAN, SANTO PATRONAL

The celebration of the day of the patron saint of Evitar takes
place on January 20. As in Spain, a community's most important
observance of the year is that of the day of its patron saint.
Although in Spain an individual may at times appeal for assistance
to the saint for whom he is named or to one who has special interest in his occupation or particular needs, in Evitar succor is
sought primarily from the patron saint of the village. It is from
his image that the milagros are hung.

San Sebastián was a Christian martyr of the third century.
There is little real knowledge concerning his life. According to
legend, he joined the Roman army as a cover for his work assisting
Christian martyrs and confessors. The Emperor Diocletian, who was
unaware of his religious activities, admired his courage and character and made him Captain of the Praetorian Guard. When Sebastián's profession of Christianity later became known to the
Emperor, he bitterly reproached Sebastián and ordered that he be
executed by archers (Butler 1956:128-30).

A basilica for St. Sebastian was built on the Appian Way and
was the goal of many pilgrims in the Middle Ages. His aid was
invoked by sufferers from the plague, who believed themselves to
be pierced by unseen arrows. Thus his cult grew rapidly following
the plagues of the seventh and fourteenth centuries. He is
important in Christian art and is usually depicted as being
pierced by arrows or merely as holding an arrow in his hand.

He was also the patron saint of soldiers and archers. According to tradition, he was "el santo de la conquista," since the
conquistadores turned to him for protection. They were, as he had
been, in danger of being killed by arrows, in their case by those
of the Indians. The image of San Sebastián found in the schoolhouse in Evitar has bloodstains painted upon its chest. Although

he is one of the saints omitted from the Roman Catholic calendar
in its revision in this century, San Sebastián is still venerated
in areas of Spain, as well as in Latin America (see p.

A priest might not come to Evitar on any other day of the year,
but one is always brought on the Día de San Sebastián, the cost
being defrayed by popular contribution. And on this day the
conjunto de cumbia of Evitar offers its services gratis to the
village. The fiesta begins with a procession through the streets.
The procession is headed by the priest, who is immediately followed by the statue of San Sebastián carried on a litter, a wooden
platform provided with handles, by several of Evitar's respected
citizens. Behind the litter walk the officials of the village,
the inspector, and the two school teachers. They, in turn, are
followed by the conjunto de cumbia.

Following the procession the priest celebrates a mass in honor
of San Sebastián. In the past this took place in the schoolhouse
for boys. More recently the ceremony has been moved to the more
commodious and prepossessing schoolhouse for girls. A general
festivity then follows. I was assured that there is always a
gran cumbia on this occasion. The conjunto de cumbia volunteers
its services, but its members will expect friends in the village
to keep them supplied with rum throughout their performance. The
bullerengue may also be danced on this occasion, and other dances
as well.

DIA DE SAN PABLO

St. Paul's Day is January 24. Since it follows St. Sebastian's
Day so closely, it is not invariably celebrated in Evitar. When
festivity does occur, it takes the form of a fandango through the
streets, the dancing of the bullerengue, or both.

It is interesting that the day of Christianity's foremost
missionary, St. Paul, and that of its chief apostle, St. Peter,
are occasions of popular celebration in Evitar. They seem to
receive less emphasis in Spain, where saints such as San Isidro
and Santa Agueda, whose positions are much less central to the
Christian faith than those of San Pablo and San Pedro, receive
much more popular acclaim (see Foster 1960:167-206).

CARNAVAL

The carnival is an ancient observance which is believed to have
as its antecedents the Dionysian rites of Greece and the Roman
saturnalia. In the Middle Ages the carnival was celebrated in
most of Europe, and it was a common fiesta in Spain until it was
banned in the present century. It was still flourishing in parts
of Latin America at the time of investigation. Although in the
past it has been celebrated at various periods of the year between Christmas and Easter, it now reaches its climax the three
days preceding Ash Wednesday, that is, the three days preceding
the Lenten season. Lent itself begins forty days before Easter.
The carnaval in Evitar traditionally begins on the Saturday or
Sunday before Miércoles de Cenizas (Ash Wednesday) and continues
through the night of Ash Wednesday. We know that the evitaleros

recognize Lent, since we were told that it is forbidden to play a
drum during *cuaresma* (Lent). However, the celebration of carnaval
on Miércoles de Cenizas is in conflict with Catholic practice.
Ash Wednesday is considered the first day of Lent, and the carnaval
extends only through the night of Shrove Tuesday or the date preceding Ash Wednesday.

The carnival as a festival is characterized by processions of
masqueraders, dancing through the streets, and tomfoolery reaching
the nuisance level. Specific aspects of its celebration in Spain
included the personification of the spirit of the carnaval (often
in the form of a straw man, which was finally ceremoniously buried)
the appearance of a man costumed as a mule or a horse, the ceremonial plowing of land, and the election of a king of the carnaval
(Foster 1960:173). None of these customs formed part of the carnaval as celebrated in Evitar. A queen was elected rather than a
king. In Spain it was traditional to elect a queen during *la
maya,* the eve of May first, but not during the carnaval. On the
other hand, the election of a queen forms part of any festival
of importance in Colombia.

Spain obviously played some part in the historical development
of la conquista, the culminating observance of the carnaval in
Evitar and the surrounding region. In the early celebrations of
the carnival in some areas of Europe, mock battles were fought
which represented the conflict of winter with emerging summer.
In Spain the antagonists in the mock battles became Christians
and Moors. In the New World they were converted into battles
between the conquering Spaniards and the indigenous population.
In Mexico, for example, the characters represented in such battles
are Cortez and his men pitted against the Indians (Toor 1947:
46-47). On the other hand, in Evitar and the region surrounding
it la conquista features mock battles between negros and Indians.
It thus represents the particular historical development in the
region rather than that of Mexico or Spain.

When I first visited Evitar, in 1964, I found that the carnaval
was no longer celebrated in the village with any regularity.
According to one informant, la conquista had not been seen in
the village since 1957. However, there seems to have been some
activity on the part of the comparsa de negros. Since one of the
functions of this comparsa was the collection of money, it would
be to the pecuniary advantage of its members to be active during
the carnaval season whether or not la conquista was celebrated.
I did, in fact, witness performances of the danza de negro in the
streets of Evitar on Sunday, February 8, 1970. This was the
first day of the carnaval in the region, and the activities
carried on were appropriate to the beginning of that festivity.
Later the same day we were accosted by a comparsa de negros in
Mahates and responded to their demand for a contribution before
we were free to go on our way. The following description of the
celebration of the carnaval in Evitar is based on interviews with
informants and therefore primarily represents what occurred
before the period of investigation. On the other hand, the
description of the danza de negro and of the activities of the
comparsa de negros in Evitar before it leaves the village are
based on my observations in 1970.

As has been previously indicated, the two principal comparsas
participating in the carnaval are those of the negros and of the
Indians. The comparsa de negros was composed entirely of men.
At times one of the men would dress like a woman and occasionally
dance with his fellows. The dancers are barefoot and wear
trousers rolled up at the bottom and secured around the waist
with a piece of rope. The body above the waist is bare, and
blue paint is often applied to the face. I was told that the
blue paint was used to indicate that the dancers represented
negros. Traditionally the chest is painted a shining black
with a mixture of soot and *miel de panela* (honey of unrefined
sugar). This miel is produced by boiling the hard cake of panela
in water until it turns to syrup. The chests of the dancers seen
in 1970 were not so painted. When I questioned the dancers concerning their lack of soot and miel de panela, they replied that
they were not as yet fully costumed but would be before they left
the village. In one hand each negro carries a long, flat stick
representing a machete. The leader is called *capitán* (captain)
and carries a longer stick than the others as emblem of his
authority.

Both men and women participate in the danza de indios. Both
sexes dress in lively colors. The men wear no shirts and
carry bows and arrows. The *jefe* (chief) paints his face in bands
of white and red. The latter color is derived from the fruit of
the *achiote* (*Bixa orellana*) tree. The women wear short skirts
decorated with varicolored ruffles formed by horizontally applied
overlapping ribbons. They wear sandals to which are attached
crisscrossed thongs reaching to the knees. The women also wear
headbands of colored paper with an erect feather thrust in the
back.

Beginning either the Saturday or Sunday before Ash Wednesday,
the comparsas leave Evitar to perform in the streets and plazas
of nearby communities. In doing so they hope to secure funds
not only to cover their expenses while they are away from home
but to cover the costs of the celebration of la conquista in
Evitar on Ash Wednesday. Before leaving the village each group
goes in a procession to the bahareque of the inspector. Here they
dance and sing as a means of requesting his permission to perform
in the streets of Evitar. Permission is always granted. In
addition, the inspector traditionally offers each group a *propina*
(gratuity). This may take any form he wishes, but it is usually
money or rum.

In 1970 the comparsa de negros gathered in the little square
in front of Abraham Herrera's rancho (fig. 7, p. 13). Two or
three songs and dances were performed here. The comparsa then
went in procession to the rancho of the inspector. In the
procession the dancers went in front in a twisting single file
while the musicians followed abreast in a single rank. They
stopped in front of the rancho of the inspector and danced and
sang (fig. 70). I heard from the distance the word *propina* being
sung and was told later by the inspector, Herculano Pimentel,
that he had given the group some rum. They then returned in procession to the little square whence they had begun. Two further
songs and dances were performed, and the group dispersed.

Fig. 70. Comparsa de negros in front of the bahareque
of the inspector. View to the west on Calle del Alambre.

Fig. 71. Dancers, danza de negro.

When dancing as a group the negros either progressed in a file in a zigzag pattern or more or less in a single rank, advancing and retiring. They swung their wooden machetes and engaged in sham battles (fig. 71). At times one would dance alone, weaving his hips as in the bullerengue and executing acrobatic leaps and whirls. When the watching crowd grew too near, a dancer would clear the street by running along the edge of the crowd with machete outstretched. Those nearby would then hurriedly withdraw, laughing as they did so.

Following the required visit to the inspector, the comparsa de negros visits another community, where it selects a site and sings and dances to attract a crowd. The dancing continues until the capitán, who is often (but not always) the soloist as well, feels that he or the dancers need a rest. He then utters a sharp cry, and the dancing and singing come abruptly to a halt. To gain money the dancers select an individual watching or passing by, then dance around and surround him. They demand money. If they are not given a small sum, they say that it is necessary to *limpiarle* (clean him). They then embrace him, dirtying him with the soot they have applied to their chests.

The comparsa de indios offers its performance in the plazas or in other locations within a community where people gather. They carry with them a pole to which are attached a number of colored streamers. Their dance is a form of the maypole dance. One Indian holds the pole erect. The others form a circle around the pole, men and women alternating, each holding the end of a streamer. The men and women dance in opposite directions, weaving past each other until the streamers form a *trenza* (braid) around the pole. They then reverse the process. After each performance contributions are solicited by the jefe, who recites a *relación*, a poem of four or more verses designed to win friendship and improve relations.

As a preliminary to the festivities of la conquista in Evitar, both a reina (queen) and a *princesa* of the Indians are elected. The queen, a virgin selected for her beauty, reigns in a palace erected for the occasion. The palace is a structure of bamboo poles with a slanting roof thatched with palm leaves. The princesa is a comely young girl approximately twelve years of age. She accompanies the comparsa de indios wherever it goes. At three o'clock in the afternoon of Ash Wednesday the queen is installed on her throne in the palace. The comparsa de indios and comparsa de negros return to the village at approximately the same time and make their way to the palace. While the queen is seated upon her throne, relaciones are recited to her, accompanied by appropriate courtly gestures. These are first addressed to her by members of her retinue, then, after their arrival, by members of the comparsa de indios and the capitán of the comparsa de negros.

The recital of relaciones completed, the two comparsas leave the palacio and begin to dance in the streets. The palace is now guarded by men representing soldiers who exact a fee from any man wishing to enter. Women enter free, but only those who at the time are not engaged in a union with a man may do so. Dancing takes place in the palace, as well as in the streets, to music provided by either the conjunto de cumbia or conjunto de gaitas.

A man wishing to dance must pay a fee for the privilege. If he wishes to dance with the queen, he must pay a much larger fee.

In the meantime the two comparsas dance through the streets and engage in mock battles at any location where they may meet. During one of these encounters the negros capture the *princesa de los indios*. The negros then take the captured princess to the house of one of their members. While awaiting the expected attempt of the Indians to rescue her, they drink rum and dance. The Indians search for their princess, checking house by house until they find her. At the approach of the Indians the negros flee. Now the Indians again search house by house, threatening anyone they meet with their bows and arrows. The negros continue to evade them.

Finally the two comparsas meet at a predetermined spot on Evitar's widest street, Calle Grande, and the final battle is joined. This lasts until someone fires a gun into the air. The chief of the Indians pretends that he is shot and falls to the ground in simulated death. The chief is then raised from the ground and dressed in a frock made of sackcloth. Thus trans- formed into a priest, he readily baptizes anyone who is accom- panied by the requisite *padrino* (godfather), *madrina* (godmother), or both. However, reversing the usual priestly procedure, he places money instead of salt into the mouths of those he baptizes. At eight or nine o'clock there is a dance for all in the palace of the queen, which ends the carnaval season. At this final dance men pay a fee only if they dance with the queen.

SABADO DE GLORIA

Lent officially ends on the Saturday before Easter. This day is known as Sábado de Gloria (Saturday of Glory). This is a joy- ful occasion, since it marks the end of the Lenten season and presages the resurrection of Christ. Music and dancing are per- mitted, but in the patios or yards of private dwellings, not in the streets, plazas, or other public places. In the past there was dancing of the cumbia or the bullerengue accompanied by musicians of the village. In more recent times music has been provided by the picó. According to custom, men pay an admission fee. The women present enter free, but only those not attached to specific men do so.

On Sábado de Gloria in Evitar two or three such dances may take place simultaneously, beginning after dark and lasting until dawn.

DIA DE SAN JUAN

The day assigned to St. John The Divine in the Catholic calen- dar is June 24. The summer solstice occurs on June 22, and the festivities of La Noche de San Juan (the Eve of St. John) exhibit many of the characteristics of pre-Christian solstice celebration both in Evitar and in the surrounding region. However, the forms of the festivities engaged in on this occasion are quite different in Spain and the Costa Atlántica. In Spain this is a night during which fire and water possess magical curing properties. Bonfires are lit, and when they have died down children leap over the embers

and are thus protected against illness. People who bathe in foun-
tains or springs at midnight or dawn receive similar protection.
There is also the belief in the efficacy of being seen dancing by
the sun as it rises (Foster 1960:198-99).

There is no evidence that such purificatory rites occur in
Evitar during La Noche de San Juan, but the value of dancing
until sunup is at least implicit in the celebration. In Evitar
and the region this is a night of *amores*, of processions from
house to house, and of dancing in the streets. It is a night of
fandango. Many evitaleros meet after dark and proceed through the
streets, singing the *gavilán* and dancing. The gavilán is considered a fandango, since it is danced through the streets. However, unlike the ritmo specifically known as fandango, it is not
accompanied by drums. At times the performance of the latter type
of fandango may be interspersed with that of gavilán. In this
case drummers would need to join the procession and play as their
services were required. There is apparently no specific pattern
of dance steps utilized in a fandango.

The dancers continue through the streets until they reach a
house where there lives a person named Juan or Juana. Upon
arriving they shout "Juancho" or "Juancha" to wake up this individual. A soloist then sings in improvised style what is known
as the *canto de gallo* (song of the cock), since it is both sung
in a high falsetto and intended to wake the person to whom it is
addressed. The individual who has been thus serenaded is obliged
by custom to provide refreshment for the celebrants. Rum is
considered the most appropriate refreshment, but food is also
welcomed. Having taken advantage of the hospitality offered,
the group now moves on, singing and dancing through the streets
until it reaches the house of another individual whose name is
Juan or Juana, where the previously described activities are
repeated.

By the time I first visited Evitar, in 1964, the canto de gallo
was no longer being performed during La Noche de San Juan, since
the only man in the village who was accustomed to singing it,
Israel Sánchez, was then old and ill and unable to do so. The
canto de gallo had therefore been replaced by a performance of a
fandango in front of the house of the individual so serenaded.
Sánchez was interviewed. He attempted to sing some verses he
might have used in the canto de gallo, but they were somewhat incoherent. I therefore give as an example of the copla of the
canto de gallo one sung for me by José Lara in San Jacinto. The
syllables in italics are lexically meaningless. The copla is
addressed to a woman.

A nana nanana nana nana	
Levántate, Juanita,	Get up, Juanita
i nana nana nana nanana	
que aquí te vengo a traer	Here I come bringing you
gallo.	cock.
O nana nana nana nanana	
Ahora por la mañanita	Now, in the early morning
i na vine con mi tocayo.	I come with my music making.

Tocayo is a word manufactured for the purpose of rhyme. It is a noun fashioned from the verb *tocar* (to play a musical instrument). Lara is a tambolero and would play his drum during La Noche de San Juan to accompany fandango.

DIA DE SAN PEDRO

The celebration of St. Peter's Day, June 28, seems to be an extension of the festivities set into motion by the summer solstice. There is a repetition of what occurred during the celebration of the Día de San Juan. However, those who are serenaded, and who are expected in return to provide refreshment for the dancers and musicians, are individuals named Pedro or Pedrona rather than Juan or Juana. When we questioned an evitalero concerning gavilán or the canto de gallo, he immediately linked these genres with St. John's Day and only later, after further questioning, with St. Peter's Day. This would indicate that the evitaleros consider the Día de San Pedro part of the same fiesta which begins with the Día de San Juan.

LA NAVIDAD (PASCUA)

La Navidad (Christmas) in Spain is a time for attending mass, joining family parties, and singing *villancicos* (carols). None of these activities take place on this occasion in Evitar. The celebration of La Navidad is a matter of music making and dancing in the yards and patios of private homes. There are no processions through the streets. As far as could be determined, the festivities at Christmas differ in only one respect from observances such as that of Sábado de Gloria. During the period of investigation it was still traditional during La Navidad for music for dancing to be provided by a conjunto of live musicians rather than by the picó.

OTHER MUSIC OCCASIONS

Certain aspects of the two music occasions to be discussed here are similar to those found in the celebration of the carnaval, Sábado de Gloria, and La Navidad. Only *señoritas* and *solteras* attend the dance held at the queen's palace during the carnaval and the dance or dances held on the other occasions previously listed. In this region the term *señorita* refers specifically to a woman who is a virgin, the term *soltera* to a woman who is not a virgin but at the time is not engaged in a union with a man.

BAILE DE CUOTA

The baile de cuota is a means by which a household raises needed cash. The man of the household pays the cost of providing the music and charges admission to the men who attend. He invites a number of unattached women as a means of attracting the men (for further detail, see p. 14). The music for the baile de cuota is provided by a picó rented for the occasion.

VELORIO DEL SANTO

A man who is in some difficulty may pray to San Sebastián for
needed assistance and promise the saint a velorio if his prayer
is granted. If the solicited milagro (miracle) occurs, the man
then feels obliged to offer the promised velorio. This may take
place in the schoolhouse for boys, where the image of San
Sebastián is kept, or the man may bring the statue to his choza
for the occasion. As night falls he lights candles placed adjacent to the saint's image and prepares to spend the required
sleepless night in his company. Women do not offer a velorio
for the saint, since custom dictates that they not spend a sleepless night alone. However, a man does not enjoy spending a night
without sleep alone. He therefore invites some male friends and
some unattached women to while away the hours with him. Since
they are his guests, he must provide both refreshments and music
for dancing. At a *velorio del santo*, tradition requires that
the music be provided by a cumbia, that is, a conjunto de cumbia
or a conjunto de gaitas. In recent years the music for a velorio
del santo has been provided by the former conjunto, since the
latter was no longer in existence.

At a velorio del santo the man sponsoring the observance is
responsible for all expenses; there is no admission charge for
the invited men. The rum and music provided for the guests are
expensive. The festive aspects of the velorio are not obligatory,
and they therefore are not usually continued through the entire
night. Candles are also expensive. Although it is obligatory,
they may not remain lit throughout the entire night.

The man's *mujer* (woman, de facto wife) or *señora* (Mrs., legal
wife) may offer prayers of thanksgiving to the saint, as may
some of his older female relatives. The man, on the other hand,
will remain outside the house or the schoolhouse the greater part
of the night, enjoying the company of his friends.

4. The Singers and Instrumentalists

THE INDIVIDUAL INFORMANTS

Listed in the following pages are the adult inhabitants of Evitar who sang or played musical instruments and who were recorded, observed, or interviewed during the period of investigation. I did not record the names of the children composing the groups that were recorded performing singing games. The names of the adults are listed in the form in which they are usually written, thus:
1. One or more given names.
2. Family name of the father.
3. Family name of the mother.

However, the names are listed alphabetically according to the family name of the father (which, for this reason, is in capital letters) and then according to the first given name. In some cases only one given name and the family name of the father were offered by the individual interviewed. In one case an initial was substituted for a given name. Both practices are common.

Where the age of the individual is given, the year in which this information was received follows in parentheses. Since births were not registered in the past, it can be doubted that the ages given are in all cases accurate. However, at a minimum they indicate the stage of life that the individual found himself in at the time of interview.

Unless otherwise indicated, the principal occupation of the men is agriculturist and that of the women is housewife. All were born in Evitar and have been in continuous residence in the village unless otherwise specified.

MEN

Pedro CUETO Pimientel (fig. 77)
Age 38 (1964). *Decimero* and singer of *vaquería* (cattle-herding songs). Worked occasionally as vaquero (cattle driver). Known for his improvisation of humorous and satiric sung verse.

Augusto ESPINOSA Torrecilla
Age 25 (1970). Player of guacharaca in danza de negro and llamador in bullerengue in 1970.

Abraham HERRERA Pacheco (figs. 67, 72 and 75)
Age 57 (1964). Cantante in bullerengue, fandango, and gavilán.
Leader of and singer in games of the velorio de angelito.
Lacks fingers on one hand and does not work the land. Is a
midwife, nurse, and tailor. Lives alone.

Andrés HERRERA
Tambolero in danza de negro in Evitar in 1970. In the past
played gaita macho and maraca or tambor mayor in the conjunto
de gaitas led by Felipe Jaramillo.

Simón HERRERA Sánchez (fig. 77)
Age 26 (1964). Decimero and singer of a game played at the
velorio de angelito. Player of llamador, bombo, and caja, the
latter in vallenato. Lived for a short period in Valledupar.
Fisherman. Bachelor. Lives with parents or relatives.

Felipe JARAMILLO
Age 53 (1971). Was the leader of two ensembles in the past, a
conjunto de gaitas in which he played gaita hembra and a sexteto in which he played marimba (marímbula). He also was
gaitero in the comparsa de indios. He lived as a young man
for a short period in Barranquilla.

Carlos JULIO Sánchez (fig. 77)
Age 35 (1964). Decimero and player of bombo. He left the
village between 1964 and 1968.

Angel OSPINO Santana (figs. 30 and 66)
Age 33 (1965). Player of llamador in conjunto de cumbia and
bombo in fandango.

Juan OSPINO Jiménez (figs. 16 and 66)
Age 45 (1965). Player of guachos in conjunto de cumbia.
Also plays bombo and llamador.

Santiago OSPINO Caraballo (figs. 42 and 66)
Age 58 (1965). Pitero and leader of the conjunto de cumbia.

Pedro Juan PACHECO Salas (fig. 78)
Age 63 (1964). Decimero and singer of coplas (vaquería).
Carpenter and builder of bahareques.

Agostín PALLARES Hernández
Age 46 (1970). Cantante in danza de negro in Evitar and in
Mahates in 1970.

José del Carmen PIMIENTEL Martínez (figs. 23 and 66)
Age 55 (1965). Tambolero in conjunto de cumbia.

Manuel PIMIENTEL Pacheco (figs. 34 and 66)
Age 38 (1964). Bombero in conjunto de cumbia and tambolero in
danza de negro, bullerenque, and fandango.

Mariano ROSADO Julio (fig. 77)
Age 40 (1964). Singer of zafras.

Reinaldo ROSADO Julio (fig. 77)
Age 39 (1964). Singer of zafras.

Enríquez SANCHEZ Palacio (fig. 13)
Age 40 (1970). Player of palmetas in danza de negro.

Israel SANCHEZ
Believed himself to be age 100 (1968). In the past had sung
canto de gallo on Día de San Juan and Día de San Pedro. Born
in Machado. Moved to Evitar at age of 12. Died between 1968
and 1970.

WOMEN

María Teresa FONTALVO
    I recorded Fontalvo on a day that she was visiting Evitar.
    She was a native of the village but had moved to Barranquilla
    eight months previously. Singer of a lullaby.
Juana GARCIA Blanquiset (figs. 67 and 75)
    Age 80 (1964). Cantante in bullerengue and contestadora in
    bullerengue, fandango, and gavilán. Born in Calamar. Moved
    to Evitar at approximately age 30. Died between 1970 and
    1971.
Basilisa HERRERA García (fig. 75)
    Age 47 (1964). Contestadora in bullerengue, fandango, and
    gavilán.
Marta Josefa HERRERA García
    Age 48 (1970). Contestadora in bullerengue and fandango.
Rosa Luisa MARTINEZ
    Age 24 (1964). Singer of lullabies and of a song of the
    velorio de angelito. Left the village between 1964 and 1968.
Ana María PACHECO (fig. 75)
    Age 26 (1964). Contestadora in bullerengue, fandango, and
    gavilán.
Juana PEREZ (fig. 75)
    Age 55 (1964). Contestadora in bullerengue, fandango, and
    gavilán.
Juana PIMIENTEL Martínez
    Age 55 (1970). Contestadora in bullerengue and fandango.
Marcelina SANCHEZ Pimientel (fig. 75)
    Age 48 (1964). Singer of lullabies and of songs of the
    velorio de angelito. Cantante in bullerengue and contestadora
    in bullerengue, fandango, and gavilán.

FAMILIAL TRANSMISSION OF MUSIC PRACTICE

    In a small village like Evitar it can be expected that many
families are related by kinship ties. Some of these families, as
identified by their patrilineages, exhibit a stronger tradition
of music making, and their members perhaps a greater talent for
this activity, than others. Thus the Ospino family has carried
on the tradition of playing the pito and the Jaramillo family
until recently that of playing the gaita. Members of the Ospino
family have been leaders of the conjunto de cumbia and those of
the Jaramillo family leaders of the conjunto de gaitas, since it
is traditional that the player of the melodic instrument or the
principal melodic instrument assume this role. The Herreras
have provided the principal cantante and the greater number of
contestadoras for the singing of the bullerengue, fandango, and
gavilán. The Pimientel family has produced the greater number
of drummers who have participated in the performance of all
ensembles which accompany dance. These statements are, of course,
generalizations. There are, for example, drummers in all four
families mentioned. Additionally, two of the four decimeros of
the village are not members of these families, nor was the player
of the musical bow nor the singer of canto de gallo.

In Evitar, learning to play an instrument or to sing or play a particular genre is primarily a matter of imitation. Some types of music making do require special skills: singing in a high falsetto in the canto de gallo, controlled inhalation of breath in playing the caña de millo, or keeping a steady beat for a sustained period of time in playing the llamador. Some ability to improvise is required in performing particular parts in the greater number of both instrumental and vocal genres. Those who possess the innate capacity to develop these skills, plus the motivation to do so, become the most successful performers. Usually the motivation is the example set by an older member of the family, who often also provides the opportunities for learning the skills which he possesses.

Watching and participating in the performances of conjuntos at fiestas play an important part in the learning process. Thus Santiago Ospino Caraballo accompanied his father, Rafael Ospino, when he went with the conjunto de cumbia to play at fiestas. Santiago listened and watched. He then made his own instrument and practiced at home. When asked, his father would offer a suggestion or two concerning how to properly play the instrument. When his father thought he was ready, Santiago was permitted to substitute for his father as pitero for a short period during performances by the conjunto.

Manuel Jaramillo Tijera was in the past the leader of the conjunto de gaitas in Evitar and played the gaita hembra in that ensemble. During Manuel's later years, his son Felipe Jaramillo played the gaita macho and the maraca in the conjunto. His father probably occasionally gave him an opportunity to play the part of the gaita hembra, but Felipe did not fully assume this role and the leadership of the conjunto until after his father's death. Felipe was possibly the third generation of cumbiamberos. He told us that his grandfather had been a _músico_ (musician) but did not specify what instrument he had played.

José del Carmen Pimientel learned to play the tambor mayor by watching his father, Manuel Pimientel Sánchez, perform on this instrument in the conjunto de cumbia. From time to time José would ask his father if he would allow him to play the instrument, and his father would do so. If asked a question concerning the manner in which the instrument should be played, his father would demonstrate by playing it himself. When his father died, José became the tambolero of the conjunto.

It can be assumed that José's son Manuel Pimientel Pacheco learned to play the tambor mayor in much the same manner as his father. There would thus be a tradition passed on from grandfather to father to son. Since his father was the tambolero of the conjunto, Manuel became the bombero in that ensemble, playing the tambor mayor in the danza de negro, bullerengue, and fandango. Manuel told me that he learned to play the bombo purely by observing various individuals playing the instrument.

Juan Ospino Jiménez informed me that he learned to play the bombo by observing the playing of his father, Pablo Ospino Caraballo, who played both bombo and pito. However, he learned to play the guachos and the llamador by watching friends play these instruments.

Angel Ospino Santana told me that he learned to play both the llamador and the bombo during performances of the conjunto de cumbia of which his father, Santiago Ospino Caraballo, was the pitero and leader. "I was always around when they were playing cumbia," Angel said. Since he was anxious to learn, his father would let him play the llamador or the bombo in the conjunto for short periods of time. "As soon as he saw I was tired, he would take it away and give it to someone else," Angel told me. Finally, he became the regular llamador player in the conjunto.

All the players made their own instruments, again learning this skill by watching their fathers, relatives, or friends make instruments for themselves. When playing in the conjunto de cumbia during the recording session in 1965, Angel Ospino made use of a llamador tuned with screws rather than wedges which had been made for him in San Jacinto. However, Angel informed me that in the past he himself had made and played instruments made in the traditional manner. All the players queried stated that they made instruments only for themselves, not to sell to others.

Since all the musical instruments except the carángano were played by men only, women participated in music performance primarily as vocalists.

THE LEAD SINGER: ABRAHAM HERRERA PACHECO

Of all the evitaleros who were recorded or interviewed, Abraham Herrera was probably the most interesting both as an individual and as a performer. He was a man of assertive character and considerable ability and one of the few men in Evitar to earn a living by means other than agriculture. These activities were unusually diversified. Of the several midwives in the village, he was the most skilled and was brought in on all difficult cases. He was also somewhat of a practical nurse and gave injections. He was, in addition, a tailor particularly skilled in the making of trousers. All this apparently brought him an income above the average. His rancho was located on a corner facing a small square and was raised above the ground by a thick concrete slab. He lived alone, the only man I knew in Evitar who did not live with a woman or with his family.

Abraham was the undisputed leader of the games of the velorio de angelito, of the bullerengue, the fandango, and gavilán. He was not a decimero and, since he did not work in the fields, did not sing zafras.

I believe Abraham's approach to performance to epitomize the music esthetic of this region of the Departamento de Bolívar, if not that of the costeño in general. Both the Latin and the African place a high value on improvisation. When Abraham so desired, he was capable of improvising copla texts. He had a large repertory of memorized coplas, and since he rarely repeated himself, he gave the impression that these were also improvised. I recorded him in performances of more than thirty coplas, and only once did he repeat a copla previously sung, and this during recording sessions which took place in different years. Abraham also had a large repertory of melodic patterns, which he frequently varied in performance.

Fig. 72. Abraham Herrera Pacheco

Like most of the costeño male musicians I recorded, Abraham did
not feel that he could offer a creditable performance unless
primed with rum. Unfortunately, he continued imbibing throughout
the recording session and toward the end of this period became
somewhat incoherent. When Abraham listened to the recordings at
a later date, he himself could not understand all the words he
had sung in the latter part of the session. In order to avoid
this problem, I arranged for a recording session in Mahates,
where I had greater control of the situation than in Evitar.
When the group of evitaleros arrived in Mahates for the recording
session, I refused to provide them with rum until the session had
been completed. After much grumbling, Abraham left and returned
with a small bottle of rum purchased with his own resources.
This was passed around so that the musicians could warm up to
their work with some semblance of normality. The recordings
made that day were, indeed, transcribable. However, when I compared them with the recordings I had made in Evitar when the
musicians were all pleasantly high, but not too high, I had to
agree that Abraham's recordings made in Mahates lacked a certain
verve and an effect which might be referred to as alcoholic
eclat!
From Abraham's lips I also heard some of the expressions which
reflect the costeño's rather dionysian approach to music performance. Once while Manuel Pimientel was playing cumbia on his tambor
mayor Abraham was moved to ejaculate: "¡Arriba! Pimientel!" This
expression not only registers approbation but urges on the performer to further flights of improvisation. When Abraham thought
he had good reason to be pleased with his own performance, he would
utter "¡Me entusiasmo!" A reasonable equivalent of this in American vernacular English might be "Man, am I cooking with gas!"

PART II
Methodology

Chapter 5. The Transcriptions and Translations

Chapter 6.   Concepts and Methods of Analysis

5. The Transcriptions and Translations

INTRODUCTION

Seventy-one transcriptions of songs and items of instrumental music are presented in chapters 7 through 12. Represented is every traditional genre which, to my knowledge, was found in the repertory of the inhabitants of Evitar during the period of investigation. Popular genres introduced through the picó, such as the ranchera, the charanga, or the tango, are not included. No evitalero offered to perform these genres for me, and I doubt that they had at the time entered the performance repertory. We did record some merengues sung by Simón Herrera, who was desirous of establishing a vallenato in the village. However, they were fragmentary in nature and were not accompanied by the customary instrumentation of the vallenato. They are therefore not represented among the transcriptions.

Transcription in music notation is provided for all instrumental items and for the majority of the songs. In most cases the music transcriptions represent only a portion of the recorded performance. Limits of time and space make it impracticable to offer full transcriptions of the music of all items. However, I have endeavored to present sufficient of the music of each genre and sufficient of each item in which music is transcribed to permit the reader to secure an adequate concept of the style and form exemplified. On the other hand, song texts have been transcribed in full in each case. Occasionally, related speech has also been transcribed. Translations into English have been provided for all song texts and speech transcribed.

In the succeeding pages I shall discuss the procedures followed in preparing the transcriptions and translations and offer keys to the meanings of the symbols and abbreviations employed. The reader who wishes to locate the discussion of a specific procedure or to find the meaning of a particular symbol or abbreviation is referred to the Chapter Outline, which begins on page 119.

I. TRANSCRIPTIONS OF THE MUSIC

A. GENERAL PROCEDURES

In purpose the transcriptions of the music are descriptive
rather than prescriptive, that is, they represent detailed descriptions of particular musical events rather than prescriptions
for performance. Only those aspects of music performance susceptible to reasonably accurate measurement are represented.
Thus the two aspects of music primarily transcribed are pitch and
rhythm. As utilized here, the latter term encompasses the phenomena of pulse, tempo, duration, and meter. However, in the transcriptions offered in chapters 9 and 10 of songs in prose rhythm,
the durational values written are only relative. The pitches
written in percussion parts are equally relative. Various signs
are employed to indicate indefiniteness of pitch in melodic parts.
Since amplitude cannot be easily measured, indications of dynamic
level and accents have in most cases not been utilized. In
general, the only description offered of timbre is the indication
that a part is sung by a man, a woman, or a child; that it is sung
by a soloist or a chorus; or that is is played on a particular instrument. However, certain differences of timbre produced in
drumming are notated. In some cases verbal descriptions of the
less-measurable aspects of the performance are given in the notes
appended to the transcriptions.

With one exception, where the transcription was developed by
frame-by-frame analysis of motion film (see I.G), the transcriptions offered were made by ear through repeated hearings of the
recorded performances. No electronic devices, such as a fundamental analyzer or stroboscope, were employed. I have indicated
elsewhere my reasons for believing that transcriptions of music
made primarily by the unaided human ear in notated form are sufficiently reliable to form the basis for scholarly study (List 1974).

For the purpose of transcription, copies of the original recordings were made in the laboratories of the Indiana University
Archives of Traditional Music, utilizing matched Ampex tape re-
corders. The copies were played back on a Sony tape recorder,
model TC-106A. The initial pitch of the recording or that of a
phrase or strophe final was determined by reference to a recently
tuned Steinway piano, the pitch level of which had been checked
with a Deagan A 440 tuning bar. The tempo indications were established by the use of a stop watch, not a metronome, although the
numbers of pulses or beats heard per minute were rounded off to
represent those commonly designated on a metronome. Pulses were
counted for 30 seconds or, occasionally, for only 15 seconds,
and the number of pulses per minute was then determined by multi-
plication.

The transcriptions of the melodic parts were initially made by
playing back the copied recordings at full tape speed, that is,
at the tape speed representing the velocity at which the music
was originally performed and heard. When difficulties arose in
the determination of pitch or rhythm, I moved to half or even
quarter tape speed, that is, from 7 1/2 ips to 3 3/4 or 1 7/8 ips.
However, when the recording is played back at a slower tape speed

than that at which it was originally recorded, pitch is distorted
by the change in octave, and phenomena can be distinguished
which are not apparent when playback is at full speed. After
working at a slower tape speed I therefore always played the recording again at full tape speed, checked the transcription, and
modified any notation made when it did not match what I then
heard. Thus, except in the case of percussion parts, the notation
in the transcriptions represents what I can hear when the recording is played back at the velocity at which it was originally
recorded.

In a number of cases I found it impossible to develop accurate
transcriptions of percussion parts while playing back the recording at full speed. Thus percussion parts may represent what is
heard at half tape speed, 3 3/4 ips, rather than full tape speed,
7 1/2 ips. Since pitch in the percussion parts is indefinite or
relative rather than exact, the pitch distortions produced by the
utilization of the lower tape speed do not materially affect the
transcription. When the transcription of a percussion part was
developed by listening to playback at less than full tape speed,
this fact is indicated in the notes appended to the transcription.

In the field I frequently recorded only the initial portion of
a performance of an item one or more times in order to adjust the
tape recorder, the microphone, and the arrangement of the performers in such a manner as to produce the best possible result.
I also at times, for one reason or another, recorded a particular
item more than once. Comparison of these partial and full performances of the same item provided much information, which is on
occasion incorporated into the transcription but more frequently
offered in the text or in the notes.

Unless otherwise indicated, I have adhered to the conventions
of Western music writing in preparing the transcriptions. The
modifications or elaborations of this system employed in the
transcriptions are discussed and illustrated below.

B. NOTATION OF PITCH

1. Establishment of a tonal center

For purposes of a comparison it is useful that the transcriptions be transposed in such a manner that the melodic contours
be represented by pitches written in the same lines and spaces
of a staff bearing the same clef. As a means of accomplishing
this purpose, the attempt was made to develop a tonal center for
each item transcribed, the tonal center thus developed serving
as the regulating factor in transposition. In determining the
melodic tonal center, the assumption was made that the majority
of the melodies transcribed were sufficiently influenced by
European musical traditions that methods utilized in the determination of such a tonal center in European music of the past
were applicable. The further assumption was made that when such
methods of establishing a tonal center were found not to be applicable, this fact was a means of differentiating genres one from
another. The following methods were utilized in establishing the
pitch which represents the tonal center.

1.1 The final as tonal center

Here the common procedure was followed in which the final
pitch of the melody is considered the representation of the
tonal center. In all cases where this method was applied, the
final of the last phrase, strophe, or section of the music performed was the same pitch as the final of previous phrases,
strophes, or sections. Thus when the entire performance was not
transcribed, the common final of several phrases, strophes, or
sections was selected to represent the tonal center.

1.2 Selection of tonal center by intervallic relationship

This method was employed when that of utilizing the final was
not applicable. In this method the pitch selected to represent
the tonal center is the lower pitch of the most commonly heard
melodic perfect 5th or the upper pitch of the most commonly
heard melodic perfect 4th. When both intervals are present, the
pitch selected is common to both intervals (see ex. 1).

Ex. 1. Common pitch of perfect 5ths and 4ths

Ex. 2. Tonally unambiguous and tonally ambiguous
melodic intervals

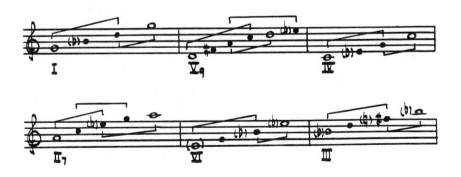

Two theoretical bases exist for the determination of a tonal center by this method. In the first the assumption is made that the melodies are related in style to European music of the so-called common practice period, roughly the eighteenth and nineteenth centuries, and that analytic techniques applicable to European music of this period can therefore be utilized in analyzing the music transcribed. In a previous study I have termed such melodic perfect 5ths and perfect 4ths *tonally unambiguous*, since they can be found in only one chord of the tonality (List 1954:60-61) (see ex. 2).

In the tonality of the G the two intervals marked in the first measure are found only in the tonic chord and are therefore "tonally unambiguous." In contrast, the 3rd found in measure 1 can also be seen in measure 5. It is therefore found in more than one chord and is thus "tonally ambiguous." The pitch *g*, found in both the perfect 5th and perfect 4th in the first measure, represents the root of the tonic chord and thus the center of the tonality as a whole.

The second theoretical basis for this method is acoustical in nature. Roots of intervals are derived from the differential or combination tones which are produced within the inner ear when two tones of an interval are sounded simultaneously (Hindemith 1945:61). By extension these roots can be associated with melodic intervals as well. In ex. 3 I give the differential tone of the first order produced by the most common perfect 5th and the most common perfect 4th found in the transcriptions. In the transcriptions these are melodic intervals. Here they are given in harmonic form.

Ex. 3.   Differential tones produced by harmonic intervals

Interval

Differential
tone

I have previously applied this method in the analysis of a performance for voice and musical bow (List 1964b:263).

2.   Transposition

All transcriptions made by the author with the exception of those offered in chapter 9 have been transposed in such a manner that the tonal center is represented by the pitch *g*. Neither method of establishing a tonal center discussed previously (1.1 or 1.2) is applicable to the items presented in chapter 9, transcriptions 19 through 23 (TR 19-23). These items are transposed an 8ve higher only in order that all melodic parts be notated in the treble clef.

When transcriptions or parts of transcriptions not made by the author are reproduced, they are transposed in the same manner unless their final pitch is already g^1. If their final is g^1, no absolute pitch is given (see 3). This applies to European melodies only, not to African or Amerindian melodies.

3. Indication of absolute pitch

The absolute pitch of the item transcribed is indicated by a stemless black note appearing at the beginning of the transcription. This note is both preceded and followed by a clef. When the black stemless note is enclosed in parentheses, it represents the absolute pitch of the final of the first phrase, strophe, or section of the item transcribed. When the note is not enclosed in parentheses, it represents the absolute pitch of the first note of the transcription. In an item performed by solo and chorus, the soloist may terminate each of his phrases on a particular pitch and the chorus terminate its sung refrain on a different pitch. In this case absolute pitch is indicated for the initial pitch heard (see TR 11 and 12, pp. 257, 261). If the pitch level changes during the performance, it is indicated in the notes appended to the transcription. Since TR 19-23 in chapter 9 do not display a clear tonality, no attempt is made to assess consistency in pitch level.

4. Accidentals

The use of double flats and double sharps has been avoided as much as possible. In TR 19-43 (chapter 9 and 10), half bars are utilized, bars extending through only the three middle lines of the staff. These bars affect the application of accidentals in

Ex. 4. Accidentals following half bars or open staves
(TR 43, v. 7-10)

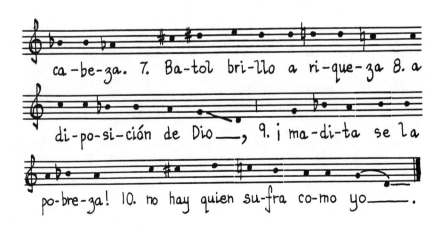

the same manner as full or regular bars; that is, an accidental
appearing before the bar no longer applies following the bar.
If no bars of any kind appear within a staff, any accidental
written applies for the entire staff. Accidentals written in
one staff do not apply in a subsequent staff. This rule applies
whether or not there is a bar line at the end of the staff in
which the accidental is found. Ex. 4 will clarify the application of accidentals when half bars or open staves are utilized.

In the first staff of the example a natural must be written
before the next-to-last note, since a sharp had previously been
written before a note in that space. Since no bar lines appear
in the staff, an accidental unless thus cancelled applies for
the entire staff. In the second staff a flat is placed before
the second note following the half bar. A flat had been placed
before a note written on the same line earlier in the staff, but
this accidental no longer applies following the half bar, and
thus the flat must be repeated. In the third staff a flat is
placed in front of the second note. A flat had been placed before a note written on this line in the previous staff (fourth
note from the end of the staff), but the accidental does not
apply in a subsequent staff, and it is thus necessary to repeat
the accidental in the third staff.

C. NOTATION OF RHYTHM

1. Indication of tempo

Where a tempo mark is given, it indicates that the performance
displays a regularly recurring pulse or beat. The pulse may be
produced directly, by clapping or accompanying percussion instruments, or it may be implied by the dynamic, agogic, and tonic
accents of a melodic part. When percussion instruments perform
alone, it may be implied by the accents and spacing of the strokes.
It is by means of this regularly recurring, directly produced or
implied pulse that tempo is measured. If the tempo changes materially during the performance, it is indicated in the notes appended to the transcription. When the tempo indication is enclosed in parentheses (as in TR 44), it indicates that the tempo
marking thus given is only approximate, since the pulse is somewhat irregular. When no regular pulse can be determined, as in
TR 19-43 (chapters 9 and 10), no tempo indication is given.

2. Metrical signatures

The metrical signatures given have two functions. Their first
function is to indicate the quantity of a particular durational
value found within a measure. Their second function is to provide in combination with the tempo marking an indication of the
pulse pattern or patterns produced or implied. Pulse patterns
are recurring groups of pulses in which one or more pulses of the
pattern receive greater emphasis than the others. The metrical
signature is applicable to a single measure, but the pulse pattern
may encompass more than one measure, as can be seen when ex. 5
and 6 are compared.

Ex. 5.   Pulse pattern encompassed within one measure
(TR 1, m. 1-2)

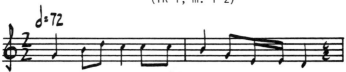

Ex. 6.   Pulse pattern encompassing two measures
(TR 8, m. 1-2)

Both melodies display the same duple pulse pattern, in which a
half note represents a pulse. In TR 1 the pulse pattern and the
metrical signature coincide; that is, the entire pulse pattern
is encompassed within one measure. In TR 8 the metrical signature does not coincide with the pulse pattern, which in this case
occupies two measures. The metrical signature utilized in TR 8
does not express the fact that the emphasis placed on the note
following the bar of the first of each group of two measures is
greater than that placed on the note following the second bar.
TR 8 is a children's song. It is conventional to employ 2/4 in
writing children's songs which are in simple duple meter. I
have followed this convention in my transcriptions of children's
songs.

Under certain circumstances durational values are indicated
before a metrical signature is given. This occurs in chapter 12
in the initial signal played on the pito at the beginning of
performances by the conjunto de cumbia. Here durational values
are derived by reference to the pulse subsequently established
when the other instruments enter and to the metrical signature
then given.

3.   Special durational signs utilized in transcribing songs in prose rhythm

The songs presented in chapters 9 and 10, work songs and
décimas, display no regularly recurring pulse and therefore may
be said to be sung in prose rhythm. Since the necessary means
by which a reasonably accurate determination of durational values
can be made is not present, the conventional methods of indicating
duration are not employed. A metrical signature is not given, and
the relative duration of pitches and pauses is indicated by special symbols (see I.E.2).

D. NOTATION OF PARTS FOR PERCUSSION INSTRUMENTS

A single line rather than a staff is utilized in writing parts
for instruments of indeterminate pitch, idiophones (including
hands struck together and poles struck against the ground) and
membranophones. Unless otherwise indicated, notes are written
on the line; that is, the line runs through the note heads. Con-
ventionally, the notation of parts for percussion instruments
represents not the duration of the sounds produced, since this is
usually indeterminate, but the points of impact and the time
lapses that occur between impact points. It is therefore possible to notate the effect produced in more than one manner. This
is show in ex. 7.

Ex. 7. Notation of percussion impact points

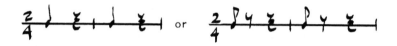

Impact, a stroke producing a sound, is indicated at the beginning
of each measure. Since the duration of the sound produced is
indefinite, the impact can be indicated by notes of different
values, in this case by a quarter note or an eighth note. The
time lapse between impacts is indicated by a combination of the
durational value of the note representing the impact and rests
of sufficient durational value to satisfy the requirement of the
metrical signature.

In performance a rapid reiteration of sound may be produced by
a roll on a drum or a shake of a rattle. In notation both are
indicated by three short, slightly oblique lines written over
whole notes or through the stems of notes of less durational
value. In the transcriptions this sign is employed only to represent the shake of the guachos (see TR 57). The rolls produced on
the tambor mayor are not very rapid, and the individual strokes
of which they are composed are therefore notated.

For the methods employed in notating other effects or changes
in timbre produced in playing the guachos, the tambor mayor, and
the bombo, see I.E.3.

E. KEY TO THE SYMBOLS UTILIZED IN THE MUSIC

1. Notation of metrical music

1.1 Tempo

♪ = 120   Number of notes of this value
                           occurring per minute.

$d(d.) = 76$

Number of either of the note values given which occur in the time space of a minute. Which durational value represents the pulse at any point is indicated by metrical signature or by triplet or duplet signs.

$(d = 152)$

The tempo indication given is only approximate, since the pulse is somewhat irregular.

1.2 Meter

$\left(\dfrac{4}{4}\right)$

The metrical signature is only generally applicable. Measures of greater or lesser durational value than indicated occur.

$\dfrac{2}{4} + \dfrac{3}{4}$

Additive meter equal to $\frac{5}{4}$.

$\dfrac{6}{8} + \dfrac{9}{8}$

Additive meter equal to $\frac{15}{8}$.

A series of vertical dashes is utilized to mark the division of the full measure indicated by the additive meter, thus:

1.3 Absolute pitch of transcription

Stemless black note indicates absolute pitch of initial pitch transcribed.

Stemless black note enclosed in parentheses indicates absolute pitch of final (see I.B.3).

1.4 Pitch signatures

Sharp placed in first space, since the majority of *f*'s nota-ted are found in this octave. However, the sharp applies to other octaves also.

1.5 Modification of pitch less than a semitone

Upward-pointing arrow indicates that note so modified is some-what sharp but not more than a quarter tone sharp.

Downward-pointing arrow indi-cates that note so modified is somewhat flat but not more than a quarter tone flat.

Due to tie, arrow continues to apply. When there is no tie, arrow applies only to note over which it is placed.

1.6 Indefinite pitch

Indication of parlando or in-definite pitch.

1.7 Glides (glissandi, portamenti)

Descending glide of definite duration. Durational value of glide indicated above it in parentheses.

Ascending glide of definite duration. Durational value of glide indicated above it in parentheses.

u - rri - a

When more than one syllable is sung to a glide, the durational value of each is given in parentheses above the glide. The small stemless notes indicate pitch of beginning and end of glide

Ascending glide of indefinite length. Durational value of glide taken from that of preceding note. Small stemless note indicates pitch at which glide ends.

1.8   Vibrato

The oscillating horizontal line indicates a pronounced vibrato.

1.9   Break in continuity

The sign placed above the staff indicates a short break in continuity, that is, a short pause.

1.10   Form

Indication of end of strophe.

Indication of end of performance.

When placed at the beginning of
transcription, this sign indicates that an initial portion
of the performance has not been
transcribed. When placed in
medial position it indicates
that a portion of the performance occurring at this point
has not been transcribed.

The performer halts abruptly at
this point without completing
the strophe and does not continue.

2. Special symbols utilized in songs in prose
    rhythm

2.1 Duration of pitch

Notes of relatively short durational value.

A pitch sustained at least
three times as long as adjacent
stemless black notes not so
modified.

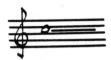

Durational value is considerably longer than that of a
black stemless note so modified.

2.2 Pauses

The half bar indicates a short
pause between phrases.

Indicates a longer pause between phrases than the half bar. Usually occurs at the end of a section.

Pause of indefinite length at end of a strophe.

2.3 Dynamic intensity

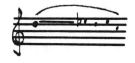

Small notes represent pitches performed with less dynamic intensity, at lower volume of tone than adjacent notes (see TR 21, v. 11).

2.4 Glides

Glide preceding note. Length of slant line indicates relative length of glide. Point where slant line begins indicates approximate pitch at which glide begins.

Glide following note. Length of slant line indicates relative length of glide. Point where slant line ends indicates approximate pitch at which glide ends.

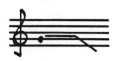

Glide following sustained pitch. Length of slant line indicates relative length of glide. Point where slant line ends indicates approximate pitch at which glide ends.

2.5 Gritos (cries)

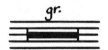

Indication of occurrence of cries or shouts (*gritos*) uttered by one or more persons. Time space occupied by cries is relatively

short in duration but may at
times occupy time space equal to
preceding sung phrase. Cries
may overlap preceding or subsequent sung phrases, that is,
occur somewhat earlier or later
than the point where the symbol
is placed.

3. Notation of parts for percussion instruments

3.1 Guachos

The notes connected by the tie
or slur represent one full cycle
of a stroke with the guachos
held in front of the body, one
in each hand. The quarter note
represents the bottom of the
stroke, the preceding eighth
note the down stroke, and the
following staccato eighth the
highest point in the upstroke.

3.2 Tambor mayor

The drum head is usually struck near the edge or near the center, a stroke near the edge producing the greatest resonance.
When the drummer is seated, a further contrast can be achieved in
the timbre or degree of resonance produced. In this position
tapado represents the timbre produced when the drum rests on the
ground or the floor and its bottom is thus closed, destapado the
timbre produced when the bottom is opened by grasping the drum between the legs and lifting it.

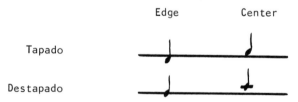

Tapado

Destapado

Other timbres produced in tapado position:

High, soft, harmonic-like tone
produced by striking the very
edge of the head with a glancing
blow of the fingers. Although
played near the edge of the drum
head, it is notated above the
line, since the tone produced

impresses the ear as being even higher in pitch than tones produced by regular strokes near the center of the drum head.

A cracking, metallic-like, penetrating sound produced by a sharp blow near the center of the head.

3.3   Bombo

Stroke on the head of the drum.

Stroke on the wood of the shell.

F.   SPECIAL TYPES OF SCORES

1.   Alternative scores

In several items presented in chapter 11, the percussion parts in the ensemble display various metrical relationships not easily recognizable in a score as it is customarily organized. Separate partial scores containing percussion parts only are therefore offered in which the score is organized in such a manner as to clarify these relationships. This is accomplished by utilizing different barring in one part than another and by assigning them different metrical signatures, as seen in ex. 8.

Ex. 8.   Alternative score (TR 45B, m. 3-5)

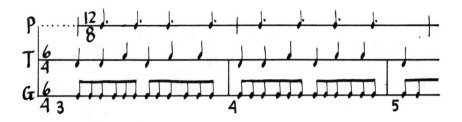

The placement of measure numbers above or below the alternative score refers to and parallels the placement of such numbers in the previously offered full score.

2. Composite scores

In the transcription of the simultaneous performance of more
than one part, one is guided by differences in pitch, rhythm, and
timbre. In the performances transcribed, more than one vocal
part is on occasion heard simultaneously. These spots present
little difficulty to the transcriber, since at least one of the
three mentioned aspects of music, and often two or all three of
them, is present as a means of differentiating one part from
another. The transcription of the simultaneous performance of
percussion parts, and four such parts are heard simultaneously in
the conjunto de cumbia (see chapter 12), presents more difficult
problems, since it may be impossible in many cases to distinguish
pitch, rhythm, and timbre with sufficient clarity to utilize any
of the three in differentiating one part from another. Although
the tones produced can to some extent be distinguished one from
another by relative pitch, pitch as an aspect of music provides
only a limited means of differentiating the parts. Nor in many
circumstances can the element of timbre be utilized as a distinguishing factor. The timbre of the guacho, a rattle or idio-
phone, can be distinguished with ease from the timbres produced
by three drums or membranophones. However, strokes upon the head
of the tambor mayor, llamador, and bombo produce tones very similar in timbre. Since the timbres are not easily distinguishable
one from another, the rhythm patterns played by the individual
instruments cannot be easily differentiated. Further difficulties in transcription are caused by the varying degrees of resonance produced by different strokes on the tambor mayor and, in
some cases, on the bombo (see I.E.3.2). Where tones have little
resonance, as those produced by strokes near the center of the
head of the tambor mayor, they are likely to be covered by more
resonant or more sharply delineated tones of the other percussion
instruments.

Transcription is facilitated when several recordings of the
same performance are made simultaneously from different vantage
points. I recorded the conjunto de cumbia of Evitar in 1965.
In 1968 I recorded a conjunto of the same type, that of Roque
Arrieta, at a radio station, Radio Bahía, in Cartagena. Three
adjacent rooms were utilized, each furnished with a microphone
connected to a different tape recorder, thus permitting three
simultaneous but separate recordings. The players of the pito,
maracas, and llamador were placed in one room, the latter the
closest to the microphone. The tambor mayor was placed in the
second room, the bombo in the third. The doors separating the
three rooms were left open, and all five instruments could therefore be heard in all three of the simultaneously made recordings.
However, in each of the three sets of tape recordings made, one
of the three drums is heard at a much higher dynamic level than
in the other two sets of recordings, since it was immediately
adjacent to the microphone leading to that particular recorder.
Utilizing these three separate sets of recordings of the same
performances (LF 173-175), it is possible in most cases to develop
an accurate score of what occurs rhythmically in the three drum
parts, but it is still impossible to determine exactly what tim-

bres are employed in playing the tambor, since the sounds of the
other drums in the background make it difficult to discern such
subtleties. (Because of their distinctive timbres, the parts for
pito or maracas are easily differentiated from those of the
drums.)

My recording of performances of the conjunto de cumbia of
Evitar took place under less favorable conditions. Only one
microphone and one tape recorder were available. Having worked
previously with other ensembles containing more than one drum, I
anticipated that I would have difficulty in transcribing the drum
parts. I therefore made additional recordings of the same item
in which only one of the three drums was recorded playing with
the pito and the guachos. I also made recordings of the same
item in which each drum was played alone or in which the tambolero
and bombero played together but occasionally one player stopped
while the other continued alone. I followed a similar policy in
recording performances of the danza de negro, bullerengue, and
fandango (see chapter 11). On occasion I found it necessary
to refer to as many as three performances of the same item in
order to reconstruct the part for tambor mayor with some accuracy.

Through transcribing the various performances recorded of the
same musical item, I was able to develop what I term a *composite
score*. When I state that the recordings are of the same musical
item, I am indicating that the performers informed me that the
performances in question were not only of the same musical genre
but that they represented a specific item within the repertory
of that genre, that is, they were given the same title. However,
in many of the genres recorded, the technique of performance is
apparently an improvisation utilizing known motifs. In such circumstances a second performance of the same musical item is not
an exact repetition of nor necessarily a reasonable facsimile of
what occurred at a previous performance. What a composite score
offers, therefore, is not a faithful reproduction of what
occurred in a particular performance but a coherent concept of
the general style plus detailed information concerning the types
of rhythmic and melodic patterns that are employed in the style.

3. Comparative scores

I use the term *comparative score* to describe an arrangement in
which two or more performances of the same musical item by the
same player or singer are compared vertically. In a composite
score a performance by the entire ensemble is at least simulated,
and I have therefore written such scores in the conventional
manner, drawing a vertical bar connecting all parts at the beginning of each score. Since a comparative score is not a score
in the full sense of this term, I have omitted this connecting
bar and indicated each performance notated of the same item by
a letter name, A, B, or C (see TR 58 and TR 68).

G. TRANSCRIPTIONS OF MOTION FILM

In only one case did I make a sufficient number of recordings
of the same item in the repertory of the conjunto de cumbia of

Evitar to permit the development of a composite score. This item
is the cumbia "No me olvides" (TR 57). The determination of the
points at which the three drums enter is the most difficult problem faced in the preparation of a composite score of a performance
by this ensemble. The entrances of the three drums cannot be
accurately related one to another when one works with recordings
of performances in which not all members of the ensemble participate. On the other hand, it is impossible when working with a
recording made through one microphone of the performance of the
full ensemble to distinguish these entrances by means of the ear
alone.

I was also desirous of checking the stylistic accuracy of the
composite score. Again, this could only be accomplished if I had
some means of developing a reasonably accurate score of several
measures, at a minimum, of the simultaneous performance of all the
instruments. As a solution to the problem in this case, I turned
to sound film. The equipment employed was a Fairchild Cinephonic
sound camera. This camera has an internal head which records the
sound magnetically on a tape strip at the edge of the film. Since
the recording head of this camera does not produce results of high
acoustic quality, I ran the line from the microphone to a Nagra
tape recorder and a second line from the output of the Nagra to
the input of the Fairchild camera. By this means a tape recording
of high acoustic quality was simultaneously obtained of the same
performance filmed, that of the cumbia "No me olvides," played by
the entire ensemble.

Utilizing a film editor, or viewer, an analysis was made of
the strokes played on the tambor mayor, the llamador, and the
bombo during 97 frames of the film, beginning just before the
first entrance of a drum. The frames were numbered and a frame-
by-frame description prepared which indicates 1) the frame in
which each of the drums is struck, 2) the hand used in striking
the drum, 3) the area or part of the drum struck, and 4) to some
extent in the playing of the tambor mayor the manner in which the
hand is held in striking.

Motion film consists of a series of still photographs separated
by intervals of darkness of the same duration. In projection the
photographic frame is usually seen for 1/48th of a second and is
then followed by a period of darkness of the same duration. On
occasion an instrument may be struck during the blank or dark
section occurring between the frames. In the cumbia "No me
olvides" both the tambor mayor and the bombo are struck during
the period of darkness occurring between frames 4 and 5. This
fact is determined by the motion of the hand or arm in the preceding and following frames. This phenomenon is indicated in
the frame-by-frame analysis by placing the word *tambor* immediately to the right of a slant line connecting the frame numbers
4 and 5.

Frame-by-frame analysis of percussion impact can be most easily
represented in graphic or tablature form, and I shall first offer
such a representation and later one in conventional musical notation. Gerhard Kubik has published impact studies of xylophone
playing in Africa in tablature form (Kubik 1965:38-48). He has
utilized a horizontal grid on which circles are placed to repre-

Frame-by-Frame Analysis

"No me olvides"

Frame	Drum	Hand	Location	Comments
1				
2	Bombo	LH	wood	
3	Tambor	LH	center	hand flat - weak
4				
/	Tambor	RH	edge	
5	Bombo	RH	head	
6	Llamador	RH		
7				
8				
9	Tambor	RH	near edge	
10				
11				
12				
13				
14				
15	Llamador	RH		
	Tambor	RH	near edge	
16				
17				
18				
19	Bombo	LH	wood	
20	Tambor	LH	edge	
21				
22				
23				
24	Bombo	LH	wood	weak
25				
*26	Bombo	RH	head	
	Tambor	RH	near center	
	Llamador	RH		
27				
28				
29				
30				
31				
32				
33	Tambor	RH	intermediate	possible cupping
34				
35				
36				
37	Bombo	LH	wood	
	Tambor	LH	near edge	
38				
39				
40	Tambor	RH	edge	fingers flat
	Llamador	RH		
41				
42				

Frame	Drum	Hand	Location	Comments
43				
44	Bombo	RH	wood	
	Tambor	LH	near edge	
45				
46				
47				
48	Tambor	RH	edge	
49				
50	Bombo	LH	wood	
51				
52	Tambor	LH	edge	
53				
54				
*55	Bombo	RH	wood?	
	Tambor	RH	center	
	Llamador	RH		
56				
57				
58				
59				
60	Tambor	LH	edge	
61				
62	Tambor	RH	edge	spread fingers
63				
64				
65	Bombo	LH	wood in front	
	Tambor	LH	edge	
66				
67				
68				
69	Tambor	RH	edge	fingers
70	Llamador	RH		
71				
72	Bombo	RH	wood	
	Tambor	LH	edge	
73				
74	Bombo	LH	wood	
75				
76	Tambor	RH	edge	
77				
78				
79	Bombo	LH	wood	
80	Tambor	LH	edge	
81				
82				
*83	Bombo	RH	head	
	Tambor	RH	center	cupping
84				
85				
86				
87	Tambor	LH	edge	

Frame	Drum	Hand	Location	Comments
88				
89				
90	Tambor	RH	edge	
91	Bombo	LH	wood	front of shell
92	Bombo?	RH	head	
93				
94	Tambor	LH	intermediate	fingers
95				
96	Llamador	RH		
	Tambor	RH	edge	fingers
97				

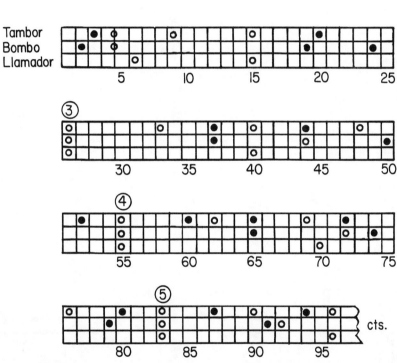

Key:

● = LH
○ = RH

Fig. 73. Graphic realization of frame-by-
frame analysis of drumming in "No me olvídes"

sent the points of impact. Each square represents one frame.
I present in fig. 73 a realization of the 97 frames analyzed
previously of "No me olvides" in tablature form adapted from
Kubik. The numbers below the graph refer to frames and coordinate with the realization in musical notation in ex. 9. Numbers
in circles above the graph refer to measures and coordinate with
TR 56 (see chapter 12). The fact that strokes on the tambor
mayor and the bombo occur during the dark period occurring between frames 4 and 5 is indicated by writing the circles representing the strokes in the vertical line separating the frames.

    Kubik's graph or tablature has a different function from that
for which it was adpated here. The grid he utilizes contains six
numbered horizontal lines, each representing a key of the xylophone. The circles are written on the lines and thus represent
not only strokes of particular hands but the production of particular pitches. Kubik offers a separate realization in musical
notation of what is presented in the tablature.

    In ex. 9 I also offer a realization in musical notation of the
97 frames of drumming previously presented. The durational values
of our Western notation system primarily involve the manipulation
of units divisible by two or three. For this reason it is impossible to represent exactly in notation some of the spatial relationships secured in frame-by-frame analysis. I therefore developed the following equivalences for duration, following a method
I had previously employed in comparing transcriptions of a single
melodic line in the form of musical notation with graphs of the
same performance made by a fundamental analyzer (List 1974:368,
372). In the latter case, equivalent note values were established for the number of millimeters of duration of a graph contour. In this case the notational value represents the frame in
which the drum is struck plus the frames intervening until the
instrument is struck again.

    Ex. 9. Realization in musical notation of frame-by-frame
                analysis of drumming in "No me olvides"

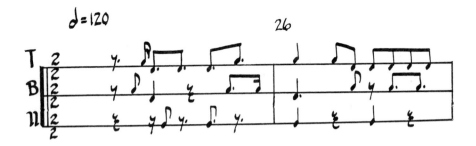

The equivalences established are as follows:

Number of frames	Notational value
1-2	sixteenth
3-4	eighth
5-6	dotted eighth
7-8	quarter
9-11	dotted quarter

The following comparison of durational values of frames and of notational values will illustrate the method employed:

Frame where stroke occurred	26	33	37	40	44	48	52	55
Durational value in frames	7	4	3	4	4	4	3	

Notational value

   A tempo indication of 120 to a half note was secured by checking the recording made by the Nagra with a stop watch. There is
thus a measure a second. Motion film is normally shot and projected at 24 frames per second. On the basis of the composite
score made by ear (see TR 57, chapter 12), I predicted that once
a pulse was established, all three drums would be struck simultaneously every 24 frames, that is, at the beginning of each
measure. Actually, as can be seen by the numbers marked with
asterisks in the frame-by-frame analysis, the simultaneous strokes
of all three drums occur in frames 26, 55, and 83. The frame
values between simultaneous strokes on all drums were thus 29 and
28 rather than 24. It is therefore obvious that the velocity of
the Fairchild camera was not the same as that of the Nagra tape
recorder. Since the Nagra recorder is a more professional
piece of equipment than the Fairchild camera, it is assumed that
the speed of the former is the more accurate. A tempo indication

of 120 pulses per minute, a half note representing one pulse, is
therefore retained.

On the basis of the composite score prepared, I had predicted
that the llamador would be struck every 12 frames. As can be
seen in the frame-by-frame analysis, it was actually struck in
frames 26, 40, 55, 70, and 83, producing frame durational values
of 14, 15, and 13. These small discrepancies in the timing of
strokes on the llamador are accommodated by the equivalences
established above for note values.

In the tablature previously presented (fig. 73), there is an
exact indication of the frame in which impact takes place plus
an indication of which hand is utilized in striking the drum.
The realization in musical notation (ex. 9) is not as exact in
its indication of the placement of impacts in time space, nor
does it indicate which hand was utilized in striking the drum.
On the other hand, a number of modes of striking the drums, and
thus the varying timbres produced, are indicated. This type of
information, that is, exactly where and how a drum is struck, is
indicated in much greater detail, and more precisely, in a
method of notating African dance drumming developed by Pantaleoni
(Serwadda and Pantaleoni 1968:47-49). Pantaleoni's notation
system is designed as a guide for performance and is therefore
purely prescriptive. It is difficult to read, and only an individual skilled in reading it can gain an impression of the
rhythm, pitches, and timbres that will be produced when it is
realized in performance. My principal goal has been to describe
a particular performance in the type of notated score which the
Western-trained musician is accustomed to reading. In doing so I
have endeavored to relate the parts one to another as accurately
as musical notation permits and simultaneously to distinguish the
principal differences in timbres heard. No descriptive score
that can be read with any ease can indicate all the subtleties of
pitch, rhythm, and timbre which are produced, but it is not
necessarily the function of a descriptive score to offer this
information.

II.   TRANSCRIPTION AND TRANSLATION OF
THE SONG TEXTS

A.   GENERAL PROCEDURES

The rural costeño speaks a particular dialect of Spanish.
Individuals native to other regions of Colombia have some difficulty in understanding the speech of the rural costeño, and I as
a foreigner experienced even greater difficulties in this regard.
In addition, the phones of speech are often considerably modified
in song. For these reasons I depended upon two individuals who
were born and raised in the region, Delia Zapata Olivella and
Winston Caballero Salguedo, to prepare initial transcriptions of
the song texts. They also assisted me in translating the texts.
In this latter task Manuel Zapata Olivella, also a native of the
region, offered further assistance. The development of adequate
translations in idiomatic English was, of course, my responsi-

bility, as was the transcription of the texts in the form in which they were associated with the song melodies.

The transcribers wrote the texts in "standard Spanish," in Spanish as it is found in dictionaries and textbooks concerned with that language, in Spanish as it is known to the educated. In my own work I used standard Spanish as a norm, and I shall follow the same course in this discussion. This is not to imply that the dialect of Spanish spoken by the semiliterate or illiterate costeño is not an equally valid means of communication. However, this dialect is not well studied and, in my experience varies somewhat in vocabulary and pronunciation from area to area within the region. The costeño dialect as such is not a written language. What I term "standard Spanish" therefore forms a known norm for use in comparison. Thus the terms *elision* and *modification* are used in a comparative sense. *Pa* in dialect or in colloquial usage is as valid and as meaningful as *para* in standard Spanish, but the first represents an elision when compared with the second. *Pueta* is as valid as *poeta*, but in comparison with the latter the former represents a modification of a vowel.

Neither Delia Zapata nor Caballero was trained as a linguist or musician. They did not attempt to transcribe exactly what they heard but to express the intent of the singer in standard Spanish. They wrote each word as it is spelled in standard Spanish no matter how the singer may have pronounced it. If the singer added phones or syllables in singing a word, these were omitted when the text was written. The transcribers, however, were asked not to modify word order or any grammatical form but to write them as they were heard.

As natives of the region, the transcribers were in most cases in a position to determine the intent of the singer, that is, the thought he wished to communicate, and thus to realize this intent in standard Spanish. In cases where intent was in doubt, we endeavored, whenever possible, to play back the recording for the singer during a subsequent visit to the village and to question him concerning his intent. When the singer was unavailable other individuals in the village were asked to express their opinions concerning the intent of the singer. When we were unable to return to the village, we questioned individuals of rural origin in Cartagena or consulted Di Filippo's dictionary of Colombian dialect and colloquial expressions (1964).

The work involved in transcribing the texts in standard Spanish and in preparing translations thereof in English was carried on at irregular intervals over a period of years. The final versions of the texts and their translations were the result of many hearings of the recordings and extended discussions. There were, of course, many disagreements, of which I was the final arbiter.

It was then my task to determine in what manner the texts should be offered when associated with the song melodies and to write them accordingly. In this all modifications, elisions, and additions had to be taken into consideration. A note must be written for every syllable sung, and none can be written for those which are not sung. Thus the song texts are presented in the following chapters in three forms: 1) in asso-

ciation with the song melodies, 2) separately realized in standard
Spanish, and 3) in translation into English.

B.   THE TEXTS ASSOCIATED WITH THE
SONG MELODIES

1.   General problems of transcription

In transcribing the song texts associated with the song melodies, I had two goals in mind. The first was to reproduce what
was heard as accurately as possible. The second was to make what
was written as immediately lexically intelligible as possible
to the reader of Spanish. The two goals to a great extent proved
to be mutually exclusive; both could not be achieved simultaneously. A discussion follows of the two basic problems involved:
the indication of elisions and the modification of phones.

A frequent form of elision is the combining of similar adjacent vowels occurring in separate syllables. Thus,

tencuentro = te encuentro

Two syllables may also be combined by the elision of one of two
dissimilar adjacent vowels:

puson = puso en

A common method of indicating this elision in Spanish song is to
write the two vowels under one note and connect them with a
ligature:

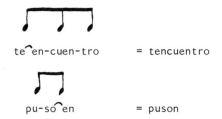

te⌢en-cuen-tro   = tencuentro

pu-so⌢en   = puson

In the first case it is obvious that one of the two similar
vowels will be elided in song. In the second case it cannot be
established which of the two vowels will be heard and which will
not. The theory is that the *o* and *e* combine to become a diphthong and will be so performed. In such circumstances in the
costeño songs I hear only one of the two vowels, not a diphthong.

There are other forms of elision, of single, medial, and final
phones, to which this method would not apply. Thus,

zúcar = azúcar

pasao = pasado

hace = hacer

Syllables containing more than one phone are also elided, as in

refina = refina*da*

We might indicate the elisions in the associated text by means of apostrophes:

pasa'o = pasa*d*o

puso'n = puso *e*n

or the elided phones might be placed in parentheses, thus,

pasa(d)o = pasa*d*o

puso (e)n = puso *e*n

However, it is questionable that this procedure would be satisfactory in representing more complex elisions, especially when it is remembered that in song texts syllables must be divided by hyphens. Let us examine, for example, the following phrase from TR 2:

de la-rrillel río = de la orilla del río

associated with the song melody.

Ex. 10.   Elisions in the associated text
(TR 2, st. VII, v.1)

The first version, utilizing apostrophes, merely informs us about the point where the elision takes place, not what is elided. The second version offers us all necessary information, but it is rather difficult to relate text and music. Nevertheless, one might opt for the second method, the use of parentheses, were it always possible to determine which phone or phones were elided. Unfortunately, it is not. There is no means, for example, of knowing which of the following is correct:

$$\text{tencuentro} = \text{t(e) encuentro}$$

$$\text{or tencuentro} = \text{te (e)ncuentro}$$

Nor can such a decision be made in the following more complex situation:

$$\text{esunto} = \text{e(s) (a)sunto}$$

$$\text{esunto} = \text{es (as)unto}$$

Thus, finding no reasonably satisfactory means of indicating elisions in the associated text, I merely write what I hear. Where the reader has difficulty in understanding what is written, he may refer to the realized text in standard Spanish which follows the music transcription.

Let us now consider the matter of the modification of phones. Such modifications may be characteristic of the dialect, they may be idiosyncratic of the speech habits of the particular singer, or they may be produced by the necessity of modifying a phone when it is produced in the higher register of the singer's voice. Many of these modifications could be reproduced by means of standard Spanish orthography. In the following examples I reproduce what I hear to the left and the equivalent in standard Spanish to the right:

$$\text{ru}y\text{ientes} = \text{ru}g\text{ientes}$$

$$\text{libe}d\text{tador} = \text{libe}r\text{tador}$$

$$\text{bu}j\text{o} = \text{bu}rr\text{o}$$

However, Spanish orthography offers no means of indicating other modifications of phones heard. Some examples follow for which equivalents are heard in English:

zh	as in	a$z$ure
a	as in	cat
i	as in	bit
ϑ	as in	$a$bout

The last is the *schwa*, commonly used in English. In English, pronunciation is dependent upon memory. In Spanish, pronunciation is regular; it can be determined by the orthography. Since Spanish orthography offers no means of representing the given four phones, they could be indicated in the associated text only by some modification of the Latin characters utilized in Spanish or by other phonetic symbols.

However, it cannot be expected that most readers of Spanish, nor of English, for that matter, will be familiar with whatever phonetic symbols are employed, and their use would therefore militate against the ready intelligibility of the text. This work is not a linguistic study as such, and the reader's ability to comprehend the associated text is already somewhat impaired by

the reproduction of the elisions made by the singers. I therefore
decided not to attempt to indicate the modification of phones
except in cases where a vowel is so modified as to become a consonant (see II.B.4).

Having discussed in some detail the principal problems faced
in reproducing the associated texts, I shall now list the specific procedures that have been followed in their transcription.

2. Orthography, accents, and syllabification

The orthography of standard Spanish is followed in both the
writing of lexically meaningful words and the writing of meaningless syllables. There is only one exception: the *ü* is employed
in initial as well as in medial position. Since *u* when it is
the initial letter of a word is never followed by a second vowel
in standard Spanish, there is no rule of orthography, nor of
pronunciation, which is applicable. To make clear that such a *u*
represents the equivalent of the English *w*, I have utilized the
diéresis in elisions (*üando = cuando*) and ejaculations (*üe*).
The letters *w* and *k* are found in Spanish dictionaries, where as
initial letters they are used almost entirely for words adopted
from other languages. For this reason I have preferred to use
the *ü* rather than the *w* as the initial letter following elisions
and in meaningless syllables.

The accents marks used in standard Spanish are written in the
associated text whether or not such verbal accents coordinate
with musical accents. It should be noted that in song in Spanish
there is not as high an expectation of such coordination as
there is in song in English.

The syllable divisions in use in standard Spanish are also
followed in the writing of lexically meaningful words, again
whether or not the result is the coordination of verbal and
musical accent. Thus in the word *cum-bia* the vowel cluster *ia*
is considered one syllable, while in *tí-a* it is considered two.
However, I write meaningless syllables or combinations of such
syllables as I hear them, employing whatever syllable division
I feel appropriate. Thus I write *u-rri-a* rather than *u-rria*,
as might be expected in standard Spanish (see TR 16).

3. Elisions and additions

No indication is given of phones or syllables elided. If
the reader experiences difficulty in understanding a passage, he
should refer to the realization of the text in standard Spanish
which follows the music transcription. The two types of texts
are coordinated through the use of parallel numbering of verses.

At times an elision may require an orthographic change in
order to render pronunciation consistent with that of standard
Spanish. Thus,

           no quentro (no kentro) = no encuentro

A *c* preceding an *e* in Spanish is pronounced differently than when preceding *ue* (in English equivalents *s* rather than *k*), and thus the orthographic change is required.

In elisions, capitalization may be changed to lower case. Thus,

$$de\text{-}vi\text{-}tar = de\ E\text{-}vi\text{-}tar$$

In some cases the initial vowel of a poetic verse is elided, and the consonant making up the remainder of the syllable is attached to the last syllable of the previous verse. Two examples (excerpted from TR 16, v.1-2 and TR 24, st. IV, v.1-2) follow:

1.	E lo-roy la lo-rai	El loro y la lora
2.	sta-ban lo-re-an-dol. =	estaban loreando.
	lo-roy la lo-rai	el loro y la lora

No hay en lo cam-po ga-la-no	No hay en los campos galanos
pal-ma que Ua-le a tu ta-llin, =	palma que iguale a tu talle,
en lo flo-ri-dos va-lle	ni en los floridos valles

In each case the elision is at the beginning of the third verse and the consonant is added at the end of the second verse. In the second example the elided vowel of the first syllable of the third verse is substituted for the last vowel of the second verse.

Although the need for an accent mark may have been obviated by an elision, it is nevertheless written. Thus,

$$tí = tí\text{-}a$$

Lexically meaningless phones or syllables added to words, as in

$$Bo\text{-}la\text{-}lí\text{-}va = Bo\text{-}lí\text{-}var$$

$$ma\text{-}no\text{-}u = ma\text{-}no$$

are transcribed, as are various non-lexically meaningful ejaculations:

$$E\ je\ je\ a\ je\ i$$

4. Modification of phones

When an individual vowel or consonant utilized in singing a lexically meaningful word is not the one employed in standard Spanish, that customarily used in standard Spanish is substituted. This rule applies whether the phone heard can be represented in standard Spanish orthography or not. On the other hand, when a vowel is so modified as to become a consonant, this modification is indicated if it can be represented in standard Spanish orthography. Thus the vowel *y* or *e* may become the consonant *y*, the vowel *o* may become the consonantal form of *u*:

$y$en = y en

re-vol-$y$ar = re-vo-le-ar

p$u$eta = p$o$eta

The latter type of modification may involve the combining of two
words or an elision:

de-ju$á$ = de-j$ó$ a

cue-lo = c$ó$-ge-lo

5. Indication of form

Strophes are identified by roman numerals, verses (lines of
the text) by arabic numerals. When strophes are so identified,
a separate sequence of verse numbers beginning with 1 is used in
each strophe. Where strophes are not identified, the numbering
sequence of the verses runs from the beginning to the end of the
transcription.

When a verse or a couplet consisting of two verses is repeated,
the verse numbers themselves are only repeated in the décimas
(see chapter 10), where such repetition is needed for formal
analysis. In all other genres when there is exact repetition of
a verse or a couplet, the verse numbers are omitted. An x following an arabic number indicates that the verse so identified
is a modified repetition of a previous verse.

The most common verse length is eight syllables, and the most
common strophic form is the quatrain. The lullabies and most of
the children's songs presented in chapter 7 have verses of a
lesser number of syllables. In order to save space in writing
the associated texts in chapter 7, I have considered the strophes
to be formed of couplets rather than quatrains and I have numbered the verses accordingly. However, I have not followed this
procedure in TR 6, since the verses of this item are octosyllabic.

C. THE TEXTS AS REALIZED IN STANDARD SPANISH

In each case the realized song text represents the entire
text sung. The associated text, on the other hand, may be incomplete, since the entire performance may not have been transcribed.

1. Elisions, additions, and modifications

In realizing the texts in standard Spanish, all material
elided in the sung texts has been restored, and syllables which
were combined have been appropriately separated. Additional lexically meaningless syllables which were embedded within or added
to lexically meaningful words have been omitted. However, separate ejaculations in the form of lexically meaningful syllables
or combinations of such syllables have been included and are
identified as such by being printed in italics. Modified phones
which were indicated in the texts associated with the song melo-

dies, that is, vowels which became consonants, are replaced by
those commonly used in the word in question in standard Spanish.

2. Word order and grammar

In the realized texts the word order heard in the sung text has
been retained. In addition, every effort was made to reflect the
grammatical construction utilized in the sung text. At times,
however, it is difficult to mirror grammatical construction, since
it is not clear whether or not an elision has taken place. For
example, *¿Quiénes son* is the grammatically correct form in standard Spanish, but *¿Quién son*, what is actually heard, seems acceptable in the dialect. In such cases parentheses have been
employed to indicate the alternative interpretations, and what
is written is *¿Quién(es) son*.

3. Indication of form

Strophes and verses are identified in the same manner as in
the texts associated with the song melodies. As indicated previously, the strophes of most of the transcriptions in chapter 7
are considered couplets in the associated text and the verses so
numbered. In the realized texts in this chapter, those in standard Spanish appearing below the music transcriptions, the strophes
have been written as quatrains rather than couplets. However, for
purposes of reference the strophes are still numbered as though
they were couplets, as in the following excerpt from TR 8 (st. 1,
v. 1-2):

> 1. Yo soy la viudita
>   del conde Laurel,
> 2. que quiero casarme,
>   no encuentro con quién.

Where strophes are identified by a roman numeral, they are
further differentiated by spatial separation. In the genres
represented in chapter 11, coplas (quatrains) are embedded in a
continuing flow of verses. The coplas are therefore identified
not by strophe numbers but merely by spatial separation, as in
the following excerpt from TR 45 (v. 1-7):

> S.   1. *E-je* la rama del tamarindo.
>
> Ch. (R) *E* la rama del tamarindo.
>
> S.   2. Tamarindo, tamarindo, tamarindo
>   paragüita. (R)
>
>   3. Yo este año voy a salir
>   4. por si acaso me muriere, (R)
>   5. para que se acuerden de mí
>   6. domingo el año que viene. (R)
>
>   7. *E-je* la rama del tamarindo. (R)

In the above, verses 3 through 6 represent a copla or quatrain embedded in the general text flow.

Repetitions of verses, couplets, and refrains are written out in the texts associated with the song melodies. In the realized text such repetitions are indicated by numerals and letters enclosed in parentheses and placed at the end of verses (see the next two examples). The capitalization at the beginning of the verse is that of the first of the repeated verses in the associated text. The punctuation at the end of the verse is that of the last of the repeated verses in the associated text. (The first example is excerpted from TR 14, v. 8, the second from TR 16, v. 3-4.)

Associated text	Realized text
8. Zúcar de la refina, zúcar de la refina, car de la refina, zúcar de la refina.	8. Azúcar de la refinada. (4)
3. Yo por la reja 4. staba mirando. Yo por la reja staba mirando.	3. Yo por la reja 4. estaba mirando. (c2)

When no punctuation appears at the end of the last repeated line of the associated text, none will appear at the end of the single verse reproduced in the realized text.

5. Antes todo preguntar, antes todo preguntar (etc.)	5. Antes todo preguntar (2) (etc.)

D. ENGLISH TRANSLATIONS OF THE TEXTS

A verse-by-verse (line-by-line) translation into English of the realized text is provided to the latter's immediate right.

1. Translation at the same level of discourse

The English does not represent a literal translation but an attempt to express the meaning of the Spanish in idiomatic English at the same level of discourse. Obviously, such an attempt will not always be fully successful. A number of levels of discourse are represented. They range from a highly literary level, in which *vagos* is translated as "languorous," to earthy levels in which *mierda* is translated as "shit."

English idioms are utilized when applicable and colloquial expressions and slang employed as needed. When exact meaning seems insufficiently reflected in the translation, further clarification may be attempted in the notes appended to the transcriptions. When the meaning of the Spanish is realized in English by an idiom, a literal translation of the Spanish may be given as well in the notes.

2. Non-translatable aspects of the texts

Certain expressive aspects of Spanish are not readily translat-
able into English. The diminutive is in common use in Spanish,
but more frequently than not it does not indicate that the object
or person to which it is applied is small. At times it may express affection or emphasis. Frequently it represents merely a
manner of speaking and has no real effect on meaning. For these
reasons the diminutive utilized in Spanish is only occasionally
reflected in the translation into English. Thus,

> lavar los pañitos   Diapers to wash

but

> Cásate, mi hijita,   Marry, my dear daughter,

The initial *que* in a Spanish phrase frequently carries no lexical
meaning but merely implies emphasis. Its use is therefore
usually not reflected in the translation.

> Que llora, gavilán,   Weep, chickenhawk,

Lexically meaningless syllables or combinations thereof in the
form of ejaculations are not usually susceptible to translation
and are not reproduced in the translation unless the same ejacu-
lation is in use in English. This rule applies also to an ejacu-
lation such as *ombe*, which is apparently derived from a lexically
meaningful word, *hombre* (man).

When no English equivalent exists for a Spanish word, the latter is used and italicized. When the names of persons living in
Evitar or in the region appear in the texts, they are not italicized.

3. Indication of form

All material found to the left of the realized text or at the end
of its constituent verses is equally applicable to the translation into English but is not repeated in the latter. The vertical spacing of the English duplicates that of the Spanish.

III. KEY TO ABBREVIATIONS AND NUMBERING SYSTEMS USED IN THE TRANSCRIPTIONS AND APPENDED NOTES

A. GENERAL

TR 1, TR 2   Identification of transcriptions.

(LF 38.3)   Identification of List Field Recordings. For
(LF 79.7)   concordance with copies on deposit in the
                  Indiana University Archives of Traditional
                  Music, see Appendix.

St. 1, st. 2-3   Strophe 1, strophes 2-3.

| V. 1, v. 2-3 | Verse 1, verses 2-3. |
| M. 1, m. 2-3 | Measure 1, measures 2-3. |

      B.   IN THE MUSIC

| 1, 2 | Identification of measures. Placed at beginning of measure. In music consisting of single staves, placed over the staff. In scores, placed above the upper staff of the score or below the lower staff of the score. |
| cts. | Placed at the end of a staff. Indicates that the performance continues past this point but has not been transcribed. |

      C.   IN THE TEXTS

     1.   Preceding strophes or verses

S.	Solo.
Ch.	Chorus.
S/Ch	Solo and chorus sing simultaneously.
(R)	Refrain.
(V)	Verse (a strophe), as differentiated from refrain.
I, II	Identification of strophes.
1., 2.	Identification of verses.
1x.	Modified repetition of the first verse.
Gr.	Gritos (cries).
(sp)	Spoken rather than sung.

     2.   Following verses or couplets

(R)	Refrain is sung after verse.
(2), (3)	The verse is sung twice, thrice.
(vr2), (vr3)	Verse and refrain are sung twice, thrice.
(c2), (c3)	The couplet, that is, the verse that this sign follows plus the preceding verse, is sung twice, thrice.

      D.   IN THE NOTES

| Perf: | Notes concerning phenomena heard in the recording or heard or observed during the actual musical event which are not indicated in the transcription. Any needed explanations of methods of transcribing music or text not offered in chapter 5 are given here. |

Text:	Notes concerning the meaning of the realized Spanish song texts and the process of translating them into English.
I -, II-III -	Reference to a specific strophe or to specific strophes.
I.1 -, 2-3 -	Reference to a specific strophe and to a specific verse or to specific verses within that strophe.
1. -, 2-3. -	In non-strophic song texts, reference to a specific verse or to specific verses.
M. 1, M. 2-3 m. 1, m. 2-3	Reference to a specific measure or to specific measures.

6. Concepts and Methods of Analysis

INTRODUCTION

In this chapter I present the methods of analysis applied in the succeeding chapters and describe the theoretical concepts which underlie them. The reader who wishes to locate the discussion of a particular concept or method should refer to the outline given earlier.

The methods employed in the analysis of music and text are often those which have been utilized by others in the past. With equal frequency, however, newly developed methods have been applied which are suggested by or have grown out of the material studied. They have been devised to provide an understanding of a particular type of sound structure or a specific characteristic thereof. Some of these methods, such as the analysis of melodic cells and melodic functions, have also as their basis many years of hearing, reading, and analyzing European and European-derived music. In some cases I have made use of methods of classification which have been widely employed but which I do not find to be fully logical. Their application was necessary, however, in order that coherent reference could be made to other published studies. Under this heading fall the classification of verse by syllable count of the realized texts and the categorization of melodies according to modal theory.

The genres presented differ in many respects, and this in itself leads to the diversity of method employed in their analysis. There are insufficient elements in common to permit a detailed statistical comparison of the various genres. Much of the discussion in the succeeding chapters is therefore concerned with the differentiation of genres, the interrelation of text and melody, and variation and stability as displayed in different performances of the same or similar items. A further purpose of the analysis is to assess the contributions made to costeño song and instrumental music by the Spanish-European, the sub-Saharan African, and the Amerindian.

Of the three parent cultures, the European has made the greatest contribution to the costeño's life in general, providing his language, his religion, and the political institutions under which he lives. It can thus be anticipated that it has made a major contribution to his song and instrumental music as well.

Two general types of European music can be distinguished: art music, which is transmitted by writing, and folk music, which is passed on by ear and memory rather than writing. Between these stands an

161

intermediate form, popular music, which shares some characteristics of each. In past centuries art and popular music were generally the product of the city and folk music of the country. Since the peasantry was conservative in nature, its music often retained some archaic features. There was always contact between rural and urban areas, however, and therefore some interpenetration of musical styles. The courts adopted and modified the dance forms of the peasantry, who in turn adopted some traits from the former. The hymnody of some Protestant sects made considerable use of folk melodies, which after their adaptation by composers and arrangers found their way back to oral tradition (Herzog 1957:1033). The plainchant of the early Catholic Church was itself partially an oral tradition until written and codified under Pope Gregory in the seventh century. Throughout the entire history of European art music, it must have existed side by side with folk music. On the basis of data gathered in more recent times, there must have been constant interaction between the two repertories, but it is impossible to determine which exerted the greatest influence upon the other at any particular time. Be that as it may, this interaction has produced sufficient correlation between these two broad types, art music and folk music, that methods of analysis applicable to one can be applied with some utility to the other. Since folk music is an oral tradition, it is not usually conceived within a theoretical framework, and in most cases the methods of analysis that can be applied are those developed for art music.

It has been ascertained that African musicians have certain structural concepts upon which they base their performance. Students of African music have discussed these in some detail and have added theoretical concepts of their own based upon the hearing and observation of music performance. These concepts are discussed in this chapter. On the other hand, there has been very little study of Indian music of northern South America. It is not known whether the Indians of this region have structural concepts upon which they base their performance, since no studies of this character have been made. Nor, to my knowledge, have scholars developed their own concepts concerning the organization of Amerindian music in this area. Most of the published data are concerned with musical instruments and ensembles and, where pertinent, have been covered in chapter 2. Thus there will be no discussion of Amerindian music as such in this chapter.

IV. ANALYSIS OF THE MUSIC

A. PITCH

1. Methods not involving the concept of tonality

1.1 Description of ambitus or range

Ambitus, or range, is described by an interval or an octave plus an interval. Thus a 10th could also be described as a 8ve plus a 3rd. In this work I use combined forms for the larger intervals. Thus a melody will be described as having a range of an 8ve plus a 4th rather than an 11th.

1.2 Designation of absolute pitch of octave registers

In general, individual pitches are represented in the running
text by italicized lower-case letters. A different means is used
to designate an absolute pitch and the octave in which it occurs:

c^2- b^2 beginning with the c in the third space of the treble
clef

c^1- b^1 beginning with middle c

c - b beginning with the c in the second space of the bass clef

C - B beginning with the c below the bass clef

All pitches occurring between the two given are designated in the
same manner.

1.3 Phrasal contours

This method provides a general characterization of contours by
indicating the relationship of pitch level of the initial and final
pitches of a phrase and the medial pitches which occur at either a
higher or lower pitch level than the former. In chapters 9 and 10
this type of contour analysis is applied to each of the numbered
verses or their repetitions. There are a small number of exceptions,
all demarcated by a short pause in the flow of the melodic line, a
pause which is represented by a half bar. These exceptions will be
discussed as needed in chapters 9 and 10.

In this analysis I employ three symbols: H, L, and M. H refers
to the highest pitch of the contour, no matter whether it is found
in the initial, medial, or final position in the melodic phrase.
Similarly, L refers to the lowest pitch found in the phrase, no
matter what its position. M, on the other hand, is a designation
which is purely relative in character. It does not refer to a
pitch exactly midway between H and L nor to an average or median of
the pitches occurring between H and L. It merely refers to a pitch
which is lower than H and higher than L. M is indicated only when
it appears in either the initial or final position in a contour or
in both. When a contour is symbolized by H-L or L-H, no M is given.
Unless the contour consists of only two pitches, there obviously will
be a pitch between the two, which could be symbolized as M, but it
does not seem necessary for purposes of contour analysis to give it.
When M is given in both initial and final positions, it represents
the same pitch unless superscripts are added. In the latter case M^2
represents the higher of the two pitches and M^1 the lower.

Since judgements made concern contours rather than exact pitch,
the beginning of an initial glide is considered an initial position
and the end of a terminal glide a final position, as is the x marking
an indefinite pitch when not followed by a glide. All these points
indicate approximate pitch. When a melodic verse is divided into
two sections by a half bar, a separate contour analysis is given for
each. The two analyses are separated by a period. The methods of
contour analysis are illustrated in ex. 1-2.

Ex. 1. Contour analysis (TR 20, st. 1, v. 1-2)

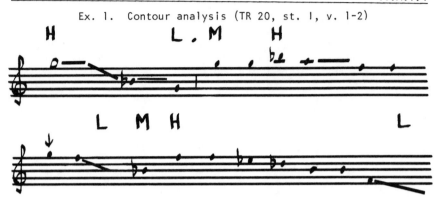

Ex. 2. Contour analysis (TR 39, v. 1)

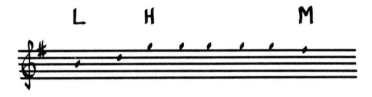

1.4 Pitch inventories, or scales

Omitting consideration of a tonal center, a scale is merely an inventory of the pitches found in a melody arranged without duplication in ascending or descending order. Such pitch inventories, or scales, are categorized by the number of their constituent pitches. Thus, pentatonic, hexatonic, and heptatonic scales contain five, six, and seven pitches, respectively. Those with fewer pitches, tetratonic, tritonic, and ditonic, containing four, three, and two pitches, respectively, occur with less frequency. Diatonic segments of scales, those composed entirely of intervals of a second, receive a different designation. Thus *gabc* and *gabdef* are respectively a tetrachord and a pentachord. This type of designation can also be applied to scales. Both *gabcde* and *gabdef♯* are hexatonic scales, since both contain six degrees. The first of the two can also be termed hexachordal, but not the second, since it contains an interval of a 3rd, *b-d*.

There are two broad types of pentatonic scales. The most common type, those which do not contain semitones, are referred to as anhemitonic. Thus *gabde* is an anhemitonic pentatonic scale and *gab♭df* is a hemitonic pentatonic scale.

1.5 Temperament, or scale intonation

Present-day keyboard instruments are tuned in a manner known as equal temperament. In this all the semitones in the octave are of the same size. In equal temperament the larger intervals are some-

what smaller in size than the so-called natural intervals. The
latter are those produced in blowing a bugle or a natural horn, one
without valves. It is impossible to arrange a diatonic scale so
that all the larger intervals found within the octave are the same
size as the natural intervals. Other methods of tuning in which
all the semitones in the octave were not of the same size were used
in Europe in the past, but the compromise of equal temperament was
finally accented.

Scales of other cultures, those of the North African and Asian
societies, divide the octave quite differently than we do. According to recent studies, the music of southern Spain, historically
influenced by the Moors, uses a scale with a range of a 6th and
microtonal intervals (Chase 1941:234). The term *microtonal* refers
to intervals smaller than the minor 2nd or semitone. Scholars
working with sub-Saharan African music have written little concerning the scales in which the music is cast. From Nketia, however,
we learn that both pentatonic and heptatonic scales are in use in
Ghana. Like European scales (see 2.2 and 2.3), these diatonic heptatonic scales contain five whole tones, a group of two and a group
of three, each separated by a semitone. The latter, however, are
slightly larger intervals than those found in European equal temperament (Nketia 1963:235-36). This obviously requires that some or all
of the whole tones be of lesser size than those of equal temperament.

1.6 Natural intervals and the overtone series

A monochord is an instrument in which a single string is
stretched over a sounding box and which is provided with a movable
bridge. When this bridge is placed exactly in the middle of the
length of string and the string is then plucked on either side of
the bridge, only the half of the string plucked will vibrate. The
pitch thus produced is an 8ve higher than that heard when the full
string is plucked. When the bridge is again moved so that the portion of the string plucked represents one-third of its length, the
pitch produced is an 8ve plus a perfect 5th above that produced
by the full string. One-fourth of the string produces a pitch two
8ves higher, one-fifth of the string two 8ves plus a major 3rd, and
one-sixth of the string two 8ves plus a perfect 5th. This can be
seen in ex. 3:

Ex. 3. Fundamental and overtones

A brass instrument such as a trombone or French horn, so constructed that the lowest pitch it can sound is G, can produce the
remainder of the illustrated pitches by overblowing. When this
occurs the tube of air will divide into two, three, four, five, or
six parts, all vibrating simultaneously. "Natural intervals" can

therefore be represented by ratios: ratio 1:2 representing the
octave, 2:3 the perfect 5th, 3:4 the perfect 4th, etc. Other
pitches can be produced by dividing the string or tube of air into
parts smaller than one-sixth, but these are beyond the scope of
this discussion.

No tone produced is a pure tone. What we hear is the fundamental
colored by much weaker overtones, which represent the possible
divisions of the string or tube of air. As seen in the preceding
illustration, one hears in addition to the fundamental (marked F
above the illustration) the five overtones plus the further higher
overtones not indicated. These weaker-sounding overtones are not
usually recognized as discrete pitches but affect the timbre or
tone color of the fundamental.

2. Methods of analysis involving the concept of tonality

2.1 Tonality in European music

European music theory developed from that of the ancient Greeks.
The latter had constructs known as harmoniai, which may be considered
scales. These were octave segments, seven diatonic tones and the
duplication of the initial pitch at the octave. The harmoniai were
primarily distinguished one from another by the intervallic relationships, that is, the location of whole tones and semitones. Thus
the Greek dorian was an octave segment descending from *e* consisting
of two similar disjunct tetrachords. The first descends from *e* to
b, the second from *a* to *e*. Each tetrachord has the interval relationship of whole tone, whole tone, semitone, and they are separated
by the whole tone *b-a*.

In classifying the chants of the Catholic Church, the early
medieval theorists adopted the octave segments of the Greeks. In
medieval theory they are termed *modes*, are written in ascending
order, and are identified by numbers or Greek names derived from but
not consistent with Greek practice. A new concept was added, that
of categorizing the mode by a particular pitch of the melody. At
first the theorists could not decide whether to use the initial or
final pitch of the melody for this purpose, but by the tenth century the pitch accepted was the finalis, or final. This decision
was basic in the establishment and development of that musical concept known as tonality, in which the mode or scale is built upon the
final tone of the melody and the other tones which occur are related to it. Although the term *tonality*, which we apply to this
concept, did not come into common use until the nineteenth century,
the concept itself was central to European music and music theory
in the subsequent ten centuries until it was opposed and negated by
the concept of atonality in the twentieth century.

The development of European written music can be divided historically into two general periods. In the first and earliest, music
was governed primarily by melodic considerations; in the second,
harmonic considerations were given equal if not greater weight.
This history began in the seventh century with the codification of
plainchant or Gregorian chant, music consisting of a single melodic
line, and then moved to a constantly evolving system in which the

association of two or more melodies, intended to be performed
simultaneously, were controlled through harmonic intervallic relationships. This finally developed into a contrasting system
involving the movement of sonorities or chords built up of 3rds over
so-called roots. The theoretical groundwork of the latter was
established by Jean-Philippe Rameau (1722). Although Rameau's
theories are based upon what he believed to be acoustical laws, they
were in fact a partial recognition of stylistic processes which had
begun in the seventeenth century. This historical period in European music, roughly covering the eighteenth and nineteenth centuries,
is termed the *common practice period* (Piston 1941:2).

2.2 Melodic functions in the common practice style

In the general musical style prevalent during the common practice
period, melodic movement is strongly influenced by the underlying
harmonies or harmonic progressions. This is particularly evident at
the beginning of a melody and at cadences. It occurs when the actual
harmonies are present or are merely implicit. The majority of folk
melodies collected in Western Europe display a similar melodic
organization and can be appropriately harmonized in the common practice style. The analysis of melodic functions is therefore an
appropriate means for determining whether or not costeño folk melodies had their stylistic sources in Western European music of the
eighteenth and nineteenth centuries.

Only two modes or scales were in use during the common practice
period, the major and the minor. These scales are transposable;
that is, any pitch in the chromatic scale can be selected as the
tonic or tonal center and a scale built above it. The term *tonic*
is the modern successor to *finalis*, and the selection of a tonic or
tonal center establishes the tonality of the melody or composition.
The bulk of the transcriptions have been transposed so that their
tonal center is *g*. I therefore give in ex. 4 the modes or scales of
G major and G minor with the numbers of the scale degrees written
above them:

Ex. 4.   Major and minor modes or scales

Brackets placed above the numbers representing the scale degrees
indicate the locations of the semitones in the scales.

The scale degrees of the major and minor modes can be considered
to represent the three primary chords of the tonality employed in
the common practice period: the tonic or I chord, the dominant or
V chord, and the subdominant or IV chord.

Scale degrees	Chords in which they occur
1	I, IV
2	$V_{(7)}$
3	I
4	IV, V_7
5	I, $V_{(7)}$
6	IV
7	$V_{(7)}$

The V or dominant appears both in the triad and as a seventh chord.
It is most frequently a seventh chord. When it occurs as the final
chord of a mid cadence, it usually takes the form of a triad. When
either form of the chord is appropriate, the subscript 7 is placed
in parentheses. The scale degrees given represent both the major
and minor modes. In the latter case it is the harmonic form of the
minor which is given. The third and sixth degrees vary according to
the mode.

The following are the functions served by these scale degrees in
the common practice period in simple melodies of one or two phrases
in the major and minor modes. If the melody has two phrases, the
initial patterns given apply to the beginning of the first phrase
only.

Initial	Mid cadence	Final cadence
1, 3, 5	2, 5, 7	2-1, $\underline{7}$-1, 5-1, $\underline{5}$-1
		2-3(-1), $\overline{4}$-3(-1), $\underline{5}$-3(-1)

Where scale degrees are found below the octave segment representing
the scale, this is indicated by underlining, as in $\underline{5}$. Inversely,
when scale degrees are found above the octave segment, this is
indicated by a line placed above the number.

The chord progression at the final cadence is always dominant
to tonic. In these circumstances the I chord always appears in root
position, with the first degree or tonic as the lowest pitch in the
chord. Since this establishes the tonality, it is not absolutely
necessary that the melody end on the first degree. It may end on
the third degree instead, as in ex. 5:

Ex. 5.   Melody closing on third degree of scale (TR 7, v. 3)

The asterisk over the 3 in the next-to-last measure indicates that this scale degree is a non-harmonic tone; that is, it is not found in the implicit underlying harmony.

Although the IV or subdominant is usually listed as one of the primary chords of the tonality, it has a much less prominent role than the tonic and dominant chords. The latter two chords alone are needed to establish the tonality, and many simple common practice melodies are based on only these two chords. The melody given in ex. 6 meets all the requirements for initial, mid, and final melodic functions as described above and represents only tonic and dominant harmonies:

Ex. 6. Melody in common practice style (TR 8, st. IV)

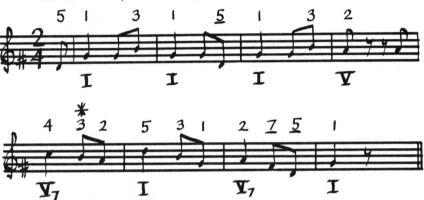

Again, the asterisk indicates a non-harmonic tone.

In common practice style, pitches specifically representing the IV or subdominant chord, 6 or 4, do not appear in initial, mid, or final positions but do occur elsewhere. The same applies to melodic patterns implying subdominant harmony, 6-8 or 8-6, 1-4 or 4-1. The cadence in ex. 7 is therefore not characteristic of common practice melodic style.

Ex. 7. Cadence not characteristic of common
practice style (TR 13, m. 1-2)

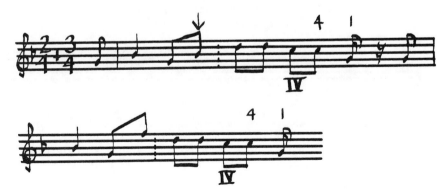

The use of accidentals not found in the key signature during the common practice period is a complex matter and will be discussed here only insofar as it is necessary for the analysis of the costeño melodies. The accidentals fall into four categories: 1) those common to the minor mode, 2) those which alter the mode, 3) those which alter the tonality, and 4) chromatic non-harmonic tones.

2.2.1 Accidentals common to the minor mode

The version of the minor mode given previously is the so-called harmonic minor, that from which the chord structures used in minor are derived. The upper tetrachord of form a, reproduced in ex. 8, was not frequently used, since it contains the interval of an augmented 2nd from e♭ to f♯. Forms containing intervals no larger than a whole tone or a major 2nd, forms b and c, were preferred. All three are framed by the fifth degree of the scale and the octave duplication of the tonic, since whether the motion was upward or downward they always moved from and/or to these framing pitches. Whether form b or c was used depended upon the implied harmony, and in either case the sixth or seventh degree or both were non-harmonic tones. The other alternative, form d, was not used, since it has modal implications. These will be discussed later.

Ex. 8. Forms of the upper tetrachord in the minor mode

The brackets again indicate the locations of the semitones.

On the other hand, when the seventh degree is employed as a lower neighbor or the sixth degree as an upper neighbor, they are taken from the harmonic minor scale. Thus, a and b in ex. 9 are acceptable in the common practice style, while c and d are not, since the latter have modal implications.

Ex. 9. Acceptable and unacceptable neighboring tones in the common practice style

As previously indicated, the sixth degree of the minor scale, e♭, represents the subdominant harmony and does not appear in initial, mid, or final positions. Nor is e♮ or f♮ used in these positions. The IV chord in the minor mode is always a minor triad and therefore cannot be represented by the e♮; the V chord is a major triad in both modes and therefore cannot be represented by the f♮. Thus both of these pitches appear only as non-harmonic tones.

2.2.2 Accidentals which alter the mode

The alteration of the third and/or sixth degrees of the scale in order to alter the modal quality is a frequent occurrence in the common practice period. The third scale degree, which controls the quality of the tonic chord, is that most frequently altered. Clear alternations between the major and minor third degree, as seen in ex. 10 from the costeño repertory, are rare in folk melodies of Western Europe.

Ex. 10. Alternation of major and minor third
degree (TR 48, m. 1-4)

2.2.3 Accidentals which alter the tonality

In this case the accidental implies a modulation, a movement to a new tonality. Melodically, this may or may not require an accidental. The most frequent modulation is to the tonality of the dominant. This is illustrated by ex. 11, taken from the costeño repertory:

Ex. 11. Modulation to the tonality of
the dominant (TR 6, m. 1-5)

The $c\sharp$ in the melody implies the dominant seventh chord (a $c\sharp$ e g) in the tonality of D. Such modulations are rare in folk music and represent a stronger influence than usual of art music. When they occur they are usually transitory; that is, after a cadence in the new tonality the melody immediately returns to that previously established.

2.2.4 Chromatic non-harmonic tones

The most common types of chromatic non-harmonic tones are the passing tone and the auxiliary or neighboring tone. Where there is

an interval of a whole tone in a scale, the chromatic tone lying
between these two scale degrees may occasionally be introduced as a
passing tone. When one tone moves to another a 2nd below or above
and immediately returns, the intermediate tone is known as an
auxiliary. When in a scale the auxiliary is a whole tone distant
from the principal tone, and an accidental is introduced to make it
a semitone distant, the result is a chromatic auxiliary. The lower
neighbor is more frequently modified than the upper.

Examples from the costeño repertory follow. In ex. 12 there is
an example of a chromatic passing tone, in ex. 13 examples of both
the chromatic passing tone and the chromatic auxiliary.

Ex. 12. Chromatic passing tone (TR 15, m. 3)

Ex. 13. Chromatic passing and auxiliary tones
(TR 24, st. II, v. 10)

2.3 Modal theory

As has been seen, many aspects of melodic movement in the common
practice period reflect or are consonant with underlying harmonies or
harmonic progressions. In contrast, the music of the previous historical period, beginning in the seventh century and continuing into
the sixteenth century, is at least supposedly based upon modal
theory. This theory is concerned with purely melodic aspects of music. Variety is achieved by the use of a number of modes or scales
differentiated by the tone upon which the melody closes, the ambitus
or range of the melody, and the arrangement of the whole tones and
semitones in the scale or mode derived from the melody.

The modes utilized in the liturgical chant of the medieval Roman
Catholic Church, in Gregorian Chant or plainchant, are eight in
number. Only four finals are recognized, d, e, f, and g. There are
two forms of the mode for each finalis: the authentic, ascending an
octave from the finalis; and the plagal or hypo form, beginning a
4th below the finalis and ascending an octave. It was later recognized that many chant melodies had an ambitus larger than an octave.
Odo of Cluny, who died in 942, extended the ambitus of the various
modes to a 9th or a 10th.

The Medieval Modes

Name	Finalis	Location of semitones in relation to finalis		Ambitus
1. Dorian	d	2-3	6-7	9th
2. Hypodorian	d	2-3	6-7	10th
3. Phrygian	e	1-2	5-6	9th
4. Hypophrygian	e	1-2	5-6	10th
5. Lydian	f	4-5	7-8	9th
6. Hypolydian	f	4-5	7-8	9th
7. Mixolydian	g	3-4	6-7	10th
8. Hypomixolydian	g	3-4	6-7	10th

Where the ambitus is a 9th, the subtonium, the tone below the octave segment, is added. Where the ambitus is a 10th, a tone is added both below and above the octave segment. The modes were known either by numbers or the Greek names.

Four additional modes were added by Glareanus in the sixteenth century: aeolian, hypoaeolian, ionian, and hypoionian, with finals on a and c (Glareanus 1547 trans. Miller 1965). The locrian and hypolocrian with finalis on b were added subsequently in order to round out the system. However, the last two modes were never in actual use, since the interval between the finalis and the pitch lying a 5th above it is not a perfect 5th. The latter in this position is found in all modes in use in Western European music throughout the nineteenth century.

The Added Modes

Name	Finalis	Location of semitones in relation to finalis	
Aeolian, hypoaeolian	a	2-3	5-6
Locrian, hypolocrian	b	1-2	4-5
Ionian, hypoionian	c	3-4	7-8

The ionian and major modes are similar in their intervallic construction, that is, in the placement of the semitones and the whole tones. They differ in that a melody in the major mode will display the melodic functions of the common practice period and one in the ionian mode will not.

Modal theory is not a fully consistent system. One finds, for example, the following ambiguities in the application of medieval modal theory:

a. There are chants with an ambitus of a 6th and others with a range of an 8ve plus a perfect 5th or larger. In the first case the mode cannot be defined, since all seven tones are not present. The second type of chant cannot be classified

as either authentic or plagal, since it encompases the ranges
of both forms of the mode (Apel 1958:148).

b.   In addition to the chants having hexatonic scales, there are
some whose scales are pentatonic. In the latter case there is
even greater difficulty in establishing the mode, since two of
the three tones usually utilized in classifying the chant modal-
ly are missing (Apel 1958:168-69).

c.   Further tonal ambiguity is produced by the use of the b^b, the
only accidental recognized in Gregorian chant. The use of the
b^b is not considered to change the mode, although it obviously
alters the relationship of the tones and semitones in the octave
segment. Some chant melodies utilize both b^b and $b^\natural$ (Apel
1958:163).

d.   The chant repertory also includes melodies which close on a, b,
or c rather than the four approved finals. This is believed to
be caused by transposition necessitated by the lack of accidentals other than the b^b. However, the melodies in question are
classified as belonging to a mode with one of the four approved
finals (Apel 1958:157).

e.   As a result of the above ambiguities, and others, in many cases
the medieval sources are in disagreement as to the mode to
which a chant melody should be assigned (Apel 1958:166).

In the sixteenth century the music performed in the Roman Catholic
Church was primarily polyphonic. Glareanus applied his system of
fourteen modes (all listed previously with the exception of locrian
and hypolocrian) to the sacred polyphonic choral music of composers
known in his day, particularly to that of Josquin Des Prez. He did
not analyze the composition as a whole, but the individual voices,
and he frequently found the various voices to be cast in different
modes (Glareanus 1547 trans. Miller 1965 II:250). The composers
whose works he analyzed made use of accidentals other than b^b.
When accidentals were present, Glareanus determined the mode through
transposition to tonality not requiring accidentals. When there
were accidentals which made this impossible, he ignored them (Miller
1965:25).

Twentieth-century scholars who have applied modal analysis to folk
music do not seem to have been aware of these ambiguities, or, if
they have been aware of them, they have not been taken into consideration. Nor have they in most cases made explicit the assumptions
underlying the modal theoretical framework they have adopted. I
discuss some of these assumptions as follows:

a.   A mode is considered to be transposable; that is, it may have
any pitch as the finalis so long as the proper relationship of
tones and semitones to the final is preserved. This obviously
is not consonant with medieval practice, but it can be said to
have some historical basis in the methods employed by Glareanus.

b.   The introduction of any accidental is considered to change the
mode, since it alters the relationship of the tones and semitones
to the final. Thus in a diatonic octave segment without accidentals beginning on a, the introduction of $f^\sharp$ would change the
mode from aeolian to dorian (transposed it would become a diatonic octave segment without accidentals beginning on d). There

is no historical justification for this practice. The presence
or absence of the *b♭* was not considered to affect the mode.
Glareanus ignored the presence of accidentals when it suited
his convenience.

c. The distinction made between the authentic and plagal forms of
the mode by both the medieval theorists and Glareanus is not
observed by most modern scholars. Thus only the name of the
authentic mode is applied, and ambitus is not considered. There
is some historical justification here, since even the medieval
theorists had recognized the fact that melodies could encompass
the authentic and plagal forms of the mode and had termed such
a phenomenon a *mixed mode*.

The modal theoretical framework just discussed has obviously been
modeled to some extent on the major and minor modes of the common
practice system. Both can be transposed without changing the mode.
Through the use of accidentals the mode can be changed without
simultaneously changing the tonality. Finally, the ambitus or range
of a major or minor melody is not a consideration in classification
during the common practice period.

Although I do not find many aspects of the described application
of modal theory to folk music historically valid, I must follow similar procedures when they are applicable in order that my conclusions
may be compared with those of other scholars and coherent reference
be made to their works. In modal analysis I shall therefore adopt
the procedures outlined in the three paragraphs designated by
letters.

2.4 Categorization of scales or modes

The application of major-minor common practice theory or of modal
theory to the costeño repertory, and to folk music in general, presents certain problems. Both sets of theoretical concepts are
applied to octave segments of diatonic scales; that is, they postulate the heptatonic mode or scale as the norm. However, the
majority of costeño melodies, and many melodies in other folksong
repertories, do not contain seven different scale degrees, but a
lesser number. They therefore cannot be fully characterized as
major, minor, aeolian, mixolydian, or other modes, since all of
these are conceived as possessing seven scale degrees. It can be
determined whether a melody displays the melodic functions of the
common practice period whether or not it has a heptatonic scale.
No similar means exists for categorizing modal melodies. The modes
do differ in ambitus and placement of the semitones, but there are,
for example, no established patterns employed in closing a melody.
The psalm tones do employ certain melodic formulae, but they do not
form part of the repertory of fully notated chants. It therefore
seems useful to use the melodic functions of the common practice
period as a norm against which to measure the melodies in the
costeño repertory.

The analysis thus proceeds in two steps. In this dual process
the melodic functions exhibited by the various items are usually
examined first, and then their scalar or modal characteristics. When
there is a melodic refrain, as TR 13r, it is always considered

individually. In these cases the verse usually consists of only
one phrase, and there is no mid cadence. When the melodic functions
differ from verse to verse or strophe to strophe, a sufficient number of alternative patterns are given to permit the placement of the
melody in a category. When a degree number is preceded by a colon,
it indicates that it occurs on a primary metrical accent; when the
indication is a period, it occurs on a secondary metrical accent
(see IV. B.1.2).

   All pitches found in the verses or strophes of each item transcribed are represented in the mode or scale offered. In the latter
the tonal center is indicated by a whole note and the remaining
scale degrees by stemless black notes.
   In the categorization the melodies are divided into three groups,
as follows:
   I. Common practice
   All items which satisfy the requirements of the common practice
system are placed here.
   II. Modal
   Melodies which do not satisfy the requirements of I are listed
under the rubric *modal*. As employed here, this term implies that in
some but not all cases, modal concepts can be applied. Items are
listed under II only when their tonal center and final are the same
pitch.
   III. Modal (Anomalous)
   Like those in II, the items listed here are non-common practice
in their melodic characteristics. However, in these items the tonal
center and the final of the entire melody or of a section thereof
are not the same pitch. They are therefore tonally "anomalous."
In the scalar or modal analysis the tonal center is given as a whole
note, the final as a black note enclosed within a square. Thus *d*
is considered the final. Since both modal and common practice theory
require that the location of the whole tones and semitones be determined in relation to the final, this pitch, although it is not the
tonal center, is indicated by the arabic number 1, and the other
scale degrees by appropriate numbers in ascending order.
   For purpose of illustration, the process of categorization which
has been described will now be applied to selected items of the
costeño repertory.

Melodic Functions

I. Common practice

Major 3rd, non-heptatonic

	Initial	Mid	Final
TR 9	5 : 1 3 . 1	2	5 . 1

Major 3rd, heptatonic

	Initial	Mid	Final
TR 2	: 1 3 5	5	2 . 1

II.   Modal

Minor 3rd, non-heptatonic, verse

	Initial	Final
TR 13	♮7 : 5	4-1
	3 : 5	
	1 : 3	

Minor 3rd, heptatonic, verse

TR 18	1 . 5	4 . 1
		5 . 4
		2 . 4

Melodic refrain only

TR 13r		: 3 . 1
TR 18r		: 3 2 . 1

III.   Modal (Anomalous)

(first scale degree represents final, not tonal center)

One-phrase melodies

TR 1	: 4 6 8	2 . 1
TR 17	: 8 6	4-1
	: 1 4	

It will be seen in I that all pitches or pitch patterns represent the tonic (I) or the dominant (V) chords. In assessing the
pitch patterns listed under II, it must be remembered that both
melodies display a minor rather than a major 3rd above the final.
The melodic functions listed must therefore be compared with those
of the common practice minor mode rather than the major. When this
is done it will be seen that a number of pitches or pitch patterns
are listed which do not represent the tonic or dominant chords in
the minor mode. The fourth scale degree is not utilized as a cadential pitch as in the final of TR 18, since it represents the IV
chord or the 7th of the dominant seventh chord. The cadence pattern
4-1, as seen in the final of both TR 13 and TR 18, represents the
IV chord and therefore is not used. Pitch patterns in which there
are intervals larger than a 2nd in which one pitch is a lowered
seventh, the seventh degree a whole tone rather than a semitone
below the tonic, cannot represent the V chord in the minor mode.
The initial pitches of TR 18 form such a pattern. With g as the
tonal center the seventh degree would be $f\natural$. In G minor when the
seventh degree represents dominant harmony, it is always $f\sharp$, not
$f\natural$.

Turning to the refrains, the cadence formula 3-1 does not provide
a pitch to represent the penultimate dominant (V_7) chord of the
expected closing formula of a common practice melody, V_7 - 1. The
cadence pattern of TR 18r, 3 2 . 1, does represent this harmonic
sequence. However, if we consider TR 18 as a full melody, combining
the verse and refrain, not all the pitch patterns are consonant with

common practice. Nor are all those seen in TR 13, whether verse and refrain are considered separately or combined to form one melody. Both TR 13 and TR 18 therefore must be listed as modal.

In III the initial patterns of both TR 1 and TR 17 represent the IV chord rather than the I or V chords. The final pattern of TR 1 represents the common practice cadential chordal progression V_7 - I, that of TR 17 does not. Thus in neither melody are all pitch patterns consonant with common practice. If we accept the tonal center as the first degree rather than the final, the pitch patterns of TR 1 and TR 17 would then read as follows:

	Initial	Final
TR 1	: 1 3 5	6 . 5
TR 17	5 : 5 3	1-5
	5 : 1	

The initial patterns now represent the tonic chord, but now both melodies close on the fifth degree of the scale. Thus the structuring of neither melody is consonant with common practice, whether the final or the tonal center is selected as the first degree of the scale. Both can be listed in only the anomalous third category.

Scales or Modes

I.   Common Practice

Major 3rd, non-heptatonic

TR 9

Major 3rd, heptatonic

TR 2

II.   Modal

Minor 3rd, non-heptatonic, verse

TR 13

Minor 3rd, heptatonic, verse

TR 18

Melodic refrain only

TR 13r

TR 18r

III.   Modal (Anomalous)

Major 3rd, no melodic refrain

TR 1

TR 17

In the preceding scales, TR 2 is in the major mode and TR 18 in the aeolian mode. TR 9 is hexatonic. If the space between d and $f\sharp$ were filled with an e, the melody would then be in the major mode. It would not be appropriate to fill this space with an $e\flat$, since there is no European mode which displays both a minor 6th and a major 3rd above the final.

I stated previously that many of the melodies placed in II and III had modal implications. By this I meant that if one added tones to scales which were not heptatonic, the resulting octave segments would represent the earlier church modes rather than the major or minor modes. Like TR 9, TR 1 is hexatonic. If the space between the e and the g is filled in, two different modes can be produced. If an f were introduced, the scale would be dorian; if an $f\sharp$ were introduced, it would be mixolydian. TR 13 is pentatonic. The introduction of various pitches would produce three different modes. When $a\flat$ and $e\flat$ are inserted, the phrygian mode is produced; when $a\natural$ and $e\flat$ are added, the aeolian mode is produced. Finally, the addition of $a\natural$ and $e\natural$ results in the dorian mode.

TR 17 displays a tetratonic scale. In this case so many additional degrees would have to be added that the modal implications of the scale are quite diffuse. It should be noted, however, that by introducing e, $f\sharp$, and $c\sharp$, a heptatonic mode would be produced with semitones between 3 and 4 and 7 and 8. Both the major and the ionian modes have this structure. TR 17 must be ionian rather than major, since its melodic organization does not conform with that of a common practice melody.

B. RHYTHM

As employed here, the term *rhythm* refers to all phenomena relating to duration and accent.

1. European rhythmic concepts

1.1 Pulse and free rhythm

Pulse is a regularly recurring accent which underlies most European music. The term *beat*, taken from the beating of time by a conductor in an ensemble, is more frequently employed than *pulse*. The term *pulse* is used here instead of *beat* because the former in itself implies regular recurrence, and no agency outside of the individual performer is assumed. When no underlying pulse is present, the music can be said to be in "free rhythm." A cadenza is an example of a type of music performed in free rhythm. If the music in free rhythm is sung to a text, it can be said to be in "prose rhythm." The recitative of opera is a form of prose rhythm. In his studies of folk music of Eastern Europe, Béla Bartók applied the terms *tempo giusto* to music which displays pulse and *parlando rubato* to music which does not.

1.2 Pulse patterns and meter

Most Western European music is metrical in character; that is, it is organized in patterns or groups of pulses in which some pulses receive greater stress than others (see chapter 5, I.C.2). Three types of pulses can be distinguished, according to their degree of accentuation: primary (P), secondary (S), and weak (W). The two basic pulse patterns are formed of primary and secondary pulses only: duple, P S, and triple, P S S. The two principal pulses, P and S, can in turn be divided into two or three parts. When the division is into two parts it is termed *binary*; when it is into three parts it is termed *ternary*. The terms *simple* and *compound* are used in the same sense.

	Simple	Compound
Duple:	P W S W	P W W S W W
Triple:	P W S W S W	P W W S W W S W W

When performing at a rapid tempo, not all performers of Western European music feel the weak pulses. They have a repertory of rhythmic patterns which will fill the time space occupied by a duple or triple pulse pattern or by the binary or ternary divisions of a principal pulse. They thus need to feel only the principal pulses, and to reproduce a known rhythmic pattern as appropriate.

The metrical signature 2/4 is usually considered a simple duple meter. It contains two principal pulses, primary and secondary, and the division is binary. The metrical signature 6/8 is usually considered compound duple meter. Like 2/4 it contains two principal pulses, but the division is ternary. However, the combinations of pulse patterns just presented do not necessarily coordinate with metrical signatures, nor are they necessarily encompassed within one measure. Tempo and tradition are also operative here (see chapter 5, I.C.2).

1.3 Accent, rhythmic patterns, and the establishment of pulse

Pulse is a regularly recurrent underlying phenomenon. Pulse patterns are produced by the degree of accentuation of their constituent pulses. They may at times be merely felt rather than realized in sound. Rhythmic patterns, on the other hand, are sound structures which contrast in duration as well as in accentuation. The durational aspect of the rhythmic patterns includes sound reproduced in transcription by notes, and silence reproduced in transcription by rests. Rhythmic patterns display two types of accentuation. The first is dynamic, the reinforcement of tone producing greater intensity or amplitude. The second type of accentuation is agogic. An agogic accent is produced when the sound in question is longer in duration than adjacent sounds.

A pulse pattern may be established by the rhythmic patterns of a single voice or part, or by two or more voices or parts being performed simultaneously. It may also be established by an accompaniment figure, whether this figure appears initially alone or simultaneously with one or more of the other parts. A pulse pattern is a psychological as well as an aural phenomenon. Once established it may exist to some extent independently of the rhythmic patterns heard, and it may continue to be felt for some time before it is necessary to reestablish it by rhythmic patterns which delineate it.

1.4 Syncopation

In the common practice period, the accents of rhythmic patterns usually coincide with those of the underlying pulses and pulse patterns. At times, however, the rhythmic pattern or parts thereof contrast with the pulse pattern or are in conflict with it. The effect produced is known as syncopation. Syncopation occurs when an agogic accent found in a rhythmic pattern does not coordinate with an underlying principal pulse. In the two illustrations of syncopation given in ex. 14, its occurrence is marked with an S placed over the staff. The pulses are indicated by letters placed below the staff.

Ex. 14. Syncopation

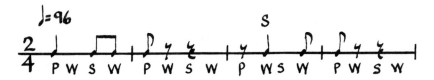

1.5 The hemiola

The hemiola is a contrast in temporal relationship in which the ratio is 2 to 3 or 3 to 2. The contrast can be horizontal or ver- tical; that is, it may occur in time space in the same voice or part or it may be displayed by two voices or parts being performed simul- taneously. Ex. 15-16 are horizontal hemiolas, ex. 17 a vertical hemiola. In ex. 15 only the principal pulses are involved; in ex. 16-17 weak pulses are also involved.

Ex. 15.   Horizontal hemiola

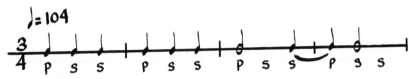

Ex. 16.   Horizontal hemiola

Ex. 17.   Vertical hemiola

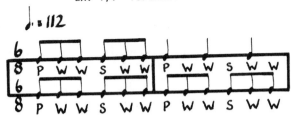

1.6 Validation of syncopations and hemiolas

Syncopations and hemiolas do not conform to the underlying pulse patterns of the music. In common practice style they therefore do not occur as individual incidents but are validated by repetition. This repetition may occur immediately, within the same phrase, or it may be duplicated in the same position in a second phrase

occurring immediately following the first. Ex. 18 illustrates the
validation of syncopation by repetition. The validation of hemiola
by repetition is seen in ex. 16.

Ex. 18. Validation of syncopation by repetition

1.7 Phrasal and strophic structures

The rhythmic patterns of the shortest and simplest phrases of
the common practice style imply a sequence of two pulse patterns.
The underlying structure is therefore either P S P S or P S S P S S.
The division of the pulse can be either binary or ternary, but the
latter division is rare in the triple pulse pattern.

The shortest strophe is composed of two of these short phrases,
thus containing four primary pulses. Adding the secondary pulses,
such a strophe would contain eight pulses if the patterns were
duple and twelve pulses if they were triple. Longer phrases are
often built up of two of the shorter phrases and are therefore of
the same length as the shortest strophe. The longer strophes are
composed of two or four of the longer phrases. No matter what the
length of the strophe, each phrase is in most cases of the same
length.

This structure applies to simple song forms. A greater variety
is seen in the more complex forms, but even in these, phrases
containing two or four primary pulses are common.

1.8 Divisive and additive rhythm

The music of the common practice period and most Western European folk melodies are cast in divisive rhythm. In divisive rhythm
the rhythmic patterns imply duple or triple pulse patterns and the
durational value of each pulse may be divided by two or three or multiples thereof. In additive rhythm the rhythmic patterns do not
provide equally spaced stresses and therefore there is no regularly
recurring pulse pattern as previously described. Instead the patterns utilized are composed of spatial units in ratio 2:3 arranged
in various combinations.

In a of ex. 19 the rhythmic pattern to the left occupies two
equal units of time space, one unit being divided into two parts and
the other unit into three parts. The pattern to the right has the
same number of eighth notes, but the two time units differ in duration in the ratio 2:3. In b both patterns occupy the same time
space and both have the durational value of eight eighth notes.
The pattern to the left, however, implies two pulses which are equal
in duration, and each of these units is divisible by two or its
multiple four. The pattern to the right, on the other hand, consists of a unit equal to two eighth notes followed by two units,

each equal to three eighth notes. It is therefore impossible to
divide the pattern into either two or three equal parts.

Ex. 19. Divisive and additive rhythm

Divisive   Additive

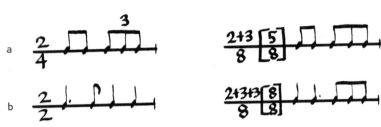

Additive rhythm is common in the folk music of Eastern Europe,
particularly in Bulgaria, Rumania, and Yugoslavia. The two durational units of which additive rhythm is composed are combined in
various permutations to form highly complex meters, as the following
from the Bulgarian repertory:

$$\frac{3 + 2 + 2 + 3}{8} = \frac{10}{8}$$

In Bulgaria such rhythmic patterns are performed at extremely rapid
tempi. Bulgarian scholars feel that at such tempi the groups of
two or three are felt as individual units and their constituent parts
are not discriminated. Thus each group of two or three becomes a
metrical unit (Kremenliev 1952:21).
     In Eastern Europe rhythmic patterns such as the 10/8 last given
may form an entire phrase. In this case each phrase of the strophe
is usually of the same length and of the same metrical organization.
In Eastern Europe, however, strophes are not always composed of an
even number of phrases. Strophes containing only three phrases, for
example, are common.
     A few examples of additive rhythm can also be found in the music
of Spain, where this phenomenon takes a somewhat different form from
its counterpart in Eastern Europe. It occurs most frequently in
instrumental genres in which a flute, bagpipe, or *dulciana* (a type
of oboe) is accompanied by a tambourine or tamboril (a small, two-
headed drum). The melodic part is built up of irregular patternings
of groups of two and three and/or multiples thereof which contrast
with the constantly repeated rhythmic pattern of the percussion
part. This genre is known as the *alborada* in Galicia and the *albai*
in Valencia (Grove's 1980:s.v. "Alborada").
     Livermore offers a transcription of a similar genre, a *pasa-calle*
played in Extremadura preceding and following a mass. The drum
repeats a figure three eighth notes in value--dotted eighth, sixteenth, and eighth--and strongly accents the beginning of each
pattern. The melody is grouped in measures of 6/8 interspersed with
occasional measures of 9/8 (1972:174). In the same region drummers
escorting a wedding party to church perform pasa-calles built up of

rhythmic patterns employing combinations of 4, 3, and 2 drum beats, the first beat of each group being highly accented. Examples of this rhythmic patterning follow:

$$4 + 3 = 7$$
$$4 + 3 + 3 = 10$$
$$4 + 2 + 3 + 2 + 3 = 14$$

Differing irregular sequences of such patterns designate the bride and the groom as they join the party. The use of such additive rhythms is believed to represent Moorish influence, since they are similar to patternings developed by Moorish musicians such as Al-Fārābī (d. 950) (Livermore 1972:173, 29).

2. African rhythmic concepts

2.1 The cycle principle

The controlling factor in most sub-Saharan African music is an underlying, reiterated cycle of pulses. This is the principle upon which both instrumental and vocal music are based. This principle has been defined by different scholars in different manners. Waterman, for example, writes of the African "metronome sense," of the theoretical framework of beats equidistant in time which form the basis of the African's performance. These beats may be represented in sound or they may merely be felt (1973:86-88). This framework of underlying pulses, anticipated and felt by both performer and auditor, is organized in cycles of eight, twelve, sixteen, or, less commonly, four pulses. Note that the number of pulses in a cycle is either four or a multiple thereof.

This cycle of felt pulses is termed by Nketia the *time-span* (1974:126). These underlying pulses or beats are almost always indicated as eighth notes. A. M. Jones, for example, in emphasizing the equal spacing of pulses in the time-span, states that a quaver always equals a quaver (1959:49). The quaver is of course the British equivalent of the eighth note. In the performance of percussion ensembles these eighth notes represent pulses which follow each other with considerable rapidity.

2.2 The realization of the cycle

In performance the cycle or time-span is of course realized in sound either in part or in full. Nketia refers to the realization of the time-span as the *time-line* (1974:131-33). The terms *time-span* and *time-line* seem to me somewhat abstruse. I shall instead employ the term *cycle* to represent the former and *realization of the cycle* or *realized cycle* to represent the latter.

With several percussion instruments--I include handclapping in this category--performing simultaneously, each may realize the cycle in a different manner. What is played by each instrument may be relatively simple, but in combination they produce a rather complex realization of the cycle. Even under these circumstances not all the pulses of the cycle are necessarily sounded or realized.

2.3 Conjunct and disjunct realizations of the cycle

Often several instruments will perform the same rhythmic patterns, which will fill the entire time space of the cycle, but they will stagger their entrances. One will enter on the first pulse, a second may enter on the third pulse, and another on the sixth pulse; or the entrances may be staggered and each instrument perform a different rhythmic pattern or patterns in realizing the cycle (Jones 1958:75 and Nketia 1974:135). A disjunct realization of the cycle is thus produced rather than a conjunct realization, which results when all instruments begin the cycle simultaneously.

2.4 Divisive and additive realizations of the cycle

Nketia applies the terms *regular* to a realization of the cycle which is divided into equal parts and *irregular* to those realizations which are not so divided. Nketia and A. M. Jones also refer to such realizations as *divisive* and *additive*. Thus a regular realization of the cycle is in divisive rhythm and an irregular realization is in additive rhythm. The most common realization of the cycle in percussion ensembles in West Africa is in additive rhythm occupying twelve pulses.

2.5 The improvisatory role

The instruments realizing the cycle repeat the same rhythmic pattern over and over again. Some variation may occur, but this remains within the bounds of the cycle. In addition to the role played by these instruments, there is one instrument (or possibly two) which does not merely repeat such a realization but provides a freer, improvised flow of rhythmic patterns. This improvisatory role can also be played by a cantor, or vocal soloist. The instrumental or vocal soloist must keep the cycle in mind and not stray from its confines for too long a period. However, he is free to shift his phrases forward and backward and to utilize both divisive and additive rhythmic patterns which will contrast with those already produced in the realization of the cycle. Thus, in fact, there are only one or two performers who have some degree of freedom in their performance. The others are constantly repeating established patterns with very little variation.

2.6 Off-beat phrasing

In the African cycle the pulses are not patterned; that is, there are no pulses which regularly receive greater weight than the rest of the pulses. Under these circumstances the term *syncopation* is not fully applicable. By advancing and delaying the beginning of his phrase, the soloist produces accents which do not coordinate with the pulse. The rhythmic patterns produced by the instruments realizing the cycle may also include accents which do not coincide with a pulse. There must, of course, be sufficient coordination of the rhythmic patterns and the pulses of the cycle so that the latter can be determined by the auditor, but there need be only a few points of coincidence to produce this result. This trait, the non-coordination of the accents of rhythmic patterns and underlying pulse, is so pervasive in African music that Waterman terms it *off-beat phrasing* (1973:88-89).

In the realization of the cycle, most of the instruments are necessarily constantly repeating the same rhythmic patterns. There is, however, no specific control of repetition in the rhythmic patterns performed by the instrumental or vocal soloist. The European principle of validation of syncopation by repetition is therefore not applicable.

2.7 Polymeter and hemiola

The rhythmic patterns employed by those instruments which constantly realize the cycle may so contrast in their internal organization that a polymetric effect is produced. This is illustrated in the conjunct realizations seen in ex. 20:

Ex. 20.   Polymeter and hemiola

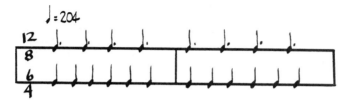

From the European point of view, the lower part can be considered a compound duple meter, the upper part a compound quadruple meter. Analyzing the upper part from the point of view of the pulse patterns common to European music, the upper part would form a simple duple meter in which there are two dotted quarter notes to a pulse. In this case the division of the half measure of the upper part is binary and that of the lower is ternary, and thus this divisive cycle produces a vertical hemiola.

The pulse of African music, like that of European music, is subject to binary or ternary division. The onset of off-beat phrasing may occur halfway between two pulses as a result of binary division, or this may occur at either of the two points in time space found between two pulses when the division is ternary. Any pulse, at any time, can be subject to binary or ternary division, particularly in the improvisatory part. The hemiolas which occur in this part are usually individual occurrences, and no attempt is made to validate them by controlled repetition.

2.8 Grading

A further principle involved in the combining of percussion parts in African music is known as grading. The rhythms combined must be graded in complexity according to the role played by this particular part in the ensemble (Nketia 1974:133). In some performances the cycle is realized by regular, equally spaced drum strokes or handclaps. These parts, which stress equidistant points in the pulse framework but do not necessarily reproduce all pulses, are of the

lowest grade in complexity. Instruments or handclaps which realize
the cycle with more complex rhythmic patterns are of a higher grade.
All must contrast with each other and can be further graded by the
degree of complexity of the patterns they display. Of the highest
grade is the free and improvisatory part of the instrumental or
vocal soloist or soloists. This part (or parts) has two prerogatives
not shared by the others. It is not necessary that it realize the
cycle by constant repetitions of the same patterns, and it is also
free to stray from the confines of the cycle.

It should not be assumed from the foregoing that those parts
which are not of the highest grade continue to realize the cycle
with the same patterns throughout the entire performance. In most
cases there are rather, at a cue from the soloist, changes to a
different set of realizations of the cycle, which, from the point of
view of European music, may or may not produce polymetric contrasts.

C. FORMAL STRUCTURES COMBINING PITCH AND RHYTHM

1. Melodic phrases

The characteristic musical phrase of the common practice style is
based on the pulse pattern P S P S. With some frequency the fourth
of these pulses is merely implicit, being represented by the sustaining of a pitch from the previous pulse or by a rest. These
concepts are illustrated in ex. 21-22:

Ex. 21. Handel: Messiah, no. 9

Ex. 22.   Beethoven: Serenade in D, op. 25,
Theme and Variations

The excerpt from Handel has been transposed for purposes of analysis.
The duration of a pulse, that time space beginning with the occurrence of a primary or secondary pulse and lasting until the following secondary or primary pulse occurs, is not necessarily determined

by the written or printed bar lines. The Viennese waltz, for
example, displays a primary pulse at the beginning of the first
measure and a secondary pulse following the bar line at the beginning of the second measure. Rather, the bar lines, the metrical
signature, and the tempo at which the music should be or was performed must all be considered. In general, the pulse, the sequences
of primary and secondary pulses, are considered to occur at a rate
of from 50 to 80 per minute. When no metronomic marking is given--
the metronome was not invented until early in the nineteenth cen-
tury--I must follow known practice or use my own judgment.

2.   Harmonic rhythm

The term *harmonic rhythm* is applied to the patterning of harmonic change, whether present or merely implied. In common practice
style, changes of harmony most frequently coincide with the primary
and secondary pulses. This fact does not indicate that such a
change of harmony must take place in each such pulse. When harmonic
change coincides with a weak pulse, such a change will also occur on
the preceding primary or secondary pulse. The application of these
principles can be seen in ex. 21-22, previously given in IV.C.1.

3.   The melodic cell

As a means of comparing the melodies of the lullabies and
children's game songs presented in chapter 7, as well as in establishing analogues in the European repertory, I employ an analytic
device which I term the *melodic cell*. A melodic cell represents
but is not identical to a half melodic phrase. It is a melodic contour offering the discrete pitches found in a half melodic phrase
beginning with that pitch coinciding with the primary pulse and
ending with that coinciding with the secondary pulse. All half
melodic phrases represented by the melodic cell display the same
sequence of pitches within this area. The half melodic phrase may
extend to the left of the primary pulse, to the right of the secondary pulse, or in both directions. The pitches found in these areas
are not considered part of the melodic cell, and the melodic half
phrases represented by the melodic cell can therefore differ from
one another in these areas. In ex. 23 two half melodic phrases
(the upper excerpted from TR 1, st. I, m.4, the lower from TR I,
st. VI, m. 8) are therefore represented by the same melodic cell:

Ex. 23.   Half phrases and resulting melodic cell (TR 1)

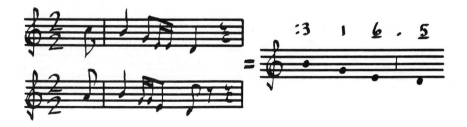

In the melodic cells, pitches are represented by stemless black
notes, and the duration of these pitches is therefore not indicated.
The first pitch of each melodic cell coincides with a primary pulse
and the last pitch with a secondary pulse. The latter is preceded
by a half bar. The numbers represent the degrees of the scale, the
punctuation the primary and secondary accents (see IV.A.2.2).

The repetition of pitches within the half bar is omitted, one
stemless black note representing a particular pitch plus any following repetitions thereof. Thus in ex. 24 the repeated d given is
that occurring on the secondary pulse:

Ex. 24.   Repetition in the melodic cell (TR 10, st. I, m. 1-2)

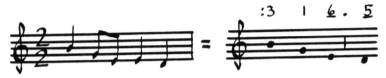

However, if a repeated tone occurring on the secondary pulse
represents an untied suspension (prepared appoggiatura), the pitch
to which it resolves is substituted for it. This can be seen in
ex. 25:

Ex. 25.   Untied suspension in melodic cell
                (TR 1, st. II, m. 4)

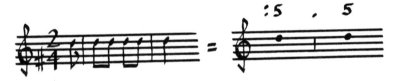

4.   Skeletal patterns

A skeletal pattern is a construct composed of those pitches of a
melodic phrase which coincide with primary and secondary pulses.
Each skeletal pattern is simultaneously a reduction of a full musical
phrase and of its two constituent melodic cells. This is illustrated
in ex. 26, in which the numbers of all pitches except those occurring on the primary and secondary pulses are placed within
parentheses:

Ex. 26.   Skeletal pattern (TR 8A, st. I, m. 5-8)

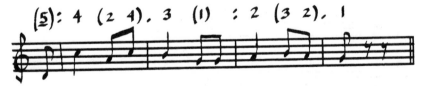

When the numbers in parentheses are elided, the skeletal pattern

:4.3:2.1 is produced. Ex. 27, taken from the Spanish repertory,
displays the same skeletal pattern:

Ex. 27. Skeletal pattern (Córdoba y Oña
1948:1:106, no. 97, m. 1-4)

V. ANALYSIS OF THE SONG TEXTS

A. METRICAL ANALYSIS (SYLLABLE COUNT)

1. Types of poetic meter

In general, there are three types of poetic meter. In the first
the verse is patterned according to the number and type of poetic
feet found in the line, as, for example, iambic pentameter. In the
second the verse is patterned according to the number of syllables
in the line, for example, hexasyllabic or octosyllabic. The third
type, known as "quantitative," was found in Old Latin poetry and is
based on the patterning of long and short vowels.

Spanish poetry is organized according to the number of syllables
in the verse or line. Although Spanish as a language has phonemic
accent, verbal accent is taken into consideration only at the cadences of the verses and in certain vowel clusters (see V.A.3 and
V.A.5).

2. General principles of Spanish poetic meter

In some Spanish poetic forms, such as the copla and décima, each
verse is composed of the same number of syllables. In other forms,
such as the *seguidilla*, there is a contrast in the number of
syllables per line. There are several devices which provide the
poet with some flexibility in arriving at the number of syllables to
be counted to a verse. Among these are the *sinalefa* and the
sinéresis. When the position of the vowels within the verse permits
him to make a single use of either of these devices, he may subtract
one syllable from his count, thus turning a verse which actually
contains nine syllables into one in which only eight syllables are
counted. If the verse or line already contains eight syllables,
and it is desirable that it be considered an octosyllabic verse,
neither device need be applied, although they may be applicable
(see V.A.4).

It is also customary that the poet count the final accented syllable of a verse as two syllables, whether or not it is followed
by an unaccented syllable. As in the sinalefa or the sinéresis,
the poet may or may not make use of these conventions, as serves
his needs (see V.A.5).

The determination of meter or syllable count in Spanish poetry is therefore not necessarily based on the actual number of syllables present in the verse. Rather, it is also determined by the conventions just described. In general, the function of these conventions is to permit the poet to regularize the meter of his verse.

3. Vowels, vowel combinations, and accented vowels

There is some difference in the way syllables are viewed in the dictionary sense and in their count in poetry. We therefore must first see how the quality of vowels affects syllable division according to the dictionary. The five vowels of Spanish are divided into two classes, the first containing the strong vowels a, e, and o, the second class the weak vowels i and u. (The y when standing alone or forming the final letter of a word is also a weak vowel.) When found within one word, two contiguous vowels of the second class are considered to form a diphthong and one syllable:

rui-do ciu-dad

Two contiguous vowels of the first class are not considered to form a diphthong and are written as two syllables:

em-ple-ar ca-o-ba

Combinations of a vowel of one class and a vowel of the other class are considered diphthongs and are written as one syllable:

a-brien-do cuan-do soy

If a weak vowel carries an accent, the cluster is now divided into two syllables:

tí-a ba-ú-les

On occasion a cluster of three vowels is also utilized. This is considered a triphthong and is written as one syllable, whether or not one of the vowels carries an accent. However, the center vowel of the three is always a strong vowel, and it is the vowel that bears the accent when it is present:

a-pre-ciáis

4. The sinalefa and the sinéresis

Syllable count of poetry differs from the dictionary method in that any cluster of two contiguous vowels in which neither vowel carries an accent may be counted as one syllable. In its most common form this involves the combining of two contiguous vowels forming part of separate but adjacent words in the same verse:

tu ma-dre fue al rí-o
1 2   3   4   5 6

In this example the *e* of *fue* and the *a* of *al* are treated as though they formed a diphthong, and the two syllables are counted as one. This process is known as the sinalefa. A sinalefa may also be formed by two similar vowels:

pa-só pa-ra a-rri-ba
1 2 3 4   5 6

The *h* is silent in Spanish and therefore has no effect:

que ten-go que ha-cer
1   2   3   4   5 (6)

The *e* of the second *que* and the *a* of *hacer* are combined to form a sinalefa. The addition of a syllable at the end of the verse will be explained later.

By extension two contiguous vowels, one forming the last vowel of one verse and the other the first vowel of the subsequent verse, may also be considered to form a sinalefa. This can be seen in the following excerpt from TR 9 (st. I, v. 2):

a-brien-do un-a ro-sa
1 2   3   4 5 6
y ce-rran-do un cla-vel.
  1 2   3   4 5 (6)

The *a* at the end of the first verse is combined with the *y* at the beginning of the second verse. A syllable is thus subtracted from the second verse. It could have been subtracted from the first verse instead. However, the purpose of the operation is to regularize verse length.

Thus a sinalefa can be formed by two similar or dissimilar strong vowels or by the combination of a weak vowel and a strong. In all cases the vowels concerned are contiguous but form parts of separate words. Less frequently two strong vowels found within a word are combined and counted as one syllable:

re-vo-le-á-ti-co   A-bra-ham
1 2 3 4 5   1   2

This process is known as the sinéresis.

Any cluster of three contiguous vowels can be counted as one syllable, whether found in one word or adjacent words:

A-ten-ción, que va a em-pe-zar
1 2   3   4 5   6 7 (8)

flor de a-hu-ya-ma
1   2   3 4

The rationale for the use of the sinalefa and the sinéresis in syllable count is that in actual speech much occurs which is not reflected in writing or print. Two contiguous similar vowels are combined to form one vowel. When one of two contiguous vowels is

strong and the other weak, they are combined to form a diphthong.
When two dissimilar strong vowels are contiguous, one may be
modified to form a weak vowel (this weak vowel frequently having a
consonantal function) and the two combined to form a diphthong.
These phenomena may or may not be heard in speech, recited poetry,
or in song, depending upon the background of the individual concerned and the particular social situation.

5.   Counting syllables at verse cadences

Further conventions are followed in the counting of syllables at
the end of a verse. Three types of textual cadences are recognized,
the *aguda*, the *grave*, and the *esdrújula*. The aguda cadence consists of a final syllable whose vowel is accented in Spanish speech.
The grave cadence adds to such a syllable a single unaccented
syllable; the esdrújula cadence adds two unaccented syllables. All
three types are counted as two syllables.

Aguda:	del con-de Lau-rel
	1 2 3 4 5 6
Grave:	Yo soy la viu-di-ta
	1 2 3 4 5 6
Esdrújula:	Fran-cis-co re-vo-le-á-ti-co
	1 2 3 4 5 6 7 8

The rationale for adding a syllable to a verse displaying an
aguda cadence is that a metrical feeling is set up which flows
through the short silence which usually occurs between succeeding
verses when they are recited or sung. When the verses are sung, it
can be expressed in music notation by rests or by the elongation of
the note on which the phrase ends, which can be seen in the first
scores of TR 1, TR 2, and TR 8. It should be noted in each case
that the final pitch plus any rests following it occupies a time
duration greater than half of the pulse.

6.   Application to folksong texts

The artifices discussed have served as forms of poetic license.
As indicated previously, they are employed by poets as means of
producing regularity of meter. The same processes are employed in
the counting of syllables in folk poetry. In this case the author
of the verse is not usually known. The original song text may
have been the creation of a particular individual, but many individuals may have participated in its modification during
transmission. Even in cases where the poet is known, it is not
easy to determine his or her intentions. The application of these
processes to folk poetry is therefore somewhat arbitrary.

Nevertheless, some scholars have attempted to indicate sinalefas
in their transcription of folksong. Such phenomena can be observed
in ex. 27 (Córdoba y Oña 1948:I:111, no. 104, m. 1-4) and ex. 28
(Marazuela Albornos 1964:141, no. 198, m. 5-8).

Ex. 27

Ca-pi-tán de bar-co me es-cri-bió un pa-pel.

Ex. 28

que quie-ro ca-sar meỹ no ten-go con quien.

In both of the preceding examples a strong vowel and a weak vowel
are combined to form a diphthong, and therefore both are represented
in the music by a single note.

I found the situation to be even more complex when making transcriptions of the songs sung in Evitar. Not only were vowels
combined, modified, and elided, but single consonants or whole
syllables were also elided. Rather than attempting to indicate
sinalefas as in the preceding examples, I wrote what I heard and
followed dictionary rules in dividing syllables (see II.B.3).

7. Procedures followed in the metrical analysis in this study

The methods of counting syllables in poetry which have been discussed are said to be based upon what is heard and felt when the
poetry is recited or sung rather than upon how it is written. From
this one could arrive at the conclusion that in this study syllable
count should be applied to the associated texts rather than the
realized texts. However, most transcribers do not indicate the many
elisions which occur in the actual performance of a song text. The
sinalefa is indeed reflected in some transcriptions in which music
and text are associated (see ex. 27-28). However, when these texts
are printed separately, there is no means of determining that the
sinalefa is indeed represented in the music by one note:

> Capitán del barco
> me escribió un papel,
>
> que quiero casarme
> y no tengo con quien.

These texts are, in fact, indistinguishable from realized texts.
Further, most studies of folksong texts are based on texts which
have been transcribed without reference to the music to which they
were sung. These texts are analogous to the realized texts offered
in this and the following chapters.

It would be interesting to compare the realized text with the associated text in those cases where both are given, but this is beyond the scope of this study. If relevant references are to be made to the results of textual studies by others, it is to the realized texts that metrical analysis must be applied. I am not applying the artifices discussed to the composition of poetry, nor do I have any means of knowing what procedures were followed in the development of the texts through oral transmission. To be consistent in my analysis, I am employing the following set procedure, which is nevertheless based, in general, on the practices observed in the associated texts but which does not include the consideration of the many elisions of syllables seen in the latter.

a. All verse cadences, aguda, grave, and esdrújula, are counted as two syllables.

b. All clusters of two or three syllables occurring within a verse are counted as one syllable. This applies to contiguous vowels found within a word or clusters formed by contiguous vowels forming part of separate but adjacent words. However, if a weak vowel carries an accent, it is considered to form part of a separate syllable. On the other hand, a strong vowel carrying an accent can form part of either a sinalefa or a sinéresis.

c. In many cases strophes which are sung as couplets are reproduced in the realized text as quatrains, since this is the manner in which students of folksong texts in Spanish customarily present them. In such cases two successive verses are encompassed in one musical phrase--the phrase in most cases being delineated by a rest or rests during which the singer breathes--and this fact is reflected in the numbering of the verses. A sinalefa composed of the final vowel or vowels of one verse and the initial vowel or vowels of the succeeding verse is not recognized unless both verses are encompassed within the same musical phrase and are thus identified by one number.

In the first of the following examples (TR 2, st. III, v. 2), a sinalefa is recognized between two successive verses; in the second example (TR 6, v. 3-4) it is not.

```
        1.   La u-na en Se-vi-lla
              1 2 3     4  5  6
        2.      y la o-tra en Ca-ta-ca.
                  1    2    3 4  5

        3.   U-no le can-ta, o-tro le pí-a
              1  2  3   4   5      6  7  8 9
        4.   O-tro le to-ca la chi-ri-mí-a.
              1   2  3   4  5  6   7  8  9 10
```

d. A sinalefa or sinéresis cannot be composed of more than three vowels. The center vowel or any cluster of three must be a strong vowel. In the excerpt from TR 2 (st. II, v. 2) the first three vowels of the second verse, y, a, and o, are counted as one syllable. They cannot be combined with the final vowel, o, of the first of the two verses, since this would form a cluster of four vowels. Nor can a cluster be formed beginning with the o (thus *oya*),

since in this case there would not be a strong vowel in the
center.

<pre>
        2.   tu ma-dre fue al rí-o
             1   2   3   4   5 6
             y a-ho-ri-ta ven-drá.
             1   2 3 4   5 6
</pre>

e.   Tables of metrical analysis based on syllable count will be
found in chapters 7 through 12. The syllable count of each verse,
of parts of a verse, or of additions to a verse is indicated by
numbers. These numbers are listed either horizontally or vertically,
depending upon circumstances. Any special means employed in indicating syllable count is discussed preceding the presentation of
the table.
f.   Exact repetitions of a verse in the associated text are not
reproduced in the realized text. The verse is given only once, and
the number of times it occurs is indicated by a number in parentheses following it. Similarly, exact repetitions of a verse are
not indicated in the syllable count. One number represents the
initial statement and subsequent exact repetitions. If the repetition is not exact, the verse number is repeated and is followed by
an *x*.

B.   RHYME

Two types of rhyme are employed in Spanish verse, assonantal and
consonantal. In order to produce assonantal rhyme, only the final
accented vowels of aguda cadences need to be the same, not any
following consonants. In grave cadences both the accented vowels
and the following vowels must be similar, not the intervening or
any following consonants. In the following example (TR 47) there
is assonantal rhyme between the first and third and between the
second and fourth verses. The assonances or rhyming vowels are
italicized.

<pre>
        1.   No quiero ser liber*a*l
        (RA) ni conservador tamp*o*c*o*,
        2.   porque no quiero vot*a*r
        (RB) ni por uno ni por *o*tr*o*.
</pre>

Here the *a* of *liberal* rhymes with that of *votar* and the two *o*'s of
tampoco with the two in *otro*. Of the three vowels involved in
esdrújula cadences, only the first and third need rhyme, but not
necessarily the second.
In consonantal rhyme the final accented vowel and all following
vowels and consonants of the rhyming verses must be the same. In
the next example (TR 49, v. 5-8) all rhymes are consonantal. The
rhyming scheme is similar to that of the previous quatrain. In
each verse that section of the final word that rhymes is italicized.

<pre>
        5.   Mañana me voy de mi ti*erra*
        6.   voy a meterme a vagab*undo*
</pre>

7. antes que venga la gue*rra*
8. me voy a ausentar del *mundo*.

Some types of verse are said to employ assonantal rhyme and others consonantal rhyme. With some frequency both forms of rhyme are found in the same poem. The rationale here may be that any consonantal rhyme can also be considered an assonantal rhyme, as seen in the following examples:

victo*r*   victo*r*
flo*r*   flo*r*

It should be noted that the term *rhyme* is usually applied only to consonance, not to assonance. At times assonance is referred to as incomplete rhyme, although usually it is not considered rhyme but a separate form of poetic color. Since assonance and consonance are intermingled in folk poetry in the Spanish language, I find it preferable to treat them both as forms of rhyme.

C. VERSE FORMS

The following are discussed here as written or recited forms. They will be discussed as song forms, implying the association of text and melody, in VI.

1. The quatrain

The quatrain, a strophe or stanza of four verses, is the most common popular Spanish poetic form. The *romance*, the Spanish classic narrative poem, was formed of quatrains with the rhyming scheme abcb.

2. The copla

The copla is a self-inclusive quatrain of a philosophic, amorous, or humorous character. It is usually octosyllabic, and the most common rhyming schemes are abcb (the *rima romancera*), abab, and abba. This poetic form had its origin in Spain. Spanish poets of the latter part of the sixteenth century referred to an octosyllabic quatrain displaying the rima romancera as a copla. Rodríguez Marín quotes several such coplas from a sixteenth-century poet, Juan Rufo, and states that these are definitely coplas, not parts of or passages from a romance. He points out, in fact, that there is some belief that the copla preceded the romance in Spanish literary history (1927:215-16).

3. The décima and the glosa

The décima is a poem or a poetic stanza concerned with a single topic which, in most cases, contains ten octosyllabic verses arranged in the rhyming scheme abbaaccddc. This Spanish poetic form underwent a lengthy development. Tracing this development according to rhyming schemes, the earliest form, *la décima antigua*, was characterized by a rhyming scheme of four plus six or six plus four. The succeeding development was known as *coplas reales*, and the rhyming scheme was five plus five. Finally came *la décima espinela*, so called because it was first introduced by Vicente Espinel in *Diversas Rimas* of 1591 (Baehr 1970:333). The décima espinela, with its rhyming scheme abbaaccddc, became the classic form, followed with few exceptions since the sixteenth century.

The glosa had a separate development. Many scholars believe the glosa to be of Arabic origin, its progenitor being the *zajel* (Menéndez Pidal 1920:310), which Carrizo believes was invented in the ninth century by Mocardum, who died in 912 (1945:109-10). However, the gloss or glosa, a paraphrase or an explanation of a text, was a form in common use in theology and philosophy in the Middle Ages. This is also a possible source of the poetic glosa (Baehr 1970:335).

In some cases the two traditions, the décima and the glosa, are combined. These forms are usually known as glosas, not as décimas. Carrizo states that this form observes two principles: 1) there are as many strophes in the *pie*, that is, in the body of the poem, as there are verses in the *cabeza*, that is, in the glosa at the beginning of the poem; and 2) all verses of the cabeza are repeated in order at the ends of the strophes of the pie (1945:127). The dominant form of the glosa since the last quarter of the sixteenth century employs a *redondilla* of four verses which is interpreted in four strophes of ten lines each, with a citation in order of one verse of the redondilla at the end of each strophe. Each strophe interprets one verse of the redondilla cabeza, and that verse forms the final verse of the strophe (Baehr 1970:333). It will be noted that TR 24 and TR 25 are in this form. The glosa with one line is called the *pie forzado* (Carrizo 1945:116) and is the form exemplified in TR 30, TR 34 and TR 35.

According to the literary sources, the décima contrasts with the romance in that the former displays consonantal rhyme and the latter assonantal rhyme. This statement is not fully applicable to costeño practice.

The *copla de arte mayor* in its most common form is a strophe of eight verses with consonantal rhyme (Baehr 1970:181-85). TR 40 is in this form.

4. The litany

The litany is a responsorial form of poetry in which there is no fixed length of verse, no strophes, and no rhyme, and a series of different verses produces the same response. The term is derived from a type of prayer used in Christian worship. This form is employed not only in church services but also in the rosarios recited at the costeño velorio for an adult. The following is such a litany excerpted from a recording I made of a performance of a rosario in the Departamento de Córdoba in 1965 (LF 146.2). The verses recited by the rezandero are given to the left, the responses by the others present to the right.

Para mayor honor y gloria de Dios sobre María	Sea la gracia concebida.
¡Viva Jesús en nuestros corazones!	¡Viva!
¡Viva María Santísima!	¡Viva!
¡Viva el patriarca señor San José!	¡Viva!
¡Viva mi padre San Joaquín de nuestra señora Santa Ana!	¡Viva!
¡Vivan todos los Santos y Santas la corte del cielo!	¡Viva!
¡Viva la gracia!	¡Viva!
¡Muera la culpa!	¡Muera!
¡Muera el pecado!	¡Muera!

VI.   RELATIONSHIPS OF TEXT AND MUSIC IN SONG

A.   SUNG VERSE FORMS

1.   Verse and refrain

The term *verse* refers to a single line of poetry or to poetry in general. It is used here primarily in the first sense but occasionally in the second. A refrain is that part of a song in which the text and melody remain in association during repetition. Refrains vary in length. They may consist of a single word sung to a musical figure or one or more textual lines sung to one or more musical phrases.

A common European form is the so-called verse and chorus. This is a balanced form in which a strophe and a refrain of approximately the same length are sung in alternation. The refrain is here called a "chorus," since it is usually but not always sung by a group of singers rather than a soloist. In this case the term *verse* has a third meaning, that of the section of the song in which the text but not the melody changes in each repetition.

Frequently both the verse and the chorus or refrain take the form of a quatrain. It is also common for the chorus or refrain to be built up of shorter lines and phrases than the verse. This form is exemplified in TR 61.

2.   The call and response pattern

The call and response pattern is a type of litany. The response is usually a choral refrain, a phrase or figure associated with the same textual material, while the call of the soloist is usually varied. The call and response pattern is known in European folk tradition, for example, the sea chanty, but is most commonly heard in sub-Saharan Africa.

B. FORMAL RELATIONSHIPS OF MELODY AND TEXT

1. The melodic refrain

In some costeño songs in quatrain form, such as TR 18 and TR 46, the soloist and chorus alternate in singing the verses. Although the stanzas sung are in quatrain form, they are treated melodically as a call and response pattern. The soloist freely varies his melody, while the chorus, with a few exceptions in TR 18, sings the same melody to each textual verse. This produces what I term a *melodic refrain*. In the refrain proper, both text and melody are similar in each performance. In the melodic refrain only the melody is the same; the verse is changed.

2. The litany with inserted coplas

Certain costeño song forms, such as the bullerengue, combine the litany and the quatrain. Throughout the performance the soloist inserts coplas within the flow of the litanic verse. In some cases each verse of the copla is treated like the call in the call and response pattern; it is sung to the same repertory of melodic phrases as the litanic verse and is followed by the same response. At other times the choral response occurs after the second and fourth verses or only after the fourth verse. Melodic phrases different from those of the calls of the call and response pattern may also be employed in singing the verses of the copla.

3. Overlapping of parts in the call and response pattern

In European folksongs cast in the call and response pattern, the chorus does not enter with its refrain until the soloist has completed his verse, and he, in turn, does not enter until the singing of the choral refrain has been completed. On the other hand, in African song built up of call and response patterns, the soloist frequently begins his call before the chorus has completed its response to his previous call. According to Waterman, the constant repetition of the choral response provides the soloist with a solid rhythmic framework over which he may vary his part (1973:90). This implies that the chorus sings its part at regular intervals and does not overlap the part of the soloist. Nketia likens the call and response pattern to an AB form often repeated with or without textual or musical variation. The most common elaboration is introduced by the leader, who often overlaps the choral response, entering early with his phrase (1974:142).

Conversely, in costeño song the choral part also overlaps that of the soloist. This overlap, however, is of a different character. In its early entrance the chorus does not sing its refrain but duplicates the latter part of the verse of the soloist and then takes up the refrain.

4. Cuing the refrain in the call and response pattern

In African song the leader or soloist often begins with the response rather than the call. This serves as a cue which alerts the chorus and refreshes their memory. This procedure is common among the Kpelle of Liberia, where the leader may also sing part or all of the response along with the chorus (data collected in the field by Ruth Stone).

C. COORDINATION OF TEXT AND UNDERLYING PULSE

1. The Spanish tradition

Although the accents of melodies of both art songs and folksongs in common practice style generally coordinate with the underlying pulse, this is not necessarily the case with the verbal accents of their texts. The degree of coordination of verbal accent and musical pulse depends to a great extent upon the language in which the song is cast. Spoken Spanish displays phonemic accent, and the simpler types of Spanish folksong, such as the game songs of children, are characterized by almost complete coordination of verbal accent and musical pulse. Possibly because Spanish versification is based upon syllable count rather than metrical feet, there is not as great an expectation of such coordination in folksong in Spanish as in English. In the latter, coincidence of verbal accent and underlying pulse is the ideal. Thus when a syllable unaccented in speech coincides with an underlying pulse, folklorists refer to it as a *wrenched accent*. In Spanish song, on the other hand, it seems quite acceptable that such coincidence should occur in only the majority of cases.

2. The African lyric tradition

A. M. Jones in his "African Metrical Lyrics" (1964:7-11) states that neither African sung poetry nor the melody to which it is sung displays what can be described as meter. Although the melodies have accent, and he believes the language to contrast long and short vowels, neither individually nor in combination do they fall in recurrent patterns. Meter is instead produced by an external factor, regular or irregular divisions of time produced by claps, drumbeats, footfalls, or recurrent kinetic impluses. Of these the clap is representative. In regular meter the time-space between two succes- sive claps can be divided into two or three equal parts or time units, and the general division of the song follows one pattern or the other. When the time-space is divided into two units, it is generally filled with two syllables; when divided into three units, with three syllables. However, this represents only the general procedure. One syllable can occupy two time units and two syllables one time unit. The last syllable of a verbal phrase may occupy all or part of the time-space of two claps.

Leaving aside for the moment the lack of coordination of melodic and verbal accent and pulse, the syllabic division of the time-space between claps described is similar to that found between pulses in

Western European song. Both African and European song are structured over a series of pulses, which may be objectified or merely
felt. In Western Europe these pulses are divided into relatively
short, repeated accentual patterns; in African music they form
cycles of various lengths in which all pulses are equal in intensity.
According to Jones, the claps or pulses underlying African lyric
song display the cyclic form. In regular meter the line of song
occupies a time-span measured by either eight, twelve, or sixteen
claps. Each succeeding line will occupy a time-span or cycle
marked off by the same number of claps but obviously may differ
exceedingly in its number of syllables. Each strophe usually consists of two lines of poetry, each in most cases containing a call
and a response. Although both lines occupy the same time-span as
marked off by the same number of claps, they may differ in their
internal organization (VI.A.2). Thus the call of the soloist and
the response of the chorus occupy different lengths of time as
measured by claps. In a strophe delineated by 16 claps, the first
may be divided into 4 + 12 claps and the second into 6 + 10 claps.
In a non-strophic call and response pattern occupying a cycle of
8 claps, the division may be 5 + 3. In irregular meter the lines
are usually delineated by 12 claps in additive rhythmic relation.
    Two other aspects of African lyric song are analogous to those of
European song if the difference in underlying structures is not
taken into consideration. According to Jones, on occasion three
syllables are sung to two time units, or three where two have usually
been sung. Relating this to the time-space of one clap, the result
is a horizontal hemiola, a phenomenon found in both Africa and
Europe. Syllables can also fall between units, intermediate to the
time-space measured by the clap. If such a syllable is sustained
longer than one time unit or, in particular, into a clap, it represents syncopation or off-beat phrasing. Since the validation by
controlled repetition characteristic of the Western European common
practice style is not present, the structuring of these phenomena
must be considered an African trait (IV.B.1.6 and IV.B.2.6-7).

3. An African narrative tradition

    In his study of the songs of the hunters' bards of the Bambara-
Maninka people in the western savannah of Africa, Bird describes
phenomena similar in some respects to but different in others from
those described by Jones (Bird 1972:208-11). Although Bambara-
Maninka is a tone language and accent is a low-level phenomenon,
Bird finds that the latter is important in the grammar of poetry.
The songs of the hunters' bards are accompanied by one or more
melodic instruments, plucked strings or a type of marimba, plus the
rasp *nárinya*, a serrated steel pipe scraped with a metal rod. In
his discussion Bird omits consideration of both the sung melody and
the parts played by the accompanying melodic instruments. His analysis is concerned with the relationship of the prosodic features of
the sung poem to the rhythmic background produced in scraping the
nárinya. In the simpler forms sung by the hunters' bards, the length
of the line of poetry is determined by and coordinated with four
strokes of the metal rod on the nárinya. Four verbal accents of the
sung line of poetry coordinate with the four pulses produced by the

rasp. Between the accented syllables are sung one or more unaccented syllables. On occasion one of the latter may be a syllable
which is accented in speech. One of the accented syllables coordinating with the strokes on the nárinya, usually the last of the four,
also may be unaccented in speech.

The underlying cycle of the Bambara-Maninka narrative songs
differs from the cycles of the lyric songs described by Jones in
having four rather than eight, twelve, or sixteen pulses. The
pulses of the former are always sounded rather than occasionally
being kinetic impulses as in the lyric songs. The expectancy of
coordination of verbal and musical accent is not too distant from
the situation in Spanish song.

Returning to Bird's description: when a call and response pattern
is utilized, the verse of the soloist may occupy four pulses produced by the rasp and the choral response a similar cycle of four
pulses. Alternatively, both parts may be encompassed in one line
and thus in one cycle, with the part of the soloist occupying three
pulses and that of the chorus one pulse. In more complex forms
the soloist speeds up his delivery, and five or more verbal accents
are sung during the period in which there are four strokes on the
nárinya. Thus the verbal accents, and the poetic line as an entity,
are now out of phase with the established four-stroke pattern of
the accompaniment. The singer may continue out of phase for some
time but will again coordinate his singing with the four-stroke
pattern of the nárinya at the beginning of sections. The art of
the bard therefore consists of producing various degrees of tension,
that is, in satisfying or evading the expectancy of the performance
of certain prosodic features in the language, such as accent and
the coordination of this accent with the recurrence of four strokes
on the rasp.

The balanced call and response, each coordinating with four
strokes on the nárinya, is analogous to European practice. The
arrangement of a call three strokes in length and a response one
stroke in length seems more African than European. The out-of-
phase singing of the soloist could be considered an extension of the
principle of off-beat phrasing by those carrying the improvisatory
role in the ensemble.

4.   Application to costeño song

The African and Spanish song texts share some prosodic features.
The African song text can be divided into verses or lines and
frequently into strophes or stanzas. In the Bambara-Maninka songs
there is an expectancy of coordination of verbal accent and underlying pulse similar to but not quite as great as that in Spanish
song. Jones believes that sung African lyric poetry is not metrical
and that the contrast in African languages is quantitative rather
than accentual. In musical terms it is agogic rather than dynamic.
Very little has been published concerning accent in African
languages, but Jones is probably overemphasizing one aspect of
accent. Linguists with whom I have discussed the matter assure me
that in Bantu languages, at least, intensity and pitch play as
important a role in verbal stress as syllable length. When melody
and languages are combined the requirements of the former often

outweigh those of the latter. Thus in verbal stress the element
of intensity is likely to be strengthened and those of pitch and
length to be diminished. In this respect, then, African and
Spanish song probably lie closer together than the respective
languages.

Both Jones and Bird agree that African sung poetry cannot be
fully understood without reference to its rhythmic accompaniment.
Like the underlying pulses of percussion ensembles, those of song are
organized in cycles of different lengths. Nevertheless, the realization of the cycles underlying the latter differs in many respects
from that of the former. In song, in most cases, all pulses of the
cycle are realized and are therefore equally spaced. Since time
must be allowed to accommodate the singing of one or two syllables
between the onset of adjacent pulses, the latter must also be more
widely spaced. The pulses underlying a song are therefore performed
at a much slower tempo than those of a percussion ensemble, the
latter often being performed with extreme rapidity.

In the chapters that follow I shall examine the relationships of
underlying pulse to both the melody and the text of the song. For
purposes of clarity it seems best to carry out the two operations
separately, relating first the song melody and then the song text to
the underlying pulse patterns or cycles.

PART III
The Music and Poetry

7. Niñez

This chapter is concerned with the songs of childhood: those sung by the mother to the child and those sung by the child or children themselves. The first are lullabies, the second primarily the songs utilized in singing games.

The songs recorded and transcribed are sung in the Spanish language, and we can therefore assume that those song texts which did not arise independently in Colombia or elsewhere in the New World were diffused from Spain. To determine whether or not such diffusion took place, I have examined published transcriptions in the Spanish literature of some 300 lullabies and approximately 500 children's songs. The sources examined were:

Córdoba y Oña, Sixto, *Cancionero popular de la provincia de Santander*, vols. I and III, 1948.

Gil García, Bonifacio, *Cancionero popular de Extremadura*, vol. II, 1956.

Marazuela Albornos, Agapito, *Cancionero segoviano*, 1964.

Schneider, Marius, "Tipología musical y literaria de la canción de cuna en España," *Anuario musical*, 1948.

This is basically the same corpus utilized in an earlier and more restricted study (List 1973b:82).

When available I shall offer after the Colombian songs analogous textual material found in Spanish sources. Consideration of the music will be deferred until later, as will, in general, that of textual form.

ARRULLOS (LULLABIES)

The singing of a lullaby is always accompanied by some rhythmic motion designed to assist in putting the child to sleep. The child is held against the shoulder while the mother walks back and forth, or she may rock herself and the child in a rocking chair. Often the child is rocked in a little hammock, which is called the *chinchorro* since it is coarse-woven like the fishing net of that name.

TR 1 (LF 79.7) ''Duérmase, Niña, que tengo que hacer''

Sung by Marcelina Sánchez Pimientel. Evitar, 1 November 1964.

2. e-res tan bue-na co-mo tu ma-ma,

e-res tan bue-na co-mo tu ma.

1. Duér-ma-se, ni-ña, que ten-go que ha-ce,

duér-ma-se, ni-ña, que ten-go que ha-ce, 2. la-

var los pa-ñi-to, po-ner-me a co-se, la

var los pa-ñi-to, po-ner-me a co-se.

1. Duér-ma-se, ni-ño, duér-me-te tú,

duér-ma-se, ni-ño, duér-me-te tú.

1. Duér-ma-se, ni-ño, que ten-go que ha-ce,

duér-ma-se, ni-ño, que ten-go que ha-ce, 2. la-

var los pa-ñi-to, po-ner-me a co-se, la-

var los pa-ñi-tos, po-ner-me a co-se.

1. Duér-ma-se, ni-ño, flor de ba-ta-ta,

duér-ma-se, ni-ño, flor de ba-ta-ta,

2. e-res tan bue-no co-mo tu pa-pa,

e-res tan bue-no co-mo tu pa-pa.

I	1. Duérmase, niña,	Sleep, child,
	que tengo que hacer, (2)	I have things to do,
	2. lavar los pañitos,	Diapers to wash,
	ponerme a coser. (2)	must get to my sewing.
II	1. Duérmase, niña,	Sleep, child,
	flor de un día, (2)	flower of a day,
	2. eres tan bueno	You are as good
	como tu tía. (2)	as your aunt.
III	1. Duérmase, niña,	Sleep, child,
	flor de ahuyama, (2)	flower of the *ahuyama*,
	2. eres tan buena	You are as good
	como tu mama,	as your mama,
	eres tan bueno	You are as good
	como tu mama.	as your mama.

IV   1. Duérmase, niña,   Sleep, child,
        que tengo que hacer, (2)   I have things to do,
     2. lavar los pañitos,   Diapers to wash,
        ponerme a coser. (2)   must get to my sewing.

V   1. Duérmase, niño,   Sleep, child,
        duérmete tú. (3)   do go to sleep.

VI   1. Duérmase, niño,   Sleep, child,
        que tengo que hacer, (2)   I have things to do,
     2. lavar los pañitos,   Diapers to wash,
        ponerme a coser. (2)   must get to my sewing.

VII 1. Duérmase, niña,   Sleep, child,
        flor de batata,   flower of the sweet potato,
        duérmase, niño,   Sleep, child,
        flor de batata,   flower of the sweet potato,
     2. eres tan bueno   You are as good
        como tu papa. (2)   as your papa.

NOTES

Perf:

The pitch level rises gradually. The final pitch of st. VII is approximately a quarter tone higher than that of st. I.

Text:

III.1 - The *ahuyama* (*Cucurbita maxima duchesne*) is a vine bearing yellow flowers.

Since Sánchez is not singing the lullaby to a particular child, she rather arbitrarily uses either the masculine or feminine form of the words for child (*niño-a*) and good (*bueno-a*). When this type of change occurs in a repeated verse, it is not indicated in the realized text.

According to Sánchez, this lullaby is the one most commonly sung in the village.

Derivation:

Looking ahead, it will be seen that this quatrain also forms st. I of TR 2. St. I of TR 5 is the same as that of TR 2, since the singer was reading from a transcription of the text of the latter. The two versions of the quatrain differ in only two aspects, the sex of the child addressed--*niña* versus *niño*--and the use of the diminutive--*pañitos* versus *pañales*.

The Spanish sources include five lullabies whose texts in part or in full are analogous to this quatrain found in the costeño repertory:

Analogue 1, Madrid (Schneider 1948:32-33, no. 11a)

Duérmete niño   Sleep, child,
   que tengo que hacer   I have things to do,
lavar los pañales   Diapers to wash,
   ponerme a coser   must get to my sewing.

Analogue 2, Santander (Córdoba y Oña 1948:III:360, no. 345)

Duérmete, mi niño,   Sleep, my child,
  que tengo que hacer,   I have things to do,
lavar tus pañales,   Washing your diapers,
  sentarme a coser.   must get to my sewing.

Analogue 3, Huesca (Schneider 1948:32-33, no. 11b)

Aduérmete niño,   Go to sleep, child,
  que tengo que hacer,   I have things to do,
lavar los pañales,   Diapers to wash,
  planchar y coser.   ironing and sewing.

Analogue 4, Huesca (Schneider 1948:30-31, no. 9d)

Ya duérmete niño   Now go to sleep, child,
  que tengo que hacer,   I have things to do,
lavar los pañales,   Diapers to wash,
  planchar y coser   ironing and sewing.

Analogue 5, Asturias (Schneider 1948:34-35, no. 14d)

Duérmete, niño,   Sleep, child,
  que tengo que hacer   I have things to do,
hacer las camas,   beds to make,
  fregar y barrer.   scrubbing and sweeping.

All of the reproduced strophes are similar in substance. The
mother wishes the child to go to sleep because she has certain
household chores to carry out. I have translated both *ponerme a
coser* and *sentarme a coser* as "must get to my sewing." Literally,
the first means "I must put myself to sewing" and the second "I
must seat myself to sew." The most striking contrast between the
texts from Evitar and those from Spain is found in the form of
the verb used to command the child to go to sleep. In the Spanish
lullabies the familiar form *duérmete* is used, in the Colombian
lullabies the more formal *duérmase*. I recorded versions of this
lullaby in three communities in the Departamento de Bolívar. All
singers used the formal *duérmase* rather than the familiar *duérmete*,
the latter representing the customary manner in which a mother
would address her child in Spanish.

The use of *duérmase* by the singers I recorded probably has its
origin in the historical development of Colombia following the
Spanish conquest. In this period the lullaby was probably most
frequently sung by a slave or a servant to the child of the
mistress. The slave or servant could not address the child in
the familiar form *duérmete*, but would have had to employ the formal
duérmase. We can assume that the latter form was carried over into
the local folk tradition, and thus costeño mothers in this rural
area still utilize the formal pronoun form (*se*, not *te*) in singing
this lullaby.

TR 2 (LF 78.3) "Duérmase, niño, que tengo que hacer"
Sung by Rosa Luisa Martínez.   Evitar, 1 November 1964.

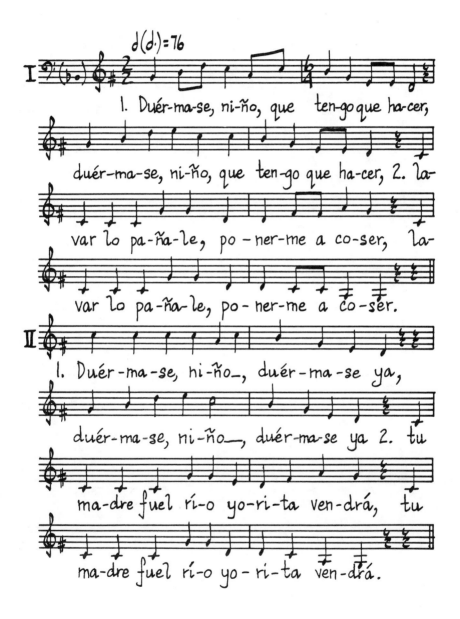

1. Duér-ma-se, ni-ño, que ten-go que ha-cer,
duér-ma-se, ni-ño, que ten-go que ha-cer, 2. lavar lo pa-ña-le, po-ner-me a co-ser, lavar lo pa-ña-le, po-ner-me a co-ser.

1. Duér-ma-se, hi-ño_, duér-ma-se ya,
duér-ma-se, ni-ño_, duér-ma-se ya 2. tu
ma-dre fuel rí-o yo-ri-ta ven-drá, tu
ma-dre fuel rí-o yo-ri-ta ven-drá.

1. Pa-pa Jo-sé___ tie-ne do va-ca,

Pa-pa Jo-sé tie-ne do va-ca, 2. La

un-en Se-vi-lli la o-tren Ca-tac,

un-en Se-vi-lli la o-tren Ca-tac.

1. Pa-to cu-cha-ro pa-só por a-quí___.

pa-to cu-cha-ro pa-só por a-quí, 2. ni

tie-ne ver-güen-za, ni sa-be sen-ti, ni

tie-ne ver-güen-za, ni sa-be sen-ti.

1. Pa-to cu-cha-ro pa-só pa-ra-rri-ba,

pa-to cu-cha-ro pa-só pa-ra-rri-ba, 2. de-

jua su mu-jer co-gien-do ba-rri-ga, de-

jua su mu-jer co-gien-do ba-rri.

VI

1. Pa-to cu-cha-ro pa-só pa-ra-ba-jo,

pa-to cu-cha-ro pa-só pa-ra-ba-jo, 2. de-

jua su mu-jer pa-san-do tra-ba-jo, de-

jua su mu-jer pa-san-do tra-ba.

VII

1. Pa-lo-mi-ta blan-ca de la-rri -lle el rí-o,

pa-lo-mi-ta blan-ca de la-rri -lle el rí-o, 2. tu

mad

I	1. Duérmase, niño,
	    que tengo que hacer, (2)
	2. lavar los pañales,
	    ponerme a coser. (2)
		Sleep, child,
		    I have things to do,
		Diapers to wash,
		    must get to my sewing.

II	1. Duérmase, niño,
	    duérmase ya, (2)
	2. tu madre fue al río,
	    y ahorita vendrá. (2)
		Sleep child,
		    now go to sleep,
		Your mother went to the river
		    and will return right away.

III	1. Papa José
	    tiene dos vacas, (2)
	2. la una en Sevilla,
	    y la otra en Cataca. (2)
		Father Joseph
		    has two cows,
		One in Seville,
		    and the other in Cataca.

IV	1. Pato cucharo
	    pasó por aquí, (2)
	2. ni tiene vergüenza,
	    ni sabe sentir. (2)
		The spoon-billed duck
		    came by here,
		He has no shame
		    nor feelings.

V	1. Pato cucharo
	    pasó para arriba, (2)
	2. dejó a su mujer
	    cogiendo barriga. (2)
		The spoon-billed duck
		    went up that way,
		He left his woman
		    getting a big belly.

VI	1. Pato cucharo
	    pasó para abajo, (2)
	2. dejó a su mujer
	    pasando trabajo. (2)
		The spoon-billed duck
		    went down that way,
		He left his woman
		    having a hard time.

VII	1. Palomita blanca
	    de la orilla del río,
	2. tu mad...
		White dove
		    on the river's bank,
		You mo...

NOTES

Perf:

During the performance there is a gradual rise in pitch level of less than a quarter tone.

The range of the melody employed by Martínez in singing this lullaby is unusually large, an 8ve plus a major 6th. Having set the melody at a low pitch level, she had difficulty in reaching the final pitch of the strophe, B♭, and her production of this pitch is poor in tone quality and barely audible. After st. II she no longer attempted to reach the B♭, ending the strophes on an alternative pitch instead.

She could not remember the rest of the text of st. VII. After the abrupt stop indicated, she tried again but could only remember v. 1. This final attempt is not transcribed.

Since that pitch which is obviously the final of the melody, B♭, is not heard in most of the strophes, the pitch of the mid cadence, the repetition of v. 1, is utilized as a guide in assessing pitch level.

At times the division of the beat is neither binary nor ternary but takes an intermediate form not reproducible in Western notation.

In transcribing in these cases I have tended to elect the binary rather than the ternary division.

Text:

III.2 - It is assumed that the name of the locality is "Cataca." Since it is coupled with Sevilla, it can further be assumed that "Cataca" is or was found in Spain. However, no community of this name can be located on a contemporary Spanish map.

IV.1 - *Pato cucharo* (*Cancroma cochlearia*) is the name given to an aquatic wading bird which frequents the shallow waters of the ciénagas. The upper part of the bird's beak is shaped like an inverted spoon.

IV-VI - These strophes register a complaint against the common practice of men leaving their women as soon as the latter become pregnant.

IV.2 - *Vergüenza* refers not only to "shame" but to a general lack of social consciousness.

V.2 - *Cogiendo barriga* is a term used when pregnancy has reached the visible stage. The literal meaning is "getting a belly."

VI.2 - *Pasando trabajo* is an idiom which indicates that an individual is in trouble. In this case, the woman is left expecting a child without a man to support her.

- - -

When questioned, Martínez informed me that this was the only lullaby melody that she knew.

TR 3 (LF 78.4) "Señora Santa Ana ¿por qué llora el Niño?"

Sung by Rosa Luisa Martínez. Evitar, 1 November 1964.

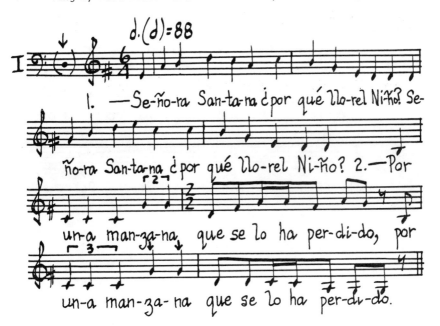

II

1. —Man-za-na de o-ro, si yo ten-con-tra-ra, man-

za-na de o-ro, si yo ten-con-tra-ra, 2. se

la die-ral Ni-ño pa-ra que ju-gar, se

la die-ral Ni-ño pa-ra que ju-gar.

III

1. Yo no quie-ro u-na—, yo no quie-ro do, 2. yo

quie-ro la mi-ma que se me per-dió—, yo

quie-ro la mi-ma que se me per-dió.

I	1.	---Señora Santa Ana ¿por qué llora el Niño? (2)	"Saint Ann, why does the Child cry?"
	2.	---Por una manzana que se le ha perdido. (2)	"For an apple that he has lost."
II	1.	---Manzana de oro, si yo te encontrara, (2)	"Golden apple, if I could find you,
	2.	se la diera al niño para que jugara. (2)	I would give it to the child to play with."
III	1.	---Yo no quiero una, yo no quiero dos,	"I don't want one, I don't want two,
	2.	yo quiero la misma que se me perdió. (2)	I want the one that I lost."
IV	1.	---Si yo fuera viudo contigo me fuera (2)	"If I were a widower I would go with you
	2.	pero soy casado ¡de veras, de veras! (2)	But I am married, without a doubt, without a doubt!"
V	1.	---Amores contigo quisiera tener (2)	"Your love I should like to have
	2.	porque el viudo sabe amar y querer. (2)	For the widower understands how to love and to cherish."

NOTES

Perf:

The pitch level drops slightly in st. V.

I asked Martínez to repeat the lullaby at a higher pitch level. She complied but in so doing had some difficulty in setting the tonality. However, she was now able to sing the final of the strophe with some ease.

Text:

Although asked to sing the same lullaby, she sang a different text.

1.1 - The reference is to the Christ Child. Saint Ann was the mother of the Virgin Mary and thus the grandmother of Jesus.

St. II is sung by the Christ Child. St. IV is sung by a man, st. V by a woman.

Derivation:

Looking forward, it will be seen that the text of TR 4 and the first three strophes of TR 3 are two versions of the same textual theme. They were sung one immediately after the other by the same woman. The text has some distribution in the Americas. Versions of it have been sung for me by women who learned it as children in Ecuador and Mexico. It is also known in Chile (Grebe 1975:57). However, I have been unable to find a version collected in Spain.

TR 4 (LF 78.5) "Señora María, Señora Isabel"

Sung by Rosa Luisa Martínez. Evitar, 1 November 1964.

I   1. ---Señora María,   "Holy Mary,
        Señora Isabel,   Saint Elizabeth,
     2. ¿por qué llora el Niño?   Why is the Child crying?"
        ---Por un cascabel. (2)   "For a rattle."

II   1. ---Cascabel de oro,   "Golden rattle,
        si yo te encontrara, (2)   should I find you,
     2. se lo diera al Niño   I would give it to the child
        para que jugara. (2)   to play with."

III 1. ---Yo no quiero uno,   "I don't want one,
        yo no quiero dos, (2)   I don't want two,
     2. yo quiero el mismo   I want the one
        que se me perdió,   that I lost,
        quiero el mismo   I want the one
        que se me perdió.   that I lost."

                              NOTES

Perf:

I again asked Martínez to raise the pitch level at which she
sang. She made several attempts but was unable to do so. She
then sang the text at a constant pitch level approximately a semitone below that utilized in TR 3.
     The false starts occasioned by Martínez' attempts to raise the
pitch level of her singing are not indicated in the realized text.

Text:

I - As in TR 3, the reference is to the Christ Child. Elizabeth was Mary's cousin and was the elder of the two. Elizabeth
was the mother of John the Baptist, who baptized Jesus. The two
women were both with child at the same time, and both births were
miraculous, Elizabeth through divine intervention having a child
past the age at which she normally could have been able to conceive.
     I-III - *Cascabel* is a feminine noun. However, the articles
and pronouns used in referring to it in the text are masculine
in gender. Thus in st. I.2 *un* is used rather than *una* and in
st. III.2 *el mismo* rather than *la misma*. St. II is sung by the
Child.

TR 5 (LF 180.1) "Duérmase, niña, que tengo que hacer"

Sung by María Teresa Fontalvo. Evitar, 4 August 1968.

I   1. Duérmase, niña,   Sleep, child,
        que tengo que hacer, (2)   I have things to do,
     2. lavar los pañales,   Diapers to wash,
        ponerme a coser. (2)   must get to my sewing.

TR 5

1. Duér-ma-se, ni - ña, que ten - go que ha-cer,

duér-ma-se, ni - ña, que ten - go que ha-cer, 2. la-

var los pa-ña-les, po - ner-me a co-ser, la-

var los pa-ña-les y po - ner-me a co-ser.

1. Duér-ma-se, ni - ño, duér - ma-se ya,

duér-ma-se, ni - ño, duer-ma-se ya, 2. su

ma-dre fuel rí-o yo - ri-ta ven-drá, tu

ma-dre fuel rí-o yo-ri-ta ven-drá.

1. Pa Jo-sé___ tie - ne dos va-cas

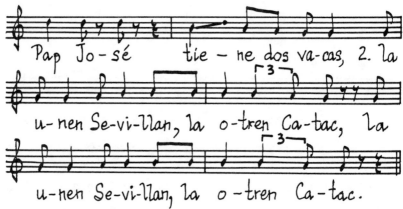

Pap Jo-sé tíe - ne dos va-cas, 2. La
u-nen Se-vi-llan, la o-tren Ca-tac, La
u-nen Se-vi-llan, la o-tren Ca-tac.

		1. Duérmase, niño,	Sleep, child,
		duérmase ya,	now go to sleep,
	1x.	duérmase, niña,	Sleep, child,
		duérmase ya,	now go to sleep.
	2.	su madre fue al río	Your mother went to the river
		y ahorita vendrá,	and will return right away,
	2x.	tu madre fue al río	Your mother went to the river
		y ahorita vendrá.	and will return right away.

III	1.	Papa José	Father Joseph
		tiene dos vacas (2)	has two cows,
	2.	la una en Sevilla,	One in Seville,
		la otra en Cataca. (2)	the other in Cataca.

IV	1.	Pato chucharo	The spoon-billed duck
		pasó por aquí, (2)	came by here,
	2.	ni tiene vergüenza,	He has no shame
		ni sabe sentir. (2)	nor feelings.

V	1.	Duérmase, niña,	Sleep, child,
		duérmase ya. (2)	now go to sleep.

NOTES

Perf:

The tempo at which Sánchez and Martínez had sung TR 1-4 seemed
to me unusually rapid for lullabies. I gave Fontalvo the realized
text of TR 2, the first lullaby sung by Martínez, and asked her to
sing the lullaby for me as slowly as she could. She had difficulty
reading the typed text and stopped a number of times. A second
recording was then made, which is represented by TR 5.

At the end of the first staff of st. II she speaks two unintelligible syllables, which are not indicated.

Fontalvo was obviously familiar with the couplets transcribed.
However, she does not sing the text exactly as it was typed, at
times substituting *niña* for *niño* and *su* for *tu*. Of most interest
is the fact that in st. III.2 she sings "Catac," like Martínez,

although the typed text read "cataca." On the other hand, in st. III.1 she pronounces the final *s* of *vacas*. The final *s* is commonly omitted in costeño speech.

- - -

Fontalvo had left Evitar for Barranquilla eight months previous to the date of recording and had returned for a visit with relatives and friends.

CHILDREN'S SONGS

TR 6 is a song taught to the children in school in Evitar. TR 7 is a traditional rigmarole sung by girls. The others, TR 8-10, are children's game songs. In a rural village like Evitar the children must depend primarily upon their own resources for amusement. For this purpose they have a large number and variety of traditional games. These games are played during school recess and at other times during the day. Often they are played on moonlit nights, when it is relatively cool in comparison with the tropical heat of the day.

A particular game is usually played by children of one sex and not by those of the other. The games played by the boys are often physically rough, and it is not thought appropriate that girls should participate in them. In general, it is the girls who play song games, not the boys. However, there are a few song games, like "Mirón, mirón, mirón," in which both girls and boys participate.

TR 6-9 were recorded only once. Only in TR 10 were the children asked to repeat their performance, and this repetition was requested primarily for the purpose of developing an accurate description of how the game is played. In singing, the children's pitch and tempo were often unsteady, and at times they did not sing together. Since in these circumstances it is impossible to notate exactly what is sung, the transcription of the melody in some cases represents what I believe to be the children's intent rather than what is actually heard. The songs follow very closely the general patterns of Western European children's songs, and the intent in most cases is therefore obvious.

TR 6 (LF 180.2) "Tres pollitos"

Sung by Catalina Vesga Fontalvo. Evitar, 4 August 1968.

1. Te-res po-lli-tos tie-ne mi tí-a,

2. tie-ne mi tí-a, tie-ne mi tí-a. 3. U-no le can-ta,

o-tro le pí-a, 4. o-tro le to-ca la chi-ri-mí.

5. A-ten-ción, que vam-pe-za 6. la gran me-rien-dan

mi co-rral. 7. Tres po-lli-to, pí-o, pí-o,

8. re-ga-la-dos, pí, pí-o, 9. pu-son dí-a

pí-o, pí-o, en mi co-rral, 10. pu-son dí-a

mi co-rral, pu-son dí-a mi co-rral.

1. Tres pollitos tiene mi tía,	My aunt has three chicks,
2. tiene mi tía, tiene mi tía.	Has my aunt, has my aunt.
3. Uno le canta, otro le pía,	One sings to her, the other peeps to her,
4. otro le toca la chirimía.	The other plays the *chirimía*.
5. Atención, que va a empezar	Attention, now begins
6. la gran merienda en mi corral.	The grand midday meal in my barnyard.
7. Tres pollitos, pío, pío,	Three chicks, peep, peep,
8. regalados. pío, pío,	Presents, peep, peep, she laid
9. puso un día, pío, pío, en mi corral,	One day, peep, peep, she laid an egg in my barnyard,
10. puso un dia en mi corral. (2)	One day she laid an egg in my barnyard.

NOTES

Perf:

The performance is by a child six or seven years of age who had not as yet developed an adequate sense of pitch. The singer begins v. 5 almost a semitone higher than she began v. 1. The pitch level then begins to descend, and at the end of the song it is approximately a semitone below that heard at its beginning.

Since the pitch level is unstable, I have offered the absolute pitch of the initial tone rather than of the final.

Text:

3. - The verb *piar* means to chirp or to peep.

4. - In Spain and in Latin America the term *chirimía* is applied to the shawm, a type of oboe (Marcuse 1975a:92, Buchner 1972:112, and Rimmer 1976:101-10). This instrument has been in use in recent times in the community of Giradota in the Departamento de Antióquia (Rimmer 1976:106). Ensembles of wind and percussion instruments known by the name chirimía are found in the Pacific littoral and the Andean regions of Colombia, but not in the Atlantic Coastal region. However, these ensembles do not contain shawms (Pardo Tovar and Pinzon Urrea 1961:9-14).

8. - *Regalados* probably refers to the food offered at the *merienda*. It could also refer to the eggs laid by the hen. In Colombia *regalado* normally refers to a gift or present. Elsewhere it may carry the meaning of "delicacy" or "bargain."

9. - *La gallina puso* is an idiom meaning that the chicken laid an egg. Here the reference is made by the use of only the verb form *puso* (put, placed).

Catalina Vesga Fontalvo is the daughter of María Teresa Fontalvo, who sang TR 5. She had been taught the song by rote by the maestra of the school for girls. Winston Caballero Salguedo, who was with me in Evitar in 1968, was at the time *rector* (principal) of the Gimnasio Bolívar, a private school in Cartagena. He informed me that one of his teachers had taught a similar song to the children in the primary grades in his school. He believed that the song was published, but in checking the textbooks in use in the Gimnasio Bolívar he was unable to find it.

Derivation:

The following is an analogue from the Spanish repertory:

Analogue 6, Extremadura (Gil García 1956:II:mus. 77, no. 164)

Treh poyitoh tiene mi tía,	My aunt has three chicks,
tiene mi tía, tiene mi tía,	Has my aunt, has my aunt,
Uno le canta, otro le pía,	One sings to her, the other peeps to her,
otro le dice la sinfonía.	The other makes up a symphony for her.

Gil García indicates that this analogue is only part of the song but does not refer to the rest. This is a song game played by little girls. One girl, the leader, imitates the playing of musical instruments. The other children must follow suit and immediately respond to her changes in motion. If one fails to do so, she pays a forfeit.

The texts differ only in their last verse. In Colombia the chick plays a chirimía, and in Spain it makes up a sinfonía. In the latter version I have translated *dice* in the sense of *decir a repente* (to improvise).

Winston Caballero believes that sinfonía rather than chirimía was used in the version of the text taught at the Gimnasio Bolívar.

Most folksong texts, even when offered in association with the music, are realized texts. There is usually no attempt to indicate the elisions or modification of phones which may occur (see chapter 6, V.A.6-7). To this practice the work of Gil García is a praiseworthy exception. In the text quoted, he endeavors to reproduce two aspects of the dialect of Spanish spoken in Extremadura. The first is the pronunciation of the consonant *ll* as *y* instead of the Castilian *ly*. The former is common throughout Latin America and a good part of contemporary Spain. According to Gil García (1956 II:15), both pronunciations are heard in the region of Extremadura. The second aspect of the dialect indicated is the use of an aspiration instead of the final *s*. The aspiration is represented by an *h*. Thus he writes *treh poyitoh* rather than *tres pollitos*.

TR 7 (LF 96.3) "El besito"

Sung and clapped by a group of girls. Evitar, 8 November 1964.

1. Dame un besito
   y vete para la escuela.
2. Si no quieres irte
   acuéstate a dormir
3. en la yerba buena,
   en el toronjil.

Give me a kiss
   and go off to school.
If you don't want to go
   lie down and sleep
In the mint,
   in the balm.

NOTES

Perf:

The clapping is uneven during v. 1 but is fairly well coordinated
beginning with v. 2. The early lack of coordination is not indicated.

I do not believe this little rigmarole to be complete in itself
but a remembered portion of a longer game song. Not only does the
melody not close on the apparent tonic (see chapter 5, I.B.1), but
the rhyming scheme is also irregular. Although *escuela* rhymes with
buena, these rhymed phrase endings do not occur in the usual order.
I have therefore indicated the absolute pitch of the initial tone
rather than of the final.

Text:

3. – *Yerba buena* (*hierbabuena*) may refer to mint in general or
specifically to peppermint. A possible English equivalent for
toronjil (*Melissa officinalis*) is "balm-gentle."

Derivation:

The following analogue is found in the Spanish repertory:

Analogue 7, Santander (Córdoba y Oña 1948:I:77, no. 68)

Ande la rueda
   con pan y canela.
Toma dos cuartos
   y vete a la escuela.
Si no quieres ir,
   échate a dormir.

Let the ring go round
   with bread and cinnamon.
Take two pennies
   and go off to school.
If you don't want to go there
   Then lie down and sleep.

According to Córdoba y Oña, after singing this little song the
girls recline on the ground and sing it again. The last three
lines of the text from Santander are analogous to lines two
through four of the text collected in Evitar. Of the two, the
Spanish analogue is better organized. It consists of a quatrain
with rhyming scheme abcb followed by a rhymed couplet dd.

TR 8 (LF 96.4) "La viudita"

Sung by a group of girls. Evitar, 8 November 1964.

S. 1. Yo soy la viu-di-ta del con-de Lau-rel 2. que

quie-ro ca-sar-me, ho quen-tro con quién.

1. Un jo-ven de Cu-ba me man-dan pa-pel, 2. man-

dan-do de-cir que me ca-se con él.

1. Y yo le con-tes-té__ con tin-ta y pa-pel: 2. yo,

sí, me ca-sa-ba pe-ro no con él.

Ch. 1. Cá-sa-te mi-ji-ta y yo te da-ré 2. za-

pa-tos y me-dia co -lor de ca-fé.

V S. 1. Ma-ma y pa-pa, le ven-go a con-tar 2. que en

los quin-ce dí-as ¡ me qui-so ma — tar !

VI Ch. 1. Ya vis-tes, mi-ji-ta, yo te lo de -cí-a 2. que

no te ca-sa-ras con el po-li-cí-a.

I	S.	1. Yo soy la viudita del conde Laurel,	I am the little widow of Count Laurel,
		2. que quiero casarme, no encuentro conquién.	I do want to get married, but I don't know with whom.
II		1. Un joven de Cuba me manda un papel,	A young man from Cuba sent me a letter
		2. mandando a decir que me case con él.	In which he said that I should marry him.
III		1. Y yo le contesté con tinta y papel:	And I answered him with pen and ink,
		2. yo, sí, me casaba pero no con él.	"I indeed will marry but not with him."

IV Ch. 1. Cásate, mi hijita,
                yo te daré
        2. zapatos y medias
                color de café.

V   S.   1. Mama y papa,
                yo vengo a contar,
        2. que a los quince días
                ¡me quiso matar!

VI Ch. 1. Ya vistes, mi hijita,
                yo te lo decía
        2. que no te casaras
                con el policía.

Marry, my dear daughter,
    and I will give you
Coffee-colored shoes
    and coffee-colored stockings.

Mama and papa,
    I've come to tell you
That after fifteen days
    He tried to kill me!

You see now, my dear daughter,
    I told you so.
You shouldn't have married
    a policeman.

NOTES

Perf:

The soloist accelerates slightly in st. II and then continues at
this tempo while singing st. III and V. However, the chorus sings
st. IV and VI at a somewhat more rapid tempo than that utilized by
the soloist.

St. IV-VI are sung to a different melody from that of st. I-III.
A different signature is required for st. IV-VI. However, the
absolute pitch level of the finals of the two sections remains the
same.

A false start by the soloist at the beginning of st. V is not
indicated.

V - Speakers of Spanish accent *mama* and *papa* on either the first
or second syllable. The second form of accentuation (*mamá, papá*)
would seem preferable here, since verbal and musical accent would
then be coordinated. However, for the sake of consistency I have
written the two words without accent in all the song texts.

Text:

III.1 - The English expression "with pen and ink" is given as
the equivalent of the Spanish expression *con tinta y papel* (with
ink and paper).

The Game:

The girls form a circle and hold hands. One girl, representing
la viudita (the little widow), stands in the center of the ring.
The girls in the ring remain standing while la viudita sings
st. I-III. They then dance while st. IV-VI are sung, beginning in
counterclockwise direction and reversing direction with each
strophe.

The game is played several times, a different girl representing
la viudita in each repetition.

Derivation:

Two analogues for TR 8 "La viudita" follow, one representing
st. I, the other st. II-III:

Analogue 8, Segovia (Marazuela Albornos 1964:141, no. 198)

Yo soy la viudita	I am the little widow
del conde Laurel,	of Count Laurel,
que quiero casarme	I wish to get married
y no tengo con quién.	but I have no one in mind.

Analogue 9, Santander (Córdoba y Oña 1948:I:111, no. 104)

Capitán de barco	The ship's captain
me escribió un papel,	wrote me a letter,
por si yo quería	Asking whether or not
casarme con él.	I wished to marry him.
Le dí la respuesta	I sent him in reply
en otro papel:	another letter:
que lo que él quería	That what he wished
no podía ser.	could not be.

The text of analogue 8 is almost identical to that of st. I of
TR 8, differing only in the last verse. In substance the two
strophes of analogue 9 and st. II-III of TR 8 are similar. The
"young man from Cuba" who seeks the hand of the little widow in
marriage is in this case a "ship's captain," and the refusal of
the offer is couched in somewhat different terms.

TR 9 (LF 96.5) "La Marisola"

Sung by a group of girls. Evitar, 8 November 1964.

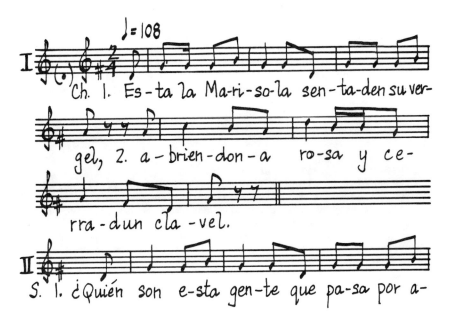

qui, 2. que ni e di-a, ni de no-che me de-jan dor - mir?

I	Ch.	1. Estaba la Marisola
		       sentada en su vergel,
			Mary was alone,
			   seated in her garden,

		2. abriendo una rosa
		       y cerrando un clavel.
			Opening a rose
			   and closing a carnation.

II	S.	1. ¿Quién(es) son esta
		       gente
		       que pasan por aquí,
			Who are these people
			   who pass this way,

		2. que ni de día, ni de
		       noche
		       me dejan dormir?
			Who neither by day nor by
			   night
			   allow me to sleep?

III	Ch.	1. Somos los estudiantes
		       que venimos a estudiar
			We are the students
			   who come to study

		2. en la gran capillita
		       de la Virgen del
		       Pilar.
			In the great chapel
			   of the Virgin of Pilar.

IV	S.	1. Platico de oro,
		       orilla de cristal,
			Plate of gold,
			   bordered with crystal,

		2. que se quiten, que se
		       quiten,
		       de la puerta principal.
			That they keep away, that
			   they keep away
			   from the main entrance.

NOTES

Perf:

The pulse is steady in st. I only.
The soloist is slightly flat at the cadence of st. II, and the chorus continues at the pitch level established at this cadence.
III - Some members of the chorus enter early, and all are not singing together for the first few pulses.
IV - The soloist cannot remember the words of the last phrase. After a slight hesitation, several girls speak rather than sing *de la puerta principal.*

Text:

Marisola is a contraction of María (Mary) and *sola* (alone).

III.2 - The reference is probably to the cathedral of Nuestra Señora del Pilar at Saragossa, Spain, or to a chapel connected with this church at which students could receive instruction. The Virgen del Pilar is the most venerated of the Spanish apparitions of the Virgin Mary. Tradition has it that during her lifetime the Virgin appeared to the Apostle St. James (Santiago) while he was praying on the bank of the Ebro River at Saragossa. St. James then built a shrine to the Virgin. In the cathedral later constructed at the believed location of the shrine, there is an image of the Virgin placed on top of a marble pillar, whence the name Virgen del Pilar (March 1911:83).

The Game:

The girls form a circle with the girl playing the part of Marisola in the center. Marisola kneels. The girls in the ring skip in one direction or another during the singing of the song. At the end of the song all run away from Marisola, who rises and chases them. Whomever she catches becomes Marisola in the repetition of the game.

In the game as played in Evitar, no action takes place which is related to the text of st. I.2. Such action does take place in a version played in Bogotá (information obtained in interview with Edelma Masa Zapata by Delia Zapata Olivella, April 1972). In this version two girls kneel at Marisola's sides and hold the hem of her skirt in their hands. While singing *abriendo una rosa* (opening a rose), the girls holding Marisola's skirt raise and spread it; while singing *cerrando un clavel* (closing a carnation), they lower the skirt to its original position.

Derivation:

I could not find analogues for TR 9, but in it one finds word associations, *rosa-clavel* (rose-carnation) and *oro-cristal* (gold-crystal), which are commonplace in the Spanish repertory. Thus in TR 9 one finds

I. 2. abriendo una rosa   Opening a rose
          y cerrando un clavel.   and closing a carnation.

and from the sixteenth-century game "Herrito de oro traigo" (Rodríguez Marín 1932:58)

          que me parece una rosa   Seems to me a rose
          escogida entre un clavel.   preferred to a carnation.

In TR 9 one finds

IV. 1. Platico de oro,   Plate of gold,
          orilla de cristal,   bordered with crystal,

and in a single game, "Atocha.---Carabí" (Córdoba y Oña 1948:I:102, no. 90) the same association of words occurring twice.

Con peinecito de oro   With a comb of gold
y horquillas de cristal.   And hairpins of crystal.

La caja era de oro,   The box was of gold,
la tapa de cristal.   The lid of crystal.

TR 10 (LF 185.3) "Mirón, mirón, mirón"

Sung by a group of girls and boys. Recorded by Winston Caballero
Salguedo and Héctor Díaz Herazo. Evitar, 20 October 1968.

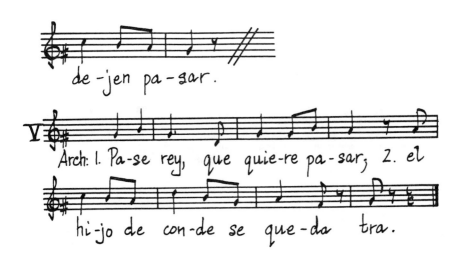

de-jen pa-sar.

Arch: 1. Pa-se rey, que quie-re pa-sar; 2. el

hi-jo de con-de se que-da tra.

			Spanish	English
I	A.	1.	Mirón, mirón, mirón ¿de dónde viene esta gente?	Onlooker, onlooker, onlooker, where do these people come from?
	F.	2.	Mirón, mirón, mirón, de San Pablo Vicente.	Onlooker, onlooker, onlooker, from San Pablo Vicente.

(The refrain *Mirón, mirón, mirón* is sung before each subsequent numbered line.)

			Spanish	English
II	A.	1.	¿Qué vendrán a buscar?	What do you want?
	F.	2.	Que nos dejen pasar.	That you let us pass through.
III	A.	1.	La puertacita está quebrada.	The archway has fallen down.
	F.	2.	Mándala componer.	Order that it be repaired.
IV	A.	1.	¿Con qué dinero?	With what money?
	F.	2.	Con cascaritas de huevo.	With eggshells.
	A.	1.	Pase el rey, él que quiere pasar;	The King may pass through and whoever may wish to;
		2.	el hijo del conde se queda atrás.	The son of the Count must remain behind.

NOTES

Perf:

The part of the Arch (A.) is initially sung by two girls, but in st. III-V it is sung by one girl only. A group of children sing the part of the File (F.).

One or two children who cannot yet carry a tune are heard in st. II-IV.

In st. II most of the children singing the File part begin to laugh, and only one child completes the verse.

V- The singer is interrupted by talking in the next-to-last measure of the song.

Text:

Although the refrain, *Mirón, mirón, mirón,* has lexical meaning in the Spanish language, the repeated word from which it is formed has no relation to the action of the game and therefore functions in the same manner as meaningless or "nonsense" syllables.

II.1 - The literal meaning of *¿Qué vendrán a buscar?* is "What are you going to come to look for?"

The Game:

Two of the larger children entwine their fingers and form the archway. The other children stand in a file leading to the arch. At first the two children making up the arch hold their grasped hands in front of them so that no one in the file can pass. As they sing *Que pase el rey* (The King may pass through), they raise their arms and the children in the file walk through the arch thus made. As the archmakers sing *se queda atrás* (must remain behind), they drop their arms, imprisoning the child passing through at that moment.

The archmakers have secretly agreed upon names for each other: moon and sun, mango and *aguacate,* or names of other fruits. The child who was caught is taken aside where the others cannot hear and is asked to choose between the two names previously selected. He then takes his place behind the individual whose secret name he has chosen and holds onto his or her waist.

In the meantime, those who had passed through the arch have circled back and taken their place at the end of the file. The game is repeated until all children have been caught and have chosen sides. The children are now arranged in two files extending back of the two archmakers. All but the archmakers are holding onto the waists of those in front of them. The two children forming the arch continue to have their fingers entwined. A tug-of-war now takes place. The game ends when either of the archmakers has been pulled into the position formerly occupied by the other.

Derivation:

Of the children's game songs, the greater number of analogues can be found for TR 10 ("Mirón, mirón, mirón"). Analogue 10 is a sixteenth-century text taken from "Baile de la Maya," which functions as a prelude to the play *La guarda cuidadosa* by Miguel Sánchez. Analogue 11 is a text taken from a twentieth-century work on Spanish folklore.

Analogue 10, sixteenth century (Sánchez n.d.:2)

---Hola, lirón, lirón,	Hello! dormouse, dormouse,
¿de dónde venís de andare?	From where have you walked?
---Hola, lirón, lirón,	Hello! dormouse, dormouse,
de San Pedro el altare.	From San Pedro *el altare*.

(The refrain ¡*Hola! lirón, lirón* is
sung before each subsequent line.)

---¿Qué os dijo don Roldane?	What did Don Roldane tell thee?
---Que no debéis de pasare.	That we could not pass.
---Quebradas son las puentes.	The bridges are fallen.
---Mandadlas adobare.	Order them to be rebuilt.
---No tenemos los dineros.	We do not have the money.
---Nosotros los daremos.	We will give it to you.
---¿De qué son los dineros?	Of what is this money?
---De cáscaras de huevos.	Of eggshells.

etc.

The literal meaning of the fourth line---*Que no debéis de
pasare*--is "That you canst not pass." This response utilizing the
second person is appropriate in Spanish. In English a response in
the first person is more idiomatic.

Analogue 11, Asturias (Cabal 1925:39)

---A la limón, a la limón,	To the lemon (tree),
	to the lemon (tree),
la puente se ha caído.	The bridge has fallen down.
---A la limón, a la limón,	To the lemon (tree),
	to the lemon (tree),
mandadla componer.	Order it to be repaired.

(The refrain *A la limón, a la limón*
is sung after each subsequent line.)

---No tenemos dinero.	We do not have money.
---Nosotros lo tenemos.	We have it.
---¿De qué es ese dinero?	Of what is this money?
---De cáscaras de huevo.	Of eggshells.
---Pasen los caballeros!	The gentlemen may pass!
---Nosotros pasaremos!	We shall pass!

A version collected in Santander (Córdoba y Oña 1948:1:23, no. 1)
has as a refrain *Al álimon, al álimon*. The first line contains
el puente rather than *la puente*, and the fourth line has *mandadle*
rather than *mandadla*. The remainder is the same as the version from
Asturias except for an additional final strophe, which is not given
here since it is not analogous to the content of TR 10.

COMMENTARY

As a matter of convenience I have offered Spanish textual analogues during the presentation of Colombian songs. Discussion of the musical sources will be deferred until later in this chapter. At this point I shall compare and differentiate the ten Colombian items and establish any relationships existing between them. I shall first consider the texts.

Three characteristics distinguish the lullabies from the children's songs. In the lullabies the first and second verses are almost without exception repeated, as are the third and fourth verses. This repetition is usually, but not always, exact. No such repetition is found in the children's songs. The only repetition of meaningful text is a half verse in TR 6. The content of the lullaby is less stable; the verses do not appear in predetermined order as in the children's songs. The singer of a lullaby enjoys much greater latitude. Although the quatrains of which the lullabies are composed are traditional, they do not customarily appear in a set sequence. Some may be related in theme and may therefore appear in a certain order within the lullaby as a whole. Other quatrains in the repertory of the singer may not be related in theme. The non-related quatrains or the groups of quatrains which are related may be sung in any order or not at all in a particular performance. The content of a lullaby may therefore differ at each singing.

Finally, some of the lullabies are related in content. TR 1 and TR 2 are related through a similar first strophe, as is TR 5, which was sung while the informant was reading from a transcription of TR 2. TR 3 and TR 4 show no thematic relationship to the other lullabies, but they are themselves versions of the same textual theme. In contrast, none of the children's songs are related in content.

A metrical analysis (syllable count) of the realized texts of all items presented in this chapter is given in table 1. The methods employed in the metrical analysis of Spanish poetry are discussed in chapter 6 (V.A.) and are followed by a statement of the procedures applied in this particular study (V.A.7). Syllable count is indicated in the following manner in table 1 only. The example is from TR 8 (st. II).

1.	Un joven de Cuba	6 = 6 6 6 7
	me manda un papel,	6
2.	mandando a decir	6
	que me case con él.	7

When the final vowel or vowels of one verse and the initial vowel or vowels of a succeeding verse are considered to form a sinalefa, in each case a syllable is subtracted from the second of the two verses involved. This is indicated by underlining the number representing the syllable count of the verse from which the syllable was subtracted. The example is from TR 2 (st. III).

2.	La una en Sevilla	5 = 5 5
	y la otra en Cataca.	5

Table 1.   Metrical Analysis of the Texts of TR 1-10

TR 1					TR 2					TR 3				
I	5	6	6	6	I	5	6	6	6	I	6	6	6	6
II	5	4	5	5	II	5	5	6	6	II	5	6	6	6
III	5	4	5	5	III	5	5	5	5	III	5	6	6	6
IV	5	6	6	6	IV	5	6	6	6	IV	6	6	6	6
V	5	5			V	5	6	6	6	V	6	6	4	7
VI	5	6	6	6	VI	5	6	6	6					
VII	5	5	5	5	VII	6	7							

TR 4							TR 5						TR 6			
I	6	6	6	6			I	5	6	6	6-7		9	10	9	10
II	5	6	6	6			II	5	5	6	7		8	9		
III	5	6	5	7	4	6	III	5	5	5	5		8	8	12	8
							IV	5	6	6	6					
							V	5	5							

TR 7				TR 8					TR 9				
I	5	7		I	6	6	6	6	I	8	7	6	6
II	6	6		II	6	6	6	7	II	6-7	7	9	6
III	6	5		III	7	6	6	6	III	7	8	7	8
				IV	6	6	6	6	IV	5	6	8	8
TR 10					V	5	6	6	6					
I	7	8	7	7	VI	6	6	6	6					
II	7	7	7	7										
III	7	9	7	7										
IV	7	5	7	8										
V	4	7	6	6										

The most common verse form utilized in folk poetry in the
Spanish language is the quatrain. The most common rhyming scheme
employed in the quatrain is the rima romancera, abcb (Magis 1969:
465). (For a discussion of the quatrain form see chapter 6, V.C.1;
for a discussion of rhyme in Spanish poetry see V.B.) The ten
items presented in this chapter are divided into two groups, those
which display these characteristics and those which do not. In
the first group are found TR 1-5, TR 8-9, and TR 10. Only st. V of
TR 10 exhibits clearly the two characteristics of this grouping.
However, the remaining strophes, with the exception of II, parallel the rima romancera in that the second and fourth verses
rhyme. The repetition of the refrain, which forms the first and
third verses, cannot be considered to form a rhyme. This seems
sufficient justification for placing TR 10 in the first group.

The second group consists of TR 6-7. TR 6 may be described as
"through composed." TR 7 contains six verses, and there is no
clear rhyming scheme.

The octosyllabic is the most common verse length in folk poetry
in Spanish. Next in importance are the hexasyllabic and pentasyllabic. The heptasyllabic and the tetrasyllabic are considerably in the minority (Magis 1969:469). Of the first group of
items, those cast in the quatrain form, only two, TR 9 and TR 10,
contain octosyllabic verses and, on occasion, a verse of nine
syllables. Of the four verses in each quatrain, never more than
two are octosyllabic. All the lullabies, TR 1-5, and the children's song TR 8 display primarily hexasyllabic and pentasyllabic
verses. The children's songs TR 9 and TR 10 contain in the main
heptasyllabic verses. Of the two items in the second group,
TR 6 displays verses which are octosyllabic or of greater length.
TR 7, on the other hand, falls within the category of texts with
verses of lesser length than the octosyllabic.

On the basis of this examination of the texts, it can be
stated that the lullabies and the majority of the children's
songs recorded in Evitar are cast in quatrain form, display the
rhyming scheme abcb, and are characterized by a verse length
shorter than the octosyllabic. Of the three items in the other
group, TR 7 shares only one of these characteristics, TR 6 none
of them. In addition, TR 6 is seemingly a composed song.

Melodic relationships can be established between the lullabies
TR 1-3. TR 4 is also related melodically to the first three
lullabies, but the music has not been transcribed. Melodic rela-
tionships can also be established between the children's songs
TR 8-9 and TR 10. No relationships in textual content or theme
were found between the lullabies and the children's songs.
However, melodic relationships can be found between TR 1-3 and
TR 8.

Note that those items listed as displaying melodic relationships fall within the first and larger group of texts, those
exhibiting a verse length shorter than the octosyllabic. As
has been previously indicated, in these items each melodic phrase
encompasses two textual verses. That part of the melody sung to
each verse can therefore be represented by a single melodic cell.
(For a description of the method of deriving melodic cells see
chapter 6, IV.C.1 and IV.C.3.)

In general, the pulses, the primary and secondary metrical
accents, are considered to occur at a rate of from 50 to 80 per
minute. The following represent a pulse in the metrical signatures employed in the transcriptions in this chapter:

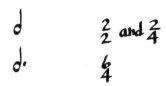

For the first two metrical signatures given, see TR 1 and TR 8,
respectively. For the third signature, 6/4, see TR 2, st. I.

Table 2 lists the melodic cells derived from all strophes transcribed of TR 1-2, TR 5, and TR 8-10. Although three strophes of
TR 3 were transcribed, they are omitted from consideration in
deriving the melodic cells. The singer had difficulty in initially
establishing her pitch level. She ran into further difficulties
in adapting a melody previously sung to one text to a second text.
The variations thus produced are not useful in establishing relationships with the other items analyzed.

St. I-III and st. IV-VI of TR 8 are sung to different melodies,
as are st. I-IV and st. V of TR 10. This is indicated by dividing
each of these items into two parts, marked A and B, respectively.
Only st. I, II, and V of TR 10 were transcribed.

Table 2. List of Melodic Cells

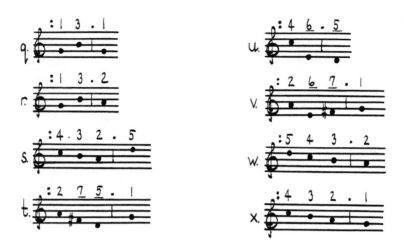

Table 3 indicates the formal organization of TR 1-2, TR 5, TR 8A-8B, TR 4, and TR 10A-10B according to their constituent melodic cells. In the lullabies both the first and second verses of the strophe are repeated, and the combination of melodic cells used in singing the first verse is different from that employed in singing the second verse. This is true in all cases but st. V of TR 1, where the same verse is sung thrice, and st. VII of TR 2, which the singer does not complete. On the other hand, the verses of the strophes of the children's songs are not repeated, and the melody of each strophe is represented by only four cells.

Table 3. Composition of Items by Melodic Cells

TR 1			TR 2			TR 5		
	1	2		1	2		1	2
I	a b a b	c b c b	I	a b d b	e f e g	I	j k j k	l k l k
II	a b a b	c b c b	II	h b d b	e f e g	II	j m j m	l k l k
III	a b a b	c b c b	III	i b d b	e f e g	III	j k j k	l k l k
IV	a b a b	c b c b	IV	h b d b	e f e g			
V	a b	c b	V	i b d b	e f e g			
VI	a b a b	c b c b	VI	i b d b	e f e g			
VII	a b a b	c b c b	VII	h b d b	e			

TR 8A		TR 8B		TR 9		TR 10A		TR 10B	
I	a b n o	IV	q r s t	I	q r s t	I	j w h x	V	q r s t
II	a b p o	V	q r u v	II	q r s t	II	j w h x		
III	a b n o	VI	q r s t						

TR 1-2 and TR 8A are related through the first musical phrase of st. I, which is composed of the melodic cells ab.

$$ab =: 1\ 3\ 5\ .\ 4 + :\ 3\ 1\ \underline{6}\ .\ \underline{5}$$

This occurs in all strophes of TR 1 and TR 8A. In TR 1 the melodic cell b also forms the second half of each musical phrase. In TR 2 it serves throughout as the melodic cadence pattern for both the first verse and its modified repetition.

TR 8B, TR 9, and TR 10B are related through a sequence of four melodic cells, qrst, which represent two musical phrases or an entire musical strophe.

$$qr =: 1\ 3\ .\ 1 + :\ 1\ 3\ .\ 2$$
$$st =: 4\ 3\ 2\ .\ 5 + :\ 2\ \underline{7}\ \underline{5}\ .\ 1$$

An exception to the above is st. V. of 8B, in which the melodic cells uv are seen rather than the cells st.

TR 5 and TR 10A are related through a single melodic cell,

$$j =: 5\ .\ 5.$$

This melodic cell is found in each strophe of the lullaby TR 5, and is of course repeated. TR 2 and TR 10A are also related through a single melodic cell,

$$h =: 4\ .\ 4.$$

None of the textual analogues presented in the first part of this chapter were sung to melodies similar to those employed in singing the Colombian texts. Thus no analogous full melodic strophes are found in the Spanish repertory. This is not an unusual situation. The association of a particular text and a particular melody is frequently dissolved in transmission. In addition, music, an abstract rather than a lexical form of communication, seems to be varied in transmission and diffusion to a greater degree than poetry. However, stylistic relationships are often maintained. Thus the Spanish repertory displays a large number of melodic patterns which are analogous to those found in the Colombian melodies, and it is at this level that comparison will be most fruitful.

In determining which melodic patterns found in the two repertories are analogous, I utilized for purposes of comparison the applicable melodic cells listed in table 2. Again, the pulses determined by metronomic markings occur approximately 50 to 80 times per minute. When no metronomic marking was offered, I used my best judgment in establishing the tempo. The meter 4/4 was treated in the same manner as 2/2 and 2/4 in the Colombian material, a half note equaling one beat. When metrical signatures displaying ternary divisions were encountered, the following durational values were considered to equal one beat:

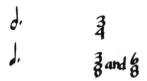

The application of these principles is illustrated in ex.1
(Córdoba y Oña 1948:1:29, no. 8, m. 1-2), ex. 2 (Córdoba y Oña
1948:1:62, no. 51, m. 7-8), and ex. 3 (Gomme and Sharpe 1909:1:8,
no. 928, m. 7-8).

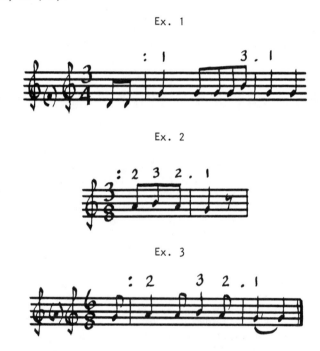

Ex. 1

Ex. 2

Ex. 3

    Those melodic cells for which analogues were found in the
Spanish repertory are listed below. The melodic cells listed
under "Initial" are those found in the first half of a musical
phrase of the items in the Colombian repertory; those marked
"Cadential" are found in the second half of a musical phrase in
that repertory.

Initial	Cadential
d = : 1 . 2	f = : 5 7 2 . 1
j = : 5 . 5	o = : 2 3 2 . 1
k = : 3 2 . 1	r = : 1 3 . 2
l = : 1 2 . 3	w = : 5 4 3 . 2
	x = : 4 3 2 . 1

A list of the analogous melodic cells found in the Spanish repertory is offered in table 4. The abbreviations employed refer to the
following publications:

CO I	Córdoba y Oña 1948, Vol. I
CO III	Córdoba y Oña 1948, Vol. III
Gil I	Gil García 1961, Vol. I
Sch	Schneider 1948

Information concerning the occurrence of each melodic cell is given
as follows, from left to right:
1. The number assigned to the transcription in the publication
   in which it is found. This is followed by a colon.
2. Following the colon is the number(s) of the page(s) on which
   the transcription is located. In Gil I this number refers
   to the music section of the volume, which is paginated
   separately.
3. After a space there follows a digit representing the number
   of times the melodic cell appears in the transcription.
   Repetitions caused by repeat signs in the music are not
   counted.
4. In some cases a melodic cell may appear in a different
   position. One which appears in the Colombian repertory in
   initial position may occur in the Spanish repertory in
   cadential position and thus be marked (C). In the reverse
   circumstance the marking is (I). When a melodic cell
   appears in initial position and is repeated immediately,
   the second occurrence is also counted as initial. When a
   melodic cell occurring first in a cadential position is
   immediately repeated, the repetition is counted as cadential.

Table 4.   Analogues of Melodic Cells

Initial Melodic Cells		Cadential Melodic Cells	
c = : 1 . 2		k = : 3 2 . 1	
CO I 75:84	2	Sch 16a:36-37	2
94:104	2		

Initial Melodic Cells

j = : 5 . 5

CO I	28:44	5
	113:117	1
	129:130	1
	134:135	3
	142:141	3
	223:218	2
	228:221	1
CO III	351:362	6

q = : 1 3 . 1

CO I	6:28	1
	8:29	4
	176:176	2
	267:250	3
	318:292	2
	319:293	1

l = : 1 2 . 3

Sch	3f:24-25	2
CO I	12:31	2
	96:106	2 (C)
	100:108	2
	106:112	3
	131:132	2
	132:133	2
	134:135	1
	141:141	2
	162:161	2
	168:166	4
	175:173	2
	197:196	1
	228:221	1
	273:256	1 (C)
	294:275	4

Cadential Melodic Cells

k = : 3 2 . 1 (cont.)

CO I	107:113	1
	108:113	3
	116:119	3
	127:128	1
	154:153	2
	168:166	3
	175:173	1
	238:228	1
	264:247	4 (I)
	269:252	1
	273:256	1

o = : 2 3 2 . 1

Sch	1f:20-21	1 (I)
CO I	2:24	5
	51:62	2
	226:220	1
	294:275	2
	336:307	4 (I)

r = : 1 3 . 2

CO I	25:41	1 (I)
	108:113	5 (I)
	272:255	2 (I)
	279:263	2 (I)

w = : 5 4 3 . 2

CO I	138:139	2
	190:188	1

x = : 4 3 2 . 1

CO I	35:50	3
	36:50	2
	104:111	1
	112:116	2

Cadential Melodic Cells

x = : 4 3 2 . 1 (cont.)

132:133	3
134:135	1
162:161	1
270:253	3
276:257	1

In the great majority of cases only one analogous melodic cell is found in each transcription, although, as indicated, it may occur a number of times in the strophe. However, two analogues were found of a full musical phrase as sung in the Colombian repertory. Both are of the following:

1k = : 1 2 . 3 + : 3 2 . 1

Ex. 4 (TR 5, st. II, m. 7-8) is from the costeño repertory, ex. 5 (CO I 168:166 m. 5-8) and ex. 6 (CO I 175:173 m. 1-4) are taken from the Spanish repertory.

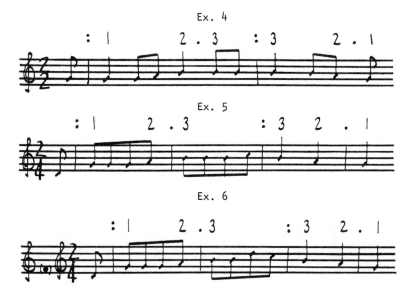

Ex. 4

Ex. 5

Ex. 6

In addition to the above, the following musical phrases composed of an initial and a cadential melodic cell are found in the Spanish repertory. The individual cells of which the musical phrases are composed are also found in the Colombian repertory, but not in these particular combinations (see table 3).

lo = : 1 2 . 3 + : 2 3 2 . 1
1x = : 1 2 . 3 + : 4 3 2 . 1

The first combination of cells is found in ex. 7 (CO I 2:24 m. 13-16), the second in ex. 8 (CO I 132:133 m. 9-12).

Ex. 7

Ex. 8

The second combination of melodic cells, 1x, is also found in CO I 162:163 m. 11-14.

As previously indicated, a melodic cell which functions as the initial part of a musical phrase in the Colombian repertory may on occasion serve as the cadential part of a phrase in the Spanish repertory. The reverse, a cadential melodic cell serving as the initial part of a musical phrase, also occurs. The first phenomenon can be seen in ex. 9 (CO I 273:256), the second in ex. 10 (CO I 108: 113 m. 1-4).

Ex. 9

Ex. 10

The entire strophe of ex. 9 is reproduced. It contains the two melodic cells which were found in ex. 5-6. However, in ex. 9 not only are the two melodic cells separated one from another, but the first of the two, 1 = : 1 2 . 3, is found in cadential rather than in initial position in the musical phrase. In ex. 10 the melodic cell r = : 1 3 . 2, which is utilized in cadential position in the Colombian repertory, is here found in initial position.

In ex. 11 (Sch 1f:20-21) the initial melodic cell, o = : 2 3 2. 1, repeated and varied by the addition of a lower neighboring tone, forms the basis of the greater part of a song.

Ex. 11

The melody of CO I 336:307 is built up in a similar fashion from the same melodic cell. It is a lullaby sung by a girl to her doll.

When the contours of the full musical phrases are reduced to skeletal form, that is, to skeletal patterns, further analogues can be established in the Spanish repertory. (For a description of the method of deriving skeletal patterns see chapter 6, IV.C.4.) Table 5 is a list of skeletal patterns derived from the items presented in the first part of this chapter for which analogues were found in the Spanish repertory. In this case the item or items of the Colombian repertory from which the skeletal patterns were derived are given, as are the measures of the transcriptions of the Spanish repertory in which the analogous skeletal patterns are found.

Table 5.   Analogues of Skeletal Patterns

1.   TR 1 II   2   c + b = : 1 . 2 : 3 . <u>5</u>
        CO I   75:84   1   m. 5-8

2.   TR 5 I   1   j + k = : 5 . 5 : 3 . 1
        CO I   275:257   1   m. 5-8
                 281:265   1   m. 1-4

3.   TR 5 I   2   l + k = : 1 . 3 : 3 . 1
        CO I   20:37   2   m. 1-4, 5-8
                 117:120   1   m. 14-17
                 168:166   4   m. 5-8, 11-14,
                                                        17-20, 25-28
                 175:173   1   m. 1-4

4.   TR 5 II   1   j + m = : 5 . 5 : 5 . 1
        CO I   21:38   2   m. 1-4, 5-8
                 33:49   1   m. 5-8
                 61:70   1   m. 1-4

5.   TR 8A I   2   n + o = : 4 . 3 : 2 . 1
     TR 8A II   2   p + o = : 4 . 3 : 2 . 1
        Sch   11a:32-33   2   m. 1-2, 2-4
        CO I   97:106   4   m. 1-4, 5-8,
                                                        17-20, 21-24
                 135:136   1   m. 5-8
                 138:139   2   m. 29-32, 37-40
                 142:141   2   m. 15-18, 5-8
                 233:224   1   m. 13-16
                 247:234   1   m. 5-8
                 267:250   3   m. 21-24, 25-28,
                                                        29-32
                 268:251   4   m. 1-4, 5-8,
                                                        9-12, 13-16

6.   TR 8B, TR 11B   q + c = : 1 . 1 : 1 . 2
        Sch   14d:34-35   1   m. 1-4
        CO I   237:227   3   m. 1-4, 9-12,
                                                        17-20
                 257:241   1   m. 1-4
                 267:250   3   m. 1-4, 9-12,
                                                        17-20

It can now be seen that although the Spanish repertory does not contain analogous full melodic strophes, a large number of melodic patterns can be found which are similar to those utilized in the songs sung in Evitar. Since these songs are sung in Spanish and have many elements in common, Spain would seem their most likely source. However, almost all the analogues listed are from collections made in northern and central Spain. As far as can be determined, there are no published collections containing transcriptions of children's songs from Andalucía. Of the four lullabies published by Schneider in which analogous melodic patterns were found, only one was collected in Andalucía. The others were collected in northern Spain. Only one analogous melodic pattern was found among the lullabies and children's songs from Extremadura published in the two volumes by Gil García. The great bulk of the listed analogous melodic patterns are contained in the transcriptions published by Córdoba y Oña in two volumes of his *Cancionero popular de Santander*. Santander is located in north central Spain and borders on the Bay of Biscay, which has France as its other shore.

It has been my observation that many Western European children's songs share stylistic elements. Evitar is located in the Caribbean coastal area of Colombia. It thus probably shares some traits of the Caribbean region as a whole, and this cultural area has been affected by English and French colonization as well as Spanish.

I have therefore applied the same analytic techniques to a small body of English and French children's songs. Five sources were utilized. The first three are believed to be representative of the English repertory, the fourth and fifth of the French. They are as follows:

Go I	Gomme	1894, Vol. I
Go II	Gomme	1894, Vol. II
Go 1	Gomme and Sharp	1909, Set 1
Marie	Marie	1975
Widor	Widor	1927

In some of the above sources the transcriptions as such are not numbered. In these cases the page numbers only are given following the colon.

Table 6. Melodic Cell Analogues in the English
and French Repertories

Initial			Cadential		
c = : 1 . 2			k = : 3 2 . 1		
Go II	:24	4 (2C)	Widor	:36	1
j = : 5 . 5			o = : 2 3 2 . 1		
Go II	:34	1	Marie	1:47	2 (1)

Initial (cont.)			Cadential (cont.)		
1 = : 1 2 . 3			x = : 4 3 2 . 1		
Widor	:20	2	Go I	:28	4
	:21	2	Go II	:41	1
			Widor	:25	2

Only one skeletal pattern, n + o or p + o = : 4 . 3 : 2 . 1,
is found in the small repertory examined. It is found in ex. 12
(Widor 39 m. 1-8), where it occurs twice as the second half of
the A part of an ABA form.

Ex. 12

This skeletal pattern forms part of a melodic formula with a
wide distribution, particularly in children's songs. Versions of
this formula,

: 1 . 5 : 6 . 5 + : 4 . 3 : 2 . 1

appear in Austria and France as early as the middle of the eighteenth century. It forms the basis of melodies to which children's
songs are sung in English, French, German, Italian, and Spanish.
The melodic formula is known both in print and in the oral tradition (List 1978:34).
    The songs recorded in Evitar presented in this chapter repre-
sent two social functions, those of lulling a child to sleep and
of accompanying a children's game. In the above discussion I have
attempted to find textual and melodic analogues in Spanish, English, and French repertories serving the same functions. The
following conclusions can be derived from the analyses made.

Texts

    Analogous textual strophes are found in the Spanish repertory
for the majority of the songs sung in Evitar. These analogues
not only are similar in content but take the same form, that of
the quatrain. Where no strophic analogues were seen, it was
possible in one case to offer analogous textual commonplaces
which are utilized in both the Spanish and Colombian repertories.
Although there was always interaction between the mother country,
Spain, and its colonies, migration was primarily from Spain to the
New World, not the reverse, and it is the carriers of tradition
who diffuse folksong. Texts utilizing similar topics and motifs
can undoubtedly be found in the repertories of other European

countries, but such texts would not be couched in idioms peculiar
to the Spanish language. We can therefore assume that some of
the song texts, or parts thereof, had their actual origin in
Spain. Those which may have developed independently in Colombia
or elsewhere in the New World still conform to Spanish tradition.

Melodies

Although a large number of Spanish migrants to the New World
came from southern Spain, from Andalucía and Extremadura, there
is little evidence of influence of the music of these regions
upon the style of the melodies of the songs sung to and by
children in Evitar. Certainly those characteristic rhythmic and
melodic patterns, those scalar structures we associate with the
cante jondo and *flamenco* of Andalucía, are not evident. Rather,
the available evidence links the melodies of the songs offered
in chapter 7 with northern Spain or, more likely, with a
general Western European tradition diffused through the Caribbean
region by English and French colonists, as well as those of
Spanish origin.

8. Velorio de angelito

This chapter is concerned with the song games played by the adults at the wake for a child. A detailed description of the velorio de angelito is given in chapter 3 (pp. 96-99) the games are played by a mixed group of men and women, and in the singing in each case there is an alternation of solo and chorus parts. Most frequently the solo part of the song is sung by the leader of the game, the chorus part by the rest of the partici- pants. In other games the solo part may be sung by an individual other than the leader or by a couple. The chorus may sing a re- frain, or it may alternate with the soloist in singing the verses of the song. The alternation of solo and chorus parts is not strictly observed. The soloist will on occasion join in singing the refrain, and the chorus may join the soloist in singing part or all of a verse. As the night wears on the men become drunk, and there is a further decrease in the delineation of the two parts.

All the songs are sung without accompaniment, with the excep- tion of "A pilar el arroz" (TR 10-11). In this one game each participant holds a bamboo pole, which he or she beats against the ground while singing and dancing. Of the song games recorded and here presented, five were sung by more than one individual, and thus the parts for solo and chorus are differentiated in the tran- scription of the music. Three performances were by a single in- dividual, who sang both the solo and chorus parts. The two parts are therefore not separately indicated in the transcription of the music. A differentiation between solo and chorus parts is made in the realized text to indicate the alternation of parts usually heard when the game is actually played. These game songs are on occasion sung out of context by an individual for his own enjoyment or that of others. Thus the songs in the latter form are not unknown in the village.

In chapter 7 three variants were presented of one lullaby (TR 1-2 and 5) and two variants of a second (TR 3-4). Considerable variation was also seen in the melodies to which these lullabies were sung, particularly in the first group. The inclusion of variants permits the assessment of the degree of stability or var- iation displayed in performing the genre. In the present chapter two variants each of two game songs, "A pilar el arroz" and "Azúcar," are offered and will serve the same purpose.

256

TR 11 (LF 78.7) "A pilar el arroz"

Sung by Simón Herrera Sánchez and Rosa Luisa Martínez. Evitar,
1 November 1964.

S.   1. Y Rosa Luisa que lo mató,   And it was Rosa Luisa who
                                                      killed him,

Ch.   Santo del día, lloro yo.   Saint of the day, I weep.

S.   2. Perfecto Martínez que le   It was Perfecto Martínez who
             enterró,   buried him,

Ch.   Santo del día, lloro yo,   Saint of the day, I weep,

(The choral refrain is repeated after each subsequent line.)

S.   3. E Felicia Polo que lo   It was Felicia Polo who
         llamó,   called him,

      4. Y Senî que lo lavó,   And it was Senî who washed
                                          him,

      5. Roberto Payare que lo   It was Roberto Payare who
         atendió,   took care of him,

      6. Lonardo Padilla lo llamó,   Lonardo Padilla called him,

      7. El compañero Polo mató,   My friend Polo killed him,

      8. Y papa Israel que lo   And it was Papa Israel who
         llamó,   called him,

      9. *Ay*, Rosa Luisa lo   Rosa Luisa took care of him,
         atendió,

     10. Martín Padilla lo llamó,   Martín Padilla called him,

     11. Y Basilisa lo lavó,   And Basilisa washed him,

     12. Y Patricia que lo   And it was Patricia who took
         atendió,   care of him,

     13. Y mama Riqueta lo bailó,   And Mama Riqueta danced him,

     14. Allí que lo atendió,   It was there that he (she)
                                          took care of him,

     15. Y Felipe lo llamó,   And Felipe called him,

     16. Y Carlos Julio lo bañó,   And Carlos Julio bathed him,

     17. El primo hermano lo   His first cousin took care
         atendió,   of him,

     18. Manuel Cachito lo golpeó,   Manuel Cachito struck him,

     19. *M-e* lloro yo,   I weep,

     20. Rosa María lo atendió,   Rosa María took care of him,

     21. Madrina Libera lo bañó,   My godmother Libera bathed
                                          him,

     22. ¡Y como Aurora lo   And how Aurora took care of
         atendió!   him!

NOTES

Perf:

The solo part of "A pilar el arroz" (Hulling the Rice) is sung
by Herrera, the refrain (which in the playing of the game would be
sung by all the other participants) by Martínez. Both Herrera and
Martínez pound bamboo poles against the floor as they sing. The
recording was made indoors, in the old schoolhouse for girls.

The beating of the poles against the floor by the two singers
is not in a steady rhythm. They are not always together, and at

Fig. 74. Girls hulling rice

times the beating of only one pole can be heard. Nor does the
singing display a steady pulse. Under these circumstances it
was impossible to accurately transcribe what occurs. I therefore
have arbitrarily indicated a steady beat of the poles and organized the vocal parts on this basis.

The pitch level rises very gradually throughout the performance
and is almost a quarter tone higher at the end than at the beginning.

The solo part of the song is improvised in such a manner that
each line ends on an accented o, that is, an $\acute{o}$. This is not
difficult to accomplish in Spanish, since most verbs in the preterite past tense, third person singular end with this accented
vowel.

In the improvisation, joking references are made to participants
in the game or to other individuals in the village. Thus in v. 1
Herrera sings that Rosa Luisa, who is singing the refrain, "is the
one who killed him."

Text:

The refrain is subject to another interpretation than that
given. There is a common costeño emphatic expression, *todo el
santo día,* meaning "all day long." Thus the refrain could be translated "I weep the whole day long."

The Game:

In the rural villages rice is still hulled by hand. Two women
or girls alternately pound the rice in a wooden mortar with two
long wooden pestles (fig. 74). The action of the game is in part
an imitation of this process. The participants form a large circle, each holding in his or her hand a pole of caña brava, a
heavy bamboo. Each player pounds his caña brava on the ground in
time to the singing, simultaneously dancing in a small circle,
or, rather, in a spiral, since the large circle rotates simultaneously.

The game is also played in Palenque, where it has greater
ceremonial significance and is played at the velorio for adults.
The participants are primarily women, and the game is played in
front of the altar, in the streets, and in the cemetery. The
players form a ring, as in Evitar, carry both pestles and sifters
woven of fiber, and pretend to be both hulling and sifting the
rice (Escalante 1954:290).

TR 12 (LF 97.7) "A pilar el arroz"

Sung by Abraham Herrera Pacheco and a group of women: Marcelina
Sánchez Pimientel, Juana García Blanquiset, Basilisa Herrera
García, Ana María Pacheco, and Juana Pérez. Evitar, 8 November
1964.

S.	1. A pilar el arroz, lloro yo,	To hull the rice, I weep,
Ch.	Santo del día, lloro yo.	Saint of the day, I weep.
S.	2. La pilada del arroz, lloro yo,	The hulling of the rice, I weep,
Ch.	Santo del día, lloro yo.	Saint of the day, I weep.

(The choral refrain is repeated after each subsequent line.)

S.	3. Manuel Pimientel pila el arroz, (2)	Manuel Pimientel hulls the rice,
	4. Juanita Pérez ventea el arroz,	Juanita Pérez winnows the rice,
	5. Marcelina Sánchez pila el arroz,	Marcelina Sánchez hulls the rice,
	6. Ya este pilón papó Dios,	This mortar of rice, God ate it,
	7. Este pilón papó Dios,	This mortar of rice, God ate it,

8. Este pilón, lo lloro yo,	This mortar of rice, I weep for it,
9. De este pilón, lo lloro yo,	This mortar of rice, I weep for it,
10. Porque en la acostada se murió,	Because he died while lying down,
11. Que en la acostada se murió,	He died while lying down,
12. Este pilón papó Dios,	This mortar of rice, God ate it,
13. A pilar el arroz, lloro yo, (2)	To hull the rice, I weep,
14. Este pilón papó Dios,	This mortar of rice, God ate it,
15. Ya que en la pilada se murió,	Since during the hulling, he died,
16. Que yo contigo pilo mejor, (2)	I hull better together with you,
17. De este pilón papó Dios,	Of this mortar of rice God ate,

(spoken) *je-pa*

| 18. Ya pilar el arroz, lloro yo, (2) | To hull the rice, I weep, |
| 19. Este pilón papó Dios, | This mortar of rice, God ate it, |

NOTES

Perf:

As in TR 11, a regular pulse is displayed in neither the beating of the poles on the ground nor the singing. Under these circumstances I have again indicated a regular recurrence of the poles striking the floor, and I have organized the vocal parts on this basis. However, it should be noted that the beat of the poles is more regular than in TR 11.

The soloist begins to raise his pitch level at the end of the first statement of v. 3, and the chorus follows his lead. By the end of v. 5 both solo and chorus are singing at a pitch level a semitone higher than that at which they began. The pitch level remains essentially constant from this point to the end of the performance.

As in TR 11 the leader again ends each verse on an accented *ó*. However, in this case the rhyme is assonantal rather than consonantal.

Text:

6. - *Papó* is the preterite past tense, third person singular of
the verb *papar*, to swallow without chewing, as pap or gruel. *Pilón*
is the mortar in which the rice is hulled. In this case the term
represents the rice contained in the mortar. Rice, as one of the
principal staples of the rural costeño, symbolizes life.

The Game:

TR 11 and TR 12 are different versions of a song utilized in
playing the same game.

Derivation:

The mortars and pestles used to hull rice in Evitar are similar
to those used in Africa (fig. 74). In Africa rice may also be
used to symbolize life either in this world or in the spiritual
world. A feast in honor of the deceased is celebrated by the
Kpelle of Liberia a few days after burial. A proper share of the
food for the departed is placed upon the grave. A bowl of rice,
a staple item in the local diet, always forms part of this offering
(data collected in the field by Ruth Stone).

TR 13 (LF 79.6) "Azúcar"

Sung by Marcelina Sánchez Pimientel. Evitar, 1 November 1964.

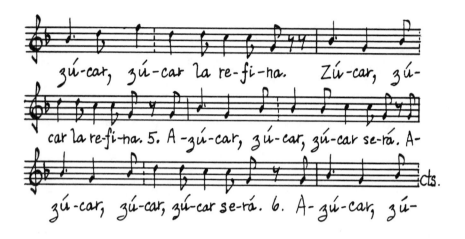

zú-car, zú-car la re-fi-na. Zú-car, zú-
car la re-fi-na. 5. A-zú-car, zú-car, zú-car se-rá. A-
zú-car, zú-car, zú-car se-rá. 6. A-zú-car, zú-

1.	Azúcar, azúcar me llamo yo. (2)	Sugar, sugar is my name.
2.	Azúcar, azúcar me puso el padre (2)	Sugar, the priest named me sugar
3.	cuando me metió la sal.	When he gave me the salt.
4.	Azúcar, azúcar, la refinada. (2)	Sugar, sugar, the refined kind.
5.	Azúcar, azúcar, azúcar será. (2)	Sugar, sugar, sugar I will be.
6.	Azúcar, azúcar, la refinada.	Sugar, sugar, the refined kind.
7.	Azúcar, la refinada.	Sugar, the refined kind.
8.	Azúcar, azúcar, azúcar será.	Sugar, sugar, sugar I will be.
9.	Azúcar, azúcar me llamo yo.	Sugar, sugar is my name.
10.	Azúcar, azúcar me han de llamar.	Sugar, they have to call me sugar.
11.	Azúcar me puso el padre,	The priest named me sugar,
12.	Azúcar, cuando me metió la sal.	Sugar, when he gave me the salt.
13.	Azúcar, azúcar, la refinada.	Sugar, sugar, the refined kind.
14.	Azúcar, azúcar, azúcar será. (2)	Sugar, sugar, sugar I will be.

Note: The first occurrence of *azúcar* in each line represents the choral refrain. When the verse is indented, as in lines 3, 7, and 11, the singer omitted the choral refrain.

NOTES

Perf:

In this game song the leader commonly begins with the refrain and often sings the refrain more or less simultaneously with the chorus

before beginning the next verse. Since Sánchez is singing both
the parts of the chorus and soloist, she finds it necessary on
occasion to omit a syllable or even a word in order to obtain
sufficient breath. Thus at times she omits the full refrain.

During v. 2 she begins to sing sharp, and she continues to
raise the pitch level throughout. The pitch level is almost a
semitone higher at the end of the transcription and nearly a whole
tone higher at the end of the performance.

In this song the refrain is two pulses in duration and the
verse three. In order to avoid changing the time signature measure
by measure, I have encompassed both refrain and verse in one measure, utilizing an additive signature (see chapter 5, I.E.2).

Text:

Since TR 13 is sung by only one singer, and the refrain is not
consistently repeated, I have not followed the scheme of punctuation and capitalization applied in songs cast in litanic verse.

The song is a long affirmation of the sweetness of the person
or persons singing.

1. - She is so sweet that she is named Sugar. Literally, she
calls herself or names herself Sugar.

2-3. - She is so sweet that at baptism the priest named her
Sugar as he placed salt in her mouth. The latter is one of the
symbolic acts of baptism, the salt representing the "salt of the
earth."

4. - She is as sweet as refined sugar, that is, white sugar,
not panela, the unrefined sugar in cake form commonly utilized by
the villagers.

5. - Literally, "sugar it will be." The meaning is that she
is as sweet as sugar and that sweet as sugar she will always be.

10. - She is so sweet that people are forced to call her Sugar.

The Game:

A circle is formed in which men and women alternate. Those in
the circle join hands and mark time to the song. Within the circle
a couple dances and sings. After each verse sung by the couple,
those in the ring respond with the refrain *Azúcar*. In dancing the
couple utilizes the motions of the cumbia (see p. 83). When the
two participants forming the couple within the ring have danced
and sung as long as they wish, they are replaced by another couple
and the game continues.

TR 14 (LF 97.10) "Azúcar"

Sung by Abraham Herrera Pacheco and a group of women: Marcelina
Sánchez Pimientel, Juana García Blanquiset, Basilisa Herrera García,
Ana María Pacheco, and Juana Pérez. Evitar, 8 November 1964.

S.	1. Mentira ha sido tu amor.	Your love has been a lie.
Ch.	Azúcar.	Sugar.
S.	2. Falso fue tu juramento.	False were your vows.
Ch.	Azúcar.	Sugar.

S.   3. Hojas que se lleva el   Leaves blown by the wind
         viento

Ch.   Azúcar.   Sugar.

S.   4. fue tu palabra de honor.   Were your words of honor.

Ch.   Azúcar.   Sugar.

(The chorus sings the refrain *Azúcar* throughout. When the
line of the soloist begins with the same word, and the line
is not indented, the soloist sings the refrain together--
but not necessarily simultaneously--with the chorus.)

S.   5. Azúcar, azúcar, azúcar será,   Sugar, sugar, sugar I will be,

      6. Azúcar, azúcar de la   Sugar, sugar, the refined
         refinada,   kind,

      7. Azúcar, azúcar, azúcar será,   Sugar, sugar, sugar I will be,

      8.   Azúcar de la   Sugar, the refined
         refinada, (4)   kind,

      9. Azúcar, azúcar, azúcar sera,   Sugar, sugar, sugar I will be,

      10.   Azúcar, azúcar sera,   Sugar, sugar I will be,

      11.   Azúcar de la   Sugar, the refined
         refinada, (2)   kind,

      12. Yo soy el gallo negro, (2)   I am the black cock,
      13. no sé que me irá a pasar.   I don't know what will
                                        happen to me.

      14. Me llevan para Bogotá,   They are taking me to Bogotá,
      15. sí, me roban de esta pueblo. Yes, they rob this village
                                        of me.

      16. Azúcar, azúcar, azúcar será, Sugar, sugar, sugar I will be,

      17.   Azúcar de la   Sugar, the refined
         refinada,   kind,

      18. Azúcar, azúcar, azúcar será, Sugar, sugar, sugar I will be,

      19.   Azúcar, azúcar   Sugar, sugar I will be,
         será, (2)

      20.   Azúcar, de la   Sugar, the refined
         refinada, (3)   kind,

      21. Azúcar, azúcar, azúcar será, Sugar, sugar, sugar I will be,

NOTES

Perf:

   Herrera's performance was influenced by the presence of Delia
Zapata Olivella, who acted as my intermediary and field assistant
in 1964. She was known throughout Colombia for her performances of
costeño folk dance on television and for her direction of *expectá-
culos,* staged performances by folk dancers and folk musicians both

Fig. 75. Contestadoras and cantante. Left to right: Ana María Pacheco, Juana Pérez, Marcelina Sánchez Pimientel, Basilisa Herrera García, Juana García Blanquiset, and Abrahama Herrera Pachecco.

in Colombia and abroad. Herrera thought she was still directing
a performing group in Bogotá (she was actually at that time residing
in Cali). He considered himself a talented performer and wished to
impress her. He therefore sang "Azúcar" as though it were a
bullerengue rather than a song game of the velorio de angelito,
inserting coplas in the flow of verses common to the song. This he
was able to do without difficulty, since the group of women singing
the refrain of the game was the same as that which sang the refrain
of bullerengues during the same recording session. (For a discussion of the copla see chapter 6, V.C.2; for examples of bullerengue
texts see TR 49-53.

   It should be noted that when the verses of the copla are being
sung, verse plus refrain equals four pulses. When the verses
common to the game are being sung, verse plus refrain equals five
pulses, as in TR 13. To this m. 13-18 are an exception.

   Text:

   The improvised second copla, v. 12-15, is a veiled suggestion
to Delia Zapata that she take him with her to join the performing
group he believed she had in Bogotá.

   The Game:

   The game is the same as in TR 13.

TR 15 (LF 79.5) "El florón"

Sung by Marcelina Sánchez Pimientel with accompanying cries by a
group of men. Evitar, 1 November 1964.

só. Por a-quí pa-só. Pa-só, pa-só, pa-só, pa-só, pa-

só, pa-só, pa-só, pa-só, pa-só, pa-só, pa-

só. Por a-quí pa-só, pa-só, pa-só.

S. 1. El florón está en la mano
    2. y en la mano está el
       florón. (c2)
    3. La patilla del sereno
    4. prima hermana del melón.

The *florón* is in my hand
And in my hand is the *florón*.

The watermelon of the *sereno*,
Cousin of the cantaloupe.

Ch. (R) Por aquí, pasó, pasó,
        pasó, etc.

This way, there it goes, there
   it goes, there it goes, etc.

Gr. ¡Allí va donde Reyes!
     ¡No pasó nadie!
     ¡No! ¡no pasó!
     ¡Allí va donde Roque!
     ¡Va para Santiago!
     ¡Acá está!
     ¡Va para él de la camisa!

     ¡Recibo!
     ¡Allí va para Tío Perucho!
     ¡La pasó él de Mahates!
     ¡La tiene Juan!

There it goes to Reyes!
No one passed it!
No! It wasn't passed!
There it goes to Roque!
It is going to Santiago!
Here it is!
It is going to the guy in
   the shirt!

I got it!
There it goes to Uncle Perucho!
The guy from Mahates passed it!
Juan has it!

NOTES

Perf:

   Beginning in the fifth staff, third measure, the tempo is slowly
accelerated, and the acceleration continues until the end of the
performance.
   The gritos (cries) begin in the first measure of the fifth staff
and continue thereafter, the last cry being heard after the singer
stops.

Text:

1. - *Florón* refers to the handkerchief or other piece of cloth
passed back and forth during the game.
3. - The term *sereno* is applied to crops planted during the dry
season in humid ground or ground subject to flooding. Such crops
depend for their maturation primarily upon the moisture provided by
the nocturnal dews of this tropical region. Thus *patilla de sereno*
is watermelon grown in this manner.

The Game:

The players sit on the ground in a circle, men and women alternating. The feet are drawn up part way, and the handkerchief is
passed back and forth under the knees. A single person in the
center of the ring sings v. 1-4 and then attempts to grab the handkerchief as it is being passed back and forth from one player to
another. Those in the circle sing the refrain, which is repeated
as many times as is necessary, or shout directions intended to
either assist or confuse the individual trying to locate the handkerchief. When the player within the ring gains possession of the
handkerchief, the person in whose hands it was last held replaces
him, and the game continues.

Derivation:

The following textual analogue is found in the Spanish repertory:

Analogue 1 (Gil II mus. 92:203)

El florín está en la mano,   The florin is in my hand,
y en la mano está el florín.   And in my hand is the florin.
De la tuya va a la mía,   From your hand it goes to mine,
de la mía ya pasó.   Now it has left mine.

The florin is an old, small coin which was used in Spain in the
past and was identified by a fleur-de-lis. The term was initially
applied to a gold coin minted in Florence, Italy which around 1500
became standard tender in Europe. The lily was Florence's insignia.
In Latin America a florón is a large paper flower. The term as
used in the game in the velorio de angelito is probably a corruption
of *florín*. A game song called "El florón" is also performed at a
velorio for a child in Puerto Rico (López Cruz 1967:173-74).

El florón pasó por aquí,   The *florón* went by here,
Yo no lo ví, yo no lo ví. (c2)   I did not see it, I did not
                                     see it.

In the Spanish children's song game "El florín" a pebble is passed
back and forth from hand to hand in back of the players in the
ring, and the child in the center must guess who has the pebble
(Gil García 1956 II:mus. 12). In the game as played in the velorio
in Puerto Rico, a handkerchief or other object is also passed back
and forth behind the players (López Cruz 1967:173-74). In Puerto
Rico a velorio for a white child is called a florón, that for a
child of color a *baquiné* (López Cruz 1967:164).

TR 16 (LF 79.3) "El loro y la lora"
Sung by Marcelina Sánchez Pimientel. Evitar, 1 November 1964.

1. E lo - roy la lo - ray 2. staban lo-re-
an - dol, lo - roy la lo - ray
sta-ban lo-re - an - do. 3. Yo por la
re - ja 4. sta-ba mi - ran - do,
Yo por la re - ja sta - ba mi -
ra. 5. —¿Qué se man-tie-ne? 6. —Con la
flor de ve - ra-no, —¿Con qué se man-
tie-ne? —Con la flor de ve-ra-no. 7. Tra-ba-ja, com-pa-
ñe-ro, 8. tra-ba-ja ¡u-rri - a___! 9. Tra-ba-

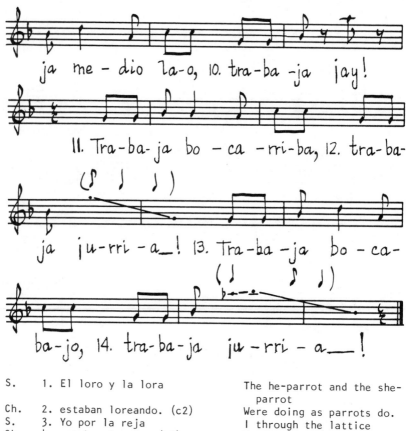

ja me - dio la-o, 10. tra-ba -ja ¡ay!

11. Tra-ba- ja bo - ca -rri-ba, 12. tra-ba-

ja ¡u-rri - a__! 13. Tra-ba -ja bo - ca-

ba-jo, 14. tra-ba-ja ¡u-rri - a__!

S.	1. El loro y la lora	The he-parrot and the she-parrot
Ch.	2. estaban loreando. (c2)	Were doing as parrots do.
S.	3. Yo por la reja	I through the lattice
Ch.	4. estaba mirando. (c2)	Was watching them.
S.	5. ¿Con que se mantienen?	What do they live on?
Ch.	6. Con la flor de verano. (c2)	On the flower of summer.
S.	7. Trabaja, compañero,	Work, partner,
Ch.	8. trabaja ¡urria!	Work!
S.	9. Trabaja medio lado,	Work to one side,
Ch.	10. trabaja ¡ay!	Work!
S.	11. Trabaja boca arriba,	Work looking up,
Ch.	12. trabaja ¡urria!	Work!
S.	13. Trabaja boca abajo,	Work looking down,
Ch.	14. trabaja ¡urria!	Work!

NOTES

Perf:

There is a slight increase in tempo at v. 5. The tempo then remains constant through the remainder of the performance.

Text:

1. - The *loro* is a small green parrot.
2. - The singer is watching the parrots mate. *Loreando* is a
verb form fashioned from the noun *loro* or *lora*.
V. 5-6 indicate that the parrots are nourished by the sexual im-
pulse rather than by food.
The section beginning with v. 7 is in double-entendre. The work
the partner is urged to carry on is coition. The terms *medio lado,
boca arriba,* and *boca abajo* (v. 9, 11, and 13) refer to positions
utilized in sexual intercourse. In medio lado (to the side) the
partners lie on their sides facing each other. In boca arriba
(looking up) the man lies facing upward, in boca abajo (looking
down) he lies facing downward. In Spanish one says "mouth (boca)
up" and "mouth down" rather than "looking up" and "looking down."
¡*Urria*! is an exclamation of pleasure, like "yippee!" ¡*Ay*! in
this context refers to sexual ecstasy.

The Game:

The games containing sexual references, TR 16-18, are played in
a similar manner. The participants form a circle, alternating men
and women. Either a man or woman goes into the center of the ring.
The chorus responds to each line sung by the individual within the
circle. Simultaneously he or she dances around preparatory to
selecting a partner, while the remaining players dance in a circle.
At the appropriate textual line, the individual in the center places
himself or herself in front of a player in the circle of the opposite sex. This is also a signal for the players in the circle to
stop dancing and to remain stationary. The man and woman facing
each other then execute various motions of the hips and loins in
imitation of coitus. At the end of the song the person within the
ring takes the place in the circle of the selected partner and the
latter goes into the center of the ring. The game is then repeated
as before, but with a person of the opposite sex within the circle.
At v. 7 in TR 16 the individual within the ring places himself
or herself in front of the partner selected from the circle. With
arms outstretched in imitation of the wings of birds, the two move
the hips and loins from side to side, simultaneously leaning to
the side, looking up, or looking down, according to the indications of the text.

TR 17 (LF 97.8) "Francisco, revoleático"

Sung by Abraham Herrera Pacheco and a group of women: Marcelina
Sánchez Pimientel, Juana García Blanquiset, Basilisa Herrera García,
Ana María Pacheco, and Juana Pérez. Evitar, 8 November 1964.

S.	1. Francisco,	Francisco,
Ch.	revoleático. (2)	revolver.
S/Ch	2. Revolear, revolear,	Revolve, revolve,
	revoleático. (3)	revolver.
(spoken)	¡Ahora entra tú!	Now you sing!
	¡Arréa! ¡arréa!	Hurry up! Hurry up!
	¡arréa!	Hurry up!

II	S.	1. Francisco,	Francisco,
	Ch.	revoleático, (2)	revolver,
	S/Ch	2. Revolear, revolear,	Revolve, revolve,
		revoleático. (3)	revolver.
	(spoken)	¡Arriba! ¡Marcela!	Get going! Marcela!
III	S.	1. Francisco,	Francisco,
	Ch.	revoleático. (2)	revolver.
	S/Ch	2. Revolear, revolear,	Revolve, revolve,
		revoleático.	revolver.
IV	S.	1. Francisco,	Francisco,
	Ch.	revoleático. (2)	revolver.
	S/Ch	2. Revolear, revolear,	Revolve, revolve,
		revoleático. (3)	revolver.

NOTES

Perf:

The recording was made quite late at night, and by this time
Herrera was drunk. There was much noise and confusion, and the
solo and chorus parts of the song are not well differentiated.
All these circumstances can commonly occur at the velorio.
Herrera sings the solo part in st. I. He then instructs Sánchez
to sing the solo part in st. II. However, it is sung by all the
women. He reiterates his command, and Sánchez is heard singing
the solo part at the beginning of st. III, but she is immediately
joined by the other women. They begin to laugh as they repeat
v. 2, and stop singing. Herrera then reenters and sings the solo
part of st. IV.
    The transcription is of st. I only plus the first phrase
spoken by Herrera following this strophe.

Text:

Revoleático = he who revolves.
Following st. II - Marcela is short for Marcelina.

The Game:

    The game is played in the same manner as that described in
TR 16, except that each verse is usually repeated a number of
times. In TR 17 the two players face each other as v. 2 is sung
and move hips and loins in a rotary motion.

TR 18 (LF 97.8) "La guacamaya"

Sung by Abraham Herrera Pacheco and a group of women: Marcelina
Sánchez Pimientel, Juana García Blanquiset, Basilisa Herrera García,
Ana María Pacheco, and Juana Pérez. Evitar, 8 November 1964.

I	S.	1. ¿Adónde está la guacamaya?	Where is the *guacamaya*?
	Ch.	2. En Palenque está. (c2)	She is in Palenque.
	S.	3. Echemela para acá	Bring her here
	Ch.	4. ¡(por) que quiero matarla!	For I want to kill her!

II	S.	1. ¡Ay! yo soy el juez,	I am the judge,
	Ch.	2. ¡él que la debe la paga!	He who owes it must pay it!
	S.	3. ¡Ay! ¡sí! que quieres que te dé	So! That's what you want me to give you!
	Ch.	4. con el papo en la cara! (c4)	The pussy in the face!
II	S.	1. ¡Ay! yo soy el juez,	I am the judge,
	Ch.	2. ¡él que la debe la paga!(c2)	He who owes it must pay it!
	S.	3. ¡Ay! ¡sí! ¡que quieres que te dé	So! That's what you want me to give you!
	Ch.	4. con el papo en la cara! (c5)	The pussy in the face!
I	S.	1. ¿Adónde está la guacamaya?	Where is the *guacamaya*?
	Ch.	2. En Palenque está. (c2)	She is in Palenque.
	S.	3. Echemela para acá	Bring her here
	Ch.	4. ¡(por)que quiero matarla! (c2)	For I want to kill her!
II	S.	1. ¡Ay! yo soy el juez,	I am the judge,
	Ch.	2. ¡él que la debe la paga!	He who owes it must pay it!
	S.	3. ¡Ay! ¡sí! ¡que quieres que te dé	So! That's what you want me to give you!
	Ch.	4. con el papo en la cara! (c6)	The pussy in the face!

NOTES

Perf:

A very gradual acceleration of the tempo begins at st. II.3 and, in general, continues throughout the performance.

Text:

In the song a woman is personified by the *guacamaya*, a large parrot or macaw with variegated plumage of blue, red, and green. On threat of death the judge tries to force the guacamaya into sexual intercourse with him. She indignantly refuses.

II.2 - ¡*El debe pagar*! is a common expression similar to the English "Crime doesn't pay," indicating that he who does wrong will usually have to pay for his transgression. Here the Spanish phrase has double meaning, serving also to express to the guacamaya the judge's intentions.

II.4 - *Papo* is a colloquial term for the vulva. It is probably derived from the verb *papar* (to swallow without chewing) and thus refers to the apparent swallowing of the penis by the vulva in sexual intercourse. An English colloquial expression for the vulva is utilized in the translation. However, the full phrase ¡*con el papo en la cara*! is an offensive expression for which there is no exact equivalent in English. An English expression at the same level of discourse, and producing a similar impact, would be "Kiss my ass!"

The Game:

The game is played in a manner similar to the two previously described. In TR 18 the imitation of coitus takes place in II.

As the person in the circle sings st. II.1, he or she hops forward
toward the partner selected in the ring. He then hops backward
and forward again, his partner advancing and retreating with him,
both imitating the hopping of a bird. Simultaneously, with hands
on hips, the partners move the loins in a forward and backward
motion. At the end of the strophe the selected partner replaces
the individual who was in the ring, and the game continues.

The repetition of st. II allows the dancing couple sufficient
time to carry out their actions and exchange places.

COMMENTARY

The items presented in this chapter are divided into sections
of various lengths which are sung by an individual, a group, or
both. In TR 13-14 the part marked "solo" is actually sung by a
couple rather than by an individual. The items offered can be
divided into two groups according to the poetic forms displayed.
The items in the first group, TR 11-14, are cast in the litany form
(see chapter 6, V.C.4); those of the second group, TR 15-18, each
contain at least one quatrain. However, quatrains are inserted
into the flow of the litanic verse in TR 14, a procedure not usually
followed in the playing of this particular song game. TR 11-12 are
versions of the same game song, and TR 13-14 are versions of a
second game song. Thus, although eight transcriptions are given,
they represent only six distinct songs.

In the first group, TR 11-14, the soloist sings a series of
verses selected from the stock of such verses in his repertory
and sung in any order that he chooses. Or he may improvise at
least part of the verse, as in TR 11-12. To each verse sung by
the soloist, the chorus responds with a refrain. Usually each
verse is independent, not requiring that a specific subsequent
verse be sung to complete the statement. Rarely, two verses are
linked, as in TR 13 (v. 2-3). In the example the refrain is
omitted.

> 2. azúcar me puso el padre
> 3. cuando me metió la sal.

Verses are repeated at the discretion of the soloist, several
times if he so desires, before a different verse is sung.

In the second group, TR 15-18, the division of material between
the soloist and the chorus is quite varied, depending in part on
the exigencies of the game the song accompanies. In TR 15 the
soloist sings a full quatrain and the chorus then sings the refrain,
or a part thereof, as many times as is necessary. In TR 16 and
TR 18 there is a constant alternation of the singing of verses between the soloist and the chorus. In TR 17 the soloist sings the
first verse, the chorus the second, and both join in singing the
third and fourth verses. The repetition of a couplet consisting of
either the first and second verses or the third and fourth is common and is controlled by the soloist who begins the couplet. TR 18
is composed of two quatrains. The order in which they are sung
also seems at the discretion of the soloist.

In the metrical analysis offered in table 7, and in similar
tables offered in subsequent chapters, the numbers representing
syllable count of verses are listed vertically rather than horizontally as in chapter 7. A number representing meaningless syl-
ables is underlined and enclosed in parentheses. Thus in TR 11,
v. 9, (1) + 8 indicates that the verse consists of one meaningless
syllable followed by eight syllables that are lexically meaningful.
In TR 13, which in the recording was sung by one individual, the
refrain is sung before the verse. At times this individual sings
the refrain plus the verse, at times the verse only. Thus 3 + 8
indicates that she first sings the three-syllable refrain and then
the verse, which in this case has eight syllables. When she omits
singing the refrain, only one number is given. TR 14 is sung by
both soloist and chorus. Since he begins with a quatrain, a
copla, the chorus does not sing the refrain until the soloist has
completed his first verse. On occasion, the soloist sings the
refrain with the chorus before singing his verse. As in TR 13,
this is indicated by 3 + 8. The length of the verse will of
course vary.

Table 7.   Metrical Analysis of Texts of TR 11-18

TR 11   TR 12

	Solo	Chorus			Solo	Chorus
1.	10	9		1.	10	9
2.	11	9		2.	11	9

(The choral refrain is repeated   (The choral refrain is repeated
after each subsequent line.)   after each subsequent line.)

3.	11		3.	10
4.	8		4.	10
5.	11		5.	11
6.	10		6.	8
7.	10		7.	8
8.	9		8.	9
9.	(1)+8		9.	9
10.	9		10.	10
11.	9		11.	9
12.	9		12.	8
13.	10		13.	10
14.	7		14.	8
15.	8		15.	10
16.	9		16.	10
17.	9		17.	8
18.	9		18.	10
19.	(2)+4		19.	8
20.	9			
21.	10			
22.	9			

TR 13

1.   3+8
2.   3+8
3.   8
4.   3+8
5.   3+9
6.   3+8
7.   8
8.   3+9
9.   3+8
10. 3+9
11. 8
12. 3+8
13. 3+8
14. 3+9

TR 15

S.   1. 8
     2. 8
     3. 8
     4. 8

Ch.   10

TR 14

      Solo Chorus
1.   9   3
2.   8   3
(The choral refrain is repeated
after each subsequent line. The
soloist sings the refrain with
the chorus as indicated.)
3.   8
4.   8

5.   3+9
6.   3+9
7.   3+9
8.   9
9.   3+9
10. 9
11. 9

12. 7
13. 8
14. 9
15. 8

16. 3+9
17. 9
18. 3+9
19. 9
20. 9
21. 3+9

TR 16

S.   1.   6
Ch.   2.   5
S.   3.   5
Ch.   4.   5

S.   5.   6
Ch.   6.   7

S.   7.   7
Ch.   8.   3+(2)

S.   9.   7
Ch.   10. 3+(1)

S.   11. 7
Ch.   12. 3+(2)

S.   13. 7
Ch.   14. 3+(2)

TR 17

I   1. S.   3
         Ch.   4
     2. S/Ch   6
                4

II   1. S.   3
         Ch.   4
     2. S/Ch   6
                4

III 1. S.   3
         Ch.   4
     2. S/Ch   6
                4

IV   1. S.   3
         Ch.   4
     2. S/Ch   6
                4

TR 18

I   S.   1. 9
     Ch. 2. 6
     S.   3. 8
     Ch. 4. 6

II   S.   1. (1)+5
     Ch. 2. 8
     S.   3. (1)+8
     Ch. 4. 7

II   S.   1. (1)+5
     Ch. 2. 8
     S.   3. (1)+8
     Ch. 4. 7

I   S.   1. 9
     Ch. 2. 6
     S.   3. 8
     Ch. 4. 6

II   S.   1. (1)+5
     Ch. 2. 8
     S.   3. (1)+8
     Ch. 4. 7

The verses of the litany forms, TR 11-14, are quite uneven in
length. On the other hand, the refrain is repeated exactly. Of
the items displaying the quatrain form, TR 15-18, only TR 15 falls
into the common octosyllabic mold. The verses of TR 16 are balanced in length, those of TR 17-18 are quite irregular. TR 16-17,
like the majority of the children's game songs in chapter 7, display verses shorter than the octosyllabic. On the other hand,
the texts cast in litanic form rarely contain a verse less than
eight syllables in length. Very frequently their verses contain a
larger number of syllables.

It should be noted that all the sinalefas taken into consideration in the syllable count in the realized text are represented
by elisions in the associated text. The text associated with the
music in this chapter, with some justification, could therefore
have been written in the conventional manner (see chapter 6,
V.A.4.6).

The litany forms do not display rhyming schemes as such, although in TR 11-12 each verse and the following refrain end on
the accented syllable ϕ. The quatrains of TR 15-16 have the
rhyming scheme abcb, the rhyme being consonantal in form. TR 17
has repetition rather than rhyme. Both strophes of TR 18 exhibit
assonantal rhyme. However, they differ in rhyming scheme. St. I
is abba, st. II abab. Another interpretation of the rhyming
scheme of TR 16 is possible. The text could be interpreted as a
strophe of six verses followed by a quatrain in which each verse
is followed by a slightly varied refrain. In this interpretation all rhyme would be assonantal. In any case, the texts of
song games played by the adults at the velorio de angelito are
much less regular in form than those of the majority of the lullabies and children's game songs offered in chapter 7.

It would seem that the form of the text, whether it be litany
or quatrain, is a useful method of differentiation. The consideration of verse length or of rhyming scheme seems to lack value
for this purpose.

I now turn to the music. I should first remind the reader
that in textual analysis arabic numerals are used to express
syllable count, while in the musical analysis they represent degrees of a scale. The music of the eight items can be divided
into two classes according to certain intervallic relationships
existing between certain scale degrees and the tonal center.
(The means by which the tonal center was selected is discussed in
chapter 5, I.B.1). In the first class, including TR 11-12, TR 15,
and TR 17, the third degree forms a major 3rd with the tonal
center below, and each verse cadences on the fifth degree, a perfect 4th below the tonal center. This refers to the verse only.
In TR 11-12 I have assigned different tonal centers to the verse
and the refrain. The second class, composed of TR 13-14, TR 16,
TR 18, and the refrain of TR 11-12, is characterized by the
existence of the interval of a minor rather than a major 3rd between the third degree and the tonal center. In this case the
tonal center is itself the final of all cadences, both of verse
and refrain. If the tonal center of the refrain of TR 11-12 in
each case is considered the tonal center of the entire song,

these two items would then necessarily be considered to belong to
the second class rather than the first. However, they would then
be the only items of the eight in which the cadence of the verse
is an incomplete rather than a full cadence.

Of the four items in the first class, all but TR 15 are related
by the cadence formula of a descending perfect 4th, 1-5. In TR 12
the seventh degree, f , is on occasion inserted between the outer
two degrees of the cadence interval. In TR 15 the cadential fifth
degree is reached by a chromatic upward movement from the third
degree.

A similar cadential interval of a descending perfect 4th functions to some extent as a cadential formula in all of the items
in the second class. In this case the pattern is 4-1 rather than
1-5. In TR 14 the flatted third degree, b , is occasionally
inserted between the two outer scale degrees forming the perfect
4th. These cadential formulae are shown in ex. 1:

Ex. 1.   Cadence formulae

Class 1

Class 2

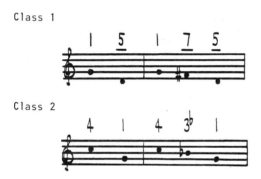

In ex. 1 repetition of pitches is omitted.

In addition there are a large number of longer melodic patterns
which appear in more than one item in the second class. These
patterns are presented in ex. 2 not as melodic cells but merely as
sequences of pitches, of which the last pitch is the final of a
phrase. Pitches given in parentheses occur in some cases but not
in others. As before, repetitions of a pitch are omitted.

Ex. 2.   Pitch sequences

Chorus

Soloist

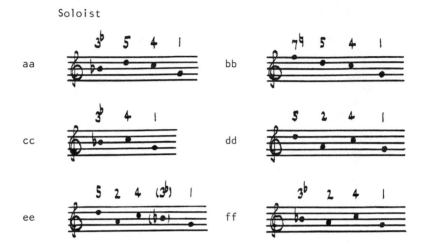

The illustrated pitch sequences are found in the following items:

xx	TR 13-14, TR 18
yy	TR 16, TR 18
aa	TR 13, TR 18
bb	TR 13-14
cc	TR 13-14
dd	TR 16, TR 18
ee	TR 14
ff	TR 16, TR 18

If the penultimate degree placed in parentheses in the pitch sequence ee is considered a non-essential tone, then the sequences dd and ee are the same pattern. In addition, in extracting the pitch sequence ff from TR 16 and TR 18, and particularly from the latter, I have considered the first pitch of the subsequent phrase to be the final pitch of the sequence. This can be seen in ex. 3:

Ex. 3. Sequence ending on first pitch of subsequent phrase (TR 16, m. 17-18)

Three different pitch sequences are utilized in the first part
of TR 16, and the same number in that part of TR 13 which was
transcribed. The form of TR 16 is quite regular.

          1-2. dd yy
                ff yy

          3-4. dd yy
                ff yy

          5-6. dd yy
                dd yy

On the other hand, the three different pitch sequences of which the
verse part of TR 13 is composed seem to occur in purely random
order.

          1.   xx aa
          2.   xx bb
          3.   cc
          4.   xx aa
          5.   xx cc
          6.   xx bb
          7.   aa
          8.   xx cc
          9.   xx aa

A larger number of pitch sequences are found in both TR 14 and
TR 18. These two songs were sung by Abraham Herrera Pacheco, who
was the regular leader of the games of the velorio de angelito in
Evitar. TR 13 and 16 were sung by Marcelina Sánchez Pimientel, who
was usually a participant in the games rather than their leader.
      Following the notes appended to TR 15 I offered a Spanish ana-
logue of the text of this song (p. 274). The analogue is a children's game song, while TR 15 is a game song which adults perform
at the velorio for a child. Although they serve different functions, the texts are obviously related. This is not surprising,
since there is evidence that many games played by children were
originally played by adults. In chapter 7, analogue 10 is a version of the text of the game song played in the sixteenth century
by adults, while analogue 11 is a version played by children in the
twentieth century (see p. 239).
      The most likely source for analogues of the songs of the velorio
de angelito would seem to be the auroro and the *baile de angelito*
of Spain (see chapter 3, p. 99). Unfortunately, I can find only
one published copla which was performed at this Spanish observance,
and it is given without the accompanying melody (Casas Gaspar 1947:
342). This copla was collected in Murcia, part of old Andalucía.

Auque la mare yora,   Although the mother weeps,
y con na encuentra consuelo,   And in nothing finds solace,
e la pobre muy dichosa   The poor one is very fortunate
porque el hijo etá ener sielo.   Since her son indeed is in
                                     heaven.

There is nothing analogous in the text except the verb *yora* (*llora*), "to weep," which is found in TR 11-12. This copla is equally applicable to the situation of the mother in the velorio de angelito in Evitar. Note also the attempt to reproduce in this copla the characteristics of the regional dialect.

In considering the possible sources of musical style and music performance, I shall first turn to Europe. The basic concept underlying European music until the twentieth century was that of tonality. (For a discussion of the historical development of European music and the concept of tonality see chapter 6, IV.A.2.1.) In chapter 7 the lullabies and children's game songs were determined to be European in melodic style through the analysis of their melodic cells, an analytic device which has as its underlying basis the concept of tonality. As will be seen, with one exception, TR 1, the melodic organization of the melodies presented in chapter 7 is consonant with compositional practice in the so-called common practice period, which roughly encompasses the eighteenth and nineteenth centuries. The melodies offered in this chapter are not consonant with this practice. In some cases the latter can be said to be "modal" in character, thus showing influences of an earlier period of European compositional practice, or at least they can be described as "non-common practice" in character. (For a discussion of modal music and the theoretical bases underlying it see chapter 6, IV.A.2.3.)

I shall now submit the bodies of melodies found in this and the preceding chapter to the same forms of analysis. By this means I shall demonstrate that those found in chapter 7 are generally consonant with common practice and those found in chapter 8 are not. This will be accomplished in two steps: in the first there will be an analysis of the melodic functions displayed by the melodies; in the second, of their scalar structure. (For an exposition of the methods of analysis to be applied see chapter 6, IV.A.2.2 and 4.) To simplify the discussion we shall consider categories I and II first and category III later. The refrain of TR 15 is omitted, since it does not display a tonal center.

Table 8.   Melodic Functions, TR 1-18, I, II

I.   Common Practice

Major 3rd, one-phrase melodies

	Initial	Final
TR 5	: 5 . 5	2 . 1
	: 1 (2) . 3	
TR 7	: 3 . 5	2 . 3 1
		2 . 3

Major 3rd, two-phrase melodies

	Initial	Mid	Final
TR 2-3	: 1 3 5	5	2 . 1
TR 6	3 : 3 (4) 5 . 8	Mod. to V	7 . 1

Major 3rd, two-phrase melodies (cont.)

	Initial	Mid	Final
TR 8A	: 1 3 5	<u>5</u>	2 . 1
TR 8B, TR 9	<u>5</u> : 1 3 . 1	2	<u>5</u> . 1
TR 10A	5 : 5 . 5	2	2 . 1
TR 10B	: 1 3 . 1	2	<u>5</u> . 1

II.   Modal

Minor 3rd, melodic verse or refrain

	Initial	Final
TR 13	♭7 . 5	4-1
TR 14	: 4 ♭7 5 . 3 5 ♭6 : 5	: 4 1 : 3 1 : 2 ♭<u>7</u> 1
TR 16	1 : 3 5	: 4 1
TR 18	1 : 5	4 . 1 5 . 4 2 . 4
TR 13-14r		: 3 . 1
TR 17-19r		: 3 2 . 1

In table 8, all pitches or pitch patterns offered under category I represent the tonic (I) or the dominant (V) chords. To this TR 6 is an exception, since it displays the chromatic tone c♯ (raised fourth degree). In m. 4 of the transcription, the c♯ indicates a modulation to the tonality of the dominant, D; the c♯ also occurs as a chromatic passing tone in m. 7 (p. 226). (Chromatic tones of these types are discussed in chapter 6, IV.A.2.2.3-4.) Such chromatic tones are rarely heard in folksong. Their presence in TR 6, plus the lack of strophic organization, indicates that this is a composed melody which has only recently entered the oral tradition. The form is too diffuse to permit the selection of a particular cadence as the mid or semicadence.

In all the items listed in II of table 8, there is at least one pitch or pitch pattern not representing the tonic or dominant chords or consonant with the movement of the sixth and seventh degrees of the scale in the common practice minor mode. These melodies therefore cannot be placed in category I. Common Practice. Some of the melodies in II can be considered to represent church modes. They are placed in the II. Modal rather than the III. Modal (anomalous) category, since the final and the tonal center are the same pitch.

I offer in table 9 a categorization by scale or mode of the same items offered in table 8. The majority of the melodies represented

are non-heptatonic and therefore cannot be categorized with complete
accuracy by their scale or mode only. Their division into category
I or II is thus based to some extent upon the analysis of their
melodic functions. In the table the items are also categorized
according to whether they display the interval of a major or minor
3rd above the tonal center and whether they are heptatonic or non-
heptatonic in character. (For the definition of terms such as
heptatonic see chapter 6, IV.A.1.3.) A transcription number followed by an *r*, as TR 16r, refers to the refrain heard in this item.

Table 9.   Scales or Modes, TR1-18, I, II

I.   Common Practice

1. Major 3rd, non-heptatonic

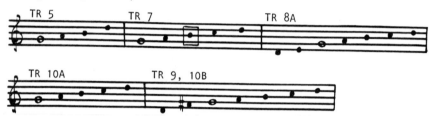

2. Major 3rd, heptatonic

II.   Modal

1. Minor 3rd, non-heptatonic

2. Minor 3rd, heptatonic

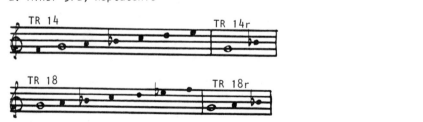

In table 9, TR 2-3, TR 6, and TR 8 are in the major mode. The chromatic tones occurring in TR 6 have already been discussed. TR 14 is in the dorian mode and TR 18 in the aeolian mode. Only these six scales are fully heptatonic. Since the non-heptatonic scales found in category I display the major 3rd above the tonic, and all their melodic functions are consonant with common practice, they can be considered to represent segments of the major scale. The situation is different in II, since each non-heptatonic scale can be considered to represent one or more church modes, depending upon which pitches are inserted to make it a heptatonic scale (see chapter 6, IV.A.2.4).

Tables 10 and 11 offer analysis of the melodic functions and the scale or mode of those melodies or parts thereof in which the tonal center and the final are not the same pitch. These are listed under III. (anomalous), and in the analysis of melodic functions the final rather than the tonal center is considered the first degree of the scale. The tonal center of the refrain of TR 11 and TR 12 is different from that of the verse of these two songs. Since the refrain does not end on *g*, it is given as transcribed and in transposition for purposes of comparison. This particular refrain is not anomalous, since its tonal center and its final are the same pitch. When the verse and the refrain of TR 11 and TR 12 are combined to produce one scale, both are transposed so that the scale may have *g* as its final. Thus the pitch *d* is considered the final in all non-transposed scales with the exception of that of TR 11-12r, where *e* is considered the final.

Table 10. Melodic Functions, TR 1-18, III

III. Modal (anomalous)

(First scale degree represents final, not tonal center)

One-phrase melodies

	Initial	Final
TR 1	: 4 6 8	2 . 1
TR 15	6 7 : 8	6 ♭7 ♯7 . 8
TR 17	: 8 6 : 1 4	4-1

Melodic verse only

	Initial	Final
TR 11	2 : 4 6	: 4 1
TR 12	6 : 8 : 2 6 : 2 8 6	3 . 1 4-1

Verse and refrain combined (first scale degree represents final of
refrain)

	Initial	Mid	Final
TR 11 + 11r	♮7-2-4	♮7	5 . 1
TR 12 + 12r	5-♮7		
	: 1♮7 5	♮7	5 : 1

Table 11.   Scales or Modes, TR 1-18, III

III.   Modal (anomalous)

1. Major 3rd, no melodic refrain

2. Major 3rd, with melodic refrain

   a. Verse only

   b. Refrain only

   c. Combined verse and refrain

    In table 10 there are many initial melodic patterns which repre-
sent not only the IV chord but the II$_7$ chord (scale degrees 2 4 6
8).   The non-common practice character of the cadence patterns 4-1
and : 3 . 1 has already been discussed, as has that of non-stepwise
patterns, including the lowered seventh degree, the natural seventh
degree in this case (see chapter 6, IV.A.2.2 and 4).   Nor can this
particular scale degree represent the V chord at the semi-cadence

in the minor mode. In TR 15 the initial pattern, 6 7 : 8, and its
chromatically varied form utilized as a final pattern, 6 ♮7 ♯7 . 8,
give the impression of a IV chord, the first and last pitches
representing that chord and the intervening pitches non-harmonic
passing tones. Thus they are not acceptable common practice
melodic functions. The patterns 5 7 : 8 or 5 6 7 . 8 would be
acceptable, since they outline the I chord, but not those listed.
If, on the other hand, the tonal center is considered the first
degree of the scale, the two patterns become 3 4 : 5 and 3 ♮4 ♯4
: 5. Representing the I chord, they are now acceptable. However,
the cadence pitch is now no longer acceptable, since in both
common practice and modal theory a melody closes in almost all
cases on the first degree of the scale, and now it closes on the
fifth degree. This anomalous situation applies to a greater or
lesser degree in all the items presented. As indicated previously,
chromatic tones are rare in Western European folk music, and
those seen in TR 15 are examples of common practice influence on
a melody otherwise displaying non-common practice characteristics.

TR 1 is a particularly interesting phenomenon. Although it is
a two-phrase melody, each phrase has the same cadential pattern.
The first phrases of TR 1, TR 2, and TR 8A show great similarity.
They are, in fact, represented by the same combination of melodic
cells, ab, in table 3 (p. 244).

The cadential pitch of the first phrase of TR 1, TR 2, and
TR 8A is the same: d^1. However, this pitch represents the final
in all phrases of TR 1, while in TR 2 and TR 8A it represents
the pitch of the mid or semi-cadence, and the second phrase of
the strophe terminates on the tonic. Indeed, the scales of TR 8A
and TR 1 are exactly the same except for the indication of the
final. (Compare tables 9 and 11.) The singer of TR 1, Marcelina
Sánchez, was active in the song games of the velorio de angelito.
She was recorded in the performance of some of the songs of this
celebration, many of which also close on a pitch a fourth below
the tonal center. Thus being accustomed to singing this type of
cadence pattern in the songs of the velorio de angelito, she may
have carried over the practice in singing the lullaby. TR 1 is
the only song presented in chapter 7 in which the final and the
tonal center are not the same pitch.

In summary, all pitches and pitch patterns listed in table 8
represent the I and V chords in the major mode and are therefore consonant with melodic functions in the common practice
period. All full items listed in II, whether one-phrase melodies,
two-phrase melodies, or verse plus melodic refrain, contain some
pitches or pitch patterns which are not consonant with common
practice melodic functions in the minor mode. It is for this
reason that these items are listed as "modal." The melodies
listed in table 10 present a more complex situation. If the
melodies are analyzed according to their selected tonal center,
all pitches and pitch patterns of all items but TR 11-12r are
consonant with melodic functions in common practice in the major
mode, with the exception of the final. In common practice
melodies the final and the tonal center are almost always the
same pitch. However, if we analyze the melodies according to

their finals, all pitches and pitch patterns except the final no longer are consonant with common practice melodic functions. Thus in neither case can the melodies listed in III be considered to fit common practice. They must instead be listed under the modal category.

The term *modal* has been used rather than *non-common practice*, since some of the melodies have heptatonic scales and therefore can be accurately classified according to mode. When the verse and refrain of TR 12 are combined, the resultant scale is heptatonic and can be classified as aeolian. Of the hexatonic scales, TR 1 has already been discussed. If the space between the d and the $f^{\#}$ in the verse only of TR 12 is filled with an $e^{\natural}$, the mixolydian mode would be produced. An $e^{\flat}$ could not be introduced, since the mode thus produced is not one which has been known in European music.

We thus find all the songs sung at the velorio de angelito, TR 11-18, to be non-common practice if not modal in character. On the other hand, the great majority of the lullabies and children's songs, TR 2-10, clearly fit within the common practice style. What then is the source of the melodies sung at the velorio de angelito? Is the style derived from Gregorian chant or from Spanish or other folksong repertories? Gregorian chant was in little use in South America after the final expulsion of the Jesuits early in the eighteenth century. Although many country people in Colombia seem not to have had access to church services, plainchant could have spread to these areas by other means and influenced folksong. Folk music in southern Spain is said to be microtonal in character (see chapter 6, IV.A.1.5), while that of northern Spain is primarily in the major mode, with some melodies in the dorian, mixolydian, and aeolian modes (Chase 1941:234). The songs of the velorio de angelito do not reflect stylistic characteristics of southern Spain, and they are characteristic, to some extent at least, of the smaller modal part of the folksong repertory of northern Spain. There was migration from Spain to Colombia for over a century before the major-minor common practice system was fully developed; there may have been a larger proportion of modal melodies in the folksong repertory during that period, and modal characteristics may have been retained in isolated rural areas like Evitar. It should also be indicated that melodies in the dorian, aeolian, and mixolydian modes have been found in the English folksong repertory, although, again, not as frequently as melodies in the major mode (Sharp 1907:69).

Some elements of African musical style may also be present in the pitch organization of these melodies. In Ghana there are pentatonic melodies in which the cadence formula 3-1 is common. Diatonic heptatonic scales are also in use. Their common cadence patterns are 2-1 or 7-1, but 4-1 and 3-1 are also heard, the former more frequently than the latter (Nketia 1963:36, 39).

African as well as European practice may have been at work in shaping the cadence formulae heard in the song melodies presented in this chapter. African influence is more strongly evident in the rhythmic and formal organization, but European stylistic elements are also always present. The call and response patterns, as such, can be considered more African than European, but the use

of a response of the same length throughout the song is more a
European than an African characteristic (see chapter 6, VI.A.1-2).
This statement applies to TR 11-14 and possibly to TR 16-18. It
is legitimate to describe the two strophes of TR 18 as quatrains,
since they contain four different verses and are linked by assonantal rhyme. To describe the four strophes of TR 17 or the first
four verses of TR 16 as quatrains is somewhat arbitrary. They are
written as quatrains in the realized texts, but these quatrains,
unlike those of TR 18, do not contain four different verses. The
first six verses of TR 16, plus their repetitions, can be considered
a form of call and response pattern, the response consisting of a
melodic refrain rather than a refrain combining the same melody and
text (see chapter 6, VI.B.1). TR 18 can be viewed in the same manner, as can TR 17, where the soloist joins in the second singing of
the refrain.

Two traits are exemplified in these songs which, as far as I can
determine, are African rather than European. Both occur during the
performance of a call and response pattern. The first is the overlap of the choral response by the leader entering early with his
phrase. This must be distinguished from the overlapping of the
call by an early entrance of the chorus, a phenomenon which occurs
in costeño but apparently not in African song (see chapter 6, VI.
B.3). In the second, the leader cues the chorus by singing the
refrain before singing his first phrase. When the chorus then
enters with the refrain, he may sing part or all of it along with
them (see VI.B.4). Although TR 13 is sung by one individual, it
can be seen in the realized text that in performance in context the
initial refrain is sung soli, by a couple rather than the chorus.
In TR 14 and TR 18 the soloist at times sings the refrain or a part
thereof along with the chorus. In TR 14 the soloist introduces
coplas within the flow of the litanic verse as though he were singing a bullerengue. Through this, and other means, he so modifies
the usual rhythmic organization of the song that the chorus must
enter after a rest of two pulses rather than three. Under these
circumstances the chorus cannot regulate its entrance according to
a regular cycle of pulses. Rather, it must determine when to enter
by reference to the text and melody sung by the soloist. This
method of determining when to enter is also followed by the chorus
in songs of the Kpelle of Liberia when the phrase sung by the leader is long or irregular in length (data collected in the field by
Ruth Stone).

I now offer examples of overlapping from the Colombian repertory.
In ex. 4 both soloist and chorus overlap in their respective entrances. However, the soloist enters early, singing his own
textual-musical phrase, while in its early entrance the chorus
duplicates the latter part of the textual-musical phrase of the
soloist. The lower line represents the beating of the poles on the
ground. In ex. 5 the leader again enters early, but this time
singing the refrain with the chorus. He does not duplicate exactly the rhythm or the pitches of the refrain melody. The second
word sung by the soloist, *zú-car*, marks the beginning of his
verse. There is a quarter note to a pulse in the first measure
and a dotted quarter to a pulse subsequently. Note that the refrain occupies two pulses and the verse three pulses.

Ex. 4.   Overlapping by soloist and chorus (TR 12, m. 8-11)

Ex. 5.   Soloist overlaps while singing refrain (TR 14, m. 11)

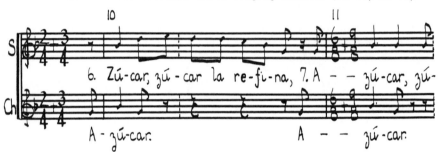

In ex. 6, the leader utilizes both methods of overlapping simultaneously. He duplicates the penultimate syllable and pitch of the choral verse and then enters early with his own verse. The chorus in turn duplicates the last syllable and pitch of the leader's verse before singing their own.

Ex. 6.   Combined methods of overlapping (TR 18, m. 15-18)

From the preceding discussion we can conclude that the overlapping techniques used in call and response in the songs of the
velorio de angelito are primarily derived from African rather than
European practice. However, we have not discussed a third possible
source, the Amerindian musical culture. Unfortunately, there are
almost no published transcriptions of songs of Colombian Indians
in which both melody and text are given. In listening to recordings of songs of the Colombian Indians, both those commercially
issued and those in the form of field recordings in the Indiana
University Archives of Traditional Music, I could hear little that
might be described as "call and response." In fact, I doubt if
there is a formal aspect of Indian musical style in northern South
America which could be described as a refrain. This point is
illustrated by fig. 76, my transcription of the first part of a
Jívaro "Victory Song," given on the succeeding page. (The transcription is reproduced from List 1973a with some modification in
the indication of the formal analysis. The transcription is based
on Turner:59-053-F, ATL 1357.5.)

The song is sung almost entirely in falsetto, the male singer
dropping into chest tone only on the final $b^\flat$. In the transcription each staff represents a musical phrase. The text line may
represent a single phrase (4, 5, 10, and 11), a repeated phrase
(2, 6, and 7), or the repetition of a single word (1, 3, 8, and 9).
The letters to the left of the music staffs and the textual lines
represent formal analysis of the music and text, respectively.
The underlined verses marked A seem to form a verbal refrain. However, this verbal refrain is sung to two melodic phrases with
diverse cadences, a^1 and a^2. Further, this verbal refrain does
not coordinate with what may be called the melodic refrain (staves
4 and 10).

I shall now examine occurrences of that rhythmic phenomenon
which can be described as syncopation or off-beat phrasing, depending upon the perspective from which it is viewed (see chapter
6, IV.B.1.4 and IV.B.2.6). Syncopation or off-beat phrasing occurs
in the majority of the items presented in this chapter. This
phenomenon is not present in TR 15, the text of which, as is indicated previously, is derived from a Spanish children's game song.
Nor is it present in TR 13, where the singer is carrying both the
solo and choral parts. It is infrequently evident in the solo
part of TR 11. It is always present when the soloist is Abraham
Herrera, the accustomed leader of the song games of the velorio de
angelito. At times it also occurs in the choral melodic response,
most notably in TR 13.

Of the following, ex. 7-9 illustrate the use of syncopation or
off-beat phrasing in the transcriptions previously presented in
this chapter and ex. 10 its use in those presented in chapter 7.
I consider this rhythmic phenomenon to be a European trait when it
is validated by immediate repetition (see chapter 6, IV.B.1.6) and
an African trait when it is not so validated. According to this
view, this rhythmic phenomenon as seen in ex. 7-8 (TR 16-17) and
ex. 10 (TR 1) represents syncopation rather than off-beat phrasing,
while that seen in ex. 9 (TR 18) represents the reverse. In ex. 7
(TR 16) there is an immediate repetition of the syncopated pattern

Fig. 76. Victory song of the Jívaro of the Ecuadorian Amazon

Ex. 7.   Syncopation or off-beat phrasing (TR 16, m. 1-2, v. 1)

Ex. 8.   Syncopation or off-beat phrasing (TR 17, m. 9-12, v. 2)

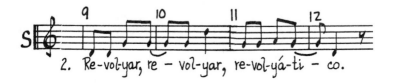

Ex. 9.   Syncopation or off-beat phrasing (TR 18, m. 8-10, v. 3)

Ex. 10.   Syncopation or off-beat phrasing
(TR 1, st. VI, m. 3-4, v. 1)

within the same phrase. In ex. 8 (TR 17) the subsequent musical
phrase repeats the same pattern of syncopations. In ex. 9 (TR 18)
the initial syncopation of the phrase is not heard in the immediately subsequent phrase, although it is heard in a later phrase
in the strophe (see p. 280).

In ex. 10 (TR 1) there is immediate repetition of the same
syncopated pattern within the same phrase. This is the only sung
item offered in chapter 7 in which syncopation occurs. In the
greater number of strophes of TR 1, the melody appears in unsynco-
pated form (p. 210). The existence of this trait in TR 1 gives
further credence to the conclusion that Marcelina Sánchez' performance of this lullaby was affected by her customary participation
in the song games of the velorio de angelito.

Considering them from the Western European point of view, all
the songs in chapter 7, and all those in chapter 8 with the exception of TR 13-14, are in duple meter, and their phrases are
four pulses in length, the most common phrase length in the common practice style (see chapter 6, IV.B.1.2-3). Examining these
songs from the African point of view, they can be assumed to be
constructed over regularly recurring cycles of four or eight
pulses which are objectified or felt and which are not patterned
into groups in which some pulses receive greater stress than
others (see chapter 6, IV.B.2.1). Keeping these two views in mind,
I shall now examine this repertory to determine the degree of
coordination existing between verbal stress and underlying pulse.
In Spanish song there is considerable expectancy that such coordination will take place, but there is little expectancy that this
will occur in African song (see chapter 6, VI.C.1-4). For purposes of this analysis I present sections of song text in which I
have underlined the vowels accented in speech and indicated the
underlying pulses by numbers. These are the texts as sung, not
the realized texts.

In the songs offered in chapter 7 there is almost complete
coordination of verbal accent and underlying pulse, as seen in
ex. 11:

Ex. 11. Verbal stress and underlying pulse (TR 8, st. I, v. 1-2)

1. Yo soy la viu-di-ta del con-de Lau-rel
        1   2   3   4

2. que quie-ro ca-sar-me, no quen-tro con quién.
         1   2   3   4

The excerpt of the music transcription from TR 1 given in ex. 10
is highly syncopated, but like the rest of the songs in chapter 7,
in which practically no syncopation is found, it displays complete
coordination of verbal accent and underlying pulse. This can be
seen in ex. 12:

Ex. 12. Verbal stress and underlying pulse (TR 1, st. VI, v. 1-2)

1. duér-ma-se, ni-ño, que ten-go que ha-ce
        1   2   3   4

2. la-var los pa-ñi-to, po-ner-me a co-se
        1   2   3   4

Here is further evidence that the source of the style of the items
presented in chapter 7 is Western Europe.

In ex. 13-15 I shall examine in more detail the initial sections
of three songs from the velorio de angelito, TR 16-18. Excerpts
from the music transcriptions of these songs in which syncopation
or off-beat phrasing is found have been given in ex. 7-9. Although
the melody with which the text given in ex. 13 is associated is
highly syncopated, there is complete coordination of verbal accent
and underlying pulse. The four-pulse melodic phrase or cycle

Ex. 13.   Verbal stress and underlying pulse (TR 16, v. 1-4)

   1.   E lo̲-roy la lo̲-ray   2.   sta̲-ban lo-re-a̲n-dol,
         1̲   2̲   3̲   4̲

      lo̲-roy la lo̲-ray sta̲-ban lo-re-a̲n-do.

   3.   Yo̲ por la re̲-ja   4.   sta̲-ba mi-ra̲n-do,
         1̲   2̲   3̲   4̲

      Yo̲ por la re̲-ja sta̲-ba mi-rá̲.

divides into two groups of two pulses each for the call and the
response. Bird describes a four-pulse cycle in which the call
occupies three pulses and the response one pulse (see chapter 6,
VI.C.3). A cycle of four pulses apparently does not occur with
great frequency in Africa, and I find no mention in the literature
of the equal division of the call and response in a cycle of this
length. The equal division of a phrase of four pulses is, of
course, common in Europe, although not necessarily as a call and
response. In addition, the four calls represented in the preceding
example constitute the melodic form abab, one sequence of pitches
being sung to v. 1 and v. 3 and another sequence of pitches when
each is repeated. This balanced form is also characteristically
European.

    On the other hand, the call is in additive rhythm, a phenomenon
common in Africa but not in Western Europe since the Renaissance.
The metrical signature given below to the left would be appropriate for each of the two measures of the call. Changing the
sixteenth notes to eighth notes, the value commonly used to represent a pulse of a cycle by students of African music, the additive
rhythmic pattern to the right is produced. This is a common
African realization of a cycle of eight pulses and, for example,
is in use among the Akan of Ghana (Nketia 1963:76).

         3 + 3 + 2   ♩·   ♩·   ♩
            16   123 456 78

Ex. 14.   Verbal stress and underlying pulse (TR 17, st. I, v. 1-2)

   1.   Fran-ci̲s-co, re-vol-yá̲-ti-co.
         1   2   3   4

      Fran-ci̲s-co, re-vol-yá̲-ti-co,

   2.   Re-vol-ya̲r, re-vol-ya̲r, re-vol-yá̲-ti-co.
         1   2   3   4

      Re-vol-ya̲r, re-vol-ya̲r, re-vol-yá̲-ti-co.

    Like ex. 14 it is highly syncopated, but the situation is
exactly the opposite as far as coordination of verbal accent and
underlying pulse is concerned. In ex. 14 not one verbal stress
coincides with an underlying pulse. In this respect African influence seems quite evident. As in African lyric songs, the number of syllables to a verse is quite irregular: 7 + 10 (see table
7, pp. 284-850). On the other hand, the melodic form is aabb, the

melody of each verse being repeated exactly. One would expect more melodic variation in an African performance.

Ex. 15.   Verbal stress and underlying pulse (TR 18, st. I, v. 1-2)

```
S.    1. ¿On-de-stá la üa-ca-ma-yen?    2. Pa-len-que  ¿On

Ch.                        ca-ma-yen?   2. Pa-len-que-stá.
               1    2    3   4                 6   7   8

S.        -de-stá la üa-ca-ma-yen?                          3.  E

Ch.                        ma-yen?         pa-len-que-stá.
               1    2    3   4  5              6   7   8

S.        -che-me-la pa-ra-cá

Ch.                       4.        ¡que la quie-ro ma-ta!
               1    2    3  4              5    6  7   8
```

In ex. 15 a number of syllables which are unaccented in speech are coordinated with pulses and are therefore accented when sung. Words of four syllables like *guacamaya* (*üacamaya*) and *échemela* have only one accent in speech. If the pattern of two syllables to a pulse is to be continued, another syllable of each word must be accented in song. In most cases speech accents coordinate with primary pulses. (Viewed as an African cycle rather than European meter, these are pulses 2, 4, 6, and 8.) Where syllables unaccented in speech coincide with pulses it is usually with secondary pulses (cycle pulses 1, 3, 5, and 7). Occasionally a syllable unaccented in speech coincides with a primary pulse, as in the third *e* of *échemela*. If, in ex. 15, a half note rather than a quarter note is counted as a pulse, there would be only one case in which verbal accent and pulse do not coincide. This would be acceptable in the Spanish tradition, but the tempo is now rather slow for a dance song.

The Western European common practice tradition and that of sub-Saharan Africa are similar in that the song melodies are constructed over an underlying framework of groups of four pulses or multiples thereof. The Spanish tradition also seems to coincide with that of Africa in the treatment of certain aspects of the song text. In ex. 15 (TR 18) there is an elision of an initial phone, the *g* in *guacamaya*. There are also sinalefas; that is, the coalescing of adjacent vowels. Thus in v. 1 one *e* represents the final *e* of *ónde* (*adónde*) and the initial *e* of *está* (*stá*), one *a* the final *a* of *para* and the initial *a* of *acá*. Immediately before v. 2 the syllable *yen* represents a combination of *ya*, the final syllable of *guacamaya* and *en*, the first word of the refrain . Somewhat similar elisions and coalescing of vowels occur in African songs (Jones 1964:10).

There remains the temporal problem presented by TR 13-14.

Ex. 16.   Verbal stress and underlying additive
pulse pattern (TR 13, v. 1)

```
A-zú-car, zú-car me lla-mo yo.
  1   2  +   1          2     3
```

This game song is in call and response form and is built over
a recurrent additive cycle of five pulses, or cast in quintuple
meter, depending upon whether its pulse organization is viewed
as an African or a European phenomenon. Nketia informs us that
in Ghana the call and its response may be disparate in length,
balance being achieved by repetition of the sequence (1963:28-30).
However, I find no mention in the literature of the use in Africa
of a cycle five pulses in length. To my knowledge, additive
quintuple meter is not found in the folk music of Spain nor in
that of the rest of Western Europe. It is in use in Eastern
Europe (see chapter 6, IV.B.1.8) and in Turkey and other areas of
the Middle East, but there certainly have been insufficient
migrants from the latter regions to affect costeño rural culture.

Although some examples of additive rhythm can be found in
Spain (see chapter 6, IV.B.1.8), they are irregular in their
organization; that is, they are not characterized by the repetition of a cycle of a certain number of pulses as in Africa nor
the repetition of musical phrases containing the same number of
pulses as in Eastern Europe. García Matos does offer a transcription of an Alborá de San Sebastián from Extremedura which is in
additive rhythm and in which the pulses are equal in length:
3/4 + 3/4 + 2/4 (1944:130, no. 151). The song was recorded in
the village of Piornal, where it is sung by the "Jarampla," a
costumed man who plays a leading role in this village's celebration of the day of its patron saint, San Sebastián (García Matos
1944:125). I find it difficult to believe that the transcription
offered is fully accurate. The text of this song consists of only
two verses, each being repeated two or three times. Ex. 17 is an
analysis of the coordination, or, rather, the lack of coordination, of verbal and musical accent in this song.

Ex. 17.   Verbal stress and underlying pulse in alborá of
          Extremadura (García Matos 1944:130, no. 151)

        1. Sa-bas-tián va-le-ro--so
             1   2   3   1

        2. Hoy es tu dí---a
             2   3   1 2

        3. To-dos te fes-te-ja--mos
             1   2   3   1

        4. Con a--le-grí-a___ .
             2   3   1 2

In this illustration I have reproduced the spelling, punctuation,
and capitalization as published.

In only three of the sixteen pulses given do verbal and musical
stress coincide. Such a lack of coordination of verbal and musical stress in a Spanish song which supposedly displays a regularly
recurring pulse seems unlikely. I suspect that the song was at
least partially sung in free or prose rhythm but that the transcriber felt it necessary to fit it within a metrical framework
(see chapter 6, IV.B.1.1 and my partial transcriptions of an
Asturian song and a *cante jondo* in chapter 9 (pp. 331, 332).

Whether regular or irregular in its organization, additive
rhythm as a general concept is found in the folk music of some
areas of Spain. This country is therefore probably the source
of the rhythmic phenomenon seen in TR 13-14. In the costeño song,
verses of the same length are followed by refrains of the same
length. Since this regularity is not characteristic of most
examples of Spanish music displaying additive rhythm, either
African or general Western European influence must also be operative. Whether applied to pulse cycles or pulse patterns, both
musical cultures emphasize regularity of repetition.

The songs sung in Evitar at the velorio de angelito display a
rather subtle and complex blend of European and African traits.
I shall now attempt to summarize the contributions of these two
parent cultures.

Texts

I have been able to find only one textual analogue of these
songs published in Spain, that of a children's game song which is
similar to the text of TR 15. The latter is the only song text
which is fully octosyllabic and which displays the rima romancera.
It is also the only song which is not in call and response form
and therefore can be described as European in all its textual
aspects. The division of a text into a call and response pattern
is assumed to be more African than European, but the equal division
of time space between call and response is assumed to be more
European than African. Of the songs in call and response form,
TR 11-12, TR 16, and TR 18 exhibit rhyme, a Spanish-European trait.
On the other hand, most of the verses within a song are quite
uneven in length and are therefore inconsistent with Spanish
poetic tradition. Of these, TR 17 is the most notable. The
assumption is that in this aspect they are related to African
practice.

Melodies

These melodies, unlike the great majority of those presented
in chapter 7, differ in scalar structure and, in general, in cadence formulae from Western European practice of the eighteenth
and nineteenth centuries. Whether this reflects earlier European
modality or African influence is difficult to determine. Song in
Africa and Europe is basically diatonic, and pentatonism is known
in both areas. Phrases four pulses in length are common in
Europe but not unknown in Africa, and groupings eight pulses in
length are common in both areas. The five-pulse grouping of
TR 13-14 seems to be derived from Spanish additive rhythm regular-
ized by African and/or European influence. In some songs there is
a strong feeling of European duple meter; in others, such as
TR 16-17, it is not strongly present, and the metrical signature
is primarily a device for the measurement of time space.

Syncopation is very evident. At times it can be related to
African practice and thus can be considered off-beat phrasing.
In most cases, it is rationalized as European tradition by vali-
dating repetition.

Relationships between text and music

Specific African traits displayed in these songs are the overlapping by the leader of the choral response and the cuing of the chorus by the leader through his singing of part or all of this response. Considerable variation is shown in the degree of coordination displayed between verbal accent and underlying pulse. Some songs, such as TR 13, show a degree of coordination commensurate with the Spanish-European tradition; others, such as TR 17, show no coordination whatsoever and are closer to the African tradition.

In summary, I believe the European to be the stronger of the two influences. The reader should note, however, that I am unable to assess Amerindian influence because of lack of data.

9. Cantos de Trabajo

The men sing zafras while working in the fields and vaquería while herding cattle. The women have no worksongs, unless the *arrullos* are so considered. In the strictest sense the terms *zafra* and *vaquería* refer to styles of singing, not to song genres. The copla is the common textual basis for both (see chapter 6, V.C.2). A further characteristic of the zafra and vaquería style is the frequent addition of lexically meaningless syllables at the beginning and end of verses. Various interjections, such as *ombe* and *por Dios*, are also added to the quatrain or inserted within the verses.

Melodically, neither the zafra nor the vaquería displays a clear tonality. The transcriptions are therefore not transposed, and no attempt is made to assess constancy of pitch level. Both forms are performed in what may be described as prose rhythm. (For the special means utilized in notating the worksongs, see chapter 5, I.C.3 and I.E.2.)

ZAFRAS

In Spain *zafra* refers to the olive harvest, in the Caribbean area in general to the harvest of sugar cane. In the Costa Atlántica the term is applied to song performed during any type of agricultural labor. In this work, whether clearing a field or cutting a crop, the long, broad-bladed knife known as the machete is employed. The men do not work together, but in various locations in the field. A man who sings a zafra does not ordinarily stop working while he sings. The zafra style is not characterized by a recurrent pulse or pulse pattern. There is therefore no need to match the rhythm of the song with the rhythm of the labor.

There is no one pattern followed in the singing of zafras. One man may sing and the others respond with gritos (cries), or two or more men may alternately sing coplas. The gritos may be lexically meaningless or they may have meaning. They may encourage others to work or they may express derision. Almost every man in the village knows a number of coplas, and most of them sing in the fields as they work. There are a few who do not think they sing well and thus confine themselves to uttering gritos. The

308

texts of the coplas are traditional; the men "sing what they
know," as one informant put it. It does not follow that in singing zafras full coplas are always utilized. Often only a couplet
from a known copla is sung, or verses from more than one copla
may be combined. Sung interjections may be added in either case.
The singing of zafras is therefore often improvisatory in nature
in that known verses and interjections are presented in new
combinations on the spur of the moment. Occasionally new verses
may be invented and inserted. In its most improvisatory form,
the zafra takes the form of a dialogue composed of verses of
irregular length unrelated by rhyme, as in TR 21.

TR 19 (LF 77.9)

Zafras sung by Mariano Rosado Julio.
Evitar, 1 November 1964.

ca - ma _____ .

III. 1. E___ a-quí tri-te de pen-sar___

2. y tri-te de pen-sa-mien-to_____ ; 3. no

me qui-sie-ra cor-dar 4. cuan-des-ta mi

tiem-po___ .

IV. 1. Om - , - - be___ , i___ i a de lo San-to___

tán-fer-ma 2. con ca-len-tu-ra ma-li-na !

3. No le va-le lo cor-dia-le 4. ni lo ca-do

de ga-lli-na___ . 3x. E___ no le va-

le lo cor-dia-le 4. ni lo cal-do de ga-lli-na___.

I. E_____ ma-ma mí-a___, tú fui-te la que

pu-si-te__ 2. tu ma-no so-bre la mí-a__.

3. Tú üi-te la que di-je 4. que nun-ca

me ol-vi-da-rí-a_____.

I	1. *A-e-i* la vergüenza del repollo	The shame of the cabbage	
	2. que en el verano se seca;	That withers in the summer;	
	3. lo siembran en tierra fresca	Even when planted in ground not lacking in water	
	4. a orillas de los arroyos.	On the banks of the brooks.	

I
1. *A-e-i* la vergüenza del repollo — The shame of the cabbage
2. que en el verano se seca; — That withers in the summer;
3. lo siembran en tierra fresca — Even when planted in ground not lacking in water
4. a orillas de los arroyos. — On the banks of the brooks.

II
1. *E* madre mía, tú eres la palma — Mother mine, you are the palm tree
2. donde mi amor se recrea. — Where my love is recreated.
3. Consuelo de mis ideas, — Comfort of my thoughts,
4. hoy te canto en paz y calma. — Today I sing to you in peace and calm.

III
1. *E* aquí triste de pensar — In this place I am sad
2. y triste de pensamiento; — With melancholy thoughts;
3. no me quisiera recordar — I do not care to remember
4. cuando estaba en mi tiempo. — How it was with me here in the past.

IV
1. *Ombe, i* ¡María de los Santos está enferma — María de los Santos is ill.
2. con calentura maligna! — She has a terrible fever!
3. No le valen los cordiales — Care does not help her
4. ni los caldos de gallina. — Nor does chicken broth.
   E no le valen los cordiales — Care does not help her
   ni los caldos de gallina. — Nor does chicken broth.

V   1. *E* mama mía, tú fuiste la que   Mother mine, you were the
          pusiste   one that put
       2. tu mano sobre la mía.   Your hand over mine.
       3. Tú fuiste la que dijiste   You were the one who told
                                                    me
       4. que nunca me olividaría.   That you would never
                                                    forget me.

NOTES

Perf:

   Mariano Rosado was asked to sing zafras alone. Without stopping,
except for short pauses between each, he sang five coplas which he
had sung in the field.

Text:

   IV.1 - *Ombe* is an exclamation derived from the word *hombre* (man).
It would not be used in speech as a substitute for *hombre*, and it
is therefore given in the realized text in italics as a meaningless
exclamation. De los Santos is a family name.

Tr 20 (LF 77.11)

Zafras sung be Reinaldo Rosado Julio with accompanying gritos by
two men. Evitar, 1 November 1964.

7. ¡ Cue-lo, por Dio ____! 8. Tú üi-
te la que pu-si-te 9. tu ma-no so-bre la
mí-a ____. 10. U je ___ je ___ i e tiempo re-cor-da-rá, ma mí ___ a. 11. Üe
i por Dió ____, em-bu-te! Tú ten-ga-ñas-
te, 12. ¡ no me muer-to to-da-ví-a, mama ____!

1. El pájaro se te fue, *je-je*

en la mano lo tuviste.

The bird has flown away
   from you,
You had it in your hand.

gr. *O-je je-je* hermano, hermano.

Brother, brother.

3. ¡Cógelo, por Dios! *je*
4. El tiempo recordará,
5. ya verás lo que perdiste.

Grab it, by God!
You will remember the time,
You will see what you have
   lost.

gr. *¡Üupa!*

6. *Üe-je* Virgen del Carmen.   Virgin of Carmen.

gr.   ¡Echa! ¡echa para acá! *Üu-vi*   Come on! Come over here!

7. ¡Cógelo, por Dios!   Grab it, by God!
8. Tú fuiste la que pusiste   You were the one who put
9. tu mano sobre la mía.   Your hand over mine.

gr. *U-ja*

10. *U-je-je-i* el tiempo recordará,   You will remember the time,
    mama mía.   mother mine.

gr.   ¡Tome de eso! ¡Tome de eso!   Drink it! Drink it!
    ¡Oiga! ¡Oiga!   Listen! Listen!

11. *Üe* por Dios, ¡embuste! tú te   By God, it's a lie! You are
    engañastes,   deluding yourself,
12. ¡no me he muerto todavía! mama.   I haven't died yet! mama.

gr. *Üu-ja-je üupa*

NOTES

Perf:

The men begin their gritos as Reinaldo sustains the final pitch of his sung verse, except in v. 10, where they enter while he is singing *mama*.

Text:

1. - The bird symbolizes an opportunity of which the person being addressed did not take advantage.
6. - The wooden statue of the Virgin Mary found in the school building for boys represents the Virgin del Carmen, one of the earliest apparitions of the Virgin. In 1251 during the reign of Pope Gregory XIII, the Virgin appeared before Saint Simon Stock, at that time head of the Carmelite Order. The Carmelites traced their origin to worship that began in a temple that the Prophet Elijah built on top of Mount Carmel 900 years before the birth of Jesus. According to Catholic theology, Elijah had prophesied the coming of both the Virgin Mary and Jesus, and he is considered the founder of the Carmelite cult. When the Virgin appeared before Saint Stock, she gave him a miraculous scapula as a gift of love and confraternity. The scapula was a symbol of health and peace, and anyone who died while wearing it was saved from the eternal fire (Comisión...Cuyo 1914:i-ii).

TR 21 (LF 78.2)

Zafras sung by Mariano Rosado Julio and Reinaldo Rosado Julio with accompanying gritos by two men. Evitar, 1 November 1964.

M: 1. *E-jia* mía *je-je*   (Mother) mine

gr.   *Jua* compañero, compadre   Friend, friend Rosado.
Rosado.

R: 2. ¡Cógelo, por Dios! Virgen del Carmen	Grab it, by God! Virgin of Carmen.
gr. ¡Ay, Reinaldo! *je-je* ¡Arréa! ¡Arréa!	Reinaldo! Get moving! Get moving!
M: 3. *E* mama mía, *fe*	Mother mine.
gr. ¡Oyelo! *aja* ¡Corte! ¡Corte! ¡Corte monte ligero!	Listen! Cut it! Cut it! Cut the field faster!
R: 4. *Üe-je-je-i* la milagrosa del mundo.	The miracle worker of the world.
gr. ¡Otro lado! ¡Al lado! ¡Echa para acá, Marianito!	The other side! To the side! Work over here, Marianito!
M: 5. *E* iarrímate para allá! *i*	Go over there!
gr. *Ajá-ju-ajá-ja*	
R: 6. *A-je* mi hermano por ser mi hermano.	My brother, because he is my brother.
gr. ¡Carlos no corta casi nada! ¡Dale! ¡Dale!	Carlos cuts practically nothing! Get going! Get going!
M: 7. *E* iarrímate para allá! 8. que aquí solo quepo yo.	Go over there! There is only room here for me.
gr. ¡Allí no más! ¡*Carajo!* ¡Corte! ¡Corte!	No more over there! Cut it! Cut it!
R: 9. *Le-je-e-i* iyo sigo pero con miedo!	I go but I am afraid!
gr. ¡Arriba, veraco! (2) ¡Arriba, Rei! (2)	Get up there, stubborn! Get up there, Rei(naldo)!
M:10. *E-je-je-i* mama mía, *ombe*	Mother mine.
gr. *Jua.*	
R:11, ¡Yo sigo pero con miedo!	I go but I am afraid!
gr. ¡Echa! ¡Echa para acá! ¡Echa para acá!	Come on! Work over here! Work over here!
M:12. *E-je* de la sierra para arriba *je* 13. ¡donde el muerto me salió!	On the heights above Where death waits for me!

NOTES

Perf:

    TR 21 represents the third part of the recording. Each of the three parts on the original tape is separated by a pause.
    In this performance there is considerable overlapping of the sung verses and the gritos. At the ends of v. 2, 3, 6, 8, and

10, the men begin their gritos shortly before the singers complete
their verses. On the other hand, the singers begin v. 4, 5, and 9
through 12 before the gritos are completed. Thus the gritos occurring between v. 3 and 4, 8 and 9, and 10 and 11 overlap in both
directions; that is, they begin before one singer completes the
first of two verses and they continue after the other singer has
begun the subsequent verse.

Text:

The two brothers, Mariano and Reinaldo, begin with exclamations
and snatches from coplas. At v. 5 they launch into a short, improvised dialogue. There are two possible interpretations of what
is sung in v. 5-12, of which the first is the most likely. The
first is that Mariano is expressing what is known in Hispanic
countries as *machismo*, a strong manifestation in one form or
another of the male ego. In this case Mariano tells his brother
that he, Mariano, can manage all this part of the field by himself and that Reinaldo should go elsewhere. Reinaldo sarcasti-
cally replies that he will do so out of deference to his brother
(Reinaldo is one year younger than Mariano) and for good measure
pretends to be afraid not to do what his brother commands. The
last verse, 12, would then be an interpolation from a known copla.
A second but less likely interpretation would be that a worker
had died or been killed in some manner in a higher portion of the
field, and thus no one wishes to work there. Mariano commands
his brother to work in this area of the field, and Reinaldo, as
the younger brother, agrees to obey his command, but expresses
his fear in doing so.

Carajo, in the gritos following v. 8, is an expression of
anger or disgust (Alario di Filippo 1964:59).

VAQUERIA

Since most of the men in Evitar work in the fields, the singing
of zafras is still common practice. Vaquería, on the other hand,
are rarely performed. Few evitaleros own cattle, and thus they
have no herds of their own to drive. The hacendados in the region
who do have large herds have their own vaqueros to handle them.
Also, for a number of years it has been a common practice to
transport cattle by truck rather than driving them. Nevertheless,
in the past, and less frequently at the time of the investigation,
hacendados apparently employed men from Evitar to drive cattle.
Pedro Cueto, for example, stated that he had been employed to
drive cattle for a considerable distance within a year of the date
he was interviewed (1968). During this drive vaquería were sung.
Other men interviewed in Evitar could not remember having heard
vaquería sung for many years. When we drove to and from Evitar
by car on the Mahates-Calamar road, I did see men driving small
herds of cattle. However, none sang as we passed.

In driving cattle, one vaquero or a group thereof walks or
rides in front of the herd and another in the rear. In form the
performance of the vaquería, like that of the zafras, is very
free. However, the interaction in singing the vaquería is always

between those in the rear and those in front of the herd. An individual in one position may sing a copla, with a response in the
form of gritos by one vaquero or the group in the other position.
Or couplets or verses may be sung back and forth, interspersed
with gritos. However, in vaquería the gritos are often directed
to the cattle, to move them forward, rather than to the other
vaquero or group of vaqueros.

TR 22 (LF 77.3)

Vaquería sung by Pedro Juan Pacheco Salas. Evitar, 1 November 1964.

I 1. En un tiempo tuve, tuve,	Once I had, I had,
2. pero ya se me acabó.	But now it is gone.
3. El consuelo que me queda	What consolation remains
4. que en un tiempo tuve yo.	Is that at one time I had
o-jo-je	it.
II 1. *E* al llegar de ayer a hoy	As yesterday became today
2. mis ilusiones perdí.	I lost my illusions.
3. De muchas la sombra fui	I was the shadow of many
4. y ya hoy ni sombra soy.	And today I am not even a shadow.

NOTES

Perf:

Pacheco was our first informant in Evitar. After he had
recorded two series of décimas for us, Delia Zapata asked him to
sing vaquería. He seemed somewhat embarrassed and reluctant, but
he did sing three coplas in vaquería style. Two of these are
transcribed as TR 22. Pacheco is a carpenter by trade and told
me in 1968 that he had never herded cattle and had never before
sung a vaquería. However, he did not wish to be discourteous to
Delia Zapata. He had heard vaquería sung many times in the past,
and he thus sang three coplas that he knew, reproducing the
vaquería style as best he could.

Text:

II.1 - This is an idiom. The literal meaning is "in order to
arrive at today from yesterday."
II.3-4 - The meaning is that he had a close attachment to many
women, but now he has none.

TR 23 (LF 179.4)

Vaquería sung by Pedro Cueto Pimientel. Evitar, 4 August 1968.

2. üe pe-re Cho-le-stá pa-sa-o. o____

je Ce com-pa-ñe-ro: ——Ja__ üe

üe ju__ i e ga-no par-lan-te__!

3. Pue__ nin-gu-no tie-ne la cul — pa

4. üe que ten-ga lo-jo pe-la-o. o jay

lle___je___ Sa u-na-si e sa-ra-mu

üe ¡pa-lan-te ga-na-do! ¡Y u-

no con más ham—bre cun lo-co!

1. *Üe* yo he visto gente maluca   I have seen ugly people
   üe-je-je-lle-ja
   he visto gente maluca   I have seen ugly people
2. *üe* ¡pero el Cholo está pasado! *e-je*   But Cholo takes the cake!

(spoken) Dice el compañero: My partner says:

   ---Ja-üe-üe-ju

(spoken) ---¡Va el ganado para adelante!   Move them on!

3. Pues, ninguno tiene la culpa   Well, no one is to blame
4. *üe* que tenga el ojo pelado.   That he's popeyed.
   o-jai-lle-je

(spoken) ¡Se va uno así de saramullo!   There goes someone who wants to be elsewhere!

   üe ¡para adelante ganado!   Move on, there!

   ¡Y uno así con más hambre que   And someone is crazy
   un loco!   with hunger!

NOTES

Perf:

Cueto interjects the gritos that would be uttered by his partner in the drive. The verses of the copla can be differentiated from the interjections by the fact that they are numbered. Cueto then expresses his exasperation at the circumstances of the work.

Text:

1. - *Cholo* in this case is a nickname.
2. - *Ganado* is a general term for cattle.
4. - *Saramullo* represents a state of mind in which one feels that he needs to be elsewhere than where he is.

COMMENTARY

It is difficult to distinguish between the zafras and the vaquería. The sample of vaquería is very small, since this form was dying out. Pedro Pacheco admittedly had no experience as a vaquero and thus in singing vaquería. That he was not accustomed to singing in this style is attested by the paucity of meaningless syllables which he incorporated into his performance.

The basic textual element is the octosyllabic copla with assonantal rhyme. When one individual sings, as in TR 19 and TR 22-23, this particular quatrain form is evident, although it may be embellished with meaningless syllables and meaningful exclamations. As soon as other individuals participate, either through cries (gritos) or singing, full quatrains no longer are clearly evident, and there is a much greater use of meaningless syllables and exclamations. Some verses form couplets which are obviously part of known coplas. Other verses may have been improvised.

Table 12 offers a metrical analysis of the items sung. Numbers underlined and placed in parentheses represent meaningless syllables. Numbers placed in parentheses but not underlined represent meaningful exclamations or interjections such as *pues, mama, mama mía, madre mía, por Dios,* and *Virgen del Carmen.* In neither case, whether lexically meaningful or not, do these form part of a verse proper of a copla. The principle of the sinalefa is not applied to contiguous vowels, one of which is found within parentheses and the other not. The principle of the aguda cadence is applied only to the copla verse proper, not to material in parentheses.

Table 12.   Metrical Analysis of the Texts
of TR 19-23

TR 19

I.   1. (3) + 8   a
      2. 8   b
      3. 8   b
      4. 8   a

II.   1. (1) + (4) + 6   a
      2. 8   b
      3. 8   b
      4. 8   a

III. 1. (1) + 8   a
      2. 8   b
      3. 9   a
      4. 7   b

IV.   1. (3) + 11   a
      2. 8   b
      3. 8   c
      4. 8   b
      3. (1) + 8   c
      4. 8   b

V.   1. (1) + (4) + 8   a
      2. 8   b
      3. 8   a
      4. 8   b

TR 20

      1. 8 + (2)   (a)
      2. 8   (b)

      gr.

      3. 3 + (2) + (1)
      4. 8   (c)
      5. 8   (b)

      gr.

      6. (2) + (5)

      gr.

      7. 3 + (2)
      8. 8
      9. 8

      gr.

      10. (4) + 8 + (4)

      gr.

      11. (1) + (2) + 8
      12. 8 + (2)

      gr.

TR 21

      1. (2) + 2 + (2)

      gr.

      2. 3 + (2) + (5)

      gr.

      3. (4) + (1)

      gr.

      4. (4) + 8

      gr.

TR 22

I.   1. 8   a
      2. 8   b
      3. 8   c
      4. 8 + (3)   b

II.   1. 7   a
      2. 8   b
      3. 8   b
      4. 7   a

TR 21 (cont.)   TR 23

5. (1) + 8 + (1)   1. (1) + 8 + (5)   a
                                       8   a
    gr.   2. (1) + 8 + (2)   b

6. (2) + 8   gr.

    gr.   3. (1) + 8   a
                                   4. (1) + 8 + (4)   b
7. (1) + 8   (a)
8. 8   (b)   gr.

    gr.

9. (4) + 8

    gr.

10. (4) + (4) + (2)

    gr.

11. 8

    gr.

12. (2) + 8 + (1)   (c)
13. 8   (b)

    gr.

When the numbers in parentheses are elided, it will be seen that
the coplas in TR 19 and TR 22-23 are quite regular. There are, in
fact, only two verses in these items which cannot be considered
octosyllabic through poetic license. These are st. II, v. 1 of
TR 19, which is six syllables in length, and st. IV, v. 1 of the
same item, which is eleven syllables in length. All other verses
in TR 19 and TR 22 which are not octosyllabic in length can be
made that length by exercising the poet's license not to consider
two contiguous vowels as a sinalefa or to assign one syllable
rather than two to an aguda cadence when these operations will
regularize the length of his verses. In this manner st. II,
v. 3-4 of TR 19 may be counted as two verses of eight syllables
rather than as one verse of seven and a second of nine.

            3. no me quisiera recordar
                1 2   3 45 67 8
            4. cuando estaba en mi tiempo.
                1   2   345 6   7 8

In v. 3 the final aguda cadence is counted as one syllable only.
In v. 4 the first cluster of contiguous vowels is combined to
form a sinalefa, the second is not. Similar license could be
applied in st. II, v. 4 of TR 22.

            4. y ya hoy ni sombra soy.
                1 2 3   4 5   6 7 8

In this case the second and third syllables are not combined. When combined they form a triphthong, *aoy*, which as a sinalefa is counted as one syllable.

Among the number of octosyllabic couplets and individual verses in TR 20, one group, v. 1, 2, 4, and 5, may be considered to form a copla. The remainder of the material sung consists of exclamations, interjections, and meaningless syllables. TR 21 contains an even greater amount of sung material which does not represent copla verses.

As indicated previously, Magis considers the octosyllabic quatrain with rima romancera to be the most common Spanish popular lyric strophic form, although he admits that at times it displays some variation in meter and rhyme (1969:465). His conclusions seem applicable to the coplas of these worksongs, although the rhyming schemes are more varied than his statement might imply. Three of the coplas display the rhyming scheme abba, three the rima romancera abcb, and one the rhyme abab. Two additional coplas exhibiting the rima romancera are implied, one each in TR 20 and TR 21.

The preceding discussion indicates that there is no accurate means of differentiating the zafra and the vaquería through their sung texts. There seems to be no particular copla theme more appropriate to one form than to the other. There is much more use of meaningful exclamations in the zafras than in the vaquería recorded, but, as indicated, the sample of the latter is neither large nor representative. When sung without accompanying gritos, no real difference is apparent. On the basis of my experience in other localities as well as in Evitar, it would seem that the only observable difference is in the type of gritos employed in each, this difference having its basis in the functions of the two types of songs. In the zafras many of the gritos admonish and encourage the other workers in actions typical of clearing a field or reaping a crop. There are thus cries of ¡corte! ¡corte! (cut it! cut it!) and ¡echa para acá! (work over here!), while in the vaquería one vaquero cries to another ¡va el ganado para adelante! (move the cattle on!) or to the herd itself ¡para adelante, ganado! (move on, then!).

Since the worksongs do not display a tonal center and are in free rhythm, the methods used in analyzing the melodies in chapters 7 and 8 cannot be applied. An attempt has therefore been made to differentiate the melodic materials utilized by means of contour analysis. All of the larger sections of the worksongs are characterized by a generally descending melodic line; that is, the initial pitch in the transcription is higher than the final pitch. Since the judgments made concern contours rather than exact pitch, the beginning of an initial glide is considered an initial position and the end of a terminal glide a final position, as is the x marking a final indefinite pitch when not followed by a glide. All these points indicate approximate pitch. The larger sections may consist of full strophes, as indicated by strophe numbers placed to the left of the staff. They may consist of the repetition of two verses, as at the end of TR 19, st. 4. In the latter case the section is demarcated by a bar line. Finally, they may consist of single verses or of groups of two or three verses which are separated by gritos.

While the larger sections of the melodies of the worksongs show
a generally descending motion, the shorter sections of the items
display a greater variety of melodic movement, which will be
demonstrated in table 13. This more detailed contour analysis is
based on the numbered verses and their repetitions (see chapter 6,
IV.A.1.3). To this there are a small number of exceptions, all
demarcated by a short pause in the flow of the melodic line, a
pause which is represented by a half bar. The first three are
found in TR 19. The initial section of meaningless syllables of
I.1 is thus separated from the remainder of v. 1, as is a similar
group of meaningless syllables at the beginning of IV.1. In
addition, a section of only two pitches sung on the vowel E is
separated from the remainder of the repetition of v. 3 in the
penultimate staff of TR 19. In TR 20 there is one such division
by a half bar. In v. 10 the initial melodic contour sung to a
series of meaningless syllables is divided from the rest of the
melodic verse. It should be noted that in TR 23 there is a half
bar at the end of the second staff which separates the repetition of the first verse of the copla from its previous performance, in which it was preceded and followed by meaningless
syllables.

Table 13.   Contour Analysis of TR 19-23

Zafras:

TR 19				TR 20		TR 21	
I.	1.	H-L . M-H-L		1.	M-H-L	1.	M-H-L
	2.	M-H-L		2.	M-H-L	2.	M-H-L
	3.	M-H-L		3.	H-L	3.	M-H-L
	4.	M-H-L		4.	M-H-L	4.	H-L
				5.	M-H-L	5.	M-H-L
II.	1.	M-H-L		6.	M-H-L	6.	M-H-L
	2.	M-H-L		7.	H-L-M	7.	M-H-L
	3.	L-H-M		8.	M-H-L	8.	M-H-L
	4.	M-H-L		9.	M-H-L	9.	M-H-L
III.	1.	M-H-L		10.	M-H-L . M-H-L-M	10.	M-H-L
	2.	M-H-L		11.	H-L	11.	M-H-L
	3.	M-H-L		12.	M-H-L	12.	L-H-L
	4.	M-H-L				13.	M-H-L
IV.	1.	M-H-L . L-H-M					
	2.	H-L					
	3.	M-L-H-M					
	4.	H-L					
	3.	H-L . M-H-L					
	4.	M-H-L					
V.	1.	H-L					
	2.	M-H-L					
	3.	L-H-L					
	4.	M-H-L					

Vaquería:

TR 22   TR 23

I.   1. M-H-L   1. H-L . M-H-L
     2. M-H-L   2. H-L
     3. M-H-L   3. M-H-L
     4. M-H-L   4. M-H-L

II. 1. H-L
     2. M-H-L
     3. L-H
     4. H-L

In the following summary of table 13, the number of each type of contour found in each genre is listed.

Contour	Zafras	Vaquería	Total
M-H-L	37	8	45
H-L	8	4	12
L-H-M	2	0	2
L-H-L	2	0	2
H-L-M	1	0	1
M-H-L-M	1	0	1
M-L-H-M	1	0	1
L-H	0	1	1
Totals	52	13	65

It will be seen that the contour most frequently employed is M-H-L and that the second in frequency of use is H-L. The contours of the melodic verses, and of the parts thereof, are similar to the larger melodic sections previously discussed in that descending motion predominates. Thus 58 out of the total of 65 contours analyzed exhibit a generally descending motion; that is, the first pitch of the contour is higher than the last pitch. There are three instances of contours, comprising L-H-M and L-H, where the final pitch is higher than the initial pitch, and four instances of contours, two of L-H-L and one each of M-H-L-M and M-L-H-M, where the initial and final pitches are the same.

There is insufficient difference in the contours employed in the two genres to utilize this means for distinguishing between them. In addition, the sample of vaquería can hardly be considered adequate. It should also be remembered that the singers of the zafras are brothers who were accustomed to singing together, while the singers of the vaquería are not related and were not accustomed to performing together. The first of the latter, Pedro Pacheco, had never worked as a vaquero. My assumption is that from the textual and melodic points of view, the two genres are stylistically similar. The only real distinction seems to be one of function. However, this distinction seems to be reflected in performance by only a differentiation of the gritos used in each case.

In chapter 7 I was able to trace a number of the song texts to Spain by means of analogues found in the repertory of lullabies and children's game songs in that country. I found it possible to do the same with one item in chapter 8, but I have found no textual analogues in Spain of the song texts presented in the present chapter. On the other hand, the poetic form most commonly employed in the worksongs, the copla, is directly traceable to Spain (chapter 6, V.C.2). The copla is employed in many types of songs. Thus its presence is only one aspect of style; it does not necessarily differentiate one genre from another.

In her *Etnología musical*, Amades includes a lengthy discussion of *cantos de trabajo* in Spain (1964:132-92). Although various types of agricultural songs are listed and discussed, there is no mention of the zafra or the vaquería. These terms are not applied to song genres in Spain as they are in Colombia. In Spain zafra refers to the olive harvest and vaquería to a drove of cattle. The names applied to the two song genres in Colombia are thus derived from related if not wholly similar social functions or activities in Spain.

I was able in chapter 7 to relate the stylistic traits of the costeño songs to similar traits in song repertories in Spain serving similar social functions. This is not possible in the case of the worksongs. Amades offers two pages of music transcriptions. All are agricultural songs, and none is similar in melodic style to the costeño worksongs.

Stock raising had precedence over agriculture in Spain during the Middle Ages and the Renaissance. Livestock was driven from pasture to pasture for distances as great as 200 miles. However, these drives were almost entirely of sheep; only a few herds of cattle were so driven. If the vaqueros made use of herding songs, they may have been transmitted to the New World, but I know of no records of this. In recent times cattle herding in Spain has been carried on primarily by the *vaqueros de alzada* (cowmen of the heights), a pastoral people whose base is the mountainous region near Luarca in northern Asturias. They are a nomadic people who move their beef cattle from place to place in areas of Asturias and northern León, depending upon the season and the weather. Their ethnic origin is different from that of the surrounding population. Their songs are called *vaqueradas*. However, this term is apparently applied to any type of song sung by any members of this group, whether men or women. I am informed that the men do have some herding songs (information from Pilar García de Diego). Unfortunately, I have been unable to secure recordings or transcriptions of herding songs of the vaqueros de alzada. The recordings and transcriptions available of vaqueradas are dance songs sung by women.

If the Indians of northern South America have worksongs, I can find no recordings or transcriptions thereof. There are some of West African worksongs, but few of them have stylistic traits analogous to the costeño songs.

In chapters 7 and 8 I attempted to relate the costeño songs to Europe or Africa through patterns of specific pitches related to

a tonal center, through the rhythmic organization of the music,
or through the relationship of stress patterns in text and melody.
Few of these methods are of utility here. Since the costeño worksongs do not display tonality, the first method cannot be employed.
The worksongs are in prose rhythm, and most types of rhythmic
analysis are therefore impossible. However, the transcriptions
do indicate the location of pitches of longer than average duration. Since the worksongs do not display a regular pulse, clear
relationships of stress patterns in text and melody cannot be
established. For the discussion of possible cultural sources, I
therefore must be concerned with traits of the costeño songs
other than those considered in the two previous chapters. These
are outlined as follows:

1. Part of the text is lexically meaningful, part is lexically
    meaningless. In addition to the usual verses there are many
    meaningful and meaningless interjections. The lexically
    meaningless parts of the song texts may include interjections
    of syllables containing both vowels and consonants or of
    syllables consisting of vowels only. Verses, particularly
    the first verse of a copla, are often preceded by the mean-
    ingless vowel *e*.
2. The songs are primarily syllabic, that is, each syllable is
    sung to only one pitch. There are occasionally short neu-
    matic passages in which a syllable is sung to two to four
    pitches. These usually occur at the beginning of a verse,
    particularly the first verse of a copla, and often are sung
    on the vowel *e*. There are no melismas, passages in which one
    syllable is sung to a large number of pitches or notes.
3. Vocal glides are employed with some frequency and are often
    of considerable length. They may move either upward or down-
    ward, but descending glides at terminal points in phrases
    are the most common.
4. The range or ambitus of the melody is unusually wide. At its
    widest it reaches an 8ve plus a major 7th. The average range
    of the worksongs transcribed is a minor 10th. Terminal vocal
    glides are included in the determination of the range.
5. Characteristic of the performance of the zafra and the
    vaquería is the use by the men of the extreme upper tessitura
    of their voices.
6. In almost all cases this upper tessitura is produced with a
    forced, somewhat strained-sounding chest tone. Falsetto is
    not employed, and vibrato is rare.
7. With considerable frequency, a high tone is sustained near
    the beginning of a phrase. This phrase is often the first
    of a group of two or more phrases. The sustained tone is
    frequently sung to a meaningless syllable.
8. Although the bulk of the melodic movement consists of 2nds,
    3rds, and 4ths, there is a fairly frequent occurrence of
    melodic 5ths and 6ths. Both the augmented 4th and the
    diminished 5th are occasionally heard.
9. The prevailing melodic movement is descending. This applies
    both to the melodic phrases sung to the individual verses and
    to the larger sections of the song. The contours most com-

monly displayed by the individual phrases are M-H-L and H-L,
the former predominating. Approximately 90% of the individual
phrases (58 out of 65) exhibit descending motion.

Performances by male singers which display some traits analogous
to those of the costeño worksongs are found in Spain, in Asturias
in the north and in Andalucía in the south. Like the costeño worksongs they are sung in the upper tessitura of the voice in a
rather forced chest tone. The range of the rural Asturian songs
examined is less than an 8ve. When not used to accompany the
dance, it is rhythmically free and melismatic. Ex. 1 is a transcription I have made of an excerpt from such an Asturian song
sung by a man.

Ex. 1. Asturian song (Lomax 1951:Side A, Band 7)

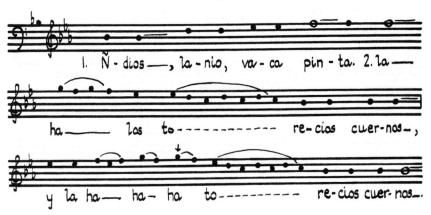

1. Adios, adios, vaca pinta,   Farewell, farewell, spotted
                                       heifer,
2. la de los torcios cuernos. (2)   You with the twisted horns.

Ex. 1 consists of the first two verses (and the repetition of
the second verse) of the first of two coplas heard in the recording. The singer utilizes the upper seventh of the normal tenor
range and sustains tones on f^1. He employs a rather intense and
forced chest tone produced with only occasional vibrato. The
performance shares a further stylistic trait with the costeño
worksongs. Seven out of ten of the phrasal contours are M-H-L,
the most common contour in the costeño songs.
    The best known song type in Andalucía is the flamenco. An
even more intense chest tone is employed than in male singing in
Asturias, but it is colored by a varied vibrato. The ambitus
of those examined is not much greater than the octave, and the
upper tessitura is emphasized. By the middle of this century
flamenco singing had become a professional or semi-professional
activity. Nevertheless, it remains primarily an oral tradition.
The older type of flamenco is sung without accompaniment and is
known by most authorities as cante jondo (deep song). Ex. 2 is my
transcription of a portion of a performance of this type of song:

Ex. 2.   Cante jondo (Murray Hill S-4360, Disc 1,
Side A, Band 2)

13.   ¡Ajai! Y así murió Juan García,   And thus died Juan García,
14.   testamento no escribió.   Having written no will.
     Y así murió Juan García,   And thus died Juan García,

Ex. 2 represents v. 13-14 and the repetition of v. 13. The song
text is not in copla form but in free verse. At this point the
melody is almost completely diatonic. Earlier a number of pitches
are sung whose relationship may be considered microtonal (see
chapter 6, IV.A.1.5). A meaningless interjection is heard at the
beginning of the excerpt. In the rest of the song there are also
two short sections of meaningless syllables. The song has a range
of an 8ve, and there are sustained tones of $f\sharp^1$.

As in the costeño worksongs, these sustained high tones are
heard near the beginning of a verse or the beginning of a group of
two verses. This phenomenon also occurs in ex. 1, the Asturian
song previously discussed. However, the Spanish and costeño songs
differ in the melodic intervals employed. The former is primarily
diatonic, and the largest interval heard is a perfect 4th. Numer-

ous 4ths, 5ths, and 6ths are heard in the latter. It would be
useful, were it possible, to compare the melodic phrases of the
cante jondo (ex. 2) with those of the zafra and vaquería (TR 19-
23). In the latter, melodic phrases are defined by the verses
to which they are sung. Thus melodic phrases and verses in
most cases are coordinated (see chapter 6, IV.A.1.3). This is
also the case in ex. 1, the song from Asturias. Such coordination is only occasionally present in ex. 2, the cante jondo.
The length of the melodic phrases requires the singer to take
frequent breaths, which do not necessarily coincide with the
ends of verses. Also characteristic of this style are short
pauses in which the singer does not breathe and repetition of
words or parts of words. Finally, the melodic phrase may end
with the first part of a word and the subsequent phrase begin
with the remainder of that word. To illustrate this last phenomenon, I give the first four verses of ex. 2, the cante jondo, as
realized in standard Spanish and then as sung. In the latter
the breaks in continuity are indicated by slashes.

     1. Fue sentenciado Juan García   2. a golpe de mosquetón,
     3. primera noche de agosto   4. sin jueces ni defensor.

     1-2. Fue sentenciao Juan / García gol- / pe de mosquetón,
     3-4. primera / noche lagoto sin jue- / ce ni defenso.

Since it is impossible to establish the boundaries of the melodic
phrases in the same manner as was done in the costeño worksongs,
no valid comparison can be made of phrasal contours.

    The Mende of Sierra Leone have at least one type of worksong
which takes the form of a call and response pattern. The verses
improvised by the soloist often contain references to other men
working in the field and words or syllables which are not meaningful in Mende speech. In a particular recorded example of this
type of worksong, the soloist is described as singing phrases
irregular in length and implying no discernible pulse. The
soloist frequently begins his phrase in the upper tessitura of
his vocal range and then descends (Schulze 1965:5 referring to
Side A, Band 2). The stylistic characteristics described are
similar to those of Liberian/Sierra Leonean style in general, in
which the rhythms of the soloist are freer than those of the
chorus and men often sing in the upper register of their voices
(Burnim 1976:36).

    I know of no available transcriptions of West African work-
songs. In addition, few transcriptions are available of any type
of West African song in which melody and text are associated.
One type of analysis made in this chapter, that of phrasal melodic
contours, cannot be carried forward unless the meaning of the text
is understood. This is best achieved by a line-by-line translation. For this reason I turn to a study of songs sung by the
Mende during the telling of tales (Burnim 1976).

    Burnim offers ten transcriptions of Mende songs. In seven of
these the soloist is a man, in three a woman. Both men and women
participate in the response. The range of the male solo parts
does not exceed a major 9th, and in two cases it is less than

an 8ve. The average range is a minor 7th. As in the general
Liberian/Sierra Leonean style, men sing primarily in the upper
tessitura of their vocal range. I have had the opportunity to
listen to the recordings upon which Burnim based her study. In
these, as in the worksong recorded by Schulze, the men employ a
somewhat forced chest tone and little perceptible vibrato. The
vocal production is therefore similar to that of the costeño
worksongs and the song from Asturias. It lacks the vibrato
heard in the performance of the Spanish songs.

The Mende songs display three other traits characteristic of
the costeño worksongs but not of the two Spanish songs. They are
primarily syllabic, and there are no melismatic passages. Melodic
intervals larger than a perfect 4th are heard with some frequency.
There are a number of ascending and descending perfect 5ths and a
few descending augmented 4ths and major 6ths. Vocal glides are
fairly frequent (they are rare in ex. 2, the cante jondo, and nonexistent in ex. 1, the Asturian song). The size of the majority
is a perfect 4th. Both ascending and descending glides are
represented. In addition, there is one ascending glide a 7th in
range and a descending glide which covers a 9th. Ex. 3 is an
excerpt from Burnim's transcriptions, the Solo Introduction of
T1, which is offered to document the presence of these traits:

Ex. 3. Mende song in tales (Burnim 1976:145, T1)

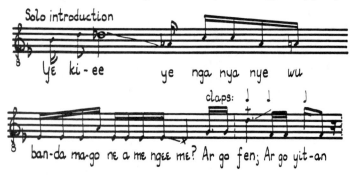

Meaningless syllables and groups of syllables are incorporated
in the Mende song texts. They are somewhat different in form
from those heard in the costeño worksongs. Some are vowels added
to verbal phrases in order to complete the musical phrase. Others
are ideophones, groups of words employed for sound effect rather
than sense. These are usually phones or groups of phones which
have meaning in speech but in song are arranged in nonsensical
order (Burnim 1976:82-83).

Traits analogous to those displayed by the costeño worksongs
are also found in the dirges of the Akan of Ghana. The dirges are
sung by women rather than by men, and the costeño has no comparable genre. However, there is some evidence that in Africa dirges
and worksongs are considered related genres. The Kpelle of
Liberia apply the term *pêle* to most types of music performance,
but do not include worksongs or funeral dirges within this category
Pêle refers to an activity carried on by a group rather than an

individual, and its function is to entertain. Although the performance of worksongs among the Kpelle is a group activity, and
more than one individual may participate in the singing of dirges,
their purpose is not considered to be entertainment, and they
therefore do not fall within the rubric of pêle (information
collected in the field by Ruth Stone).

The texts of the Akan dirges are traditional, but there is
variation in performance. Interjections are added at the beginning and the end of the dirge. The vowel e is often used at the
beginning of the dirge, sung to more than one but generally not
more than four pitches. Melodic movement is primarily by 2nds,
but some 4ths and 5ths are heard. The range of pitches within
the individual phrase is limited and is controlled by the tones
of the language. The individual phrases follow various melodic
contours, but the general melodic motion is descending. The
final pitch is always lower than the initial pitch (Nketia 1955:
153-55).

An examination of Nketia's transcriptions of the dirge melodies
indicates that their average range is slightly less than an 8ve.
The largest ambitus seen is a minor 10th and the smallest a minor
6th. However, these dirges sung by women are analogous to the
costeño worksongs in several respects. Of these the most obvious
is the use of sung interjections using fairly large intervals
in initial and final position. The second possibly analogous
trait is the use of the vowel e in singing the interjectory
melodic pattern. However, Nketia does not give the phonetic
equivalent of the vowel e as employed in the dirges, and I am
not sure it is the same phone as that represented by e in
Spanish. A third similar trait is the combining of lexically
meaningful and lexically meaningless textual material in song.
Finally, the melodic motion as a whole in both the Akan dirges
and costeño worksongs is descending.

The search among the songs of the Amerindians for traits analogous to those of the costeño songs proved very difficult. Although recordings are available, there is no published stylistic
study of Indian music of the Atlantic coastal region of Colombia.
An attempt was therefore made to find analogous traits by means
of sampling the recordings available in the Archives of Traditional Music. Music of the Chocoan tribes of the Pacific coastal
region was also sampled. The northern part of the Departamento
de Chocó borders on the Caribbean Sea. However, the greater part
of this area drains to the south, into the Pacific Ocean. Tran-
sit between the two coasts can be achieved primarily by waterways,
and the Cuna and the Chocó thus have musical instruments in common. The songs of the Jívaro men of the Ecuadorian Amazon range
as high as d^2 and are sung almost entirely in falsetto (fig. 76,
p. 300). Men of the Cuna living in Colombia sing in an equally
high tessitura. However, it is difficult to determine whether
they are singing in falsetto or using chest tone (see, for example,
Moser-Tayler 1972:MC 3.A, item 3b). The male descendants of the
Atánquez Indians, now living in a village of that name on the
eastern slope of the Sierra Nevada de Santa Marta, sing dance
songs with Spanish texts known as *chicotes*. The singing is in a
high, strained-sounding chest tone very like that used in the

worksongs recorded in Evitar (see Moser-Tayler 1972:MC 1.A, 3e
and LF 127-128).

Ex. 4-5 are transcriptions which I have made of short sections
of two Indian songs. Ex. 4 is of the Ika of the Sierra Nevada
de Santa Marta and ex. 5 of the Noanamá Chocó of the Guapi River
basin near the Ecuadorian border. Both were selected primarily
because of their wide range, an 8ve plus a perfect 4th. Ex. 4,
the Ika song, consists of short vocal sections heard between
longer sections of performance on the jaw's harp. The sex of the
singer is not given in the documentation. I cannot determine
whether it is a woman singing or a man singing in falsetto. Ex 5,
the Chocó song, is sung by a man. I have omitted the last few
pitches. At this point he is joined by another man and they sing
in heterophony. The final pitch is B.

I am not familiar with the languages of the Ika or the Chocó,
and the texts as transcribed cannot be expected to be wholly
accurate. Nor do I know the meaning of the texts or whether or
not they are meaningful. I shall use the transcribed texts to
determine whether the songs shall be described as syllabic,
neumatic, or melismatic. However, I cannot be certain that the
placement of my half bars correctly indicates textual-melodic
phrases, and I therefore shall not attempt to analyze the contours
of these phrases. The staff notation represents only an approxi-
mation of the pitches sung, since they often are not stable.

A few Amerindian songs of the general geographic area do show
traits similar to those of the costeño worksongs, a high tessitura in male singing and a wide melodic range. These characteristics are even more pronounced in the songs of the Plains-Pueblo
Indian group of North America. Among the Arapaho, for instance,
men often begin their songs at a very high tessitura and return
to it repeatedly (see, for example, Salzman ATM Pre'54-016-F,
ATL 230.4). Hopi songs have ranges as great as an 8ve plus a 7th
(see List 1968a:51). Although it may exist, or may have existed,
I know of no comparable body of Indian song in northern South
America which displays these traits to the same degree.

Ex. 4.   Ika song (Garibello 1962:ATM 66-212-F, EC 3958)

Ma dei mda yem mei go ka na yen

ma ga ka la dei mei-la dei nai ka

Ex. 5.   Chocó song (Universidad Nacional de Colombia-Instituto
         Popular de Cultura de Cali, ATM 67-190, ATL 4870, Item1)

An analysis of the melodic contours of the individual phrases
of the costeño worksongs was offered in table 13 and then followed by a summary (pp. 327-28). In table 14 I give a similar
analysis of one Spanish song, five African songs, and the first
section of one Indian song from northern South America. Spain
is represented by the song from Asturias, which is partially
transcribed in this chapter in ex. 1. Since verbal and melodic
phrases do not coordinate in the cante jondo (partially transcribed in this chapter in ex. 2), it could not be utilized in
this type of analysis. Sub-Saharan West Africa is represented
by a song sung by the Mende while telling tales (Burnim 1976:
145-46, 150-55). The analysis is of the solo parts only. (The
first of these songs has been partially transcribed in ex. 3.)
The songs selected for analysis were those in which there was no
question of coordination of verbal and melodic phrases. Such
coordination could not be determined in the Mende worksong nor
in the Akan dirges, and they therefore could not be utilized.
Amerindians are represented by only one song, that of the Jívaro
(fig. 76, p. 300). I can be sure of the accuracy of the text of
this song, since it was transcribed by a Jívaro trained by a
member of the Summer Institute of Linguistics.

Table 14.   Phrasal Contours of Spanish, African,
            and Amerindian Songs

Asturias

I.	1.	L-H		II.	1.	L-H
	2.	M-H-L				L-H
		M-H-L			2.	M-H-L
	3.	M-H-L			3.	M-H-L
	4.	M-H-L			4.	M-H-L

Mende

T1. 1. M-H-L . M-H-L   T5. 1. L-H-M . H-L-M
     2. M-H-L   2. M-H-L
     3. L-H-M . M-H-L   3. M-H-L
     5. H-L-M . M-H-L   4. L-H-L . H-L . H-L .
     7. L-H   H-L
     8. L-H   5. L-H-M

T3. 1. H-L-M . L-H-M   T6. 1. H-L
     2. H-L   2. H-L
     3. L-H . L-H   3. M-H-L . H-L . H-L .
     4. L-H . L-H-L . H-L   H-L . L-H-L . H-L
                                      4. L-H-L
T4. 1. H-L-M   5. H-L
     2. L-H-M
     3. L-H-M . M-H-L . M-H-L
     4. H-L-M . H-L . L-H-M
     5. L-H-M
     6. M-L-H-M . L-H . L-H-M

Jívaro

     1. L-H   7.   M-H-L
     2. L-H-L   8.   L-H
     3. M-H-L   9.   H-L
     4. L-H-M   10.   L-H-M
     5. L-H-L   11.   L-H
     6. H-L-H

Verses 4 and 6 of Mende T1 were omitted in the analysis, since
there was simultaneous singing by the soloist and chorus. Table
14 is summarized below and compared with the summary of the phrasal
contours of the costeño worksongs which follows table 13.

Contour	Asturias	Mende	Jívaro	Costeño
M-H-L	7	10	2	45
H-L	0	13	1	12
L-H-M	0	9	2	2
L-H-L	0	4	2	2
H-L-M	0	5	0	1
M-H-L-M	0	0	0	1
M-L-H-M	0	1	0	1
L-H	3	6	3	1
H-L-H	0	0	1	0
Totals	10	48	11	65

M-H-L is the most frequent contour heard in the song from
Asturias, as it is in the costeño worksongs. The second contour

employed in the song from Asturias, L-H, is heard only once in the
worksongs. The contours of the Mende songs are relatively analogous to those of the costeño worksongs. The majority of the contours descend, but this majority is by no means as large as in the
costeño songs. Again, as in the costeño songs, M-H-L and H-L are
the most frequently heard contours. However, the rate of frequency
is reversed, H-L occurring more often than M-H-L. The latter is
found only slightly more often than the ascending contour L-H-M.
Although the Mende songs display a greater variety of contours,
the two contours most frequently heard in the costeño songs, M-H-L
and H-L, account for almost half of the contours sung (23 out of
48).

On the other hand, the majority of the phrasal contours
employed in the Jívaro song are of the ascending type. Thus the
Jívaro song and the costeño worksongs are quite disparate in this
respect. The analysis of the Jívaro song is also evidence that
not all melodic repertories display a preponderance of descending
phrasal contours. The type of analysis made therefore has some
utility in determining relationship of melodic styles.

After this short tour of four continents, I shall summarize
the accumulated evidence concerning the existence in other musical
cultures of stylistic traits analogous to those heard in the
costeño worksongs. In so doing I shall follow the nine-point outline of the traits displayed by the costeño worksongs (pp. 330-31).

1. In Spain, meaningless syllables and interjections are
heard in the cante jondo but not in the Asturian song. In the
former, groups of meaningless syllables seem to form a prelude
and an interlude. Continuants, vocables used to fill in or continue melodic phrases, are also employed. The Mende songs display both ideophones and continuants. In the former, meaningful
words or syllables are sung in nonsensical order. In the Akan
dirges interjections are sung both at the beginning of the dirge
and at the ends of phrases. Meaningless syllables or vocables
are commonly employed in North American Indian songs. I do not
have such information concerning the songs of the Indians of the
Atlantic coastal region. The Jívaro song consists of meaningful
text only. Of the songs discussed here, the Akan dirges seem
most analogous to the costeño worksongs in the use of interjections and meaningless syllables.

2. Rural Asturian song and cante jondo are characteristically
melismatic. The Mende songs, the Akan dirges, and the Amerindian songs transcribed are all primarily syllabic. Some neumatic passages are heard in all but the Amerindian songs. The
costeño songs and the Akan dirges possibly share an additional
trait, an initial neumatic passage which is often sung on the
vowel *e*. However, in the dirges such passages are occasionally
melismatic.

As far as this trait is concerned, the dirges again seem the
most analogous to the worksongs.

3. Glides sufficiently definite to be transcribed are not
heard in the two Spanish songs discussed. If the women who sang
the Akan dirges performed glides, Nketia has not indicated them
in his transcriptions. There are a number of glides in the Mende
songs, and, as in the costeño worksongs, they occur most fre-

quently at the terminal points of phrases. In the Amerindian
songs glides occur only in that of the Chocó, and they are not
terminal glides.

In this trait the Mende songs are most analogous to the costeño songs.

4. The rural Asturian songs examined have a range of less
than an 8ve. The one transcribed has the range of a major 7th.
The cante jondo transcribed has the range of an 8ve. The ambitus
of most flamencos does not seem to exceed a major 9th. This is
also the case of the Mende songs in tales and the Mende worksong.
The average range of the Mende songs in tales sung by men is a
minor 7th. The Akan dirges transcribed by Nketia range from a
minor 10th to a minor 6th. Only two have a range larger than an
8ve. Both the Ika and Chocó songs have the range of an 8ve plus
a perfect 4th, the Jívaro song a major 10th.

Although none of the Amerindian songs reach the extreme range
of one of the worksongs, their average range is slightly wider
than that of the costeño songs.

5. The Spanish male singers employ the upper tessitura of
their voices, the singer from Asturias sustaining f^1 and the
singer of the cante jondo $f^{\sharp 1}$. Mende men also sing in the upper
register of their voices, reaching a^1. The Cuna men also employ
their upper tessitura, reaching $a^{\flat 1}$ and $b^{\flat 1}$. The Ika sing as
high as $b^\flat$, the Jívaro as high as d^2. The singers of Atánquez
begin one chicote on a^1 and return to this pitch level with
frequency.

Only the Jívaro singer reaches a pitch higher than Mariano
Rosado's $c^{\sharp 2}$. Some of the African singers and the Ika singer
ascend to pitches as high as those sung by the other three singers
of costeño worksongs.

6. In producing their high register, the Spanish singers employ
a rather forced chest tone. The singer of the cante jondo makes
use of an intense and variable vibrato, which is less pronounced in
the performance of the singer from Asturias. The Mende men also employ a rather intense chest tone and, like the Spanish singers, make
no use of falsetto. Of the Indian songs under discussion, both the
Cuna and the Jívaro sing almost entirely in falsetto. If the Ika
song is sung by a man, it is also in falsetto. The Chocó singer,
as far as I can determine, employs chest tone. The singers of Atánquez utilize the same rather strained-sounding chest tone as the
evitaleros. The population of Atánquez includes not only acculturated Indians but a number of individuals with African racial inheritance. The vocal production employed in singing the chicote may
therefore have been derived from costeño rather than Indian tradition or, at least, may have the same sources as the former.

Only the Spanish singers employ vibrato. It is primarily the
Amerindians who utilize falsetto. The vocal production of the
Mende men is the most analogous to that of the costeño.

7. A high, sustained pitch near the beginning of a phrase is
heard in the Spanish and Mende songs but not in the Akan dirges
or in the Amerindian songs. It occurs with considerable frequency in the Spanish songs, less frequently in the Mende songs.
When it occurs in the cante jondo or the Mende songs it is usually
in the first of a group of phrases.

This analogous trait is thus found in both Spain and Africa.

8. Most of the intervals in the Spanish songs are 2nds or 3rds, the perfect 4th occurring rarely. The Mende songs transcribed by Burnim employ larger intervals, major 6ths, perfect 5ths, and augmented 4ths. The Akan dirges also contain 5ths and 4ths. The perfect 4th is the largest interval heard in the Amerindian songs, if the 8ve leaps occurring in the Ika and Chocó songs are omitted from consideration.

In the use of large melodic intervals, the Mende songs in tales are most analogous to the costeño worksongs.

9. Only the Jívaro song displays a generally ascending motion; that is, the final pitch is higher than the initial pitch. In both of the Spanish songs the initial and final pitches are the same. The remaining songs display a prevailing descending motion; that is, the entire song or a portion thereof begins with a pitch which is higher than the final pitch.

As far as individual pitch contours are concerned, 70% (7 out of 10) of those of the Asturian song descend. In the Mende songs used in telling tales, 58% (28 out of 48) are of the descending variety. The seven descending contours in the Asturian song are all M-H-L. In the Mende songs H-L is the most frequent melodic contour, M-H-L the second in frequency.

Since the Mende songs display both prevailing descending motion and a majority of descending contours, they are the most analogous to the costeño worksongs from the point of view of melodic motion.

There are two factors which limit the conclusions which can be derived from the above evidence: the first is that not only is the sample inadequate as a representation of the cultural-geographic areas involved, but the songs discussed do not serve the same social function as the costeño worksongs. The second factor to be taken into consideration is that some of the traits discussed have a very wide distribution. The use of interjections and meaningless syllables is well documented in Europe, Africa, and North America and certainly occurs to some extent elsewhere. The terminal glide is found in the songs of many cultures (see List 1963), as is general descending motion (see Kolinski 1957). Traits which are this widespread are not very useful in determining the cultural source of a particular style.

If we assume that the available evidence is representative of the music cultures involved, it will be seen that the greater number of traits characteristic of costeño worksongs will be found in West Africa rather than in Spain or among the Indians of northern South America. Nevertheless, one or more traits of the costeño songs are more evident in the last two areas than in West Africa. In addition, most of the traits discussed are more strongly evident in the costeño songs than in the songs of the other cultures with which they have been compared. Thus Manuel Rosado utilizes a wider range than any Spanish, African, or Amerindian singer. There is a greater use of interjections and meaningless syllables in the worksongs than in any of the other songs discussed, and the costeño songs display a larger percentage of descending individual phrasal contours.

My conclusion, therefore, is that the zafra and the vaquería

Fig. 77. Male singers. Left to right:
Simón Herrera Sánchez, Reinaldo Rosado
Julio, Mariano Rosado Julio, Carlos Julio
Sánchez, (front) Pedro Cueto Pimientel.

represent an independent musical development in this area of the
New World which, nevertheless, is based in part on traits found
in the three parent cultures.

An analogous development is found in another area of Latin
America. The *aboios*, the herding or cattle driving songs of the
aboiaderos or *vaqueiros* of northeastern Brazil, represent a similar phenomenon. They consist primarily of sustained tones in a
very high tessitura which are connected by vocal glides. More
meaningless syllables are heard than meaningful text, and they
do not display tonality in the sense in which that term is employed here (information based on the study of field recordings
made by Gerard Béhague in the state of Bahía, Brazil). According
to Cascudo, the traditional aboios of the northeast were sung to
vowels only (1972:3-5). The recordings heard would therefore
represent a more recent development. In addition, at times two
men are heard singing in parallel 3rds. The word *boi* in Portuguese means ox. According to Cascudo, the Portuguese scholar
Sampaio has made a study of worksongs in the Province of Minho
in Portugal which he also refers to as aboio. However, these are
harvest songs with meaningful texts sung by solo and chorus. The
oxen referred to in this case are draft animals. Sampaio indicates that the Portuguese aboio is cast in the major mode. We
can therefore assume that, in contrast to the Brazilian aboio, it
displays tonality (Sampaio 1940:xx-xxvi).

Thus, we have again the transference of a term from the Old
World to the New, but little relationship between the two genres
so named.

10. Décimas

Décimas are not sung to accompany dancing or work or at particular fiestas. Rather they are performed by men for their own enjoyment or for the enjoyment of others, most frequently when the men get together to drink on Sundays and other holidays. In this society emphasis is placed upon the ability to recite poetry or to perform it in the form of song. Those who can compose poetry are held in high esteem, but even greater prestige redounds to those who can improvise poetry in song form. Since the décima is the most complex poetic form in traditional use by the costeño, the ability to improvise a décima carries the maximum of social prestige. It is therefore usually said that one is "improvising" a décima rather than "singing" one, although it is apparent in most cases that what is occurring is the repetition of a poem that has been memorized. Contests between decimeros, known as *piquerías* (from the verb *picar*, to bite), are also traditional in the region. In a piquería two or more decimeros vie for the plaudits of their auditors by improvising on a given theme. Experienced decimeros usually have a fund of décimas concerning common themes which they utilize as a whole or with some improvised changes in a piquería. I heard a decimero from one of the larger towns of the region supposedly improvise a décima at a piquería and later found that he had previously written down the text, had it published, and sold copies of it. This sale of printed sheets of locally composed décimas is a fairly common practice.

Upon inquiring in Evitar, we were told that piquerías had taken place in the village in the past, but not in recent times. There were few decimeros now, since most of the younger men had little interest in learning to perform décimas. A further reason was given by Simón Herrera, the youngest of the men who performed décimas for us. He stated that he did not know a sufficient number of décimas to engage in a piquería. This statement offers some corroboration of my belief that even in a piquería a decimero is primarily performing from memory rather than improvising.

When Pedro Pacheco, the first decimero of Evitar presented in this chapter, was asked to define the décima, he replied that it consisted of *diez palabras* (ten words). This is a poetic phrase implying that it is a form composed of ten verses. The décima

exhibits almost without exception a single rhyming scheme,
abbaaccddc (see chapter 6, V.C.3).

Each décima is concerned with a particular textual theme, and
this theme is often expressed in capsule form in the tenth and
last verse. When a piquería takes place, the theme upon which the
decimeros improvise may be expressed in a pie forzado (forced foot),
an obligatory last verse. TR 30, TR 34, and TR 35 are examples of
this usage. TR 24 and TR 25 are examples of a more complex method of
thematically binding together groups of décimas. In this case an
initial four-verse glosa (gloss) stating the theme is sung. Four
décimas concerned with the same theme then follow, each of the four
décimas concluding in order with one of the four verses of the
glosa.

The two forms just discussed are combinations of the décima and
the glosa (see chapter 6, V.C.3). The terms applied to the second
form by the costeño are different from those applied in Spain. In
my transcriptions I have followed costeño practice.

In 1968 in Cartagena I recorded four decimeros in a piquería.
They were José Manuel Palacio Coronado and José Aguedo Vibanco Palacio of Villanueva, Julio Gil Beltrán Simanco of Arjona, and Manuel
Alvarez Frías of Cartagena (LF 164). In the interview following the
piquería they informed me that most decimeros of the region utilized
the same melody in performing décimas and that this melody differed
from that used elsewhere, as in Panamá or Cuba. Upon questioning it
became clear that what they were referring to was a general pitch
contour rather than a melody in the sense of a particular pattern of
pitches and rhythm. According to these decimeros it was the custom
in the region when singing a décima to begin at a high pitch level,
to then descend, and to cadence at a low pitch level. On checking
the recordings of the performances of these four decimeros, I found
that they do indeed begin each décima at a high pitch level and cadence at a low. However, there are always two such cadences, one at
the end of v. 4 and the other at the end of v. 10. Melodically, the
décima is therefore divided into two sections, the first containing
four phrases and the second six. The pitch level at which phrase
five, the beginning of the second melodic section, is sung is higher
than the pitch level of the cadence of phrase four but not usually
as high as that of phrase one.

A reading of the transcriptions of the décimas given in the
following pages will indicate that the decimeros of Evitar follow
this general melodic pattern. However, within this broad outline
each decimero seems to employ particular shorter melodic formulae.
The latter are most apparent at the beginning and end of the two
sections into which the décima is divided. I therefore in some
cases have transcribed only the first, fourth, fifth, and tenth
phrases of the décima. Since melodic phrases and textual verses
coincide, identification can most easily be made by the numbered
verses (see TR 28-29 and TR 35-36).

TR 24 and TR 25 each contain four décimas integrated by the glosa
which precedes them. TR 32 contains two décimas. Not only are both
concerned with the same textual theme, but the second does not exhibit at its beginning the usual rise to a higher pitch level. I
therefore have considered the second a melodic continuation of the
first. In all other cases the décimas, although they may be

concerned with the same textual theme, and may have been sung
successively, are given separate transcription numbers.

Almost without exception, the décima, like the zafra and
vaquería, is sung in prose rhythm, and the same methods of indicating durational values are employed (see chapter 5, I.C.4 and I.E.2).
However, unlike the zafra and the vaquería, the décima does exhibit
a tonal center. Thus the absolute pitch of the final is indicated
unless the décima concludes with a glide. In the latter case the
absolute pitch of the initial tone sung is given.

TR 24-25

Décimas sung by Pedro Juan Pacheco Salas.   Evitar, 1 November 1964.

Pacheco informed us that he had not sung the décimas for eight or
nine months, since he had been en luto for a daughter who had died.
He also told us that he had no schooling and could neither read nor
write. When asked how and when he had learned these highly literary
décimas, he replied that in the 1930's some men in the village had a
book of décimas which they read aloud. He liked them very much, and
at his request they were read to him until he had memorized them.
However, the melody was his own. He had never heard these décimas
sung.

When asked if he knew the author of the décimas, he replied that
it was Gabriel Córceza (our interpretation of his pronunciation).
We asked if the book could still be found in the village, and he
replied in the negative. Pacheco was probably referring to Gabriel
Escorcia Gravini of Soledad, near Barranquilla, who is best known for
his cycle of décimas *La gran miseria humana*. This work is still to
be found in pamphlet form in the region. We were unable to locate
other published poems by Escorcia and do not know whether or not the
décimas sung were of his authorship. However, judging by the style
of his *La gran miseria humana*, they seem to be of an earlier vintage.

Pacheco did not understand the meaning of every word he sang, and
his pronunciation of a number of them is doubtful. We have done our
best to reconstruct the poem. Our efforts may or may not be fully
successful.

TR 24 (LF 77.1)

ci - nes co-mo mis ver-so d. ni si-re-na

co - mo tú _____.

I. 1. Y do-lor de mi pa-sión____, 2. mu-jer

de mis es-pe-ran-za, 3. Dio pu-so en

tus o lan-za 4. pa he-rir mi co-ra-

zón___. 5. E-re tú de mi-lu-sión, 6. la

lám-pe-ra re-flec-to-ria, 7. mi e-

ter-no sue-ño de glo-ria, 8. tre-lla

pre-san-te nie-ve 9. cuan-do an-te mí

te mue-ve 10(a). lle-na de lu mi me-

mo - ria ___ .

II 1. Cuan-do me cre-o má ven-ci-do

2. es cuan-do es-toy má triu-fan-te 3. por-

que tú i-ra-man-te 4. le-van-tal po-e-ta

ca - i - do ___ . 5. Por mí so-lo no he le-i-

do 6. len-sue-ño la cruz___, 7. vi-te de

o-ro y e tu 8. la mu-sa que tie-ne

fa-ma, 9. don-de el sol su luz e-rra-ma

ver - so.

IV.

1. No hay en lo cam-po___ ga-la-no___

2. pal-ma que ŭa-le a tu ta-llin, 3. en lo flo-

ri-dos va-lle 4. vio-le-ta co-mo tu ma-no-

ŭ, 5. nien lo ru-gien-te o-cé-a-no, 6. en

don-de cre-cel bam-bú, 7. el a-zu-lo-so ti-

zur 8. de lo as-tro fu-gien-te, 9. no hay

per-las co-mo tu dien-te 10(d). ni si-re-

ha co-mo tú___ ___.

Glosa

a.	Llena de luz mi memoria,	Full of light, my memory,
b.	allá en el mar siempre azul	There in the ever-blue sea
c.	no hay cisnes como mis versos	There are no swans like my verses
d.	ni sirena como tú.	Nor sirens like you.

I

1.	Y dolor de mi pasión,	Affliction of my desire,
2.	mujer de mis esperanzas,	Woman of my aspirations,
3.	Dios puso en tus ojos lanzas	God gave your eyes lances
4.	para herir mi corazón	With which to wound my heart.
5.	Eres tú de mi ilusión,	You are my illusion,
6.	la lámpara reflectoria,	The reflecting lamp,
7.	mi eterno sueño de gloria,	My eternal dream of glory,
8.	estrella presa entre nieves	Star imprisoned in snow
9.	cuando ante mí te mueves	When I see you before me
10(a).	llena de luz mi memoria.	Full of light, my memory.

II

1.	Cuando me creo más vencido	When I feel myself vanquished
2.	es cuando estoy más triunfante	Then I am most triumphant
3.	porque tu mirada amante	Because your beloved glance
4.	levanta el poeta caído.	Raises the fallen poet.
5.	Por mí solo no he leído	I alone cannot comprehend
6.	el ensueño de la cruz,	The mystery of the Cross,
7.	viste de oro y de tul	Clad in gold and tulle
8.	la musa que tiene fama,	Muse of fame,
9.	donde el sol su luz derrama	Where the sun sheds its light
10(b).	allá en el mar siempre azul.	There in the ever-blue sea.

III

1.	En el mundo donde alojo	In this world in which I live
2.	se encuentran los que son sabios;	One finds those who are wise;
3.	no hay rosas como tus labios	There are no roses like your lips
4.	ni estrellas como tus ojos.	Nor stars like your eyes.
5.	Sueñan los jazmines rojos	The red jasmine drowses
6.	con tus pies nievos e tersos;	At your snow white feet;
7.	se besan los vagos cierzos,	Kissed by the languorous north winds,
8.	se adormecen mis cantares	Hushed are my songs
9.	porque en los líricos mares	For in the murmuring seas
10(c).	no hay cisnes como mis versos.	There are no swans like my verses.

Fig. 78. Pedro Juan Pacheco Salas

IV

1. No hay en los campos galanos	There is not in the most beautiful field
2. palma que iguale a tu talle,	A palm equal to you in bearing,
3. ni en los floridos valles	Nor in the flowering valleys
4. violetas como tus manos,	Violets like your hands.
5. ni en los rugientes océanos	Nor in the roaring oceans,
6. en donde crece el bambú,	Where grows the bamboo,
7. el azugoso tizú	The silvery, iridescent cloth
8. borda los astros fulgentes,	Embroiders the refulgent stars,
9. no hay perlas como tus dientes	There are no pearls like your teeth
10(d). ni sirena como tú.	Nor sirens like you.

NOTES

Text:

III.1 - Literally, *alojo* means "I lodge."

III.7 - In a tropical climate the north wind is not the same as in a temperate climate.

III.5-8 - The relation of these verses one to another is problematical.

TR 25 (LF 77.2)

Glosa

a. Para vivir sin criterio,	Rather than to live without rectitude,
b. siendo el baldón de una raza,	Being a disgrace to your people,
c. mejor el tiempo se pasa	It is better to pass the time
d. durmiendo en el cementerio.	Sleeping in the cemetery.

I

1. El que pierde la vergüenza	He who loses his honor
2. mejor que pierda la vida,	Had better have lost his life,
3. que la vergüenza perdida	For the loss of honor
4. es la mancha más inmensa.	Is the greater misfortune.
5. Se va como nube densa	Like a dense cloud it fades away
6. y no vuelve a su hemisferio;	And never returns to your hemisphere;
7. la hace tornar en serio	It is really regained
8. el oro con su poder,	Only through the power of gold,
9. y más vale no nacer	It is better not to have been born
10(a). para vivir sin criterio.	Than to live without rectitude.

II

1. Mujer que pierde candor	A woman who loses her virtue,
2. de origen sus ricas alas,	The origin of her beautiful wings,
3. es mariposa sin alas,	Is like a butterfly without wings,
4. flor marchita sin olor.	A withered flower without scent.
5. En el fuego del amor,	In the fire of love,
6. desvergonzante se abraza,	Shamelessly embracing,
7. cuando el honor fracasa	When honor fails
8. ¿de qué sirve la mujer	Of what value is it
9. vestir cual la reina Ester,	To be clad like Queen Esther,
10(b). siendo el baldón de una raza?	Being a disgrace to your people?

(Apparently not remembering décima III, he
repeats décima II instead, also repeating
the last two lines of the latter.)

IV

1. El que ya pierde el decoro	He who has lost his honor
2. debe que ponerse entonces	Must therefore disguise himself
3. una máscara de bronce	In a mask of bronze adorned
4. con cascabeles de oro;	With little golden bells;
5. debe de convertirse en toro	He must convert himself into a bull
6. como el cuerno amenaza;	With menacing horns;
7. el mundo no le rechaza	The world will not reject him
8. para sí vivir.	For thus living.
9. Muerte sin ver ni sentir	Dead without sight or feeling
10(d). mejor el tiempo se pasa.	It is better to pass the time.

NOTES

Perf:

TR 25 is sung at a pitch level a semitone lower than TR 24.

In décima III, v. 7, which is the same text as décima I, v. 7, he sings *la ce* (*la ce* = *la hace*), stops, and then repeats *la ce* in singing the entire verse.

Text:

a. - *Criterio, vergüenza* (I.1), *honor* (II.7), and *decoro* (IV.1) are terms with approximately the same meaning. They refer to social responsibility, to the sense thereof possessed by the individual, and to the reputation he or she bears based upon his or her actions.

II.9 - The reference is to the heroine of the Book of Esther in the Old Testament. She was Queen of Persia and was instrumental in foiling a plot against her people, the Jews, an action which is celebrated in the Jewish festival of Purim.

IV.4 - *Cascabeles* refers to what are known in English as "jingle bells."

TR 26-29

Décimas sung by Carlos Julio Sánchez. Evitar, 1 November 1964.

Julio had left the village by the time I returned in 1968, and there was no opportunity to question him concerning the sources of the décimas he performed. At least one of the texts of these décimas was known to others in the village (TR 43).

Julio sang the four décimas successively, with a short pause between each.

TR 26 (LF 77.5a)

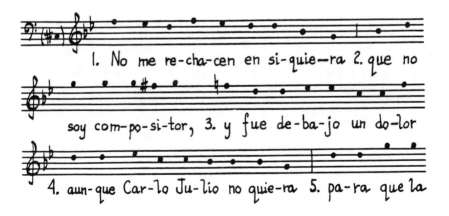

1. No me re-cha-cen en si-quie—ra 2. que no soy com-po-si-tor, 3. y fue de-ba-jo un do-lor 4. aun-que Car-lo Ju-lio no quie-ra 5. pa-ra que la

gen-te vie-ra_ 6. a-don-de da mi ca-be-za.

7. Cual-quier bri-llo la ri-que-za 8. a li-po-si-ción

de Dio, 9. ¡ ma-di-go se-a la po-bre-za!

10. no quen su-fra co-mo yo____.

9. ¡ ma-di-go se-a la po-bre-za! 10. no

quen su-fra co-mo yo____.

1. No me rechacen siquiera
2. que no soy compositor,
3. y fue debajo un dolor
4. aunque Carlos Julio no quiera
5. para que la gente viera
6. adonde da mi cabeza.
7. Cualquier brillo la riqueza
8. a la disposición de Dios,
9. ¡maldigo sea la pobreza!
10. no hay quien sufra como yo. (c2)

Do not reject me even though
I am not a composer,
And one is under pressure
Even though Carlos Julio did not want
To let the people see
How capable I am.
Whatever shining riches
At the disposition of God,
Cursed be the poverty!
There are none that suffer more than I.

NOTES

Perf:

As indicated by the double bar, there is a pause of considerable length before he repeats v. 9-10.

Text:

3. - This is an idiom. The literal meaning is "I was under a pain or an affliction." In standard Spanish the idiom is *fue debajo de un dolor*. In the décima the preposition *de* is missing.

6. - This is an idiom. The literal meaning is "whither my head delivers."

TR 27 (LF 77.5b)

sí le can-ta Car-le-ra 8. con to-da la me-lo-
dí-a. 9. E-sun-to de mis a-le-grí-a,
10. mu-cha-chas e-vi-ta-le-ra.

1. ¡Oh, joven! siempre te miro	Oh, young one! always I look upon you
2. con dolor en mi corazón; (c2)	With an aching heart;
3. por tí tengo una pasión,	For you I have a passion,
4. de mando y de suspiros.	I need you and for you I sigh.
5. Como la mente en el nido	Like the mind in the nest
6. para que la gente viera	In order to let the people see
7. que así le canta Carlera	That thus Carlos sings to you
8. con toda la melodía.	With all the melody.
9. Es asunto de mis alegrias,	It is a matter of my happiness
10. muchachas evitaleras.	Girls of Evitar.

NOTES

Text:

1. - In this case *joven* refers to a woman. She could be similar in age to the singer (he was 35 at the time) or younger.
5. - This verse has little meaning in this context and apparently was inserted to produce a rhyme.
7. - Carlera = Carlos. It is an affectionate term applied to an individual with the latter name; the feminine form is used for purposes of rhyme.

TR 28 (LF 77.5c)

1. Y la jo-ven con-sen-ti - da,

4. dan-del ca-lo-re mi vi-da. 5. E-res tú la pre-fe-ri-da, 9. me des-pi-do co-ra-zón.

1. Y la joven consentida,	And the girl upon whom I dote,
2. porque te adoro y te estimo,	Because I adore and admire her,
3. siempre a tí arrimo,	I wish her always to be near me,
4. dando el calor de mi vida.	Bringing warmth to my life.
5. Eres tú la preferida,	You are my favorite,
6. dueña de mi corazón.	Mistress of my heart.
7. Por tí tengo una pasión	For you I have a passion
8. que no puedo soportar;	Which I am unable to endure;
9. mañana en este lugar	Tomorrow in this place
10. me despido, corazón.	I say goodbye, sweetheart.

NOTES

Text:

1. - See the note for v. 1 under TR 27. Here *joven* is translated as "girl." In v. 10 of this décima it is translated as "sweetheart," although there is no specific indication that the woman being addressed has looked with favor upon the singer.

TR 29 (LF 77.5d)

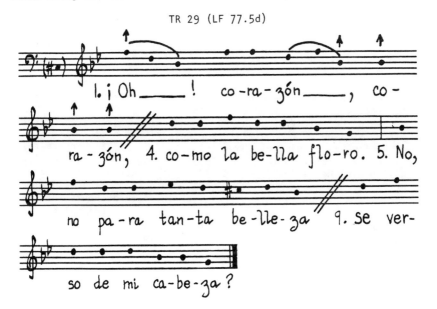

1. ¡Oh___! co-ra-zón___, co-ra-zón, 4. co-mo la be-lla flo-ro. 5. No, no pa-ra tan-ta be-lle-za 9. se ver-so de mi ca-be-za?

1. ¡Oh! corazón, corazón,	Oh! sweetheart, sweetheart,
2. ¿porqué me tienes sufriendo?	Why do you make me suffer?
3. Y poco se va muriendo	And little by little my love is dying
4. como la bella flor.	Like a beautiful flower.
5. No, no por tanta belleza	It is not that you are so beautiful
6. si no tienes la grandeza,	Nor are you my womanly ideal,
7. que me haces sufrir,	Yet you still attract me,
mi vida.	light of my life.
8. ¿Te tienen entretenida	You are entertained
9. ese verso de mi cabeza?	By my poem?

NOTES

Perf:

5. - There is a false start at the beginning of this verse consisting of one syllable. This is not indicated in the transcription.

8. - There is a slight pause between syllables of the last word of the verse. He sings *entre tenida* rather than *entretenida*.

TR 30-37

Décimas sung by Simón Herrera Sánchez

Herrera learned both the texts and the music of the décimas he sang for us by listening to men in the village sing them. He said that he had learned them at the age of fifteen or sixteen. Since he was 26 years of age at the time of the first recording session, 1964, he learned them in 1953 or 1954.

TR 30-35

Evitar, 1 November 1964.

On this date Herrera sang two groups of décimas, TR 30-32 (TR 32 containing two décimas) and TR 33-35. An additional décima was sung following TR 35 which has not been presented here, since the text is somewhat garbled and I found it impossible to offer an intelligible translation. Within each group sung, only short pauses were made between the constituent décimas.

Since the melody of each décima ends with a glide, the absolute pitch is given of the initial tone rather than of the final.

During his singing of the first group, TR 30-32, Herrera raises his pitch level a whole tone. TR 31 is sung at a pitch level a semitone higher than TR 30. TR 32 is begun at the same pitch level as TR 31, but the singer is slightly sharp at the end of ·décima I, v. 10. He gradually raises the pitch level throughout. At the end of décima II it is a semitone higher than at the beginning of décima I. TR 33-35 are sung at the pitch level at which TR 32 ends. However, the final cadence of TR 35 is slightly sharp.

TR 30 (LF 77.7a)

1. Si tienes a Chepa y Catana	If you have only one shirt and one pair of pants
2. y mandas a hacer la paloma	And you send them to be washed
3. llueve, y el sol ni se asoma,	Then it rains, nor does the sun shine,
4. porque no le da la gana.	For it is not worth the trouble.
5. Dura hasta una semana,	This lasts a whole week,
6. en tu casa encerrado;	You are cooped up in your house;
7. y si eres invitado	And if you are invited out
8. de tus amigos de la barra	By the gang
9. que mal suena la guitarra	How poorly sounds the guitar
10. cuando el pobre está salado.	When one is poor and thus unlucky.

NOTES

Text:

1. - This is an idiom or slang expression in use in the region in the early part of this century.

2. - Idiom. The *paloma* (dove or pigeon) is the symbol for whiteness. The literal meaning is "to make it white."

8. - Idiom. *Amigos de la barra* (friends of the bar) = your cronies, the group of friends to which you belong.

10. - Idiom. Literally, *está salado* means "to be salted." The reference is to an individual who is not only poor, which is bad enough, but who also is unlucky.

TR 31 (LF 77.7b)

1. Quien tiene un padre bueno	He who has a good father
2. y intenta de casarse	And intends to get married
3. que sepa que va a entregarse	Must know what he's getting into
4. a amansar un duro freno.	And keep a tight rein.
5. Mejor que me mata un trueno	I had better be killed by lightning
6. que moriría sin dolor	And die without pain
7. y no manchar mi honor	And not have my good name stained
8. con una 'señorita.'	By a 'lady.'
9. ¡Ay! si te sale maldita	Ay! if it turns out badly
10. ¡es el enemigo peor!	She will be your worst enemy!

NOTES

Text:

1. - The implication is that he has a good home where all necessities are provided.

3. - An English idiom is utilized in translating the latter part of the verse.

4. - The literal meaning is "to tame with a strong bridle or bit." An equivalent English idiom is used in translation.

5. - The singer is putting himself in the position previously described.

8. - By implication it is indicated that the "señorita" in question may be unfaithful or turn out to be a prostitute.

TR 32 (LF 77.7c-d)

1. Vie-nun po-bre a su-pli-car___ 2. en casa de un sa-cer-do-te, 3. re-zan-do-lu pa-
te-nos-te___. 4. —E-to ven-go a de-cla-
rar___: 5. Pa-dre, me quie-ro ca-sar 6. y
no ten-go por a-ho-ra; 7. yo ven-go con
mi se-ño-ra 8. pa-ra que me ca-se de
bal-de. 9. En-ton-ce con-tes-tel pa-dre:
10.—Hom-bre po-bre en en-a-mo-ra___.

II

1.—Pa-dre, le pi-do por Dio 2. que no me niegue los au-xi-lio; 3. aun-que no ten-gun
cuar-ti-llo 4. e-to que-den-tre lo do.
5. El pa-dre le con-tes-tó: 6. — Que-so e-
rim-po-si-ble ha-cer-lo; 7. que se üe-ra
pre-ve-hien-do 8. ha-ta con-se-guir lo re-
al-e. 9. La vo de po-bre no va-le;
10. la ver-dad la_ voy di-cien-do_.

1. Viene un pobre a suplicar	A poor man came to beg
2. en casa de un sacerdote,	At the house of a priest,
3. rezándole un paternóster.	Reciting for him a paternoster.
4. ---Esto vengo a declarar:	"This is what I wish to tell you:
5. Padre, me quiero casar	Father, I want to get married
6. y no tengo por ahora;	But I do not have it now;
7. yo vengo con mi señora	I come with my intended
8. para que me case de balde.	So that you will marry me without charge."

9. Entonces contesta el   Then the priest answered:
   padre:
10. ---Hombre pobre no se   "A poor man should not fall
    enamora.   in love."

II

1. ---Padre, le pido por   "Father, I beg you in God's
   Dios   name
2. que no me niegue los   That you do not deny me the
   auxilios   sacrament;
3. aunque no tengo un   Although I do not have a cent
   cuartillo
4. esto quede entre los dos.   This would be between us two."
5. El padre le contestó: The priest answered:
6. ---Que eso era imposible   "It is impossible to do this;
   hacerlo;
7. que se fuera previniendo   You must be cautious
8. hasta conseguir los   Until you have the money."
   reales.
9. La voz del pobre no vale;   The voice of the poor does
                                    not count;
10. la verdad la voy diciendo.   The truth I am telling you.

NOTES

Text:

I.6 - That is, he does not have money to pay the priest's fee.

I.7 - *Señora* is employed here as a rhyme for the previous verse. The term is usually applied to a woman who is married, but it obviously does not have this implication here.

II.3 - A *cuartillo* is a coin no longer in use in Colombia which was worth 2-1/2 *centavos*.

II.7 - The implication is that the supplicant should take care of himself until he is able to pay the priest's fee.

II.8 - A *real* is a Spanish coin worth 1/4 of a *peseta*. In Latin America the term *los reales* refers to money in general.

II.10 - Literally, "I am going around telling the truth."

TR 33 (LF 77.8a)

1. Si debes, y te andan   If you are in debt, they keep
   cobrando   trying to collect from you
2. de mañana y oscurito;   From morning till night;
3. si tocas te rompe el pito,   If you play your flute it breaks,
4. y te quedas vacilando.   And you don't know what to do.
5. Si entonces te andan   If then they come looking
   buscando   for you
6. para amarrar una res,   To lasso a steer,
7. él sale con mucho interés   He goes out with enthusiasm
8. pero de pronto fracasa.   But he soon fails.
9. Vive lleno de amenazas   One lives full of fears
10. cuando el Cristo está   When Christ has turned away.
    al revés. (c2)

NOTES

Perf:

9-10. - There is a pause before the repetition of these verses.

Text:

4. - An idiom. Literally, "and you remain vacillating."
6. - That is, to find a runaway steer, lasso it, and return it to the owner.
7. - There is a grammatical change from second to third person, but the reference is still to the same individual.

TR 34 (LF 77.8b)

1. Si en la Empresa Nacional	If in the National Company
2. están buscando veinte obreros;	They are looking for twenty workers;
3. el pobre no andarse ligero	The poor one does not hurry
4. y cerraron el personal.	And they have closed the employment office.
5. Dijo el pobre: ---Menos mal,	Says the poor one: "All right,
6. ahora me iré a pasitos contados	Now I'll take it easy,
7. para coger el pescado	I'll go fishing
8. para vender esa la lata.	And sell a bucketful."
9. Se le vuelve alcanfor la plata	Money evaporates like camphor
10. cuando el pobre está salado.	When one is poor and thus unlucky.

NOTES

Text:

5. - The last part of the verse is an idiom. The literal meaning is "less bad."
6. - An idiom. The literal meaning is "I leave by steps (of the feet)." The translation is an equivalent English idiom.
7. - Translated with an English idiom.
8. - *Lata* in this context signifies "bucket."
9. - Literally, "money turns out to be camphor."

TR 35 (LF 77.8c)

te sa-le   con vi-rue-la . 5. Son

in-fier-no   can-de-la 10. cuan-del

po-bre-stá sa-la-do___.

10. cuan-del po-bre — stá sa-la-do___.

1. Si tu mujer te revela	If your wife suggests
2. que compres un cerdo y lo mates,	That you buy a pig and slaughter it,
3. se convierte en disparate	It turns into a disaster,
4. y te sale con viruela.	Your pig has smallpox.
5. Son infierno de candela	There is a hellish fire
6. que sale por todos cuatros costados;	Which surrounds you on all four sides;
7. ya no camina de frente,	You can't go forward,
8. ya no camina de lado.	You can't go to the side.
9. Todo queda en accidente	Everything turns into misfortune
10. cuando el pobre está salado. (c2)	When one is poor and thus unlucky.

NOTES

Text:

2. - Butchering a pig and selling the meat in the village is one means of securing cash.

TR 36-37

Recorded by Winston Caballero Salguedo and Hector Díaz Herazo. Evitar, 22 September 1968.

TR 36 and 37 are not sung successively. A short conversation between Caballero and Herrera is heard between them.

TR 36 (LF 184.4)

I was not present at this recording session. Before singing the
décima Herrera says:

Como nosotros somos negros y
hay blancos que quieren poco
más o menos - sentirse más que
nosotros, me entiendo yo siempre
me aprendí esta decimita que oí,
que dice así:

Since we are negros and there
are whites who think better of
themselves than of us, and I
have always been aware of this,
it brings to mind a decima which
I heard and learned and which
goes like this:

1. El negro hace mochila,
2. silla, taburete y sillón;
3. también, maneja un camión,
4. un burro y un caterpila.

The *negro* makes bags,
Chairs, stools, and armchairs;
Also he handles a truck,
A burro, and a tractor.

5. Su color, morado lila,	His color, dark purple,
6. sirve para ornar los santos;	Is useful to ornament the saints;
7. y si llega al campo santo	And if he goes to a cemetery
8. y cava una sepultura;	He can dig a grave;
9. y si le dan lectura	And if he is given education
10. el negro se pasa el blanco.	The *negro* surpasses the white man.

NOTES

Perf:

There is no glide at the cadence. The absolute pitch of the
final tone is therefore given rather than that of the initial.

Text:

4. - *Caterpila* is utilized in referring to tractors in general.
The Caterpillar was apparently the first make of tractor in use in
Colombia.

5. - The reference is primarily to the color of the robes adorn-
ing the images of saints found in the churches.

TR 37 (LF 184.5)

yo me sté mu-rien-do 8. le di-ré a
mi ma-es-ta: 9.—É que no tie-ne que
dar 10. no de-be an-dar pi-dien-do___.

1. Yo sé todos los sacramentos,	I know all the sacraments,
2. para todo en general.	You name it and I know it.
3. Para el rico se cobrar	As for the rich, they are covered
4. que tenga merecimiento.	Which is only just.
5. Yo solito me lamento	I only complain
6. y suspirando me mantengo.	And keep on sighing.
7. Cuando yo me esté muriendo	When I am dying
8. le diré a mi Majestad:	I will tell my God:
9. él que no tiene que dar	He who does not have to give
10. no debe de andar pidiendo.	Ought not to go around asking.

NOTES

Text:

2. - An English expression is used in translation. The literal meaning of the Spanish is "for everything in general."

9-10. - That is, since God has nothing to give to the singer, God should ask nothing of him in return. Specifically the singer should not have been required to pay for the performance of sacraments by the priests.

TR 38-42

Décimas sung by Pedro Cueto Pimientel

Only the last two of the five performances by Pedro Cueto reproduced below are actually décimas in form. All five are included, since some similar melodic formulae are utilized in each item. Cueto is known in the village as a jokester and a singer of humorous songs. He was never specifically questioned concerning the sources of his verses or melodic material. However, his performances suggest that he does attempt some improvisation of verse.

TR 38-39

Evitar, 1 November 1964.

Cueto was one of those who volunteered to sing décimas for us at this recording session. He was drunk, and the verses he sang did not form décimas. He also addressed Delia Zapata, who was acting as my intermediary, with greater familiarity than was appropriate to the occasion. I have transcribed the first and third of the three performances recorded.

TR 38 (LF 77.6a)

1. Ni-ña De-lia___, co-mo a-mi-go, yo le di-go_____, 2. di-ri-jo-mus-te-de do_____. 3. Pa-che-co_____, a la mu-jer de mi her-man-o 4. yo se les-ta-ba me-tien-do_____, 5. a la mu-jer de mi her-man-o 6. yo se les-ta-ba me-tien-do 7. un es-tan-te a la co-ci-na 8. que se les-ta-ba sa-lien-do___.

1. Niña Delia, como amigo
    yo le digo,
2. diríjome a ustedes dos.
3. Pacheco, a la mujer de
    mi hermano
4. yo se lo estaba metiendo,
5. a la mujer de mi hermano
6. yo se lo estaba metiendo
7. un estante a la cocina
8. que se lo estaba saliendo.
	Delia, as a friend, I say
	    to you,
	I address myself to you both.
	Pacheco, for my brother's
	    wife
	I was putting in,
	For my brother's wife
	I was putting in
	A shelf in the kitchen
	That was coming out.

(risas)	(laughter)
Un estante es un horcón. ¡No cojan la cosa por mal camino!	An *estante* is a pillar. Do not take it the wrong way!

NOTES

Perf:

He begins with the phrase *A la mujer de mi hermano*. I interrupt to adjust the recording level. This verse is not transcribed. He then begins again as given above.

Text:

1. - In this region *niña*, which generally refers to a female child, is also utilized as a term of respect in addressing a woman, as *doña* would be elsewhere. Like *doña*, *niña* in this case is followed by the given rather than the family name of the woman addressed. There is no equivalent in English.

3-8. - This is in double-entendre. *Metiendo* is the present participle of *meter* (to put in, to insert or introduce). This verb is also commonly used to express the act of coition. The singer is therefore implying that he has had sexual intercourse with his brother's woman. This implication is reinforced by v. 5-6, which are basically a repetition of v. 3-4. A different and more socially acceptable meaning is then supplied by v. 7-8. However, the last two verses only partially offset the original impression, since *colocar* rather than *meter* would commonly be used to express the action of fastening a shelf to the wall. The double-entendre aspect of what was sung is then further reinforced by his spoken statement *Un estante es un horcón*. An *estante* can be either a pillar (*horcón*) or a shelf or a set of shelves. A pillar may be a phallic symbol.

TR 39 (LF 77.6c)

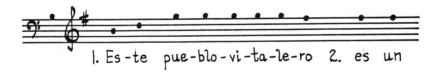

1. Es-te pue-blo-vi-ta-le-ro 2. es un

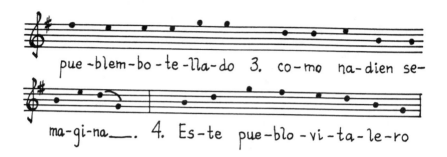

pue -blem-bo -te -lla-do 3. co-mo na-dien se-

ma-gi-na___. 4. Es-te pue-blo -vi -ta -le-ro

Cueto pauses, apologizes, and then continues.

5. Es -te pue -blo -vi-ta -le -ro___ 6. ¡ Oh, to-do

le a-gra-de-ce-mo 7. al doc -tor Si- món

Ló-pez Bo-sa___! 8. es un ti-po   ma-

te -ro 9. co-mo na-dien se-ma-gi-na___.

10. E-run pue-blo em-bo -te-lla -do, 11. y

e -run pue -blo em-bo-te -lla -do_____;

12. ya ca-rre-te-ra te-ne-mo 13. por me-dio de

1. Este pueblo evitalero	This village, Evitar,
2. es un pueblo embotellado	Is an embottled village
3. como nadie no se imagina.	As no one can imagine.
4. Este pueblo evitalero	This village, Evitar,

- - -

5. Este pueblo evitalero	This village, Evitar,
6. ¡Oh, todos le agradecemos	Oh! everyone is grateful
7. al doctor Simón López Bossa!	To Doctor Simón López Bossa!
8. es un tipo mahatero	He is a fellow from Mahates
9. como nadie no se imagina.	As no one can imagine.
10. Era un pueblo embotellado;	It was an embottled village,
11. y era un pueblo embotellado;	And it was an embottled village;
12. ya carretera tenemos	Now we have a road
13. por medio de...	Due to...

¡Termíneme usted este verso!	Finish this verse for me!
¡Termíneme! Acompáñeme ese	Finish it for me! Join me in
versito para ver.	this verse to show me what you can do.

NOTES

Perf:

The pitch level at the beginning is slightly sharp in comparison with that of TR 38. At v. 10 he begins to raise the pitch level further. V. 11-12 are sung a semitone higher than v. 1.

Text:

7. - The reference is to a politician who was instrumental in having the present road to Evitar constructed. His name is actually Simón Bossa López. Cueto reversed the two family names.
8. - Bossa López was not a resident of Mahates. He did have relatives who lived there.
13. - This verse is incomplete. He asks his listeners to complete it.

TR 40-42

Evitar, 4 August 1968.

TR 40 (LF 179.1)

nio 3. que a-man-ce dia-blo pri-me-ro
4. lo-con un ma-ni-co-mio__. 5. An-tes to-
do pre-gun-tar__, an-tes to-do pre-gun-
tar__ 6. ¿ de-que-llas sus con-di-cion-es,
7. si es mu-la que va do-mar 8. con fal-
das y pan-ta-lo-ne__?

1. Don Jorge, el joven que esté soltero	George, he who is a bachelor
2. y piense en el matrimonio	And thinks of marriage
3. que amanece el diablo primero	Must first tame the devil
4. loco en un manicomio.	Or be crazy in a madhouse.
5. Antes todo preguntar (2)	First of all you must ask
6. ¿de aquella sus condiciones,	What is she like,
7. si es mula que va a domar	If she is a mule you must break in,
8. con faldas y pantalones?	With skirt and pantaloons?

NOTES

Text:

1. - *Don* is an expression of respect. Like *doña* it precedes the given name. The singer is addressing the author. Jorge is the equivalent in Spanish of George.

4. - The "Or be" is understood.

6. - *Condiciones* refers to the physical, mental, and emotional characteristics of the individual referred to.

8. - It would make better sense in English if this verse followed the word *mule* in v. 7. The reference is apparently to the long drawers decorated with ruffles worn by women under their skirts in the nineteenth century.

TR 41 (LF 179.2a)

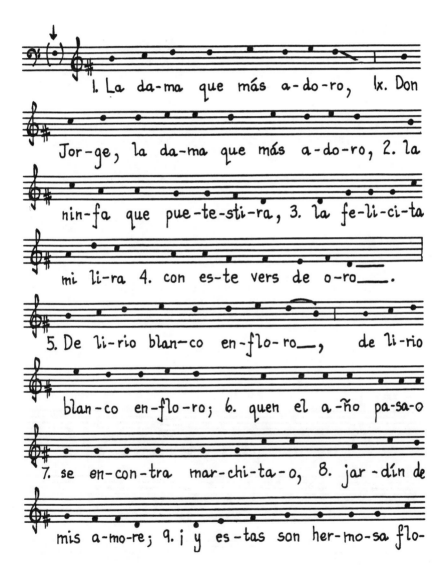

1. La da-ma que más a-do-ro, lx. Don Jor-ge, la da-ma que más a-do-ro, 2. la nin-fa que pue-te-sti-ra, 3. la fe-li-ci-ta mi li-ra 4. con es-te vers de o-ro___.

5. De li-rio blan-co en-flo-ro___, de li-rio blan-co en-flo-ro; 6. quen el a-ño pa-sa-o 7. se en-con-tra mar-chi-ta-o, 8. jar-dín de mis a-mo-re; 9. ¡ y es-tas son her-mo-sa flo-

re! 10. Don Jor-ge, i de mi ta-len-to in-spi-ra-do___!

	English
1. La dama que más adoro,	The lady whom I most adore,
1x. Don Jorge, la dama que	George, the lady whom I
más adoro,	most adore,
2. la ninfa que el poeta estira,	The nymph the poet extols,
3. la felicita mi lira	She my lyre congratulates
4. con este verso de oro.	With this verse of gold.
5. De lirios blancos la	With white lilies I bedeck
enfloro; (2)	her;
6. que en el año pasado	As in the past year
7. se encontraba marchitado,	One finds it withered,
8. el jardín de mis amores;	The garden of my love;
9. iy estas son hermosas	And those are beautiful
flores!	flowers!
10. Don Jorge, ide mi	George, of my inspired
talento inspirado!	talent!

NOTES

Text:

2. - The verb *estirar* means "to stretch" or "to extend." I
assume there is a poetic usage which can be translated as "to extol."

10. - Like v. 4, this is an affirmation of pride in his skill as
a poet. One is supposed to believe that he has either composed or
improvised the décima. In this case, the verse is directed to the
author.

TR 42 (LF 179.2b)

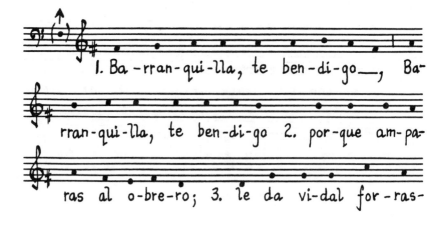

1. Ba -rran-qui-lla, te ben-di-go___, Ba-
rran-qui-lla, te ben-di-go 2. por-que am-pa-
ras al o-bre-ro; 3. le da vi-dal for-ras-

te-ro 4. co-mo si fue-ron tus hi-jo___. 5. Sí, a tu som-bra me co-bi-jo___, 5. sí, a tu som-bra me co-bi-jo. 6. Yer la-stre-lla do-rien-te; 7. ¡oh, vi-da re-plan-de-cien-te! 8. cuan-do na-ció Je-su-cri-to, 9. hoy pa-re po-bri pa-re ri-co. 10. Don Jor-ge, ¡tie-nes e pan su-fi-cien-te___!

1. Barranquilla, te bendigo (2)	Barranquilla, I bless you
2. porque amparas el obrero;	Because you protect the worker;
3. le das vida al forastero	You give life to the stranger
4. como si fueron tus hijos.	As if they were your own children.
5. Sí, a tu sombra me cobijo. (2)	Yes, in your shade I shelter myself.
6. Y eres la estrella de oriente,	And you are the star of the East;
7. ¡oh, vida resplandeciente!	Oh, splendid life!
8. cuando nació Jesucristo,	When Jesus Christ was born,
9. hoy para el pobre y para el rico.	Today for the poor and for the rich.
10. Don Jorge, ¡tienes el pan suficiente!	George, you have bread enough!

NOTES

Perf:

The singer begins to sharp during v. 5. He then gradually raises
the pitch level, which is a quarter tone higher at the final cadence
than at the beginning of the décima.

Text:

6. - The implication is that as the Magi found Jesus in Bethlehem,
those who journey to Barranquilla will find a type of salvation
there. The analogy is continued through v. 9.

10. - This is addressed to the author and is related to v. 9. As
a *gringo* he must have sufficient wealth to assure his welfare in
this world or the next.

TR 43 (LF 184.6)

Décima sung by Abraham Herrera Pacheco.

Recorded by Winston Caballero Salguedo and Hector Díaz Herazo.
Evitar, 22 September 1968.

According to Caballero this was the only décima that Abraham
Herrera knew. It is similar in text to TR 26 sung by Carlos Julio
in 1964 (see p. 353-54). Caballero recorded Abraham Herrera
singing this décima in order to document the fact that others in
the village knew this text and that Julio had thus not in fact composed or improvised it.

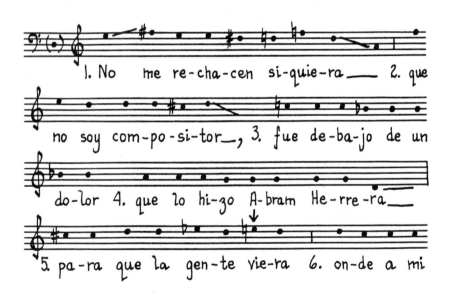

ca-be-za. 7. Ba-tol bri-llo a ri-que-za 8. a

di-po-si-ción de Dio___, 9. ¡ ma-di-ta se la

po-bre-za! 10. no hay quien su-fra co-mo yo___.

1. No me rechacen siquiera	Do not reject me
2. que no soy compositor,	Even though I am not a composer,
3. fue debajo de un dolor	It was under pressure
4. que lo hizo Abraham Herrera	That Abraham Herrera did it
5. para que la gente viera	In order to let the people see
6. donde va mi cabeza.	How capable I am.
7. Bastó el brillo o la riqueza	Without brilliance or wealth
8. a la disposición de Dios,	Or whatever be God's disposition towards me
9. ¡maldita sea la pobreza!	Cursed be the poverty!
10. no hay quien sufra como yo.	There are none that suffer more than I.

NOTES

Perf:

Abraham Herrera is obviously not accustomed to singing décimas. His pitch is at times uncertain and the tonality of the melody at times not clear. The cadence at v. 4 is somewhat flat in comparison with that at v. 10.

Text:

3, 6. - See notes to TR 26.
7. - The literal meaning of *bastó* is "to suffice."

COMMENTARY

This is the only one of the six chapters in which the discussion of the music and the poetry is concerned with one genre only, namely, the décima. However, certain of the items presented are not actually décimas. They are included because they were sung in res-

ponse to a request for decimas and because their inclusion may
assist us in establishing the norms and limits of the *décima evita-*
lera. The three items which are not décimas in poetic form are TR
38-40, all sung by Pedro Cueto. TR 38 contains a copla in double-
entendre. TR 40 is a double copla. TR 39 is somewhat formless.
This can be seen in the metrical analysis of the realized texts offered in table 15. The standard rhyming scheme of the décima is
abbaaccddc. The cadences of the melodies to which the décima is sung
divide the text into two unequal sections, thus: abba accddc. The
rhyming scheme is offered with the syllable count only when it differs from the norm given above. The rhyming scheme for TR 26, TR 35,
and TR 43 is given because the second section of each does not follow
the usual pattern of rhyme. That for TR 29 is given because it contains only nine verses. V. 5 is apparently missing. On the other
hand, the rhyming scheme for TR 41 is offered because there is a
modified repetition of v. 1. When it exists, the rhyming scheme of
all three of the non-décima items is given. When a verse does not
rhyme, this is indicated by a hyphen. It should be noted that exact
repetitions of a verse are omitted in the syllable count.

Approximately 75% of the verses listed in the metrical analysis
are octosyllabic. The majority of the remaining verses contain seven
or nine syllables. In five instances an address or salutation is
added to the beginning of a verse. All these occur in performances
by Pedro Cueto. Thus "Niña Delia," "Pacheco," or "Don Jorge" is
added, depending upon who is being addressed. These salutations are
given separate numbers. Thus the syllable count of

> Don Jorge, el joven que esté soltero

is written 3 + 8.

Although assonantal rhyme is occasionally employed, the rhyme in
the great majority of cases is consonantal. In the actual performance, however, there are many elisions of consonants following the
final stressed vowel of a verse. The consonant most frequently
omitted is *s*. Thus *Dio* is sung rather than *Dios* and a rhyme is produced with *yo*. This is acceptable either as a consonantal or an
assonantal rhyme.

As indicated at the beginning of the chapter, the décimas are
characterized by a general descending melodic movement; that is, the
pitch of the initial note sung is higher than that of the final note.
In this the décimas are similar to the worksongs presented in the
previous chapter. This characterization is applicable to the two
sections of the items in décima form except for the second section of
TR 32 II, where the initial and final pitches are approximately the
same, the final pitch being represented by the end of a terminal
glide. In the repetition of v. 9-10 of TR 26, the initial and final
tones are the same. Both cases are, of course, exceptional. TR 32
I-II are concerned with the same textual theme. The two are joined,
and the usual pitch contour of the décima form is therefore not
followed in TR 32 II. In the case of TR 26 there is an addition to
the décima form proper.

Table 15. Metrical Analysis of the Texts of TR 24-43

TR 24		TR 25		TR 26		
Glosa:		Glosa:		1.	8	a
a.	8	a.	8	2.	8	b
b.	8	b.	8	3.	8	b
c.	8	c.	8	4.	9	a
d.	8	d.	8	5.	8	a
				6.	8	c
I 1.	8	I 1.	8	7.	8	c
2.	8	2.	8	8.	9	d
3.	8	3.	8	9.	8	c
4.	8	4.	8	10.	8	d
5.	8	5.	8			
6.	8	6.	8	TR 27		
7.	8	7.	7	1.	8	
8.	8	8.	8	2.	9	
9.	7	9.	8	3.	7	
10.	8	10.	8	4.	7	
				5.	8	
II 1.	8	II 1.	8	6.	8	
2.	8	2.	8	7.	8	
3.	8	3.	8	8.	8	
4.	7	4.	8	9.	10	
5.	7	5.	8	10.	8	
6.	8	6.	8			
7.	7	7.	7	TR 28		
8.	8	8.	8	1.	8	
9.	8	9.	8	2.	8	
10.	8	10.	8	3.	5	
				4.	8	
III 1.	8	II repeats		5.	8	
2.	8			6.	8	
3.	8	IV 1.	8	7.	7	
4.	8	2.	8	8.	8	
5.	8	3.	8	9.	8	
6.	8	4.	7	10.	8	
7.	8	5.	9			
8.	8	6.	7	TR 29		
9.	8	7.	8	1.	8	a
10.	8	8.	6	2.	8	b
		9.	8	3.	8	b
IV 1.	8	10.	8	4.	7	a
2.	8			5.	8	c
3.	7			6.	8	c
4.	8			7.	8	d
5.	8			8.	8	d
6.	8			9.	9	c
7.	8					
8.	8					
9.	8					
10.	8					

TR 30

1. 9
2. 9
3. 8
4. 8
5. 7
6. 7
7. 7
8. 8
9. 8
10. 8

TR 31

1. 7
2. 7
3. 8
4. 8
5. 8
6. 8
7. 7
8. 7
9. 8
10. 9

TR 32

I 1. 8
   2. 8
   3. 8
   4. 8
   5. 8
   6. 7
   7. 8
   8. 9
   9. 8
   10. 9

II 1. 8
   2. 9
   3. 8
   4. 8
   5. 8
   6. 8
   7. 8
   8. 8
   9. 8
   10. 8

TR 33

1. 9
2. 8
3. 8
4. 8
5. 8
6. 8
7. 9
8. 8
9. 8
10. 8

TR 34

1. 8
2. 9
3. 9
4. 9
5. 8
6. 10
7. 8
8. 9
9. 9
10. 8

TR 35

1. 8   a
2. 9   b
3. 8   b
4. 8   a
5. 8   a
6. 11   c
7. 8   d
8. 8   c
9. 8   d
10. 8   c

TR 36

1. 7
2. 9
3. 8
4. 8
5. 8
6. 8
7. 8
8. 8
9. 7
10. 8

TR 37

1. 9
2. 8
3. 7
4. 8
5. 8
6. 9
7. 8
8. 8
9. 8
10. 8

TR 38

1. 4 + 8   a
2. 8   a
3. 3 + 8   b
4. 8   c
5. 8   b
6. 8   c
7. 8   -
8. 8   c

TR 39

1. 8   a
2. 8   b
3. 8   c
4. 8   a
5. 8   a
6. 8   c
7. 9   -
8. 7   a
9. 8   -
10. 8   d
11. 8   d
12. 8   c
13. -   -

TR 40

1. 3 + 8   a
2. 8   b
3. 9   a
4. 7   b
5. 8   c
6. 8   d
7. 8   c
8. 8   d

TR 41			TR 42			TR 43		
1.	8	a	1.	8		1.	8	a
1x.	3 + 8	a	2.	8		2.	8	b
2.	8	b	3.	8		3.	8	b
3.	8	b	4.	8		4.	7	a
4.	7	a	5.	8		5.	8	a
5.	8	a	6.	8		6.	8	
6.	7	c	7.	8		7.	8	
7.	8	c	8.	8		8.	9	d
8.	8	d	9.	9		9.	8	c
9.	9	d	10.	3 + 8		10.	8	d
10.	3 + 8	c						

Table 16 offers a contour analysis of certain verses of items presented in this chapter. (For the methods used in this analysis see chapter 6, IV.A.1.3.) In all cases but TR 38 and TR 39 the verses selected for analysis in each item were the first, fourth, fifth, and last. In TR 38 and TR 39 the verses selected were the same as those utilized in the analysis of melodic patterns in table 17 (pp. 385-86).

Table 16. Contour Analysis of TR 24-43

Pedro Juan Pacheco Salas

TR 24

St. I-IV, v. 1; gl. (a):

I.	L-H-L
II.	M-H-L
III.	M-H-L
IV.	M-H-L
gl. (a)	M-H-L

St. I-IV, v. 4; gl. (d):

I.	H-L
II.	M-H-L
III.	M-H-L
IV.	M-H-L
gl. (d)	M-H-L

St. I-IV, v. 5:

I.	L-H
II.	L-H
III.	L-H-M
IV.	L-H-M

St. I-IV, v. 10:

I.	H-L
II.	M-H-L
III.	H-L
IV.	M-H-L

Carlos Julio Sánchez

TR 26-29

TR 26-29, v. 1:

TR 26	H-L
TR 27	H-L-M
TR 28	L-H-L
TR 29	H-L

TR 26-29, v. 4:

TR 26	M-H-L
TR 27	M-H-L
TR 28	H-L
TR 29	M-H-L

TR 26-29, v. 5:

TR 26	M-H-L
TR 27	L-H-L
TR 28	L-H-M
TR 29	L-H-L

TR 26-28, v. 10;
  TR 29, v. 9:

TR 26	M-H-L
	M-H-L
TR 27	M-H-L
TR 28	M-H-L
TR 29	M-H-L

Simón Herrera Sánchez

TR 32 I-II, TR 35-37

TR 32 I-II, TR 35-37, v. 1:

TR 32 I	M-H-L
TR 32 II	M-H-L
TR 35	M-H-L
TR 36	M-H-L
TR 37	M-H-L

TR 32 I-II, TR 35-37, v. 4:

TR 32 I	M-H-L
TR 32 II	M-H-L
TR 35	M-H-L
TR 36	M-H-L
TR 37	M-H-L

TR 32 I-II, TR 35-39, v. 5:

TR 32 I	H-L-H
TR 32 II	L-H
TR 35	H-L-H
TR 36	L-H-M
TR 37	H-L-H

TR 32 I-II, TR 35-39, v. 10:

TR 32 I	M-H-L
TR 32 II	M-H-L
TR 35	M-H-L
TR 36	M-H-L
TR 37	M-H-L

Herrera Pacheco

TR 43

v. 1	M-H-L
v. 4	H-L
v. 5	L-H-M
v. 10	M-H-L

Pedro Cueto Pimientel

TR 38, TR 39, TR 40-42

TR 38:

v. 1	M-H-L
v. 4	M-H-L
v. 8	M-H-L

TR 39:

v. 1	L-H-M
v. 4	M-H-L
v. 9	M-H-L
v. 11	M-H-L

TR 40-42, v. 1; TR 41, v. 1x:

TR 40	L-H-L . L-H-M
TR 41	M-H-L
	L-H-M
TR 42	L-H-L

TR 40-42, v. 4:

TR 40	H-L
TR 41	H-L
TR 42	H-L

TR 40-42, v. 5:

TR 40	L-H-M
TR 41	L-H-L
TR 42	M-H-L

TR 40, v. 8; TR 41-42, v. 10

TR 40	M-H-L
TR 41	M-H-L
TR 42	M-H-L

A summary of table 16 is given below

	Pacheco	Julio	S. Herrera	Cueto	A. Herrera	Totals
M-H-L	10	9	15	11	2	47
H-L	2	3	0	3	1	9
L-H-L	2	3	0	3	0	8
L-H	2	0	1	0	0	3
L-H-M	2	1	1	4	1	9
H-L-M	0	1	0	0	0	1
H-L-H	0	0	3	0	0	3
Totals	18	17	20	21	4	80

In comparing this summary with that of table 13 in chapter 9 (pp. 327-28), it will be seen that descending melodic motion is not as preponderant in the décimas as it is in the zafras and vaquería. In the décimas there are 23 contours which do not descend. There are 11 which ascend, comprising L-H and L-H-M, and 12 whose initial and final pitches are the same, comprising L-H-L and H-L-H. In the decimas 28% of the verse contours do not descend, in the work-songs, 10%. In all the genres discussed, the verse contour M-H-L predominates. It comprises over half of the verse contours of the décimas and over two-thirds of the contours found in the zafras and vaquería. The summary also indicates that all decimeros make the greatest use of the melodic contour M-H-L. It forms at least half of the contours analyzed in the repertory of each decimero. It is most predominant in the repertory of Simón Herrera, the youngest of the group. He was 26 when his first group of décimas was recorded in 1964. In that year Pacheco was 63, Julio 35, Cueto 38, and Abraham Herrera 57. Simón told us that he had learned the texts of the décimas he sang and the melody to which he sang them from other men in the village some ten years before the first group was recorded. Pacheco, on the other hand, had never heard the décimas he performed sung and said that the melody he used was his own. The décimas sung by Simón Herrera are more melodically consistent than those sung by the other decimeros. Whether this is a result of his having learned the melody with the texts, whether it is due to his age and lack of experience or possibly to a lack of talent for improvisation, cannot be determined. In any case, the melodic contour M-H-L forms three-quarters of the melodic verses analyzed in his repertory. Of the other three contours he uses, one, H-L-H, occurs three times. It is not utilized at all by the other decimeros and appears only once in the worksongs. It should also be noted that he is the only one of the group who employs a terminal glide, an effect common in the worksongs. Cueto is next in melodic con-sistency, making use of only four contours and each at least three times. Both Pacheco and Julio utilize five different contours. Abraham Herrera sings only one décima. The distribution of con-tours in this case is not very meaningful.

The performance styles of the decimeros can be more easily dif-ferentiated by means of the similar melodic patterns which they utilize in v. 1, 4, 5, and 10 of their décimas. These similari-ties are most frequently found in the cadences of these verses, but in certain cases they extend through the entire verse. Where the item has only nine or eight verses, as in TR 29 and TR 40, respectively, this last verse was selected to compare with v. 10 of the other items in décima form. Since TR 38 and TR 39 display no clear form, those verses were selected whose cadence patterns matched those sung by Cueto in his items in décima form. These similarities in melodic patterns are presented in table 17, organized when feasible in numerical order of item. Melodic pat-terns are given only when they are similar in all cases or in the majority of cases. Otherwise no pattern is given. There is, for example, no consistency in the melodic patterns sung by Pacheco in v. 5 of his décimas nor by Julio in v. 1 of his décimas. No

pattern is therefore offered in table 17 in either case. When only
a majority of the melodic patterns are alike, this fact is indicated in two manners. In the first note heads are placed in parentheses, thus indicating that these pitches occur in the minority of
cases. When this is not feasible, as in Julio v. 5, the pattern
which occurs in the majority of cases is given first followed by
that occurring in the minority of cases. The relationship, however, is usually three to one. In Julio v. 10 the procedure has
of necessity been reversed, and the first version sung is given
second, as indicated by the following single bar. When it is indicated that the pattern is found in more than one position, as v. 4
and 10, the pattern may be followed by both a single and a double
bar, as needed, in the respective verses. S. Herrera's TR 36 is
given separately, since its tonal center is different from that of
the remaining décimas.

An examination of table 17 will indicate that each decimero has
particular melodic patterns of which he constantly makes use.
Pacheco uses the same cadential pattern, a descending major 3rd
ending on the tonal center, in v. 1, 4, and 10. In v. 1 it occurs
in the upper octave, in v. 4 and 10 in the lower octave. A passing tone connects the b and g in some performances of v. 4.
Julio prefers the cadence pattern of a descending minor 3rd, also
terminating on the tonal center. This occurs at the ends of sections, v. 4 and 10. In his first performance of v. 10 in TR 26,
the movement is instead a descending perfect 5th. He then repeats
v. 9-10 and again concludes with the minor 3rd. Other cadences
of a descending 3rd are utilized in v. 5.

In contrast, S. Herrera utilizes a cadence pattern of a descending major 2nd followed by a glide in all items but TR 36. This
occurs in all cases in v. 10 and in most cases in v. 4, both verses
representing the ends of sections. S. Herrera shows much greater
consistency than the other decimeros in the pitch patterns utilized
in v. 1 and 5. The patterns in most of the performances of v. 1 and
of at least three pitches in performances of v. 5 are similar. In
transcription, TR 36 was given a tonal center different from that of
the remainder of the items sung by S. Herrera. This was done in
order to make clear its melodic relationship to the other décimas.
The final cadence pattern of TR 36 is the same as that employed by
Pacheco, the descending major 3rd. Nevertheless, all but the last
two pitches of v. 1, TR 36 can be found in sequence in v. 1 of TR 32 I,
TR 35, and TR 37. All but the last two pitches of v. 4 and 10 of
TR 36 can be found in sequence in v. 10 of the remaining décimas sung
by S. Herrera. Although it possesses a different tonal center, TR
36 displays considerable relationship to the other décimas. In the
recordings I cannot hear a definite pitch at the end of the terminal
glide utilized in the majority of the cadences. However, the glide
terminates in the vicinity of c. If the terminal point of the glide
is considered the tonal center in the items in which the glide occurs, then all items sung by S. Herrera could be conceived as having
the same tonal center. Thus the descending major 3rd of TR 36
might be considered a substitute for the glide. On the other hand,
TR 36 is sung at a much lower tessitura than the other décimas per-

Table 17. Melodic Patterns, TR 24-43

Pedro Juan Pacheco Salas

TR 24, gl. (a), I-IV

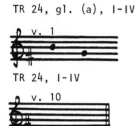

TR 24, I-IV

TR 24, gl. (d), I-IV

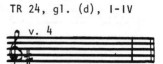

Carlos Julio Sánchez

TR 26-29

TR 26 repeat, TR 27-29 (v. 9), TR 27

TR 26-27, TR 29, TR 28

Simón Herrera Sánchez

TR 32, I, TR 35, TR 37

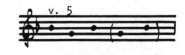

Simón Herrera Sánchez (cont.)

TR 32 I-II, TR 35, TR 37

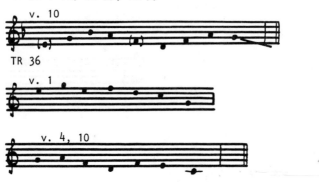

Pedro Cueto Pimientel

TR 38, v. 1, 4; TR 39, v. 4, 11

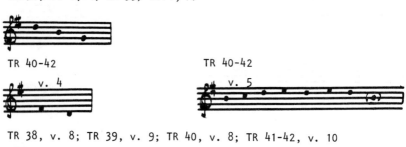

Abraham Herrera Pacheco

TR 43

formed, and the singer may have felt it difficult to perform a glide
in this range of his voice. Placing speculation aside, if TR 36 is
considered to have a different tonal center, it is a good example of
how melodies can be related by their constituent patterns and yet
exhibit differing tonal centers.

The performances by Cueto and A. Herrera differ from those of the
first three decimeros in that their cadential melodic patterns close
on the fifth degree rather than on the tonal center. They differ
from one another in that Cueto utilizes a cadential pattern of a
descending major 3rd, while A. Herrera employs a descending perfect
4th. It should be remembered, however, that A. Herrera was not accustomed to singing décimas and that this cadence pattern of a
descending perfect 4th occurred frequently in the melodies of the
songs sung at the velorio de angelito, of which he is the leader.

Cueto sang TR 38 and 39 in 1964, TR 40-42 in 1968. All performances
are within a quarter tone of the same pitch level, possibly indicating that Cueto had perfect pitch. In TR 40-42 the cadence patterns
of v. 4 and 10 are similar. In the latter, however, the patterns are
extended to include a third pitch. Larger melodic patterns are seen
in v. 5 of TR 40-42 and in a number of different verses of TR 38 and
TR 39. These last patterns occur in one time period or another.
Those occurring in TR 40-42, recorded in 1968, are not found in TR
38 and 39, recorded in 1964, and vice versa. However, the cadence
pattern of a descending major 3rd is utilized in both time periods.

The décimas of S. Herrera were also recorded in two groups, TR 32
I-II and TR 35 in 1964 and TR 36-37 in 1968. The patterns utilized
in TR 37, recorded in 1968, are the same as those employed in the
décimas recorded in 1964. TR 36, as indicated previously, employs
different cadence patterns, but much of the remainder of v. 1, 4, and
10 is similar.

In summary, three stylistic levels can be distinguished in décima
performance through the consideration of pitch contours or patterns.
The characteristics of each of the higher levels apply to the level
or levels below it.

1. The macro or regional style. Each décima is divided into two
large pitch contours, each ending on the lowest pitch of the melody.
The first contour cadences at the end of the fourth verse, the second
contour at the end of the tenth verse. The first contour begins on
or reaches the highest pitch of the melody. The second contour begins on a pitch lower than the highest pitch of the melody but higher
than the cadence pitch.

2. The micro or village style. An analysis of the individual
phrases sung in Evitar indicates not only a preponderance of descending motion but the preponderance of the use of a particular melodic
phrasal contour, M-H-L. It is possible, of course, that this trait
is common in other communities in the region or is characteristic of
the region as a whole, but this has not been investigated.

3. The idiosyncratic or individual style. The melodic styles of
the five decimeros recorded can be differentiated by the cadence
formulae employed by each and, in some cases, by larger pitch patterns occurring within the verses.

The historic development of the décima as a Spanish literary form
is discussed in chapter 6 (V.C.3). It has also been in widespread
use as a popular form. The popular form may have a memorized text

sung to a known tune or text, or either or both the text and melody
may be partially or wholly improvised. In Spanish-speaking America,
to the best of my knowledge, the décima is always sung. It may be
sung unaccompanied or accompanied by instruments, as in the *seis* in
Puerto Rico (López Cruz 1967:4). In Spain the décima is both recited and sung. In Galicia the décima is recited (information from
D. Jesús Bal y Gay). In the Canary Islands it is sung to the melody
of the *habanera* (information from José Pérez Vidal). Décimas are
also sung in Murcia. A type of décima sung in much of Spain, but
particularly in Andalucía, is the *guajira*, which at times lacks one
verse (information from D. Arcadio de Larrea Palacín). It has been
noted that TR 29 has nine verses rather than ten.

Contests in which decimeros improvise on a given theme are also
known in Spain. In the Basque region in northern Spain both text and
melody were improvised in the past. In more recent times the text
is improvised to a known melody (information from D. Gaizka Barandiaran). Puig Campillo describes such a contest which took place
between two decimeros in the city of Cartagena. At one point they
sang 20 décimas alternately, in immediate succession, on the theme
of *la mentira* (the lie), given to them by a spectator (1953:34-36).

Unlike the worksongs, the décimas display tonality. We therefore
can discuss their possible sources from the point of view of the
melodic functions and their scalar or modal organization. The categorization of a melody is dependent upon both its melodic functions
and its scalar organization. On the basis of the analysis of only
their melodic functions, it would seem that some décima melodies
should be categorized as I. Common Practice although they have been
placed in II. Modal (see table 19). Their placement in the latter
category was dictated by their scalar organization. I therefore
shall begin with analysis of scalar or modal organization and then
move to the analysis of melodic functions.

Table 18 offers the former type of analysis of those décimas for
which music transcriptions have been provided.

The scale or mode of TR 36 is the only one listed which is consonant with common practice. In TR 24, a glosa in décima form sung
by Pedro Pacheco, the accidentals $c\sharp$, $a\sharp$, and $f\natural$ occur. The $c\sharp$
occurs as a chromatic passing tone, the $a\sharp$ as a chromatic auxiliary
(raised lower neighbor) (see chapter 6, IV.A.2.2.4). In most cases
the $f\natural$ is found near the end of the second section of the décima and
is not followed by an $f\sharp$. In common practice style this $f\natural$ would
represent a change in tonality, a modulation to the tonality of C
(see chapter 6, IV.A.2.2.3). However, there is no cadence on c, and
the melody closes on g. Where the $f\natural$ occurs, this part of the
décima therefore gives the impression of being in the mixolydian
mode. I have given a separate scale for décima III. There is no f
of any kind in the first section of this décima, and only an $f\natural$
appears in the second section. This décima, therefore, can be considered as a whole to be in the mixolydian mode.

The scales representing the décimas sung by Carlos Julio, TR 26-
29, contain both an $f\natural$ and an $f\sharp$. Judging from their scales only,
these décimas might be considered to be in the minor mode. An examination of table 19, however, will indicate that their melodic
functions place these décimas within the modal rather than the common practice category.

Table 18.   Scales or Modes of TR 24-43

I.   Common Practice

Major 3rd, heptatonic

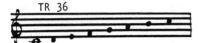

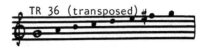

II.   Modal

Major 3rd heptatonic

Minor 3rd, heptatonic

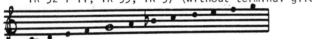

III. Modal (anomalous)

Major 3rd, heptatonic

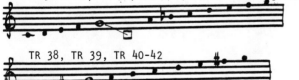

Indeterminate 3rd, heptatonic

TR 43

The décimas sung by Simón Herrera listed under II. Modal (TR 32 I-II, TR 35 and TR 37) all cadence on g^1. With one exception, the g^1 is followed by a descending glide which ends approximately at c^1. TR 36 does cadence on a definite pitch, and this pitch is c^1. If we ignore the glide and accept g^1 as the final, all the décimas sung by Simón Herrera with the exception of TR 36 can be considered to represent the dorian mode. In category III. Modal (anomalous) I have considered the final of these same décimas to be the c upon which the cadential glide seems to terminate rather than the tonal center g. When the final is considered to be c, the items in question are then cast in the mixolydian rather than the dorian mode. According to their final, the décimas sung by Cueto also fall within the mixolydian mode.

The one décima sung by Abraham Herrera (TR 43) contains too many accidentals to permit a modal analysis. It is placed in the III. Modal (anomalous category, since the final and the tonal center are not the same pitch.

The melodic strophe of the décima is divided into two sections, which in almost all cases encompass four and six verses, respectively. Each section concludes on the final of the melody, and there are no intermediate or mid cadences as previously defined. In table 19 the melodic functions designated are therefore initial, final 1, and final 2.

Table 19.   Melodic Functions, TR 24-43

I.   Common Practice

Major 3rd

	Initial	Final 1	Final 2
TR 36	3 5 3	4 3 1	4 3 1

II.   Modal

Major 3rd

	Initial	Final 1	Final 2
TR 24 glosa	♯2 3 4 2		5 3 2 1
I	1 4	5 3 1	♮7 5 3 1
II	4 5 3	4 3 1	3 ♯2 3 1
III	3 4 5	5 3 2 1	5 4 3 1
IV	3 4 5	5 3 1	♮7 5 4 3 1

Minor 3rd

	Initial	Final 1	Final 2
TR 26	♮7 5 3	6 4 3 1	♮7 2 4 3 1
TR 27	♮7 5 3	6 4 3 1	♮7 5 3 5 3 1
TR 28	3 5 8 ♯7	4 5 3 1	♮7 5 3 5 3 1
TR 29	♮7 5 3	♮7 5 3 1	♮7 5 3 1
TR 32 I	♮6 ♮7 8 ♮6	5 ♮7 2 1	5 ♮7 2 1

	Initial	Final 1	Final 2
TR 32 II	3 4 ♮7 ♮6	1 ♮7 ♮6 5	5 ♮7 2 1
TR 35	♮6 ♮7 8 ♮6	5 ♮7 2 1	5 ♮7 2 1
TR 37	♮6 8 ♮6	5 ♮7 2 1	5 ♮7 2 1

III. Modal (anomalous)

(First scale degree represents final, not tonal center)

Major 3rd

TR 38	6 1 4		♮7 5 2 3 1
TR 39	6 1 4		4 2 3 1
TR 40	1 4	♮7 5 3 1	♮7 5 3 2 3 1
TR 41	6 ♮7 8	♮7 5 3 2 3 1	6 5 4 2 3 1
TR 42	3 4 5	♮7 5 3 2 3 1	♮7 5 3 2 3 1

(First scale degree represents terminal point of glide at
cadence, not tonal center)

Minor 3rd

TR 32 I	3 5 3	4 6 5 1	4 6 5 1
TR 32 II	♭7 8 4 3	4 2 1	4 6 5 1
TR 25	3 4 5 3	2 4 6 5 1	4 6 5 1
TR 37	3 5 3	2 4 6 5	4 6 5 1

(First scale degree represents final, not tonal center)

Indeterminate 3rd

TR 43	2 3 2 ♯1	5 4 1	5 4 1

The only item included under I. Common Practice, TR 36, satis-
fies all the criteria previously presented. Of the décimas contained in the glosa sung by Pedro Pacheco (TR 24), only the melodic
functions of III. are consonant with common practice. However, as
has already been indicated, the only f which occurs in this particular décima melody is an f♮. This décima is therefore in neither
the major nor minor mode but in the mixolydian mode. The remaining
décimas found in category II. Modal have been placed there rather
than in category I. Common Practice, since all have a seventh
degree located a whole tone rather than a semitone below the eighth
or first degree in either initial or cadence patterns.

Of those décimas included in category III. Modal (anomalous)
the first group is not consonant with common practice in its initial
melodic patterns, the second group in the patterns representing
final 1, and the last décima in the patterns representing final 2.
Thus of all the décima melodies analyzed, only that of TR 36 falls
clearly within the common practice style. The remainder are non-
common practice. Some may be considered modal, displaying the
characteristics of either the mixolydian or the dorian mode. It

should be noted that TR 36 is concerned with a racial theme, and it
is the only one of this type sung by any of the decimeros recorded.
Simón probably did not perform this text with any frequency. It
was sung with some hesitation while he and Winston Caballero were
along. The melody utilized is possibly a blend of the melody to
which Simón had heard the décima sung and the melodic patterns
which he himself was accustomed to using.

The ranges of the melodies employed in the décimas are very
wide, although none reach the extreme range utilized by Manuel
Rosado in the worksongs. One of the décimas sung by Pacheco in TR
24 has the range of an 8ve plus a major 6th, the remaining four
have the range of an 8ve plus a perfect 5th. The ranges of the
décimas sung by Simón Herrera are nearly as wide. Three of his
décimas also display the ambitus of an 8ve plus a perfect 5th,
while the fourth has the range of an 8ve plus a perfect 4th. Of the
décimas sung by Cueto, three have the range of an 8ve plus a perfect
4th and two a major 9th. The one décima sung by Abraham Herrera
displays the range of a major 10th. The décimas sung by Julio are
the most restricted in range. Two have a range of a major 9th, one
an 8ve, and one only a minor 7th. The average range of the décimas
transcribed is a little less than an 8ve plus a perfect 4th. It is
interesting to note that Cueto utilized a narrower range, a major
9th, when singing texts which fit the décima form (TR 41-42) than
that, an 8ve plus a perfect 4th, used in singing items in which the
text does not follow that form (TR 38-40).

I have been able to locate only one transcription of a popular
décima collected in Spain which includes notation of the music. This
décima, ex. 1, was sung by an elderly woman in the southern half of
the present Provincia de Ciudad Real, which can be considered to form
part of the general region of Andulacía. It has a literary text
and is sung during Lent. The transcription is given here in transposed form and with verse numbers added. A contour analysis of each
melodic phrase is given above the staff. The method of analysis employed is the same as that which was utilized in table 16. The
transcription is followed by the scale, or mode, which I have extracted from it.

Ex. 1. El Credo (Echavarría Bravo 1951:371)

4. a to do-gé-ne-ro hu - ma - no! 5. A - sí, to-do fiel cris-
tia - no, 6. por-que nues-tro a-mor os cua-dre, 7. pues vues-
tra gra-cia nos a - bre 8. con-tra el in-fier-no victo - ria, 9. pa - ra con-se-guir la glo - ria, 10. de-ci-
mos: Cre - o en Dios pa - dre _____ .

Scale

The melody of the *décima española* is cast in the common practice
harmonic minor mode. It displays one accidental, the $b^{\natural}$, which
occurs twice. Both times it represents what is known as a raised
lower neighbor, a device in frequent use in the common practice
period. The triplets preceding the cadence pitches of phrases are
a common element in Andalusian melodic style. The range of the
melody is a minor 9th. Of the décimas recorded in Evitar, all but
two, TR 26 and TR 29, sung by Carlos Julio, have a wider range.
However, the scale or mode in which the décima española is cast cannot be found in the repertory in Evitar.

In the earliest form of the décima, *la décima antigua*, one of the
rhyming schemes utilized was 4 + 6 (see chapter 6, V.C.3). This

rhyming scheme, as such, no longer applies in the *décima espinela*.
However, this division seems to have had its influence on the
development of the melody to which the décima espinela is sung.
As previously indicated, in Evitar and elsewhere on the Atlantic
coast, the décima is divided into two sections of four and six
verses, respectively. In addition, the same melodic cadence is
commonly employed at the end of the tenth verse as that heard at
the end of the fourth verse. These are characteristic traits
of the *décima costeña*. The décima española has very much the
same formal melodic organization. The melody of the first four
verses descends, and the cadence pitches are well differentiated,
being *c*, *b♭*, *a*, and *g*. The tenth verse also cadences on *g*. However, the melodic phrase cadences of the second section of the
décima are not as well differentiated as those of the first. The
sequence is *a*, *g*, *e♭*, *g*, *e♭*, and *g*. In this latter aspect of its
melodic organization the décima española differs considerably from
that of the décima costeña.

The décima española also differs from the décima costeña in the
degree of descending motion displayed. It does, indeed, close at
a lower pitch than that at which it begins, and seven of its
phrasal contours descend, while only three ascend. However, there
is very little similarity in the contours employed. In the
décimas recorded in Evitar, 47 out of the 80 contours analyzed
follow the pattern M-H-L. None of the ten melodic phrases of the
décima española follow this contour. Of the remaining contours,
the two most frequently utilized in the décimas costeñas are H-L
and L-H-M, each occurring nine times. The first contour occurs
three times in the décima española, the second contour once.
Otherwise there is no duplication of contours. The contour M^2-
H-L-M^1 occurs three times in the décima española but not at all in
those recorded in Evitar. Correlation is found only in the contour representing purely descending movement, H-L. However, the
contour which is preponderantly characteristic of the Colombian
genre, M-H-L, is not present in the décima española.

Both the décimas and the worksongs are cast in free or prose
rhythm, and both derive their poetic form from Spain. While the
worksongs are not always cast in the copla form, the poetic form
of the décimas is similar in almost every respect to that in use
in Spain. On the basis of the one transcription available, it
seems that the melodic form of the décima is also Spanish in
origin. The principal difference between the décimas and the
worksongs is that the former exhibit tonality, a European trait,
and the latter do not. The two genres have many other traits in
common. It thus will be useful to compare the two types of song
and simultaneously to discuss the possible stylistic sources of
the décimas. For this I shall employ the same numbered outline
of characteristics as in the previous chapter.

1. Fewer interjections are found in the décimas than in the
worksongs, and all are in initial position. These include the
meaningless interjection *oh* and the meaningful interjections addressed to a particular individual, Niña Delia and Don Jorge.
There are no cries from other participants or the audience. The
type of interjections heard and the lack of participation are more
characteristic of European than African or Amerindian practice.

2. Like the worksongs, the décimas are primarily syllabic.
They display fairly frequent neumatic passages, but none that are
melismatic. In this they are analogous to the Mende and the
Amerindian songs discussed in the previous chapter but not to the
cante jondo of southern Spain or the rural Asturian folksong.
They also share this trait with a good part of the Gregorian
Chant repertory and with folksong of other areas of Spain.

3. As in the worksongs, vocal glides occur with some frequency
in the décimas. In character these are usually terminal and descending. The occasional ascending glide is usually found in
initial position. Vocal glides do not seem to form part of performance tradition in Spain, nor in the performance of Gregorian
Chant. They are found in the Mende songs and some Amerindian
songs. The glides seem to form a non-European characteristic of
the décima melodies.

4. The ranges of the décima melodies are quite wide, reaching
the ambitus of an 8ve plus a major 6th. They lack only a major
2nd in reaching the extreme range of the worksongs. In this they
differ from all of the Spanish, African, and Amerindian songs discussed. They also differ in this respect from other genres of
costeño song. However, two of the Amerindian songs presented have
ranges as wide as the average of the décimas.

5. At the beginning of the décima, and on occasion at other
points as well, the singer employs the highest tessitura that his
voice is capable of producing. The highest pitches sung in the
décimas are only slightly lower than those sung in the worksongs.
Where Mañuel Rosado reaches $c^{\sharp 2}$, Simón Herrera climbs to $b^{\flat 1}$. In
singing vaquería Cueto reaches a^1, in his décimas only g^1. Only
the Jívaro singer employs a tessitura higher than any of those
of the decimeros.

6. The same intense, rather forced chest tone is utilized in
singing both the décimas and the worksongs. No use is made of
falsetto or vibrato. Male singing in a high tessitura is found
in southern Spain, in Liberia and Sierra Leone, and among the
Indians of northern South America. However, these groups differ
in the type of vocal production employed. Of the areas discussed
in chapter 9, only in Liberia and Sierra Leone does there seem to
be comparable male singing.

7. In the décimas, as in the worksongs, high sustained tones
are heard with some frequency near the beginning of a phrase. In
the décimas these occur almost entirely in their first verse. Of
the various types of songs examined in the previous chapter, this
occurs only in the Spanish and Mende songs.

8. The décimas display even larger melodic intervals than the
worksongs. There are two ascending minor 7ths, a descending minor
6th, an ascending augmented 5th, and numerous ascending and descending perfect 5ths. Of all the types of songs discussed in
chapter 9, only those of the Mende contain intervals of commensurate size.

9. Like the worksongs, each décima as a whole exhibits descending motion. Further, in almost all cases each of the two
sections of the décima displays such motion. Only 72% of the
phrasal contours of the décimas exhibit descending motion, while
90% descend in the worksongs. In the décima española and the

song from Asturias 70% descend, as do 56% of the phrasal contours
of the Mende songs in tales. The phrasal contour M-H-L predominates in both the décimas and the worksongs. It comprises over
half of the phrasal contours of the décimas and over two-thirds
of those found in the zafras and vaquería. It is completely absent in the décima española. Of the non-costeño songs analyzed
in the previous chapter, only the song from Asturias shows a
predominance of this contour. In the Mende songs H-L is predominant and M-H-L is second in number of occurrences. The opposite
is the case in both the décimas and the worksongs.

I shall now summarize my conclusions concerning the cultural
sources of the décimas:

Texts

The term *décima*, unlike the terms *zafra* and *vaquería*, has the
same connotation in Spain as in the Atlantic coastal region of
Colombia. In meter, rhyme, and combination of glosa and décima
its poetic forms are similar to those which have been in use in
Spain. The décima of nine verses sung by Julio (TR 26) is similar
to the décima guajira of Spain; the item with eight verses sung by
Cueto (TR 40) is similar to a related form, the copla de arte
mayor, in use at the time that the décima espinela came into being.
The only meaningless interjection employed, *oh*, is characteristic
of European rather than African or Amerindian song.

Performance Practice

Contests among decimeros in which two or more individuals improvise décimas on a given theme have been in vogue in both Spain
and Colombia. In Spain décimas may be either sung or recited;
among the rural costeños they are sung. Whether or not the initial interjections in the form of salutations as sung by Cueto are
part of Spanish practice, I do not know.

An intense chest tone is used in singing the décima costeña.
Neither vibrato nor falsetto is employed. This is analogous to
West African practice.

Melodies

The décima possesses tonality in the sense in which this term
is applied here. Tonality in the décima, as in European song, is
defined by a recurrent pitch at the end of sections or strophes.
Some of the décimas collected in Evitar can be considered to be
cast in the dorian or mixolydian modes. This introduces the
possible influence of old Spanish folksong or Gregorian Chant.
Diatonic, heptatonic scales are also known in Africa, but they do
not display tonality as the term is defined here. No evidence is
available concerning the scalar organization of the melodies of
Indian songs of northern South America.

On the basis of the one transcription available, it also seems
that the melody to which the décima is sung shares at least two
traits with the Spanish form: it is composed of two sections which

encompass four and six verses, respectively, and each section
concludes on the same pitch.

The highest pitches of the décima melody are usually found in
its first melodic phrase, which employs the highest tessitura of
the singer's voice. The pitches sung in this first phrase are
higher than any sung by the Spanish singers but are matched or
exceeded by West African or Amerindian singers.

General descending motion is predominant, as are descending
phrasal contours. Analogous stylistic traits are found in both
Spain and West Africa. Other aspects of melody, such as a wide
range and descending terminal glides, are found in cultural areas
other than Spain.

Relationships of Text and Melody

The décimas are primarily syllabic but display a few neumatic
passages. In this they differ from Spanish songs from Andalucía
and Asturias but are similar to some Spanish songs from other
areas and most Western European songs, as well as West African
and Amerindian songs. A further trait, the occurrence of a high,
sustained pitch near the beginning of a verse and/or musical
phrase, is found in both Spain and West Africa but not among the
Amerindians.

Although the primary cultural source of the décimas is obviously Spain, some traits displayed seem to have their source in
West Africa or among the Amerindians. At least one trait, that
of a wide vocal range, is more pronounced in the décimas costeñas
than in Spanish, West African, or Amerindian songs. To some
extent, therefore, the décimas, like the worksongs, must be considered an independent development of this area of the New World
rather than purely an amalgam of traits derived from the three
parent cultures.

II. Cantos de las Fiestas

Presented in this chapter are transcriptions of four vocal genres performed at various fiestas. All are sung by a soloist and a chorus. The first, gavilán, is performed by voices only and is used as a processional. The remaining genres, danza de negro, bullerengue, and fandango, are accompanied by various percussion instruments. The *danza de negro de la calle* is a processional, while the *danza de negro de la plaza*, the bullerengue, and the fandango provide the musical accompaniment for dancing. Where transcriptions of the music of the last three genres are offered (TR 45-46, TR 48 and TR 54), they are in each case presented in the form of a composite score; that is, the score has been developed from more than one recording of the same musical item (see chapter 5, I.F.2). For each of these performances an alternative score is also offered, that is, a partial score containing only percussion parts which is designed to clarify the rhythmic and metrical relationships of the parts (see chapter 5, I.F.1). The regular score and the alternative score are given the same transcription number and are marked a and b, respectively. Thus TR 45a identifies the regular score of "La rama del tamarindo" and TR 45b the alternative score drawn from the regular score. The measure numbers given in the alternative scores coordinate with those of the regular scores.

In examining the notated parts for percussion instruments it should be remembered that what is indicated is impact points in time space, not sustained tones (see chapter 5, I.D.). For the meaning of particular forms of notation or of signs utilized in the percussion parts see chapter 5 (I.E.3).

All the genres presented in this chapter are open-ended; that is, there is no predetermined point at which they end. Performances actually accompanying a procession or dancing would generally be of greater duration than most of those recorded.

GAVILAN

Gavilán is performed during the celebration of the Día de San Juan and the Día de San Pedro (see pp. 107-9).

TR 44 (LF 96.7) "Gavilán"

Abraham Herrera Pacheco and a group of women: Marcelina Sánchez
Pimientel, Juana García Blanquiset, Basilisa Herrera García, Ana
María Pacheco, and Juana Pérez. Evitar, 8 November 1964.

1. Yo no quie-ro que te va-ya, ¡llo-ra, vi-lán___!

ya, ¡llo-ra, vi-lán___! (R) Pió, pió, pió_____, ga-vi-lán.

2. ni tam-po-co que te que-de, ¡llo-ra, ga-vi-lán___!

que-de, ¡llo-ra, ga-vi-lán___! (R) Pió, pió, pió_____, ga-vi-lán.

3. ni que me de so-li-to, ¡llo-to, ¡llo-

S.	1. Yo no quiero que te vayas,	I don't want you to go away,
S/Ch	¡llora, gavilán!	Weep, chickenhawk!
Ch.	(R) Pió, pió, pió, gavilán.	Cluck, cluck, cluck, chickenhawk.
S.	2. ni tampoco que te quedes,	Nor do I want you to stay,
S/Ch	¡llora, gavilán!	Weep, chickenhawk!
·Ch.	(R) Pió, pió, pió, gavilán.	Cluck, cluck, cluck, chickenhawk.

(Following each subsequent line sung by the soloist he
and the chorus jointly sing ¡*llora, gavilán*! and the
chorus then sings the refrain.)

S.	3. ni que me dejes solito,	Nor do I wish you to leave me here alone,
	4. que ni tampoco me lleves.	Nor that you take me with you.
	5. Gavilán, garrapatero,	Chickenhawk, tick eater,
	6. Que gavilán, garrapatero,	Chickenhawk, tick eater,
	7. Mañana me voy para Rocha,	Tomorrow I'm going to Rocha,
	8. a pescar con los rocheros,	To fish with the *rocheros*,
	9. a comer la arenque frita,	To eat fried herring,
	10. y sábalo gambotero,	And the shad of Gambote,
	11. Gavilán, garrapatero,	Chickenhawk, tick eater,
	12. Llora, llora, gavilán,	Weep, weep, chickenhawk,
	13. Gavilán, garrapatero,	Chickenhawk, tick eater,
	14. ¿Cómo quieres que me vaya	How can you expect me to leave
	15. sin esperanza ninguna?	With no hope whatsoever?
	16. Aquí me dejes parado	You leave me here stranded
	17. como garza en la laguna,	Like a heron in a lagoon.
	18. Gavilán, garrapatero,	Chickenhawk, tick eater,
	19. Que gavilán, garrapatero,	Chickenhawk, tick eater,
	20. Llora, llora, gavilán,	Weep, weep, chickenhawk,
	21. Adiós para tí no quiere, (2)	I don't want to say goodbye to you,
	22. yo les digo a mis amigos,	I say to my friends,
	23. a mis hermanos queridos,	To my dear brothers,
	24. que por si caso yo muriere.	Just in case that I die,
	25. Que gavilán, garrapatero,	Chickenhawk, tick eater,
	26. Gavilán, garrapatero,	Chickenhawk, tick eater,
	27. Llora, gavilán, garrapatero,	Weep, chickenhawk, tick eater,
	28. Gavilán, garrapatero,	Chickenhawk, tick eater,

29. En la pascua hizo un año	Christmas it was a year
30. pero de tí me enamoré.	Since I fell in love with you.
31. Me esperas en nochebuena,	You wait for me on Christmas Eve,
32. que mira, sí, me acordaré.	See, I do remember you.
33. Gavilán, garrapatero, (2)	Chickenhawk, tick eater,
34. Que llora, llora gavilán,	Weep, weep, chickenhawk,
35. Gavilán, garrapatero, (2)	Chickenhawk, tick eater,

NOTES

Perf:

For the meaning of the metrical signature in parentheses see chapter 5 (I.E.1.2).

Beginning with v. 7 only the initial phrase of the soloist's part is transcribed; ¡llora, gavilán! and the refrain sung by the chorus are omitted. The melodic phrase sung to v. 21 (m. 82) is included as a rare example of the use of the lowered third degree.

As indicated in the transcription of the music, but not in the realized text, the chorus enters in each case before ¡llora, gavilán! is sung, joining the soloist in the singing of one or more previous syllables. Beginning with v. 7 (m. 26) the syllables of the initial phrase, which are sung by both the soloist and the chorus, are indicated by underlining. In the syllable che in m. 30 the upper note is sung by the soloist, the lower by the chorus.

The entrance of the chorus seems to be controlled by pitch rather than text; that is, the chorus generally enters when the soloist reaches the pitch b^1 toward the end of his phrase. However, when the soloist sings the word garrapatero (see v. 13), the chorus joins in singing the entire word, although the soloist has not as yet reached the b^1.

Text:

5. - The gavilán (sparrowhawk) is colloquially known as the chickenhawk because of its propensity to attack domestic fowl. However, in this region this predator does not seek out chickens, but lives on ticks which infest cattle. A symbiotic relationship has developed in which the cattle accept the presence of the hawks as a means of ridding themselves of ticks.

21. - The verb form should be quiero. Quiere is substituted for purposes of rhyme.

DANZA DE NEGRO

The danza de negro is performed during the celebration of carnaval (see pp. 102-7). The ensemble utilized is described in chapter 2 (pp. 84-87).

TR 45-47

Cantante, Agustín Pallares Hernández; palmetas, Enríquez Sánchez
Palacio; bombo sticks, Angel Ospino Santana; tambor mayor, Manuel
Pimientel Pacheco; guacharaca, Augusto Espinosa Torrecilla.   The
instrumentalists also form the chorus.   Mahates, 12 April 1970.

Of the three following transcriptions of this genre, TR 45 is
of the type known as de la calle (for the street), which is performed while the dancers and musicians go in procession through
the streets (see pp. 104-6).   TR 46 and TR 47 are of a second type
known as *de la casa* (for the house) or de la plaza (for the
plaza), which is used to accompany dancing in one location, in
front of a house or in a plaza.

TR 45 (LF 188.3) "La rama del tamrindo"

S.	1. *E-je* la rama del tamarindo,	The branch of the tamarind,
Ch.	(R) *E* la rama del tamarindo.	The branch of the tamarind.
S.	2. Tamarindo, tamarindo, tamarindo paragüita, (R)	Tamarind, tamarind, umbrella tamarind,
	3. Yo este año voy a salir	This year I'm going away
	4. por si caso me muriere, (R)	Just in case I should die,
	5. para que se acuerden de mí	In order that they remember me
	6. domingo el año que viene. (R)	On Sundays next year.
	7. *E-je* la rama del tamarindo, (R)	The branch of the tamarind,
	8. Tamarindo, tamarindo, tamarindo, tamarindo,(R)	Tamarind, tamarind, tamarind, tamarind,
	9. Tamarindo, tamarindo, tamarindo paragüita, (vr2)	Tamarind, tamarind, umbrella tamarind,
	10. *E-je* la rama del tamarindo, (R)	The branch of the tamarind,
	11. Tamarindo, tamarindo, roble, campano y guayabo, (R)	Tamarind, tamarind, oak, bell tree and guava,
	12. Yo este año voy a salir	This year I'm going away
	13. por si caso me muriere, (R)	Just in case I should die,
	14. para que se acuerden de mí	In order that they remember me
	15. domingo el año que viene. (R)	On Sundays next year.

TR 45a (composite score)

ta-ño voy a sa-lir 4. por sí ca — so me mu-rie — re,

E_____ la ra-me ta-ma-rin-do.

5. pa-ra

cts.
cts.
cts.

que se cuer-den de mí 6. do-min-go la que vie — ne.

E_____ la ra-me ta-ma-rin--do.

je_____ la ra-ma de ta-ma-rin-do_,

E_____ la ra-me ta-ma-rin-do.

rin-do, ta-ma-rin-do, ta-ma-rin-do, ta-ma-rin-do_,

E_____ la ra - me ta-ma-rin - do.

ma-rin-do, ta-ma-rin-do, ta-ma-rin-do pa-ra-güi-ta,

E_____ la ra - me ta-ma-rin - do.

rin-do, ta-ma-rin-do, ta-ma-rin-do pa-ra-güi-ta___,

16. La rama del tamarindo, la
    rama del tamarindo, (R)

The branch of the tamarind,
    the branch of the tamarind,

17. Tamarindo, tamarindo,
    roble, campano y
    guayabo, (R)

Tamarind, tamarind, oak,
    bell tree and guava,

18. E-je la rama del
    tamarindo, (R)

The branch of the tamarind,

19. Tamarindo, tamarindo,
    tamarindo paragüita,
    (R)

Tamarind, tamarind,
    umbrella tamarind,

20. Los negros evitaleros se van para Barranquilla, (R)	The *negros* of Evitar are going to Barranquilla,
21. *E-je* la rama del tamarindo, (R)	The branch of the tamarind,
22. Tamarindo, tamarindo, tamarindo paragüita, (vr2)	Tamarind, tamarind, umbrella tamarind,
23. *E-je* la rama del tamarindo, (R)	The branch of the tamarind,
24. *E-je* roble, campano y guayabo, (R)	Oak, bell tree and guava,
25. Yo quise una prima hermana	I wanted to have a cousin,
26. y una tía y una sobrina; (R)	An aunt, and a niece;
27. la vieja se me escapó	The old one got away from me
28. de la sala a la cocina. (R)	From the living room to the kitchen.
29. *E-je* la rama del tamarindo, (vr2)	The branch of the tamarind,
30. Tamarindo, tamarindo, tamarindo paragüita, (R)	Tamarind, tamarind, umbrella tamarind,
31. *E-je* la rama del tamarindo, (R)	The branch of the tamarind,
Gr. ¡*O-o-u*!	

NOTES

Perf:

All parts but that of the tambor mayor were transcribed from LF 188.3. I was unable to hear the strokes played near the center of the drum head in this recording. They were reconstructed by reference to LF 98.3, which was recorded 8 November 1964. The tambolero in the latter recording was also Manuel Piemientel. Since neither the palmetas nor the guacharaca was played in LF 98.3, it was possible to distinguish the strokes played near the center of the head of the tambor mayor.

In beating together the sticks of his bombo, Angel Ospino played the same rhythm as that performed with the paletas by Enríquez Sánchez. The beating together of the bombo sticks is not specifically indicated in the score.

In the playing of this type of danza de negro the tambolero carries his drum by means of its rope sling. The bottom of the drum shell is therefore always open, and the change from destapado to tapado cannot be made (see chapter 5, I.E.3.2). In any case,

it is not customary to utilize this contrast in resonance in performing the danza de negro (see notes to TR 46).

Each eighth note in the part for guacharaca represents either
an up or down stroke of the trinche.

It frequently happens that the percussion players do not
settle into their usual patterns until a few beats have elapsed.
This can be seen in m. 2 (see also m. 2 of TR 56, chapter 12,
p. 481).

There are gritos (cries) during the performance by the men
playing the percussion instruments. These gritos are composed of
meaningless syllables such as *je*. During the performance in
street or plaza these gritos may also be uttered by the dancers.

The performance ends with a descending cry by the soloist. In
the street or plaza this cry would be given by the capitán of the
comparsa as a signal that the performers should stop and rest.

The recording is 2:09 (two minutes and nine seconds) in duration.

Text:

2. - *Paragüita* is the diminutive of *paragua* (umbrella) and
refers to the shape of this particular tamarind.

11. - The *campano* (*Samanea saman*) is a bell-shaped tree for
which there is apparently no term in English.

25-28. - The implication is that he tried to make love to a
first cousin, to an aunt, and to a niece. The aunt escaped from
him. The verb *querer*, of which *quise* is the first person singular, preterite past tense, means to want, to like, and to love.

TR 45b (alternative score)

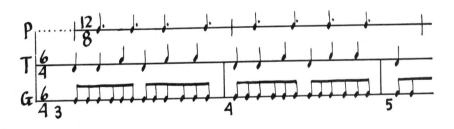

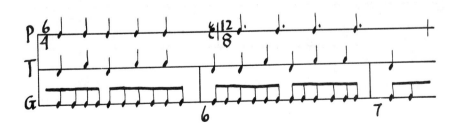

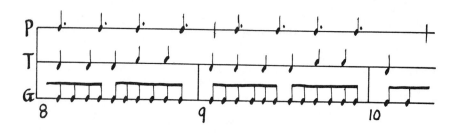

In the two scores, the regular score (TR 45a) and the alternative score (TR 45b), I have offered two realizations in notation
of the part played by the palmetas. In the regular score I interpreted the rhythms played by the palmetas from the European
point of view and adapted them to the prevailing 6/4 meter. In
the alternative score I viewed the palmetas part as an African
rhythmic phenomenon and represented it as the realization of a
disjunct cycle (see chapter 6, IV.B.2.1-3). The two interpretations are made possible by the fact that a percussion score in
actuality represents impact only, the note value given to any
impact point being arbitrary. The distance in time space between
impacts remains the same in both versions. In my opinion, the
realization offered in the alternative score reflects more
accurately the effect produced.

In TR 45b each cycle of twelve eighth notes is represented by
a measure. The tambor mayor and the guacharaca are performing
in conjunct cycles which are divided into two equal parts. Each
of these parts is in turn divisible by three or its multiple six.
The palmetas, on the other hand, are performing a disjunct cycle
of the same length, since their first stroke occurs two eighth
notes later in time than those of the tambor mayor and the
guacharaca. Their realization of the cycle is also divided into

Ex. 1.   Rhythmic organization of the palmetas
part (TR 45b, m. 3)

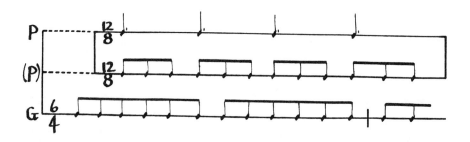

two equal parts. However, these parts are divisible by two rather
than three. The effect produced by this combination of three
cyclic patterns is off-beat rhythmic accents or phrasings caused
by not only the disjunctness of the cycle but the ensuing juxtaposition of groupings of two and three. To clarify the effect
produced in ex. 1, I have given the part for palmetas both in
its original dotted quarters and in the equivalent eighth-note
triplets.

   Note that in TR 45b in the third measure of the part for
palmetas a change is made in the realization of the cycle to six
quarter notes rather than four dotted quarters. For the period
of this one cycle there is no off-beat phrasing and no contrast
of two against three. The quarter notes of the palmetas coincide
with those of the tambor mayor and the commensurate two eighth
notes of the guacharaca.

TR 46 (LF 188.5) "Mama Inés"

S.	1. Mama Inés,	Mama Inez,
Ch.	2. Papa José, (c4)	Papa Joseph,
S.	3. todos los negros	All of us *negros*
Ch.	4. tomamos café. (c40)	Drink coffee.

TR 46a (composite score)

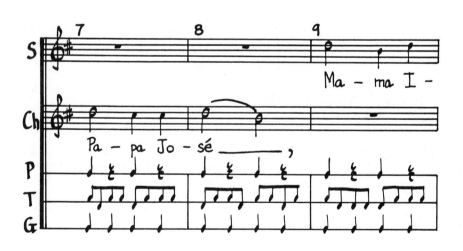

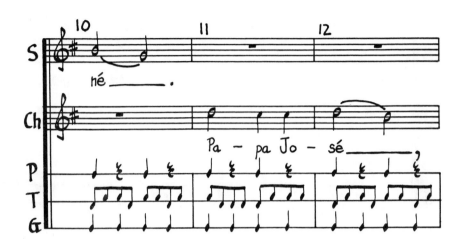

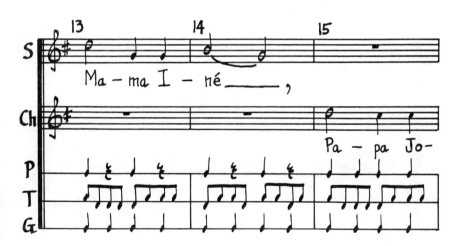

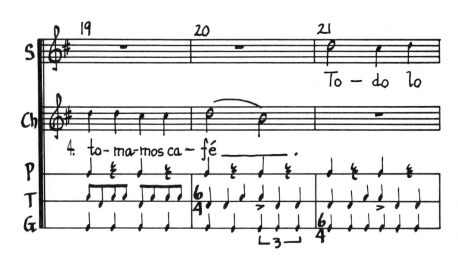

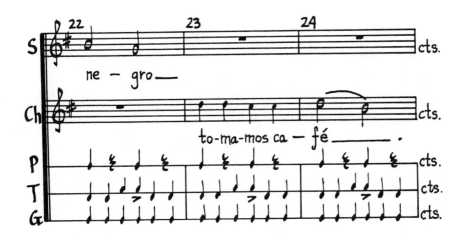

NOTES

Perf:

    All parts but that of the tambor mayor were transcribed from LF 188.5. The strokes played near the center of the drum head could not be distinguished in that recording. The patterns played by the tambor were therefore determined by reference to LF 188.8, a recording made of the percussion parts performed in the danza de negro de la plaza, omitting voices and clapping. In the latter recording I could determine with clarity the strokes directed toward the center of the drum head when it was played at a quarter of the velocity at which it was recorded, 1 7/8 rather than 7 1/2 ips.

    In m. 14 strokes by the bombo sticks are heard which do not match those of the palmetas. The player of the bombo sticks apparently changes to four quarter notes at this point. Finding that he is not in concert with the palmetas, he becomes uncertain in his rhythm. These additional strokes are therefore not transcribed.

    In this type of danza de negro the tambolero first plays a cycle of sixteen eighth notes, then, after repeating it a number of times, shifts to a cycle of twelve quarter notes, which, because it is composed of four triplets, occupies the same time span as the sixteen eighth notes. The cycle of eighth notes occurs in two forms. The first can be seen in m. 2-3 and the second in m. 8-9. They differ in the placement of the third and fourth strokes (third and fourth eighth notes) of the second

measure of the cycle. In the first form of the cycle these two
strokes are played near the center of the drum head, in the second
form they are played on the canto. In TR 46b this variation in
the form of the two cycles is seen in the fifth and sixth eighth
notes in the second measure of 6/8.

The number of times the cycle of eighth notes occurs before
there is a shift to the quarter-note cycle, and the order in
which the particular forms of the cycle are utilized, were determined by listening to LF 188.5. In LF 188.8 the tambolero plays
the cycle of eighth notes five times before moving to the cycle
of quarters. In LF 188.5 he plays the cycle of eighth notes nine
times before shifting to the contrasting cycle. The cue for the
change is obviously the move by the soloist and chorus from the
first to the second half of the copla. In LF 188.8 no copla was
sung, thus no cue was provided the tambolero which would advise
him when to shift from one cycle to another.

There is apparently no fixed order in which the two forms of
the eighth-note cycle should be performed. In LF 188.8 the two
forms are utilized in this order: 1 1 2 1 2. In LF 188.5 they
appear in the following order: 1 1 1 2 2 2 2 1 1.

In the danza de negro de la plaza the tambolero may perform
standing or sitting. In the latter case the drum remains tapado;
it is not raised from the ground.

In the part for guacharaca a quarter note represents an up
or down stroke of the trinche.

The guacharaca shifts to a ternary division of the pulse in
the second half of m. 20. From this point on there are no
changes in the patterns played by the percussion instruments.

During the performance the instrumentalists utter gritos, including *ju-pa*, *jupa je*, and *a-ja*.

All participants join in the descending cry which signals the
conclusion of the performance.

The duration of the recording is 2:09.

TR 46b (alternative score)

The excerpt from TR 46b represents two cycles of sixteen eighth notes each. Note that the omitted guacharaca part consists solely of repeated eighth notes. When the difference in resonance produced by the performance of strokes on the canto versus strokes played near the center of the drum head is taken into consideration, the internal rhythmic organization of the eighth-note cycle played by the tambor mayor becomes apparent. The cyclic organization is conjunct, but the realization of the cycle by the tambor is in additive rhythm, a rhythmic phenomenon characteristic of African but not Western European music (see chapter 6, IV.B.2.4). This realization of the additive cycle consists of four groups of three eighth notes and two groups of two eighth notes. For convenience in reading I have written the cycle as two groups of six eighth notes and one group of four. The result of the contrasting cycles is again off-beat rhythmic accent or phrasing produced by the juxtaposition of groups of two, represented by the quarter notes of the palmetas part, and groups of three, as heard in the part of the tambor mayor.

TR 47 (LF 188.7) "No quiero ser liberal"

S.	1. No quiero ser liberal		I don't want to be a Liberal
Ch.	2. ni conservador tampoco, (c5)		Nor a Conservative either,
S.	3. porque no quiero votar		Because I don't want to vote
Ch.	4. ni por uno ni por otro. (c24)		For either one or the other.

NOTES

Text:

1-2. - The reference is to the two Colombian political parties.

BULLERENGUE

The bullerengue is not associated with a particular fiesta, but is performed under various circumstances (see chapter 3, "Music Occasions"). It may be performed at *fiestas familiares*, that is, at private parties on occasions such as birthdays. It is less expensive than the cumbia, since there are fewer musicians to employ and no candles to purchase. For a description of the ensemble that performs the bullerengue and the dance which it accompanies see chapter 2 (pp. 87-88). The following six bullerengues were performed on different dates and by different groups of musicians:

TR 48-49 and TR 51-52

Cantante, Abraham Herrera Pacheco; cantadoras, Marta Josefa Herrera García and Juana Pimentel Martínez; tambor mayor, Manuel Pimientel Pacheco; llamador, Augusto Espinoza Torrecilla. Mahates, 12 April 1970.

TR 50 and TR 53

Cantante, Abraham Herrera Pacheco; cantadoras, Marcelina Sánchez
Pimientel, Juana García Blanquiset, Basilisa Herrera García, Ana
María Pacheco, and Juana Pérez; tambor mayor, Manuel Pimientel
Pacheco; llamador, Simón Herrera Sánchez (in TR 50 only). Evitar,
8 November 1964.

TR 48 (LF 188.13) "Tres golpes"

S.	1. Tres golpes, nada más,	Three blows, no more.
	2. Estos fueron los tres golpes	Those were the three blows
Ch.	(R) Tres golpes, nada más.	Three blows, no more.
S.	3. que le dieron al tambolero, (R)	That they gave the drummer,
	4. Bolívar, libertador (vr2)	Bolívar, liberator
	5. de la nación colombiana, (R)	Of the Colombian nation,
	6. que de la noche a la mañana (R)	In no time at all
	7. se metió en el Ecuador. (R)	He got into Ecuador.
	8. Mama, estos fueron los tres golpes, (R)	Mama, those were the three blows,
	9. Estos fueron los tres golpes, (R)	Those were the three blows,
	10. Mañana por la mañana (R)	Tomorrow morning
	11. riega tu casa de flores (R)	Strew your house with flowers
	12. que te viene a visitar (R)	For the one who is coming to visit you
	13. el dueño de tus amores (vr2)	Is the master of your heart.
	14. Mama, estos fueron los tres golpes, (vr2)	Mama, those were the three blows,
	15. Aquel doble de campana (R)	The tolling of the bell
	16. no fue para él que murió (R)	Was not for he who died
	17. sino para que sepa yo (R)	But to let me know
	18. que me he de morir mañana. (R)	That I am going to die tomorrow.
	19. Mama, estos fueron los tres golpes, (R)	Mama, those were the three blows,

TR 48a (composite score)

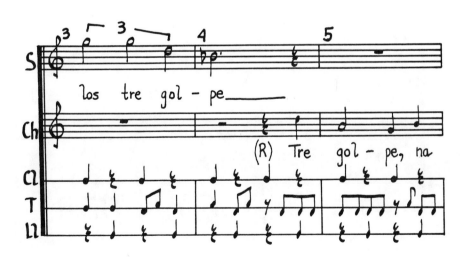

S: 5. de na-ción____ co-lom-bia — na____,

Ch: na má____.

S: 6. que de le la no-che la ma-

Ch: Tre gol-pe, na má____.

S: ña-a____ 7. se me-tien el

Ch: Tre gol-pe, na má____.

S: E-cua-dor____. 8. Ma-

Ch: Tre gol-pe, na

NOTES

Perf:

The vocal parts and clapping were transcribed from LF 188.13.
The first two strokes of the parts for tambor mayor and llamador
are also derived from LF 188.13. It is assumed that two initial
strokes are played by both instruments. However, it is difficult
to distinguish one timbre from the other, and the llamador may
not enter until the fourth quarter of m. 2. The other parts for
tambor and llamador were transcribed from LF 188.15, a recording
in which the two instruments at first play simultaneously and
then one continues without the other. Reference was also made to
LF 97.1, recorded 8 November 1964, to ensure that the parts for
clapping and the llamador are accurately related one to another.
In LF 98.1 there is a short initial section in which only clapping
and the llamador are heard.

As notated, the drums begin on the beat and then shift to off-
beat patterns. Initially the chorus coordinates its refrain with
its clapping; that is, the accents of each coincide. The soloist
at times coordinates the accents of his sung phrases with those
of the clapping and at other times with the strokes of the
llamador. Thus either the clapping or the strokes of the llamador,
which occur half a beat apart, may be considered the controlling
factor. To illustrate this point I have introduced a 3/4 measure
at m. 10 and have thus shifted the bar line so that the strokes
of the llamador are now written on the beat and the clapping off
the beat. The phrases sung by the soloist in m. 10-12 and 14-16
can now be seen to be coordinated in accent with the percussion
parts rather than the clapping, while the choral refrain remains
coordinated with the latter. In m. 18-20 the soloist is again
in phase with the clapping rather than with the percussion.
Beginning at m. 21 the chorus truncates the refrain, the first
accent now coordinating with their clapping and the final accent
of the refrain with the stroke of the llamador. The syllable
gol coordinates with a clap and the syllable *má* with a stroke
of the llamador.

In the bullerengue the tambolero plays in seated position.
He raises the drum into destapado position with some frequency,

thus producing a contrast in resonance. While the drum is raised
most strokes are directed at the canto rather than at the center
of the head.

There is an occasional grito by one of the women who sing the
refrain. This is usually *je*.

The cantante may give either a hand or voice signal when he
wishes the performance to stop. In this case a hand signal was
given.

The duration of the recording is 1:17.

Text:

4-7. - This copla concerns an incident during Colombia's struggle for independence from Spain in which the movement's leader,
Bolívar, escaped capture.
6. - An equivalent English idiom is given for a Spanish idiom.

TR 48b (alternative score)

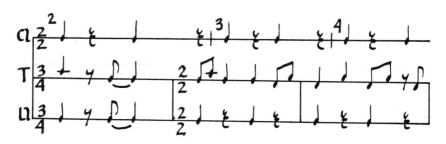

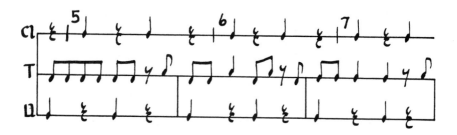

The alternative score, TR 48b, is presented as a further clarification of the rhythmic relationship existing between the clapping and the drum parts. In preparing and discussing the composite score, TR 48a, I have taken the European point of view and
attempted to correlate the solo vocal part with either the clapping or the strokes on the llamador. I shall now apply the African point of view. The women who sing the refrain also clap, and
they coordinate the two parts. Combining the time space occupied

by the verse of the soloist and the refrain of the chorus, it can
be seen that they are performed over a repeated cycle of eight claps.
If the llamador is also performing a cycle of eight strokes, the two
cycles can be seen to be in disjunct relationship, the cycle of
clapping beginning a half pulse behind that of the llamador.
This is a common phenonmenon in African rhythmic organization.

It can be objected that a similar phenomenon is present in
most European dance music of the common practice period, a bass
note being sounded on the beat and an accompanying chord on the
off-beat. This is rarely as regular as the alternation between
strokes on the llamador and the claps seen in TR 48. In European
dance music of the period indicated there is usually some variation in the bass line and in the rhythm of the accompanying chords
at the ends of sections, if not at the ends of phrases. Nevertheless, for purposes of discussion let us assume that the alternation seen in TR 48 represents the bass and accompanying chord
relationship of European dance music. Which then represents the
bass and which the off-beat chord? Since the llamador enters
first, and the rhythmic patterns of the tambor mayor are coordinated with its strokes, let us asume that it represents the bass
and the claps the accompanying chords. But this requires that
the melodic accents of the choral refrain always occur on the
off-beat, and this is inconceivable in European music. If we
reverse the roles and consider the strokes on the llamador to
represent the off-beat, the accents of both of the percussion
parts will then coordinate with the off-beat throughout the performance. This is equally inconceivable in European music. In
any case, in European music the great majority of the melodic
accents of the solo part would coordinate with the primary and
secondary pulses represented by the bass. No matter whether the
strokes on the llamador or the claps are considered to represent
the bass, the soloist does not consistently coordinate with
either. It is obvious, therefore, that TR 48a is not an adequate
representation of what is occurring and that the phenomenon being
observed is an African rather than a European trait.

A further understanding of the principles underlying the rhythmic organization of TR 48 can be gained through an analysis of the
relationship of verbal and musical accent. In this, consideration
of the percussion parts is omitted. In ex. 2, as in similar examples in chapter 8, the accented vowels are underlined and the
claps realizing the cycle of eight pulses are indicated by arabic
numbers.
Note that this is the text as sung, not the realized text.

Ex. 2. Verbal and musical stress
(TR 48, v. 1-4)

S.   1. Tre gol-pe, na má.

S.   2. sto fue-ron los tre gol-pe____   3. que
Ch.   Tre gol-pe, na má.
Cl.   1   2   3   4 5   6   7   8

```
S.   le die-ron a tam-bo-lero_____,                        4. Bo-
Ch.                                    Tre gol-pe, na má.
Cl.       1          2        3  4 5    6   7      8

S.   lí-va, li-ber-ta-da-dor____,                         Bo-la-lí-
Ch.                                    Tre gol-pe, na má.
Cl.       1          2 3          4 5    6   7      8

S.   va, li-ber-ta-dor_____
Ch.                                    Tre gol-pe, na má.
Cl.  1      2     3     4     5          6   7      8
```

Considering this as European duple meter, the primary pulses
are 2, 4, 6, and 8 and the secondary pulses are 1, 3, 5, and 7.
Thus, the beginning of the cycle coincides with a secondary pulse.
Throughout the example the verbal accents of the choral refrain
coordinate with both primary pulses and claps. Even when the
chorus truncates its response, as it does in m. 21 of TR 48a, it
continues to coordinate its initial accented syllable with both a
primary pulse and a clap.

The situation is quite different in the verses sung by the
soloist. Where speech accents do coordinate with claps, it usually
occurs on secondary pulses. On the other hand, all syllables
which coincide with primary pulses are unaccented in speech.
Further, a number of syllables which are accented in speech fall
between claps. This situation occurs in v. 2 with the syllable
gol in *golpe* and in v. 4 with the syllable *lí* of the word *Bolíva*.
What is sung by the soloist is similar to what is sung by the
cantor in the African lyric songs described by Jones. Although
he restricts his utterance to his allotted time space within the
established cycle of pulses, neither stress nor accent in the
text nor in the melody to which it is sung is necessarily coordinated with the claps (see chapter 6, VI.C.2). The soloist in
the bullerengue is, in fact, playing the improvisatory role common
to the leading singer or instrumentalist in an African ensemble
(see chapter 6, IV.B.2.5).

This performance is in duple meter in the sense in which Jones
applies this term to African song; that is, the time space delineated by each clap is divided into two equal units. However,
in the realization of the second cycle, in v. 3, three equally
spaced syllables are sung to one clap. In v. 2 three equally
spaced syllables are sung within the time space of two claps,
claps 1 and 2 of the first cycle. Jones indicates that both
types of hemiola are found in African song. I believe these
hemiolas to represent an African rather than a European trait,
since they are not validated by repetition (see chapter 6, IV.B.
1.6 and IV.B.2.7).

The final syllable of the verse of the soloist is at times
prolonged and encompasses more than one clap. This occurs in
African song, according to Jones, but is also characteristic of
European song. The refrain or response of the chorus occupies
three claps, the verse or call of the soloist five or six claps,
depending upon whether or not the latter overlaps the choral
refrain. According to Jones, this uneven division of the time

space of the cycle between soloist and chorus is common in African
lyric song.

In Jones's study of African song (1964) the time space delineated by one clap is occupied by not more than three time units.
Although the strokes on the llamador are in disjunct relationship
with the claps, the lapse of time between two strokes or two
claps is the same. However, the time space between claps can be
divided into more than three units. The tambor mayor frequently
performs four strokes to one of the llamador. The tempo of the
pulses of the cycles underlying the performances of percussion
ensembles is usually extremely rapid. The claps, footfalls, or
other kinetic impulses which realize the cycles underlying song
must of necessity occur at a slower tempo. The possibility
therefore exists that the cycle realized by the clapping and the
choral response and that realized by the llamador and the tambor
mayor are not only in disjunct relationship but may also differ
in tempo and thus in length.

When the tambolero enters he requires a few pulses before he
is able to settle into an appropriate rhythmic pattern performed
in proper relationship with the other parts. In the bullerengue,
as in the other genres discussed in this chapter in which there
is participation by percussion instruments, the performance is
begun by the vocal soloist. In the bullerengue the percussion
parts enter next and are followed almost immediately by the
clapping of the chorus. Judging from the rhythmic patterns performed by the tambor mayor from approximately the fourth measure
on, the cycle performed by the percussion instruments is eight
eighth notes in length. The majority of these pulses are realized
by the tambor mayor, only two by the llamador. I previously
stated that the accents of the parts for the tambor mayor and
llamador were coordinated. In this case the tambor part begins
with an anacrusis or upbeat, an unaccented eighth note. Thus
the notation of the two percussion parts in TR 48b still reflects
the European point of view. In African practice no one pulse of

Ex. 3.   Disjunct cycles of llamador and
          tambor mayor (TR 48b, m. 4-7)

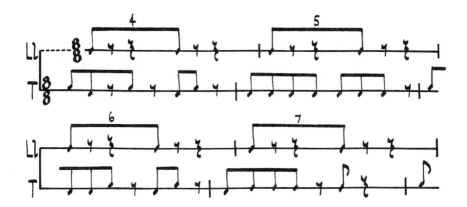

the cycle is conceived as receiving more stress than another.
The coordination of the various parts realizing the cycle is
therefore not a consideration. If the entrance of each percussion
instrument is conceived as the beginning of a cycle, the two
realizations of the cycle are in disjunct relationship. This is
shown in ex. 3.

We thus have a very complex situation. Rhythmic contrast is
produced not only by varying lengths of cycles but by two levels
of disjunctness in which these cycles are realized. The first
cycle realized by the two vocal parts and the claps as a group
is in disjunct relationship with either of the two realizations
of the cycle of the percussion instruments. In the second the
percussion instruments themselves are in disjunct relationship
in the realization of a cycle of the same length. It should be
noted that the tambor frequently gives the impression that it is
realizing a cycle of sixteen rather than eight pulses or eighth
notes. This can be seen in m. 4-5 and m. 6-7, if each group is
considered to represent one rhythmic pattern. On the other hand,
the tambor frequently repeats an eight-pulse pattern comparable
to m. 4 or m. 6.

TR 49 (LF 188.14) "Tres golpes"

S.	1. Y estos fueron los tres golpes,	And those were the three blows,
Ch.	(R) Tres golpes, nada más.	Three blows, no more.
S.	2. Mama, estos fueron los tres golpes, (R)	Mama, those were the three blows,
	3. los que le dieron al tambolero, (R)	The ones they gave the drummer,
	4. que le dieron al tambolero, (R)	That they gave the drummer,
	5. Mañana me voy de mi tierra, (vr2)	Tomorrow I am leaving my land,
	6. voy a meterme a vagabundo; (vr2)	I am going to become a wanderer;
	7. antes que venga la guerra (R)	Before the war starts
	8. me voy ausentar del mundo. (R)	I am going to leave this world.
	9. Mama, estos fueron los tres golpes, (R)	Mama, those were the three blows,
	10. estos fueron los tres golpes, (R)	Those were the three blows,
	11. que le dieron al tambolero, (vr2)	That they gave the drummer,

12. Adiós, por sí no volviere, (R)	Goodbye, in case I don't return,
13. yo les digo a mis amigos; (R)	I say to my friends;
14. y a mis hermanos queridos (R)	And to my beloved brothers
15. por si caso yo muriere. (R)	In case I should die.
16. Entrego estos tres golpes, (R)	I gave those three blows,
17. estos fueron los tres golpes, (R)	Those were the three blows,
18. Mama, estos fueron los tres golpes, (R)	Mama, those were the three blows,
19. Mama, me voy, vidita mía, (vr2)	Mama, I am going, my dear one,
20. al campo a llorar mis penas; (vr2)	To the fields to lament my sorrows;
21. yo me voy para tierra ajena (R)	I am going to a strange land
22. porque en la mía no cabía. (vr2)	Because I do not fit in mine.
23. Mama, estos fueron los tres golpes, (vr2)	Mama, those were the three blows,

NOTES

Text:

19. - The literal meaning of *vidita mía* is "my life." *Vidita* is the diminuitive of *vida* (life).

TR 50 (LF 98.2) "Tres golpes"

S.	1. *E-le-le* tres golpes,	Three blows,
Ch.	(R) Tres golpes, nada mas.	Three blows, no more.
S.	2. estos fueron los tres golpes (R)	Those were the three blows
	3. que dió el tambolero, (R)	That were given by the drummer,
	4. *E* Abraham Herrera, (R)	Abraham Herrera,
	5. Abraham Herrera se va (R)	Abraham Herrera is leaving
	6. junto con Manuel Pimientel; (R)	Together with Manuel Pimientel;
	7. Simón Herrera creo, (R)	Simón Herrera thinks,
	8. ¡Marcelina y los demás van al carajo! (R)	Marcelina and the rest are going to hell!
	9. Estos fueron los tres golpes (vr2)	These were the three blows

10. que dió el tambolero, Herrera, (vr2)	That were given by the drummer, Herrera,
11. *E-le-le-le-le-le* (R)	
12. ¿Cómo te vas y me dejas? (R)	Why do you go away and leave me?
13. Solo siento que no quedarme; (vr2)	I'm only sorry that I can't remain;
14. el alma me vas arrancarme, (R)	You are going to leave me soulless,
15. yo no sé de sí, preciosa, me vaya. (R)	I don't know for sure, darling, that I am going.
16. Estos fueron los tres golpes (R)	These were the three blows
17. que dió el tambolero, Abraham Herrera, (R)	That were given by the drummer, Abraham Herrera,
18. ¡Ah! tres golpes, tres golpes, (R)	Three blows, three blows,

Gr.   ¡E!

NOTES

Perf:

This performance was recorded late at night, and Abraham Herrera was drunk.

Text:

7-8. - What is implied is: "Simón Herrera may think he is going with us, but he isn't, and as far as I am concerned, Marcelina and the rest can go to hell!"

13. - Since she is leaving, and he is very much in love with her, he must leave also.

14. - Literally, "You are going to tear out my soul." The reference is to his attachment to the place that he must leave.

TR 51 (LF 188.11)   "Palo grande"

S.	1. Me gusta ese palo grande	I like that big tree,
	2. para oirle su zumbido. (c2)	To hear it murmuring.
	3. La mujer cuando se casa	A woman when she marries
	4. la gobierna su marido.	Is governed by her husband.
S/Ch	(R) Ña María.	María.
S.	5. Alístame el pantalón,	Get my pants ready,
Ch.	(R) Ña María.	María.
S.	6. Alístame el pantalón (R)	Get my pants ready
	7. que me voy para Colón, (R)	For I am going to Colón,

8. Alístame de verdad,   Be sure to get them ready,
(vr2)

9. Cipriana Villarreal,   Cipriana Villarreal,
(vr2)

10. El sapo quiere volar,   The toad wants to fly,
(vr2)

11. Bailecito de mi tierra,   Dance of my land,
(vr2)

12. mañana venid por mí. (R)   Come for me tomorrow.

13. Yo no soy para este   I am not for this world
tierra (R)

14. ni esta tierra es para   Nor is this world for me.
mí.

S/Ch (R) Ña María.   María.

S.   15. Alístame el pantalón,   Get my pants ready,
(vr2)

16. Yo me voy para Colón,   I'm going to Colón,
(R)

17. Me voy para Colón, (vr2)   I'm going to Colón,

18. Alístame la camisa (vr2)   Get my shirt ready

19. que mañana me voy para   For tomorrow I'm going to
misa, (vr2)   mass,

20. Mañana me voy para misa,   Tomorrow I'm going to mass,

S/Ch (R) Ña María.   María.

21. Alístame el pantalón,   Get my pants ready,
(vr3)

22. Me voy para Colón, (R)   I'm going to Colón,

23. Yo me voy para Colón,   I'm going to Colón,
(vr2)

24. Que yo con mi tambolero   My drummer and I
(vr2)

25. atreve de amanecer.   Can keep going till
(vr2)   daybreak.

26. Espéreme, compañero, (vr2)   Wait, friend,

27. ¡no me lleves al tropel!   Don't rush me!

S/Ch (R) Ña María.   María.

S.   28. Alístame el pantalón,   Get my pants ready,
(vr2)

29. Ya me voy para Colón, (R)   I'm going to Colón,

30. ¡Mira! ¡me voy para   Look! I'm going to Colón!
Colón! (R)

31. Alístame de verdad,   Be sure to get them ready,
(vr2)

NOTES

Perf:

The litanic verses of "Palo grande" are much shorter than those of "Tres golpes." Each litanic verse of "Palo grande" together with the short refrain encompasses a cycle of four claps, the first of these apparently coordinating with the final accented syllable of the choral refrain.

Text:

2. - *Zumbido* refers to the sound made by a light wind disturbing the leaves of a tree.

R. - *Ña* is short for *doña*.

7. - Panamá was once part of Colombia, and Colón is Panamá's principal city on the Caribbean coast. In the past it was very fashionable to travel there. Young men wished to visit Colón because its women were reputed to be the most beautiful in Colombia.

11. - The reference is to the bullerengue.

13-14. - *Tierra* could also be translated as "land" or "country."

16. - The addition of the pronoun *yo* makes this verse more emphatic than v. 17.

25. - The literal meaning is: "I venture to daybreak."

TR 52 (LF 189.7)   "Palo grande"

		Spanish	English
S.	1.	Me gusta ese palo grande	I like that big tree,
	2.	para oirle su zumbido.	To hear it murmuring.
	3.	La mujer cuando se casa	A woman when she marries
	4.	la gobierna su marido.	Is governed by her husband.
S/Ch	(R)	Ña María.	María.
S.	5.	Alístame el pantalón,	Get my pants ready,
Ch.	(R)	Ña María.	María.
S.	6.	Alístame el pantalón, (R)	Get my pants ready,
	7.	Me voy para Colón, (R)	I'm going to Colón,
	8.	Yo me voy para Colón, (R)	I'm going to Colón,
	9.	Alístame, de verdad, (vr2)	Be sure to get them ready,
	10.	Cipriana Villarreal, (vr2)	Cipriana Villarreal,
	11.	El sapo quiere volar, (vr3)	The toad wants to fly,
	12.	Acordeón barranquillera,	Accordion of Barranquilla,
	13.	¿quién te trajo por aquí (R) (c2)	Who brought you here
	14.	para darle en que sentir	To mortify all those
	15.	a todas las bullerengueras?	Who perform the *bullerengue?*

S/Ch (R) Ña María. | María.

S. 16. El pantalón, (vr2) | My pants,

17. ¡*Ay*! me voy para Colón, (R) | I'm going to Colón,

18. Yo me voy para Colón, (vr2) | I'm going to Colón,

19. Mañana me voy para Colón, (vr2) | Tomorrow I'm going to Colón,

20. Alístame el pantalón, (vr12) | Get my pants ready,

21. Me voy a dejar el mundo (vr2) | I'm going to leave this world

22. antes que el mundo me deje; (vr2) | Before this world leaves me;

23. que me venga algún hereja (R) | Before some heretic comes to me

24. a someterme a vagabundo, (R) | To make a wanderer of me.
    a someterme a vagabundo.

S/Ch (R) Ña María. | María.

S. 25. El pantalón, (R) | My pants,

26. *E* el pantalón, (R) | My pants,

27. Alístame el pantalón (vr4) | Get my pants ready

28. pero que tenga almidón, (vr2) | But be sure they are starched,

29. Este pantalón, (vr3) | These pants,

30. Relámpago vino al suelo | A lightning bolt fell to earth

31. que bailando lo empujaron. (c2) | Pushed over by those dancing.

32. ¡Mira! que anoche formaron | Look! last night they had

33. un bullerengue en el cielo. | a *bullerengue* in the heavens.

S/Ch (R) Ña María. | María.

S. 34. El pantalón, (R) | My pants,

35. *E* el pantalón, (R) | My pants,

36. Yo me voy para Colón, (R) | I'm going to Colón,

37. Yo me voy para Colón, | I'm going to Colón,

NOTES

Text:

See notes to TR 51.

12-15. - In this copla the accordion represents the sophistication of the popular music of the city.

21-24. - The meaning of this copla is that the singer had better change his ways before someone comes who will make him do so.

31. - The lightning bolt was not thrown, but involuntarily pushed over the edge of the sky by the dancers.

TR 53 (LF 97.4) "Palo grande"

S.	1. Me gusta ese palo grande	I like that big tree,
	2. para oirle su zumbido.	To hear it murmuring.
	3. La mujer cuando se casa	A woman when she marries
	4. la gobierna su marido.	Is governed by her husband.
	(R) Ña María.	María.
	5. El pantalón,	My pants,
Ch.	(R) Na María.	María.
S.	6. Me voy para Colón, (R)	I'm going to Colón,
	7. Alístame de verdad, (vr2)	Be sure to get them ready,
	8. Cipriana Villarreal, (R)	Cipriana Villarreal,
	9. El sapo quiere volar, (vr2)	The toad wishes to fly,
	10. Si no te da dolor	If you do not feel pity
	11. mereces una corona. (c2)	You deserve a crown.
	12. ¿Cómo te llevas mi voz	How can you carry my voice away
	13. y dejas a mi persona?	And leave the rest of me here?
Ch.	(R) Na María.	María.
S.	14. El pantalón, (vr4)	My pants,
	15. Me voy para Colón, (R)	I'm going to Colón,
(sp)	¡Ay!	
	16. El pantalón, (vr2)	My pants,
	17. Me voy para Colón, (R)	I'm going to Colón,
	18. Alístame de verdad, (R)	Be sure to get them ready,
(sp)	¡Mierda! Julio Pimientel.	Shit! Julio Pimientel.
	19. Verdad, (R)	Be sure,
	20. Yo me voy para Colón, (vr4)	I'm going to Colón,
	21. El pantalón, (vr2)	My pants,

22. Este pantalón, (vr3) | These pants,

23. Me pesa de haberte amado | I am sorry to have loved you

24. y el haber pensado tr. (R) (c2) | And that my thoughts have dwelled upon you.

25. Considero el infeliz | I contemplate the unfortunate one

26. que tengas encadenado. (R) | Whom you have chained.

S. 27. El pantalón, (vr2) | My pants,

28. Me voy para Colón, (R) | I'm going to Colón,

29. Yo me voy para Colón, (vr2) | I'm going to Colón,

30. Me voy para Colón, | I'm going to Colón,

31. Alístame de verdad, (vr4) | Be sure to get them ready,

32. Cipriana Villarreal, (vr4) | Cipriana Villarreal,

33. El sapo quiere volar, (vr3) | The toad wants to fly,

34. El pantalón, (R) | My pants,

NOTES

Perf:

We had waited some time for someone to bring a llamador and finally began recording without one. Abraham Herrera was already somewhat drunk.

Text:

See notes to TR 51.
10. - The literal meaning is: "If it does not give you pain."
13. - Literally, "And leave my person."
10-13. - This improvised copla is directed at Delia Zapata. This is again a suggestion that Delia take the singer to join the performing group he believed she had in Bogotá (see pp. 270, 272).
25. - The literal meaning of *el infeliz* is "the unhappy one."

FANDANGO

The term *fandango* has many meanings. Here it is applied to a particular genre and to the ensemble that performs it (see p. 88). The dance fandango is apparently performed during the Día de San Juan and the Día de San Pedro, but I was unable to establish the particular pattern of dance steps utilized (see pp. 107-9).

TR 54-55

Cantante, Abraham Herrera Pacheco; cantadoras, Marta Josefa
Herrera García and Juana Pimientel Martínez; tambor mayor, Manuel
Pimientel Pacheco; bombo, Angel Ospino Santana. Mahates, 12 April
1970.

TR 54 (LF 188.17) "Francisco"

TR 54a (composite score)

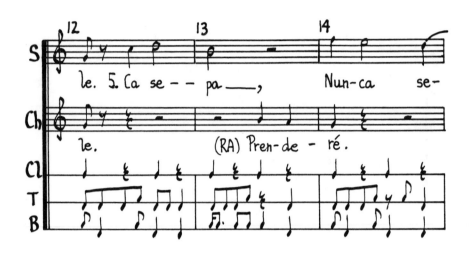

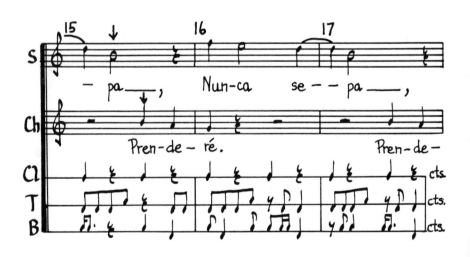

S.	1. Francisco, señor,	Francisco,
S/Ch	2. tu mama te va a vender. (c2)	Your mama is going to sell you.
S.	3. ¿Por qué?	Why?
S/Ch	¿Por qué?	Why?
	4. Porque no sabes moler.	Because you don't know how to mill.
S.	5. Nunca sepa,	I'll never learn,
Ch.	(RA) Aprenderé. (vr3)	But I'll try to.
S.	6. Dale, dale,	Give it to it, give it to it,
Ch.	(RB) ¿Para beber?	To drink?
S.	7. Dale agua,	Give it water,
Ch.	¿Para beber? (vr2)	To drink?
S.	8. Vuelve y dale,	Give it to it again,
Ch.	¿Para beber?	To drink?
S.	9. Vuelve y dale,	Give it to it again,
Ch.	(RC) ¿Con el pie? (vr2)	Kick it?
S.	10. Dale agua,	Give it water,
Ch.	(RB) ¿Para beber? (vr7)	To drink?
S.	11. Dale, dale,	Give it to it, give it to it,
Ch.	(RC) ¿Con el pie? (vr5)	Kick it?
S.	12. Cuando tengo el pecho claro	When I am in good voice
	13. hago lo que me da la gana.	I do whatever I want to.
Ch.	(1.) Francisco, señor, (2.) tu mama te va a vender.	Francisco, Your mama is going to sell you.
S.	14. De mi pecho hago una torre	Of my chest I make a tower
	15. y de mi lengua una campana.	And of my tongue a bell.
Ch.	(1.) Francisco, señor, (2.) tu mama te va a vender.	Francisco, Your mama is going to sell you.
S.	(3.) ¿Por qué? ¿Por qué?	Why? Why?
Ch.	(4.) Porque no sabes moler.	Because you do not know how to mill.
S.	16. Nunca sepa,	I'll never learn,
Ch.	(RA) Aprenderé. (vr2)	But I'll try to.

S.	17. Dale, dale,	Give it to it, give it to it,
Ch.	(RC) ¿Con el pie?	Kick it?
S.	18. Vuelve y dale,	Give it to it again,
Ch.	(RC) ¿Con el pie? (vr2)	Kick it?
S.	19. Dale ¡y dale!	Give it to it but give it to it!
Ch.	(RC) ¿Con el pie?	Kick it?
S.	20. *E-le-le-i-la-le-la-le-le-la*	
Ch.	(1.) Francisco, señor, (2.) tu mama te va a vender.	Francisco, Your mama is going to sell you.
S.	21. Aquel doble de campana 22. no fue para él que murió	The tolling of the bell Was not for he who died
Ch.	(1.) Francisco, señor, (2.) tu mama te va a vender.	Francisco, Your mama is going to sell you.
S.	23. sino para que sepa yo 24. que me he de morir mañana.	But to let me know That I am going to die tomorrow.
Ch.	(1.) Francisco, señor, (2.) tu mama te va a vender.	Francisco, Your mama is going to sell you.
S.	25. *E*---Santísimo Sacramento,	"Sacred Sacrament,"
Ch.	(1.) Francisco, señor, (2.) tu mama ta va a vender.	Francisco, Your mama is going to sell you.
S.	26. *E*---Santísimo Sacramento, 27. ¿para dónde vas tan de mañana?	"Sacred Sacrament, Where are you going so early in the morning?"
Ch.	(1.) Francisco, señor, (2.) tu mama te va a vender.	Francisco, Your mama is going to sell you.
S.	28. ---A visitar un enfermo 29. que tengo grave en la cama.	"To visit a sick person Who is in bed very ill."
Ch.	(1.) Francisco, señor, (2.) tu mama te va a vender.	Francisco, Your mama is going to sell you.
S.	(3.) ¿Por qué?	Why?
S/Ch	¿Por qué?	Why?
Ch.	(4.) Porque no sabes moler.	Because you do not know how to mill.

S.	30. Nunca sepa,	I'll never learn,
Ch.	(RA) Aprenderé. (vr3)	But I'll try to.
S.	31. Dale, dale,	Give it to it, give it to it,
Ch.	(RC) ¿Con el pie? (vr2)	Kick it?
S.	32. Dale agua,	Give it water,
Ch.	(RB) ¿Para beber? (vr3)	To drink?
S.	33. Dale agua,	Give it water,

NOTES

Perf:

The vocal parts and the clapping were transcribed from LF 188. 17. The entrances of the tambor mayor and the bombo were also determined from this recording. The tambor part given was tran- scribed from LF 189.2, a recording of fandango by only the two drums. It is taken from a section of the recording where the two drums play simultaneously. However, in m. 2-3 the patterns de- rived from LF 189.2 are modified to be consonant with what can be heard in LF 188.17 before the bombo enters.

There are two types of fandango. The first, de la calle, is used in processions; the second, de la plaza, is played when the dancing takes place in one location. Both TR 54 and TR 55 are of the latter type. The tambolero is seated and does at times raise his drum to destapado position. However, he does not do so at the beginning of LF 188.17 nor in that section of LF 189.2 from which the greater part of the tambor part was derived. The bombo part is given as transcribed from a section of LF 189.2 where the bombo plays alone.

In TR 54a, as in TR 48a, the score is organized from the European viewpoint. Although not indicated, the quarter notes preceding the bar lines in the bombo part receive slightly greater stress than the remaining notes of the measure. Thus these stressed notes played on the bombo precede by half a pulse the strokes on the llamador which occur immediately following the bar line. For the first twelve measures the parts of the chorus and the soloist are coordinated with the claps. The melo- dic accents of the choral refrain continue to coincide with the clapping. The soloist, however, now sings very freely, some of his melodic accents being coordinated with the percussion and others with the claps.

There are intermittent cries of *ja*, *ja-je*, and *lle-ma* from the women who sing the choral refrain.

At midpoint in the recording there is a slight acceleration of the tempo which continues to the end. The tempo at the latter point is between 144 and 152 to a half note.

The duration of the performance is 2:16.

Text:

Francisco is a young boy who is lazy and does not wish to work at the mill. An attempt is made to frighten him into working by telling him that his mother will sell him. The last is a reference to the days of slavery in Colombia. The boy tries to avoid being kept at work at the mill by pretending not to understand the orders given him. This is facilitated by the fact that *dale*, the order given, has a large number of meanings. It can mean that the person so commanded should give something to a person, an animal, or a thing or that he should move an object or put a vehicle into motion. It may be used to incite one individual into physical attack on another, or it may be employed to indicate that it is the turn of the person commanded to carry out some action.

The mill referred to is probably one employed in grinding cereals. A long pole is attached to the upper millstone. A burro or mule is harnessed to the end of the pole and turns the mill by walking in a circle around it.

There are three different refrains, marked (RA), (RB), and (RC). V. 3, v. 5, and the three refrains represent questions or statements by Francisco whether sung by soloist, chorus, or both.

1. - In this case *señor* is a term of address affectionately directed at a child. There is no counterpart in English, and it is therefore omitted in the translation.

6-7. - The significance of the command is that Francisco pour water on the millstones to cool them. Since the command is susceptible to several interpretations, Francisco pretends not to understand. His question in reply is also subject to more than one interpretation. He may be asking whether he should water the animal turning the millstones or whether he should bring drinking water to those working at the mill.

9. (RC) - Again, the boy pretends not to understand the command. His question in reply is again subject to two interpretations. He is asking whether he should kick the animal turning the millstones or the mill itself.

14. - That is, to produce the greatest possible resonance.

26-29. - In this case *Santísimo Sacramento* (Sacred Sacrament) refers to the vessel in which the priest carries the host. The person who is ill is afraid that he may die and wishes to be given communion.

Like TR 48b, the alternative score TR 54b, which is given on the succeeding page, demonstrates that the realizations of cycles by the claps and the percussion instruments are in disjunct relationship. In this case, as can be seen in ex. 4, which follows TR 54b, the cycle is of four rather than eight pulses. Above the cycle of four claps the soloist or chorus may sing a full verse, as in the first four verses, or there may be a short call followed by a short response, as in v. 5-7. However, the first clap of the cycle does not coordinate with the first accented syllable of the verse, as in TR 48. Rather, in the initial copla it coordinates with the last accented syllable of each verse and in the following call and response pattern with the last stressed syllable of the response.

TR 54b (alternative score)

Ex. 4.   Verbal stress and musical pulse
(TR 54b, v. 1-4)

```
S.    1. Fran-cis-co, se-ñor___, 2. tu ma-ma te va ven-de ___.

Ch.                               2. tu ma-ma te va ven-de ___.
Cl.                   1   2          3      4    1    2


S.    Fran-cis-co, se-ñor ___, tu ma-ma te va ven-de ___.

Ch.                           tu ma-ma te va ven-de ___.
Cl.      3   4    1   2         3      4    1    2


S.    3. ¿Por qué?___ ¿por qué ___? 4. Por-que no sa-be mo-le.

Ch.                   ¿por qué ___? 4. Por-que no sa-be mo-le.
Cl.      3    4        1    2         3      4    1


S.    5. Ca se-pa___.      Nun-ca___ se-___pa___.  Nun-ca___

Ch.          (RA) Pren-de-ré.              Pren-de-ré.
Cl.       2   3      4     1    2      3     4     1


S.    se-___pa___. 6. Da-le, da-le.      7. Da-le a-___gua. Da-le

Ch.          Pren-de-ré.      (RB) ¿Pa be-be?      ¿Pa be-be?
Cl.      3      4     1     2   3      4    1     2   3   4    1
```

The cycle realized by the percussion parts is eight eighth
notes in length. As seen in ex. 5, the realizations of this cycle
by the bombo and the tambor mayor may also be considered to be in
disjunct relationship.

Ex. 5. Disjunct cycles of bombo and tambor mayor
(TR 54b, m. 4-7)

For short periods during the performance of the fandango one has
the impression that either the bombo or the tambor mayor, or both,
is realizing cycles of sixteen rather than eight eighth notes.
This effect is produced by almost exact repetition of two measure
groups, such as m. 4-5 and m. 6-7.

The fandango, TR 54, thus displays the same complex rhythmic
fabric as the bullerengue, TR 48. There are, again, two lengths
of cycles and two levels of disjunctness.

TR 55 (LF 189.1) "Ño Díaz"

S.	1. Que te pica, que te pica,		It's going to bite you, it's going to bite you,
	2. ¡mira! que te va a picar.		Watch out! It's going to bite you.
	Que te pica, que te pica,		It's going to bite you, it's going to bite you,
S/Ch	¡mira! que te va a picar.		Watch out! It's going to bite you.
S.	3. ¿Quién tiene la culpa de eso		Whose fault is it
S/Ch	4. que Sincelejo y Corozal?		That Sincelejo and Corozal?
S.	5. Este es ño Díaz,		This is Mr. Díaz,
Ch.	(R) A navegar.		To navigate.
S.	6. ¡Arriba! ño Díaz,		Keep it up! Díaz,
Ch.	(R) A navegar. (vr3)		To navigate.

(The choral refrain is repeated after each
subsequent line sung by the soloist or its
repetition.)

S. 7. Navegación,   Navigation,

    8. La navegación,   Navigation,

    9. La vela, el timón,   The sail, the rudder,

   10. Dale la vela al bote (2)   Set the boat's sail

   11. para el enfoque, (5)   In order to be on course,

   12. Este es ño Díaz, (8)   This is Mr. Díaz,

   13. ¡Arriba! ño Díaz, (4)   Keep it up! Díaz,

   14. Este es ño Díaz, (3)   This is Mr. Díaz,

   15. Es ño Díaz, (3)   It is Mr. Díaz,

   16. Este es ño Díaz, (2)   This is Mr. Díaz,

   17. ¡Arriba! ño Díaz,   Keep it up! Díaz,

   18. Se va el ño Díaz, (2)   Díaz is on his way,

   19. Es ño Díaz, (2)   It is Mr. Díaz,

   20. Este es ño Díaz,   This is Mr. Díaz,

   21. Hermana mía, (3)   My sister,

   22. Yo vi una hembra, (2)   I see a woman,

   23. me da la lengua, (4)   She gives me her tongue,

   24. Este sí es ño Díaz, (4)   This indeed is Mr. Díaz,

   25. La navegación, (3)   Navigation,

   26. Dale el timón, (3)   Manage the rudder,

   27. Vela el bote, (4)   Trim the boat's sail,

   28. Hermano, varón, (3)   Brother, man,

   29. coje el timón, (2)   Take the rudder,

   30. ¡Ño Díaz no podía (2)   Díaz couldn't do it

   31. con dos mujeres! (2)   With two women!

   32. ¡Ño Díaz no puede! (2)   Díaz can't do it!

NOTES

Perf:

   As in TR 54, the vocal parts realize a cycle of four claps. The
first clap of the cycle coordinates with the final accented syllable of the refrain.

Text:

The text of this fandango is to a great extent couched in double-entendre. It concerns a man from whom much is expected but who is unable to rise to the occasion. One interpretation of the text could be that the man is attempting to manage a small sail-boat overburdened by having two women aboard. A second interpretation could be that he is attempting to sexually satisfy two women in immediate succession. V. 23 indicates that the second interpretation is the one the listener is expected to derive from the performance.

4. - This is an incomplete statement. The meaning is unknown. Corozal is a town located a short distance from Sincelejo, the capital of the Departamento de Sucre.

5. - *Ño* is short for *señor* and is commonly used as a term of address in the countryside.

(R) - The verb *navegar* and the noun *navegación* employed later by the soloist have the same general meaning as their English equivalents "to navigate" and "navigation," but in the more specific sense they refer to transport by a sailboat or sailing vessel.

6. - The term of address is omitted, since it would not be employed in English in these circumstances.

9. - The meaning is: "watch the helm."

21. - The reference is not to a sister but to a woman who is a friend.

22. - The reference is to an attractive and capable woman. *Hembra* equals "female."

23. - The reference is to kissing with the tongue.

28. - Again, the reference is not to a relative, not to a brother, but to a man who is a friend. *Varón* refers to the male sex in general but may refer specifically to a male adult.

COMMENTARY

There are various means by which the genres presented in this chapter can be differentiated. They can be divided into two groups according to their function or according to whether men or women sing the choral refrain. TR 44-45 are processionals; the rest of the items presented accompany dancing. The choral refrain in TR 45-46 is sung by men, who also form the repercusión, the percussion section of the ensemble. In the remaining items the chorus is composed of women. In all cases the soloist is a man.

In the danza de la plaza form of the danza de negro, TR 46-47, the text consists of one quatrain only. All other items are cast in litany form with a choral refrain. In all but TR 55 coplas are inserted within the flow of the litanic verse.

A metrical analysis of the items presented in this chapter is given in table 20. It will be noted, however, that while a syllable count is given for the first version of "Tres golpes," TR 48, none is given for the following versions, TR 49-50. The same holds true for versions of "Palo grande." A syllable count is given for the first, TR 51, and not for TR 52-53. However, TR 49-50 and TR 52-53 will be considered in a later discussion of variation.

Table 20. Metrical Analysis of the Texts
of TR 44-55

TR 44

S.	1.	8	a
S/Ch		6	
Ch.	(R)	7	
S.	2.	8	b
	3.	8	c
	4.	8	b
	5.	8	
	6.	9	
	7.	9	a
	8.	8	b
	9.	8	c
	10.	8	b
	11.	8	
	12.	8	
	13.	8	
	14.	8	a
	15.	8	b
	16.	8	c
	17.	8	b
	18.	8	
	19.	9	
	20.	8	
	21.	8	a
	22.	8	b
	23.	8	b
	24.	9	a
	25.	9	
	26.	8	
	27.	10	
	28.	8	
	29.	7	a
	30.	9	b
	31.	8	c
	32.	9	b
	33.	8	
	34.	9	
	35.	8	

TR 45

S.	1.	$(\underline{2})$+8	a
Ch.	(R)	$(\overline{1})$+8	
S.	2.	$\overline{16}$	
	3.	8	a
	4.	8	b
	5.	9	c
	6.	8	b
	7.	$(\underline{2})$+8	
	8.	$\overline{16}$	
	9.	16	
	10.	$(\underline{2})$+8	
	11.	$\overline{16}$	
	12.	8	a
	13.	8	b
	14.	9	c
	15.	8	b
	16.	16	
	17.	16	
	18.	$(\underline{2})$+8	
	19.	$\overline{16}$	
	20.	16	
	21.	$(\underline{2})$+8	
	22.	$\overline{16}$	
	23.	$(\underline{2})$+8	
	24.	$(\underline{2})$+8	
	25.	8	a
	26.	8	b
	27.	8	c
	28.	8	b
	29.	$(\underline{2})$+8	
	30.	$\overline{16}$	
	31.	$(\underline{2})$+8	

TR 46

S.	1.	4	a
Ch.	(RA)	5	b
S.	2.	5	c
Ch.	(RB)	6	b

TR 47

S.	1.	8	a
Ch.	(RA)	8	b
S.	2.	8	a
Ch.	(RB)	8	b

TR 48

S.	1.	7	
	2.	8	
Ch.	(R)	7	
S.	3.	9	
	4.	8	a
	5.	8	b
	6.	9	b
	7.	8	a
	8.	$(\underline{2})$+8	
	9.	8	
	10.	8	a
	11.	8	b
	12.	8	c
	13.	8	b
	14.	8	
	15.	8	a
	16.	8	b
	17.	9	b
	18.	8	a
	19.	$(\underline{2})$+8	

TR 51

S.	1. 8	a
	2. 7	b
	3. 8	c
	4. 8	b
S/Ch	(R) 4	
S.	5. 8	
	6. 8	
	7. 8	
	8. 8	
	9. 7	
	10. 8	
	11. 8	a
	12. 8	b
	13. 8	a
	14. 8	b
	15. 8	
	16. 8	
	17. 7	
	18. 8	
	19. 10	
	20. 9	
	21. 8	
	22. 7	
	23. 8	
	24. 8	a
	25. 8	b
	26. 8	a
	27. 8	b
	28. 8	
	29. 8	
	30. (2)+7	
	31. 8	

TR 54

S.	1. 6	a
S/Ch	2. 8	b
S.	3. 3	
S/Ch	3	c
	4. 8	b
S.	5. 4+(RA)5	
	6. 4+(RB)5	
	7. 3+(RB)5	
	8. 4+(RB)5	
	9. 4+(RC)4	
	10. 3+(RB)5	
	11. 4+(RC)4	
	12. 8	a
	13. 9	b
Ch.	(1.) 6	
	(2.) 8	
S.	14. 8	c
	15. 9	b
Ch.	(1.) 6	
	(2.) 8	
S.	(3.) 5	
Ch.	(4.) 8	
S.	16. 4+(RA)5	
	17. 4+(RC)4	
	18. 4+(RC)4	
	19. 4+(RC)4	
	20. (10)	
Ch.	(1.) 6	
	(2.) 8	
S.	21. 8	a
	22. 8	b
Ch.	(1.) 6	
	(2.) 8	
S.	23. 9	b
	24. 8	a
Ch.	(1.) 6	
	(2.) 8	
S.	25. (1)+8	
Ch.	(1.) 6	
	(2.) 8	
S.	26. (1)+8	a
	27. 10	b

TR 54 (cont.)

Ch.	(1.) 6	
	(2.) 8	
S.	28. 8	a
	29. 8	b
Ch.	(1.) 6	
	(2.) 8	
S.	(3.) 3	
S/Ch	3	
Ch.	(4.) 8	
S.	30. 4+(RA)5	
	31. 4+(RC)4	
	32. 3+(RB)5	
	33. 3	

TR 55

S.	1. 8	a
	2. (2)+6	b
	8	
S/Ch	(2)+6	
S.	3. 8	c
S/Ch	4. 9	b
S.	5. 5	
Ch.	(R) 5	
S.	6. 6	

TR 55 (cont.)

7. 5
8. 6
9. 6
10. 7
11. 5
12. 5
13. 3+(3)
14. 5
15. 4
16. 5
17. 3+(3)
18. 5
19. 4
20. 5
21. 5
22. 4
23. 5
24. 7
25. 6
26. 5
27. 4
28. 3+(3)
29. 5
30. 7
31. 5
32. 6

Table 20 indicates that the majority of verses are octosylla-bic. This holds true whether the verse is litanic or forms part of a copla. Refrain lines, on the other hand, frequently contain fewer syllables. The litanic verses in TR 54 are exceptionally short. When combined with the equally short refrains which fol-low them, they form lines of eight or nine syllables.

Some 33 coplas are found in the items presented. In both TR 46 and TR 47 the entire text consists of only one copla. In the other items the text is composed of a combination of coplas and litanic verse. The great majority of coplas are easily defined as such by means of meter and rhyme. Others are so irregular in these aspects that they are considered to be coplas only because it is obvious that they do not form part of the litanic text. The rhyming schemes utilized, in order of their frequency, are abab, abcb, and abba. However, six of the 33 coplas here presented are somewhat irregular. For example, a rhyme, if it may be called that, is produced by the repetition of the same word, *tierra*. In another case *vayas* is offered as a rhyme for *dejas*. In other coplas no rhyme occurs when one might be expected, thus resulting in the rhyming schemes abbc and aabc. The type of rhyme employed may be assonance or consonance or a mixture of the two. There seems to be no preference for one type over the other.

In general, considerable variety is shown in the relationship between verse and refrain. In TR 44 there are actually two refrains. I have not marked the first one as such since it is sung by both soloist and chorus. Both follow in sequence a generally octosyllabic verse. In TR 45 the solist begins with a slightly modified form of the refrain, which he also sings at intervals throughout the performance. This is followed by the choral refrain. However, in all other circumstances the choral refrain follows a sixteen-syllable utterance by the soloist. This may form a single verse of the litany or it may consist of two copla verses.

The copla forming the text of TR 46 is not octosyllabic but is composed of three verses of five syllables and a fourth verse of six. The copla of TR 47 is octosyllabic. Although the texts of TR 46-47 are in quatrain form, the soloist and chorus alternate in singing the verses. The choral part is thus a melodic refrain, as in TR 18.

In TR 48-50, the three versions of the bullerengue "Tres golpes," the choral refrain is sung following each verse of the litany and each verse of the inserted coplas. In TR 51-53, the three versions of the bullerengue "Palo grande," the situation is more complex. This can be seen in table 21.

Table 21. Verses of Coplas after Which
Refrain Occurs, TR 48-53

	TR 48	TR 49	TR 50	TR 51	TR 52	TR 53
I. C.				4	4	4
C. 1	1(2)	1(2)	1	1(2)		
	2	2(2)	2	2	2(2)	
	3	3	3	3		
	4	4	4	4	4	4
			5			
C. 2	1	1	1	1(2)	1(2)	
	2	2	2(2)	2(2)	2(2)	2(2)
	3	3	3	3(2)	3	
	4(2)	4	4	4	4(2)	4
C. 3	1	1(2)				
	2	2(2)				
	3	3				
	4	4(2)			4	

In each version of "Palo grande" (TR 51-53) the soloist sings the same initial or introductory copla from which the title of this bullerengue is taken. The choral refrain is sung following only the fourth verse, and in two cases, TR 51-52, the soloist joins the chorus in singing the refrain at this point. In some coplas the chorus responds as it did following those found in TR 48-50, singing the refrain after each verse. In other coplas the choral refrain is heard following only the second and fourth verses or only the fourth verse. In TR 51-53 there are two examples of each of the last two types of responses. Considering what occurs in similar circumstances in the fandango "Francisco" (TR 54), one is led to believe that the occurrence of the choral refrain after the second and fourth verses, rather than after all four verses, is caused by a change in melodic contour in the performance of the soloist. The soloist ends the melodic contours to which he sings the litanic verses on the first scale degree or tonal center, which in most cases is the lowest pitch of the contour. When he wishes the choral refrain to be sung following a single verse of an inserted copla, he utilizes a melodic contour similar to those employed in singing a litanic verse. If he wishes the chorus to respond after he has sung two verses rather than one, he sings the first verse and the beginning of the second verse in a middle range and postpones dropping to the lowest and cadential pitch of the contour until the end of the second verse. This procedure is illustrated in ex. 6-8. Ex. 6 is a litanic verse, ex. 7 a copla verse, and ex. 8 consists of two copla verses:

Ex. 6. Contour, litanic verse (TR 52, v. 5)

a-lís-ta-me pan-ta-lón

Ex. 7. Contour, copla verse (TR 52, v. 21, repetition)

Me voy de-jar e mun-do

Ex. 8. Contour, two copla verses (TR 52, v. 12-13, repetition)

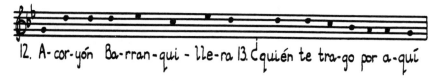

12. A-cor-yón Ba-rran-qui - lle-ra 13. ¿quién te tra-go por a-quí

Each of the preceding examples sung by the soloist is followed by the choral refrain Ña María, all four syllables of which are sung on b♭. As indicated previously, the call and response pattern of the bullerengue "Palo grande" realizes a cycle of four claps, the first of these coinciding with the only accented vowel of the choral refrain. Since the verse of the soloist often begins with this clap, there is constant overlapping of the two vocal parts. This is shown in ex. 9, as is the lack of choral response following a verse when the melodic contour is altered as illustrated in ex. 8.

Ex. 9.   Verbal stresses and claps
(TR 52, v. 11)

```
S.    11. El    sa-po quie-ro-lar,         El  sa-po quie-ro-lar,
Ch.      rí-a.                        Ña Ma-rí-a.
Cl.       1        2      3       4        1      2      3

S.          El  sa-po quie-ro-lar,      12. A-cor-yón ba-rran-
Ch.  Ña Ma-rí-a.                     Ña Ma-  rí-a.
Cl. 4      1        2      3       4        1      2           3

S.    qui-lle-ra, 13. ¿quien te tra-go por a-qui          A-
Ch.                                        Ña Ma ría.
Cl.           4             1      2    3    4      1

S.    cor-yón ba-rran-qui-lle-ra,      ¿quién te tra-go por a-quí
Ch.                                                             Ña
Cl.      2        3         4            1      2      3      4
```

In ex. 9, as in most of the performances of the bullerengue
"Palo grande," the verbal accents of the verses sung by the soloist
coordinate with the strokes of the llamador rather than with the
claps of the chorus. The strokes of the llamador precede the
claps by half a pulse. Nevertheless, the chorus continuously coordinates its cycle of claps with its sung refrain.

As indicated previously, the choral refrain is heard after
only the fourth verse in two of the inserted coplas. One of
these, the first inserted copla of TR 53, v. 10-13, is improvised.
Lack of familiarity with this text may therefore be a factor
inhibiting the reaction of the chorus. The cadence of the contour to which the third and fourth verses are sung is also exceptional. After reaching the first scale degree, the soloist
returns to and ends upon the third degree. The chorus hesitates
before entering. This hesitation may be caused by lack of familiarity with the text and/or the unexpected cadence. However, the
third inserted copla of TR 52, v. 30-33, does not seem to be improvised. Although the soloist in each case encompasses two
verses in his melodic contour, as he did in the first copla of
TR 51, the chorus enters only following the fourth verse. The
only explanation that can be offered is that complete consistency
in response is not expected. The musicians of Evitar do not re-
hearse. In the recordings it can be heard that at times only
part of the chorus sings the choral response, the remaining members either uttering gritos or merely clapping. The fact that
only part of the chorus responds is not indicated in the transcriptions. The disjunct cycles of claps and strokes on the
llamador continue whether or not the chorus responds to a particular verse or a particular set of verses sung by the soloist.
The soloist is therefore able to continue without pause and the
chorus again to respond with its refrain in the proper relationship.

In this chapter I have presented three versions each of the
texts of the bullerengues "Tres golpes" and "Palo grande." I
shall now analyze and compare these six texts in order to assess
what is variable and what is stable in the performance of a

bullerengue. I first offer in table 22 a comparison of the repetitions of copla verses in the six items. Only the verses that
are repeated are given. A horizontal line indicates that no
verses are repeated in this copla. Only the texts of TR 48-49
and TR 52 contain a third inserted copla.

Table 22.   Repetition of Copla Verses,
TR 48-53

	TR 48	TR 49	TR 50	TR 51	TR 52	TR 53
I. C.				v. 1+2	————	————
C. 1	v. 1	v. 1	————	v. 1	v. 1+2	v. 1+2
		v. 2				
C. 2	v. 4	————	v. 2	v. 1	v. 1	v. 1+2
				v. 2	v. 2	
				v. 3	v. 4	
C. 3	————	v. 1			v. 1+2	
		v. 2				
		v. 4				

An examination of this table will indicate that in this aspect
of the organization of the texts there is little parallelism,
variety seeming to be the more important consideration. The only
parallels in the repetition of verses are found between the introductory and first coplas of TR 52 and TR 53. It is interesting
to note that the first of these was recorded in 1970, the second
in 1964.
    None of the fifteen coplas found in these six bullerengue texts
is a repetition of another. All are different. The first inserted coplas of TR 50 and TR 53 are improvised. The first copla
of TR 53 meets the standard requirements of the form in number of
lines, number of syllables per line, and rhyming scheme. That in
TR 50 does not. It has five verses, is uneven in verse length
(5 8 7 7 12), and displays no clear rhyming scheme.
    In table 23 I offer a comparison of litany sections of the six
items. The comparison of the three texts of each bullerengue is
preceded by a key. In the keys the litanic verses are arranged
in complementary pairs, A and B, C and D, E and F. The numbers
following the letters represent variants of the particular verse,
A1, A2, A3, for example. M stands for a meaningless syllable or
for a group of meaningless syllables. M may appear by itself or
associated with another letter. In the latter case, the meaningless syllable or syllables form only part of a verse. In "Tres
golpes" there are only two types of verses, A and B. The A verse
represents the three blows (*tres golpes*) and the B verse the receiving or the giving of the three blows by the drummer. In
"Palo grande" there are three pairs of complementary verses. The
A verse refers to preparing the singer's trousers and the B verse
to his going to Colón. I have added to the variants of the B
verses the admonition to starch his trousers, B8, since it refers
to the same general subject and rhymes. C and D, rhyming *camisa*
(shirt) and *misa* (mass), are in subject matter variants of A

and B. They have been given separate letters because they display
a different rhyme. E and F always appear in sequence. One infers
that the singer is addressing his woman and informing her of his
desire for a change.

Table 23. Comparison of the Sections of
Litanic Text, TR 48-53

Example 1, "Tres golpes"

Key
A1 = estos fueron los tres golpes
A2 = mama, estos fueron los tres golpes
A3 = y estos fueron los tres golpes
A4 = entrego estos los tres golpes
MA1= ¡Ah! tres golpes, tres golpes
MA2= E-le-le, tres golpes

B1 = que le dieron al tambolero
B2 = los que le dieron al tambolero
B3 = que dió el tambolero
B4 = que dió el tambolero, Herrera
B5 = que dió el tambolero, Abraham Herrera

M = E-le-le-le-le-le

Comparison

TR 48	TR 49	TR 50
A1, B1	A3, A2, B2, B3	MA2, A1, B1
COPLA 1	COPLA 1	COPLA 1
A2, A1	A2, A1, B1(2)	A1(2), B4(2), M
COPLA 2	COPLA 2	COPLA 2
A2(2)	A4, A1, A2	A1, B5, MA1
COPLA 3	COPLA 3	
A2	A2(2)	

Example 2, "Palo Grande"

Key

A1 = alístame el pantalón
A2 = el pantalón
A3 = este pantalón
A4 = alístame de verdad
A5 = verdad
MA = e el pantalón

B1 = me voy para Colón
B2 = que me voy para Colón
B3 = yo me voy para Colón
B4 = ya me voy para Colón
B5 = mañana me voy para Colón
B6 = que mañana me voy para Colón

B7 = ¡mira! me voy para Colón
B8 = pero que tengas almidón
MB = ¡Ay! me voy para Colón

C = alístame la camisa

D1 = mañana me voy para misa
D2 = que mañana me voy para misa

E = Cipriana Villarreal

F = el sapo quiere volar

Comparison

TR 51	TR 52	TR 53
INTRO COPLA	INTRO COPLA	INTRO COPLA
A1(2), B2, E(2), F(2)	A1(2), B1, B3, A4(2), E, F	A2, B1, A4(2), E, F
COPLA 1	COPLA 1	COPLA 1
A1(2), B3, B1(2), C(2), D2(2), D1, A1(3), B1, B3(2)	A2(2), MB, B3(2), B5(2), A1(12)	A2(4), B1, A2(2), B1, A4, A5, B3(4), A2(2), A3(3)
COPLA 2	COPLA 2	COPLA 2
A1(2), B4, B7, A4(2)	A2, MA, A1(4), B8(2), A3(3)	A2(2), B1, B3(2), B1, A4(4), E(4), F(3), A2
	COPLA 3	
	A2, MA, B3(2)	

In "Tres golpes" the A verse is varied by adding a word initially, by changing the wording but retaining the idea (as in A4), by repeating the phrase *tres golpes*, or by substituting meaningless syllables. In verse B variation is achieved by adding a word and/or by a grammatical change causing the drummer to give the blows rather than to receive them. The latter is also extended by the addition of Herrera's name in final position. An entire verse is also constructed of meaningless syllables. There is much greater variation of verse in "Palo grande." Verse A is varied primarily by the omission of words rather than by their addition. In verse B, on the other hand, variants are principally secured by the addition of words in initial position. In both titles most changes in a particular verse are small, and the original idea is usually retained. A varied form of the verse is not usually heard until the verse has been sung several times in its original form. For the listener, then, the altered versions symbolize the gestalt represented by the verse in its original form.

At the beginning of the first section of litanic verse in each of the six texts, the complementary paired verses A and B appear in sequence. The variants employed are not necessarily A1 and B1, and a second variant of A may occur before the statement of the B. Subsequent litanic sections may or may not follow this pattern. Some, as in "Tres golpes," contain one or more variants of A only. In each of the three performances of "Palo grande" the complementary paired verses E and F appear in sequence at the end of the first litanic section. The repetition of either of two complementary verses does not affect their relationship. Verses C and D also appear in sequence. However, there is more than one variant of D, and the two follow each other. It should be noted that

the complementary pair E and F appears in the first litanic sections of only "Palo grande" and that the complementary pair C and D
appears only once, in the second litanic section of TR 51. Except
for the parallels just listed, the bulk of the litanic text seems
to be organized on the basis of random selection as a means of
producing variety. It should, of course, be remembered that the
greater part of the textual material consists of minor variations
on the complementary verses A and B.

Before comparing the texts in their entirety, we should consider the circumstances under which they are performed and those
under which they were recorded. The items which accompany processions, TR 44-45, continue until the procession reaches its
destination. Those which accompany dancing continue as long as
the soloist wishes to sing or, as in the case of the danza de
negro, until the capitán gives the signal to stop. As far as
formal organization is concerned, there is therefore no particular point at which any one of these items is supposed to terminate. All are open-ended. The performances of the two types of
danza de negro with Pallares as soloist were approximately of the
length of those I heard performed in Evitar on Ash Wednesday in
1970. In recording the bullerengues and fandangos, Herrera sang
only as much of each item as he felt necessary to give me an
adequate concept of its character. When performed to accompany
the dance, the duration in each case is normally much greater.

Table 24. Number of Verses per Section Including
Repetitions, TR 48-53

	TR 48	TR 49	TR 50	TR 51	TR 52	TR 53
INTRO. COPLA				6 (24)	4 (16)	4 (16)
Lit. vrs. 1	2 (16)	4 (32)	3 (24)	7 (28)	8 (32)	6 (24)
Copla 1	5 (40)	6 (48)	4 (32)	5 (20)	6 (24)	6 (24)
Lit. vrs. 2	2 (16)	4 (32)	5 (40)	16 (64)	19 (76)	19 (76)
Copla 2	5 (40)	4 (32)	5 (40)	7 (28)	7 (28)	6 (24)
Lit. vrs. 3	2 (16)	3 (24)	3 (24)	6 (24)	7 (28)	15 (60)
Copla 3	4 (32)	6 (48)			6 (24)	
Lit. vrs. 4	1 (8)	2 (16)			4 (16)	
TOTALS	21 (168)	29 (232)	20 (160)	47 (188)	61 (244)	56 (224)
DURATION	1.17	1.50	1.33	1.22	2.07	1.52

Table 24 is a summary of the number of verses, including repetitions, sung in each section of the six performances, as well as the
total number heard in each. In combination, each verse and refrain
of TR 48-50 encompass eight pulses, while those of TR 51-53 encompass only four pulses. Further, each verse of the latter represents a cycle of four pulses whether or not a refrain is sung.
Verses indicated for TR 51-53 therefore occupy half the time space

of those indicated for TR 48-50. In order that a comparison can
be made not only of the actual number of verses sung, but of the
time space occupied, two figures are given. The first represents
the number of verses sung. The second figure, placed in parentheses, represents the number of pulses. The last line of the
table offers the duration of each performance in minutes and
seconds.

It can be seen that the formal organization of all six texts is
approximately the same. Each contains two or three inserted
coplas, each copla being preceded and followed by a section of
litanic verse. The performances of "Palo grande" (TR 51-53) differ
in two respects from those of "Tres golpes" (TR 48-50). The former
begin with an introductory copla not found in the latter, and the
second section of litanic verse is considerably longer in performances of "Palo grande" than in those of "Tres golpes." Otherwise
there is considerable variation in the length of the sections
making up the whole. The length of the entire performance depends
upon a number of factors: the number of inserted coplas sung, the
number of repetitions of copla verses, and the length of the sections of litanic verse. For example, the length of the first two
sections of litanic verse of TR 53 is roughly comparable with the
length of those of TR 51-52, but the third section of litanic
verse is much longer. Nor is tempo a constant factor. Although
the total number of verses or pulses in TR 50 is smaller than in
TR 48, the former is of greater duration.

In summary, there is much more consistency in the organization
of the full text than in the detailed material found therein.
There are parallel aspects in the organization of the three versions of each bullerengue, as well as a general pattern into which
all six are cast.

I have been discussing variation produced by changes in the
text. The melodic contours to which the verses are sung are also
modified. Such modifications are particularly useful for securing variety when the same textual verse is repeated many times.
In the second litanic section of TR 52 the last variant sung is
A1. It is sung twelve times. Since the same text is incessantly
repeated, variety is achieved by changes in the pitches utilized
in the melodic contour. As shown in ex. 10, ten such variants of
the melodic contour are employed in singing the twelve repetitions
of the text. The melodic form is thus a b c c d e f g h i j j.

Ex. 10.   Variation in contour sung to repeated
verse (TR 52, v. 20)

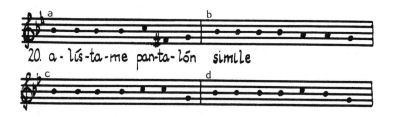

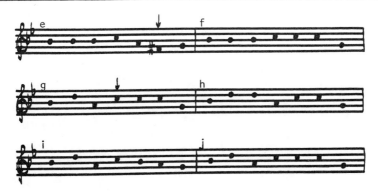

Note that the first two pitches and the last pitch of the contour
remain the same throughout; only the remaining pitches change.

Finally, we come to the two fandangos transcribed. In the
second of these, "Ño Díaz" (TR 55), a choral refrain follows each
verse as it does in the three versions of "Tres golpes" (TR 48-
50). Except for the introductory copla, if the first four verses
can be so described, TR 55 is composed entirely of litanic verse
and choral refrain. There are no inserted coplas. Of those
items in litany form presented in this chapter, it is therefore
the simplest and the most straightforward. On the other hand,
the first fandango, "Francisco" (TR 54), exhibits the most complex organization of any of the litany forms presented. The
introductory copla also serves as a choral refrain in part or as
a whole. Melodically it is divided into halves, the second
phrase of each half being identical. In "Francisco," as in the
bullerengue "Palo grande" and the fandango "Ño Díaz," the litanic
verse and the following refrain encompass a cycle of four claps.
These litanic verses are quite short and, as previously indicated,
combine with one of the equally short following choral refrains to
form a text line of eight or nine syllables.

In singing the inserted coplas the soloist encompasses two
verses in a single musical phrase. The first and second verses
of the copla are thus sung to one melodic phrase and the third
and fourth phrases to a second melodic phrase. The chorus then
responds at the end of each of the two musical phrases, that is,
following the second and fourth verses of the inserted copla. It
responds by singing the first two verses of the introductory copla:

      1.   Francisco, señor,
      2.   tu mama te va a vender.

Once the full inserted copla has been sung and responded to, the
soloist sings the third verse of the introductory copla,

      3.   ¿Por qué? ¿por qué?

the chorus answers with its fourth verse,

      4.   Porque no sabes moler.

and the soloist returns to the singing of litanic verse. How this
process relates to the underlying cycle of four claps is illustrated in ex. 11 (this excerpt begins with the second syllable of
the fourth statement of v. 11):

Ex. 11. Verbal stresses and claps (TR 54, v. 11-14)

```
S.       -le, da-le____,   Da-____ le, da-le____,      12. Cuan-do
Ch.  pie?               ¿Con el pie?           ¿Con el    pie?
Cl.   1        2      3   4     1     2     3   4          1

S.   ten-go pe-cho cla-ro  13. lo lo que me da ga-na___  .
Ch.                                              (1.) Fran-cis-
Cl.   2      3    4    1           2     3    4  1  2         3

S.                              14. De  mi pe-cho un-a to-rre
Ch.  co, se-ñor___,  (2.) tu ma-ma te va  ven-de.
Cl.    4     1   2           3        4      1  2    3    4    1

S.   15. de mi len-gua-na cam-pa-na.
Ch.                        (1.) Fran-cis-co, se-ñor___,  (2.) tu
Cl.        2      3     4   1  2     3    4    1   2

S.                     (3.) ¿Por qué ___? ¿por-qué ___?
Ch.  ma-ma te va ven-de.                          (4.) Por-que
Cl.   3       4     1           2    3        4  1 2         3

S.       16. Ca se-___ pa,    Nun-___ca se-pa___,
Ch.  no sa-be mo-le.      (RA) Pren-de-ré.            Pren-de
Cl.   4        1     2   3   4       1     2      3  4
```

Note that in order to bring in the choral refrain at the proper
point in the cycle of claps, the soloist must extend his double
verse (v. 12-13 and 14-15) through the time space of nine or ten
rather than eight claps.

The first couplet of the introductory copla is also heard as a
choral refrain under two other circumstances. In the first it follows a series of meaningless syllables:

20.   *E-le-le-i-la-le-la-le-le-la*

In the second a sustained meaningless syllable is followed by a
single verse:

25.   *E* Santísimo Sacramento

In the previous discussion of the choral refrains following inserted coplas in TR 52-53, the last two versions of the bullerengue "Palo grande," I offered the opinion that the occurrence of
the choral response after the second and fourth verses rather
than after every verse is caused by a change in the melodic contour employed by the soloist. In the versions of "Palo grande"
there was insufficient evidence to prove this point, since the
chorus was inconsistent in its response, responding at times at

the end of only the fourth verse. Since in this fandango the same
choral response is elicited by verses and by meaningless syllables, it is obvious that it must be cued by means other than the
text. The evidence indicates that this cue is the type of melodic
contour sung. In singing the short litanic verses, the soloist
ends each contour on its lowest pitch, in these circumstances the
third scale degree. The chorus then sings its short refrain,
which ends on the first scale degree. When singing two verses of
an inserted copla as one musical phrase, the soloist does not drop
to the lowest pitch of the melodic contour until the end of the
second verse. In such cases he cadences on the pitch pattern 3-1,
thus ending at a lower pitch level than in the contours employed
in singing litanic verse. This is shown in ex. 12-13:

Ex. 12. Contour, litanic verse (TR 54, v. 11)

Ex. 13. Contour, two copla verses (TR 54, v. 12-13)

As can be seen in ex. 14, a similar melodic contour sung to meaningless syllables produces the same choral response.

Ex. 14. Contour sung to meaningless syllables
(TR 54, v. 20)

TR 54-55 are the only items presented in the chapter which, to
some extent at least, are narrative in character. The fandangos
can therefore be differentiated from the other genres by this
characteristic. In the first, "Francisco," a boy employs various
subterfuges to avoid work. There is, however, little development
and no conclusion to the narrative. In "Ño Díaz," which is in
double-entendre, the narrative is developed through the occurrence
of various incidents, or implied incidents, and it comes to a
rather explicit conclusion. The inclusion of coplas would produce discontinuity in the suspense of the narrative, and it is
probably for this reason that coplas are omitted. As previously
indicated, it is the only item in litany form offered in this
chapter in which coplas are not inserted.

Table 25. General Characteristics of the Cantos de las Fiestas

	Function	Sex of Chorus	Verse Form	Lyric or Narrative	Instrumentation	Tempo
Gavilán	processional	women	litany	lyric	voices only	♩ = 152
Danza de negro						
de la calle	processional	men	litany	lyric	P, T, G	♩. = 75
de la plaza	dance	men	quatrain	lyric	P, T, G	♩ = 160
Bullerengue	dance	women	litany	lyric	C1, T, L1	♩ = 126
Fandango	dance	women	litany	narrative	C1, T, B	♩ = 138

There is one further means, instrumentation, by which the
genres can be distinguished from one another. "Gavilán" (TR 44)
is sung without instrumental accompaniment. Both types of danza
de negro are accompanied by tambor mayor, guacharaca, and palmetas. The part for palmetas is duplicated by the beating together
of bombo sticks. The bullerengue is accompanied by tambor mayor,
llamador, and clapping; the fandango by tambor mayor, bombo, and
clapping. The instrumentation of the last two genres is therefore quite similar. During my first recording of the fandangos
in Evitar, on 1 November 1964, no bombo was apparently available.
Both "Francisco" and "Ño Díaz" were performed for me at that time
but were accompanied by tambor mayor, llamador, and clapping. I
made previous arrangements for the session in which the same
genres were again recorded in 1970, and what I had been assured
was the proper instrumentation, tambor mayor and bombo, was indeed
provided. In 1964 "Ño Díaz" had been announced as a bullerengue
rather than a fandango. I queried Abraham Herrera concerning
this in 1968 and was assured that the announcement was an error.
Herrera then sang a few verses of "Ño Díaz," and another evitalero
who was present said that it was without question a fandango and
not a bullerengue. I then asked what the difference was between
a fandango and a bullerengue. Herrera replied that "one throws
oneself more into a fandango" and that it was performed *más alegre*.
In other words, the fandango is performed in a more energetic manner and more rapidly than the bullerengue. Judging by the two
fandangos transcribed, they can be partially differentiated from
the bullerengues by their non-octosyllabic litanic verse. The
soloist probably needs to enunciate the shorter verses with
greater vigor in order to trigger the entrance of the chorus with
its refrain. Concerning the second aspect of the performance,
the fandango transcribed is indeed performed at a somewhat more
rapid tempo than the bullerengue transcribed, although the contrast, 126 to the half note versus 138 to the half note, is not
very great.

A summary of the characteristics of the various genres presented is offered in table 25. The two processionals, "Gavilán"
and the danza de negro de la calle, display almost exactly the
same tempo. When changed so that a half note would be considered
a beat, the marking of the former would be 76. Of the items
which accompany dancing, the most rapid is the danza de negro de
la plaza.

Two of the *cantos de las fiestas*, TR 44 and TR 54, are complex
in their organization from both the textual and musical views.
TR 44 has two refrains, the second immediately following the
first. In the litanic section of TR 54 three textual refrains
are sung to the same melodic refrain. This item has, in addition,
an initial section in the form of an introductory copla which, as
previously indicated, is itself, either in part or in full, used
as a refrain. Viewed separately, some of these sections of TR 44
and TR 54 represent different scales and display different tonal
centers and/or finals. This diversity is made manifest in
table 26.

Table 26.   Scales or Modes of TR 44-54

I.   Common Practice

Major 3rd, non-heptatonic
    TR 54, 1st section

II.   Modal

Minor 3rd, heptatonic
    TR 45, verse and refrain

Indeterminate 3rd, heptatonic
    TR 54, 2nd section, verse and refrain

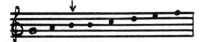

    TR 54, 1st and 2nd sections combined

III.   Modal (anomalous)

Major 3rd, non-heptatonic
    TR 46

III.   Modal (anomalous), cont.

Indeterminate 3rd, non-heptatonic
    TR 44
        a.   verse and refrain 1

        (transposed)

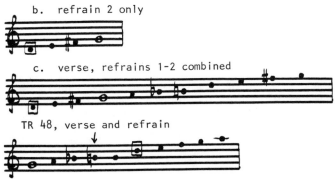

b. refrain 2 only

c. verse, refrains 1-2 combined

TR 48, verse and refrain

In table 26 the one scale which is consonant with common practice has been extracted from the first section of TR 54. The
scale of the second section of TR 54, the litanic verse, plus its
refrain is the second item listed under II. Modal. If we elide
the neutral third, the b with the downward-pointing arrow above it,
the scale can be considered to represent the mixolydian mode.
Immediately below, both sections of TR 54 plus the refrain are
combined. The resultant scale has both an $f♮$ and an $f♯$, and it
is therefore both non-common practice and non-modal; that is, it
does not fit the requirements of the major and minor modes nor
any of the church modes.

The first scale listed under II. Modal was derived from TR 45.
The $e♮$ occurs infrequently. If we elide it, TR 45 can be said to
be cast in the aeolian mode.

As before, those items placed in III. Modal (anomalous) have
one pitch as their tonal center and another pitch as their final.
TR 46 is a rather unusual type of pentatonic scale, since it
includes a semitone between b and c. Scales of this nature are
extremely rare if not nonexistent in Western Europe. For TR 44
a scale is first given which represents only the verse and first
refrain. This is then transposed for ease in comparison. This
scale has no pitch corresponding to a sixth degree and has two
forms of fifth degree. However, the $b♭$ ($d♭$ in the transposed
version) only occurs once in the transcription. If the latter is
elided and a $c♮$ is added, the aeolian mode is produced. If the
$b♭$ is elided and a $c♯$ is introduced, the mode produced is the
dorian. The scale representing the second refrain has only four
pitches. According to the combination of whole tones and semitones displayed, this tetrachord fits the requirements of the
lower half of either the major or mixolydian modes. The verse
and both refrains of TR 44 are then combined to form one scale
in which the final pitch differs from that of the tonal center.
Considering the final as the first degree, as I have done in each
case previously, the scale displays two forms of sixth degree and
has no degree corresponding to the seventh degree of a heptatonic
scale. By eliding the $b♭$ and adding a $c♮$, we produce the mixolydian mode. By adding a $c♯$ we produce the major mode. In this
case it is not necessary to elide the $b♭$ since this modification
of the sixth degree, a borrowing of the flatted form from the minor
mode, is a fairly frequent occurrence in common practice style.

TR 48 again has different pitches as the final and tonal center.
It also lacks a pitch corresponding to the seventh degree of a
heptatonic scale but has a minor third degree and three varieties
of sixth degree. If we elide all forms of the *b* except *b*♮ and add a
c, we produce the dorian mode. If we elide all forms of the *b* except the *b*♭ and add a *c*, we produce the aeolian mode.

Due to the complexity of the formal organization of TR 44 and
TR 54, I have, as in chapter 10, preceded the discussion of melodic functions with one of scalar or modal organization. Table 27
offers a comparison of the melodic functions of the items previously discussed.

Table 27.   Melodic Functions, TR 44-54

I.   Common Practice

Major 3rd, one-phrase melody

	Initial		Final
TR 54, 1st section	3 : 5		<u>5</u> . 1

II.   Modal

Minor 3rd, verse and refrain

	Initial	Mid	Final
TR 45	: 3 ♮7 . 5	4 .3 1	4 . 3 1
	5 : 5		
	♮7 : 5		
	♮6 : ♮7 5 3		

Indeterminate 3rd, 2nd section, verse and refrain combined

	Initial	Final
TR 54	4 : 5 3	3 2 . 1
	: ♮7 6 5 3	

Indeterminate 3rd, 1st and 2nd sections

	Initial	Mid	Final
TR 54	3 : 5	<u>5</u> : 1	3 2 . 1

III.   Modal (anomalous)

(First scale degree represents final, not tonal center)

	Initial	Mid	Final
TR 46, verse and melodic refrain	: 4 . 2	: 1 . 6	3 . 1
	: 3 . 1 3		

III. Mὸdal (anomalous), cont.

                    Initial   Mid   Final

TR 44

a. verse and refrain 1 (first scale degree represents final
    and tonal center, e)

                    8 : $\overline{3}$ 8   ♮7 . 5   4 : 1

                    2 : 4   4 . 5 4   4 3 : 1

                    3 5 : ♮7   5 . 5 3

                    ♮7 : 8 $\overline{3}$ 4 : 5

                    ♮$\underline{7}$: 2 4   ♮7 : ♭5

b. refrain 2 only (first scale degree represents final, d)

                                                    4 3 2 : 1

c. verse, refrains 1-2 combined (first scale degree repre-
    sents final, d)

                    $\overline{2}$: $\overline{4}$ $\overline{2}$ 5 : 2   4 3 2 : 1

                    3 : 5   5 4 : 2

                    4 6 : 8

                    8 : $\overline{2}$ $\overline{3}$

                    1 : 3 5

TR 48, verse and refrain (first scale degree represents final,
    not tonal center)

                    1 : 5   ♭6   . 4 6 : 8

                    1 : ♮3   ↓
                                         6

                    : 1 . 4   6

The melodic functions of the first section of TR 54, like its
scalar organization reproduced in table 26, are consonant with
common practice. This is not the case in any transcription considered as a whole. The melodic functions of TR 54 as a whole,
which is the last item under II. Modal, meet the requirements of
common practice to some extent. However, both cadence patterns
given, the mid and the final, close on a pitch representing the
tonic chord. The one cadence I have omitted, that of the verse,
closes with the third degree and therefore also represents the
tonic chord. A basic characteristic of the common practice style
is the alternation of tonic and dominant harmonies. It is unlikely that all three cadences of a melody would close on the
tonic harmony, that is, that none would close on a scale degree
representing the dominant chord.

With the possible exception of TR 54, all the transcriptions
contain some melodic patterns not utilized in their particular
position in the common practice period. Several of the initial
patterns found in TR 45 include a natural seventh degree, that is,

one located a whole tone below the tonic. The fourth initial pattern, having a sixth degree a whole tone above the fifth degree
and a seventh degree a whole tone below the eighth degree, is
characteristic of the dorian rather than the major or minor modes.
The mid-cadence of TR 46 is on the sixth degree of the scale and
thus represents the subdominant rather than the tonic or dominant
chords. When TR 44 is considered as a whole, one initial pattern
will be found to represent the subdominant chord. Finally, both
the mid and final cadences of TR 48 represent this chord rather
than the tonic or dominant.

The preceding discussion has indicated that none of the melodies
transcribed when considered as a whole are consonant with common
practice in either scale organization or melodic functions. Nor
can any of them be considered to be cast in a church mode without
elisions and/or additions. Both heptatonic and non-heptatonic
scales are found in African music as well as in European folk
music. Nketia indicates that some vocal music in Ghana is also
cast in a diatonic heptatonic scale, which, however, differs
slightly in intonation from that of the European major scale (see
chapter 6, IV.A.1.5). This is very much like the European major
scale, except that there are wider spaces between the seventh and
eighth degrees and between the third and fourth degrees, that is,
in the places where the semitones occur in the European major
scale. Nketia does not define the term *scale* as he uses it and
also states that African melodies end on any degree of the scale
(1963:36). If the latter is true, how does he determine what
tones form the seventh and eighth degrees of the scale or what
tones form the third and fourth degrees? In European practice,
scale degrees are numbered in relation to the melodic final or
to a determined tonic or tonal center.

Be that as it may, let us assume that the transplanted
African, influenced by his European master, adapts the principle
of the final or tonal center to his traditional diatonic scale.
The final or tonal center, the first or eighth degree, will now
become a point of reference by which relationships within the
scale or mode are established. However, the intonations of both
the seventh and third degrees of the scale still differ from those
of the European major and minor scales. Accepting g as the tonal
center, the seventh degree lies between $f^\sharp$ and $f^\natural$ and the third
degree between $b^\natural$ and $b^\flat$. We can therefore postulate that it is
the influence of this African scale which causes the indeterminate
nature of the seventh and third degrees of the scale in three of
the performances transcribed.

In TR 44 the seventh degree is $f^\sharp$ and the third degree is $b^\natural$.
There is one $b^\flat$, which appears in m. 82. In TR 48 the seventh
degree is $f^\natural$ and there are three forms of the third degree, $b^\natural$,
$b^\flat$, and the neutral third midway between them. The latter is
indicated by a $b^\natural$ with a downward-pointing arrow above it. In
TR 54 there are two forms of the seventh degree and two forms of
the third degree. In that part of the performance transcribed,
the seventh degree occurs as $f^\sharp$, the third degree as $b^\natural$ and the
neutral third. As the performance of TR 54 progresses, however,
the $f^\sharp$, which forms the first pitch of the melodic phrase to which

v. 2 and v. 4 are sung, is slowly flatted and is finally produced
as an $f\natural$.

Since the modification of the third degree occurs only once in
TR 44, let us direct our attention to the scales and performances
of TR 48 and TR 54. The first is a bullerengue and the second a
fandango. As has been indicated, they have a number of characteristics in common. The bullerengue is performed primarily in the
negro villages of the region and is believed to have originated
in Palenque. There the bullerengue apparently had as its progenitor the *lumbalú*, a song and dance accompanied by two hand-beaten
drums, which is performed as part of a funerary rite. There is
also historical evidence that an ensemble similar to that which
performs the bullerengue accompanied the currulao, a dance of the
negros in the Costa Atlántica in the early part of the nineteenth
century (see pp. 93-94).

Common to these two forms, the bullerengue and the fandango
(TR 48 and TR 54, respectively), is the singing of a flatted
seventh degree, that is, a seventh degree a whole tone below the
eighth degree, and an indeterminate third degree, that is, a
major third, a neutral third, or a minor third degree. Why the
neutral third degree was at least in part retained and the neutral
seventh degree not, I have no means of knowing. However, it will
be noted that there is some ambivalence concerning the pitch of
the seventh degree in TR 54 which is resolved in favor of the
flatted seventh. In transcribing songs of the Blacks of North
America, I have found the scale commonly utilized to exhibit similar characteristics. Here, however, the indeterminate third degree, the so-called blues note, often takes the form of a glide
between the minor and major third degrees. It is perhaps the
fusion of the African scale described by Nketia and European
modality which produced these similar characteristics of scalar
patterns in the music of the North American Black and that of the
costeño.

A further African trait is the occurrence of a short section of
harmonic intervals within what is otherwise a single melodic line.
This phenomenon is illustrated in ex. 15-16:

Ex. 15. Vocal harmonic intervals (TR 44, m. 5-6)

Ex. 16. Vocal harmonic intervals (TR 45a, m. 3-4)

In Western European art music a chorus may sing a phrase in unison, in two or more parts, or in imitative counterpoint. In the
last two styles a unison may occur, but the insertion of a short
section of harmonic intervals within a musical phrase which is
primarily sung in unison is quite rare. Nor is the latter common in Western European folksong, which in most cases consists of
a single melodic line. This phenomenon, however, is quite common
in the choral parts of African music. According to Nketia, such
harmonic intervals appear when choice in melodic movement is
possible, and they should be considered purely decorative. Although the single line may briefly break into two voices, the
basic concept remains mono-linear (1963:30). It should be indicated, however, that such sections of harmonic intervals do not
occur with any regularity within a performance of African music.
Ex. 15, taken from TR 44, is consonant with African practice,
since it occurs only once in that part of the song transcribed.
On the other hand, the choral refrain reproduced in ex. 16 is sung
in exactly the same manner in each of its seven occurrences in the
transcription. This aspect of the performance is a European rather
than an African stylistic characteristic.

    Two other aspects of the performance of the call and response
pattern in these songs represent, as far as I can determine,
African rather than European traits. The first is the overlapping
of the call and the response, the second the cuing of the chorus
by the soloist through his singing of their refrain (see chapter
6, VI.B.3-4). These traits are also present in the songs of the
velorio de angelito and are discussed at some length in chapter 8
(pp. 297-99). Two examples of overlapping follow. In ex. 17
the call of the soloist overlaps the response of the chorus,
while in ex. 18 the opposite situation is represented.

Ex. 17.   Overlapping of choral part by soloist
(TR 44a, m. 14-15)

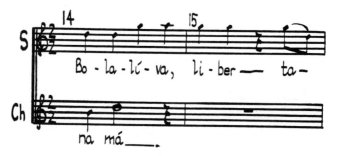

    In ex. 17 the soloist enters with his call before the chorus
has completed its response to the previous call. Note that harmonic intervals are produced in this situation also. Harmonic
intervals of a major 2nd, a minor or major 3rd, a perfect 4th, and
others are common in African music. When, as seen in ex. 18, the
chorus enters before the soloist has completed his verse, the
former does not sing the refrain, but duplicates the text sung by
the soloist. As previously indicated, this seems to be a costeño

trait. I have no knowledge of this phenomenon occurring in African music.

Ex. 18. Solo part overlapped by chorus
(TR 44, m. 5-7)

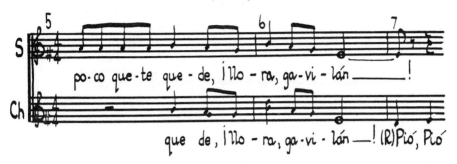

In order to cue the first entrance of the chorus, the soloist on occasion begins with the response or refrain before singing his first call or verse. This can be seen at the beginning of TR 45a and TR 48a (pp. 405, 421). Since these initial refrains are sung by the soloist rather than the chorus, I have given them verse numbers. In TR 52 the soloist sings the refrain simultaneously with the chorus following the last verse of each copla. This may be a form of cue or assurance when it follows the introductory copla or it may be merely a reinforcement of the choral part when it follows the inserted coplas (see the realized text of TR 52, pp. 434-35).

A further African trait is the use of the non-validated hemiola (see chapter 6, IV.B.2.7). In the two examples which follow, ex. 19, taken from TR 54a, is necessarily a horizontal hemiola, since I have given only the soloist's part. Ex. 20 is an example of vertical hemiola (see chapter 6, IV.B.1.5). The hemiola in ex. 20 has already been presented in ex. 2, an analysis of the relationships existing between verbal and musical accent in TR 48 (see pp. 427-28). However, the 2:3 ratio upon which the hemiola is based is more accurately represented by music notation.

Ex. 19. Horizontal hemiola (TR 54a, m. 1-4)

A further African rhythmic trait discussed in chapter 8 is off-beat phrasing (pp. 299-304). *Off-beat phrasing* is a term invented by Waterman in order to describe the African phenomenon roughly equivalent to the European *syncopation* (see chapter 6, IV.B.2.6). In chapter 8 the majority of the songs are unaccompanied, and melodic rhythm and verbal accent are contrasted with felt under-lying pulses, which are considered to represent either European

Ex. 20. Vertical hemiola (TR 48a, m. 3-4)

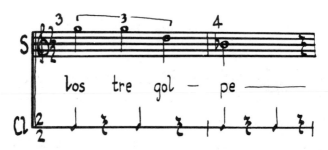

meter or African cycles. All the songs discussed in this chapter
with the exception of TR 44 are accompanied by percussion instruments, and there is little doubt that the instrumental and vocal
parts are organized according to the African cyclic principle.
The realization of the majority of the cycles is disjunct, and
where the realization is conjunct, as in TR 46, there is a contrast of additive and divisive rhythm. Analysis has also indicated that in the improvisatory part of the soloist neither melodic nor textual accent is necessarily coordinated with the pulses
of the cycle. Under these circumstances, *off-beat phrasing* or
hemiola are merely terms which categorize the end results of the
underlying principles of African cyclic organization. The performance of each part is coordinated with the cycle as a whole,
not necessarily with the individual pulses thereof.

Nevertheless, rhythmic contrast is an important element in
African music. In fact, a principle of African musical organization which Nketia terms *grading* exerts at least a partial control on rhythmic contrast (see chapter 6, IV.B.2.8). In each of
the four genres represented in this chapter in which percussion
instruments play a part, at least one is of the lowest grade.
In the danza de negro de la calle it is the guacharaca, and in
the danza de negro de la plaza it is the guacharaca and the
palmetas. Conversely, in the bullerengue it is both the llamador
and the handclapping, and in the fandango it is handclapping only.
The choral refrain, with its constant reiteration, may also be
said to lie at this lower grade. The tambor part in the two types
of the danza de negro is also of the lowest grade but somewhat
more rhythmically complex. The parts for the tambor in the
bullerengue and the fandango, as well as for the bombo in the
latter, are of a higher grade. They realize the cycle in a more
varied manner but do not stray from its confines. The part of
the palmetas in TR 45 is of this grade but less complex in its
variation. Only the part of the vocal soloist is of the highest
grade. Not only is it freer rhythmically, but it frequently
begins its call before the choral response is completed. In the
items presented in this chapter the soloist exercises more freedom
in both respects in performing the bullerengue and the fandango
than in the two types of danza de negro.

The cantos de las fiestas, like the songs of the velorio de
angelito presented in chapter 8, display a complex blend of Afri-

can and European traits. For reasons previously stated, I can
find no evidence of Amerindian influence. The pervasive presence
of the call and response pattern and the use of a group of percussion instruments in all items transcribed but one suggest a
greater African influence than that found in the items presented
in chapter 8. It is therefore necessary to modify somewhat the
organization of the following summary of the contributions made
by the two parent cultures.

Texts

The European heritage is most manifest in the song texts. I
know of no Spanish analogues of the texts presented in this chapter. It contains thirty-three coplas and the rhymed quatrain, of
which the copla is one form, is probably the most common verse
form in the folksong of Western Europe. Although the litany form
is most frequently heard in Africa, it is also known in Europe.
Thus, one cannot rule out European influence even when the performance consists entirely of unrhymed litanic verse. Another
specifically Spanish influence is the pervading octosyllabic verse.
Quatrains with verses of shorter length also form part of the Spanish repertory, especially in children's songs. When the litanic
verse is shorter than the octosyllabic, and uneven in length, as it
is in the fandango, one suspects African influence.

Melodies

None of the melodies of these songs as a whole are cast in the
major or minor modes of the common practice period. Nor can any
of their scales be said to represent any of the earlier church
modes except by considerable modification by means of additions
and/or elisions. Nor are the melodic functions of any song as a
whole consonant with common practice. Some of the cadential patterns, such as 4-1 and 3-1, are found in Gregorian chant, modal
European folk music, or African song.
The indeterminate nature of the seventh and third degrees, particularly in the bullerengue and the fandango transcribed, may
result from the fusion of African and European scales.

Relations of Verbal and Musical Stress

In the items accompanied by musical instruments, verbal and
musical accents are almost always coordinated in the choral refrains. Since TR 44 has no accompaniment, and is somewhat irregular in pulse, such a determination concerning it cannot be easily
made. In the performances of the bullerengue and the fandango the
soloist does not regularly coordinate his verbal stresses with
either handclaps or the accompanying drums. The Spanish tradition
requires considerably more coordination than is shown, and the
African tradition therefore predominates. There is much more coordination in this respect in the danza de negro. This occurs in
TR 45 between the part of the soloist and strokes on the canto of
the tambor mayor and in TR 46 between the former and the strokes
of the palmetas. Although the coordination displayed in TR 45 is

somewhat less than that seen in TR 46, both would seem to fall
within the Spanish tradition.

Formal Aspects

Omitting consideration of the handclaps, the percussion parts
in the items presented fall into cycles of eight, twelve, and
sixteen pulses. In number they are thus typical of African
cycles. Except for their rapidity of movement they might be interpreted as groups of two, three, or four European phrases of
four pulses each. In the danza de negro de la calle, the
bullerengue, and the fandango the cycles are in disjunct relationship. This is a typically African trait which is not found in
European music. In the danza de negro de la plaza the cycles are
in conjunct relationship, but one cycle is in additive rather than
divisive rhythm. Additive rhythm is primarily an African rather
than a Western European trait. It is found in traditional music
in some areas of Spain, where, however, it lacks the cyclic organization characteristic of African music (see chapter 6, IV.B.1.8).
Thus, all items containing percussion parts are primarily African
rather than European in their organization. If the performances
were fully African in style, one would expect a much greater use
of additive rhythm.

In the bullerengue and the fandango the vocal parts have been
analyzed as having been built upon underlying cycles of eight or
four claps. Phrases or cycles encompassing four pulses are more
common in Europe than in Africa. On the other hand, the uneven
division of the time space of the cycle between call and response
is an African trait. In the danza de negro the call and response
are equal in length. This is accomplished in the danza de negro
de la plaza by turning the copla, a European form, into a call and
response pattern, primarily an African form, by the use of the
melodic refrain. Nevertheless, in both TR 45 and TR 46, the vocal
parts can be conceived to represent four-pulse European phrases
sung alternately by solo and chorus. Thus, from the formal point
of view vocal parts which are primarily European in character are
performed simultaneously with percussion parts which are predominantly African.

One proof of the cyclic character of the vocal parts in the
bullerengue and the fandango is the use by the soloist of a different melodic contour as a means of postponing the entrance of
the choral refrain until the end of the second of two verses, each
verse encompassing one cycle of claps. In TR 54 there are refrains of different lengths. When in this case the soloist delays
the entrance of the chorus until after the second of two verses,
he finds it necessary to extend his contour to ten pulses, that
is, to encompass two pulses of a third cycle in order to bring in
the chorus at the proper time. Near the end of his performance
the soloist extends his contour to twelve pulses and thus brings
the choral refrain in two pulses late. From this point on the
parts continue as before, in cycles of four pulses. This is seen
in ex. 21.

The change in cycle relationship may have been purposeful or it
may have been in error. The form of TR 54 is sufficiently complex

Ex. 21. Shift in cycle of verbal stresses
and claps (TR 54, v. 28-29)

```
S.      28. A vi-si-tar un-fer-mo____29. que ten-go gra-ven
Ch. -de.
Cl.  1          2   3   4   1 2 3              4       1

S.  ca-ma____.
Ch.          (1) Fran-cis-co, se-ñor___, (2) tu ma-ma te va
Cl.  2  3   4        1    2   3  4         1         2
     1     2         3    4   1  2         3         4

S.  (3) ¿Y ¿por qué ____?  ¿por qué ____?
Ch.     ven-de.                          (4) Por-que no sa-
Cl.          3       4  1      2  3  4       1      2
             1       2  3      4  1  2       3      4

S.  30. Nun-____ ca se-pa____.
Ch.     be mo-le.
Cl.          3      4   1  2
             1      2   3  4
```

to permit the latter conclusion. The shift in the position of
the cycle is facilitated by the fact that the eight-pulse cycle
of the percussion parts covers a time-span equal to half of the
four-clap cycle. On the other hand, one could consider the
phenomenon discussed as proof that the song is cast in European
duple meter. Thus the cycle of the percussion parts in reality
represents one measure of duple meter, the tambor entering in each
case before the first beat of the measure. The soloist extends
his phrase by one measure, and the chorus continues, as before,
to conclude its refrain on the first beat of the measure. However, since this is the only case of its kind, I find it more
realistic to consider it an error and thus to maintain the African
rather than the European viewpoint concerning the organization of
the time as a whole.

Other aspects of the performance reinforce the impression of
African influence. Among these are the overlapping of the vocal
parts and cuing of the chorus by the soloist through his initial
singing of the refrain. One may conclude that the African and
European contributions to the cantos de las fiestas are fairly
well balanced, but the fact that the texts are sung in Spanish
tends to emphasize the latter.

12. Cumbia

The term *cumbia* in its various meanings is discussed in some detail in chapter 2, and a description is offered of the dance of that name (pp. 83-84). Here we are concerned primarily with the ensemble known as cumbia or conjunto de cumbia and the ritmos which it performs to accompany dancing.

Santiago Ospino Caraballo is the leader and pitero of the cumbia of Evitar. His father was the leader of a cumbia, which disintegrated after his death in 1952. Santiago formed a new ensemble very soon thereafter and has been its leader since that time. It is he who decides who shall be a member of the group and when and where they shall perform. The cumbia volunteers its services for the celebration, on January 20, of the day of the patron saint of the village, San Sebastián. Otherwise it performs infrequently in the village itself. This is due not only to the competition of the picó (see p. 92) but to the fact that in a village of this size the members of the conjunto are necessarily related to most other individuals in the community by ties of blood or marriage or as *compadres*. When they are individuals with whom one has such ties, it is difficult to charge for one's services. With the exception noted, members of the cumbia therefore make it a policy not to play in Evitar unless they receive remuneration. Their most frequent engagement in Evitar is to play at a velorio del santo (see p. 110).

When the services of the cumbia are desired, whether in the village or elsewhere, the negotiations concerning the details are handled by Santiago. When asked what the usual fee was for a night of cumbia, Santiago informed me that under exceptional circumstances it could be as low as 250 *pesos*. (At the time, 1965, the exchange rate was approximately 16 Colombian pesos to the U.S. dollar.) In addition, the musicians are always provided with rum. Male musicians do not feel they can perform adequately without the assistance of rum. If the engagement is outside the village, food and lodging must be provided in addition to the cash fee and rum.

Santiago exerts only a minimum of control over the performances of the individual members of the group. Most of the members of the cumbia are related, having either Ospino or Pimientel as patrilineage (see chapter 4). If they do not perform adequately,

478

there are other relatives who could replace them, but Santiago
obviously has to exercise discretion in such matters. Like all
piteros, Santiago gives a musical cue for the other instruments
to begin. His signal is a sustained b^1, given in transposition
in the transcriptions as g^1, the lowest tone in the agudo register of the caña de millo. This tone is difficult to sustain
since all fingerholes are closed, and a fluctuation of pitch is
produced which is apparently a characteristic of the musical cue
(see p. 58). To end a performance Santiago merely stops playing,
and the other players then follow suit. Like the performances
of the cantos de las fiestas discussed in chapter 11, those by
the cumbia are open-ended. There is neither an agreed-upon
point at which the performances should end nor formulas utilized
as closing devices.

One aspect of the performance of the ensemble is the use of
the *revuelo*, the only musical concept for which the costeño
musician seems to possess a technical term. As generally employed
in Spanish, *revuelo* means "uproar" or "commotion." Although all
costeño musicians are familiar with the term, it is much easier
for them to perform a revuelo than to express the meaning of the
term in words. In general, the term seems to refer to virtuosic
display occurring at intervals during the ritmo. Its purpose
seems to be to maintain or increase the excitement of the performance. Periodic gritos by the performers serve the same function.
All the instrumentalists perform revuelos except the player of the
llamador, whose function is to hold the ensemble together by means
of his steady beat. The cuartetos (see TR 61 and TR 65) are
usually sung by a member of the repercusión, the percussion section. This individual may continue to play his instrument while
he sings, as in TR 61, or, in order that he may devote full attention to his singing, a substitute may play his instrument during
this particular item, as occurs in TR 65. Each cumbia usually
has one or more substitute players who serve the above purpose or
relieve players when they are tired. The pito is usually silent
while a cuarteto is sung. In TR 61 the singer follows his
cuarteto with an *estribillo* (refrain). During the latter the
pitero does play.

There are four ritmos in the traditional repertory of the conjunto de cumbia: the cumbia, gaita, porro, and puya. As indicated
previously (pp. 83-84), the first two are utilized to accompany
the same dance, the cumbia. I was unable to establish specific
kinetic patterns for dances called porro or puya, dances that
would be accompanied by the ritmos bearing these names. According
to published sources, the term *porro* is applied in the Costa
Atlántica to the tambor mayor or a smaller but similar drum. The
term is believed to be derived from the verb *aporrear* (to beat).
The dance of that name is similar to the cumbia in that it is
danced around the musicians seated in the center, but it is more
rapid in tempo (Perdomo Escobar 1963:380-81). The puya is described as a type of waltz in which the couples dancing must exhibit considerable skill if the music is to be properly interpreted (Perdomo Escobar 1963:382).

Transcriptions follow of performances of these four ritmos by
the cumbia of Evitar. Because of the length of the performances,

only a partial transcription is offered in each case. The difficulties encountered in transcribing performances in which several
drums are playing simultaneously (see chapter 5, I.F.2) have led
me to offer a full score of only one item, the cumbia "No me
olvides." The transcriptions of the remaining items offer the
part played by the one melodic instrument, the pito, plus the
vocal part if cuartetos are sung. This is followed by transcriptions of recordings made of only the tambor mayor or the bombo,
in which they perform the patterns they customarily utilize in
playing the particular ritmo. TR 57 is a composite score and TR 58
and TR 68 are comparative scores (see chapter 5, I.F.2-3).

The following are the five regular members of the conjunto de
cumbia of Evitar:

> Pito, Santiago Ospino Caraballo
> Tambor mayor, José del Carmen Pimientel Martínez
> Bombo, Manuel Pimientel Pacheco
> Guachos, Juan Ospino Jiménez
> Llamador, Angel Ospino Santana

Simón Herrera Sánchez on occasion acted as substitute bombero.
All the items transcribed were recorded in Cartegena, 10 March
1965.

CUMBIA

TR 56 (LF 115.4) "No me olvides"

NOTES

Perf:

This transcription represents the first six seconds of LF 115.4,
"No me olvides" (Do Not Forget Me). It is not a composite score.
All the parts have been derived from LF 115.4, but by two means.
The performance was simultaneously filmed with a sound camera and
recorded by a tape recorder. The parts for pito and guachos were
transcribed by ear from the tape recording. The parts for tambor,
bombo, and llamador were first transcribed in tabular form through
frame-by-frame visual analysis (fig. 73) and then converted into
music notation. (For the methods employed in transcription from
motion film see chapter 5, I.G.) In TR 56 the two parts transcribed by ear are combined with the three parts realized in music
notation from the frame-by-frame analysis (chapter 5, ex. 9) to
form a full score. The coordination of the entrances of the various parts was determined by ear. (For the meaning of the notation employed in writing the parts for tambor mayor and guachos
see chapter 5, I.E.3.)

Since the pitero's opening formula does not exhibit pulse, the
players of the percussion instruments upon their entrance cannot
immediately coordinate their rhythmic patterns. However, it requires less than a second for them to do so. At this tempo each
measure represents the duration of a second.

The total duration of LF 115.4 is 2:43. Only one grito is
heard during the recording, at 1:10.

TR 56

TR 56 is presented as a means of validating the percussion patterns reproduced in the composite score, TR 57. By this I mean that a comparison of the two transcriptions will establish that the patterns represented in TR 57 are customarily utilized in the performance of this genre and item. Such a comparison will also indicate that the relationship of the parts exhibited is equally characteristic of the style.

TR 57 "No me olvides" (composite score)

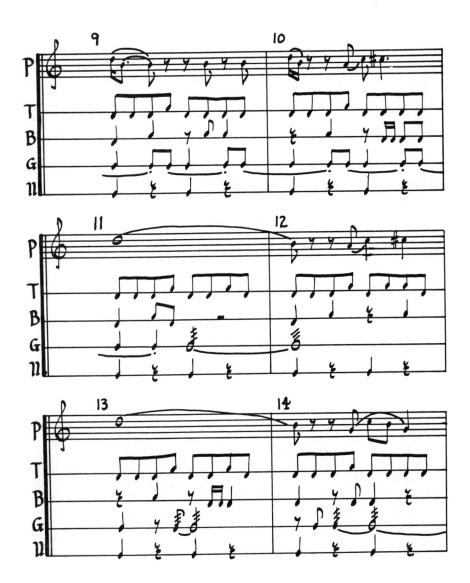

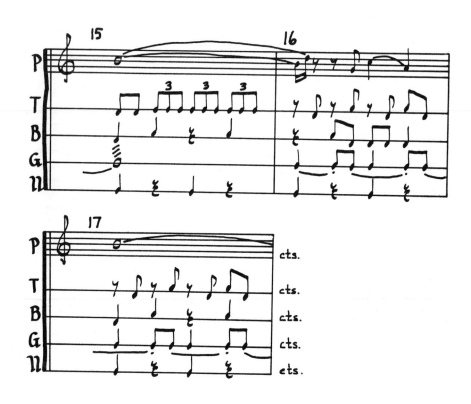

NOTES

Perf:

    Since m. 1-2 are given in TR 56 and the parts do not coordinate their patterns until m. 3, TR 57 begins with the latter measure.

    This score combines transcriptions made by ear from four different recordings of "No me olvides." The pito part was transcribed from LF 115.4, a recording of the full ensemble. The part for tambor mayor was transcribed from LF 118.6, a performance in which only the pito, tambor, and guachos participated. The part for bombo was transcribed from LF 118.5, a recording made of pito, bombo, and guachos only. The parts for guachos and llamador were transcribed from LF 118.7, a performance in which only these two percussion instruments and the pito participated.

    Effects which fall under the rubric of revuelo will be seen both in the parts of the tambor mayor and guachos. The triplet pattern played by the tambor in destapado position in m. 15 is such an effect. In LF 115.4 the tambor plays a similar roll-like pattern in m. 16. The shakes by the guachos in m. 13-15 also represent a revuelo. In LF 115.4 the guachos play the same pat-

tern throughout. A transcription of LF 118.7 was therefore utilized in the composite score in order to illustrate a revuelo as
produced by the guachos.

TR 58   "No me olvides"   (pito part,
comparative score)

NOTES

Perf:

TR 58 compares the first seventeen measures of the pito part of
three different recordings of "No me olvides." Version A is
transcribed from LF 115.4, version B from LF 118.1, and version
C from LF 118.5.
   An examination of TR 58 will indicate that there is a substan-
tial relationship between the three versions beginning at the end
of m. 1 and extending through the first part of m. 7. Following
this point there is greater variation in what is performed, and
relationships are more diffuse.

TR 59 (LF 115.5) Tambor mayor:
accompaniment for cumbia

NOTES

Perf:

TR 59 is a further illustration of the patterns utilized by the
tambolero in playing a cumbia. In this recording the tambor mayor
is heard alone. (For the meaning of the signs in m. 7 see chapter
5, I.E.3.2.)

TR 60 (LF 115.13) Bombo: accompaniment
for cumbia

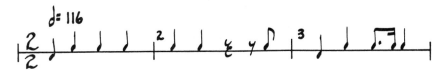

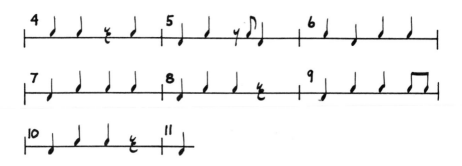

NOTES

Perf:

TR 60 is a further illustration of the patterns used by the
bombero in playing a cumbia. The recording is of the bombo playing alone.

The principal effect which seems to represent a revuelo as
played on the bombo consists of syncopated strokes on the head
which contrast with the established duple meter. Such syncopated
patterns can be heard during the latter part of LF 115.4 and can
be seen in m. 5-6 of TR 60. The division of these two measures
into three uneven groups of three, two, and three quarters rather
than into two even groups of four quarters is illustrated by
ex. 1:

Ex. 1. Revuelo played by bombo

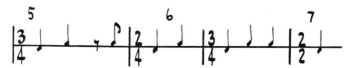

It should be remembered that the strokes upon the head have
greater carrying power and thus have more impact on the ear
than strokes upon the wood.

Derivation:

Thus far the cumbia has been considered entirely from the
European point of view, and it has been so notated. The African
viewpoint concerning temporal organization can also be applied
and the cumbia "No me olvides" be considered to be structured
over an underlying cycle of sixteen eighth notes. The illustration excerpted from TR 60 is an example of the bombero realizing
the cycle in additive rhythm, an African rather than a European
trait. The bombo apparently also realizes a cycle of the same
length since it plays a stroke on the head of the drum at the be-

ginning of each group of sixteen eighth notes.   However, no such
dynamic delineation is heard at the onset of an African pulse
cycle.   The cycle is also realized by the steady strokes played
on the llamador and by the performance by the guachos of a repeated
pattern eight eighth notes in length.   The division of the realized
cycle into two equal parts by a percussion instrument is not un-
common in Africa (Nketia 1974:126).   Over this repetitive structure
of conjunct cycles the pito and tambor mayor play improvisatory
roles.   The pito remains within the confines of the cycle while
providing frequent off-beat phrasing.   The tambor mayor provides
the same by means of random contrast between strokes upon the
center of the head and the canto.   In its random patterning the
tambor mayor sounds the great majority of the eighth-note pulses
of the cycle.

TR 61 (LF 117.5)   "Veinte de enero"
(pito and vocal solo parts only)

Sung by Juan Ospino Jiménez.

I (V) 1. Cuan-do me pon-go to-car

2. yo no me des- es- pe- ro. 3. La cum-bia de-vi-

tar 4. se lla-ma Vein-te de-ne- ro

(R) 1. ¡Oh! 2. ¡To- quel pi- to

3. ¡To- que li- ge- ro___! 4. ¡To-

quel pi- to___!

II.(v) I.En-

la cumbia de- vi- tar_____   2. lo

doc-to-re son de jui- cio__. 3. Cuan-do me pon-go

to- car 4. por- que co-noz-quel o- fi- cio____

_____. (R)1.¡Oh   ! 2.¡To- que pi- to__

__! 3.¡To- que____ li-ge-ro___!   4.¡To- que

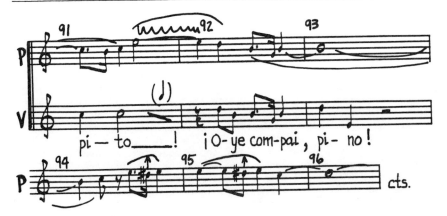

I. (V)	1. Cuando me pongo a tocar	When I am playing
	2. yo no desempero.	I allow nothing to annoy me.
	3. La cumbia de Evitar	The *cumbia* of Evitar
	4. se llama: Veinte de enero.	Is called "The Twentieth of January."
(R)	1. ¡Oh!	Oh!
	2. ¡Qué toque el pito!	Play, *pito*!
	3. ¡Qué toque ligero!	Play it now!
	4. ¡Qué toque el pito!	Play, *pito*!
II. (V)	1. En la cumbia de Evitar	In the *cumbia* of Evitar
	2. los doctores son de juicio.	The players are competent.
	3. Cuando me pongo a tocar	When I am playing
	4. porque conozco el oficio.	I know my business.
(R)	(As in I)	
III. (V)	1. ---Mama, me quiero casar.	"Mama, I want to get married."
	2. ---Pero, mi hija ¿con quién?	"But who with, my daughter?"
	3. ---Con Santiago Moreno	"With Santiago Moreno
	4. porque toca muy bien, mama.	Because he plays very well, mama."
(R)	2. ¡Qué toca el pito!	Play, *pito*!
	3. ¡Qué toque el pitero!	Play, *pitero*!
	4. ¡Qué toque el pito!	Play, *pito*!
IV. (V)	1. Me gustaría preguntar,	I would like to ask you,
	2. porque ignorante ha venido,	Since we arrived in ignorance,
	3. quiero que me den contesta	I should like you to let me know
	4. si seré mal recibido.	Whether I will be well received.
(R)	(As in I)	

NOTES

Perf:

I had worked with the conjunto for a full morning before this
item was recorded. I had filmed, photographed, and recorded the
ensemble as a whole, each member individually, and two or three
members playing as a group. During this entire period they had
been asked to continue playing one item, the cumbia "No me
olvides." I had also carried on extensive interviews with individual members and with the group as a whole.

These were new experiences for the members of the conjunto.
They had never before been interviewed, nor had they ever been
asked to perform under such circumstances. Through Manuel Zapata,
who was acting as my intermediary, I had contracted for their services for the day. They wished to please us, but they were not
sure what our requirements were. One incident during the interview had upset them. Upon learning that the villagers were reluctant to pay for their services (see p. 676), Manuel Zapata suggested that in this case perhaps the other evitaleros did not
consider them to form a fully professional cumbia. This suggestion was obviously resented.

Before recording "Veinte de enero" I had asked them to again
perform "No me olvides" as an entire ensemble. At its conclusion
they were asked if they knew a *cumbia cantada*, a cumbia in which
cuartetos were sung. Again taking this comment as a slur on their
abilities, they replied that cuartetos could be sung in "No me
olvides" if I so desired. I explained that this was not what I
desired. Rather, I wanted them to perform a cumbia in which
cuartetos were customarily performed. They then performed TR 61,
in which they made every effort to demonstrate their competence as
cumbiamberos. Simultaneously, Juan Ospino skillfully improvised
cuartetos in which he courteously but unmistakably informed us
that the group did not feel that we were according them the proper
respect (see st. IV of the realized text of TR 61).

The guachos enter on the second pulse of m. 2, the remaining
percussion instruments at the beginning of m. 3. Juan Ospino,
the *guachero*, continues to play as he sings the cuartetos. The
pitero is silent during the cuartetos but plays during the refrains. The tambolero begins with a pattern of eighth notes similar to that seen in TR 56 and TR 57. During the singing of the
cuartetos he plays a simpler pattern, at times seeming to duplicate the strokes of the llamador. An emphatic stroke upon the
head of the bombo can be heard on the first pulse of every second
measure beginning with m. 5.

Below are listed in chronological order by measure number the
revuelos and gritos utilized to maintain the level of tension in
the performance. I have isolated as effects representing revuelos
the following: the roll in the form of triplets on the tambor
mayor in destapado position (see TR 57, m. 15), sustained shakes
by the guachos (See TR 57, m. 11-15), and a syncopated pattern of
strokes on the head of the bombo (see TR 60, m. 5-6). A revuelo
played on the pito would seem to be a sustained and vibrated tone
in the sobreagudo register (see TR 61, m. 21-22).

Measure(s)	Revuelo	Grito
2	pito	
14-15	tambor	
21	pito	
22-25	guachos	
35	pito	
55	tambor	
56-57		*au*
60		*iuupa*
66-67		¡Arriba, Juancho!
73-74	tambor	
77		*jau*
91	pito	
92-93		¡Oye, compai, pito!
94		*ua*
95	tambor	

¡Arriba, Juancho! = Get going, Juan!
¡Oye, compai (compadre), pito! = Listen, compadre, to the pito!
The pitches in this last grito were sufficiently definite to per-
mit transcription in notation.

Following that section of the performance transcribed, revuelos
are performed by the pitero with more frequency, and the gritos
also increase in number. During this period three revuelos are
performed by the tambor and one each by the guachos and the bombo.

The percussion instruments are heard for six pulses after the
pitero stops playing.

The duration of the performance is 4:15.

Text:

I (V) 1-2. - The meaning the singer wishes to convey is that
when he is playing he "keeps his cool." He knows what to do, and
he will do it no matter what the provocation.

I (V) 4. - The twentieth of January is the day of the patron
saint of Evitar, San Sebastián. This cumbia is dedicated to the
celebration of that occasion (see pp. 101-2).

I (R) 3. - The meaning of *ligero* in this case is that the act
be carried out immediately.

II (V) 2. - *Doctores* is an old usage and refers to people
possessing knowledge. The holding of a degree is not specifically
indicated. Thus the members of the cumbia of Evitar are individuals with knowledge and judgment.

II (V) 4. - Literally, he knows his craft.

IV (V) 1-4. - The entire cuarteto is a subtly voiced complaint against the treatment the group has received. They did not know that they would be insulted when they came to play for us, and they wish to know if they are really welcome.

IV (V) 2. - The "we" is editorial. Grammatically as sung it is "he has come."

Derivation:

As far as I can determine from the one recording made, the patterns performed by the percussion instruments in the cumbia "Veinte de enero" are similar to those transcribed from the performances of "No me olvides." The only exception is the simpler pattern played by the tambor mayor during the singing of the cuartetos. Since there was no singing of cuartetos during performances of "No me olvides," it cannot be determined whether this was or was not the usual practice. In any case, the percussion parts of both cumbias can be readily viewed as realizing cycles of sixteen eighth-note pulses.

In TR 61, however, the pito part does not easily fall into cycles of sixteen eighth notes, or, phrasing it from the European point of view, into groups of two measures. The refrain sung by the soloist does fall into such a grouping. If we relate this refrain to the strokes played on the llamador in the same manner in which the refrain in the bullerengue was related to the claps, it can be considered to be constructed over a cycle of four pulses. The cuartetos do not fit as comfortably into this scheme, since in each the first and last verse occupy the time space of six rather than four strokes on the llamador. The relationship of the cuarteto, or Verse, and its following estribillo, or refrain, to the strokes of the llamador is shown in ex. 2. When no text appears above the numbers representing the strokes, as in strokes 1, 3, and 4 in v. 1 of the refrain, they coincide with rests.

Ex. 2. Verbal stress and strokes on the
llamador (TR 61, m. 38-56)

I. (V) 1. Cuan-do me pon-go to-car____ 2. yo no me des-es-pe-ro.
             1   2   3   ‾4 1 2   3   4   1   ‾2

3. La cum-bia de-vi-tar__ 4. se lla-ma vein-te de-ne-ro____.
     3   4   ‾1 2   3   ‾4   1 ‾2 ‾3 ‾4

(R) 1. ¡Oh! 2. ¡To-quel pi-to__! 3. ¡To-que li-ge-ro__.
       1   ‾2 3 4   ‾1 ‾2 ‾3   4   ‾1   ‾2 ‾3

4. ¡To-quel pi-to____!
   4   ‾1 ‾2 ‾3 ‾4

Note that the cuarteto as a whole, the four lines, or verse, of TR 61, occupies five rather than four cycles. The vocalist is out of phase with the cycle of four strokes of the llamador by the end of v. 1 but is back in phase by the end of the cuarteto. This may be considered an extension of the improvisatory role of the soloist in African music.

The pitero and vocalist perform the refrain in heterophony; that is, they simultaneously perform variations of the same melodic formulae. The melodic material of the refrain is also extended by the pitero's playing a fifth two-measure phrase similar to the first and third phrases, which he performs while the vocalist is singing the refrain. One member of the conjunto always utters a grito during the playing of this fifth two-measure phrase. Thus both the cuartetos or Verses and their following refrains realize five cycles of four strokes on the llamador.

Alternatively, each cuarteto and each refrain may be considered to be composed of five phrases of two measures each, forming a section of ten measures. In Western European music both Verses and Refrain are more likely to contain four phrases or eight measures. Thus the vocal and percussion parts may be considered to be conjunctly realizing cycles of one or more lengths, but there remains the lack of a clear cyclic construction in the performance by the pitero.

In ex. 3 it can be further observed that the great majority of verbal accents, as indicated by the underlined vowels, do not coordinate with the strokes played on the llamador. This is even more pronounced in the refrain than in the preceding cuarteto. A lack of coordination to this degree between verbal and musical stress is characteristic of the African rather than the Spanish tradition (see chapter 6, VI.C.2-3).

GAITA

TR 62 (LF 118.2) "Mariana"
(pito part only)

cts.

NOTES

Perf:

At least one drum enters at the last quarter of m. 2. The guachos and the other drums enter at the beginning of m. 3. The pattern played by the guachos is the same as that played in the cumbia (see TR 56), and it is not varied throughout the performance. A stroke on the head of the bombo is heard on each pulse, that is, twice in each measure. The additional strokes played on the bombo and the patterns played on the tambor mayor cannot be distinguished with any clarity. The llamador, as always, plays only on each pulse.

At one point the pitero lost control of his reed. He himself brought this to my attention at the end of the performance. He began to lose control in m. 15 but continued playing, although with rather poor intonation, until m. 29. He then stopped, adjusted his reed, tested it, and began anew with the upbeat to m. 35. During this period the other instrumentalists continued playing without interruption. Since pitch is uncertain, I did not find it useful to transcribe what was played on the pito from the second pulse of m. 15 through m. 29.

I have previously indicated what effects I believe constitute revuelos as played on the different instruments (see p. 479). In the portion of the performance transcribed, which is 1:08 in duration, revuelos are heard only in the parts for pito and tambor mayor. Revuelos by the pitero are seen in m. 51 and m. 53. Similar revuelos are heard in a like passage in m. 26-29, a passage which is not transcribed. The tambolero performs a revuelo in the usual form of a roll beginning on the second pulse of m. 53 and continuing through m. 54.

No revuelos were played by the bombero in this performance. I asked Manuel Zapata to inquire whether no revuelos were performed because it was not the custom to do so when playing a gaita or whether in this case the bombero did not wish to play revuelos. He couched the question in a somewhat different manner than I intended. He asked Manuel Pimientel, who was the bombero in this performance, whether he did not play revuelos because it was not the custom to do so when performing a gaita or whether he did not know how to play revuelos. Pimientel replied that it was not customary to play revuelos on the bombo in a gaita. However, in the subsequent gaita recorded, "Me voy con dolor" (LF 118.3), which is not transcribed, Pimientel proceeded to perform numerous revuelos. I assume that he was doing so to prove that he did indeed know how to play revuelos. Later I was informed that revuelos are not performed on the bombo during the playing of a gaita because this ritmo is properly that of the conjunto de gaitas and there is no bombo in this ensemble. In a gaita the bombero restricts himself primarily to marking the pulse.

In TR 64, in which the bombero was recorded playing alone, no revuelos are seen. TR 64 was recorded much earlier in the recording session than either gaita played by the full ensemble.

In neither of the two gaitas recorded were cuartetos customarily sung. We were told, in fact, that the ensemble did not have in its repertory a gaita with which cuartetos were associated.

However, in the recording made of "Mariana" the pitero stops
playing almost immediately after the end of that portion of the
performance transcribed and sings two or three short phrases.
He then plays for a while, stops again, and at 1:45 sings six or
seven additional phrases. He then continues playing the pito
until the end of the recording. When asked why he had sung during
a performance of a piece in which we had already been informed
that cuartetos were not customarily sung, Santiago replied that it
was an inspiration of the moment. No other instance has come to
my attention of a pitero singing during any of the four traditional ritmos performed by the conjunto de cumbia. It is my view
that Santiago's singing in this particular performance was a response to my previous questions concerning whether cuartetos were
customarily sung in one ritmo or another. He was, I believe,
under the impression that we did not feel his group was competent
unless there was singing in each ritmo performed. He was therefore attempting to satisfy us by improvising *letras* (song verse)
in an item for which none existed.

His sung phrases do not form either one or more cuartetos, and
the words are at times unintelligible. Since I do not believe
his singing to constitute a usual aspect of the performance of
"Mariana," it is not transcribed. What he sings is apparently a
somewhat varied repetition of the following:

> Adiós, Mariana,   Goodbye, Mariana,
> Va con Dios, Mariana.   God be with you, Mariana.

The pitch formula used in all phrases sung is given in ex. 3:

Ex. 3. Pitch formula sung in "Mariana"

The pitero performs three revuelos between his two snatches of
song. The third of these is somewhat higher in pitch than the
first two. He repeats the three revuelos in the same order in
the passage which he plays subsequent to the second portion of
his improvised song. The tambolero performs a revuelo immediately
after the second sung improvisation by the pitero. He also plays
a long roll accompanying the first two revuelos which are played
by the pitero in the following section. As indicated previously,
neither the guachero not the bombero plays revuelos during the
entire recording.

The duration of the performance is 2:41.
                               - - -

Transcriptions follow of recordings made of the tambolero and
bombero playing patterns utilized in performing a gaita. Both
instrumentalists were recorded playing alone.

TR 63 (LF 115.12)   Tambor mayor:
accompaniment for gaita

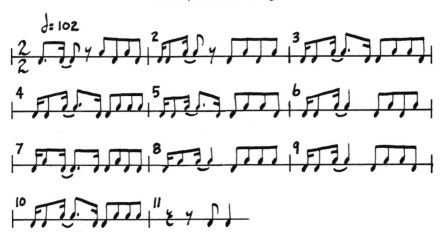

NOTES

Perf:

This performance is characterized by the playing of various
types of syncopation during the first half of the measure and four
eighth notes during the second half of the measure, the beginning
of each group thus coinciding with a stroke of the llamador.

TR 64 (LF 115.21)   Bombo:
accompaniment for gaita

NOTES

Perf:

It can be seen in TR 64 that in the gaita a stroke is played on
the head of the bombo on each pulse and that no revuelos, as previously defined, are performed. The additional strokes, which cannot be easily distinguished in the recording of the full ensemble,
can be seen here. They are fairly evenly distributed between
strokes on the wood and those on the head.

Derivation:

The gaita presents a somewhat different aspect than the cumbia
when viewed as a cyclic structure. The pito's two-measure phrases
are even more clearly defined than in the cumbia and thus represent a realization of a cycle of sixteen eighth notes. On the
other hand, the bombo and llamador perform a stroke on the head
at the beginning of each group of four eighth notes, while the
tambor mayor and guachos repeat patterns eight eighth notes in
length. Since the division of a cycle into two equal parts is
common in Africa, all will fit within the sixteen-pulse cycle.
As in the cumbia, all cycles are in conjunct relationship.
Nevertheless, an alternative European interpretation is feasible, wherein a melody built up of phrases of four pulses is structured over an accompaniment built up of measures of two pulses.
This interpretation is weakened by the fact that there seems to
be no dynamic differentiation between the two pulses making up
the measure.

PORRO

TR 65 (LF 117.7) "Ven acá"
(pito and vocal solo parts only)

Sung by Manuel Pimientel Pacheco

I. 1. Cha-cha ¿ dón stá ta‑bue‑la ____ ?

2. —De_ la cho - za stá_, —Cha-cha ¿ dón stá ta-bue-la_____? —De_ la cho - za stá_,

3. ga-nan-do re-al y me-dio 4. pa-ra ma-ña-na mo-zar_, ga-nan-do re-al y me-dio_____

pa-ra ma-ña-na mo-zar_.

I. 1. ---Muchacha ¿dónde está   "Little girl, where is
        tu abuela?   your grandmother?"
   2. ---Detrás la choza está, (c2) "She's back of the house,
   3. ganando un real y medio   Earning a *real* and a half
   4. para mañana almozar. (c2)   For tomorrow's lunch."

II. 1. ¡Déjala que baile!   Let her dance!
    2. ¡Déjala bailar! (c2)   Let her dance!
    3. Cumbia evitalera   The *cumbia* from Evitar
    4. se puede gozar. (c2)   She may enjoy.

III.   (Same as I)

NOTES

Perf:

The guachos and the llamador enter at the beginning of m. 3, the former playing on each pulse in that measure like the llamador. In m. 4 the guachero begins to play the same pattern performed in the cumbia and the gaita. The tambor mayor and the bombo apparently enter on the first pulse of m. 6. However, the patterns played by the percussion instruments do not seem fully coordinated until the beginning of m. 9.

The pitero does not play while the cuartetos are sung. In the porro "No te vayas" (Don't Go Away), LF 117.6, which was recorded immediately preceding "Ven acá" (Come Here), the pitero makes frequent use of d^1 (transposed to $f^{\#1}$). He utilizes this pitch with less frequency in "Ven acá" (see m. 13-14 and m. 62) and not at all in the other items transcribed or analyzed. Thus it is apparently the only pitch in the grave register of which Santiago makes use. As can be seen in fig. 43 (p. 61), this pitch can be produced with all fingerholes open or by the use of only the first finger. The melodic patterns utilized by the pitero at the beginning of the performance are similar to those sung by the vocal soloist in st. I, except that the vocalist cadences on f^1 (transposed a^1) and the pitero does not. Following st. I the pitero twice attempts to cadence on this pitch, on the second beats of m. 54 and m. 58. As can be seen in fig. 43, this pitch is not easily produced. Santiago is playing by ear, and when he attempts the cadential f^1 the pitch produced is indefinite. This is represented by an x rather than by a note head (see chapter 5, I. E.1.6). In the second case the subsequent tremolo is also affected. St. I and st. III are sung to similar melodies. However, the vocalist sings st. III at a somewhat lower level than st. I, and in his subsequent imitation of the vocal part the pitero manages to reach a pitch approximating that of the vocal cadence, but not one of very good tone quality.

The section beginning with the latter part of m. 62 and extending through the first part of m. 68 has been omitted to shorten the transcription.

The number of revuelos or gritos heard in this performance is not very large. Manuel Pimientel does not play the bombo while he sings. Simón Herrera is the bombero in this performance. I noticed that a different individual was now playing the bombo in the ensemble. I also noticed that he played on every pulse, as if he were performing a gaita, and seemed not to play revuelos. After the recording had been completed, Herrera was asked if he had played revuelos, and he replied that he had not. This inquiry may have had some bearing on Pimientel's later performance of revuelos in the second gaita recorded (see pp. 497-98). In the recording session the porro "Ven acá" was performed earlier than the two gaitas.

The initial thematic material played by the pitero, which is repeated later in various guises, begins with pitches in the sobreagudo register. However, they are not sustained, and vibrato is utilized in only one passage, which occurs between the singing

of st. II and st. III. The tambolero performs only five short
revuelos throughout the recording, each beginning on one pulse
and ending on the subsequent pulse. The first begins on the
second pulse of m. 7, the second on the first pulse of m. 89.
Of the remaining three, the first begins before st. III, the
second during this strophe, and the third following it. The
guachero performs a revuelo beginning on the second pulse of
m. 34 and sustains it through m. 35. His only other revuelo is
heard at the conclusion of the performance.

In the section not transcribed, m. 62-78, the grito *iuupa* is
heard. Some time after the singing of st. II, *jai* is heard. This
is followed by ¡*Oye, compadre Alonzo*! Following st. III one first
hears *iuupa* and then ¡*Oyelo, Juancho*!

At the end of the performance the guachero begins a revuelo.
The pitero stops playing almost immediately, but the guachero
continues for several pulses. The drums continue also, stopping
only when the guachero discontinues his shake.

The duration of the performance is 3:19.

Text:

I.3 - A real is an old Spanish coin no longer in use in Colombia. *Real y medio* is an idiom used to describe the general cost
of a meal.

II.2 - V. 1 and 2 of st. II have the same meaning. The *que* in
v. 1 merely adds emphasis.

TR 66 (LF 115.8) Tambor mayor:
accompaniment for porro

NOTES

Perf:

Two porros were recorded, the first, "No te vayas" (LF 117.6),
immediately before "Ven acá." It is difficult in both recordings
to distinguish the patterns played on the tambor mayor. If the
tambolero is playing the patterns shown in TR 66, a recording
made of him playing alone, this is understandable. The tone
produced by the glancing blow of the fingers on the canto is very
soft, and such tones would be covered by the louder strokes of
the other drums. In both porros recorded the tambolero occasionally performs revuelos in the form of triplets with sufficient
dynamic force to be distinguishable from the patterns played by
the other two drums. Such revuelos can be seen in TR 66 beginning
with the first pulse of m. 9 and the second pulse of m. 11. In
each case a stroke played on the llamador would occur on the initial rest, thus producing the effect of a four-note pattern. This
can be seen in ex. 4:

Ex. 4.   Combined pattern of llamador and tambor mayor
(TR 66, m. 9 and m. 11)

TR 67 (LF 115.18)   Bombo: accompaniment
for porro

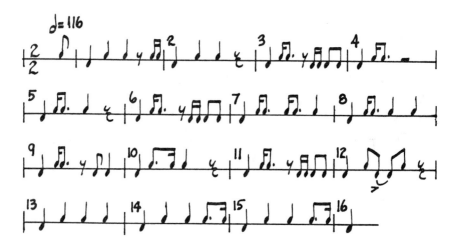

NOTES

Perf:

This recording was made of Manuel Pimientel playing the bombo alone. It will be noted that he plays a stroke on the head of the bombo at the beginning of each measure, that is, on every second pulse. He can be heard to do the same in "No te vayas" (LF 115.6), in which he rather than Simón Herrera is the bombero.

The syncopation seen in m. 12 may or may not be considered a revuelo. It is heard once near the very end of "No te vayas." In my opinion it would have to be repeated several times to produce sufficient effect to be considered a revuelo.

Derivation:

In cyclic organization the porro is similar in many respects to the cumbia and gaita but also differs in certain of its aspects. Again, the realization of the cycles by the pito and the percussion instruments can be considered to be sixteen or eight eighth-note pulses in length and the vocal parts four half-note pulses in length. The guachos and the llamador play the same patterns as heard in the other two genres. As in the gaita, the cycle realized by the tambor mayor seems to be eight eighth notes in length, but two patterns are involved rather than one. In the porro the bombero strikes the head of the bombo with some emphasis at the beginning of each group of eight eighth notes, while in the cumbia this effect is heard at the beginning of each group of sixteen eighth notes. For reasons previously given, no similar effect is heard in the gaita.

The pito part is extremely free and improvisatory. At times there seem to be phrases two measures in length, but these are often in disjunct relationship with the cycles of the percussion parts. The cuartetos sung, on the other hand, are clearly two measures in length and coordinate with cycles of four strokes performed on the llamador. This is shown in ex. 5:

Ex. 5.   Verbal stress and strokes on the
llamador (TR 65, m. 35-50)

I. 1. Cha-cha ¿dón stá ta-bue-la_? 2. ---De la cho-za stá__,
    1   2   3   4   1   2   3 4

  ---Cha-cha ¿dón stá ta-bue-la_? ---De la cho-za stá __,
     1   2   3 4   1   2   3 4

  3. ga-nan-do re-al y me-dio_ 4. pa-ra ma-ña-na mo-zar__,
     1   2   3   4   1   2   3 4

  ga-nan-do- re-al me-dio__ pa-ra ma-ña-na mo-zar__ .
    1   2   3   4 1   2   3 4

Various interpretations of the cyclic structure of the porro are possible. The two-measure phrases of the cuartetos are sixteen eighth notes in length. Thus it can be considered that the fundamental cycle is of this length and that all of the percus-

sion instruments with the exception of the llamador realize this
cycle by repetition of patterns half its length. The vocalist
matches this time-span by coordinating his phrases with four
strokes of the llamador. Simultaneously the pito carries forward
an improvisatory role even freer than that common in African
music, since it is not bound by the confines of the underlying
cycle.

Alternatively, as before, the two-measure phrases sung by the
vocalist and the free improvisation by the pitero can be conceived
as being structured over an accompaniment built up of measures two
pulses in length. The lack of a clear dynamic differentiation of
the two pulses of the measure plus the unevenness in the part of
the tambor mayor, caused by both off-beat phrasing and off-beat
hemiola, militates against this conception.

As can be seen in ex. 5, the majority of the verbal stresses,
sixteen out of twenty-six, coordinate with the strokes of the
llamador. There is thus a higher degree of coordination than is
seen in the cuartetos sung in TR 61. This still seems to be somewhat closer to the African than the Spanish tradition, but perhaps
may be said to lie midway between the two.

PUYA

TR 68 "La jaquimita"
(pito part, comparative score)

NOTES

A *jaquimita* is a mount composed of wooden slats placed over a base of cloth or sacking. When set on the back of a burro, mule, or horse it provides not only a rude type of saddle for a rider but a means of securing bags or bundles of produce or other cargo. The evitalero seen in fig. 3 (p. 9) is perched upon produce attached to a jaquimita, which he is taking to market.

Perf:

The bombero in this performance is Simón Herrera. The transcriptions were made by playing back the recordings at 3 3/4 ips. Due to the rhythmic complexity of the accompanying percussion parts, it was impossible to prepare transcriptions of any adequacy at the tape speed at which the recordings were originally made, 7 1/2 ips.

Version A represents the first section of the pito part of LF 118.9, a performance of "La jaquimita" which is 1:15 in duration. Version B represents the pito part of LF 118.8, a test recording of "La jaquimita" made immediately preceding LF 118.9. In what would be m. 12 of version B, I cut off the tape recorder. It will be seen that except for slight variations, the patterns played in the first eight measures of each version are similar. At m. 9 somewhat different melodic material is introduced in version B. This does not appear in version A until m. 12. Beginning at m. 5 all patterns played by the pitero utilize only the three pitches of the major triad. The rapid playing of figures composed of these three pitches is facilitated by spec al fingerings which are used for this particular purpose (see fig. 44, p. 61).

What is played through m. 11 by the instruments of percussion seems to be very much the same in both versions, with one exception, which will be noted. The guachos and llamador enter on the second pulse of m. 4 (i.e., on the fourth quarter) and play two quarter notes to a pulse. In version A the bombo enters on the first pulse of m. 3; in version B it enters on the second pulse of that measure, and also plays quarter notes. The tambor mayor enters immediately after the second pulse of m. 3, playing a series of syncopated quarter notes, which occur an eighth-note value behind those of the bombo. At m. 4 the guachos move to a pattern of four eighth notes to the pulse, eight eighth notes to the measure. At m. 6 the drums to a great extent coordinate the patterns played, displaying a ternary division of the pulse. This contrasts with the binary division of the pulse heard in the parts for pito and guachos. In m. 10-11 the guachos are heard in a series of three shakes. Each shake begins before or after the pulse and is approximately a half note in duration.

During the remainder of version A the pitero plays only triadic patterns. He does not repeat the initial passage of m. 2-4, in which he utilizes pitches in the sobreagudo register. The guachero performs an additional series of longer shakes in m. 17-18. Almost immediately following the end of the section transcribed, the tambolero again plays a series of off-beat quarter notes, a

pattern similar to that he had previously played beginning on the
second pulse of m. 3. This continues for a short period, and the
drums again coordinate their patterns in a ternary division of
the pulse. They then continue in this manner to the end of the
recording. Somewhat later the guachero again performs a series
of shakes of longer duration than his standard eighth notes.

The more sustained shakes of the guachos, and possibly the
syncopated quarter-note patterns of the tambor, may be considered
revuelos. However, the greater part of the performance could
itself be considered a type of "commotion" or "uproar." The concept of revuelo therefore is perhaps not applicable in the performance of a puya.

TR 69 (LF 115.9) Tambor mayor:
accompaniment for puya

TR 70 (LF 115.20) Bombo:
accompaniment for puya

NOTES (TR 69 and TR 70)

Perf:

TR 69 and TR 70 are transcriptions of recordings in which the instruments are heard alone. TR 70 was played by Manuel Pimientel.

Each instrumentalist repeats a particular rhythmic pattern, with only slight variations. At this tempo there is only one principal pulse in the measure, the primary pulse. This is marked by a stroke played on the canto of the tambor mayor or on the head of the bombo. The tambor mayor also plays such a stroke on the first of the two weak pulses, the second pulse of the measure, and the bombo on the second of the weak pulses, the third pulse of the measure (see chapter 6, IV.B.1.2). Strokes on the canto or the head are played on all three pulses, the primary and both weak pulses, in each part in only one measure. This occurs in the tambor part in m. 11 and in the bombo part in m. 6.

In TR 71 I have endeavored to illustrate the relationship of parts at a point in the recording where they seem most fully co-ordinated.

TR 71 "La jaquimita" (composite score)

NOTES

Perf:

The part for pito is taken from TR 68, version A, the tambor part from TR 69, and that for bombo from TR 70. The part for the guachos was transcribed from the same recording as that of version A of the pito, LF 118.9. The part for llamador is surmised on the basis of its usual function in other ritmos.

In a second puya recorded but not transcribed, "Vente para acá" (Come Over Here), LF 119.1, the rhythmic relationship of the parts is even more difficult to ascertain. The performances of the two puyas are alike in a number of respects. The entrances of the drums and the quarter-note patterns played, including the syncopated pattern of the tambor, are very similar. However, the pito part seems to display a binary division of the pulse throughout, and there are no sustained shakes of the guachos, only repeated eighths. The syncopated pattern played by the tambor is heard more than once. On the other hand, at no point in the recording do the drums seem to coordinate their patterns in a ternary division of the pulse. In sum, I am unable to establish the relationships of the various parts through listening to this recording made with one microphone and one tape recorder.

I was informed that neither of the puyas performed contained letras. There were, however, puyas in which cuartetos were sung.

Derivation:

The pito part in TR 68, and the excerpt from TR 68 reproduced in TR 71, divides rather clearly into one-measure phrases eight eighth notes in length. It can be seen in TR 71 that the guachos realize each eighth note in this cycle, while the strokes on the llamador occur, as usual, on the first and fifth eighth notes of the cycle. Two of the patterns played by the tambor mayor and bombo fit within the time space of the eight-pulse cycle, but their realization involves six pulses rather than eight. All of the cycles are of course in conjunct relationship. However, in both puyas recorded there is an introductory section in which the tambor mayor enters an eighth-note value earlier, or later, as the case may be, than the other percussion instruments and continues playing an equally spaced series of strokes in the same relationship for some time. I suspect that the tambor mayor is performing the same cycle as the other percussion instruments but in disjunct relationship.

A multi-linear, polyrhythmic structure in which groups of two and three are juxtaposed either horizontally or vertically, or both, is characteristic of African music, especially of ensembles containing percussion instruments. However, such a structure usually is characterized by the use of additive rhythm, which is not present in TR 71. Here each part is divisive. Each measure can be divided into equal halves and the parts thereof divided into two, three, or multiples thereof. When the measures of TR 71 are divided into halves, the part for the guachos is in 2/4 and that for the bombo in 3/4, thus producing a vertical hemiola in the ratio 2:3. The part for the tambor mayor is now in 9/8, and thus a quarter in the bombo part equals a dotted quarter in that of the tambor mayor, again producing the ratio of 2:3. The latter can most easily be seen in the last of the three pulses. In the bombo part this pulse is divided into two eighth notes, while in the tambor part it is divided into three eighth-note values.

In rhythmic structure the *puya evitalera* certainly displays more African than European traits. European influence is evident in the lack of additive rhythms and, to a lesser extent, in the realization of the cycle by two similar patterns, which suggests a two-pulse measure. The lack of dynamic differentiation between these two pulses tends to diminish this effect. On the other hand, the long passages in which the pitero utilizes only the three pitches of a major triad certainly suggest European melodic influence.

COMMENTARY

It is difficult to establish the characteristics by which the four ritmos--cumbia, gaita, porro, and puya--can be distinguished one from another. They are all played by the same ensemble, the conjunto de cumbia, and the instrumentation is therefore the same in each case. In some cases there are vocal solos in the form of cuartetos or coplas. As can be seen in table 28, these coplas do not differ markedly from those sung in other genres. The majority of the verses are octosyllabic, and the remaining verses seldom vary from this norm by more than one syllable.

Table 28.   Metrical Analysis of the Texts
of TR 61 and TR 65

TR 61

TR 65

I. (V)	1. 8 a	III. (V)	1. 8 a	I.	1. 7 a
	2. 6 b		2. 7 b		2. 7 b
	3. 7 a		3. 7 c		3. 8 a
	4. 8 b		4. 8 a		4. 8 b
(R)	1. 1 a			II.	1. 6 a
	2. 4 b	(R)	2. 4 b		2. 6 b
	3. 5 c		3. 5 c		3. 6 c
	4. 6 b		4. 4 b		4. 6 b
II. (V)	1. 8 a	IV. (V)	1. 9 a	III.	= I.
	2. 8 b		2. 8 b		
	3. 8 a		3. 8 c		
	4. 8 b		4. 8 b		
(R)	= I.	(R)	= I.		

It is primarily in these ritmos, however, that the four-line estribillo, refrain, or chorus is heard. The verses of the estribillo are in almost all cases shorter than those of the cuarteto proper. In content and meter the second cuarteto of TR 65 gives the impression of originally having been an estribillo. However, the copla forming the text of TR 46, a danza de negro de la calle, also contains hexasyllabic verses. In the ritmos of the

conjunto de cumbia the cuartetos are sung by one member of the
repercusión. Both words and melody of the cuartetos are usually
composed by a member of the conjunto and most frequently sung by
him. I was told that Manuel Pimientel, the bombero, was the composer of all the cuartetos used in performances by the conjunto de
cumbia of Evitar. However, they are at times improvised by whoever is singing.

During my field work I questioned members of conjuntos de cumbia
in Evitar, Cartagena, and Soplaviento concerning the characteristics which differentiated the four ritmos: cumbia, gaita, porro,
and puya. The majority were able to express themselves concerning
only one chararactersitic, tempo, and they were not very consistent in their judgments. During our first recording session in
Evitar, in 1964, Manuel Pimientel played the tambor mayor in performances of the danza de negro, the bullerengue, and the fandango.
At that time I was unaware of the fact that his role in the conjunto de cumbia was that of bombero rather than tambolero. At the
end of the recording session I asked him to play for me the part
played on the tambor in the four different ritmos performed by the
conjunto de cumbia. After he had played a short section of cumbia, followed by one of a gaita, I asked him if there was a difference in the accompaniment played by the tambor mayor for these
two ritmos. ¡*Como no*! (Of course!) was his reply. I then asked
him to describe how the two ritmos differed. After some hesitation he replied that I had seen him play the ritmos and that I
had them on tape. He then performed the two ritmos again so that
I could see and hear what the difference was. I returned to the
questioning and asked which of the two ritmos was the *más rápido*
or the *más alegre*. He replied that the gaita was the faster of
the two ritmos. As will be seen later, his assertion was not consonant with practice as I have been able to determine it.

The most extensive characterization of the four ritmos which I
received from an informant was given me by Erasmo Arrieta. As
previously indicated (p. 57), he is a native of Mahates, where he
learned his art, and later moved to Bogotá. This pitero of considerable experience informed me that the players primarily differentiate the four ritmos according to the speed at which they
are performed. The cumbia is the slowest in tempo, the puya the
most rapid, and the porro is intermediate in tempo. The gaita is
performed at about the same tempo as the cumbia. He informed me
that all have the same *compás*. In Spanish this last term refers
to measure, time, or meter. Erasmo Arrieta further stated that
the cumbia is the most sentimental of the ritmos; that in it "the
most emotion" is shown; that the cumbia is more melodic than the
gaita and that the porro and the puya display more the characteristics of the dance. It was his opinion that the repercusión, the
players of the percussion instruments, did not utilize particular
rhythmic patterns in playing a particular ritmo, but used the same
patterns in playing all the ritmos.

I shall use this outline of the characteristics of the four
ritmos offered by Erasmo as a basis for the following discussion
and compare his statements with the results of my own investigations. At times the conclusions that I draw from the analysis of
the data available will differ from those based upon his exper-

ience; our two views will not necessarily coincide. This is not to say that his view is incorrect. The first is the view of the insider or the bearer of the tradition. The second is that of the outsider, of the scholar-observer. In applying the tools and skills of his discipline, the outsider may not find the concepts offered by the insider to represent objective reality. Nevertheless, the concepts of the insider are valid in their own right, and as reflections of cultural values they shed light upon the esthetics of the group. Anthropologists utilize the terms *emic* and *etic* in referring to these two views, the first representing that of the insider and the second that of the outsider.

In forming conclusions about the characteristics of the four ritmos, I have studied not only the performances of the conjunto de cumbia of Evitar but those of similar groups in Cartagena and Soplaviento. However, I have made detailed transcriptions of the performances of only the Evitar ensemble. The ensemble in Soplaviento, of which Antonio Manjarrea was the pitero, was recorded in 1964; that in Cartagena, of which Roque Arrieta was the leader, in 1968. As previously indicated (p. 57), Roque originally led an ensemble in Mahates and later moved to Cartagena. When we recorded his conjunto in 1968, some of the players were still living in Mahates and had come to Cartagena for the purpose of playing with the group. This is the same conjunto I recorded at Radio Bahía in Cartagena, using three adjacent rooms with connecting doors open and three microphones, each leading to a separate tape recorder (see pp. 140-41).

Of the various characteristics of the ritmos, I shall initially discuss the one first mentioned by Erasmo Arrieta, that of tempo. This is the one aspect of the ritmos upon which all the players consulted had an opinion. I give in table 29 tempo indications for performances of the various ritmos of the three conjuntos previously mentioned. The tempo indications are given in the form of metronome markings according to the number of pulses per minute and were determined by a stop watch.

Table 29. Tempi of Ritmos Played by
Conjuntos de Cumbia

	Conjunto de Evitar	Conjunto de Cartagena	Conjunto de Soplaviento
Cumbia	120, 116	96	104
Gaita	116, 112	92, 88	
Porro	120, 116	92	112
Puya	144	152	132

The conjunto de Soplaviento did not perform a gaita for me. It will be seen that the three ritmos recorded by this ensemble follow the schedule given by Erasmo Arrieta. The marking for the cumbia, 104 pulses per minute, is the slowest of the three tempi, and that of the puya, 132 pulses per minute, is the most rapid. The tempo of the porro lies between those of the other two ritmos. The gaitas were performed by the other two conjuntos at slightly slower tempi than their cumbias. The difference in tempo is not great, and Erasmo's statement that the cumbia and gaita are played at the same speed would seem applicable. However, the conjunto de Evitar performed porros at exactly the same tempo as cumbias, and the conjunto de Cartagena performed porro at a slower tempo than cumbia. This is definitely not consonant with the scheme of tempi as enunciated by Erasmo Arrieta.

Erasmo further stated that the cumbia was the most "sentimental" of the ritmos. In it the most emotion is displayed. It is more melodic than the gaita. In contrast, the porro and puya are more dance-like in character. I know of no objective means by which the degree of sentimentality or emotion expressed in music can be measured. Nor does a similar measurement exist by which one can determine that one piece of music is more melodic than another. The pitero seems to use more chromatic tones in the performance of a cumbia than in the performance of the other three ritmos. Perhaps it is this characteristic which is implied by the terms *sentimental* or *more emotion*. When Erasmo states that the cumbia is the most melodic of the ritmos, and that the porro and the puya display more the characteristics of the dance, I can only assume that he is making a distinction between a performance in which there are many long or sustained pitches and one in which there are many short, running notes. Since he employed the term *melodic*, I also infer that he is referring to a performance on the pito, the only melodic instrument in the conjunto. In listening to the recordings I find that the pitero of the conjunto de Soplaviento does utilize more sustained tones in his performance of the cumbia than in those of the porro or the puya. The same contrast can be heard in the performances by the pitero of the conjunto de Cartagena. In addition, there are clearly more sustained pitches in his performance of the cumbia than in that of the gaita. On the other hand, although he contrasts cumbia with porro and puya, the pitero of the conjunto de Evitar seems to utilize as many sustained pitches in his performances of gaitas as in his performances of cumbias. I therefore can agree only partially with the differentiation made in this regard by Erasmo Arrieta as I understand it.

Erasmo also stated that all the performances were in the same compás. If this statement indicates that all are cast in duple meter, they can indeed be so interpreted. On the other hand, it cannot be stated that they are at all times cast in simple duple or compound duple meter, that is, that there is a binary or ternary division of the principal pulses (see chapter 6, IV.B.1.2). In the part of the llamador there is no division of the pulse, and in that of the guachos the division is always binary. Ternary divisions of the pulse occur under some circumstances in the performances of all three of the remaining instruments. In order of their frequency of occurrence, they are seen or heard in the parts of the tambor mayor, the bombo, and the pito. In these three parts there is a frequent shifting of the division of the pulse from two to three, or the reverse. The change in division may be temporary, as in an individual triplet performed by the pito, or in the rolls consisting of repeated triplets played by the tambor in most of the ritmos. There may also be a contrast of meters between the parts, some instruments playing in simple meter, some in compound meter.

I do not hear this contrast, this continuous juxtaposition of
binary and ternary divisions of a pulse, in any of the ritmos performed by the conjunto de Soplaviento. In the performances by the
conjunto de Cartagena it occurs in the gaita and the puya, in those
of the conjunto de Evitar in the puya only.

The puya "La jaquimita" as played by the conjunto de Evitar
(TR 68-71) is the most rhythmically complex of all performances of
the ritmos transcribed. I shall therefore employ it to illustrate
the problems raised by Erasmo's statement that all of the ritmos
are performed in the same compás. In its transcription, as in
those of all ritmos in this chapter, the principal pulses have
been represented by the value of a half note or a dotted half note.
The part played by the pito is in simple duple meter, except for a
short introductory section which is in compound duple meter. Thus
in the first case the pulse has a value of a half note and in the
second case of a dotted half note. For purposes of clarity, when
transcribing the puya played alone by either the tambor or the
bombo I have notated them in triple meter, each measure representing one principal pulse. The tambor part is thus written in 9/8
and the bombo part in 3/4. By this means the required duple signature of the tambor part of 18/8 is reserved for the short composite score TR 71, in which all five parts are combined. Even
when written in triple meter it can be seen that the tambor and
bombo utilize various combinations of simple and compound division
of the three pulses postulated.

When the tempi of the parts played by the tambor and bombo are
matched to the performance of the pito and all parts are related
in a composite score, the tambor and bombo can be considered to
be performing in a complex form of compound duple meter. To
avoid difficulties in reading, it would have been logical to have
written the entire score in such a manner that a measure would encompass one principal pulse only. The part of the tambor would be returned to 9/8, that of the bombo to 3/4, and the remaining parts
written in 2/4. In this case two parts would perform in triple
meter and three parts in duple meter. I therefore cannot fully
agree with Erasmo's statement that all ritmos are performed in
the same compás. In general, they are performed in duple meter.
However, there are occasions when an individual part can be interpreted as a performance in triple rather than duple meter.

I remind the reader that the foregoing discussion was carried
on from the European perspective. It is a cyclical rather than a
metrical concept which is operative in African music. In an African percussion ensemble any instrument operating at a lower grade
may repeat patterns which display a particular division of the
pulse or a group of pulses. There is therefore no requirement
whatsoever that all parts maintain either duple or ternary division of the pulse.

The last statement made by Erasmo was that all the percussion
instruments utilize the same rhythmic patterns in playing all the
ritmos, that there are no rhythmic patterns which are characteristic of particular ritmos. The llamador plays on only the principal pulses. The guachos, or the maracas if these are used instead, perform a binary division of the pulse or shakes of some
length. Rhythmic patterns of any complexity are played by only

the tambor mayor and the bombo. The revuelo and its function in
this music have already been discussed. In all ritmos but the
puya, the revuelo employed by the three tamboleros is a roll which
has been transcribed as triplet eighth notes. In such rolls there
are six strokes to the pulse, whether the pulse is represented by
a half note or a dotted half note (see p. 484). It would thus
seem that rhythmic patterns characteristic of a particular ritmo
as played on a particular instrument will be those performed when
the instrumentalist is not engaged in performing a revuelo. As a
group the tamboleros of the three conjuntos do not seem to reserve
any particular rhythmic pattern for use in any one ritmo and not
in the others. This is documented in table 30, in which I contrast
common patterns utilized in the four ritmos played by the tamboleros of the conjuntos de Evitar and Cartagena. These are representative patterns, not the only ones employed. As indicated previously (pp. 140-42), in transcribing the performance of the tambolero of Cartagena, I can vouch for the accuracy of the rhythm
but not always for the timbres employed.

In the rhythmic pattern played in the cumbia by the tambolero
of Cartagena, there are probably more strokes on the canto than
indicated. It would thus display greater similarity to the pattern
played by the tambolero of Evitar. On the other hand, a rest
follows the second eighth note of every measure or every second
measure in the performances by the tambolero of Cartagena--it is
the latter case in the illustration--and this differentiates the
patterns played by the two tamboleros. In the gaita the tambolero
of Evitar uses a syncopated pattern, that of Cartagena a pattern
in compound duple meter with strong accented strokes in the center
of the head. In the porro the tambolero of Evitar employs a particular tone quality, a harmonic-like sound produced by striking
the edge of the drum with the fingers. The tambolero of Cartagena,
on the other hand, makes use of off-beat triplets. I have indicated these by the grouping of the eighth notes. Finally, in the
puya the tambolero of Cartagena plays in compound duple meter,
while that of Evitar is apparently playing in compound triple
meter.

There is some consistency shown, however, in the rhythmic patterns utilized by the three bomberos. As indicated previously,
the bombo is played with two sticks. Most blows are struck upon
the shell of the drum, on the wood. Less frequently blows are
struck on the right head of the drum. In the cumbia, when not
performing a revuelo all three bomberos struck an accented blow
upon the head at the beginning of every second measure. Viewed
as European meter, this occurs at the beginning of every group of
four pulses. There is no such consistency in placing blows upon
the head of the drum in playing the porro or puya. However, in
performances of the gaita, the bomberos of both Evitar and Cartagena struck an accented blow on the heads of their instruments on
every pulse. Also, neither bombero performed revuelos while playing the gaita.

Although no consistency was observed in the rhythmic patterns
played in any particular ritmo by the tamboleros as a group, there
is some evidence that an individual performer may associate a
particular rhythmic pattern with one ritmo rather than another.

Table 30.   Comparison of the Rhythmic Patterns
Utilized by the Tamboleros of
Evitar and Cartagena

Cumbia

Evitar, TR 57, m. 3-4

Cartagena, LF 173.1

Gaita

Evitar, TR 63, m. 3-4

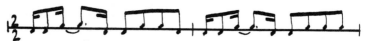

Cartagena, LF 173.2

Porro

Evitar, TR 66, m. 3-4

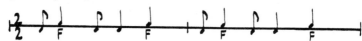

Cartagena, LF 173.3

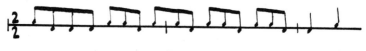

Puya

Evitar, TR 69, m. 3-4

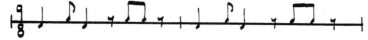

Cartagena, LF 173.4

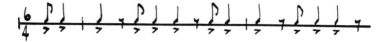

Thus in all cumbias recorded by the conjunto de Evitar the tambolero played a pattern of running eighth notes characterized by an
apparent random selection of points at which strokes are played in
the center of the head rather than on the canto (see TR 56-57 and
TR 59). I also found that the bombero of the conjunto de Evitar
struck an accented blow on the head of his instrument on the first
of each group of two pulses in the porro. Thus when not producing
revuelos, he consistently struck such blows on the first of each
group of four pulses in the cumbia, on the first of each group of
two pulses in the porro, and on each pulse in the gaita (see TR 60,
TR 67, and TR 64).

I now turn to the melodic parts of the ritmos--the performances
of the pito and the few vocal solos which are introduced. The
repercusión provides the rhythmic background for the dancing, and
the pitero is therefore free to mold his part as he wills. It is
thus often very free in its phrasing and rhythmic structure. The
pitero is restricted in his performance by the limitations of his
instrument. Tones in the grave register do not carry well, and
those in the sobreagudo register are difficult to produce. Arpeg-
giations of the G major triad are the easiest of all patterns to
execute, and they figure to some extent in all performances. Because of the free and improvisatory nature of the performances on
the pito, an examination of the transcriptions of those by the
pitero of Evitar offers little additional information concerning
the characteristics which differentiate the four ritmos. It is
clear, however, that in the performance of a particular piece,
that is, of a particular ritmo with a particular title, the
pitero has in mind certain melodic phenomena which are representative of this particular piece rather than another. It is
possible, for example, to distinguish between the pito parts of
the two cumbias, TR 58 "No me olvides" (pp. 485-86) and TR 61
"Veinte de enero" (pp. 489-93), by means of the tones sustained
in each case. In "No me olvides" d^2 and b^1 are the tones sustained, in "Veinte de enero" b^1 and c^2. There is no c^2 of any
length in the former. In both items, and in almost all cases,
the sustained tones listed are heard alternately.

TR 61 is also characterized by a particular cadence formula
which appears with some frequency. Three such cadences are offered
in ex. 6:

Ex. 6.   Cadence formula employed by pitero in TR 61

The two cuartetos transcribed in TR 61 are similar only in their
cadential patterns. This pattern, a descending major 3rd from e^2
to c^2, is the same as that frequently employed by the pitero.
While the vocalist sings the estribillo, the pitero plays a more
florid version of the same melody. The melody of the estribillo
is related to the pito part as a whole. It displays the same
alternating succession of sustained tones, b^1 and c^2.

There are also certain pitch sequences which are characteristic
of the pito part of TR 58, "No me olvides." These are not found
at cadence points, as in TR 61, but in the first three of the two-
measure phrases which follow the opening signal. In the three versions given in TR 58, these two-measure phrases are not similar in
every respect. Nevertheless, the pitch sequence given in ex. 7 is
found in all three (the pitches of longer duration are indicated
by white notes, those of shorter duration by black notes; as before, pitches given in parentheses do not occur in all versions):

Ex. 7.   Pitch sequence played by pitero in
versions A-C of TR 68

The pito part in the two puyas recorded, TR 68 "La jaquimita"
(pp. 510-11) and "Vente para acá" (LF 119.7), can also be easily
differentiated by the melodic patterns performed. The pito part
in "La jaquimita" is based almost entirely on the three pitches
of the G major triad, g^1 b^1 d^2 while "Vente para acá," which is
not transcribed, frequently repeats the pattern b^1 a^1 g^1, in half-
note values. This last melodic pattern is highly reminiscent of
the old English round "Three Blind Mice."

The preceding section of the commentary has been devoted to
discussion of the means by which the various genres performed by
the conjunto de cumbia can be differentiated. In summary, this
can be accomplished with some ease in the cumbia, gaita, and puya,
but it is rather difficult in the case of the porro. Cumbia and
gaita are performed at approximately the same tempo, the puya at
a more rapid tempo. My best informant was of the opinion that the
porro is performed at an intermediate tempo, but my analysis does
not confirm this opinion. The use of sustained tones is common in
both the cumbia and the gaita. However, more chromatic tones are
found in the performance of a cumbia than in a gaita. A stroke on
the head of the bombo is heard at the beginning of every group of
four pulses in the cumbia and on every pulse of the gaita. All
four ritmos can be interpreted as being cast in duple meter. All
but the puya would be in simple duple meter, with some, but not
continuous, ternary divisions of the pulses. The puya would than
be polymetric in character, since there is almost constant contrast
of binary and ternary divisions.

There is some evidence that a tambolero may associate particular rhythmic patterns with a particular ritmo. There is also evidence that there are melodic characteristics in the parts played
by the pitero and sung by the vocalist which distinguish one piece
in a particular genre from another in the same genre.

I now proceed to the consideration of repetition and variation
as structural devices in the performance of the conjunto de cumbia.
I first return to the three versions of the pito part of the cumbia
"No me olvides" given in TR 58 (pp. 485-86). Through m. 7 the
pitch inventory in all three versions has been limited to the
pitches found in the G major triad plus e^2 and $d^{\sharp 2}$. New material

is now introduced in versions A and B which includes the use of a^1, c^2, and, in some cases, $c^{\#2}$. In version C additional pitches are not introduced until m. 14. Once the new pitches, and the pitch patterns they form, are introduced, they are repeated at two-measure intervals, often in varied form. This is shown in ex. 8:

Ex. 8.   New material and variations thereof in
versions A-C of TR 58

It is interesting to note that all three versions were recorded during the same day, version A in the morning and versions B and C in the afternoon, the last two within half an hour of each other. Nevertheless, version C is quite disparate in form from version B. At the same time, its use of new material, of the pitches a^1 and c^2, is similar to that of version B.

In TR 68 I have compared in part two versions of the same puya, "La jaquimita" (pp. 510-11). The B version, a test, was recorded immediately before the A version. In the two versions m. 2-4 are almost identical and m. 5-8 are identical in every respect. As shown in ex. 9, m. 6 is an exact repetition of m. 5, and I shall call the pattern contained in each x. M. 8 is a repetition of m. 7, and I shall call this different pattern y.

Ex. 9.   Patterns x and y of TR 68

Pattern: x   y

In m. 9 versions A and B part ways. Version B immediately be-gins to present pattern x in various guises. Version A, on the other hand, states pattern y for a third time in m. 9 before be-ginning to present variants of pattern x. One could, of course, consider what occurs in m. 10-11 of version A and m. 9-11 of ver-sion B to be a varied combination of patterns x and y. Examining

the continuation of version A, it will be seen that basically the
same melodic material is utilized. There is also repetition of
measures containing the same pattern. Thus m. 13 and 14 are identical, as are m. 20, 21, 24, and 25.

    In the performances by the tambolero and the bombero, somewhat
different processes of repetition and variation are operative.
The tambolero may establish a pattern, which he then repeats a
number of times. There is usually some irregularity before the
pattern is fully established, and in most cases minor variations
occur in its repetition. The tambolero may then perform a revuelo,
after which he returns to the original pattern or establishes a new
one. In an alternative procedure he contrasts two patterns, one
performed with considerable regularity and the other quite irregular in its presentation (see TR 66, p. 507). In the cumbia the
tambolero plays a series of running eighth notes (see TR 57, pp.
482-84). Occasionally a dotted eighth and sixteenth are employed
instead of two eighth notes (see TR 59, p. 487). As previously
indicated, the selection of the area of the head to be struck,
the canto or the center, seems to be random. At least, there is
no discernible pattern of repetition. In the gaita (TR 63, p. 501),
a pattern is immediately established and the rhythm as such remains the same throughout. The transcription, of course, represents only a small section of a full performance by a tambolero
in a gaita. Variation occurs in the strokes representing the
last four eighth notes of the measure. There is again an apparently random selection of the part of the head, that is, the
canto or center upon which the strokes are placed. The variants
produced and the order in which they occur in m. 1-10 are illustrated in ex. 10:

Ex. 10.   Random variation in the tambor part of TR 63

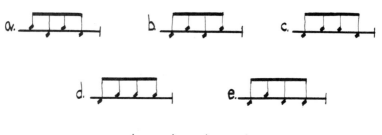

                    a   b   c   d   c   b   e   d   c   c

    In the porro (TR 66, p. 507), the tambolero uses two contrasting
patterns. The first consists of triplets formed of quarter notes
and quarter rests. The second is a partially syncopated pattern
utilizing a special timbre produced by striking the edge of the drum
with a glancing blow of the fingers. The second pattern is heard
seven times in succession without modification. The first pattern
is varied in almost every occurrence. Only twice does it appear in
the same form. The first is in m. 9-10, the second begins on the
second pulse of m. 11. The second entrance is therefore shifted
so as to occur one pulse later. In the puya (TR 69, p. 513)

the pattern played on the tambor is almost identical throughout.
On the third pulse of each 9/8 measure, however, one hears either
three eighth notes, or two eighth notes followed by an eighth
rest. Except in m. 11, all notes represent strokes upon the
center of the head. Again, the variants seem to be performed in
random order. In ex. 11 I give the three variants and the order
in which they occur:

Ex. 11. Random variation in the tambor part of TR 69

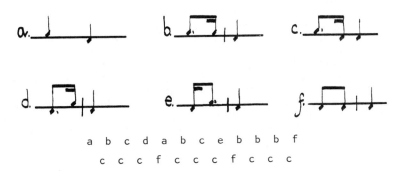

a   a   a   a   b   a   b   a   b   a   b^1 a

Since in the cumbia the bombo strikes an accented blow on the
head at the beginning of every second measure, it seems appropriate to employ two-measure groups in assessing repetition and
variation. In the short transcription of the bombero playing
cumbia alone (TR 60, pp. 487-88), there are no two groups of two
measures each which are exactly alike. However, m. 3-4 can be
considered a modified repetition of m. 1-2 and m. 9-10 a modified
repetition of m. 7-8. The bombero strikes the head of his instrument on every pulse in the gaita. It would therefore seem
that he would be somewhat restricted in the variation he could
produce in performing this ritmo. This, however, is not the
case. If we divide the gaita played by the bombero alone (TR 64,
p. 501) into groups representing two quarter-note values, the
second receiving the pulse, it will be seen that six different
figures are utilized. The six different patterns and the order
in which they occur are given in ex. 12. As before, the analysis
reads from left to right, but in this case continues on the second line.

Ex. 12. Random variation in the bombo part of TR 64

a   b   c   d   a   b   c   e   b   b   b   f
c   c   c   f   c   c   c   f   c   c   c

In the porro (TR 67, p. 508) a blow is struck upon the head at
the beginning of each measure. I shall therefore consider the
measure to delineate the rhythmic pattern, although, musically

speaking, it extends to the first note of the subsequent measure.
There are only two measures in all which are similar in every respect, m. 6 and m. 11. M. 9 could be considered to represent a
variant of the same pattern. In the puya (TR 70, pp. 513-14)
the bombero plays a repeated pattern, which fills a measure of
triple meter. Repetition is exact throughout except for a slight
variation in m. 6.

To summarize, there is repetition in all five parts forming the
conjunto de cumbia. The repetition is unvaried in the part for
llamador and within each ritmo almost entirely unvaried in the
parts for guachos, except for revuelos. In the other three parts
modified repetition is preponderant, exact repetition less frequent. Variations often succeed themselves in what seems to be
random order.

The type of repetition and the degree of variation displayed
in each of the instrumental parts in the four ritmos can also be
categorized according to the African principle of grading (see
chapter 6, IV.B.2.8). Applying this principle to the cumbia,
gaita, and porro, it can be stated that the part of the llamador
is of the lowest grade, since its function is to realize the cycle
by means of regular, equally spaced strokes. The guachos are at a
somewhat higher grade. Their function is also to realize the
cycle through the means of a slightly more complex pattern, occasionally enlivened by a revuelo. The bombo brings both greater
order and more diversity to the realization of the cycle. It
delineates the length of the cycle in the cumbia and the porro
and duplicates the strokes of the llamador in the gaita. It fills
in the remaining space with improvised rhythms. The function of
all three of these instruments is thus to realize the cycle through
primarily repetitive patterns. The bombo is of the highest grade
of the three, since it produces not only the most complex rhythms
but the greatest variety in timbre, playing on both the head and
the wood.

The tambor mayor must of course be graded the highest of the
percussion instruments. It serves a dual function: it combines
with the other instruments in realizing the cycle, or it may play
an independent improvisatory role. In the cumbia it serves both
purposes simultaneously, realizing the cycle with a stroke on almost every eighth note and simultaneously producing random off-
beat phrasing. In the gaita it joins the other instruments in performing repeated patterns. In the porro it alternatively plays
accompaniment and improvisatory roles. In all three cases it produces off-beat phrasing or vertical hemiola. The pito is primarily an improvisatory part, although in the cumbia and the gaita it
generally aligns its phrases with the cycle. In all three ritmos
the realization of the cycle by the percussion instruments is conjunct. All the percussion instruments, with the exception of the
llamador, perform revuelos. If the principle of the revuelo
exists in African music, it has not come to my attention.

In the puya the tambor mayor apparently joins the remaining
percussion instruments in realizing the cycle through the playing
of repetitive patterns. There seem to be two such realizations,
an introductory one in which the tambor mayor enters in a disjunct
cycle one eighth note before or after the remaining percussion

instruments and a realization used throughout in which all the
percussion instruments are in conjunct relationship. However, as
has been seen, the realization of the cycle in the puya is rhythmically very dense.

The melodic aspects of a performance by the conjunto de cumbia
are provided primarily by the caña de millo or pito and secondarily
by the male voice. The caña de millo has a limited gamut, and
triadic patterns utilizing g^1, b^1, and d^2 are very common; g^1 would
seem to be the instrument's natural tonal center. This pitch is
accoustically the first overtone, and the d^2 a perfect 5th above is
the second overtone. The differential tone produced by this interval is g, which is also the fundamental of the instrument. The
perfect 4th with c^2 as the upper pitch and g^1 as the lower is also
quite commonly performed. The differential tone produced by this
interval would be c rather than g (see chapter 5, I.B.1.2). In
the scales of the various items played by the pito, table 31, I
have therefore written g^1 as a square rather than a circle in

Table 31.   Scales, Pito

TR 58 (A-C), Cumbia

TR 61, Cumbia

TR 62, Gaita

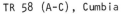

TR 65, Porro

TR 68 (A-B), Puya

order to indicate its anomalous character. No arrows are given above notes of the scale. Considering the frequency of pitch modification of some of the scale degrees, such indications do not seem useful. Although the f$\#^1$ in the first space is included in the scale, it does not really represent a scale degree, but rather a modification of pitch occasioned by the difficulty of performing a sustained overtone, g^1, as an introductory signal. Note that the cumbias display more chromatic tones than the other ritmos.

Performance on the pito is very free, and phrasal cadences are difficult to distinguish. It is open-ended, and there are no repeated finals. For these reasons no table of melodic functions is offered.

In table 32 c^2 is given as the tonal center for the vocal part of TR 61. It is also the final as far as melodic function is concerned. Since the pito frequently cadences on and/or sustains this pitch, we may consider it to represent the tonal center of the entire cumbia. In TR 65 the tonal center of the vocal part, f^1, differs from that of the pito. The hyphens found within the groups of figures of the melodic functions represent ties across bar lines.

Table 32.   Scales or Modes and Melodic Functions,
Vocal Part of TR 61 and TR 65

TR 61

TR 65

	Initial	Mid	Final
TR 61			
Verse I	5 : 1 3	. 2 3̽ 1	2 . 3 1
Refrain	7	1 . 7 - 5	1 5 . 1
Verse II	5 : - 1 3	. 2 5	2 3̽ . 3 1
Refrain	7	3 1 7 . - 5	5 1 . 1
TR 65			
Verse I	6 #6 7 : 8 ♮6	: 5 6 5 4 3 . 1	: 1 3 5 6 ♭4 3 . 1
Verse II	: 8 5 ♭4 5	: 6 5 1	: 5 ♭4 3 1

TR 61 is cast in a type of pentatonic scale rarely if ever met in Western European music. Like the scale of TR 46 (pp. 413-17),

one of the intervals is a semitone. In TR 61 the semitone is between *b* and *c*, in TR 46 between *c♯* and *d*. Since we consider the
c to be the tonal center of TR 61, the semitone is therefore between the seventh and eighth degrees. There are only two European
modes which the scale of TR 61 could represent, the major, or
ionian, and the lydian. It would become the major mode if *f* and *a*
were added, the lydian if *f♯* and *a* were added. However, the
lydian mode is not in use in Western European folksong. An *a♭*
cannot be added because there is no European scale containing both
a♭ and *e♮*. Since the melodic functions of the vocal part of TR 61
are almost entirely consonant with common practice, we can therefore consider this scale to represent the major mode. On the
other hand, the scale of TR 65 contains nine pitches. Since the
b♮ does not occur as a chromatic passing tone, this scale cannot
be considered to be a major scale.

The melodic functions of the vocal part of TR 61 are almost
completely consonant with common practice. The only exception is
the mid cadence of Verse I, which closes on the tonic. All final
cadences move appropriately from dominant to tonic, with the exception of the final cadence in the refrain following Verse II,
which arrives at the tonic pitch too early.

The situation in TR 65 is quite different. The tonal center
and final of the vocal part is f^1, a pitch which the pitero is
unable to produce on his instrument. In TR 65 there are repetitions of the verses of coplas. The initial pitch pattern represents only the first statement of that pattern. The mid and final
patterns represent those sung in the repetition of the couplets.
In the initial pattern of Verse I the sixth degree moves to the
eighth degree and then back again, producing the impression of a
subdominant chord rather than a tonic chord. The initial pattern
of Verse II is 8 5 4 5. The fourth degree coincides with the
second pulse of the measure. The movement from the fifth degree
to an unmodified fourth degree and back to the fifth degree does
not occur with any frequency in common practice melodic style.
The mid and final cadences all close with tones or intervals representing the tonic chord. None of the mid cadences close on a
pitch representing the dominant chord. It requires a short time
for the singer to set his tonality. Immediately before the singer
enters, the pitero has played the tones of the G major triad, *g b
d*, which apparently influences the singer, who sings a *b♮* rather
than a *b♭* in his first cadence, m. 41-42.

Ex. 13. Final patterns in vocal part of TR 65

Verse I

Verse II

Verse III

The fact that a melodic sequence at the cadence is 4 3 1 does not necessarily ensure that it will form a proper common practice cadence. It is also necessary that appropriate harmonic rhythm be observed (see chapter 6, IV.C.2). Thus the fourth degree, representing the dominant chord, must occur before the principal pulse, and the third degree, representing the tonic chord, on this pulse. In m. 49-50 the resolution to the a, and thus to the I chord, occurs too early, since it precedes the pulse. In m. 94-95 the entire cadence is shifted forward by off-beat phrasing. Even the final f appears too early. None of the three cadences is consonant with common practice, that of Verse I because of the $b^\natural$ which does not represent the dominant seventh chord, those of Verses II and III because the resolution from the dominant to the tonic chord occurs too early due to off-beat phrasing.

The ritmos performed by the conjunto de cumbia, like the songs of the velorio de angelito offered in chapter 8 and the cantos de las fiestas presented in chapter 11, display a blend of European and African traits. As in the case of the genres discussed in the other two chapters cited, I am unable to find evidence of Amerindian influence. In the following I therefore attempt to summarize the contributions of the African and the European to the performance of the cumbia, gaita, porro, and puya.

Texts

The texts of the few vocal solos are completely Spanish-European in character. The cuartetos are rhymed quatrains and are primarily octosyllabic, like the coplas previously discussed. The estribillo, or refrain, is, in this case, also a quatrain. Although somewhat uneven in length, it displays the rima romancera.

Melodies

The caña de millo has a limited gamut, and the pitches produced in performance are quite irregular in intonation, as judged from the European viewpoint. Two tonal centers can be determined by interval relationship, but not by repeated finals as in European music. On the other hand, there are frequent rapid passages using only the three pitches of the G major triad, a phenomenon which

would tend to indicate European influence. Thus Europe has obviously made some contribution to pito performance tradition, but
whether the remaining elements of this tradition have been contributed by the African or the Amerindian, or have developed independently, I have no means of determining. The few recordings
of performances on African analogues of this instrument which I
have had the opportunity of hearing do not display similar tonal
or scalar characteristics.

European influence is clear in the scalar organization and
melodic functions of the vocal part of TR 61, which is almost
entirely consonant with common practice. Such influence is less
evident in the vocal part of TR 65. Here both scale and melodic
functions are not consonant with common practice, although some
pitch formulae at cadence points seem quite European. The chromatic tones utilized do not permit a modal interpretation, and
the fact that the vocal and pito parts do not share the same
tonal center is hardly a European characteristic. Nevertheless,
Europe seems to have made a somewhat larger contribution to the
pitch structure of the vocal part than to that of the pito.

Relations of Text and Melody

In the Verses, or cuartetos, and the refrains, or estribillos,
the great majority of verbal stresses do not coordinate with the
strokes of the llamador. The highest degree of coordination is
seen in the cuartetos of TR 65, the least in the estribillos of
TR 61. There is little question that the African rather than the
Spanish tradition is predominant here.

Formal Aspects

The pito and percussion parts of the four ritmos discussed in
this chapter can be conceived as being structured in cycles of
sixteen or eight eighth notes. The common African twelve-pulse
cycle is absent. In cyclic organization each ritmo is almost
entirely conjunct and divisive. There is an occasional additive
realization of the cycle by the bombo in the cumbia and a disjunct
realization by the tambor mayor in the puya. The additive and
disjunct realizations of cycles characteristic of African music
are otherwise absent. The polymetrical structure of the puya is
certainly derived from African practice, but remains divisive.
The tambor mayor is fully improvisatory in the cumbia and partially
so in the porro. The pito plays an improvisatory role in all four
ritmos, but in the porro does not seem bound to the underlying
cycle.

Like a number of items presented in chapter 11 which realize a
cycle outlined by four claps, the cuartetos of the ritmos presented in this chapter realize cycles delineated by four strokes
on the llamador. In the porro, as in the fandango (TR 54),
the vocalist manipulates phrase lengths in such a manner that he
first moves out of and then back into phase with the cycle of four
strokes.

The formal structure is also subject to an alternative European
interpretation, wherein the ritmos are conceived to be cast in

duple meter, with each stroke of the llamador representing a principal pulse. The majority of the percussion instruments perform
a generally repetitive pattern beginning on the primary pulse of
the cumbia, gaita, and porro and on each pulse of the puya. Above
this the pito and the vocalist, in the main, execute two-measure
phrases. Such phrases are four pulses in length, the most common
phrase length in European music. Militating against this European
interpretation are the polymetric character of the puya and the
occasional presence of additive and disjunct rhythmic structures.
To this must be added the absence of differentiation in stress
characteristic of the primary and secondary pulses of Western
European duple meter.

In the aspects so far discussed, Europe has probably made as
large a contribution as Africa. However, the majority of the instruments forming the ensemble had their progenitors in West Africa,
and a percussion ensemble of this size and type is characteristically African rather than European. These factors tend to emphasize the African contribution to the conjunto de cumbia.

PART IV
Synthesis

13. Style and Content

The preceding six chapters have been devoted to the genres of song and instrumental music in the repertory of the evitaleros. Examples of each genre have been presented and described. They have been differentiated by whatever means I have found useful, and various aspects of their structure and style have been discussed. Finally, in each chapter I have endeavored to assess the contributions made to each genre by the Hispanic-European, the African Negro, and the Amerindian, and also to distinguish those aspects of the performances which may represent an independent development in the New World. This discussion will be continued in the following pages but will be concerned with the style and content of the repertory as a whole rather than of particular genres.

THE SONG TEXTS

Since the Spaniards provided the language spoken in Evitar, it is not surprising to find that the poetic and literary traditions of Spain have had the greatest influence upon the content and form of the texts of the songs. As indicated in chapters 7-8, I have been able to trace specific texts of lullabies and children's songs to Spanish sources by means of their themes and content. To my knowledge, *el canto a lo divino,* a song on a sacred subject, as contrasted with *el canto a lo humano,* a song on a secular subject, does not exist in Evitar. Nevertheless, the Roman Catholic form of the Christian religion established by the Spaniards in this area so permeates the culture that references to it or to themes taken from it are found in many secular songs. In the lullabies TR 3-4 there are references to the Christ Child, the Virgin Mary, and Saint Elizabeth. In the children's song TR 9 there is a reference to the chapel of the Virgen del Pilar, which is located in Spain. In TR 13, a song sung at the velorio de angelito, a humorous reference is made to the custom of baptism when the priest places salt in the mouth of the person being baptized. Of the zafras, TR 19 alludes to a woman with the family name of de los Santos (of the Saints), and in TR 20-21 there are references to the Virgen del Carmen, the oldest of the apparitions of the Virgin Mary. In the décimas, TR 24 contains the phrase "the mystery of

the Cross," and in TR 42 there are references to the star of the
east and the birth of Christ. A negative view is expressed in
TR 32, where it is declared that a priest will not marry a couple,
no matter how poor, without pay, and in TR 37, where it says that
the poor should not pay for sacraments, since God offers them
nothing in return. Finally, in TR 54, a fandango, there is a
reference to sacramento santísimo (holy communion).

Other common themes of the song poems are relationships between the sexes, poverty, the singer's desire to leave his community or this world, and his premonition of death. References to
sexual intercourse, whether overt or disguised in the form of
double-entendre, are common both in Africa and in European rural
societies untouched by puritanism. Affection of man for woman and
woman for man undoubtedly existed and continues to exist in African, Amerindian, and European cultures. However, romantic love,
the characterization of the relationship in glowing terms rarely
consonant with actuality, is typically a European concept. It
receives its full-blown literary expression in the décimas sung by
Pacheco, TR 24, and is expressed in a somewhat less literary form
in three of those sung by Julio, TR 27-29. Cueto in TR 41 sings
ecstatically of the nymph he adores, but this romantic expression
is perhaps satirical, since it follows immediately upon TR 40, a
diatribe against womankind and marriage. A number of the coplas
sung by Abraham Herrera, particularly those found in the cantos
de las fiestas, deal with romantic love, but in a more succinct
fashion. V. 23-26 of TR 53 form a copla concerned with unrequited
love, a frequent theme in the texts previously mentioned.

Julio in TR 26 and Abraham Herrera in TR 43 complain of their
poverty. Simón Herrera equates poverty and poor luck in TR 30 and
TR 33-34. The contrast between wealth and poverty is less pronounced in tribal societies than in those which form larger units
and are more technologically advanced. This contrast has always
been obvious in Christian Europe and is reflected in Cueto's
statement at the end of TR 42 that Christ came to save both the
poor and rich. There have probably been individuals in all three
cultures who at one time have desired a change of venue, whether
it be in this world or that to come. Thus I doubt that expressions
such as "tomorrow I leave this place" or "tomorrow I leave this
world" can necessarily be traced to a particular cultural source.
However, in TR 48, v. 15-18, and in TR 54, v. 21-24, Abraham
Herrera sings of the tolling of the bell. Before European contact no bells tolled in sub-Saharan Africa or among the Amerindians.

It is possible that some of the song poems represent themes
common among the Amerindians and the Africans which have been re-
shaped and stated in the Spanish language. However, we have as
yet little knowledge concerning what the common themes are of
African sung poetry and next to nothing in the way of information
concerning the sung poetry of the Amerindians of this area. Obviously, some of the themes of the song texts represent present-
day rural social conditions and cannot be easily traced to particular past influences. Of such nature are the copla sung in TR 47
expressing the campesino's disillusionment with both political

parties and that in TR 52 complaining of the intrusion of the
city's accordion upon the music of the countryside.

Meaningless syllables or words which are lexically meaningless
in the context in which they are employed are found in some song
texts in all six of the previous chapters, most frequently in the
worksongs presented in chapter 9. At times these form a full
verse, as

E-le-le-le-i-la-le-la-le-le-la,

in TR 54, v. 20, and

Mirón, mirón, mirón,

in TR 10. There are, in addition, both meaningless and meaningful
interjections. Meaningless interjections such as *o, e,* and *ay*
usually appear in initial position; meaningful interjections such
as *por Dios* or *mama mía* appear in other positions as well. The
meaningless syllables or interjections are usually an integral
part of the verse; that is, when the text displays reasonably regular meter, their occurrence does not lengthen it. On the other
hand, in the décimas sung by Cueto, interjections such as *Niña
Delia* precede a full verse.

Interjections or meaningless syllables are found with some frequency in European or European-derived folksong, the meaningless
syllables usually forming part or all of a refrain. In the non-
strophic texts of Spanish flamenco, meaningless syllables occasionally serve as interludes marking off sections of meaningful
verse. Interjections and meaningless syllables are also heard in
African song. The former may also be markers, as in the Akan
dirges, delineating the beginning and end of the dirge. Words
which are meaningful in speech are also employed in a meaningless
context in Mende songs. Lexically meaningless syllables (usually
referred to as vocables) are commonly employed in the songs of the
North American Indian, but I have no data concerning their use in
the songs of the Indians of northern South America. The use of
meaningless interjections of *o* or *ay* would seem to be a European
trait, as would the employment of meaningless material in refrains,
as in TR 10. The use of the vowel *e* as an initial interjection,
especially in neumatic form, seems more likely to have been derived
from African practice, as does the copious use of interjections in
the worksongs. There are, however, insufficient data available to
arrive at adequate conclusions concerning the sources of the phenomena discussed.

In chapter 6 the verse forms copla and décima were traced
to Spain (see V.C.2-3). The litany is found in both Europe
and Africa but in its sung form as a call and response pattern is
much more common in the latter (see chapter 6, V.C.4 and VI.A.2).
The litanic verse with inserted coplas as found in chapter 11 thus
shares both European and African traits (see chapter 6, IV.B.2).

Prosodic features such as the verse or line, the strophe, and
the refrain are found in both European and African song. The items
presented in chapters 7-8 and 11-12 display all three of these prosodic features, those in chapters 9-10 only verse and strophe. If

the prosodic features of the Amerindian songs of the region have
had some influence on those sung in Evitar, there are insufficient
data to document this fact. The only text of an Amerindian song
of northern South America available to me with translation is one
of the Jívaro of the Ecuadorian Amazon (fig. 76, p. 300). As defined by the musical phrases, this song text may be said to have
verses or lines, although at times this verse may itself consist
of two short statements of the same material. There is one verse
which might be considered a refrain because of the number of times
it occurs. However, its occurrence seems to be random; that is,
each occurrence is not preceded by a specific number of verses.

Meter and rhyme are European traits; they are not found in the
texts of either African or Amerindian songs. Litanic verse, as,
for example, found in the ritual of the Catholic Church, does
not display rhyme. In the European sung call and response pattern
the verses usually do rhyme, as in the following examples from sea
chanteys (Lomax and Lomax 1934:490-91).

"Blow the Man Down":   As I was walking down Paradise Street
                        A saucy young policeman I chanced for
                        to meet.

"The Black Ball Line": I served my time on the Black Ball Line,
                        On the Black Ball Line I served my time,
                        Once there was a Black Ball ship
                        That fourteen knots an hour could clip.

The verses of the African call and response pattern do not display
rhyme. The lack of rhyme in the litanic verse of chapter 11 and
in TR 13-14 of chapter 8 is thus an African rather than a European
trait. There are other cases in the song repertory of Evitar
where the verses are not rhymed, but the greater part of the non-
litanic verse does exhibit this European trait. In addition, the
great majority of all verses, whether they display rhyme or not,
are octosyllabic or hexasyllabic, the two most common verse lengths
in Spanish folk poetry (Magis 1969:469).

Thus in cultural inheritance the song texts are primarily
Spanish-European. The two prosodic features, strophe and refrain,
are characteristic of both African and European sung poetry but
apparently not of that of the Amerindian. The verse, defined as a
self-contained section of textual material sung to one musical
phrase, is found in all three cultures, but only in European sung
poetry are the verses necessarily related by meter and rhyme. As
far as poetic forms are concerned, the quatrain is a widespread
Western European form, the copla and décima specifically Spanish,
and the call and response pattern is found in Europe and Africa.
The principal African contribution to the formal structure of
costeño verse is the non-rhymed litanic verse. The litanic verse
with inserted coplas seems to be an independent development which
fuses European and African traditions.

VOCAL STYLE

Whether an informant's utterance is song or speech or a form intermediate thereto is basically a cultural distinction (List 1963:1-16). The informants and the investigator may differ in this categorization. Here I am interested in the informant's viewpoint as it can be best determined. In almost all cases, those items presented in the last six chapters in which vocal production is involved represent what the evitaleros consider song. It should be noted, however, that decimeros do not employ the verb *cantar* (to sing) to describe their performances but rather the verb *improvisar* (to improvise). However, in all the genres presented they do make a distinction between *las palabras* or *las letras* (the words or the text) and *la tonada* or *la melodía* (the tune or melody). The decimas can therefore be considered to be sung rather than recited. The verb *gritar* (to shout or to cry) is used to describe those random utterances which are not considered an integral part of the song. The soloist is usually too occupied with his part, but the members of the repercusión or chorus may utter gritos, as may participants in the work or the game, as well as onlookers. Although these gritos are fairly melodic, I have notated only one of them, and this where it seemed to play a part in the structural form of the refrain (see TR 61, m. 49, 85). I have transcribed only the text of the other gritos.

In European song the vocal range of a woman is normally an octave higher than that of a man. Thus in European song, and in European-derived song, when men and women sing the same melody they normally sing in parallel octaves. Not so in Evitar. As table 33 indicates, the vocal ranges of the men and women in Evitar differ considerably from those of their European counterparts. The absolute pitch of their ranges is approximately the same. When they sing the same melody, men and women sing in unison rather than in parallel octaves. The women sing in the lowest possible tessitura of their voices, the men in their highest possible tessitura. Thus in some items where there is a male soloist and a female chorus, as, for example, in TR 11-12, the choral part is sung in a lower tessitura than that of the soloist. There is only one case in which a man sings pitches lower than those sung by a woman, that of Pacheco in TR 24.

Women rarely sing above g^1. The melody employed by Martínez in singing TR 2-3 has the range of an 8ve plus a major 6th. When she had difficulty in emitting $B^\flat$, the second line of the bass clef, I asked her to repeat the song at a higher pitch level. The result was TR 3. However, her voice broke when she attempted to sing b^1, the third line of the treble clef. As indicated, the men show a preference for singing in the upper range of their voices. Those who had naturally low voices, Pacheco, Julio, and Reinaldo Rosado, could reach only d, e, and f in the treble clef. Those with more flexible voices sang as high as $c\sharp^2$. All these pitches were sung in chest tone, not in falsetto.

As indicated in chapter 9, I have found a number of recorded examples in which Indian men of northern South America sing in a very high vocal range. These observations were made while seeking analogues for the wide-ranged melodies of the worksongs. In the

Table 33.   Vocal Ranges

I.   Female Solo

Name of Singer	TR No.	Range
Sánchez	1	$e\flat-e\flat^1$
	13	$g-f^1$
	15	$g\sharp-e^1$
	16	$a-e^1$ (glide to $c\sharp^2$)
Martínez	2	$B\flat-g^1$
	3	$d-b^1$
Fontalvo	5	$f-c^1$

II.   Male Solo

M. Rosado	19	$f-b\flat^1$
	21	$d-c\sharp^2$
R. Rosado	20	$c\sharp-c\sharp^1$
	21	$d-f^1$
Pacheco	22	$f\sharp-e^1$
	24	$F-d^1$
Cueto	23	$a-a\flat^1$
	38, 39, 40	$d-g^1$
	41-42	$f-g^1$
Julio	26-29	$c\sharp-d\sharp^1$
S. Herrera	32 1-11, 35, 37	$d-b^1$
	36	$B\flat-f^1$
A. Herrera	43	$d-f\sharp^1$

III.   Male Solo and Female Chorus

S. Herrera	S.	11	$g-e^1$
	Ch.		$e-d^1$
A. Herrera	S.	12	$a-a^1$
	Ch.		$f-f^1$
	S.	14	$g-f^1$
	Ch.		$a-c^1$
	S.	18	$b\flat-a\flat^1$
	Ch.		$b\flat-f^1$
	S.	44	$f-b^1$
	Ch.		$f-e\flat^1$
	S.	48	$e-f\sharp^1$
	Ch.		$e-b$
	S/Ch	54	$c-e^1$

IV.   Male Solo and Male Chorus

Name of Singer		TR No.	Range
Pallares	S/Ch	45	$f-f^1$
	S.	46	$g\flat-e\flat^1$
	Ch.		$b\flat-d\flat^1$

few performances by Indian women to which I listened, some use was
made of a low tessitura, but it is not as prominent as in the songs
recorded in Evitar. Male singers in Spain, particularly those who
sing flamenco, also employ a high tessitura, but the vocal range
of female singers is roughly comparable to that employed by women
in other Western European countries. This can be seen in the
décima española presented in chapter 10 (pp. 392-93).

In the Liberian-Sierra Leonean region of West Africa, as in
Evitar and the surrounding region, men sing in their highest register and women in their lowest, placing both within approximately
the same pitch boundaries (Knott 1973:163-64, van Oven 1970:20-27,
71, and Burnim 1976:107). Thus this characteristic of costeño song
seems to be derived from the vocal style of this area of West
Africa.

Costeño men sing with an intense, rather strained-sounding chest
tone. Amerindian men in northern South America in most cases employ falsetto when singing in a high register. In Andalucía and
Asturias men singing in a high tessitura employ vibrato. It is
only in the recordings of Mende men of Sierra Leone that I have
heard singing in a high tessitura in which the tone production is
analogous to that of costeño men (see paragraphs 5-6, p. 330).
Whether the use of an intense chest tone in singing in a high
register is characteristic of male singing in the entire Liberian-
Sierra Leonean region, I do not know, but it obviously is not
typical of Africa as a whole. Waterman cites singing in falsetto
as a common African trait (1973:89). In her study of the music
of Central Africa, Brandel also stresses the frequent use of
falsetto in male singing (1961:96). On the other hand, Nketia indicates that many types of vocal production are utilized in the
various regions of Africa (1974:145-46).

The male singers of Evitar also employ extremely wide vocal
ranges. This is particularly evident in the worksongs and the
décimas, in which Mariano Rosado displays a vocal range of an 8ve
plus a major 7th and Simón Herrera an 8ve plus a major 6th. Some,
but not all, of these very wide ranges include a terminal glide.
There are, however, performances by male singers not involving
glides in which the range is an 8ve plus a perfect 5th or an 8ve
plus a perfect 4th. Only one of these, TR 44, is neither a worksong nor a décima. The melodies of these male performances are,
at least to some extent, improvised. Female singers, on the
other hand, primarily sing set melodies which rarely exceed an
8ve in range. The one exception, the melody of TR 2-3, has a
range of an 8ve plus a major 6th, which is past the capacity of
its singer.

As far as I can determine, such wide-ranged singing by men in chest tone is not common in Spain, sub-Saharan West Africa, or among the Indians of the Costa Atlántica. The singing of wide-ranged worksongs is also known in Brazil, where falsetto is employed in the high register. Thus this particular costeño trait, wide-ranged male singing employing chest tone in the high tessitura, seems to be an independent development peculiar to this region.

Another characteristic of the song style of the evitaleros is the tendency to gradually raise the pitch level. This tendency is found in the singing of both men and women and is probably due to the tenseness of vocal production of both sexes. Marcelina Sánchez concludes the lullaby TR 1 at a pitch level a quarter tone higher than that at which she began. In TR 13, a song of the velorio de angelito, she gradually raises her pitch level throughout. It is nearly a semitone higher at the end of the transcription and nearly a whole tone higher at the end of the performance. The rise in pitch level in the singing of the lullaby TR 2 by Rosa Luisa Martínez is not as pronounced. By the end of the performance she has raised her pitch level not quite a quarter tone. On the other hand, in singing TR 3 she lowers her pitch level slightly during the last strophe. This probably occurred because I asked her to sing the lullaby again at a higher pitch level than that at which she was accustomed to singing it, and she could not maintain it (see p. 221).

A rapid rise in pitch level is also heard in most performances by Simón Herrera. His pitch level is a quarter tone higher at the end than at the beginning of his performance of TR 11, a song of the velorio de angelito. In his first group of décimas, TR 30-32, he gradually but unevenly raises the pitch level a whole tone. By the time he begins his second group of décimas, TR 33-35, he seems to have reached the limits of his range, since the pitch level at which he concludes TR 35 is only slightly sharp in comparison with that at which he begins TR 33. The pitch levels of the décimas sung by Pacheco and Julio remain fairly constant. There is a gradual rise in pitch level in only one of Cueto's décimas, TR 42, that of a quarter tone. Abraham Herrera also usually maintains a fairly stable pitch level. In TR 12, however, by v. 5 he and the chorus are singing at a pitch level a semitone higher than that at which they began. There is no further rise in pitch level throughout the rest of the performance.

Thus there are songs in which the pitch level remains reasonably constant, but there are none in which the pitch level is lowered as the performance progresses. To my knowledge there are no studies of Western European or Western European-derived folksong in which data concerning change in pitch level are given. Bartók does offer such information in some of his studies of folksong of Eastern Europe (Bartók and Lord 1951). Due to the more open and less tense vocal production preferred, performances by singers of Western art music are characterized by a tendency to lower rather than raise the pitch level.

The concept of the final apparently cannot be applied in determining a tonal center in African music. In her study of Mende song Burnim establishes as the tonal center that pitch which

occurs the most frequently, especially at cadences (1976:142).
However, she offers no information concerning change in pitch
level during performance. Thus I have no means of relating this
particular aspect of costeño vocal style to any of the parent
cultures.

MELODIC MOTION AND MELODIC CONTOUR

In the following discussion I employ three terms: *descending
motion, ascending motion,* and *equality of motion.* These terms
are applied to entire songs or to sections or strophes of songs.
If the initial pitch is higher than the final pitch, descending
motion is displayed. If the reverse is true, it is ascending
motion. If the initial and final pitches are the same, the term
equality of motion is used, no matter what the intervening pitches
may be. Most of the worksongs and décimas display descending
motion. This type of motion characterizes the larger sections of
the worksongs and is true of the décimas as a whole and of each
of the two sections of which they are composed. In chapter 7
all the lullabies exhibit descending motion, while in the children's songs it is found only in TR 10A. The remaining children's
songs are characterized by ascending motion or equality of motion.
Since TR 6-7 are not strophic in form, melodic motion has been
determined by the initial and final pitches of the entire song.
The majority of the items in chapter 8 are not strophic in structure. The initial quatrain of TR 15 displays ascending motion,
the first strophe of TR 17 descending motion, and the first strophe
of TR 18 equality of motion. Since all of the items presented in
chapter 11 are open-ended, this type of analysis cannot be applied.
In chapter 12 the two cuartetos in TR 61 show equality of motion
and the two in TR 65 descending motion.

Thus the lullabies, the worksongs, and the décimas form one
group, in which descending motion predominates. A second group,
comprising the game songs of both the children and the adults,
shows a preponderance of other than descending motion. The third
group, the cuartetos, is equally divided between descending motion
and equality of motion.

The melodic contours displayed by the individual verses of the
worksongs and décimas are listed and summarized in tables 13 and
16 (pp. 327-28, 381-82). The methods of analysis employed are discussed in chapter 6 (see IV.A.1.3). A listing of the melodic contours of the individual verses found in the items presented in
the remaining four chapters is given in table 34.

In these four chapters the melodic contours M-H-L and H-L pre-
dominate, as they do in chapters 9-10, which contain the worksongs
and the décimas. M-H-L comprises approximately two-thirds of the
verse contours found in chapter 9, over half of those found in
chapter 10, and approximately two-fifths of those found in the
remaining chapters. The items presented in chapters 7-8 and 11-12
employ four descending contours, M-H-L, H-L, H-L-M, and M^2-H-L-M^1;
three ascending contours, L-H, L-H-M, and M^1-L-H-M^2; and three
contours displaying equality of motion, L-H-L, H-L-H, and M-H-L-M.
There are 151 descending contours, 49 ascending contours, and 45

Table 34. Melodic Contours, Chapters 7-8 and 11-12

| | Chapters | | | | |
Contours	7	8	11	12	Totals
M-H-L	47	19	20	6	92
H-L	13	5	16	6	40
L-H-L	9	21	1	7	38
L-H	2	1	4	4	11
L-H-M	17	12	5	2	36
H-L-M	2	5	4	1	12
H-L-H	1	0	3	0	4
M-H-L-M	2	1	0	0	3
M^1-L-H-M^2	2	0	0	0	2
M^2-H-L-M^1	7	0	0	0	7
	102	64	53	26	245

contours which display equality of motion. There are therefore 94 contours which do not descend.

In the worksongs (chapter 9) only 10% of the contours do not display descending motion; in the décimas (chapter 10) 28% do not display descending motion; and in the remaining material 38% of the contours are of the non-descending type. Thus the worksongs can be differentiated from the other genres by their preponderant use of descending motion and the verse contour M-H-L. The décimas occupy an intermediate position between the worksongs and the remaining genres as far as these two characteristics are concerned. However, it should be indicated that in chapter 8 there are a larger number of the verse contour L-H-L than M-H-L, twenty-one versus nineteen. In chapter 11 one finds an unusual number of the contour H-L, although not reaching that of M-H-L, sixteen versus twenty. Finally, as discussed earlier, in chapter 7 the lullabies can be differentiated from the children's songs by the fact that the former are characterized by general descending motion while the latter display all three types of melodic motion discussed.

Any attempt to trace the discussed traits to other cultural sources depends upon the availability of accurate transcriptions in which the melody can be segmented by means of established textual groupings comparable to the verses of European song texts. The few data I have available of this type are offered in chapter 9 in the summary of table 14 (p. 338). The table offers insufficient material from Spain and from the Amerindians of northern South America to made an adequate comparison. There are somewhat more data from the Mende of Sierra Leone, whose songs display traits similar to those of the costeño. M-H-L and H-L are the predominant verse contours in the Mende song, but in reverse order; that is, there are a larger number of the latter than the former. Some

40% of the contours do not descend, a somewhat larger percentage
than is found in the costeño songs.

Considering the physiological processes involved, particularly
the problem of breath support when the bulk of air has been ex-
pelled from the lungs, it seems likely that the song of most cultures would display more descending than ascending motion. In this
case, this particular trait would not be too useful in determining
the cultural sources of costeño song. The Jívaro song, however,
does emphasize ascending motion. Therefore the individual contours
employed would seem to be a more likely means of determining cultural sources. In this trait the Mende songs are reasonably
analogous to those of the costeño. The two most common contours
employed in the costeño songs form almost half of the total contours utilized in the Mende songs. They form a little over one-
fourth of those utilized in the Jívaro song.

PITCH INVENTORIES, TONALITY, AND MODALITY

Table 35 lists the type and number of pitch inventories or
scales displayed by the sung melodies presented in the six previous
chapters. I have omitted TR 19-23 because of the indefiniteness of
pitch. Separate pitch inventories have been given for TR 8A and 8B
and for TR 10A and 10B, since two distinct melodies are employed in
each song. When a song is composed of verse and refrain, both are
combined in the pitch inventory. Octave duplications are not taken
into consideration when deriving the pitch inventory from the transcription. If the final note of a melody is followed by a glide,
the latter is not taken into account. In the table the transcriptions are represented only by their numbers. When chromatic tones
are present, they are indicated by numbers in parentheses, and a
microtone, a pitch modified by an arrow, by m. Thus 48 (1 plus m)
indicates that the pitch inventory of TR 48 contains one chromatic
tone and one microtone. Pentatonic pitch inventories marked with
an asterisk are hemitonic, those not so marked are anhemitonic
(see chapter 6, IV.A.1.4).

Forty percent of the pitch inventories are non-heptatonic. Of
these, three are tetratonic, six are pentatonic, and seven are
hexatonic. The melodies of Western European art music rarely contain less than seven diatonic scale degrees. Non-heptatonic scales
are common in Western European folk music, and are also found in
sub-Saharan African music. The scales of Jívaro song are primarily
tritonic in character, and those of the Indians of the Peruvian and
Ecuadorian Andean region are reputed to be built upon pentatonic
scales. One can therefore conclude that the non-heptatonism displayed in the costeño songs represents influences other than those
of Western European art music, although the specific influences
cannot be designated. In Western Europe and, to the best of my
knowledge, in the New World, pentatonic melodies are anhemitonic
in character; they display no semitones. TR 46 and TR 61 display
hemitonic pentatonic scales. Such scales are definitely non-
European and probably are not characteristic of Amerindian music.
I have no knowledge as to whether or not such scales occur in sub-
Saharan Africa.

Table 35.   List of Pitch Inventories or
Scales According to Type

A. Non-heptatonic

1.   Diatonic

 Tetratonic   5   12

 Pentatonic   7   10A   13   16   46*   61*

 Hexatonic   1   8A   9   10B   11

2.   Plus chromatic tone(s)

 Tetratonic   15(1)

 Hexatonic   44(1)   48(1 plus m)

B.   Heptatonic

1.   Diatonic

 2   3   8B   12   14   18   32   35   36   37   38   39   40   41   42

2.   Plus chromatic tone(s)

 6(1)   24(3)   26(1)   27(1)   29(1)   43(5)   54(1 plus m)   65(2)

Totals

	1. Diatonic	2. Plus chromatic tone(s)	Totals
A. Non-heptatonic	13	3	16
B. Heptatonic	15	9	24
Totals	28	12	40

A somewhat smaller proportion of the pitch inventories, 30%, contain chromatic tones. The remainder are diatonic. Only three of the melodies exhibit more than one chromatic tone, TR 24, TR 43, and TR 65. Two pitch inventories, those of TR 48 and TR 54, display a chromatic tone plus a microtone. The remaining seven transcriptions contain only one chromatic tone. Chromatic tones are rarely found in European folk music, nor are they common in sub-Saharan African or Amerindian music. Except in the case of the variable third degree, as will be noted later, and in the uncertain performance by A. Herrera in TR 43, they can be attributed to the influence of Western art music.

In the preceding discussion pitch inventories or scales have been considered without reference to the concept of tonality (see chapter 6, IV.A.1.4 and IV.A.2.1). Using the term in its broadest sense, tonality is produced when a particular pitch of the inventory is considered to be the tonal center, that is, the pitch of

the inventory which serves the most important function. Depending
upon the system, the remaining tones then function in some type of
subordinate relationship to the tonal center. In this study I have
employed two means to establish the tonal center. The first utilized was that conventional in Western art music until approximately the beginning of this century, the selection of the final
pitch of the melody as the tonal center. In the second I established the tonal center by means of the melodic intervals of a perfect 4th and a perfect 5th most commonly found in the transcription (see chapter 5, I.B.1.1.2). Burnim made use of a third
method of establishing the tonal center, which had been developed
by German scholars early in this century (Abraham and von Hornbostel 1909-10:24-25). In this method, whose principal utility
is in the analysis of non-European music, the tone to be selected
as the tonal center is determined by the frequency of its occurrence and the points at which it occurs within the melody. As
described by Abraham and von Hornbostel, the method is not very
precise. Frequency, for example, could indicate the number of
occurrences of the particular pitch within the melody or the total
time value occupied when the individual time values of the various
occurrences are added together. Nor do the authors state how much
weight should be given to the occurrence of a particular pitch in
initial, medial, or final positions. This method, therefore, cannot be employed with any precision without assigning arbitrary
weights to these several factors. For these reasons I have not
utilized this method when the first two mentioned means of establishing a tonal center were not applicable, as in the worksongs,
TR 19-23.

Once a tonal center is established, a pitch inventory becomes
a mode. (In the common practice period the terms *mode* and *scale*
are relatively interchangeable.) Modes are distinguished one
from another by the intervallic relationships existing between
their constituent tones. With the Greek harmoniai as the model,
the heptatonic mode was established as the norm in European music
(see chapter 6, IV.A.2.1). The European heptatonic modes fall
into two groups, the so-called church modes plus the additions
made by Glareanus and the major and minor modes of the common
practice period (see chapter 6, IV.A.2.2-3). In both groups of
modes the final of the melody is, with certain exceptions, the
tonal center to which the other degrees of the mode are related.
In order to establish a clear relationship with European tradition, I have followed this method in table 36 in listing the heptatonic modes into which the items of the costeño repertory are cast.
Modes are defined only by their intervallic structure. Harmonic
implications are not taken into consideration, and only the chromatic tones common to the minor mode are accepted (see chapter 6,
IV.A.2.4). Again, the transcriptions are identified only by the
numbers.

Using this rather simplistic procedure, nineteen of the forty
melodies listed in table 36 can be related structurally to modes
historically in use in the art music of Western Europe. The
greater proportion of Western European folk melodies are cast in
the major mode; the minor mode is much less frequently employed.
Folksongs utilizing the dorian, mixolydian, and aeolian modes are

Table 36.   List of Heptatonic Modes
According to Type

Group 1

						Totals
1.	Major	2	3	8B	36	4
2.	Minor	26	27	28	29	4

Group 2

							Totals
1.	Dorian	14	32	35	37		4
2.	Mixolydian	38	39	40	41	42	5
3.	Aeolian	12	18				2

	Totals
Group 1	8
Group 2	11
Total	19

found in Central and Northern Spain, England, and other areas in Western Europe. These songs are believed to represent an older stratum of folk melodies because of their structural similarity to modes employed in the Gregorian chant. Such a historical connection, of course, cannot be proved, since folksong is an oral tradition characterized by constant change.

If melodic functions are taken into consideration, the pitch inventories of TR 5, TR 7, TR 8B, TR 9, TR 10A, TR 10B, and TR 61 must be viewed as segments of the major mode. Following this procedure, however, TR 26-29 can no longer be considered to be cast in the minor mode. Accepting further harmonic implications, TR 6 can be added as an example of a melody cast in the major mode and displaying one modulatory chromatic tone. We have thus gained eight major melodies and lost four minor melodies. The score now reads: major 12, dorian 4, mixolydian 5, and aeolian 2, or a total of 23. To this TR 45 might be added, since it is aeolian except for one occurrence of a raised sixth degree. In any case, the majority of the melodies transcribed are characteristically Western European in their modal structure. It is interesting, however, that such a large proportion of the melodies, approximately one-half, fall into group 2, representing the modes in use in the earlier period of Western European art music. Of the remaining sixteen pitch inventories listed in table 35, I can comment concerning specific source or sources for only four. TR 46 can be considered non-European in character because of its hemitonic pentatonic scale. Since TR 61 can be considered a segment of the major mode, it no longer falls in that category. In

chapter 11 I discuss the possibility that the variable seventh and
third degrees heard in TR 48 and TR 54 represent the influence of
an African scale differing in intonation from the European (pp.
(pp. 470-71). In his work on the music of Ghana Nketia noted the
existence of such a scale. Waterman states that the "blues" scale
with variable seventh and third degrees has been occasionally
noted in West Africa, but he does not indicate the regions in
which it is found (1973:90).

The cadential pitch patterns 4-1 and 3-1 occur in both modal
European folk music and African melodies (Nketia 1963:36-39).
The first cadential pattern is not consonant with common practice
because of the implied subdominant harmony. Whether or not the
second cadential pattern would be employed during the common practice period depends upon its relationship to the underlying pulse
patterns. Thus :3.1 is unacceptable because of the lack of an
implied penultimate dominant harmony (see chapter 6, IV.A.2.2 and
4, and pp. 177-78). Some elements of African musical style therefore may be present in the costeño repertory, especially in chapters 8 and 10, where a number of melodies display these cadential
patterns. Alternatively, these patterns may represent the influence of modal European folksong or of European art music of
earlier periods.

USE OF PERCUSSION

According to Waterman, there is a dominance of percussion in
African music, since these instruments are the type required to
elaborate the complex rhythmic structure of this music. Handclapping serves the same function. Even melodic instruments like
the *mbira*, or lamellaphone, are used because of their percussive
value (1973:87). In chapter 11 only percussion instruments and
handclapping are employed to accompany the voices. In the conjunto de cumbia the majority of the instruments are of the percussion family, as are those found in the conjunto de gaitas.
The same holds for the sexteto, in which the marímbula, or thumb
piano, plays the bass part.

Although percussion instruments play an important role, the
bulk of African music is vocal rather than instrumental (Merriam
1962:121-22). Characteristically, African song is accompanied by
handclapping and/or one or more percussion instruments (see chapter 6, VI.C.2-3). In Europe in earlier centuries percussion instruments were employed in music accompanying both the folk dance
and the dance of the court. The tambourine, castanets, and side
drum have been in use in recent times to accompany folksong and
folk dance in Spain. Percussion instruments, especially rattles
and drums, are also employed by the Amerindians to accompany song
and dance. African influence therefore cannot be discerned in
the dance songs in chapter 11 solely because the latter are accompanied by percussion instruments. Rather, the African influence
is apparent in the type of percussion employed, the manner in
which the instruments are played, and the structure of the music
they perform.

Percussion instruments are without question dominant in the
ritmos found in chapter 12. This aspect of the music must have

its source in Africa, since analogous ensembles of percussion instruments are charactertistic of neither European folk music nor
Amerindian music. Throughout West Africa drums are usually played
in groups of three (Merriam 1962:119). Of the ensembles recorded
in Evitar, three drums were employed in only the conjunto de
cumbia, although there is some evidence that three drums rather
than two were utilized in the fandango (see p. 88).

Almost all of the songs sung in the remaining four chapters,
chapters 7-10, are unaccompanied. There is handclapping in TR 7
and the beating of poles upon the ground in TR 11-12. In both
cases there is a mere reiteration of a pulse, a phenomenon which
is seen and heard in all three parent cultures.

REPETITION, CONTRAST, AND VARIATION

There are three principles by which music and some poetry are
organized in time space: repetition, contrast, and variation.
Continued exact repetition of the same material produces monotony.
This is avoided by introducing contrasting new material or by
varying in some manner the material being repeated. The following
discussion is primarily concerned with two contrasting forms found
in the costeño repertory, the strophic songs found in chapter 7 and
the songs organized in call and response pattern found in chapters
8 and 11. The former are consonant with European practice; in
many aspects the latter are not.

In the lullabies and children's game songs presented in chapter 7,
the length of the verses is approximately the same throughout. In
addition, each strophe contains the same number of verses and usually displays the same rhyming scheme. Contrast is produced by change
of text from strophe to strophe, variation by change of phones which
form the rhymes. In most cases the same melody is employed in singing each poetic strophe. This melody is itself composed of two contrasting phrases. In the lullabies each verse plus its associated
melodic phrase is repeated. In TR 2-3 the melodic phrase is varied
in repetition. In addition, there will be some variation in the
melody as sung from strophe to strophe. This is caused in most
cases by a change in the number of syllables sung. The melodic variation produced may be purely rhythmic, accommodating a greater or
lesser number of syllables. The addition of a syllable to a verse
may also cause the introduction of a new pitch, particularly when
the added syllable is sung as an upbeat. Variation which is purely
melodic may also occur; that is, variation not caused by a change
in the text.

Two specific types of variation of a melodic phrase or pattern
are characteristic of the common practice period of Western European
art music. The first is known as the sequence, the second as modified repetition. In the first the same melodic phrase or pattern is
repeated at a different pitch level. In the second the same pitch
level is maintained, but the pitches and/or the rhythm are modified
in some manner. Both of these variation techniques can be seen in
the lullabies and children's game songs offered in chapter 7 and
further link them to European practice. The melodic sequence occurs
in only the children's songs, not in those of the adults. Modified
repetitions of a melodic pattern do occur elsewhere, but in a dif-

Ex. 1. Melodic sequence (TR 10A)

Ex. 2. Modified repetition of a phrase (TR 2)

Ex. 3. Modified repetition and sequence (TR 9)

ferent manner and under different circumstances. Ex. 1 is an example of a melodic sequence, ex. 2 of a modified repetition of a
phrase; in ex. 3 both techniques are applied to shorter patterns.

Songs which are fully or partially cast in the call and response
pattern are TR 11-14 of chapter 8 and TR 44-45 and TR 48-55 of
chapter 11. Their verses, like those of the strophic songs of
chapter 7, are fairly regular in length but do not display rhyme.
Although there is a regular and usually unvaried response by the
chorus, the part of the soloist is at least partly improvisatory
in nature and often represents a different application of the principles of repetition, contrast, and variation from that seen in
the songs in strophic form. The part of the soloist in songs cast
in the call and response pattern at times seems to be composed of
a limited number of verses and melodic phrases. These textual and
melodic elements placed one after another in some chronological
order form the solo part of the song or of a section thereof.
They are usually independent in their relationship; that is, a
particular textual element and a particular melodic element do
not necessarily remain associated. Nor are the individual verses
or melodic phrases presented in any discernible pattern of repetition. They are heard chronologically in such a manner that, con-
sciously or unconsciously, the effect of randomness is produced.
Thus any feeling that there is a pattern in the repetition is
negated. Documentation of this particular formal organization
will follow.

In ex. 4 I offer an analysis of TR 13, a simple example of the
type of formal structure discussed in the previous paragraph. A
formal analysis of the music has already been given in chapter 8
(p. 289). For ease in comparing the music and text, I have
changed the original designation of the musical elements in TR 13
from double to single lower-case letters, and I am indicating the
elements of the text by capital letters. Consideration of the
textual refrain and the melody sung to it is omitted.

Ex. 4.   Random variation, music and text
of verses (TR 13)

Music: a   b   c   a   c   b   a   c   a

Text: A   A   B   B   C   D   D   E   E

The alphabetical order in which the letters appear designates
the order in which these elements are heard in this particular
version of the song. They would not necessarily occur in the same
order in a subsequent performance. Ex. 5 is an analysis of TR 14.
According to the informants, it is the same song as TR 13. I omit
v. 1-4 since these verses represent an inserted copla. The verses
analyzed are the same as those found in TR 13 and are therefore
given the same letter names. D1 and D2 represent slight variations
of the same text. The musical phrases are different from those
heard in TR 13. In this case the letters used in the analysis represent the cadence formulae employed in the phrases. Thus a
represents the cadential pitch formula 5 4 1, b = 4 3 1, and

c = 2 7 1. The superscripts refer to the varying pitch sequences
making up the rest of the phrase.

Ex. 5.   Random variation, music and text
of verses (TR 14)

Music: a b^1 b^2 c^1 b^3 b^4 b^5 c^2 c^3

Text: E   D1   E   D2   D2   D2   D2   E   E

Further and more complex examples of this type of random variation can be found in the repertory of Evitar. An analysis of
textual variation in several versions of the same song was offered
in table 23 (pp. 457-58). In ex. 6 I reproduce from this table the
following section of TR 51. This is the litanic section following
COPLA 1. The analysis is again of only the solo part. Repetitions
are written out rather than being indicated by numbers in parentheses as they are in the table.

Ex. 6.   Random variation, verses (TR 51)

A1 A1 B3 B1 B1 C C D2 D2 D1 A1 A1 A1 B1 B3 B3

A similar random organization of varied and unvaried rhythmic
groups is found in some performances by the tambolero and the
bombero in the ritmos presented in chapter 12. Ex 7 is an analysis
of the part of the tambor mayor in the cumbia "No me olvides"
(TR 57). This section of the performance, m. 3-14, consists of an
equally spaced, running series of strokes. The strokes near the
edge of the head are marked e, those struck near the center of the
head are marked c. In the cumbia the melodic phrases of the pito
are two measures in length, and this structural division is emphasized by the bombero, who plays an accented stroke on the head of
his drum at the beginning of each two-measure phrase. These two-
measure phrases coincide with the lines representing the tambor
part given, m. 3-4, 5-6, and so on.
When we examine the two-measure phrases of the tambor part,
represented by the letters A through F, we find that there is no
exact repetition. However, there is some repetition in the constituent parts of the phrases. Thus, if we examine the tambor
part measure by measure, we find that there are five different
patterns, which I have marked a through e. Some of these measures
occur more than once in the section, and there is some immediate
repetition of a measure. There is, however, no discernible over-
all pattern of repetition. If we further analyze by half measure
or pulse, designated by italicized a through e, we find that there
is a great preponderance of a. In fact, all lines but one begin
with a, and the first pulse of each of the second measures begins
with a.
Similar random patterning is found in the parts for the tambor
mayor (TR 63) and the bombo (TR 64) in the gaita "Mariana" (see
pp. 526, 527).
This randomness in variation can also be seen in at least one
case in larger aspects of musical form. In the first section of

Ex. 7.   Random variation, tambor part,
                        cumbia (TR 57)

```
              A
              a                    b
              a      b      a      c
m.    3-4.    e e e c e e e | e e e c e c c e |
```

```
              B
              c                    c
              a      d      a      d
m.    5-6.    e e e c e e c e | e e e c e e c e |
```

```
              C
              d                    e
              b      d      a      e
m.    7-8.    e e e e e e c e | e e e c c e e e |
```

```
              D
              a                    a
              a      b      a      b
m.   9-10.    e e e c e e e e | e e e c e e e e |
```

```
              E
              c                    b
              a      d      a      c
m.  11-12.    e e e c e e c e | e e e c e c c e |
```

```
              F
              c                    a
              a      d      a      b
m.  13-14.    e e e c e e c e | e e e c e e e e |
```

Ex. 8.   Random variation, tambor part,
                        gaita (TR 63)

```
        a   b   c   d   c   b   e   d   c   c
```

Ex. 9.   Random variation, bombo part,
                        gaita (TR 64)

```
        a   b   c   d   a   b   c   e   b   b   b   f
            c   c   c   f   c   c   c   f   c   c   c
```

performances of the danza de negro de la plaza (TR 46-47) the
tambolero randomly shifts from one realization of the cycle of
sixteen eighth notes to a second, slightly varied realization
(see p. 418). The random order in which these two variants
appear in the tambor part in two performances of this genre is
shown in ex. 10:

Ex. 10.   Cyclic variation, tambor part, danza de
          negro de la plaza (TR 46-47)

LF 188.8   1 1 2 1 2

LF 188.5   1 1 1 2 2 2 2 1 1

Before attempting to establish possible cultural sources for the
formal organization under discussion, I think it useful to again
summarize its characteristics:

1. A small number of musical and/or textual elements, often in
    variant forms, are consciously or unconsciously strung to-
    gether in such a manner as to produce the effect of random-
    ness; that is, there is repetition of a number of elements
    in exact or varied form, but this repetition follows no
    discernible pattern.
2. If the item is a song, there is not necessarily a coordination
    of textual and musical elements; that is, a particular textual
    element and a particular musical element do not necessarily
    remain associated.
3. If the same textual and/or musical elements are employed in
    what may be considered a second performance of the same item,
    they do not necessarily appear in the same order as in the
    first performance.

In the repertory of Evitar neither all the solo parts of songs
cast in the call and response pattern nor the parts played by the
tambor mayor and the bombo in all ritmos display this particular
structural organization. Nevertheless, it is sufficiently common
to rank it as a stylistic characteristic of this repertory.
Whether or not it is a common trait in West African music, I am
not in a position to determine. Certainly, it is not strongly
evident in the Mende songs in tales transcribed by Burnim (1976:
145-62). The Mende songs, like many of the costeño, consist of a
series of calls and responses. The calls of the soloist, unlike
those of the costeño songs, may contain more than one phrase. In
ex. 11 I offer a formal analysis of the part of the soloist in two
of the Mende songs in tales. In the performance the numbered
calls are preceded by the responses of the chorus.
In some cases in the two items analyzed, textual and musical
elements do not remain in association. However, whether it is
varied or not, there is repetition of only one element. In all
the illustrations from the costeño repertory there is repetition
of at least two elements, whether in varied form or not. Although
I am not certain that it is found in West Africa, this random
structuring in the repetition of a number of elements is common in

Ex. 11.   Formal analysis, soloist's part,
Mende songs in tales

Calls	Music	Text
Intro	a	A
2	b	B
3	c + d	C + D
4	e + f	E + F
5	g^1	G
6	$h + i + g^2$	H + I + J

Mende T6 (Burnim 1976:155-56)

Intro	a	A
2	b^1	B^1
3	$c + d + b^1$	$C + D + B^2$
4	b^2	E
5	b^3	F

the songs of the Jívaro Indians of the Ecuadorian Amazon.   The
formal analysis presented in ex. 12 is reproduced from the transcription of a Jívaro victory song given earlier (fig. 76,
p. 300).

Ex. 12.   Random variation, music and text,
Jívaro victory song (fig. 76)

Music: a^1 a^2 a^1 b a^4 a^1 a^5 a^1 a^3 b a^6

Text: A   B1   A   B2   C   B2   B1   A   A   B1   C

The formal analysis found in ex. 12 should be compared with
those of TR 13-14 given previously (pp. 554-55). In the Jívaro song
at least two elements in both the melody and the text are repeated.
Again, the textual and melodic elements do not always remain associated.   Thus A, which might be considered a textual refrain, is
associated with more than one melodic element.   In ex. 13 I offer
an analysis of two sections of the melody of a second Jívaro song
(see List 1964a:16 and Turner:59-053-F, ATL 1357.4).

Ex. 13.   Random variation, music,
Jívaro song

1. a^1 a^1 b^1 c b^2 b^1 a^1 b^1 c b^2 a^1 b^1 c b^1 c b^1
2. a^2 a^3 a^2 b^2 c b^1 a^2 b^1 c b^1 c b^1

Again, a small number of varied elements are repeated in random order. There are other Jívaro songs which are much simpler in form (List 1964a:15). However, as in the repertory of Evitar, this formal phenomenon occurs with sufficient frequency to be considered a stylistic trait.

The Jívaro Indians live in the Ecuadorian Amazon to the east of the Andes. Their songs are basically tritonic in character, consisting almost entirely of the three pitches of the major triad. In this respect their songs differ in style from those of the Indians of the Atlantic and Pacific coastal regions of Colombia. I have studied both costeño and Jívaro song. Whether or not the Indian music of the coastal regions of Colombia displays similar principles of formal organization, I am not in a position to determine. There are insufficient published studies or documented recordings of any one tribe to make feasible the kind of study I made of Jívaro music. Nor have I found sufficient data concerning West African music to throw light upon this problem. I therefore can only state that since there is a large group of Indians in northern South America whose songs display principles of formal organization similar to those found in the songs and instrumental music which I recorded in Evitar, the possibility exists that this aspect of costeño music has been derived from Amerindian sources.

Looking at the matter from a broader perspective, what seems to be involved is a principle which might be described as continuous variation. Thus in those songs of Evitar discussed earlier it is extremely rare that one finds more than one unvaried repetition of associated textual and musical elements. In one case the same textual phrase is sung successively twelve times. The melodic phrase to which this textual phrase is sung is almost continuously varied, there never being more than one immediate repetition of the same variant of the melodic phrase (pp. 460-61). Western European music is characterized by a much greater emphasis on exact repetition, although this repetition is usually in the form of a sequence, a phenomenon rare in costeño melodies (see pp. 552-54). On the other hand, some semi-literate or non-literate societies seem to show a preference for continuous variation utilizing a small number of elements. To my knowledge no broad studies bearing on such matters have yet been attempted.

PULSE, METER, CYCLE, AND PHRASING

The worksongs and décimas presented in chapters 9-10 display no regular pulse and are therefore in free rhythm (see chapter 6, IV. B.1.1). Free rhythm is a phenomenon common to many music cultures. It is found, for example, in the cante jondo of Spain, the Akan dirges of Ghana, and the shaman's chants of the Cuna Indians of Colombia (Moser and Tayler 1972:MC3 Side A Band 2[b]). It is a useful trait in distinguishing one genre from another in a particular repertory, but it is so widespread that it cannot be a primary means of determining the cultural source or sources of a specific genre within that repertory. The same statement applies to the phenomenon of a regularly recurring, equidistant pulse. This is a trait common to dance music of Western Europe and West Africa and among the Amerindians.

Thus neither free rhythm nor a regularly recurring, equidistant pulse is a trait peculiar to Western European music. On the other hand, the occurrence of a repetitive pulse pattern, as distinguished from a repetitive but non-patterned pulse, is a characteristic of most Western European music in the common practice period and of Western European dance music in earlier and later periods (see chapter 6, IV.B.1.2). Western European folk music which accompanies the dance shares this trait.

Several aspects of music structure serve either singly or in combination to produce the effect of meter. A single percussion instrument can establish a pulse pattern or meter by the rhythmic patterns it performs. In a single melodic line meter can be established by a combination of rhythmic patterns and melodic phrasing. In the common practice period harmonic rhythm, whether produced by two or more voices or merely implicit in the melodic structure, can serve to establish meter.

When there is a regularly recurring pulse in African music, these pulses remain equal in value. They are not molded into metrical patterns by dynamic, agogic, or tonic accents. As far as I can determine, the same situation applies in Amerindian music. The equally stressed and equidistant pulses are often objectified by handclaps or strokes upon a drum. In other cases pulses are merely implied; that is, they are felt rather than heard. Much African music is structured above an underlying cycle of a certain number of pulses. It is objectified in part or in whole by voices, handclapping, or instruments (see chapter 6, IV.B.2.1). Most of the instruments realizing the cycle--in most cases instruments of the percussion family--perform the same rhythmic and/or melodic patterns or variants thereof during each repetition of the cycle. There is a free use of either binary or ternary divisions of the pulse, which at times produces hemiola or the effect of polymeter (see chapter 6, IV.B.2.7). The cycle may be realized disjunctly rather than conjunctly or in additive rather than divisive rhythm (see chapter 6, IV.B.2.3-4). One or two solo instruments or voices provide a freer improvisatory realization of the cycle. They may phrase their parts so that they at times begin before the onset of the cycle or continue past its conclusion (see chapter 6, IV.B.2.5). If the item is a song cast in the call and response pattern, and the soloist enters with the call before the cycle is completed, he overlaps the part of the chorus (see chapter 6, VI. B.3).

In most cases both European and African music are constructed over segments of time space measured by four equidistant pulses or multiples thereof. The phrase four pulses in length is common in Europe, and a cycle four pulses in length is known in Africa (see chapter 6, VI.C.3). A call and response pattern occupying eight pulses is common in both Europe and Africa. Groupings of four or eight pulses can therefore represent either European or African practice, depending upon whether or not the performer and/or auditor feels a repetitive pulse pattern. Such a determination may at times be somewhat difficult. In some of the songs in chapter 8 there is a strong feeling of European duple meter, while in others, such as TR 16-17, this effect does not seem to be strongly present. In both TR 18 of chapter 8 and TR 48 of chapter 11 the call and response pattern occupies eight pulses, which are evenly divided between the call and the response. Thus this call and response pattern can be considered to represent the realization of a cycle of eight pulses or a group of two musical phrases, each of the latter being structured over two duple-pulse patterns. Whether this musical segment represents the metrical or cyclic principle depends upon the effect on the auditor. Unless considerable care is exercised, the determination will be affected by the cultural background of the auditor and will not necessarily represent an objective judgment. The difficulty of arriving at such an objective judgment is an indication not only that the musical styles of the two cultures, the European and the African, display like traits but that in certain items of the costeño repertory acculturation has produced such a blending of styles that it is difficult to isolate one trait from another.

There are, of course, some means of differentiating the influence of one culture from that of another. Some of these have been mentioned above. When found in items in the costeño repertory, disjunct and additive realizations of cycles, polymeter, and overlapping of call and response patterns can be assumed to represent African influence, since all are African traits and are not characteristic of Western European music. The even division of time space between call and response, although occasionally found in Africa, is primarily a European trait and therefore represents that cultural influence. On the other hand, the uneven division of time space between call and response can be considered primarily an African influence.

"Azúcar," a song game played in the velorio de angelito (TR 13-14), is an exception to which none of the statements just made fully apply. Although it is cast in additive rhythm, the call and response are uneven in length, and thus it cannot have its source in Africa. If it is built over a cycle, the cycle is five pulses in length, while African cycles consist of four pulses or multiples thereof. Viewed as European music it is cast in quintuple meter, which is characteristically found in Eastern rather than Western Europe. Thus, TR 13-14 apparently represent an independent development which may have been influenced by the irregular form of additive rhythm found in some areas of Spain (see chapter 6, IV. 8.1.8).

There are two other means by which the influences of the two cultures can be differentiated. The metrical effect of European music is produced by the placement of dynamic and agogic accents at the points where pulses are desired. This effect will be dissipated if syncopation is not controlled. Thus in most European music of the common practice period, syncopation is validated by repetition. Since the same division of the pulse, whether binary or ternary, is usually maintained throughout a complete phrase, and more frequently throughout an entire composition or a large section thereof, hemiolas are validated in the same manner (see chapter 6, IV.B.1.4-6).

In African music there need be only properly placed strokes or pitches in sufficient number to realize the cycle. There is no requirement that one pulse receive greater stress than another. Further, any pulse is subject to either binary or ternary division at any time. Under these circumstances there is a profusion of dynamic and agogic accents which do not coincide with the pulses of the cycle, a phenomenon so common in African music that Waterman has termed it *off-beat phrasing* rather than *syncopation* (see chapter 6, IV.B.2.6). The individual hemiola, that is, the hemiola unvalidated by repetition, is also a frequent occurrence in African music. Realistically viewed, off-beat phrasing and the hemiola are end results of the cyclic principle, in which each part coordinates with the cycle as a whole, not necessarily with particular pulses.

In summary, then, European music is characterized by the frequent occurrence of syncopations or hemiolas, which, when they do occur, are validated by repetition. African music, on the other hand, makes frequent use of off-beat phrasing and hemiola not validated by repetition.

In all items transcribed in chapter 11 with the exception of TR 44, and in the two items in chapter 12 containing cuartetos (TR 61 and TR 65), I have assumed that two cycles are realized simultaneously and therefore occupy different but overlapping segments of time space. Thus the vocal parts in relation to hand-clapping or strokes on the llamador may realize a cycle of eight pulses, this cycle occupying the same time space as two or four cycles of eight pulses realized by the other percussion parts. The postulated two-tiered cycle represents a combination of the vocal cycles described by Jones and Bird (see chapter 6, VI.C.2-3) and the instrumental cycles described by Nketia and Jones (see chapter 6, IV.B.2.1). There is, to my knowledge, no study of African music in which the simultaneous performance of two cycles of different lengths is either described or assumed.

The degree to which the various discussed stylistic traits are exemplified by the genres presented in chapter 7-8 and 11-12 will not be discussed. They contrast with the worksongs and décimas presented in chapters 9-10 in that in almost all cases they display a regular, recurrent pulse. The lullabies and children's game songs found in chapter 7 are characteristically European. All are in duple meter and are divided into phrases four pulses in length. There is very little syncopation, and when it does occur it is validated by repetition. The remaining genres exhibit a mixture of European and African traits. In the songs of the velorio de angelito presented in chapter 8, some songs are obviously metrical in character and others are not. The four-pulse phrase is dominant. When a song is cast in the call and response pattern, each part is four pulses in length. Melodic stresses which do not coordinate with the underlying pulse are at times controlled by validation in the European manner. At other times they are not so controlled and are so frequent as to be considered African off-beat phrasing. The African trait of overlapping is present in two items.

In the cantos de las fiestas offered in chapter 11 and the ritmos of the cumbia presented in chapter 12, the European influence is to be heard primarily in the organization of the vocal and pito parts into phrases four pulses in length. There are, of course, some exceptions. The refrain of TR 51-53 and some refrains of TR 54 are of shorter duration, and the pito part in TR 62 is not consistently organized in four-pulse phrases. The greater number

of the items in these two chapters can be conceived as being cast
in duple meter, but their structuring over cycles of eight, twelve,
or sixteen pulses seems a more likely interpretation. Three items
in chapter 11 and one in chapter 12 display disjunct realizations
of cycles and one in chapter 11 an additive realization of the
cycle. Both are African traits not characteristic of European
music. However, there is much less use of the additive cycle in
costeño than in African music. Of other specifically African
traits, polymeter can be seen in TR 71, overlapping of call and
response patterns in all items of chapter 11. Finally, off-beat
phrasing is common in the parts of the tambor mayor and the bombo
in chapter 12 and in the vocal parts of TR 44, TR 48, TR 54, and
TR 61. It occurs with less frequency in TR 45-46 and TR 65.

Considering only the stylistic traits discussed in this section
of this chapter, the lullabies and children's songs are characteristically European; the songs of the velorio de angelito display an uneven mixture of African and European influences; African
traits are predominant in the cantos de las fiestas; and African
influence is somewhat stronger than European in the ritmos of the
cumbia.

ENSEMBLE FUNCTIONS

The principle of grading, which controls the structure of an
African percussion ensemble, whether led by a solo instrumentalist
or vocalist, affects not only the realization of the underlying
cycles but also the degree of repetition, contrast, or variation
produced (see chapter 6, IV.B.2.8). The principle of grading can
be applied only to the genres presented in chapters 11 and 12,
where the performance of each item except TR 44 requires the participation of a group of percussion instruments.

There are basically three grading levels: the lowest is applied
to a part consisting of recurrent, equidistant strokes or handclaps, the intermediate to the repetition in variant forms of similar rhythmic patterns in each cycle, and the highest to the performance by an instrumental or vocal soloist of what has been
termed the *improvisatory role* (see chapter 6, IV.B.2.5). This is
somewhat analogous to the arrangement of European ensembles which
accompany dances or marches. The principal elements are the bass
part, the accompaniment part, and the leading melodic part. The
latter differs from the leading part in the African ensemble in
that it is not usually improvisatory in nature.

In the cantos de las fiestas the vocal soloist carries the improvisatory role. In the ritmos of the cumbia this role is primarily played by the pito but is also assumed on occasion by the
vocalist singing the cuartetos. Of the percussion instruments,
the tambor mayor and the bombo on occasion shift from accompaniment to improvisation, the former more frequently than the latter.
I have no certain knowledge that this shift in roles occurs in
West African music, but I assume that it does. The constant,
almost unvaried repetition of the choral refrain in the cantos de
las fiestas also places the choral part in the lowest grade.
Waterman believes this exact reiteration of the choral refrain to
be characteristic of African music (1973:90). Jones is not in

agreement with this view (see chapter 6, VI.B.1). Nor is Bird or
Burnim (see chapter 6, VI.C.3 and Burnim 1976:98-99). Although
the even division between call and response does occur in Africa,
its common use in the cantos de las fiestas suggests a stronger
European than African influence.

Finally, there is one ensemble function found only in performances of the conjunto de cumbia for which, as far as I can determine, there are no analogues in African, Amerindian, or European
music. This is the revuelo, a short virtuosic display by an individual instrumentalist which, like the random cries uttered, is
designed to increase the emotional intensity of the performance.
Although there seems to be no predetermined order in which any instrumentalist may execute a revuelo, it is noteworthy that such
performances rarely overlap. The other instrumentalists apparently
concede the right of whoever has begun a revuelo to continue and
complete his tension-producing display before engaging in the same
activity on their own part.

In the African ensemble the instrumentalist or vocalist carrying
the improvisatory role also acts as the leader of the group. If
the soloist is a vocalist, he may cue the chorus by singing their
response before his first call and at times may sing the response
with them to assure their entrance (see chapter 6, VI.B.4). This
African trait is displayed in both the songs of the velorio de
angelito and the cantos de las fiestas (TR 13-14, TR 45, and
TR 48). A second type of cue given by the soloist in African
ensembles informs the players of the instruments of the lowest
grade that they should change from one prescribed rhythmic pattern
to another (see chapter 6, IV.B.2.8). This occurs in the part of
the tambor mayor in the danza de negro de la plaza (TR 46-47), the
cue being the movement by the soloist to the third verse of the
copla (see p. 418). A third type of cue is given by the soloist
in performances of the bullerengue and fandango when he wishes the
chorus to withhold their response until he has sung two verses
rather than one. This is accomplished by modifying the melodic
line in such a manner that the expected cadence does not occur
until the end of the second rather than the first verse (see
pp. 453-54, 462-63). I find no mention of this type of cuing in
the literature concerning African music. It would seem to me to
be based on European practice, since the concepts of both tonality
and verses even in length are involved.

RELATIONS OF TEXT AND MELODY

The song genres comprising the costeño repertory are almost
completely syllabic, with the exception of the worksongs and the
décimas, which contain fairly frequent neumatic passages. The latter trait is again too widespread to offer much assistance in itself in determining cultural sources. The degree to which verbal
stresses coordinate with recurrent underlying pulses does offer
such evidence. It is conventional in Spanish song that at least
the majority of verbal accents coordinate with the pulses of the
music. No such convention exists in African song (see chapter 6,
VI.C.1-3).

Considering the genres from this point of view, the lullabies and children's songs are purely European in character. They exhibit almost complete coordination of verbal and musical stress. The songs of the velorio de angelito again display an uneven mixture of European and African traits. Coordination of verbal accent and musical pulse is at times complete, as in TR 16, or almost completely lacking, as in TR 17, or it may lie between these two extremes, as in TR 18. African influence is stronger in the songs in chapters 11-12. Lack of coordination of verbal and musical stress is a frequent occurrence in TR 48, TR 54, and TR 61. It occurs with less frequency in TR 45-46 and TR 65. As far as this trait is concerned, then, European influence is dominant in the lullabies and children's songs and African influence in the cantos de las fiestas. Both influences are apparent in the songs of the velorio de angelito and in the cuartetos sung in the ritmos of the conjunto de cumbia.

A song in which syncopation or off-beat phrasing frequently occurs also commonly displays a lack of coordination between verbal and musical stress. However, the correlation of these two phenomena in any particular song is by no means absolute. Thus, TR 1 and TR 16 display considerable syncopation, but there is, nevertheless, complete coordination of verbal and musical pulse. On the other hand, this correlation is clearly evident in the vocal parts of TR 48, TR 54, and TR 61 and serves to emphasize the African influence in these particular items.

14. The Tri-Cultural Heritage

Of the three parent cultures which influenced the development of the costeño, that of the Spanish-European was without question historically dominant. It has left the greatest imprint on Evitar and the region, providing the legacy of the language, the religion, and to some extent the bases of economic and political organization. The contributions of the African Negro and the Amerindian, on the other hand, are to be seen in personal and social behavior and, in particular, in the arts and crafts. Thus the custom of a man having more than one family is probably based on polygamous practices in Africa, and that of men becoming drunk at almost all festivities probably has its basis in similar practice among many Indian groups in northern South America. The mortar and pestle in which rice is hulled in Evitar are analogous to those in use in Africa, and the hammocks to those woven by the Indians.

None of the musical instruments presently in use in Evitar or known to have been in use in the past, with the exception of the accordion, are totally derived from European sources. The two gaitas and the maraca are without question indigenous instruments. It is equally certain that the marímbula (lamellaphone), marimba (costeño musical bow), and carángano (earth bow) had their source in Africa. The tambor mayor, llamador, and caña de millo are primarily derived from African progenitors but display some European or Amerindian traits. The bombo, on the other hand, has been derived principally from European analogues but displays a number of African traits. Analogues of the guacharaca (rasp) and the guacho (cylindrical rattle) are found among both the Amerindians and the Africans. The guacho possibly exhibits European influence as well. Again, Europe cannot be considered the full source of any of the instruments played in the countryside, with the exception of the accordion (see chapter 2, esp. p. 93). At least one evitalero, Abraham Herrera, considers the accordion to be an urban rather than a rural instrument, not indigenous to the countryside (see TR 52, v. 12-15, p. 434). Some of the rural musical instruments, as distinguished from those in use in urban centers, are derived entirely from non-European sources, and the remainder, with the exception of the bombo, primarily from such sources.

566

Spain has provided not only the language in which the songs are
sung but in the majority of cases the forms into which they are
cast. Characteristic of these forms are rhyme and the octosyllabic
verse. The lullabies and children's songs almost without exception display the traits of simple European songs of the eighteenth
and nineteenth centuries. This has been determined by their
strophic structure, the presence of a recurrent pulse pattern or
meter, the prevalence of the major mode, the harmonic implications
of their initial and cadential pitch patterns, and their use of
melodic-rhythmic devices such as the sequence. Most importantly,
they have been related to this European tradition through the
existence of analogous melodic cells and skeletal patterns in
lullabies and children's songs collected in Spain, France, and
England. Although European influence is evident in all the genres
discussed, only the lullabies and children's songs are purely
European in character. All other genres, and any instruments or
ensembles involved in their performance, are the result of syncretism; that is, they result from the combination or blending of
the traits of more than one parent culture.

The contribution of Africa is second in importance to that of
Europe. It is the largest as far as musical instruments are concerned, and it has also resulted in an emphasis on the use of percussion instruments and handclapping. The greatest African contributions have been in aspects of rhythm and accentuation, all growing
out of the underlying cycle principle, which is evident in the phenomena discussed in chapters 11 and 12, "Cantos de las Fiestas" and
"Cumbia," and to a lesser extent in chapter 8, "Velorio de Angelito."
The disjunct and additive realizations of the cycle as found in
chapter 11 and the polymetrical realization of the cycle in the puya
of chapter 12 are characteristically African. Other African traits
which result from the cycle principle, and which are seen in all
three of these chapters, are the non-coordination of verbal and musical stress, off-beat phrasing, overlapping in the call and response
patterns, and the unvalidated hemiola. The pervasive use of the
call and response pattern and some of the methods used by the soloist in cuing the chorus are also derived from African practice. In
addition, the African principle of grading seems to apply in the
organization of the ensembles in their performances of the genres
presented in chapter 11 and 12.

The Amerindian culture, although indigenous, has apparently
played a relatively minor role in the syncretism which has produced costeño song and instrumental music. Only three of the
instruments in use, the two gaitas and the maraca, are fully indigenous, and only one ensemble, that employed to accompany the
danza de indio, is composed entirely of these instruments. Some
characteristics of the Indian rasp and rattle may be incorporated into their costeño equivalents. The caña de millo, whose
progenitor is African, may have been provided with four fingerholes in imitation of the Indian gaita. It is possible that the
Amerindian made some contribution to the development of the bombo,
but the evidence is very sparse and inconclusive.

Although Amerindian sources can be established for some of the
instruments, this is not possible in the case of the music and
song texts due to the paucity of information available. With some

frequency Indian men sing in a high tessitura, and the melodies
sung occasionally display wide ranges. These traits are analogous
to those characteristic of the costeño genres presented in chapters
9 and 10 and therefore may possibly represent Indian influence.
The data available, however, indicate that it is more likely independent development in the region. The random patterning of repetition and variation in both the text and melody of song may also be
partially derived from Indian practice.

In some cases the specific distribution of an analogous trait
can be determined; in others it cannot. The commercially fabricated
bass drum has been in use throughout Europe in this century. It
seems to have existed as a folk instrument primarily in Portugal.
The copla and décima have continued to be employed as folk verse
forms in Spain, and textual analogues of costeño lullabies and children's songs are also extant in that country. Melodic analogues of
the lullabies and children's songs are found primarily in central
and northern Spain, France, and England.

The single-headed drum displaying a tension system analogous to
that of the tambor mayor and the llamador has its distribution primarily in the southern region of West Africa, ideoglottic clarinets
analogous to the caña de millo in the western Sudanic region of the
continent. The mouth bow has a wide distribution, but the closest
analogues are again found in the southern region, as are those of
the earth bow. Traits in vocal style analogous to those of the
costeño are found in the Liberian-Sierra Leonean region, where men
also sing in their highest tessitura and women in their lowest. In
this area the men also employ only chest tone in producing their
high register.

The maraca or a similar rattle has a wide distribution among
Amerindian groups, but the particular perforated pattern characteristic of the maraca costeña seems to be derived from the Indians of
that particular region. Flutes analogous to the gaita hembra and
gaita macho are found almost entirely among Indian people living in
the Atlantic and Pacific coastal regions of Colombia and in an adjacent area of Panamá.

The traits derived from Europe or Africa were not necessarily
transmitted directly from these geographic areas to the Caribbean
coastal region of Colombia. English and French folk and popular
music was also exported to colonies on the islands of the Caribbean.
There was then interaction with the Spanish colonies on the islands
and on the mainland. Modified African traits were diffused from
the islands to the mainland in much the same manner. Large populations of Africans were brought to the Caribbean islands, where various modifications of African practice took place. An example of
this is the marímbula, a Cuban form of the lamellaphone, for which
there seems to be no exact equivalent in Africa. This instrument
diffused to the Costa Atlántica in the 1920's through audio-visual
means (p. 90).

Now that the contributions of the three parent cultures to costeño music and poetry have been summarized, it will be of interest
to examine the probable reasons why each has exerted the types and
degrees of influence indicated. Why, for example, did the African
and the Indian supply almost all of the instruments used in the
rural ensembles? Why did the dominant Spaniard have so little in-

fluence in this direction? Conversely, why are the lullabies and
the children's songs so completely European in style? Why can so
few traits of the indigenous Indian be distinguished, while a
large number of African traits are readily apparent? Were adequate data available, it would still be impossible to satisfac-
torily address these questions in a few pages. Nevertheless, it
will be useful to consider, if only briefly, some of the historical forces and sociological processes which bear upon these problems.

In an earlier study of the acculturative process as it relates
to music, I discussed three of the principal factors which determine the degree of acculturation which occurs:

1. The vitality of each of the competing cultures, i.e., the
   degree to which the individuals in each accept and maintain
   their allegiance to the values of their particular culture.
2. The degree to which the dominant culture accepts or shows
   tolerance of the values of the culture upon which it impinges.
   Religious attitudes are important in this connection.
3. The degree of disparity existing between values or aspects of
   the juxtaposed cultures or between similar aspects such as
   musical style (List 1964c:18).

The situation under discussion is complex in that historically
there were three competing cultures. That of the Spaniard was
dominant, and those of the African and the Indian were subordi-
nant. The dominant culture as such had the least difficulty in
maintaining its values, while the two subordinate cultures had
to compete not only with the dominant culture but with each
other. In this competition the African had certain advantages.
The Africans had been engaged in the mining and smelting of iron
for a millennium and a half by the time of European contact. They
were skilled in its fabrication into tools and weapons. The Amerindians, on the other hand, had gone through neither a bronze nor
an iron age. Many of the Africans came from societies which had
experienced complex political development. There had existed in
the Sudanic region, in particular, large states such as Ghana,
Mali, and Songhay, the latter persisting until the end of the
sixteenth century. These states possessed standing armies and
large bureaucracies. Some of the members of the latter were
literate in Arabic. Other centralized states or kingdoms which
were in existence in the early period of European contact were the
Wolof in Senegal, Benin on the southern coast, and Bakongo at the
estuary of the Congo.

We have ethnographic data concerning only ten of those tribes
that occupied the lowlands when the Spaniards arrived: the Calamari,
Turbaco, Tolú, Urabá, Cenú, Utibara, Yapel, Mompox (Malebú),
Tamalameque, and Bonda (Hernández de Alba 1948:329). Although the
Chibcha of the Andean highlands of Colombia had reached a degree
of centralized political development comparable in some respects
to that of the Incas in the south and the Aztecs to the north
(Kroeber 1946:887), the political organization of the coastal
tribes was at the level of chiefdoms. They were, however, skilled
in agriculture and weaving.

The enslavement of captives had been a common custom in Africa before the period of the European slave trade, as was the sale or exchange of servile persons. In the large states in the western Sudan the status of servitude could be inherited. The African, having had some experience with the institution of slavery in addition to that in mining and tropical agriculture, was in a better position to bear up under the harsh conditions of colonial slavery than the Indian. The Spaniards, finding the Africans more suitable to their purposes, began to import them in large numbers and eventually gave up the attempt to work the Indians as slaves.

In the early period of the western slave trade the majority of the individuals shipped from Africa had experienced a previous period of enslavement. By the middle of the seventeenth century most had been newly captured in warfare (Davidson 1966:218-21). They were thrust into a servitude much more onerous than they had experienced or expected in Africa, where in most societies slaves were eventually absorbed into the kinship system. In Africa they never became racial outcasts as they did in the Americas. Thus there were frequent revolts of African slaves, which at times resulted in independent communities such as Palenque in Colombia. Here the African's inherited military and political skills enabled him to remain relatively free of Spanish domination.

The indigenous Indians had a further disadvantage. They had never had an opportunity to build up any immunity to the diseases carried by the European. As many died of smallpox, influenza, typhus, measles, and other maladies as from warfare or harsh conditions of labor (Morner 1967:32-33). Many of the diseases carried by the Europeans were common to the entire Mediterranean community. Over the centuries they had been brought south, in particular, by Berbers traveling the trade routes of the Sahara or attempting conquest of the Sudan. Thus some Africans brought to the New World had developed partial immunity to the diseases which so easily ravaged the Indian.

The Indians were considered pagans who had never had previous opportunity to accept Christianity. Great efforts were made to convert them and to cause them to forsake their traditional values for those of the Catholic faith. The Africans were considered infidels rather than pagans, possibly because many were taken from Islamic-influenced areas during the early period of the trade. As infidels they were assumed to already have refused the offer of the Cross, and very little effort was expended to convert them (Morner 1967:112). Rather, they were considered expendable. Nevertheless, the Africans were under much less pressure than the Indians to forsake their traditions.

In Palenque the Africans could of course preserve whatever traditions they chose. This settlement was established on lands appropriated from the Indians. Since the early palenqueros were mostly male, they also raided the Indian villages for women. This, plus the effect upon the Indian's self-esteem of the superior adaptability of the African to colonial life, produced ill will between the races, which the Spaniard aggravated for his own purposes.

In the area which is now rural Bolívar, the negro is still

considered the superior of the Indian. Although there are now very few rural costeños whose racial inheritance is not mixed, this feeling that the Indian is inferior to the negro still persists. It is exemplified in la conquista, the concluding action of the carnaval, in which the negros conquer the Indians. It persists in subtler manners as well. In my early work in Bolívar each informant was queried concerning the race of each of his parents and grandparents. I soon discovered that my informants were loath to admit any strong Indian strain in their ancestry, and I discontinued this type of questioning.

The African's music had greater survival powers, since it had many traits in common with that of the European which Indian music did not share. The diatonic scales of African music are in some cases similar to those employed in Europe, and both musics make use of the harmonic intervals of the 3rd, 4th, 5th, and 6th. The structures of both musics are commonly based on groups of four pulses or multiples thereof. Binary and ternary divisions of these pulses are also common in both musics. The organization of various parts of an ensemble according to the African principle of grading is in some respects similar to the relationships of melodic line, bass, and accompaniment in ensembles performing European and European-derived march and dance music.

The Indian, of course, did not desert all his cultural values. The fact that there has been so little study of the music of the extant Indian groups in the Costa Atlántica may have caused me to underestimate their contribution to costeño rural music. However, the Ika and Kogi retain to this day the ensemble of two duct flutes and maraca. We have testimony that acculturated Indians employed the gaitas to accompany their dancing as late as the first half of the nineteenth century (p. 93).

Judging by the present situation, the church did not place a chapel and priest in every village, as is the current custom in Spain. Nor, again judging by the present, was there strong political control of country life. Thus the pressure upon both subordinate races for cultural change was probably less strong in rural than in urban areas. The rural public schools, which offer instruction in the Catholic religion as well as in other subjects, were not established until the second quarter of this century. The rural population therefore has been to a great extent dependent upon its own cultural resources. These circumstances tend to explain the strong retention of musical instruments with African and Indian progenitors and, conversely, the limited number of European traits adopted in their fabrication.

There remains the question of why the children's songs and lullabies, unlike the other genres presented, display no African traits but rather are purely European in character. In most cases, their texts can be traced to Spain. Melodically they not only are wholly European but fall within the common practice style of the eighteenth and nineteenth centuries. I shall first consider the children's songs. Why, it is legitimate to ask, is there such a great disparity in style between the songs of the adults and those of the children? Should not the children be expected to model their behavior on that of the adults around

them? When questioned, the children told me that they did sing
some game songs found in the repertory of the adults, in particular those used in the velorio de angelito. However, the adults
did not wish the children to play such games, and they therefore
were not played when adults were present. Adults were present
when I recorded the children playing games, and thus I have no
recordings of this type of game song sung by the children.

In checking the repertory of children's songs published in
Spain, I noted that the great majority of them, approximately
90%, had melodies which were consonant with common practice. The
remainder were non-heptatonic and had one or more modal characteristics such as a whole tone between the seventh and eighth
degrees. A melody in the minor mode displaying a leading tone is
an extreme rarity. Equally rare are neumatic cadence patterns
like those seen in the décima española (p. 392-93).

Of the Spanish lullabies examined, approximately half fell
within the common practice style, and the remainder are modal in
character and display the type of cadences found in the décima
española just cited. One can conclude that in Spain the children's repertory also differs greatly from that of the adults
and that the lullabies represent a form partaking of both styles.
The preponderance of the common practice style in the lullabies
recorded in Evitar may therefore be accidental.

Since children's songs differ from adult songs in both Spain
and the Atlantic coastal region of Colombia, it may be assumed
that a similar force has been operative in both cases. Most of
the Spanish songs were recorded in rural areas or in small towns.
We know that in Evitar some of these songs were taught in school.
We can assume that the same practice existed in Spain. Most
teachers in rural schools cannot read music, and the melodies,
if not the texts as well, were taught by rote. The teachers
themselves had been taught by individuals with a higher degree
of education, who probably molded the tunes according to the
styles of art music prevalent in their time.

Public schooling has not been available in Evitar for an extended period of time. Before 1963 only two years of education
were offered to the children, and none of my informants remembered there being schools in the village before the early 1940's.
Most of the older adults were illiterate. Since the majority of
the children's songs seem to have been learned at school, this
may be a repertory adopted in relatively recent times which
superseded one in which the songs were more stylistically similar to those of the adults.

EPILOGUE

In the spring of 1978 Winston Caballero travelled to Evitar for the first time since February 1971. In the summer of 1978 he came to the United States, and when we met he reported to me concerning his observations. On his visit to the village he carried with him a disc album, *Cantos Costeños* (List 1973), containing recordings made in Evitar and photographs of some of the singers. I had sent this album to Caballero in Cartagena, and I had asked him to deliver it to Domingo Polo, maestro of the school for boys.

Caballero found that the road to Evitar had lately been improved and, for a dirt road, was in excellent condition. The reverse was true of the village itself, which was in a sorry state. It had diminished considerably in population. Although it was Sunday, very few young or middle-aged adults of either sex were to be seen. Upon inquiry Caballero was informed that most of these had left the village for larger communities, and that Evitar was now primarily populated by the older adults and children. The almacén was no longer in existence, and Caballero could see that many of the chozas were not occupied and were in disrepair. Indeed, some were falling down.

Maestro Polo was nowhere to be found. He had taught for a while in Mahates and then moved elsewhere. He had no family left in the village, and no one knew where he could be located. Caballero then went to see one of our chief informants, Abraham Herrera. By this date Herrera had reached age seventy. He was senile and did not recognize Caballero. Not knowing what else to do, Caballero left the disc album with him. Upon inquiring concerning other informants, he was told that Simón Herrera, Abraham's nephew and decimero, had left the village, as had Herculano Pimientel, who had been inspector in 1970. Pedro Pacheco, also a decimero and our oldest informant, had died, as had Pedro Cueto, also a singer of décimas, at a rather early age. The other informant in addition to Abraham Herrera whom Caballero was able to locate was Felipe Jaramillo, who had been leader of the conjunto de gaitas. Jaramillo, now in his late fifties, had been deserted by his wife and was attempting to rear several children.

Neither Santiago Ospino, who was apparently still active, nor any other member of the conjunto de cumbia was in the village that day. There was now a great demand for their services, and they were out of the village as much as they were in it. At this time there was a recrudescence of interest in the performance of costeño folk music at fiestas of all types. In 1968 I had recorded in Cartagena a group of urban youth who had formed a conjunto de gaitas. This seems to have been an early manifestation of a folk music revival movement, which in 1978 was in full flower.

573

APPENDIX

Sources of the Transcriptions

1. CONCORDANCE OF ITEMS TRANSCRIBED WITH COPIES ON DEPOSIT IN THE INDIANA UNIVERSITY ARCHIVES OF TRADITIONAL MUSIC

All copies of the original List field recordings (LF) on deposit in the Archives of Traditional Music (ATM) are earliest copies (EC). The latter indication is therefore omitted. In the identification of the recordings from which the transcriptions were made, the number following the period--(LF 77.1), (LF 77.2)--represents the musical item. These are given in the order in which they occur in the tape roll. Tests are included in this number series, false starts usually are not. When items have been performed successively but have been separated in transcription, as have many *décimas*, their relationship is indicated by lower-case letters following the item number: (LF 77.5a), (LF 77.5b), etc. Each tape copy represents the full original tape roll. When the original tape was recorded on two tracks, each copy represents one full track thereof. The item numbers and the division letters have been omitted below since they are the same in both original and copy.

LF No.		ATM No.	
77		1060	
78		1061	
79	(1st pt)	1062	(1st pt)
96	(2nd pt)	1079	(2nd pt)
97		1080	
98		1081	
115	(2nd pt)	2679	(2nd pt)
117		2681	
118		2682	
146		2717	
179	(tr. 2)	3154	
180	(1st pt)	3155	(1st pt)
184	(tr. 1)	3240	
185	(tr. 1, 2nd pt)	3242	(2nd pt)
188		4653	
189		4654	

In some cases only the first or second part of the tape roll may have been utilized in a recording session with the *evitaleros*,

575

the remainder containing other materials. The part of the tape
from which the transcription or transcriptions were derived is
therefore identified above by (1st pt) or (2nd pt). When the
original recording is dual-track, the track in which the recordings transcribed is found is also indicated: (tr. 1) or (tr. 2).

The following is a concordance of other List field recordings
mentioned but not transcribed.

LF No.	ATM No.
127	2691
128	2692
164	3136
173	3147
174	3148
175	3149

2. CONCORDANCE WITH *CANTOS COSTEÑOS*, 12'' LP DISC
(SEE AUDIOGRAPHY, LIST 1973a).

TR No.	LF No.	Side	Band
1	79.7 (1st pt)	A	1a
2	78.3	A	2a
3	78.4	A	2b[1]
4	78.5	A	2b[1]
8	96.4 (2nd pt)	A	6a
9	96.5 (2nd pt)	A	4a
10	185.3 (tr. 1, 2nd pt)	A	5b
11	78.7	B	4
13	79.6 (1st pt)	B	5a
15	79.5 (1st pt)	B	5b
16	79.3 (1st pt)	B	6a
17	97.8	B	7a
18	97.9	B	7b
21	78.2	A	8b[3]
23	179.4 (tr. 1)	A	7b

Partially transcribed but not assigned TR number

| 146.2 | | A | 1 |

---

[1]The first three strophes of A2b were copied from LF 78.5,
the last two strophes were copied from LF 78.4.

[2]Only three of the four strophes given in TR 10 are heard in
A6b, and in the following order: I-III-II.

[3]Verses 1-4 given in TR 22 are omitted in A8b, which begins with
the last *grito* preceding verse 5.

AUDIOGRAPHY

Battle, Francisco, and Battle, José María
  n.d.   *The History of Cante Flamenco; An Archive.* Murray-Hill
        S-4360.

García Matos, Manuel
  n.d.   *Antología del folklore musical de España.* Hispavox
        HH 10-107/8/9/10.

Himmelhaber, Hans
  1968   *Playing a Musical Bow.* Encyclopaedia Cinematographica,
        Göttingen: Institut für den Wissenschaftlichen Film,
        E1534.

List, George
  1973   *Cantos costeños: Folksongs of the Atlantic Coastal
        Region of Colombia.* Ethnosound EST-8003.

Lomax, Alan
  1951   *Spanish Folk Music.* Columbia World Library of Folk and
        Primitive Music. Vol. 15. Columbia SL216.

Moser, Brian, and Tayler, Donald
  1972   *The Music of Some Indian Tribes of Colombia.* The British
        Institute of Recorded Sound MC 1/2/3.

Pérez Piñango, Agustín
  n.d.   *Música indígena venezolana 1: música guajira.* Editado
        por el Ministerio de Justicia, Comisión Indigenista.
        Caracas, Venezuela.

Rouget, Gilbert, ed.
  1946   *Musique Bantou d'Afrique Equatoriale Francaise: Mission
        Ogooue-Congo.* Musee de L'Homme, LD 324.

Schulze, Gary
  1965   *The Music of the Mende of Sierra Leone.* Folkways FE 4322.

FIELD RECORDINGS IN THE INDIANA UNIVERSITY
ARCHIVES OF TRADITIONAL MUSIC

Colombia
  1963-64 Instituto Popular de Cultura de Cali and Universidad
        Nacional Cauca. 67-190-F, ATL 4870.

Garibello, Carlos
  1962   Ika Indians. 66-212-F, EC 3958.

Salzmann, Zdenek
  1949   Northern Arapaho Indians. Pre '54-016-F, ATL 230.

Turner, Glen Davis
  1957   Jíbaro Indians. 59-053-F, ATL 1357.

BIBLIOGRAPHY

Abraham, Otto, and Hornbostel, Erich Moriz von
1909-10 "Vorschläge für die Transcription exotischer Melodien."
Sammelbände der Internationalen Musikgesellschaft,
pp. 1-25.

Alario di Filippo, M.
1964 *Lexicon de colombianismos.* Cartagena: Editora Bolívar.

Amades, Joan
1964 "Etnología musical." *Revista de dialectología y tradiciones populares* 20:113-200; 289-331; 480-526.

Ankermann, Bernard
1901 "Die afrikanischen Musikinstrumente." *Ethnologishes
Notizblatt* 3:1-134.

Apel, Willi
1958 *Gregorian Chant.* Bloomington: Indiana University Press.

Aretz de Ramón y Rivera, Isabel
1967 *Instrumentos musicales de Venezuela.* Cumana: Universidad
de Oriente.

Baehr, Rudolf
1970 *Manual de versificación española.* Translated and
adapted by K. Wagner and F. López Estrada. Biblioteca
Románica Hispánica, 3: Manuales, vol. 25. Madrid:
Editorial Gredos. (Translated from *Spanish Verslehre
auf historischer Grundlage.* Tubingen: Max Niemeyer
Verlag, 1962.)

Ballanoff, Paul A.
1971 "Origen de la cumbia: Breve estudio de la influencia
intercultural en Colombia." *América Indígena* 31, no. 1:
45-49.

Bartók, Bela, and Lord, Albert B.
1951 *Serbo-Croatian Folk Songs.* New York: Columbia University
Press.

Béart, Ch.
1955 *Jeux et jouets de l'Ouest africain.* Vol. 1. Memories de
l'Institut français d'Afrique noire, no. 42. Dakar: IFAN.

Bebey, Francis
1975 *African Music: A People's Art.* Translated by Josephine
Bennett. New York: Lawrence Hill & Co.

Bermúdez-Silva, Jesús, and Abadía M., Guillermo
  1966   *Algunos cantos nativos, tradicionales de la región de Guapi (Cauca)*. Bogotá: Imprenta Nacional.

Bird, Charles S.
  1972   "Aspects of Prosody in West African Poetry." In *Current Trends in Stylistics*, edited by Braj B. Kachru and Herbert F. W. Stahlke, pp. 207-15. Champaign, Illinois: Linguistic Research.

Boone, Olga
  1951   *Les tambours du Congo belge et du Ruanda-Urundi*. Tervuren: n.p.

Boulton, Laura
  1957   *African Music*. Record liner notes. Folkways FW 8852.

Bowdich, T. Edward
  1966   *Mission from Cape Coast Castle to Ashanti, 1819*. 3d ed., edited, with notes and an introduction by W. E. F. Ward. London: Cass.

Brandel, Rose
  1961   *The Music of Central Africa: An Ethnomusicological Study*. The Hague: Martinus Nijhoff.

Buchner, Alexander
  1972   *Folk Music Instruments of the World*. Translated by Alžběta Nováková. New York: Crown Publishers.

Burnim, Mellonee
  1976   "Songs in Mende Folktales." Master's thesis, University of Wisconsin.

Butler, Alban
  1956   *Lives of the Saints*. Edited, revised, and supplemented by Herbert Thurston and Donald Attwater. New York: Kenedy & Sons.

Cabal, Constantino
  1925   *El individuo*. Madrid: Edición del Excmo. Ayudamiento de Oviedo.

Capmany, Aurelio
  1931   "El baile y la danza." In *Folklore y costumbres de España*, directed by F. Carreras y Candi, vol. 2, pp. 167-418. Barcelona: Casa Editorial Alberto Martín.

Carrizo, Juan Alfonso
  1945   *Antecedentes hispano-medioevales de la poesía tradicional argentina*. Buenos Aires: Estudios hispánicos.

Casas Gaspar, Enrique
  1947   *Costumbres españolas de nacimiento, noviazgo, casamiento y muerte*. Madrid: Editorial Escelicer.

Cascudo, Luis da Camara
  1972   *Dicionário do folclore brasileiro*. 3d ed., rev. and enl. Brasília: Instituto Nacional do Livro.

Chase, Gilbert
   1941   *The Music of Spain*. New York: W. W. Norton.

Comisión Pro Coronación de la Virgen del Carmen de Cuyo
   1914   *Coronación de Nuestra Señora del Carmen de Cuyo*. Buenos
           Aires: Casa Editoria, Imprenta y Libería "Alfa y Omega."

Córdoba y Oña, Sixto
   1948   *Cancionero popular de la provincia de Santander*.
           Santander: Aldus.

Davidson, Basil
   1966   *Africa: History of a Continent*. New York: Macmillan Co.

Davillier, Jean Charles
   1881   *Spain*. Translated by J. Thompson, illustrated by Gustavo
           Doré. London: Bickers & Son.

Djenda, Maurice
   1968a   "L'Arc-en-terre des Gbaya-Bokoto." *African Music* 4,
           no. 2:44-46.
   1968b   "Les Pygmées de la Haute Sangha." *Geographica* 14:27-43.

Echevarría Bravo, Pedro
   1951   *Cancionero musical popular manchego*. Madrid: Consejo
           Superior de Investigaciones Científicas.

Escalante, Aquiles
   1954   "Notas sobre el Palenque de San Basilio, una comunidad
           negra de Colombia." In *Divulgaciones etnológicas*.
           Barranquilla: Universidad del Atlántico, Instituto de
           Investigación Etnológica.
   1964   *El negro en Colombia*. Monografías sociológicas, no. 18.
           Bogotá: Universidad Nacional de Colombia.

Foster, George McClelland
   1960   *Culture and Conquest: America's Spanish Heritage*.
           Chicago: Quadrangle Books.

Garay, Narciso
   1930   *Tradiciones y cantares de Panamá, ensayo folklórico*.
           Brussels: Presses de l'Expansion belge.

García Matos, Manuel
   1944   *Lírica popular de la Alta Extremadura*. Madrid: Unión
           musical española.

Gil García, Bonifacio
   1956   *Cancionero popular de Extremadura*. Vol. 2. Badajoz:
           Imprenta de la Excma. Diputación.

Glareanus, Henricus
   1965   *Dodecachordon*. Translation, transcription and commentary
           by Clement A. Miller. 2 vols. Musicological Studies and
           Documents, 6. American Institute of Musicology. Origi-
           nally published in 1547.

Gomme, Lady Alice, collector and ed.
   1894   *Children's Singing Games, with the Tunes to Which They
           Are Sung*. 1st and 2d ser. London: D. Nutt.

Gomme, Lady Alice, and Sharp, Cecil, eds.
1909   *Children's Singing Games*. Set 1 of 5 sets. London:
        Novello.

Grebe, María Ester
1974   "Instrumentos musicales precolombinos de Chile."
        Revista musical chilena 28, no. 128:5-55.
1975   Review of *Cantos costeños. Folksongs of the Atlantic
        Coastal Region of Colombia*, recorded and with notes by
        George List and collectors. Ethnosound EST-8003, 1973.
        Revista musical chilena 29, no. 132:56-59.

Hernández de Alba, Gregorio
1948   "Tribes of the North Colombia Lowlands." In *Handbook
        of South American Indians*, edited by Julian H. Steward,
        vol. 4. Bureau of American Ethnology Bulletin no. 143.
        Washington, D.C.: Smithsonian Institution.

Herzog, George
1957   "Song: Folk Song and the Music of Folk Song." In
        Standard Dictionary of Folklore, Mythology, and Legend,
        edited by Maria Leach, vol. 2, pp. 1032-50. New York:
        Funk & Wagnalls Co.

Hindemith, Paul
1945   *The Craft of Musical Composition*. Vol. 1. Rev. ed. New
        York: Associated Music Publishers.

Hornbostel, Erich Moritz von
1933   "The Ethnology of African Sound-Instruments." *Africa* 6,
        no. 2:129-257; no. 3:277-311.

Howard, Joseph H.
1967   *Drums in the Americas*. New York: Oak Publications.

Instituto Geográfico Augustín Codazzi
1967   *Atlas de Colombia*. Bogotá: Litografía Arco.

Izikowitz, Karl Gustav
1935   *Musical and Other Sound Instruments of the South
        American Indians*. Göteborg: Elanders.

Jones, A. M.
1958   *African Music in Northern Rhodesia*. Occasional Papers.
        No. 4. Livingstone: Rhodes-Livingstone Museum.
1959   *Studies in African Music*. Vol. 1. London: Oxford Univer-
        sity Press.
1964   "African Metrical Lyrics." *African Music* 3, no. 3:6-14.

Karsten, Rafael
1935   *The Head-Hunters of Western Amazonas: The Life and Cul-
        ture of the Jibaro Indians of Eastern Ecuador and Peru*.
        Commentationes Humanarum Litterarum, vol. 7. Helsinki:
        Societas Scientiarum Fennica.

Knott, Arnold
1973   "Music of Liberia." In *Liberian Educational and Cultural
        Materials Research Project*, pp. 151-92. Monrovia: Depart-
        ment of Education.

Kolinski, Mieczyslaw
  1957   "Ethnomusicology, Its Problems and Methods." *Ethnomusi-cology Newsletter*, no. 10:1-7.

Kremenliev, Boris
  1952   *Bulgarian-Macedonian Folk Music*. Berkeley and Los Angeles: University of California Press.

Kroeber, A. L. (Alfred Louis)
  1946   "The Chibcha." In *Handbook of South American Indians*, edited by Julian H. Steward, vol. 2, pp. 887-909. Bureau of American Ethnology Bulletin no. 143. Washington, D.C.: Smithsonian Institution.

Kubik, Gerhard
  1965   "Transcription of Mangwilo Xylophone Music from Film Strips." *African Music* 3, no. 4:35-51.
  1968   *Mehrstimmigkeit und Tonsysteme in Zentral-und Ostafrika*. Vienna: Österreichische Akademie der Wissenschaften.
  1979   *Angolan Traits in Black Music, Games and Dances of Brazil: A Study of African Cultural Extensions Overseas*. Estudos de Antropologia Cultural, no. 10. Lisbon: Junta de Investigações Científicas do Ultramar.
  1980   "Marimba." In *New Grove Dictionary of Music and Musicians*, vol. 11, pp. 681-83. Washington, D.C.: Dictionary of Music.
  n.d.   "Instruments de Musique Mpyemo." Unpublished manuscript.

Kurath, Gertrude P.
  1949   "Dance: Folk and Primitive." In *Standard Dictionary of Folklore, Mythology, and Legend*, edited by Maria Leach, vol. 1, pp. 276-96. New York: Funk & Wagnalls Co.
  1956   "Dance Relatives of Mid-Europe and Middle America: A Venture in Comparative Choreology." *Journal of American Folklore* 69, no. 273:286-98.

List, George
  1954   *An Analysis of the Relationship of Non-Stepwise Melodic Movement to Tonality in Selected Works of W. A. Mozart*. Doctoral dissertation, Indiana University. Ann Arbor: University Microfilm Publication no. 10, 151.
  1963   "The Boundaries of Speech and Song." *Journal of the Society for Ethnomusicology* 7, no. 1:1-16.
  1964a   "Music in the Culture of the Jíbaro Indians of the Ecuadorian Montaña." *Inter-American Music Bulletin* 40-41:1-17.
  1964b   "Transcription III" in "Symposium on Transcription and Analysis: A Hukwe Song with Musical Bow." *Journal of the Society for Ethnomusicology* 8, no. 3:252-65.
  1964c   "Acculturation and Musical Tradition." *Journal of the International Folk Music Council* 16:18-21.
  1966   "The Musical Bow at Palenque." *Journal of the International Folk Music Council* 18:36-49.
  1968a   "The Hopi as Composer and Poet." In *Proceedings of the Centennial Workshop in Ethnomusicology, 1967*, pp. 43-53.

Vancouver: Government of the Province of British
Colombia.
1968b   "The Mbira in Cartagena." *Journal of the International
Folk Music Council* 20:54-59.
1973a   "El Conjunto de Gaitas de Colombia: la herencia de tres
culturas." *Revista musical chilena* 27, nos. 123-124:
43-54.
1973b   "A Comparison of Certain Aspects of Colombian and
Spanish Folksong." *Yearbook of the International Folk
Music Council* 5:72-84.
1974   "The Reliability of Transcription." *Journal of the
Society for Ethnomusicology* 18, no. 3:353-77.
1978   "The Distribution of a Melodic Formula: Diffusion or
Polygenesis?" *Yearbook of the International Folk Music
Council* 10:33-52.
1979   "Ethnomusicology: A Discipline Defined." *Journal of the
Society for Ethnomusicology* 32, no. 1:1-4.
1980   "Colombia, II: Folk Music." In *New Grove Dictionary of
Music and Musicians,* vol. 4, pp. 570-81. Washington,
D.C.: Dictionary of Music.

Livermore, Ann
1972   *A Short History of Spanish Music.* New York: Vienna
House.

Lomax, John A., and Lomax, Alan, comps.
1934   *American Ballads and Folksongs.* New York: Macmillan Co.

López Cruz, Francisco
1967   *La música folklórica de Puerto Rico.* Sharon, Connecti-
cut: Troutman Press.

Magis, Carlos H.
1969   *La lírica popular contemporánea.* México: El Colegio de
México.

Marazuela Albornos, Agapito
1964   *Cancionero segoviano.* Segovia: Jefatura Provincial del
Movimiento.

March, José María, S. J.
1911   "Pilar, Nuestra Señora del." In *The Catholic Encyclo-
pedia,* edited by Charles G. Herbermann *et al.,* vol. 12,
p. 83. New York: Robert Appleton Co.

Marcuse, Sibyl
1975a   *Musical Instruments: A Comprehensive Dictionary.* Cor-
rected ed. New York: W. W. Norton.
1975b   *A Survey of Musical Instruments.* New York: Harper & Row.

Marie, Cécile
1975   *Anthologie de la chanson occitane.* Paris: G. P. Maison-
neuve et Larose.

Meek, Charles Kingsley
1925   *The Northern Tribes of Nigeria.* London: Milford.

Menéndez Pidal, Ramón
　1920　*Estudios literarios*. Madrid: Atenea.

Merriam, Alan P.
　1962　"The African Idiom in Music." *Journal of American Folklore* 75, no. 296:120-30.

Morner, Magnus
　1967　*Race Mixture in the History of Latin America*. Boston: Little, Brown.

The New Grove Dictionary of Music and Musicians.
　1980　Edited by Stanley Sadie. London: Macmillan & Co., Washington, D. C.: Grove's Dictionaries of Music.

Nketia, J. H. Kwabena
　1955　*Funeral Dirges of the Akan People*. New York: Negro Universities Press.
　1963　*African Music in Ghana*. Evanston: Northwestern University Press.
　1974　*The Music of Africa*. New York: W. W. Norton.

Okie, P. L.
　1955　*Folk Music of Liberia*. Record liner notes. Folkways FE 4465.

Oliveira, Ernesto Veiga de
　1966　*Instrumentos musicais populares portugueses*. Lisbon: Fundação Calouste Gulbenkian.

Ortiz, Fernando
　1954　*Los instrumentos de la música afrocubana*. Vol. 4. Havana: Dirección de Cultura de Ministerio de Educación.

Pardo Tovar, Andrés, and Pinzon Urrea, Jesús
　1961　*Rítmica y melódica del folclor chocoano*. Bogotá: Universidad Nacional de Colombia.

Perdomo Escobar, José Ignacio
　1963　*Historia de la música en Colombia*. 3d ed. Bogotá: Editorial ABC.

Piston, Walter
　1941　*Harmony*. New York: W. W. Norton.

Posada Gutiérrez, Joaquin
　1929　*Memorias histórico-politícas*. Bogotá: Imprenta Nacional.

Puig Campillo, Antonio
　1953　*Cancionero popular de Cartagena*. Cartagena: Gómez.

Rameau, Jean Philippe
　1722　*Traite de l'harmonie a ses principes naturels*. 4 vols. Paris: Ballard.

Reichel-Dolmatoff, Gerardo
　1945　"Los Indios Motilones (etnografía y lingüística)." *Revista del Instituto Etnológico Nacional* (Bogotá) 2:16-115.

Reymond, Eduardo
1942   *Compilación de los estudios geológicos oficiales de
        Colombia. Informe sobre una misión, geológica en los
        Departamentos del Magdalena y Atlántico.* Vol. 5.
        Bogotá: Ministerio de Minas y Petroleos (Imprenta
        Nacional).

Rimmer, Joan
1976   "The Instruments Called Chirimia in Latin America." In
        Studia Instrumentorum Musicae Popularis, vol. 4, pp. 101-
        10. Stockholm: Musikhistoriska Museet.

Rodríguez Marín, Francisco
1927   "La copla: estudio folklórico." In *Miscelánea de
        Andalucía*, by D. Francisco Rodríguez Marín, pp. 203-54.
        Madrid: Biblioteca Giralda.
1932   *Pasatiempo folklórico, varios juegos infantiles del
        siglo XVI.* Madrid: Tipografía de Archivos.

Sachs, Curt
1928   *Geist und Werden der Musikinstrumente.* Berlin: Riemer.

Sampaio, Conçalo
1940   *Cancioneiro minhoto.* Oporto: Tipografia Costa Corregal.

Sánchez, Miguel
n.d.   "La guarda cuidadosa." In *Dramáticos contemporáneos a
        Lope de Vega*, edited by Ramón Mesonero Romanos, p. 2.
        Biblioteca de autores españoles, vol. 43. Madrid: Real
        Academia Española, 1951. Originally published 1857.

Schneider, Marius
1948   "Tipología musical y literaria de la canción de cuna en
        España." *Anuario musical* (Barcelona) 3:3-54.

Schwab, George
1947   "Tribes of the Liberian Hinterland." Papers of the Pea-
        body Museum, Harvard University, vol. 31. Cambridge,
        Mass.

Serwadda, Moses, and Pantaleoni, Hewitt
1968   "A Possible Notation for African Dance Drumming."
        African Music 4, no. 2:47-52.

Sharp, Cecil
1907   *English Folk-Song, Some Conclusions.* London: Simpkin
        & Co.

Stone, Ruth, and Stone, Verlon
1972   *Music of the Kpelle of Liberia.* Record liner notes.
        Folkways FE 4385.

Tayler, Donald
1968   "The Music of Some Indian Tribes of Colombia." *Journal
        of the British Insitute of Recorded Sound* 29-30:supps.
        I-XXII.

Thomas, Louis V.
1959   *Les Diola.* Vol. 2. Dakar: IFAN.

Thompson, Donald
1971   "The Marímbula, an Afro-Caribbean Sanza." *Yearbook for Inter-American Musical Research* 7:103-16.

Toor, Frances
1947   *A Treasury of Mexican Folkways*. New York: Crown Publishers.

van Oven, Jacoba
1970   "Music of Sierra Leone." *African Arts* 3, no. 4:20-27, 71.

Waterman, Richard Alan
1973   "African Influence on the Music of the Americas." In *Mother Wit from the Laughing Barrel*, edited by Alan Dundes, pp. 82-94. New Jersey: Prentice Hall. Originally published in *Acculturation in the Americas*, edited by Sol Tax, pp. 207-18. Chicago: University of Chicago Press, 1952.

Widor, Charles M.
1927   *Vieilles chansons pour les petits enfants*. Paris: Typographic Plon.

Wieschhoff, Heinrich Albert
1933   *Die afrikanischen Trommeln und ihre ausserafrikanischen Beziehungen*. Stuttgart: Strecker und Schroder.

Zapata Olivella, Delia
1962   "La cumbia, síntesis musical de la Nación colombiana. Reseña histórica y coreográfica." *Revista Colombiana de Folclor* 3, no. 7:187-204.

Zečević, Slobodan
1974   *Rusalke i todorci u narodnom verovanju*. Vol. 37. Belgrade: Glasnik Etnografskog Museja.

INDEX